The Letters of Stephen A. Douglas

THE

Letters

O F

Stephen A. Douglas

Edited by Robert W. Johannsen

University of Illinois Press

Urbana 1961

Contents

LETTERS OF STEPHEN A. DOUGLAS

[xi]

[xiv]

[xvi]

[xx]

Introduction

===

Stephen A. Douglas, declared one of the Senator's eulogists, played so important a part in the "progress and renown of his State and the Nation, that the history of the one would be incomplete without that of the other." Taking into consideration the customary eulogistic exaggeration, this obituary estimate was strikingly accurate. During the years preceding his untimely demise in June, 1861, no man occupied a more prominent and controversial role in American politics than did the "Little Giant." Douglas is remembered chiefly as the opponent of Abraham Lincoln. That Douglas was also the antagonist of proslavery Southern leaders, like Jefferson Davis, has not always been appreciated. Indeed, Douglas had more in common with Lincoln, a fellow Illinoisan, than he did with many in his own political party. In his last years, he was caught in a bitter three-cornered political struggle that shook the very foundations of the nation; he died soon after the crisis of civil war had arrived. Douglas' role in prewar political life was thus overshadowed by the war and his career was either misinterpreted or neglected by the generation of postwar historians. Many cast him into the shadow of his former antagonist who had been given the awesome responsibility of guiding the nation through its fiery time of trial. Not until the turn of the twentieth century was Douglas considered deserving of biographical study. His private papers and public utterances have never been published, although many lesser figures of Douglas' generation who survived the great national struggle have been accorded this treatment.

I

Douglas' life spanned the formative years of American nationalistic development, a period sometimes referred to as America's adolescent age. Born during the conflict that first gave vivid and fervent expression to American nationalism, Douglas died just as that nationalism met its most serious test of survival. The test proved to be the price of maturity. The letters presented in this collection cover the years of Douglas' mature life, from 1833, when the twenty-year-old Douglas, newly arrived in Illinois, recorded his first impressions of his new home, to 1861, three weeks before his death, when as a national leader he sought to rally his section and his party to the cause of the Union. Born in the green hills of Vermont in 1813, Douglas combined the New England tradition of stubborn independence with the boisterous individualism of the frontier. From his first entrance on the political arena, he was a fighter. Standing five feet four inches tall, with a large head and short, stubby legs, he soon earned the sobriquet, "Little Giant." He was a person who never shrank from controversy, a person who was frequently at his best when in the thick of the fray. "He loves furor," commented one newspaper. To some he possessed the qualities of a prize fighter, "pluck, quickness and strength; adroitness in shifting his positions, avoiding his adversary's blows, and hitting him in unexpected places in return." "He is a plucky, hard, unscrupulous, conscienceless fellow," continued this observer, "who will be a hard man to meet in debate. . . . His strong point is his will to have his own way." As a master of debate, he won praise from even his opponents. "His language," commented a person who witnessed one of Douglas' forensic efforts in the Senate, "is always sharp and clear, and strong, and knotty; never soft; seldom beautiful."

As a youth, Douglas adopted the Jacksonian faith for his own and for the rest of his life he espoused the ideals of Jacksonian democracy. The "Old Hero" was the object of Douglas' adulation and devotion— the guiding star to his career. The organization of the Jackson party in Illinois was to a large extent the result of the youthful exertions of Douglas. The apparent ease with which he won political office in Illinois fed his ambition; each office was but a step toward the achievement of his ultimate goal, service in the Congress of the United States. In the relatively brief space of a decade, he held the positions of State's Attorney, member of the state legislature, Register of a Federal land office, Secretary of State, and finally, in 1841, he became, at twenty-seven, the youngest justice ever to sit on the state Supreme Court. Two years later, he was elected to his first term in Congress. Between 1843 and his death in 1861, Douglas was elected three times to the House of Representatives and three times to the Senate.

Douglas was a pragmatist in politics. He distrusted ideologies and doctrinaire thinkers, partly, one suspects, because he proved unable himself to argue effectively from abstract grounds. His political actions were based on a strong sense of realism and practicality. This is not to say that Douglas lacked principles, for he was a man of principle as well as of action. His principles were always tempered in their expression, however, by his determination never to seek more than he thought politically possible. For Douglas, the statesman was he who would "adapt his laws to the wants, conditions, and interests of the people to be governed by them." "A wise man," he said on another occasion, "always conforms his actions to a policy which he cannot prevent."

"I am a radical & progressive democrat," Douglas wrote in 1852. His political creed rested on two basic principles which had been shaped in the "radical & progressive" democratic mold of frontier Jacksonian politics: a strong belief in national expansion and the integrity of the Union, and an equally strong faith in man's ability to govern himself. Manifest destiny and popular sovereignty were the principles which motivated his actions. He was a champion of Texas annexation, of "all of Oregon or none," and of the Mexican War. By expansion, Douglas meant not only the extension of the boundaries of the United States but also the growth and development of the American nation in other ways, politically, economically, and socially. The nation, he said, was growing "with a rapidity unequalled in the history of the world." Its free institutions were progressive, adapted to the happiness of man, and could not be restrained. Through expansion, and by fulfilling the promise of democracy, he said, the nation can increase "in wealth, in population, in power, and in all the elements of greatness, until we shall be the admiration and terror of the world."

Expansion, however, was closely related to popular sovereignty. Only by combining the two could the United States "perform that great mission, that destiny which Providence has marked out for us." Popular self-government became an obsession to Douglas. The right of a people to determine the character and nature of their own local institutions was to him an inalienable right. In the context of the sectional conflict, Douglas was convinced, popular sovereignty had an additional practical significance. By allowing the people to determine their own institutions, including that of slavery, Douglas believed that the nation would not only be fulfilling its God-given obligation to expand free institutions but it could also be spared what might very well prove to be its death struggle.

During the decade of the 1850's, Douglas focused his energies on the application of popular sovereignty to the sectional issues of the time. His efforts brought him national fame and a recognized position of leadership in the Democratic party but they also plunged him into bitter controversy. An increasing number of Americans denied that slavery was an institution which could be decided by a majority vote on the local level. Douglas' failure to appreciate the increasing moral

[xxv]

commitment of many Americans to the restriction of Negro slavery was a weakness in his political attitude. Nothing has so influenced the image of Douglas in the American mind as his neutralist position toward slavery. He had little patience with those who argued that slavery was a moral question. To him, the question had no practical value within the framework of American politics; indeed, it was a question fraught with danger to the very existence of the Union. "I do not know of any tribunal on earth," he once told an audience, "that can decide the question of the morality of slavery or any other institution. I deal with slavery as a political question involving questions of public policy." Slavery, to Douglas, was an institution of local significance only and therefore one that must be decided on the local level. He did not care, he said, whether it was voted up or down. Douglas was not proslavery. He frequently registered his personal distaste for the institution and condemned it as a "curse beyond computation." Popular sovereignty, moreover, would result in the extension of freedom and the restriction of slavery. Slavery, he thought, had reached its natural limits of expansion; the circumstances of geography, as well as the greater tendency of free Northerners to emigrate to the West, would effectively prevent the spread of the institution. The leader of a national party, Douglas had perforce to formulate a national solution to the slavery problem. As a national solution, Douglas' scheme had of necessity to recognize the possibility, remote as he might regard it, that slavery could be expanded. As the sectional controversy deepened, he became more convinced that popular sovereignty was the only hope for the Union. Having made his commitment, he fought for it with a single-minded zeal that approached the fanaticism of some of his opponents. In pursuing his course of indifference toward the moral question of slavery, however, he sowed the seeds of his own political repudiation, for he satisfied neither those who regarded slavery as immoral and desired its restriction above all else, nor those who looked on slavery as a positive good and sought to guarantee its expansion.

When the Union foundered in 1860-61, Douglas, rightly or wrongly, attributed the disaster to the nation's inability to recognize and accept what he regarded as a logical extension of democratic self-government. With secession and disunion an accomplished fact, the "Little Giant" saw his duty and, in the last effort of his life, urged that party differences be subordinated to the cause of patriotism and union. "There are but two sides to the question," Douglas declared, "and every man must be on the side of the United States or against it. There can be none but patriots or traitors." He contemplated the destruction of the Union, he said, "with sad heart—with a grief I have never before experienced," but he was spared the four years of bloodshed that followed. On June 3, 1861, Douglas died. John J. Crittenden, respected Senator from Kentucky, lamented several weeks later, "I know of no man who might have been more useful in this crisis."

II

Douglas was a political leader toward whom few people could be neutral. He was praised and condemned, vilified and idolized, a man who inspired fierce loyalty on the one hand and bitter hatred on the other. One newspaper editor of the time wrote that Douglas enjoyed "a higher degree of popular regard than any other statesman in America," but that he was also "hated, feared and abused more heartily than any other statesman." Few Americans could regard the Illinois Senator with apathy. Yet few Americans also really knew Douglas. "Never was a man really less known, appreciated and estimated at his actual value" than Douglas, commented a New Englander in 1857.

The situation has not changed markedly in the century since Douglas' time. In 1859, as Douglas encountered bitter attacks from members of his own Democratic party as well as from Republicans, he received a reassuring word from one of his correspondents: "If the present generation does not do you justice, posterity will." Posterity, however, seemed reluctant to grant Douglas the recognition he deserved. Not that Douglas has been neglected in the annals of American historiography or that he has been without his admirers, for historians and biographers have accorded him considerable attention. Nonetheless, he has seldom inspired the kind of balanced treatment essential to an understanding of the man and of his role in nineteenth-century American politics. Douglas has often been portrayed either as the archvillain of the sectional struggle or as the unsung hero, whose perspicacity had correctly diagnosed the nation's ills and whose admonitions, if heeded, would have spared the American people the holocaust of civil war. "No man in the whole nation," wrote Henry Adams, "has done so much as he to degrade the standard of political morality and to further the efforts of the slave power." George Fort Milton has described Douglas as a great patriot and statesman: "Great in friendship, great in mind, great in purpose, his was the greatest effort to make intelligence the arbiter of American affairs." Neither version does credit to the "Little Giant."

One handicap to the study of Stephen A. Douglas has been a dearth of personal papers. The discovery of a large body of Douglas manuscripts in the early 1930's, utilized principally by Milton in his *Eve of Conflict: Stephen A. Douglas and the Needless War* (Boston, 1934), aided in placing Douglas more accurately in the perspective of his own time, but the collection (now deposited in the University of Chicago Library) has certain limitations. In the first place, it does not encourage an even treatment of Douglas' total career, since the great majority of the papers covers only the last four years of his life. Second, it contains virtually no letters written by Douglas himself, but includes only the Senator's incoming correspondence. A study of the collection bears out the conclusion that Douglas' mail came principally from people who agreed with him; consequently, a heavy and too-exclusive reliance on the papers is apt to result in a distortion of Douglas' story.

Letters written by Douglas himself have remained relatively scarce and widely scattered. Aside from the papers still in the possession of the Douglas family, the largest collections are in the Illinois State Historical Library, the Chicago Historical Society, the National Archives, and the Library of Congress.

This edition represents an attempt to bring together Douglas' own letters, a project that developed out of the editor's work on a new biographical study of Douglas. Although the collection is the result of several years of searching in libraries, historical societies, newspaper files, and private collections, no claim of completeness is or can be made. Obviously, a man as politically active as Douglas on both state and national levels would have written many more letters than are here included. One can only conclude that these letters have been destroyed or that they yet lurk in unnoticed or hidden depositories. It is hoped that this collection of Douglas' correspondence will succeed in "flushing out" additional Douglas letters. The editor is also hopeful that this collection may aid in an understanding of Douglas and his activities.

III

The decision to include in this edition only the letters written by Douglas was based on practical considerations of time and space, and on the belief that these most urgently required collection. The incoming correspondence has been omitted, partly because of the magnitude of the collection and partly because the collection is available in one manuscript depository. Douglas' speeches, delivered over a period of some twenty-seven years, have also been omitted, although a full appreciation of Douglas' character and influence cannot be gained without them. Some of his speeches are well known and have been widely reprinted; many of them are yet buried in the columns of forgotten newspapers. Legal briefs, drafts of speeches, resolutions and bills, and other manuscripts of various kinds have been located but have not been included in the interest of compactness and unity.

All the letters written by Stephen A. Douglas which have been located are printed in full, except those which are so routine as to be relatively devoid of historical interest. The latter have been calendared in their proper chronological order. In some cases, allusions to Douglas letters have been found but the originals could not be located. These letters are noted and briefly summarized (where summaries were available) in their chronological sequence. The calendared letters and the notations to letters not found are enclosed in brackets. Documentation has been kept to a minimum, restricted to the identification of persons (where this has seemed essential to an understanding of the letter) and to an explanation of situations and events without which the document would not be completely intelligible.

Each letter, whether reprinted in full, calendared, or merely noted, has been preceded by a heading indicating the name of the addressee, if known; in the few cases where documents, not strictly letters, have been reprinted, brief descriptive statements have been supplied. Each letter is followed by a source identification, indicating the nature of the source from which the letter was copied and the present ownership or location of the source. An identification of the addressee, if this was considered necessary, and other information pertinent to an understanding of the letter have been supplied in an explanatory note following the source identification. All other editorial identifications or comments have been included in the footnotes. The date of each letter or document has been uniformly presented at the beginning of the text, regardless of its position in the original; where the date was originally elsewhere, or was missing in the original, it has been enclosed in brackets. The complimentary closing has been included in the texts of the letters, and has not been set off from the texts as frequently was the case with the originals. The internal address, usually following the text of the letter in the original, has been deleted where it simply repeated the heading supplied by the editor for the letter.

The original spelling and punctuation of the letters have been faithfully retained, except that periods have frequently been supplied at the ends of sentences. In many cases, paragraphing has been provided by the editor. Where words or portions of words were omitted by Douglas, the missing letters or words have been inserted, where these seemed obvious, and have been enclosed in brackets. Where the missing letters or words were not obvious and the editor has had to resort to conjecture, the editorial insertions have been followed by a question mark. In cases where the original manuscript has been mutilated, where words have been obscured by ink blots, or where the handwriting is illegible, the editor has supplied the missing words, if possible. Where the missing words have not been ascertainable, even by conjecture, they have been indicated by brackets and ellipses, thus: [...]. Editorial insertions of a directive character have been enclosed in brackets and italicized, as [*In the margin*]. In some instances, the only copies of Douglas letters located were the author's rough drafts, with interlineations and deletions. The interlineations have been incorporated in the texts; the words or lines crossed out by Douglas have frequently, but not always, been supplied and enclosed in brackets, with an explanatory footnote.

IV

A project of this type obviously could not succeed without the full cooperation and generous assistance of many persons. Acknowledgment is here made to all who responded to the editor's appeal for Douglas letters and who, through their interest, make possible this edition. To name each of them would take more than the space allowed. The editor, however, wishes to express his sincere gratitude to Martin F. Douglas, grandson of the "Little Giant," who not only gave the project his strong encouragement by allowing the editor to examine his collection of his grandfather's papers, but who also extended to the editor the gracious hospitality of his home and family. It is no exaggeration to state that without his encouragement, the project would have faltered long ago. A special debt of gratitude is also due the two universities with which the editor has been associated during the completion of the project, the University of Kansas and the University of Illinois. Grants from the research funds of these two institutions enabled the editor to travel and made possible the reproduction of Douglas' letters on microfilm or photostat, the research necessary for the identification of men and events, and the many typing chores involved in bringing Douglas' letters to publication.

The editor also extends his appreciation and thanks to his colleagues at the University of Illinois, Arthur Bestor and Robert M. Sutton, who read portions of the manuscript, and to those individuals who rendered valuable assistance to the project at various stages in its development: Clyde C. Walton, Miss Margaret Flint, and S. Ambrose Wetherbee, of the Illinois State Historical Library; Mrs. Marion D. Pratt, of the Illinois State Archives; Miss Blanche Jantzen, Miss Margaret Scriven, Miss Ruth Cibulka, and Mrs. Mary Frances Rhymer, of the Chicago Historical Society; Robert Rosenthal, of the University of Chicago Library; Ralph Newman, of the Abraham Lincoln Book Shop, Chicago; Philip M. Hamer, Clarence E. Carter, and Harold W. Ryan, of the National Archives; Mrs. Ralph O. Stratton, of the Ontario County Historical Society, Canandaigua, New York; Mrs. Charles Shons, of the Watertown, Connecticut, Library Association; Arthur W. Thompson, of the University of Florida; E. Merton Coulter, of the University of Georgia; Wallace Farnham, of the University of Alberta; Holman Hamilton, of the University of Kentucky; E. B. Smith, of Iowa State University; and Philip S. Klein, of Pennsylvania State University. Finally, the editor is grateful to George Pilcher, graduate student at the University of Illinois, who served as research assistant; and to Mrs. Don E. Dulany, Jr., and Donald D. Jackson, of the University of Illinois Press, for encouragement and valuable suggestions.

Robert W. Johannsen

Symbols Used in Describing the Letters and Documents:

AD	Autograph Document
ADS	Autograph Document Signed
ADf	Autograph Draft
ADfS	Autograph Draft Signed
AE	Autograph Endorsement
AES	Autograph Endorsement Signed
AL	Autograph Letter
AL Copy	Retained copy
ALS	Autograph Letter Signed
ALS Copy	Retained copy
AN	Autograph Note
ANS	Autograph Note Signed
Copy	Copy, not in Douglas' hand
D	Document
DS	Document Signed
Df	Draft
DfS	Draft Signed
ES	Endorsement Signed
LS	Letter Signed
NS	Note Signed
RG	Record Group

T H E
Letters

―――――

To Julius N. Granger

Dear Sir   Cleveland Sep 20th 1833

You may be somewhat surprised to receive a letter from me at the present time dated at Cleveland;[1] but no one can foresee what tomorrow will bring forth. A few days after mailing my last letter I was taking down with an Inflammatory fever accompanied with the rheumatism, from the effects of which I have not yet entirely recovered.

Both my fever and rheumaties left me a number of days since, so at present I have no disease about me, and may confidently expect to regain my strength so as to be about in a few days. By the attention and skill of my Phisician and the kindness of my friends here I was rendered as comfortable during the whole time as the nature of the disease would admit. Even Mother herself could not have taken better care of or exhibited more kindness towards me than Mr[s] Lathrop the lady with whom I board, had ever since I was taken. Your letter of the 2nd inst. reaced me some two weeks ago, but I was so low that I did not open it till a few days since, when I sent the check to the Bank which they accepted. As for St. Louis, I cannot make any calculation now upon going there or any other place; I shall put off all those things untill I get entirely well and then take a new start. From what I have written I trust that you will all be free from all axiety about me even if I should [not] happen to write quite so often as you may wish or expect; since I am comfortably situated, free from all pain or diseas, in good spirits, gaining strength fast, and in a fair prospect of being about in a very few days. I see some of my Canandaigua friends almost every day, more particularly has this proved true since I have been sick; Messers Payne & Willson, who were reading law at Canandaigua when I left, arrived here a few days since to continue their studies with Mr Andrews:[2] I am expecting also Mr Thomas M Howell son of Judge Howell, every hour from Michigan who may possibly take charge of this Mr. Howell does not arrive; I therefore send this by mail—[3]

AL, owned by Martin F. Douglas, Greensboro, North Carolina. This letter contains no signature. Julius N. Granger was Douglas' brother-in-law,

[1]

having married Douglas' elder sister Sarah on February 14, 1830. Later in the same year, Granger's father, Gehazi Granger, married Douglas' widowed mother. Douglas lived at the Granger home near Canandaigua, Ontario County, New York, from December, 1830, until June, 1833, when he left for the West.

¹Douglas arrived in Cleveland in the latter part of June, 1833, intending to remain there a short time visiting with a first cousin, Daniel P. Rhodes. He determined to lengthen his stay when the opportunity to study and practice law

in Cleveland offered itself. These plans were cut short by the sickness described in this letter. Soon after his recovery, in October, 1833, Douglas set out once again for the West.

²Sherlock J. Andrews, a distinguished Cleveland lawyer and subsequently a member of Congress, took an immediate interest in Douglas and offered him the use of his office and library to further his law studies.

³Payne, Willson, and Howell were classmates of Douglas at Canandaigua Academy. Marcius Willson was Douglas' roommate there.

To Julius N. Granger

December 15th 1833
Winchester Morgan County Illinois

Dear Brother & the rest of the folks—I fear that my negligence in writing has occasioned you great axiety for my safety and welfare. I confess that under existing circumstances such gross remiss on my part was almost unpardonable and that my own sconscience has condemed me, yet, I have put it off from time to time with the promise to myself, that I would write as soon as I should becomed located at any place a sufficient time to write and receive an answer at the same place.

When I wrote you on the 22nd of last September I lay sick with the inflamitory billious fever at Cleveland Ohio. I have since sent you papers from Chilocotha, Cincinatti, Louisville Ky, St. Louis Jacksonville Illinois &c to let you know that I was still in the land of the living— but making some progress towards the "far west"—now you find me in the little town of Winchester in the Sucker State.¹ You may feel anxious to know what has brought me here, my object, motives, future plans and prospects &c—as an answer to which you must be content for the present to learn that I found myself here just at night a few weeks since tired and hungry and after a good supper findind I had fallen into good hands I concluded to take up my winter quarters here, and so here I am as Jack Douning² would say. I am aware that this answer will be far from satisfactory, but to tell the truth I have not yet selected any place for a permanant residence, and finding the season far advanced, determined to pitch up on some place where I could live cheap this winter, do business enough to bear my expenses and pursue my studies until spring, and then accompany the Circuit Court, through their Northern part of the State in their April term, particularly at Galena and Chicago which places are growing into great importance and bid fair to rival *your* Eastern cities. I say *your* Easter[n] cities for

[2]

as far as any division can be said to exist between the East and West I have become a *Western* man have imbibed Western feelings principles and interests and have selected Illinois as the favorite place of my adoption, without any desire of returning to the land of my fathers except as a visitor to see my friends and the improvements that may be made from time to time in the country. As to the country here I can only say that those places I have visited, in fertility of soil, the beauty of location and the ease with which it can be reduced to cultivation exceed all the favorable reports I had ever heard of it, and that as far I have been able to learn will warrant all the apparently extravagant accounts which have been circulated by those who have visited this country. So upon the whole I must say that I am highly pleased with the Western country particularly Illinois—notwithstanding it possesses many disadvantages which time alone can overcome. The impression is very general to the East that this state is very unhealthy, and that Eastern people coming here would be liable to d[is]eases. In part this is true—there are diseases prevalent here which are not at the East, and again there are disease there which are entirely unknown here. Persons coming into the Western States are liable to billious fevers and the fever & ague which is owing in part probably to the decomposition of vegitable matter and decay of timber on the [low] lands or bottoms as they are here called upon [the] banks of the streams and rivers—but is more to [be] attributed to the change of climate and living [or] to the exposure consequent upon such a [journey.] Yet I cannot bring myself to believe that Ill[inois] is any more sickly than all the other new states [or] than the other states are when they were first se[ttled] all of which were subject to billious fevers and the ague more or less and these may be said to be the only diseases known here as far as I can learn. So I feel satisfied that this cannot be considered a sickly state and will as soon as the soil is once brought into cultivation be one of the most healthy portions of the Union. I have only been in the State about six weeks and have never enjoyed better health than during this time, and in fact I may say than since I left Cleveland at which place I had the rubber of which you shall hear hereafter—Be so kind as to write as soon as you receive this for I have not heard from any of you since my last letter—send papers also as often as you can for I am destitute of news. Your affectionate brother

S. A. DOUGLASS[3]

ALS, owned by Martin F. Douglas.

[1]Douglas arrived in Jacksonville around the middle of November, 1833, but finding his finances almost exhausted and with little prospect for employment, he moved on to the small town of Winchester, where he spent the winter teaching school.

[2]Major Jack Downing was a fictitious character invented by Seba Smith, of the Portland (Maine) *Courier*, and widely copied by a number of other

[3]

writers. He was known for his humorous, homespun comments on the events of the day. Smith's most successful imitator was Charles Augustus Davis, who converted Downing into a critic of Jackson.

[3]Douglas spelled his name with a double *s* until the summer of 1846.

To Julius N. Granger

Dear Brother   Jacksonville March 11th 1834

I have delayed answering your letter of Jan 12th until I could ascertain what place on the inhabitable Globe was destined by the Fates to become my future and permanant abode. That point however being settled and Jacksonville having been fixed upon as the favorite place, I am happy to inform you that your humble servant has become permanently located as an attorney and counseller at law and Soliciter in chancery under the most favorable auspices. Upon a full survey of events for the last year I cannot but be forcibly struck with the vicissitudes of fortune and how much the most important events in a persons life depend upon very trifling circumstances. Yet, notwithstanding the changes of fortune to which I have been exposed by sickness and otherwise and the bold steps I have taken within the last year (and perhap many of them were rash and inconsiderate of which my friends must be the judges) I say notwithstanding all these facts and circumstances, yet I am confident in the belief that all of these things will operate to my benefit and these very movements will prove the most fortunate in my life. Perhaps you have not had a full account of my affairs and sickness whilst at Cleveland; and my reason for not informing you was to prevent that anxiety which I knew it would occasion in the bosom of my friends. The sickness to which I alluded was likely for some time to prove fatal, so violent was it that on the third day I was given over by my Phisicians and remained in that hopeless condition for some weeks, and months befor I was able to walk. In this critical condition you may imagine the feeling with which I received your letter at that time containing two hundred dollars. With the money I paid off the demands against me viz two Doct bills 50 dollars each and my board which during my sickness was ten dollars per week and other incidental expenses reduced my funds to the sum of thirty dollars, by an economical use of which I bore my expenses to Illinois and on my arrival in Jacksonville had about five dollars in my pocket. Finding my resources diminished and my health equally as much improved, I took a school in Winchester a small town in this county, where when out of school I was either mingling with the people and forming acquainances or pettifoging in the Justices Court. At the end of the quarter I found myself pretty generally known as a lawyer in that part of the County, popular (as I think) among the "Suckers" and with money

[4]

enough to pay off my expences and purchase a small library. Under these what I call favorable auspicies I have just opened a law office in Jacksonville the county seat of Morgan Co. and probably the finest village in the State. I have been thus minute that you may judge of my true condition, of the course I have taken under the existing circumstances and of my probable success or failure in the future. I repeat what I said above that I do not regret in the least the course I have taken, for wherever I have erred, I have a good lesson before me for the future—in being absent from friends in time of peril I realize their worth and importance—at all times and circumstances—and from every similar state of facts a corresponding lesson can be drawn and will be drawn which I shall make a living guide during my whole life. I have now been in this country long enough to judge with some degree of correctness of the manner in which I shall be pleased with it as a *home*. In my first letter I give you the first impression its apearance made upon my mind; I now add that those opinions have since been confirmed and stregthened by observation and mingling among the people. After all that has been said and that can be justly said of the beauties and natural advantages of Illinois, yet persons who have been accustomed to the older and more densely settled States, must expect to experience many inconveniences and perhaps I may add hardships, if they come here. So without extoling the Country too highly, or inducing you [to] form too favorable an opinion of it I sincerely hope and as confidently expect that you or father or both of you will visit Illinois this coming Summer with a view of moving here. That you might the better understand the Geography of the State, I sent you a map a few weeks ago which I hope you received. I am happy to learn that you settled with Doct Douglass[1] with regard to our claim upon my Grand Father's Estate, and when you come to Illinois you will be so kind as to bring me my share after paying L. L. Morse for another years subscription to his paper and have him send the paper hereafter to Jacksonville Ill.[2] If any thing should happen that you should not come out this Summer perhaps you will have an opportunity of sending to the U. S. B. Bank a[t] Buffalo and getting of them a check on the U. S. B. Bank at St. Louis and then send the check to me here. My love and best wishes to Mother, Sarah, Father and all the rest of the folks. Your affectionate B[r]other

S. A. Douglass

ALS, owned by Martin F. Douglas.
[1]Beriah Douglass, uncle of Stephen. In a letter to Douglas dated June 10, 1832, Beriah discussed the settlement of the estate of Douglas' grandfather, Benajah Douglass, who died in 1829.

The original of Beriah's letter is owned by Martin F. Douglas.
[2]Probably the *Ontario Messenger*, published in Canandaigua, which Douglas continued to read for a time after his arrival in Illinois.

To Nathan Barlow

Dear Sir   Jacksonville Illinois May 14th 1834

    I received a letter a few days since from my Step-Father Mr Granger who states that he had depoisited for me in the Savings Bank at Canandaigua ninety five dollars until further orders concerning it were received from myself. Doct. E H James[1] of Virginia who has been spending a few weeks in Illinois, but is now returning home by way of Canandaigua has been so kind as to advance me the money here, and take a check for the above named ninety five dollars upon the Savings Bank at your place, which check will be presented for payment in the course of one or two days. Upon the receipt of this letter I wish you would do me the favor to send word *immediately* to Mr Granger that he may stand ready to pay off the said check or direct the Bank to do it whenever Doct James shall arrive at Canandaigua. Dr James will take charge of this letter as far as Buffalo where he will put it into the office together with one to Mr Granger,[2] and then visit Niagara falls for a day or so and then proceed upon his journey home, so you will perceive that he will be in your town in one or two days after the arrival of this. Permit me earnestly to press my request upon you as a matter of great importance to me and assure you that my Father & Mother will cheerfully compensate you for your trouble; for I should dislike very much to have the check protested and my friend Doct James discommoded in consequence of his kindness to me. I remain truly your friend

STEPHEN A. DOUGLASS

NB Dr. James will call upon you when he arrives at Canandaigua, and I hope that the business will be so arranged between my Father yourself and the Bank that he will not be detained on his journey. Yours &c

S. A. DOUGLASS

ALS, owned by Martin F. Douglas. Nathan Barlow was a merchant in Manchester, six miles from Canandaigua and not far from the Granger farm.

[1] Edwin H. James had been an assistant surgeon in the United States Army between 1823 and 1833, stationed in Wisconsin and Michigan. A native of Vermont, he was botanist, geologist, and surgeon to Major Stephen H. Long's expedition to the Rocky Mountains in 1819. Following his resignation from the Army in 1833, he was associated for a time with a temperance journal in Albany, New York. Just prior to this, his residence had been in Annapolis, Maryland, not Virginia as Douglas states.

[2] The letter was postmarked at Buffalo on May 29.

Bank Draft

Jacksonville Illinois; May 14th 1834

    The officers of the Savings Bank at Canandaigua will pay E. H. James o[n] order ninety five dollars out of the monies deposited in the

Bank for my use by Gahazi Granger of Manchester Ontario Co NY for value received of me

STEPHEN A. DOUGLASS

ADS, owned by H. F. Sherwood, West Bloomfield, New York. The draft is endorsed by Edwin H. James.

To Julius N. Granger

My Dear Sir   Jacksonville Illinois July 13th-34

I have been kept in anxious suspense for a long time in expectation of receiving news from you. Some six weeks ago I wrote in great haste to Doctor James of Virginia on the subject of that money coming to me from my Uncle at Albany. I have heard nothing either from you or Doctor James, whether he obtained the money or not when he passed through Canandaigua. By informing me upon that point you will relieve my [mind] from the painful apprehensions arrising from the uncertainty in which I am placed.

Up to last week I remained ignorant of all that was agoing on in Old Ontario, except what I could gather from your letters, and from the Newspapers; but I have now the pleasure to informing you that Mr Samuel B Knapp, formerly of the Utica Branch Bank Canandaigua, has just arrived and has given me a pretty good idea of what is passing in Canandaigua. Mr Knapp is so highly pleased with Illinois, that he says he can never think of returning again *only as a visitor*. In refference to the superior natural advantages of this country over any other he has ever seen, or of which he can have any conception, Mr Knapp joins in the common sentiment expressed by all who visit us, that he can never content himself hereafter in any other region. And it seems to him a matter of surprise how he has contented himself so long in New York, whilst there was a country like this at so short a distance abounding in all that can be made subservient to the wants, and that can conduce to the comfort and happiness of man. Nor is this feeling perculiar to Mr Knapp or myself; but is the common sentiment and spontaneous expression of every person who visits Illinois, and who possesses penetration enough to distinguis between what is and what is not calculated to promote his happiness. Under this view of the subject, if I can pursuade you and father to come and see the country for yourselves the rest of my object will be very easily accomplished. For I do not pretend to deny that I am particularly anxious to have you all move to Illinois. I cannot doubt for a moment that Mother & Sarah would be pleased with the idea, and as for you and father you could not but discover that your own interests, your happiness and your *future prospects* all require it. So well am I convinced of this as far as it relates to myself,

[7]

that I can say with the utmost sincerity that no motives of interest, pleasure, ambition or of any other nature could induce me to abandon Illinois. As often as I reflect upon this subject I congratulate myself upon having been so fortunate as to have located in the Paradise of the world. It is now harvest time, and the farmers are busily engaged gathering in their crops. Crops of all kinds are generally good, particularly corn. There will be corn enough raised in Illinois this season to supply the who[le] western country. Farmers raise from fifty to five hundred acres of corn, which will produce from fifty to seventy five bushels per acre. Wheat and corn have been materially injured by the frosts in Ohio & Kentucky and some of the other western States, all of which will opperate to our benefit. Some two or three weeks ago we had very heavy [rains?] which it was feared would produce sickness, but happily our country has never been more healthy at this season of the year than at the present time. I am succeeding here far beyond my expectations, and the prospect before me is fair and flattering. Permit me to urge my resquest that you all come out here. If you have an opportunity of selling your farm immediately, be sure and embrace it, and all come on at once. The law establishing two new Land Offices in the northern part of this State has just passed the house and will probably pass the Senate this session. There are greater bargains to be had now and better locations than there will be at any future time. Land far superior to yours in beauty, in fertility, in location and in every other respect may be had at one dollar & twenty five cents per acre. And these very land five or ten years hence will be worth from five to fifty dollars per acre. The land that was entered at congress price one mile from Jacksonville five years ago is now selling at thirty dollars per acre. Yours &c.

STEPHEN A. DOUGLASS

ALS, owned by Martin F. Douglas.

To Julius N. Granger

Jacksonville Morgan County Illinois

My Dear Sir,   September 21st 1834

A few days since I received a copy of the Ontario Messenger containing your remarks to the Republicans of Manchester, which have served as food, drink, and lodging to me ever since. The pleasure I experienced from their perusal was real and irresistable, arrising from the recollection of former times, and of persons and things connected with them, together with anticipations of the future. The past with all of its attendant circumstances, from the principles of association, rushed upon the mind; whilst the principles asserted in your Speech, and the ability and talent with which you advocated them give the most unequivocal assureances of a glorious future. This was the first intimation, I had received of the manner you stood affected by the Distress, Pressure, and Panic that has prevailed throughout the Union since the Reign of Terror[1] commenced. I perceive however that the same attachment to Democratic principles, and the same deadly hostility to the Aristocracy, which animated you at Coonsville, excites the Republican party to action not only throughout Old Ontario, but the whole State. On this head I have only to say to you that you are certainly right, so "go ahead". In this State the Election resulted favourable to the cause of Democracy Liberty—our three Congressmen all being friendly to the Administration and opposed to *the* Bank, although one of them may be in favor of *a* Bank, unless Gen Jackson tells him better.[2] In the Legislature we have a decided majority, and therefore feel sure of electing a Jackson Senator. Indiana remains sound to the core, the "Whig" papers to the contrary notwithstanding. Noble[3] formerly a Clay man, but now a Johnson[4] man has been reelected Governor in consequence of his being in favor of their Canal, and his opponent being opposed to it. In the Legislature however the Jackson Anti Bank ticket has succeeded by a large majority. In Missouri too we have succeeded equally large majorities, although a local question injured our ticket considerable. Kentucky has gone for the Bank by a small majority. These are all of the Western States in which the Elections have taken place, except Louisiana where we have gained one Congressman. So much for the Elections & Politics—

Now My Dear Sir let me give you a gentle gog that you may wake up and see if you can remember when you wrote me last. I do not claim any great credit for punctuality myself, but it is now a month or two since I wrote a letter, and have since written one or two, and then torn them up because you did not answer my others. In your next I hope you will let me into your secrets as it respects your intention of ever coming to Illinois; and also Father & Mother's and Sarah's feelings on this subject. I forbear at this time to recommend the Country, for as fi[ne] a country as this ought to recommend itself. Just tell Father to write once a year at least, that [I] may see how his pulse beat. As to Mother & Sar[ah] I do not expect them to write, but one would suppose that they might get yourself and father at it some Sunday after having your heads well combed. It is getting late, my lamp is going out and I am growing sleepy, and will therefore quit without any other ceremony than—

STEPHEN A. DOUGLASS

ALS, owned by Martin F. Douglas.
[1]The withdrawal of government funds from the Second United States Bank by President Jackson had caused the bank to contract its credit, a policy which was especially felt in the specu-

lative atmosphere of Illinois. Opponents of the bank accused it of deliberately creating financial uncertainty and hardship in order to impress the public with the need for its recharter.

[2]The three Illinois Congressmen elected in 1834 were John Reynolds, Zadoc Casey, and William L. May.

[3]Noah Noble, a nominal Whig and strong supporter of an internal improvements policy, was elected to his second term as Governor of Indiana in 1834.

[4]Richard Mentor Johnson, a member of Congress from Kentucky, later served as Vice-President under Martin Van Buren.

To Julius N. Granger

My Dear Sir   Jacksonville November 14th 1834

Yours of the 15th Oct is just received. There was one feature of your letter that was particularly interesting and gratifying to me, if I interpreted it right. You know that we are apt to put that construction, upon everything of a doubtful nature, which is most conformably to our wishes. I was under the influence of such feelings that I contrued the following passage in your letter as an intimation that your [family?] were all about to come to Illinois. "We wish you to write soon and give us information of the practicability of [in]vesting capital in that State". Now my Dear Sir, you are aware of the interest I feel in getting you to come to this Sate, and will consider, as you have heretofore, all that I may say of the superior advantages of this country, as mere fictions, existing only in my imagination, or perhaps as exagerations made for the purpose of inducing you to move here. However, what I shall say on this subject shall be my honest opinions, formed from a residence of more than a year in this country. I still entertain the same opinion which I have often expressed, and which I believe is the opinion of every individual who visits this country with an impartial mind that Illinois is the best Agricultural State in the Union; that it contains a greater quantity of good Land; that the Land is of a superior quality; that it presents a more regular, rolling, and beautiful surface; that the Timber and prairie are interspersed in better proportions; that it affords greater facilities for Internal Improvements; and that in short, Illinois possesses more natural advantages, and is destined to possess greater artificial and acquired advantages, than any other State in the Union or on the Globe. The population of this State in 1830 was about 160,000. It is now estimated at from 250 to 300,000. Such has been the increase of population for three or four years past, and the emigration is supposed to be double this year what it has been at any year previous. The emigration to this State this year is of a much better character than that it has been heretofore being composed of the most wealthy, intelligent, and enterprising citizens of almost every State in the Republic, or country on the Globe. Every kind of business here is good, except professional business; for we have Lawyers, Doctors, and Ministers here in abundance. Every man that is industrious and economical gets rich, at any kind of business. Farming however is the most proffitable. Money can be invested to a good advantage in almost any way. The legal interest here is six per cent when no particular bargain is made; but you are not allowed to take over twelve per cent. So a man can do better here than to loan out his money. Money here to carry on any kind of business or to enter Land and depent upon the rise in value is worth twenty five per cent. Land within two miles of this place which was entered four years ago at $1.25 per acre is now worth from $15. to $30. per acre. Town Lots which sold for $10 and $15. eight years ago are now selling at $1,5[oo] [fif]teen hundred. Lands in the Towns and Counties [...] parts of the State have risen in value in nearly the same, and in some places in a great proportion. Do not suppose that all the good land is yet taken up, for not more than two thirds of the Land in this State has yet been brought into market, and a great proportion of that which has not yet been sold is in the very heart of the State, and even superior to any except Morgan & Sangamo[n] Counties. Not more than two thirds of the land in this county are yet entered, ten thousand acres of Land of the very best quality may be found in a body unentered. The County Seats to the New Counties are not yet all settled, now Towns are being laid out every few days, and Lots sold for a mere trifle which soon become valuable. Money makes the more go, and will command any thing. My health is good, and that of the people generally. Yours &c

S. A. DOUGLASS

[*In margin*] The Lands in the upper part of the State are expected to be brought into market between this and next fall, then fortunes can be made easily—

ALS, owned by Martin F. Douglas.

To Julius N. Granger

Jacksonville February 22nd 1835

J. N. Granger, and the rest of our folks, (for all of our correspondence passes under this title). I must apologize for not answering your letter of Decm'r the 23rd sooner, by informing you that I have spent a considerable portion of the Winter at Vandalia,[1] and consequently did not receive it so soon as I otherwise should have done. Our Legislature has now adjourned however, so that I shall hereafter be at home unless absent on the Circuit. You have probably seen from the papers I have sent you that the Legislature, in addition to the important bills the[y] have passed for the good of the State at large, have done something for the

"Widows youngest and only Son." I allude to my election by the Legislature to the office of "*States Attorney*" for the first Judicial Circuit of this State, composed of the Counties of Morgan, Sangamon, Macon, McLean, Tazwell, Macoupin, Green, and Calhoun.[2] The duties of the "States Attorney" are to prossecute all criminals in each county in the Circuit, and also all civil actions in which the People are concerned, the Pres & Directors of the State Bank, any county, or the Auditor of Public &c. The States Atty for compensation receives a Salary of two hundred and fifty dollars for annum, and the fees besides; which, (varying from five to ten dollars in each case, according to the nature of the crime or suit) will make a Sallary of about five or six hundred dollars a year. In addition to this I have the privilege of attending to all other suits the same as my brother Lawyers. From this you will perceive that I can answer Mother's enquiry in the P.S. of your letter; That I am doing as well in my "*profession*" as could be expected of a Boy of twenty one. In my Election I had to run against one of the strongest men in the State. My opponent John J. Hardin,[3] having held the Office two years, and being a descendant of one of the greatest families in *Kentucky* (which in this country is the strongest recommendation a man can have for Office) and also having the influence of the Governor in his favor. But as the *Lord*, and the *Legislature*, and *Gen Jackson* would have it, I beat him four votes on the first ballot. I was sorry to learn that I had in the midsts of my zeal, put a wrong construction on certain passages of your letter in relation to your removal to this country. However I am in some measure consoled with the hope of a visit from yourself, and perhaps father, sometime in the Spring. I trust that you will not disappoint me in this hope. My health has been extraordinarily good, and still contunes the same. In Politics I can only say that the cause of *Democracy* is triuphant, and that the *People* are disposed to retain the advantage they have gained over the aristocracy. Illinois still remains sound to the core, although she has got a *Traitor* for Governor.[4] Tell father, and Mother and Sarah that they must consider, what I say to you in my letters, as said to each of them, as I am compelled to consider your letters as their letters. Give my respects to all of my friends and tell them I should like to see them in the *Sucker* State. Let me hear from you as often as possible. I remain your affectionate Brother.

STEPHEN A. DOUGLASS

P.S. the Notice of my election in the Newspaper calls the office *Circuit* attorney, but the Law terms it "*States*" attorney &c

ALS, owned by Martin F. Douglas.
[1]Vandalia was at this time capital of the state of Illinois.

[2]This was Douglas' first political office. He described the circumstances of his election in a subsequent letter. See

below, Douglas to Granger, May 9, 1835.

[3]John J. Hardin, a Whig and an able Jacksonville lawyer, had been appointed State's Attorney by Governor John Reynolds in 1832. He later served one term in the national House of Representatives. During the Mexican War he recruited a regiment of infantry and was killed at Buena Vista in 1847. In spite of their political disagreement, Douglas and Hardin remained friends throughout the latter's lifetime.

[4]Joseph Duncan, also a resident of Jacksonville and once an ardent supporter of Andrew Jackson, had split with the President over the latter's bank and internal improvements policies.

To Julius N. Granger

Dear Brother & the rest of the folks.   Jacksonville April 25th 1835

I have just returned from the circuit after a tour of about six weeks and am greatly disappointed at not finding a letter in the Office from you, as I wrote just before I left. My Official duties require me to be absent a great share of the time and are of just such a kind as a young man ought to perform to learn him the Practice of the Law in all its various branches and to keep him steady and regularly employed in his profession. I have had so far remarkably fine success since I entered upon the duties of my office. Whilst on my present Tour I have sent two men to the State Prison and have not had an Indictment quashed, to the great mortification of my enemies, and the gratification of my friends. I shall have to leave again tomorrow for the Northern Part of the State to be gone about two weeks, which will close my labors on the Circuit for this Term. I find myself on a new theatre of action, and I may say a very important and critical one, when conducting an important trial alone, with three or four of the best Lawyers in the State on the opposite side ready to take advantage of every circumstance, neither asking favors nor granting them. But I think I shall be able to give general satisfaction. So much for myself, which I acknowledge seems a good deal like Egotism; but I trust you will excuse me upon the ground that I have no body else to write about but myself. Our State is in an exceedingly prosperous condition at the present time. Emigration from all quarters is immense. Money is more plenty[ful] than usual. Our produce brings a fine price and above all our Country [is] very healthy. Capitalists are rushing in from all quarters to take our Bank stock which it is supposed will be very proffitable. The stock [has] all been taken and the Bank will soon go into opperation. Here I must remark by way of explanation that I am no friend to the Banking System but on the contrary am in favor of the real *Bentonian Shiners;*[1] But under existing circumstances a Bank may be necessary in this State in self defense. We collect in the State about seven hundred thousand dollars of Public moneys at the Land Officers which together with a like sum from Missouri is deposited in the Bank of Kentucky at Louis-

[13]

ville and from that place distributed again to the Indian Agents & the Officers of the Army. It was in view of the Public Deposits and Disbursement of Public moneys that our State Bank was established. It is not allowed to issue notes under five dollars, and after a certain period may be restricted to ten. So much for the Bank &c. Now for Politics—and in the first place Huzza for Martin Vanburen & the National Convention. The whigs are making a tremendous effort here to divide the Democratic party by bringing out Judge White.[2] But it wont do. We are determined to all go together and act in concert with our brethern in other parts of the Union. I expected to have seen or heard from you or some of you before this. Owing to some cause—probably the failure of the mails (for I cannot suppose for a moment that you have neglected to write) I have not been greeted with a single line from your pen since sometime in the Winter. You must write in you[r] next particularly about Father & Mother & Sarah and the rest of our folks. And Tell them to answer my letters for they must consider my letters to you as directed to them also. I remain [as] usual your friend & Brother in Politics, Religion, and every thing else.

STEPHEN A. DOUGLASS

ALS, owned by Martin F. Douglas.
[1]A "shiner" was a gold or silver coin. Douglas here refers to the hard-money policy supported by Thomas Hart Benton, Democratic Senator from Missouri.
[2]Hugh Lawson White, United States Senator from Tennessee and former jurist in that state, was a former Jacksonian who broke with the administration over Jackson's support of Martin Van Buren. In 1835, White was nominated for the Presidency by the Alabama and Tennessee legislatures.

To Julius N. Granger

My Dear Brother   Jacksonville May 9th 1835

On yesterday I returned from Court at Pekin after visiting Bloomington, Peoria, and some of the other Northern Towns and upon my arrival I found a letter from you bearing date April 9th 1835, the perusal of which has afforded me a great deal of satisfaction, and has inspired me with the confident hope of much more pleasure in the Fall.[1] Your "Congratulations upon my success" are gratefully received and duly appreciated; fearing however that you in your anxiety for my welfare have drawn conclusions too favorable to my "character abilities and eminence" as a Lawyer and my "diligence, close application, and ardent desire of knowledge" as a Student. I say I fear you may draw too favorable conclusions from the past results, (which I presume have quite equaled the anticipations of my friends) and may imbibe hopes of the future too high to be realized; yet I adhere to the same resolution, with which I left Home nearly two years ago—"never to be a disgrace to my friends nor a nuisance to the community in which I reside" if "diligence, close application, and an ardent desire of knowledge" can "overcome" the "many obstacles" to that "eminence" which you describe with so much felicity in your letter. Neither must you suppose that I am making money so very fast as to become rich, for in this there is a great mistake. Out of the long list of Lawyers that come to this country and settle, there is not one out of an hundred who does *one half* business enough to pay his expenses the first year nor *enough* to pay his expenses for three of the first years. Last year I *charged* more than sufficient to pay my expenses, but find it very difficult even now to collect money enough to pay my little debts when they become due, but as yet I have been able to get along without ever being sued in my life. From this you will perceive that practicing Law in the Sucker State will not make a man rich the first year or two, and that honor is what is termed, *"honor without proffit"*. You "wish to learn the radical & primary cause" of what you are pleased to call "this singular good fortune" "this gratifying preeminince" and you also "wish to learn whether to attribute it to a *real* eminence you (I) have gained over your competitors" or whether like Telemachus you (I) are attended by the inimitable Mentor &c. Now My Dear friend I confess you have put rather a hard question, which I supposed I had answered by telling you that the Lord, the Legislature, and Gen Jackson would have their own way. To be candid, I will tell you the secret. Soon after my arrival in this State, whilst I was keeping School in Winchester the "Panic" alias the "Reign of Terror" of the Bank commenced. When I left my School & came to this place just about a year ago the "Pressure" was in its maridian, and there was the most tremendous excitement here I ever witnessed. All the *weak bretheren* among the friends of the Administration *deserted* and many others were scared, and the party were about to be used up. Some of the *real* friends of Gen Jackson called a public meeting to organize the party, and came to me & solicited me to make a Speech on the occasion to the "Boys" as our Suckers call the "Sovreign People". I took a part in the Meeting and made as good a Speech as I could.[2] The opposition rallied their forces also in order to vote us down, and called all their Lawyers together to the number of twelve and Selected their best to answer me.[3] After he had closed I replied. When he attempted to answer me, but was hissed down by the People and our Resolutions were adopted approving of the Administration & denouncing the Bank. The opposition were much chagrined at this result, and from that time made me the particular object of their malice & abuse. The next week their paper the "Patriot" [of] this place devoted a who[le] column to my benefit for all of which I felt very grateful to the Editor.[4] Judge Lockwood[5] the Judge of this circuit took part in this matter and John J. Hardin then States Attorney, and a newphew of Henry Clay was one of their leaders and he & the Judge did the writing & worked the wires. Things remained in this situation until the August Election and the excitement increased as the Election approached when we carried as we supposed three out of four of our Representatives but lost our Senator in this County. Soon after the Election we discovered that we had been deceived in two of our Rep, they having secretly pledged themselves to the Opposition— leaving only one Rep & no Senator favorable to Gen Jackson. When this result was discovered the opposition were more abusive than ever & bragged that the *"Jackson Party was used up"*. Up to this time I had never dreamed of being a candidate for any Office, but had acted the part I did because I conceived it to be right. But seeing the opposition were determined to put me down, and to starve me out as they expressed themselves, I thought it best to carry the war into "Africa" as of old. I then consulted my friend John Wyatt (remember his name for it ought to be written in letters of gold) one of our Rep and the only on[e] who proved true to the Democratic cause.[6] At that time the States Attorneys were appointed by the Governor with the advice of the Senate for the Term of four years. Hardin had been in office two years and had two more to serve, with the assurance of reelection as Gov Duncan is known to be favorable to him & hostile to any Democrat. Under these circumstances my friend Wyatt & myself were of the opinion that if we could repeal Hardin out of Office & confine Judge Lockwood to the Supreme Bench alone & have a new circuit Judge appointed the opposition would be used up in this part of the State. Accordingly the day before the members started for Vandalia to attend the Legislature Capt Wyatt came to my office & I wrote a Bill repealing the Old States attornies out of office, and making them Elective by joint ballot of both houses of the Legislature. We went to Vandalia together and in the second day Wyatt introduced my "Atty Bill" which after awhile passed both houses and went to the Governor & counsel of Revision for their approval (here let me remark that the Gov & the Judges of the Supreme Court constitute a counsel of Revision a majority of whom can veto a Law) and the Counsel of Revision being a majority of them in favor of Hardin & opposed to the Administration, and knowing that this Bill was intended for Hardin alone as all the other offices of States Attornies were vacant, vetoed the Bill & sent it back to the House of Rep with their objections. Then my friend Wyatt made a speech in favor of the Bill & against the gov &c and then the Bill passes by a constitutional majority it was then sent to the Senate where it passed also with an increased vote & was consequently a Law, the objections of the Counsel of Revision to the Contrary not-

withstanding. Then came the "tug of war" (i e) the election which resulted as you have already seen, although the Gov. two out of the four
Judges of the Supreme Court, our Senator whom I had opposed at
Home in his Election and our two recreant Rep all opposed me with all
the violence usual to the opposition. Whilst at Vandalia I also helped
draft a Bill by which the Judiciary System was revised and the Judges
of the Supreme Court (who formerely held circuit courts in each
county & then met and all together hold a Supreme Court & decided all
cases which had been decided by each of them separately whilst sitting
as a circuit Court) were relieved from the trouble of holding Circuit
Courts & a new set of circuit judges were elected & as a natural consequence we got an impartial and pretty clear fellow in the place of
Lockwood my old enemy & the opposition considered themselves
pretty near *used up* (I use this term because it precisely expresses my
meaning). From these facts you can judge for yourselves "whether this
unexampled success is to be attributed to a *real* eminence over your
(my) competitors" or "whether like Telemachus you (I) are attended
by the inimitable mentor". Perhaps these details of minute circumstances may be tiresome & uninteresting to you, but I am thus particular, that you may see the real cause of my *election*, the *course* I have
pursued since my residence in this State, and the *opposition* I have met
with from the self stiled "Whig Party", and finally that you may see
the result of the whole contest, and then you can judge of the *extent of
the victory* I have gained over them, and the position I now occupy in
regard to the present political situation of the State. Those who
hitherto have been my most violent enemies, have now laid down their
weapons & sued for peace. From my experience here I have found that
no person can be independent in the expression of his sentiments, without incurring the disapprobation of the Opposition. Or in other words
the opposition make it a[n] article of their creed to put down every
person who dares think for himself or has talents & the confidence of the
People, so that he may [not] be in their way hereafter. So confident
am I in this belief that I feel under great obligations to my *opponents*
for "past favors" and sincerely hope that they will continue the same
hereafter. As long as they will do this I shall always know I am right,
and shall have the confidence of the people, and can carry a majority
of them with me. I must confess that although the opposition have
given me "tribulation" heretofore, at the present time I occupy precisely the position I have long wished for *Politically* and *Professionally*.
Since my Election I have devoted myself strictly to the duties of my
office, and to my other business, not omitting however to spend a portion of my time to my Books, which is absolutely necessary of a young
Lawyer. I have now been once around the circuit & have not lost an

Indictment, whereas my friend Hardin used to loose from one third to one half. I do not mention these circumstances by way of *boasting*, but merely that you may have a full account of my whole course since I have been here both good & bad, I confess that I have

AL, owned by Martin F. Douglas. The letter is not complete.

[1]Granger had apparently announced his intention of visiting Illinois later in the year.

[2]Jackson's withdrawal of the government deposits from the Second United States Bank had caused considerable defection among the ranks of Jackson men in Illinois. The meeting described by Douglas was called in March, 1834, for the express purpose of bolstering the Jackson organization in Jacksonville and Morgan County. It was on this occasion that Douglas was said to have received his nickname, the "Little Giant."

[3]Josiah Lamborn, subsequently Attorney General of Illinois.

[4]James G. Edwards.

[5]Samuel Drake Lockwood, member of the state Supreme Court and former Attorney General of Illinois, had examined Douglas in March, 1834, for his license to practice law.

[6]John Wyatt, a Democratic member of the state legislature, had determined to seek Hardin's removal as State's Attorney because of the latter's refusal to support his candidacy for the legislature.

To Julius N. Granger

My Dear Sir   Jacksonville May 24th 1835

When I concluded my last letter, I promised to write you again in a few days and give you my opinions in relation to the course you should pursue in the event of your moving to this State. In relation to this matter, I confess I am at a loss what to advise you. Not, that there are no inducements here for engaging in business, nor opportunity for successfully conducting it, but because you can lay out your money here to a good advantage in almost any kind of business. The most money is made here by speculating in Lands, for which this year presents the finest opportunities that have ever been afforded in this State. A great portion of the Northern part of the State will be brought into market next month by public Sale which will continue 20 days, and then all lands indiscriminately will be sold for $1.25 per acre. Many of the farms which are entered at $1.25 per acre will in a short time sell for $10.00 per acre. Lands about this Town have been entered from 4 to 10 years, and are now selling from six to twenty five dollars per acre say at an average of $12.50. Large fortunes are made by laying out Towns and selling the Lots. By purchaseing Lots in the most flourishing Towns and letting them lay & rise in value as the Towns improve. Money is realy worth twenty five per cent here to invest in either of the above ways. Farming is also a grand business here—raising wheat-corn-& all sorts of produce &c. Money can be made here by raising cattle, horses, sheep, and particularly hogs, all of which can be raised with comparatively but little labor. If a person wishes to labor for [a] living and make money fast he would go to farming. Merchandizing is a tolerably good business, for those who understand it well, and have a sufficient capital to meet all of their engagements. We have but a few such merchants here however, and consequently merchandizing among the Suckers is considered rather a dangerous business. Distilling & retailing Liquors is very proffitable but in these days of Temperance not very honorable, particularly among you Eastern People or "*Yan-kees*" as the Suckers call you. You must come here & choose an occupation for yourself. With the capital you can bring with you, you will be able to make a fortune in Lands without laboring any yourself. I think you had better sell out where you now are and all come along together this fall. If you once come and see this country you will be sure to remove here. By settling your business there and bringing your money along with you, you will save a good deal and also have an opportunity of purchasing here this fall. It is probable that Traveling would improve Sarahs health, and this climate may be beneficial as a change of climate usually is to sick persons. I have no doubt that if Father would come here, he would recover from his *Rheumatism*, for I have never been troubled with them since I have been here. And as for yourself and Mother I believe you now enjoy good health, and I am sure you would have nothing to fear if you should come here, unless it might be a touch or too of the *ague & fever*. During the whole time I have been here I have enjoyed better health than I ever did before for the same length of time. I have not even had a shake of the ague a touch of the Rheumatism nor even of the head ache. I do therefore as sincerely hope that you will all come for good this fall, as I do believe that it would be for your interest to do so. If you conclude to all com[e] this fall, just let me know it, and I will have a house ready for your reception. Tell mother that board is from $1.50 per week to $3.00 avarage about $2.00 per week. I have paid all of these prices since I have been here. When at Vandalia last Winter I paid $[. . .]o. When on the circuit my expenses are about $1.00 per day or a little more. I should have given you this Suplement to my answer to your letter before this but have been absent apart of the time since & the great Spring Races came on in the mean time, which is a time of great interest here. In your next give me a general view of things as they really are in Old Ontario. Remember me particularly [to] father & mother & Sarah and generally to all the other people with whom I am acquainted. Permit me again to take an affectionate farewell until you hear from me again.

S. A. Douglass

ALS, owned by Martin F. Douglas.

To Joseph Duncan

[September 22, 1835, n.p.; DS, Illinois State Archives, Springfield. Petition to Governor Joseph Duncan, asking that Charles Emerson, a Decatur attorney, be appointed to the office of Probate Judge for Macon County. The petition is in the hand of Dan Stone, and was signed by Stone, Thomas Lord, Josephus Hewett, Joseph Williams, Edward Dickinson Baker, Stephen A. Douglas, and ten others.]

To Gehazi Granger

Dear Father   Jacksonville Nov 9th 1835

I embrace the opportunity afforded by Julius return, to write you a few lines. It is unnecessary for me to say to you that I was greatly rejoiced to see Brother Julius in this Country, and to learn from his lips those behind, who are dear to me above all others in this world, are in good health and enjoying all the blessings of prosperity. I had been absent from Town on a long and wearisome tour on the circuit in the discharge of my official duties, and had just returned to take a week or two of leisure and ease, when to my great surprise and satisfaction, as if it had been so decreed by Him who rules the universe, I met no other than Brother Julius to enjoy my leisure with me and delight me with a detail of what had happened to our friends in distant lands. But I am sorry to say that his stay here is to be as short as it has been pleasant to me. I shall not attempt to say anything in this Letter about myself, and my situation, and prospects. Julius has been here and he can give you more satisfaction upon that subject than I can. Perhaps I may say the same in reference to the country, its delightful climate, its beautiful roling surface, its rich productive soil, and the great and unexampled advantages it offers to those who may choose to emigrate to it. But Julius' visit here has been at an unhappy time for him to form a favorable opinion of it. It is true [he] has rode over the Prairies and has seen their black and luxurient soil, fields of corn containing from fifty to five hundred acres, and yielding from sixty to eighty bushe[l]s to the acre. He has seen the stubble where the wheat had been gathered, which would show him where a similar crop had been raised. He has seen large farms for raising stock composed of a part Prairie and a part Woods with brooks of ever living water winding their way through them. But he has not been here in the month of June to see the Country in its bloom, to see the Prairies covered with young cattle feeding upon the green grass to see the fields of corn and wheat and Oats and Potatoes and every kind of fruit that can be raised in a Temperate Climate. I say he has not seen this Garden of the World in its beauty and its loveliness nor can he see it unless he comes here at a different season

[20]

of the year, and remains more than one week at a time. I will not for I cannot anticipate what may be Julius' opinions of this Country, unless I conclude that he is like all other intelligent and well informed men and consequently he must like the country, and concur with them in saying that it is superior to any other they have ever seen. There is another subject I wish to say a few words about and that is the subject of Politics. The people of this country are more thoroughly Democratic than any people I have ever known. They are democratic in principle and in Practice as well as in name. For every body is willing to assume that name, for the purpose of accomplishing his designs. But here equality and equal rights prevail. And no man acknowledges another his superior unless his talents, his principles and his good conduct entitle him to that distinction. Democratic principles and Democratic measures as professed and acted upon in New York are popular and becoming more popular every day among the People of this Country. The people of this State have ever give[n] Gen Jackson and his administration a warm and enthusiastic support, and will give Van Buren and Johnson a larger majority than they ever did Jackson. Perhaps I place an undue importance upon this Democratic character of the People of this State. If so it is to be attributed to my ardent and fervent attachment to that character and the principles which are the result of it. However this may be, I am firmly and decidedly of the opinion that those are matters not to be overlooked by a young man who feels an interest in the Politics and Political fate of his Country. I am free to confess that the character of the People of this Country, the Political principles that prevail here, and the bright and allureing prospects that greet and cheer on a young man and invite him to action, had a great influence on my mind in inducing me to remain here. And I will also confess *to you* that these considerations weigh upon my mind and add an additional charm and a brighter lustre to the beauty of the rolling Prairies and majestic woods with which our Country abounds. You may consider this vanity in me, and I confess it is. But it is a feeling that will obtain a place in every persons bosom who comes to this country and has a taste for those things, and who sees the advantage to be derived from them, and the benefits he can bestow upon others and upon his country. Whilst on this subject I cannot help expressing the pleasure I have experienced dureing the last year or two in watching the course, of Julius and the progress he has made, improvement and the reputation he has deservedly obtained for talents. Perhaps you are not aware of the fact that I have received in the New York Evening Post each of Julius' Speeches in the Ontario Co Conventions. On this subject I can say to you what it would not do to say to him for he would think I was flattering him. But I do think I perceive something in *Julius' mind* and in the *Speeches* he has made, which indicate greater intellectual powers than is common for a man of his age and opportunities to possess. If he applies himself to study as closely and improves as rapidly as he had done for the last few years, I confidently expect to see him one of the brightest ornaments of the Democratic Party of your State. He certainly possesses sufficient genius and natural powers, if once cultivated and brought into action, to make one of the first men in the country. I hope therefore that you will encourage him to press forward in the same course he has so nobly begun that he may rise to that station for which nature intended him. There is no necessity for yourself or Julius either, laboring and toiling to make money. You have already emassed sufficient to support yourself and Mother during your lives, and then leave enough for you[r] Children. And as for Julius there is no probability of him and Sarah's having any body besides themselves to support. I ask then what is the necessity for toiling and wearing yourselves out for the sake of wealth when you do not need it. And more especially when Julius by perseverence and study may become one of the most eminent and most useful of America's Sons. I have been threatening in my own mind to write to you on this subject ever since I received Julius Speeches in the Post. I have been more frank and free on this subject to you that I would have dared to be to any one else. I would not wish Julius to see that part of this letter which refers to himself, because even a just tribute of praise and commendation to merit is apt to have an unhappy effect on the subject of it, by inspiring him with the belief that there is no more need of further application. I do not belief that Julius has even as great a share of vanity as most young men, but I can say from what experience I have had, that the expression of approbation has its effect. Julius is naturally rather modest and it may be necessary for you to push him forward sometimes in your public meetings and conventions, for I am sure his services may be of great importance to the democratic Party, and if exerted will be appreciated by the Party. I have already spun this letter out to too great length, but the truth is, when I get to writing and particularly on the subjects touched upon in this, I never know when to stop, for I cannot say enough. Before I close I wish to say a word or two to you about coming to this country. It is true that I feel so great an interest about your coming here I am liable to take a one sided view of things, that is, it is possible that I fancy the advantages to be greater than they really are, and pass the disadvantages over unheeded. But if I do err in this particularly the error is unintentional. I am candidly of the opinion that this country offers greater inducements to emigrants than any other on the Globe. There is this difference between emigrating to this country and to any other or between this country and the first settlement of New York. There you have to make roads into the wilderness, cut down the Woods and clear the land before you could raise a crop. Here the Prairies furnish good natural roads which without any working except bridges across some of the small creeks and Rivers furnish a safe and easy passage to travellors. The Country is divided into woods and Prairies in just proportions and better cleared and more easily cultivated than even your beautiful farm in Old Ontario. The population of the country is different from that which usually settles new countries. In short this country as soon as settled enjoys all the benefits of Old settled countries. Society, Schools, Churches, News papers and all the appendences of an old settled Country are to be found here. But of this Julius can give you more satisfaction than I can. If perchance he should happen to agree with me. For I am not able to say what description he will give of this Country only I feel confident it cannot be unfavorable. The rage for speculation in Lands runs high. Fortune after fortune is made as it were magic, by entering Lands at $1.25 per acre and selling them again at advanced prices. Without performing a particle of labour you might make four fold the money you now do off your farm by all your labor and industry. More money can also be made at raising grain, cattle, horses, Sheep, hoggs, or at any branch of Agriculture than can by the same amount of labor by one half in New York. A man of your capital here can make money with or without work. I know these statements have sounded in your ears time and time again, and have been published in the public prints until they are familiar to every School Boy. But the truth cannot be told too [much], tis' for that reason I reitterate them. I have [...] trespassed too long upon your time and patience, and will conclude by asking you to come and see for yourself, for I speak of things which eye hath heard and which being seen and heard can be understood. I wish to be affectionately remembered to Mother and Sarah, and wish you to say to them that I gratefully acknowledge the receipt of those articles and the money they forwarded to me by Julius. Give my best respects to Maria & Miller, Ermino & Henry, and all the rest of my friends and acquaintances. I have ordered to be sent to you the Illinois State Gazette printed at this place, supposing it would be interesting to you and sincerely hoping that it will be received each week in remembrence of me. I wish you would write to me and give me your views of matters and things in general. Although heretofore I have generally directed my letters to Julius I intended them for each and all of you, and hope they were received as such. Until you hear from me again permit me to subscribe myself your affectionate son and obedent servant.

STEPHEN A. DOUGLASS

ALS, owned by Martin F. Douglas.

To the Democratic Republicans of Illinois

[December 31, 1835]

To the Democratic Republican citizens of Illinois:—With a view to urge upon the republican party of this state, concert of action, to promote harmony, and to dissipate objections, as well as to represent to the people the motives of the members of the state convention, which recently assembled at Vandalia to nominate candidates for electors friendly to the election of Martin Van Buren to the presidency, and Richard M. Johnson to the Vice Presidency, the undersigned, in compliance with the directions of said convention, address their fellow citizens and political friends; asking of them a candid scrutiny into their conduct and motives; believing, as they do, that the origin and proceedings of the convention are to be found in the purest principles of democracy; and are to be sustained, by the lovers of the institutions of our happy country—

That "the people have a right to assemble together in a peaceable manner; to consult for their common good," is a noble declaration of the constitution of our state; and contains in it the best gem of democracy, and is of so exhalted a character, and of such essential utility, as to place its propriety beyond all controversy. The depositories of liberty, and of power, the people, by frequent exercise of this constitutional privilege will be sure to maintain their just influence in the management of the political affairs, and will always preserve that ascendency over aspirants for power and dangerous distinction, which unholy ambition and love of glory too often instil into the hearts of men who, perhaps without being fully aware of it prefer personal aggrandizement to the happiness, and prosperity, and liberties of their country.

The convention which assembled at Vandalia, met in obedience to the will of the constitution, was respectable to numbers, consisting of delegates from a very large portion of the state; and unquestionably through them was made a very fair expression of the feelings of the democracy of those parts of the state, from which those delegates respectively were sent; and it is not to be doubted but that they expressed, not only their own opinion, but the opinion of those by whom they were delegated. They acted in a representative character, responsible to the will of the people, and bound by every tie of honor, confidence, and personal esteem, to regard their wishes.

To guard against misrepresentations, and the clamor of our political opponents, who to swell their numbers and defeat the objects of the friends of Martin Van Buren and Richard M. Johnson, are very vehement in the condemnation of conventions, and who, to raise and court the prejudices, of the people of this State, happily always watchful of their rights and liberties, are associating conventions with the words "caucuses," "juntos," and "dictation;" it is thought advisable to warn our friends against the misrepresentations of their opponents, and to declare, that our only object is to induce the friends of democracy to act together; to embody and give effect to the popular will; to maintain their ascendency, to unite their efforts; and general union, to triumph in the maintenance of those genuine principles of democracy, which the people love, and which will continue the power in their own control, to be exercised at their pleasure, obedient to their desires, and under their direct and positive influence. To this end it is recommended, that care be taken that these conventions emanate directly from the people, be held at some central point, and at a time of which all shall be aware. The republican party, friends to the administration, and to the adoption of conventions, would in defence of themselves, (if defence can be considered necessary) remonstrate against being connected with the use of "caucuses," those midnight and dangerous instruments in the employ of our opponents by which they effect their control over the public mind; we would urge upon our friends to avoid caucuses and to resist their influence, by which candidates, apparently coming from the desires of the people, are frequently the tools of those caucuses, pledged to a few, and opposed to the popular will, and, by secret concert, defeating it. Our desire is, that our republican friends should not participate in caucuses; but, when advisable, to act in concert by use of primary meetings, and consultations, publicly notified, and regulated in a manner, which every citizen in the state, may exercise his legitimate influence in the control of the party and its candidates.

Before the system of conventions are condemned, we would ask an enquiry into the political character and conduct of those who for the most part reprobate it, (for we admit that there are honorable and worthy exceptions.) Are they not men who have for a long time been enlisted in the federal ranks? acting in concert among themselves, to take advantage of any divisions which might happen in our political party, to ride into power against the will of a majority? If those who object to conventions would point out some other plan of promoting concert of action, we would cheerfully adopt it; but until that is done, we see no impropriety in frequently recurring to first principles; freqently holding primary meetings, frequently consulting together, and uniting by means of conventions, conducted by fair open and honorable principles, to preserve union and harmony among the people.

In the early stages of our government, when the name of Washington was in itself a rallying point for all parties, and no one thought of disputing his claims for the presidency, and while the struggles of that good man in favor of the liberties of the people, were yet fresh in their minds no effort was necessary to concentrate public attention upon a single individual as the most desirable person to fill the highest office in the gift of a free people; but as time imparted its changes to men and things, it soon became apparent, that an office of so elevated a character as that of president of the U. States, would not fail to be sought after by the most eminent of our citizens, from different parts of the Union, of different political principles, and to reconcile and obviate the difficulties which might ensue from a too great and violent competition for this office, caucuses were first held by members of congress, to nominate candidates. This course was pursued for a number of years; and as it was found objectionable, since it might lead to corruption and bargain, by which the members might be seduced from the true course of patriotism, conventions were then resorted to, as a means by which caucuses might be put down, and the views and desires of the people, through delegates fresh from them and expressly instructed, could be best ascertained. This proceeding, experience has sanctioned, and its usages in some shape or other have been adopted by all the states of the union. In May last, a convention respectable in numbers, and composed of members eminent in capacity and possessing a large share of the confidence of their fellow citizens, met at Baltimore, and nominated as the most suitable candidates for the presidency and Vice presidency, Martin Van Buren and Richard M. Johnson. These individuals were selected not only on account of their distinguished merits which have been long known to the people of this union but as the persons best calculated and endowed by habit, education and practice, to carry out and support those essential principles of liberty and justice, defined by the constitution, and known to be the will of the people,—principles which have marked, distinguished and elevated the political course of Andrew Jackson, with whom, in the prosecution of his effective and well advised measures, they have been efficient and cheerful coadjutors; sustaining him in peril, and cooperating with him in the great contests for the integrity of the union, and for the preservation of the constitutional liberties of the people; whether against the impending, insidious, and dangerous doctrines of nullification, or against the aristocratic and baneful influence of a monied institution, which was striving by the most industrious, fascinating and ingenious maneuvers, to coil itself around the liberties of the people, to control or crush them.

To secure the election by the people, of the nominees of the Baltimore convention, ought to be a primary consideration; and to effect this, the only course is for the friends of democracy to sustain the choice of their delegates, to unite in their efforts, and to keep a steady eye upon the great principles which they are desirous to foster; watching with caution, the exertions of those who are struggling to divide, that they may the more easily conquer. To promote our disunion every stratagem of the wily politician is exercised, local prejudices have been appealed to, envy has been excited, pride and ambition have been courted, candidates of every political party have been brought into the field, urged upon the people without success, and finally abandoned; upon any of which candidates, no matter how opposed to each other in principle, they are all willing to unite; if by that means the candidate of the people, selected by the Baltimore Convention, can be defeated. —White, Webster, Harrison and others are in turn lauded and sought to be raised; unquestionably with a view to withdraw from the democratic ranks, a sufficient number to bring the presidential election before the H. of Representatives; and there by bargain & corruption, and a course by which the most daring and vicious is most certain of success, to secure the election of some person who will distribute favors to new aspirants, change the unpolluted course of the free stream of democracy which now runs thro' every act and rule of the administration, and taint it with the rancor of bitter and illiberal federalism.

The cry of "no party" is raised to disarm the people, and to lull to sleep that eternal vigilance which is the price of liberty. Yet we see in the exertions and actions of our opponents, all that anxiety and industry to unite in party discipline, which, if not resisted, is sure to be successful, and will overthrow the laudable exertions of others, who may rely with too much safety upon the purity and integrity of their motives and thereby fail to act with sufficient concert and energy. It is not our intention to censure opposing partizans. We only invite union among ourselves, to prevent their success; we appeal to the democracy of the country to sustain their principles, and caution them not to be thrown off their guard by the cry of "no party," and the alarm of "dictation," raised to exite their prejudices and to arouse their fears. That is not dictation, which the people demand, and which has emanated spontaneously from themselves.

To "divide and conquer," has been an old artifice, and however specious the means which may be used to effect this purpose, it is hoped, that the scheme will be penetrated and defeated, and that neither the cunning nor the treachery of our opponents will be allowed to prevail.

Mr. V. Buren has, from Attorney Gen. for the state of N. York, risen step by step until he has occupied every intermediate post to that of governor. In the senate of the United States he has been a distinguished actor; and was appointed by our present venerable chief Magistrate, who is authorized, as the only exhalation he requires, in the hearts of his people, and whose entire confidence and esteem he possesses, first to act in the responsible character of secretary of state, and next as minister to the court of St. James, from which latter office he was recalled by the manifestation of a spirit in the senate, which it is hoped will never again suffer itself to prevail. But the people, to evince their estimation of his merits, and their marked disapprobation of his enemies, soon repelled any imputation of fault which such a proceeding was calculated to elicit, by elevating him to his present distinguished standing in our government.

His opponents deny him any merits, and are so extravagant in their abuse, as to render it almost unnecessary to enter into a refutation of their aspersions. In the malevolence of their opposition, they would rob him of every claim to confidence from the democracy of his country, and the illiberal spirit of all uncharitableness, overreached and defeated their own ends. But his upright, and able, independent course in sustaining Gen. Jackson in the distinguishing events of his popular administration, added to the numerous other evidences before the people, of his ability to fill the highest office in the union, recommend him to our support. The "magician" who had capacity and power but a short time since to work miracles in the public mind, and to control and direct the president himself, is now condemned as a man possessing but moderate attainments, and is denied the meagre praise of mediocrity in talents. But such sudden and unaccountable changes in the expressed opinions of his opponents, only serve to show that their opposition does not proceed from any well grounded objections to the individual, but to the principles which have controlled and distinguished his actions.

In pursuing their violent opposition, it is repeated, that the friends of Mr. Van Buren endeavor to bolster his claims and support them upon the merits of Gen. Jackson. Although we associate the name of Martin V. Buren with that of Gen. Jackson, it is not from any deficiency of merit in Mr. V. Buren. The leaders of parties who contend for principles, become for some time identified with those principles, and their names are used as an index to the leading measures which they have sustained. We often say of a man, he is of the Jefferson or Jackson school; but these are mere terms of discrimination, adopted for convenience. The supportors of Mr. Van Buren connect his name with that of Jackson because Andrew Jackson is the most recent and prominent of those brilliant men who have most eminently sustained the great principles of liberty, and extended their benefits; therefore their names are associated—they have been co-workers in the good cause—striving together and repelling with perfect unanimity the efforts of the aristocratic and federal organs of the land.

Richard M. Johnson, the candidate for Vice President, has also received numerous proofs of the confidence of the citizens of his state, and the uniform course which he has pursued in the councils of the nation, marked as it has been by the most pertinacious adherence to the rights of the people, and bearing the highest evidence of attainments of a most elevated character, eminently entitle him to the confidence of the people. In truth, so unanimous is public opinion in his favor, that the old leaven of aristocratic federalism, which is stirring the scattered fragments of opposing parties, to concentrate them against the democratic candidate for the presidency, does not attempt to bring out any individual to defeat his claims.

To enumerate in brief terms the principles of political action, which have won enduring civic laurels to grace those which are already adorning the brows of our present chief magistrate as a military chieftain and which his friends demand should be carried out and perpetuated by his successor, we would simply remark, that he has been governed by a strict construction, preserving the rights of the states, and the supremacy of the general government, avoiding that dangerous latitudinal course, which would lead, no one knows whither, which has no definable bounds, and which is pregnant with the most dangerous consequences. He has conducted our foreign relations in a manner, which has strengthened the bonds of amity, and extending our commercial prosperity, opening new avenues for the enterprize of our citizens, and unfolding an extensive field for personal and national aggrandizement.—The rights and claims of our citizens he has vindicated with a firmness and propriety, which while it commands respect abroad, awakens the admiration and warmest patriotism of our citizens at home.

The policy, alike humane and wise, of removing from within the borders of civilizations, the remnants of the aboriginal tribes, who were learning the vices of the whites without imitating their virtues, thereby adding to their native ferocity, the worst depravities of civilized life, cannot but meet the approbation of all. It commends itself to the head and heart of every politician and christian.

To afford the agriculturalist those advantages which his pre-eminent importance to society entitle him to claim, as well as to extend the settlement of our western country, and to add to our revenue, it has been the settled policy of the present administration to effect a reduction in the price of public lands; an object which it is hoped will soon be accomplished.

The United States bank, that powerful instrument in the hands of an aristocracy, wielding an immense amount of capital and furtively endeavoring, by the most unwarrantable means, to mould and direct public opinion, and to cripple the independence and energies of the government, is now expiring. A timely and firm resistance has subdued its influence and the few who at first doubted, are now free to admit, that the union is well rid of a dangerous engine, which had too great a control over the happiness and liberties of the people. A resistance to monopolies is a principle which will be sure to fasten itself upon the affections of the people and to restrict their illegitimate influence, will always be the aim of the genuine patriot. By a judicious course of economy, in the administration of affairs, the public debt has been paid off, and we now see the unparalleled instance of a large and widely extended government, free from debt and possessing a surplus revenue!!!

The candidates which we commend to the support of the democracy, are bound by the strongest ties of obligation and honor, as well as by education and inclination, to continue in the same wise and beneficent course which has gained for Andrew Jackson so much honor and esteem. It is to perpetuate the same course, that we desire to see the elevation of Martin Van Buren and Richard M. Johnson. Their devotion to the genuine principles of democracy and good government, guaranteed to us by the constitution, are unquestionable. Having always acted in conformity with the interests and wishes of the people, they will undoubtedly regulate their future conduct by the same rules and motives of action; as it is only by such a course that they can gain honor or regard. Therefore we would appeal with the most sincere earnestness, to the democracy of our country, to unite for the support of those principles, which have sustained us in our prosperous and happy condition, pressing upon them the propriety of concert of action, and union in effort; warning them to guard against the artifices and intrigues of opponents, no matter how concealed under specious pretexts and pretenses. We would as the lovers of freedom and the unimpeachable principles of democracy, urge upon them to discard sectional pride and jealousies, to relinquish personal preferences, to the support of principles, which if abandoned, would deprive our government of its power and usefulness, and would hazard the peace and repose of society. Let the democracy offer up all prejudices and predilections upon the alter of principle, and making a generous sacrifice, rally around the constitution and those distinguished individuals selected by a majority of their friends as the most competent and best calculated to support and sustain it in all its pristine force and efficacy.
Vandalia, Dec. 31, 1835.

JAMES TURNEY
S. A. DOUGLASS
E. PECK
DANIEL GREGORY
JAMES SEMPLE
EDWARD SMITH[1]

Vandalia *Illinois Advocate,* February 17, 1836. At a state convention of the Democratic party, held in Vandalia, December 7, 1835, to nominate Presidential electors favorable to Van Buren and Johnson, Douglas was appointed to the committee to prepare an address to Illinois Democrats. The address has usually been attributed to Douglas' authorship. This meeting was one of the early steps taken by Democratic leaders to introduce the convention system into local politics, as a means of enforcing party unity and regularity. The convention met at the capital on the opening day of the legislative session, since most of the delegates were also members of the legislature. Douglas played a leading role throughout this formative period in persuading his fellow Democrats to adopt the convention system, eventually forcing the opposition to follow suit.

[1]Turney (of Greene County) and Semple (of Madison County) were former Attorneys General of Illinois; Ebenezer Peck had arrived in Chicago from Canada early in 1835 and took an immediate part in Cook County political affairs. Turney, Semple, and Smith (of Wabash County) were members of the state legislature. Gregory (of Shelby County) had been an unsuccessful candidate for the legislature in 1834.

To Julius N. Granger

My Dear Sir   Jacksonville Jan 7th 1835 [1836]

I owe you an apology for neglecting to write you so long. I went to Vandalia soon after you left to attend the Supreme Court & a Special Session of the Legislature and only returned Home day before yesterday. Whilst there I could hear nothing from you and when I returned I went to the Post Office in vain. I received a letter from you dated at St. Louis informing me of some very flattering compliments bestowed upon my character and that of my friend John Wyatt. My friend permit me to make this request of you. When you travel in the western country again be sure for my sake that you do not ride on a Steam Boat, for judging from what you heard near Louisville and on the Illinois River I infer that my character does not stand very fair on the water. Your suspicions in regard to the man abusing me on the Steam Boat are correct. He is a notorious desperado, devoid of character, was arrested for whipping his wife it became my duty to prosecute him, and had him fined $50. under the Corporation Law of the town and also convicted in the circuit court and divorced from his wife. The threats of such men do not frighten me. I come in contact with them too often to be intimidated by this blustering. I go prepared for such animals in real *"Kentuck style"*. I[n] relation to the money you deposited in my hands at the time I can only say that the week after you left I went and examined a number of tracts in this county and made choice of two 80 acre Lots under the Bluffs near the Illinois River below Naples, and immediately proceeded to Springfield to enter them, but on arriving at the Land Office I ascertained that they were attached to the Edwardsville District, and could not be entered until the Office at Edwardsville should be opened again. The tracts selected are situated under the Bluffs, extending out into the Prairie Bottom, and also up on to the points of the Bluffs, composed of about one third timber and the rest Prairie. I shall invest your money as soon as I can conveniently. Our Legislature have been engaged a great portion of the time in political Matters. You will observe from the News papers that Resolutions have passed both Houses in favor of Bentons expungeing Resolutions.[1] And that our State Senate have nominated Hugh L. White of Tennessee for President.[2] This fact unexplained is calculated to leave the impression that this State is favorable to the Judges pretentions. The nomination was obtained by the most fraudulent means. Two of the Senators who voted for the nomination were Van Buren men up to the time they gave the vote, and were immediately placed upon the White Electorial Tickett, from which facts the conclusion is irristable that they were bought up, and so it will be received by the people. One Van Buren Senator was absent by sickness. Under these circumstances White was nominated by one Majority. In the Lower House Van Buren is supposed to have a majority. The Canal Bill[3] has passed the Lower House its fate in the Senate is uncertain. You must write to me often, but do not use a silver Pen as I am now doing, for if you do I cannot read your letter. Give my love to Father & Mother & Sarah and the rest of the folks, the fact is I am in great haste so good Bye.

S. A. DOUGLASS

ALS, owned by Martin F. Douglas.
[1]Both houses of the legislature approved resolutions in December, 1835, instructing Illinois' Senators to support Thomas Hart Benton's proposal to "expunge" from the record Clay's earlier resolutions censuring President Jackson for his removal of the government deposits from the Second United States Bank. Clay's resolutions were adopted in March, 1834; Benton first introduced his "expunging" resolution at the end of the session, in June, 1834.
[2]On December 19, 1835, the Illinois Senate, by a vote of 13 to 12, nominated Hugh Lawson White for the Presidency. Many of White's supporters claimed to be true Jackson men, but disliked Martin Van Buren.
[3]The canal bill referred to by Douglas was one of many such bills during this period designed to implement construction of the Illinois and Michigan Canal. This particular bill would authorize the Governor to borrow $500,000 upon the faith and credit of the state in order to commence construction of the canal immediately.

To Henry Howe

My Dear Friend and Teacher.   Jacksonville, Illinois Jan 14th 1836.

Judging from the kindness that I have heretofore received at your hands, and of the many proffs you have given of a desire for the prosperity of all your pupils, I have presumed that you would feel an interest in perusing a few lines from one who is free to acknowledge that he is indebted to your instruction, your counsels and advice more than anything else for what little success he may [have] had in his outset in life. I have this motive in writing to you; the first and principal one of which is to inform you where I am, to the end that you will find time, notwithstanding your arduous duties, to write to me and inform me of your own health and that of your family, and of the success of the Academy and its students, and of the progress you are making in the many benevolent and moral Institutions with which you are connected. Since I left Canandaigua I have been able to learn a very little of what was transpiring there. I saw Mr. Samuel B. Knapp[1] here last year who was the only person I have seen from Canandaigua. You will probably recollect Bryant[2] who was at the Academy whilst I was there and left to visit his friends in Kentucky. I am happy to have it in my power to tell you that he entered the Transylvania Law School at Lexington Ky and pursued a regular course of studies and at the recent Commencement received his *Diplomy*. Mr. Bryant is now in this place looking for a place to permanently locate himself. I cannot doubt Bryant will do well from the evidence he now exhibits. He often speaks of you and expresses his gratitude for the course of instruction and discipline that you established in the Academy. I sincerely hope that all of my old schoolmates will succeed as well, for I have not been able to hear from any of them. I would really be glad to hear what has become of Bull, Germaine, Griswold, Adams, *Ambrose Spencer,* Codding, Bennett &c &c. I also feel a great interest in the class of younger men or Boys, among whom are John Bull, George Hubbell, Selden Marvin &c &c.[3] You will indulge me in saying a few words about myself, although I may *smatter* of the *Egotist*. I left Canandaigua as you will recollect in June 1833 for Cleveland in Ohio where after a few weeks I was taken sick with the Billious fever and was confined to my bed until sometime in October, when I took a boat for Cincinatti thence to Louisville, St. Louis and to this place where I have since remained. Upon my arrival here I was reduced in funds to less than five dollars, and was under the necessity of teaching a Common School for one Quarter at the expiration of which time I obtained a License to practise Law and opened my Office in March 1834. I pursued my proffession with sufficient success to yield me a handsome support until February 1835 when I was elected by the State Legislature to the Office of States Attorney which station I now occupy. In the discharge of my official duties I am required to be absent on the circuit a great portion of the time. Whilst at Home however I enjoy the advantages of good society and of Literary and Religious Institutions. I must excuse myself or rather you must excuse me for having become the Hero of my own Story. I have done so however hoping that it might be interesting to you after the wearisome labors of your School. You can say to my acquaintances in the Academy that I have been as successful as could reasonably have been expected, and sufficiently to afford me a comfortable support. It is useless for me to attempt to give you a description of this country for I discover the public prints are filled with articles upon this subject. You will find the most accurate information about Illinois in the works of Judge Hall of Cincinatti formerly of this State.[4] I will add however that Illinois actually sustains a more elivated character in Morals and Religion than she is generally represented to do. In this Town we have a College with about one hundred and twenty five students—one Female Academy with a large number of young Ladies in it a number of good Common Schools,—a Presbyterian, a Congregationalist, a Methodist, a Baptist and an Episcopal Church. Each of these denominations have comfortable Houses and respectable congregations. We have also many benevolent Societies, among which are the Temperace, Education, missionary societies and a Lyceum &c &c. I must beg your pardon for having trespassed so long upon your patience. Permit [me] to close by earnestly requesting that you will favor me with a reply, and by subscribing myself your pupil and friend

STEPHEN A. DOUGLASS

P.S. Please send me the reports of the Lyceums &c other societies from time to time in New York.

Copy, owned by Mrs. Morgan Phelps Noyes, Dorset, Vermont. The original of this letter has not been located. Henry Howe was Principal of the Canandaigua Academy at the time Douglas was a student there.

[1]Knapp had been a Canandiagua banker. See above, Douglas to Granger, July 13, 1834.

[2]Probably Henry L. Bryant of Rushville, New York, who attended the Canandaigua Academy in 1831-32.

[3]The names referred to by Douglas in this and the preceding sentence were students from Canandaigua or its vicinity who attended the academy at some time during Douglas' stay there.

[4]James Hall was the author of several books describing Illinois, among them being his two-volume *Sketches of History, Life, and Manners in the West*, published in 1834 and 1835. An attorney by profession, Hall had resided in Illinois from 1820 to 1833, during which time he held appointment as a circuit judge. While in Illinois, he founded the *Illinois Monthly Magazine*, the first literary periodical west of Ohio.

To Gehazi Granger

Dear Father,   Jacksonville Feb 28th 1836

I have been wating with a great deal of patience, and of late with a good deal of anxiety to hear from you all, but more particularly of Julius' arrival home. It is now nearly four months since he left this place for home under a positive promise to write to me immediately upon his arrival. He wrote me a few lines from St. Louis bearing date the 12th Nov last as near as my recollection serves me, which is the last I have heard from him. I wrote a letter directed to him at Manchester Centre Ontario Co. N.Y. about the first of January last, supposing that if he had not arrived from any accident which might have befallen him, in that case you would have answered the letter and communicated the facts. So it is however I [have] been able to hear nothing from any of you and from that circumstance *do feel a great anxiety for the fate of Julius,* or fear that some misfortune has befallen the rest of the family. Do write immediately and relieve my fears, or let me know the *worst!* Remember me to Mother and Sarah, and to all friends in general & assure them of my good health, and that my business has been more proffitable than usual this winter and is increasing. I am with great respect your affectionate

S. A. DOUGLASS

ALS, owned by Martin F. Douglas.

To Julius N. Granger

My Dear Sir   Jacksonville April 8th 1836

Having just returned from the circuit I have the pleasure to acknowledge the receipt of two Letters from you which afford me a good deal of relief and happiness in learning that you arrived Home in safety and are now together with Sarah, Father & Mother in the enjoyment of usually good health. On relation to the Qr section of Land alluded to in your & my formerly letter, I regret to inform you that I have had my labour for my pains. As I informed you before I selected a Qr Sec & went to Springfield to enter it & there found that there was a mistake in the Office, this was at the time I was about starting to attend the Supreme Court at Vandalia, and before I could go to a[n] Edwardsville Office I ascertained that some persons living near the Land had seen me examing it & immediately went & entered it at Edwardsville before I could get there. That your money might not remain idle & without proffit to you I invested it in town Lots in this place until I could have an opportunity to do better for you by selecting some more Congress land. I am happy to inform you that I can now sell your Lots at from fifty to an hundred per cent advance—or for between three & four hundred dollars—which by the by is a pretty good interest. Unless I receive contrary instructions I shall sell them & invest the proceeds in Congress Land as soon as I think I can make a better investment for you. In relation to Politics I think there is no doubt of the success of the Electorial Ticket friendly to Van Buren & Johnson in this State. In our own county we have formed a tickett for the Legislature of which I am one as the ticket is now shaped as you will perceive by our paper.[1] I confess that this arrangement is much against my will, for I did not desire to be a candidate this year, but rather make money—In this as in other things I yielded to the solicitations of my friends. Judging from the prospects at present I ent[ert]ain no doubt of my success in the election. I find no difficulty in adopting the Western mode of Electioneering by addressing the people from the Stump. John J. Hardin who was my opponent for States Attorney is now my principal opponent for Representative. We have already had a number of pitiched battles on the Stump in addressing the People, in which my friends & I believe his say I came out conqueror. We shall have a warm contest however—warmer the better for I like excitement. Tell Sarah that I will purchase for her the first s[. . .] Skin I can get & bring it to her when I come—if I do not have an opportunity to send it before. When I shall come I am unable to say at present. I will write you from time to time & you must do the same. I remain your affectionate Brother

STEPHEN A. DOUGLASS

ALS, owned by Martin F. Douglas.

[1]Douglas had not been included in the original legislative slate nominated by the Democrats of Morgan County. However, after the nomination of Hardin for the state legislature by a Whig convention, the Democratic ticket was reorganized, one of the nominees dropped from the slate, and Douglas' name substituted. This move was made, it was said, to allow Douglas to oppose Hardin before the voters of the county. In the August election, Douglas was elected. Among his colleagues in the lower house during the subsequent session was Abraham Lincoln.

To James Semple

[N.d., n.p.; cited in Frank E. Stevens, "Life of Stephen Arnold Douglas," *Journal of the Illinois State Historical Society,* XVI (October, 1923–January, 1924), 394. In 1836, Semple, who had been a member of the state legislature and Attorney General, was a candidate for the United States Senate. Douglas, according to Stevens, wrote Semple "that the use of his name would add strength to the party in Morgan County. . . ." Semple was not successful in his bid for the Senate. The original of this letter has not been located.]

To the Editor of the *Illinois Patriot*

[March 8, 1837]

Mr. Editor:—In your paper of the 22d of February last, there appears an editorial in which you make the specific charge that I had made an arrangement with the Sangamon delegation by which they were to use their influence to secure my appointment as Register of the Land Office and that in consideration of their services I had abandoned the interests of my own constituents and was acting in concert with the Sangamon delegation in supporting Springfield for the seat of government.[1]

Whilst I freely admit that the Representative who would be guilty of so flagrant an abuse of the trust reposed in him by a generous people would justly merit, as he would certainly receive, the execration of every honest man, I also hold that the man who would make and publish a false charge of that magnitude for the purpose of blasting the character of a political opponent who was absent on public duty, and consequently unable to defend himself, should meet with the same scorn and indignation of a virtuous people. Having made the charge, one which impeaches my integrity as a man and my fidelity as a Representative, you are bound by every principle of honor and honesty to exhibit the evidence to substantiate its truth, or publicly retract the slander, and the failure on your part to do so must be taken as conclusive evidence of the falsity of the charge and malice in which it had its origin. Conscious of my own innocence and of the rectitude of my conduct, I am impelled to demand the proof, so that the people may see whether I have been the traitor or you the slanderer.

It is not true that any arrangement was made or any understanding existed between the Sangamon delegation and myself in relation to a land office, the seat of government, or any other measure. It is not true that one solitary member of that delegation signed a recommendation in my favor, or was in any way concerned in it. That recommendation was got up by my friends without my solicitation or knowledge, and when the fact was communicated to me I told them that I did not desire that or any other appointment under the government, that I looked to the people and not the government for any favor I might ask. So far from there being any arrangement or concert of action between the Sangamon delegation and myself, it was my misfortune to differ on almost every important question that came before the Legislature, and more especially on the location of the seat of government. That was the all-absorbing topic with them, and with that view they used every exertion and made every necessary sacrifice to secure the passage of the bill, which recently became a law, on that subject. To that bill I was opposed in every form and shape it assumed, from its first appearance in the House up to its final passage. My decided and uncompromising opposition to that bill, and to the object intended to be accomplished by its passage, arrayed the Sangamon delegation *en masse* against me. So notorious was this fact at the seat of government at the time your paper containing the above charge was received that [there was] no person of any political party who hesitated for an instant to pronounce it a base slander. I defy you to find any one of my colleagues, or any member of either branch of the Legislature, or any individual who will, in the slightest degree, confirm the charge and become responsible for its truth. I make the statement with the more assurance and fearlessness, because I feel confident that each and all of them must know and will do me the justice to say that the whole charge is a mere fabrication, false as the heart that conceived it and the hand that penned it. I therefore call upon you to establish its truth or admit its falsity.

In relation to your remark that you had, 'before the last August election, told the people that S. A. Douglas was an office hunter,' I will only say that when I shall have applied for and accepted an office at the hands of the government, it will then be time enough for you to talk about office hunters.[2]

Jacksonville, March 8, 1837.   S. A. DOUGLAS

Printed in Joseph Wallace, "Stephen A. Douglas: Some Old Letters by, and Relating to, the Distinguished Statesman," *Transactions of the Illinois State Historical Society, 1901,* pp. 111-112. This letter, with some minor variations chiefly in punctuation, was also printed in Frank E. Stevens, "Life of Stephen Arnold Douglas," *Journal of the Illinois State Historical Society,* XVI (October, 1923–January, 1924), 308-310. In the latter version, Douglas' name is spelled with the double *s.*

[1] The Illinois legislature, in joint session, had chosen Springfield as the new and permanent state capital on February 28, 1837. The victory for the Springfield forces was in large part due to the exertions of Abraham Lincoln, then a member of the lower house. Douglas was consistent in voting against the move to Springfield, in spite of the charges brought by the editor of the *Patriot.*

[2] Douglas' appointment as Register of the Land Office at Springfield was dated March 13, 1837.

To Joseph Duncan

[March 15, 1837, n.p.; DS, Illinois State Archives. Petition, probably addressed to the Governor, Joseph Duncan, asking that William Brown be appointed to the office of Judge of the First Judicial District, in place of Stephen T. Logan, who had resigned. The petition is in the hand of John J. Hardin, and is signed by Hardin, Douglas, and nine others. Brown, a Jacksonville attorney, received the appointment.]

[Stephen A. Douglas held office as Register of the Springfield Land Office from his appointment on March 13, 1837, until March 2, 1839. During his term, he wrote many routine letters dealing with Land Office business to the Secretary of the Treasury, the Commissioner of the General Land Office, and others. These letters have been listed and described in Appendix II.]

To Lewis W. Ross

My Dear Sir   Springfield August 12th 1837

I have delayed answering your favor of the 20th ult in order to obtain and send at the same time a copy of the Private Acts of last winter Session of the Legislature. I have [made] enquiry at every place in Town where I would suppose they might probably be found, and have thus far been unable to obtain a copy. If I should be so fortunate as to procure one I will send it to you by the first opportunity. In answer to your enquiry as to what I think of the difficulty between our Senator & Representative in Congress, I will tell you frankly that I think there can be but one opinion upon the subject, and that is favorable to Judge Young[1] and adverse to Col May.[2] The fact is our Party will never support Col May again for Congress, unless public sentiments takes a great change. I am unable to say or even imagine who will be our Candidate for Congress. I am decidedly in favor of a District Convention to nominate a Candidate, and then let us all unite and elect him, be he who he may. As you sugest the name of Judge Ford,[3] I will take occasion to say that there is no man in the District whom it would give me more pleasure to support, than the Judge. I am informed however by his friends that he does not wish to run, but is anxious to remain on the Bench. You have probably seen the proceedings of a meeting of the Democratic Party at Vandalia, at which a State Convention was recommended to be held in December next to nominate Candidates for Governor & Leut Gov.[4]

In your views of the Banking system as expressed in your last letter, I most cordially concur. I believe the whole system is founded in error, and must undergo a thorough & radical reform, or be entirely abandondoned, before the currency of our country will return to a prosperous state. There should be a Divorce granted between the Banking system and the Government, and the Public revenue should be collected in the current coin of the U.S. as fixed by the Constitution. Such I have no doubt are the opinions of Mr Van Buren & his cabinet. Our County Election is over and resulted most gloriously for the Democrats. There was no contest for Co Clerk & Treasurer in consequence of there being but *one* candidate for the former, and four for the latter of whom *three* were Democrats. The battle was consequently fought on the Probate Justice of the Peace. Gen James Adams[5] was our Candidate & Doct A. G. Henry[6] the opposition. Henry is a prominent man in their ranks, assistant Editor of the Journal, and a very active devoted partizan, and hence their anxiety to Elect him. But we had the satisfaction of beating him about 300 votes. We do [not] *claim* it as a *party* victory, altho we [...]er it so in fact. A day or two ago [...] the pleasure of seeing a *Mrs* —— somebody I dont recollect who; but it was she who was once the beautiful, lovely Miss Mary Price. She & her husband were here on their way to Philadelphia. Remember me to Each of my acquaintances in your region and accept the best wishes of your friend who at all times will be glad to hear from you, and that a little oftener than heretofore. I remain your friend

S. A. DOUGLASS

ALS, Illinois State Historical Library, Springfield. Lewis W. Ross had attended college and studied law in Jacksonville at the time Douglas lived there. In 1839, he returned to Lewistown, Fulton County, a town founded by his father and named for himself, where he commenced the practice of law. A staunch supporter of Douglas, he held several terms in the state legislature in the 1840's, and was elected to Congress in 1862.

[1]Richard Montgomery Young was United States Senator from Illinois from 1837 to 1843. He had practiced law in Illinois since 1817; later he sat in the state legislature, and for twelve years served as a circuit judge of the fifth Illinois circuit.

[2]William L. May was Representative in Congress from the Third District, in which Springfield was located. He had been elected in 1834 and re-elected in 1836; in November, 1837, at a district convention in Peoria, he lost the Democratic nomination to Stephen A. Douglas. The "difficulty" between May and Senator Young, referred to by Douglas, grew out of May's repudiation of Van Buren's financial policies, and the attempt by Young and Douglas to read him out of the Democratic party.

[3]Thomas Ford, an early resident of Illinois, was serving as a circuit judge at the time this letter was written. He was not nominated for Congress but was later elected to the governorship of Illinois. A district convention was one of the means by which Douglas

hoped to defeat May's aspirations within the party.

[4]On July 10, 1837, a group of Democratic members of the legislature, then meeting at Vandalia in special session, determined to call a state convention for the following December to nominate candidates for the state offices and to strengthen the party organization. Although Douglas had resigned his seat in the legislature to accept appointment to the Springfield Land Office, he went over to Vandalia, attended the meeting, and was appointed to the committee to prepare an address to the Democrats of Illinois. This was a period of crisis for the party. Many hitherto faithful Democrats, like May, had dropped away from the party over disagreement with the administration's fiscal program. The Whigs, sensing an opportunity to disrupt the Democratic party, offered support to the bolters. The convention system, Douglas felt, would effectively enforce party regularity and unity.

[5]James Adams was a pioneer attorney of Sangamon County and a resident of Springfield. He had held appointment as justice of the peace for many years before his election as probate justice of the peace.

[6]Anson G. Henry, a Springfield physician, was an important Whig politician in central Illinois. His candidacy for probate justice of the peace was supported by Abraham Lincoln. The *Sangamo Journal*, of which Henry was assistant editor, was the Whig party organ in Springfield.

To Levi Woodbury

Sir   Springfield October 6th 1837

I have the honor to acknowledge the receipt of your letter of the 20th ultimo and a copy of a note received by you from the Hon Wm Lilley, in which you request me to give such explanation as I may consider it proper to submit in relation to a charge prefered against me by Mr May of being and having been "engaged in a political electionering tour through his District in getting up [a] meeting of the voters to organize a Convention of delegates to nominate a Candidate for Congress who are to be pledged against him" &c. Upon what authority Mr May founds his charge I am unable to conceive, unless it is a short paragraph in a late number of the Sangamo Journal an opposition paper in this Town which seizes every opportunity to impugn the motives, and misrepresent the acts of every member of the Democratic Party. That you may better understand the nature of this charge and the circumstances out of which it had its origin I will give the facts which are as follows. Previous to my appointment to this office last Spring I devoted myself to the practice of Law in all the counties in this Judicial Circuit, and had considerable unfinished business which rendered it necessary to attend the late Terms of the Courts to attend to the business in which I had been previously engaged. I accordingly did so and confined myself *exclusively* to this Judicial Circuit a part of which is in Mr May's Congressional District and a part in Mr Snyder's.[1] No political meetings were held and of course no delegates were appointed and pledged as stated by Mr May, in any county that I was in during the time I was there; nor have I attended or in any manner participated in the proceedings of any political meeting in Mr May's District since I have held an Office under the General Government.[2] From the facts you will perceive that the charge is not only destitute of any foundation in truth; but is the production of a suspicious jealous mind operated on by the slang of a petty newspaper managed and conducted for political and selfish purposes. I do not wish the department to construe my denial of all participation in political meetings recently as an admission that I would deem such a course culpable or in any degree improper, or that I have been prevented from doing so by the fact of holding Office. On the contrary, I feel myself as free to mingle with my fellow citizens and express my opinions of men and measures (not even excepting Mr May) as I should if I had never received an Office at the hands of the Government. If any other charges or complaints should be made to the Department against me I would feel myself under peculair o[bli]gation if you would give me noti[ce of] them as you have in this instance. I remain very respectfully your obedient servant

STEPHEN A. DOUGLASS

ALS, RG-56, National Archives, Washington, D.C. Levi Woodbury was Secretary of the Treasury.

[1]Adam W. Snyder had been elected to the House of Representatives in 1836.

[2]Douglas, in spite of his denial of open participation in political meetings, had been actively working against May's renomination.

To the Democratic Republicans of Illinois

[November, 1837]

FELLOW-CITIZENS:—In accordance with a resolution adopted in July last, by a large and respectable portion of the Democratic Party of Illinois, assembled at Vandalia, the undersigned as a committee appointed for the purpose, have now undertaken to address the members of that party wherever they may be in the State, upon the subject of a State Convention to be held at that place on the first Monday of December next.—The object of which will be to nominate candidates for the offices of Governor and Lieutenant Governor, to be supported by the Democratic Party, at the next August election.

The most limited view that we could take in justice to the important subject assigned for our discussion, would require us at least to notice briefly the organization and the distinguishing principles of the parties of this country. The rule of conduct of the one, which of late days is styled whig; and the necessity at this juncture, of the organization of the Democratic strength by Convention.

It is not, fellow-citizens, to be disguised, that in this country as well as in those less happy and free, there are two opposing parties. The one, the advocates of the rights of the People; the other, the advocates of the privileges of Property.

This difference has been the touch stone of political controversy and party feuds in all ages and in all countries, and will continue to be as long as men shall permit the selfishness of ambition and avarice to influence their intercourse with each other; yes, as long as these passions shall find favor, whether through interest or conscience, with our public men.

As endless as are the modifications of parties, yet still do they all relate to these two antagonist principles.—They may change their guise as often as the camelion his hues, or their attitudes as often as Proteus ever changed his shape, yet still either the power of the many or the few is the magnetism of their attraction—it constitutes the grand *dissideratum* of their labors.

The success of these principles has been alternate. At one time the dominion of the few and the franchises of property, has been firmly established, exacting in the turn of their fortune the tributes of natural liberty and personal rights. At another time the voice of the many, and the doctrine of equal rights have exerted their mild sway and happy influences over a free and self governed people. But now, to the pride and joy of every American citizen, the abstract question of ascendancy, as between the Democracy of numbers and the Aristocracy of wealth, no longer exists. The advance of civilization, science, and experience has entrenched the rights of the many with the affections and enlightened judgments of the civilized world.

The one common object of liberty, which was paramount in its importance served to bind the patriots of the revolution together as a unit, during its continuance. All minor differences of whatsoever nature, were merged in this common consideration. And it was only after that glorious struggle had been so gladly closed, that those political and party differences of which we have spoken, disclosed themselves in our happy country.

They were kept down to a great extent during the Presidency of GEN. WASHINGTON,—because of his great personal popularity, and the surpassing esteem in which he was held by the nation for which he had done so much. But upon the close of his public career, there was no longer a citizen to be found, who, for his distinguished military and civil services, could harmonize in his character, all the numerous and angry differences which were soon destined to distract and divide the public mind. So in the canvass that preceded the election of the elder ADAMS to the Chief Magistracy, as well as during the term of his administration, these opposite principles were brought in direct competition with each other. And from that period to the present time there has been an unceasing warfare between them; and an untiring effort on the part of the Federalists, (who under all their varying names,) have been the steady advocates of strong government and exclusive privileges, to supplant the constitutional supremacy of the "many".

Whilst the party of the people, the Democratic Republican party, from its organization to the present time has been uniform and consistent in its name and course, its old and inveterate enemy the *privilege party* has been as remarkable for the multitude of its names and the vascillation of its members.

Having been overthrown in their efforts to re-elect the elder Adams, they deemed it expedient (one of the text words of their creed,) to drop the name of Federalist, and adopt such as might deceive the confidence of the people into their support. And from that time to the present, they have used at different periods according to the exigency of the times the cognomens of "Federalists," "National Republicans," "Republicans," "Whigs," and "Nullifiers." Under all these names have the enemies to the power of the many contended against the success of the Democratic Republican party, vainly thinking that such a change of mere sound would shield them from the odium of their principles, and the condemning judgment of an enlightened people.

If there were any doubt as to the anti-republican character and tendencies of their principles, those thus sceptical we would refer to the replete history of the past.

[43]

We would refer them to their opinions relative to the principles of Democracy as they were publicly expressed during the late war— "That democracy was a cursed delusion, *adopted by traitors and recommended only by sycophants.*" We would refer them to the paternity of the alien and sedition laws—their devotion to the United States Bank, and to the principles of monied monopolies and exclusive privileges,—their identity with exorbitant tariffs and all the chimeras of the American system. They have been in favor of taxing our community to make roads and canals elsewhere. They resisted to the last the removal of the public deposites from the Bank of the United States, when it was every where known that that odious corporation was using them as the means of oppressing the people, and driving them to the necessity of its recharter, when it was known that it was in an unholy alliance with the monarchists of England—and that it was unblushingly expending its money for the publication of angry and inflamatory attacks upon a republican administration. The same party refused during the late war to vindicate the national honor or to assert our injured rights against the wanton and lawless practices of a foreign nation.— When our seamen had been impressed, and our commerce destroyed, they refused to furnish our navy the necessary supplies for our defence; and our soldiery who were offering up their blood and their lives in the repulsion of a savage foe, they denied the food and raiment necessary to shield them against hunger and cold.—Yes! this is the party that rejoiced in the bloodshed of the Western States during that struggle, as a just retribution to Heaven. At a later period they refused an appropriation, the object of which was to fortify our sea-board against foreign aggression, the prospect of which was then most imminent.

In fact their political weight and influence has been always found in the scale adverse to the popular will and those measures approved by public opinion. They have ever courted the influence of wealth rather than the just approbation of the people. And now most certainly, it cannot be contended that there will be any consistency or propriety in yielding up the principles which have been so long and so anxiously contended for by the great Republican party of the Nation, and under the influence which our country has so much prospered, either as the earnest of an illicit compromise of principle, or for the favor of those who have ever been and must continue to be, our political enemies.

To do so would be to acknowledge to the world, that the great and distinguishing measures which have hitherto marked the political creed of the Republican Party, and in virtue of which our Government has grown and flourished, are vain delusions, and the time-serving schemes of power—which would be a deed as repulsive to every Democrat as it would be inconsistent and void of truth. Let it be remembered by the

[44]

Republicans of Illinois, that the principles of the Constitution are the principles of the Democratic Party—that the success of the latter is the safety of the former—that the principles of the whigs, as they are self-styled, as being friendly to strong government, distinctions in society, and exclusive privileges, are in subversion of both.

Under the sanction of political friendship, we would admonish our Democratic brethren of Illinois, to beware of the false fights of their old enemies—to examine narrowly the numerous plans and subtle devices of a scheming opposition, to divert them from the cause in which they have embarked, and that it is now identified with the success of liberal principles.

If there is any thing in the political history of our fathers, or aught in the principles of the Republican Party, or in those measures of policy which have so eminently fostered the glory, the power, and wealth of our nation, worthy of preservation, the time has now arrived when it is necessary that the strength of this party should be put forth in its behalf in the most unquestionable manner.

Our adversaries, the Whigs, have been organizing the force of their party, for some time past, by means of State Conventions, as the most effectual method of ensuring concert of action, and the elevation of their political leaders.

If the general success of the distinguished principles of the Democratic party were not a sufficient stimulus for the adoption of the same system, by the latter, the most decisive reason for it could be found at this juncture, in the settled design and varying schemes of their enemies, to defeat and proscribe them. If our principles are as valuable as we would represent, if they are worth preserving, they are worthy of the means necessary to preserve them, whether by Conventions or otherwise.

What are the plans put on foot by the Whigs to gain the 'haven of power' that would convince us of the necessity of party organization? Have not the opposition of every hue and dye joined in one common crusade against the success of the Democratic Party? Has not every constituent element of anti-republicanism, however jarring and incompatible, been harmonized in one battle array, to subvert the principles and supremacy of the people? Convinced that they were in the minority, did they not in the struggle that preceded the last Presidential election, under the motto of "Divide and Conquer," put forth a candidate in the North, the South, and the West for this office, who were severally the political antipodes of each other, who had been at one time the leaders of different and opposing political parties?

Did they not run Mr. Webster to rally the once powerful but now routed phalanx of Federalism, in the North—Gen. Harrison to embody its few and scattered adherents in the West—and Judge White in the South, to bring to their common object the aid of the Nullifiers, and a seceding and deluded portion of the Democratic Party of the Nation? And did they not thus lose sight of principle, in order to so divide the people in the support of the numerous candidates, that the popular voice would be ineffectual to the election of any one, and that the election should be thus referred to the House of Representatives, where the result might be controlled by intrigue and management rather than by the virtue and intelligence of the people? Can the virtuous of any party regard these inconsistencies without regret and remorse? There was no unity of principle between Judge White on the one side and Gen. Harrison and Mr. Webster on the other. Their theories of our Government were as variant as opposite extremes. If Judge White's political doctrines were orthodox, those of Gen. Harrison and Mr. Webster were not. If the Whig party could find a justification in the support of the former, they could not in that of the latter.

Judge White had been held up by his partisans as a friend of General Jackson, and as a prominent member of the party of which that distinguished individual was then a leader. The Democratic party were invited to his support because he was opposed to the Tariff, the Bank, and a latitudinarian construction of the constitution. On the other hand the public were invited to the support of Gen. Harrison, because he had been a supporter of the administration of the elder Adams, and because as a fearless and consistent Federalist he had on a notable occasion, as the supporter of the Alien and Sedition laws, publicly declared in "thanks to his God that he was a member of that party." It was said that the people would support Gen. Harrison because he was in favor of a strong Government—because he was for a high tariff—the U.S. Bank, and all the leading doctrines of the Federal party.

Great must have been the anxiety and blind the zeal of the members of the Whig party, when one of its most distinguished leaders, Mr. Clay, could be brought to say at one time that he would rather see "war, pestilence, and famine desolate the country, than a Military Chieftain elevated to the Presidency,"—and at another to exert all his influence and talent for a gentleman of this character for the same place.

After the defeat they have experienced in the election of our present Chief Magistrate, have they ceased their warfare, or their exertions to force themselves into power? They have not.—You find them sowing the seeds of discord and dissention with the same zeal and untiring industry that has ever characterized their political conduct. You now find them compassing every means that ingenuity can devise, or that calamity, and a sleepless vigilence can furnish, to possess themselves of the administration of the Government. Again they are endeavoring to fix upon the people the oppression of the U.S. Bank; an institution the creature of their will, and against the re-establishment of which, the public judgment has been most decisively pronounced in the two last presidential elections. If the Republicans of Illinois would guard against the revival of so great an evil as the U.S. Bank, an institution which has fattened upon their substance, and sported at their sufferings, they must decree concert and unity of action among themselves. Are not the whigs now openly resisting the patriotic efforts of the Chief Magistrate of our choice, to separate Government from all Banks, and thereby to free it from all the embarrassments incident to a fiscal relation with these institutions? they are;—and why so? because to place the fiscal operations of the Government upon a footing that would be self-dependent and self-directed, would be to diminish the chances as also the reasons for the re-charter of their favorite institution.

Such are the plans and the efforts, and such the zeal and anxiety of our old political adversaries to re-establish themselves in office. And if we would preserve and perpetuate the principles of Washington, Jefferson, Madison, Monroe, Jackson and Van Buren, we must follow their advice, and conform to their usages.

For this purpose the Democratic Republicans of Illinois, propose to meet in General Convention, at Vandalia, on the second Monday of December next, to choose candidates from their number to be supported by them for the two highest offices in the gift of the people, viz: Governor and Lieut. Governor.—They propose this method of organization because it has been successfully tried heretofore, and because it has been sanctioned by the long usage of the party to which they profess to belong. If caucuses were justifiable, in the language of the Democratic members of Congress, in 1808—"from the necessity of the increase"—much more so are the free and voluntary Conventions of the People, spontaneously gotten up and disinterestedly conducted, and designated only for the union of the party and the conservation of the public interests. Even caucuses were sanctioned by Mr. Jefferson, Mr. Madison, and Mr. Monroe. In truth the history of the times fully establish the fact that their election to the Presidency was essentially attributable to the conciliatory influence of this, then, Democratic usage.

If, then, the exigencies of the past created a necessity and justification for the organization of the Democratic strength by means of caucuses, certainly it cannot now be denied that the extraordinary exertions and deceptive schemes of the opposition, would place the propriety of Conventions, fairly gotten up and designed for proper objects, beyond all manner of question.

It is now understood that the Federalists of this State, who have recently adopted the cognomen of Whigs, have already brought forward their candidates for these offices—and that too through the instrumentality of caucuses; a system of organization much more objectionable than Conventions, and against which they have said so much and clamored so long. Indeed it is irreconcilable with consistency that a party which has so unequivocally condemned all manner of party concert and unanimity, could bring themselves to consent to the employment of the most exceptionable individuality for the accomplishment of the same purposes.—They have brought forward their candidates by a secret, and as it is said, a "midnight caucus." The Democratic Republicans of Illinois propose to bring theirs forward by the free and consentaneous voice of every member of their political association. The candid of all sides will readily decide which of the parties are most consistent, and which of the methods are most objectionable.

In the variety of their schemes for the attainment of their object, one not less remarkable, is the peculiar formation of their ticket for these offices; for Governor (if report is aright) they have brought forward a gentleman who has been long and invariably identified with the Federalists—who has always acted with that party, and from whom the democratic party of this State can reasonably expect nothing. For Lieutenant Governor, they have brought forward a gentleman who was an original democrat, and who at one time was a supporter of Gen. Jackson's administration, but who has since seceded from his old political friends, and is now completely incorporated with their old and inveterate enemies,—in evidence of the fact, we might refer to the result of his canvass in 1834, for a seat in Congress; on that occasion, as the whig candidate for the 2d Congressional district, he was overwhelmed with defeat; the public judgment was pronounced against him in the most decisive manner.[1]—The apparrent design of this arrangement would seem to be to unite the dissevered fragments of their party for the greatest possible effect;—in a word, if by possibility it can be done, to defeat the Democratic party. Such being the case, the latter will beware of these subtleties—they will reflect that to counteract them they must yield all minor differences, and co-operate in generous fellowship; and that to effect this desideratum they must resort to the efficacious instrumentality of a State Convention. They will recollect that, in "Union there is Safety"—and that to triumph over our enemies, we must guard against divisions among ourselves.

[48]

The Republicans of Illinois have every motive for cordiality of feeling—mutual concession—and concert of action. Their Republicanism has ever been above suspicion; their weight and influence has always been cast in the scale of Constitutional Democracy, nor is it now believed that they will flag in the cause with which they have been so long identified, and for the establishment of which they have so long struggled—If they would be consistent, they cannot now yield to the illusive semblancies of their adversaries; and to preserve the principles they, in conjunction with the republicans of the nation, have adjudged wise and sound under the administrations of Jefferson and Jackson, and for the maintenance of which President Van Buren is committed; they must rally to the standard of their common cause, and sleep not while the enemy is in the field.

It is a just pride of the republicans of Illinois, that, whilst their old compeers in the same cause in other of the States of the West, have been confused and misled by the arts and intrigues of the modern Whigs, that they have been steadfast to their political integrity—neither the threats nor promises of their enemies, having been adequate to deter them from the support of their principles and the faithful discharge of their duty. By the election which is to take place for these high stations, it is to be ascertained whether Illinois is to remain true to her interests, 'her State pride, and the republican faith to which she has long since subscribed: for the election of these officers will be sure to be put upon the question of Whig or Democratic ascendency. The principles of 'consolidation,' 'monopoly,' and "property privilege" will be in issue on one side; on the other, those of a strict construction of the Constitution—equal distribution of the favors of the Government —and equal rights; yes, all those principles, the influence of which, have so eminently distinguished our country for prosperity, character, and power; which have vindicated the national honor, and exacted our rights from foreign powers; which have paid off the national debt, and freed the people from the burdens of a high tariff; which have extended our trade and commerce to ports and nations that were closed to the negociations of our political adversaries; which had condemned geographical discriminations, and seditious practices; which has put down the United States Bank, and would forbid any improper interference in the elections of the people, are to stand or fall according as the support of Illinois may be material to their success, in the great struggle of parties.

We would, therefore, impress upon the minds of our Democratic brethren the necessity of organization, the duty of due attention to the Convention proposed, and in conclusion, adjure them under the sanctions of the public interests, their consistency, and the State pride, to discard all petty differences and to unite for the cordial support of the principles they so esteem, and that are so valuable to our common country.[2]

Vandalia *Illinois State Register*, November 4, 1837. As a member of the committee chosen to prepare this address, Douglas exerted a strong influence in perfecting the first real Democratic party organization in the state.

[1]The Whigs had met in caucus during the special legislative session the previous July and had nominated Cyrus Edwards for governor and William H. Davidson for lieutenant governor.

[2]The address was signed by twenty-nine persons, including Douglas.

To Julius N. Granger

Dear Brother,   Springfield Dec 18th 1837

Your kind Letter of the 12th ult came to hand during my absence at Vandalia attending the Supreme Court or it would have received an earlier answer. You keep me making apologies in my Letters for my remissness in writing, and making fair promises to do better in future; but in this instance I believe I have a little the advantage of you. Although I confess I have been almost unpardonable in not writing to you since last Spring, yet I must say that I have never received an answer to that letter except your later letter dated the 12th Nov, and have been anxiously expecting one from you. If therefore you did write to me, your letter must have been miscarried as it never came to hand. Be this as it may I am disposed to blot out all old matters, and begin anew. I am very happy to receive the Congratulations you say you expressed at my good fortune in this world, and will return the compliment by congratulating you upon your election to the office of Justice of the Peace and the acquisition of the title of "Esq" as distinctions and titles seem to be the great objects of our aspirations in this world. Tell Sister Sarah that I acknowledge the justice of her chidings and reprimands for being so actively engaged in politics that I have neglected my friends who are bound to me by all the dear ties of blood and kindred, and I will *promise* to do better in the future. I suppose this will be entirely satisfactory as *promises* are all that is expected of politicians in these days if the Whigs are to be believed. I am afraid that she has turned politician; or found some other fascinating employment that occupies all her time; for I believe I have not received a single line from her before since I have been in Illinois. I will not criminate however for fear that she may recriminate, and that I should find myself no better off than when I began. It is unnecessary to say to you that I enjoy first rate health as I have not had scarcely a days sickness since I have been in the State. You seem to take it for granted that I have been fortunate in the acquisition of honors if not of riches, and I will not take the pains to deny it as it is flattering to ones vanity, and gratifying to dear friends to think so, whether true or imaginary. This leaves me to your enquiry about your investment here, and where it is, and in what it consistes? You certainly cannot take much interest in the matter if you have forgotten whether I ever told you. I believe I told you in my last letter that it consits in real Estate in Jacksonville, and that I would give you six hundred dollars for it if you thought it a bad bargain. At all events such is the fact, and I believe the property very cheap at that price. A Rail Road is now in progress of completion from the Illinois River to Jacksonville which will have the effect to raise the price of property,[1] and I think it would be well for me to sell the land for you as soon as times become more Easy, and invest the proceeds in Congress land for you. My situation in this office will enable me to make a better investment now than I could have done at any previous period for you.[2] Unless you give me specific instructions I shall m[anage] it in such manner as I shall think [most] conducive to your interests. Ask Mother what she should think if the People of Illinois should be so foolish as to send her "prodigal Son" to Congress, and give him an opportunity to visit her on his way. If she has no serious objection to it, I believe the people have some idea of doing so at the next August Election just for the fun of the thing.[3] Tell Father that I want him to write me a long letter, and give me the aid of his advice to assist me along in the rugged path I have to tread. I have not even heard enough from him to know for a certainty whether he is among the living. Give my respects to all my friends and write soon & often. I am &c yrs &c

S. A. Douglass

ALS, owned by Martin F. Douglas.

[1] The Northern Cross Railroad, scheduled to connect Quincy with the eastern boundary of the state, was one of the many internal improvement projects approved by the state legislature during these years.

[2] Douglas refers to his position as Register of the Springfield Land Office.

[3] Douglas' campaign against May's renomination was successful. At the Third District convention held in Peoria in November, 1837, he defeated May and was himself nominated for Congress, although he had not yet attained the legal age for a seat in the House of Representatives.

To George R. Weber

[January 30, 1838]

Mr. Weber: The enclosed communication was prepared for the Journal, and sent to the house and twice to the office of the editor to ascertain if he would publish it.[1] But as my friends were so unfortunate as not to be able to see him, I wish you would insert it in your paper, and hope the editor of the Journal will do me the justice to transfer to his columns, as it is a reply to an article containing charges against me which originally appeared in his paper. Yours respectfully, Springfield, Jan. 30, 1838.   S. A. DOUGLASS

TO THE PUBLIC.

FELLOW CITIZENS:

Nothing is more disagreeable to me than to be under the necessity of appearing before you in the defence of my character against false accusations. I had indulged the hope that the wanton personal abuse and detraction, which sometimes characterize political contests, and are so disgraceful to those who indulge in them, would not have been resorted to in the present canvass, and that a regard for truth, honor and dignity becoming gentlemen, would have been preserved. In this, I regret to say, I have been disappointed. Kind, courteous, and conciliatory deportment towards those differing with me in opinion have failed to secure for me that kind of treatment which such a course deserves, and I had a right to expect from those who claim to be *honorable* opponents. My nomination as a candidate for Congress seems to have been the signal for a systematic and simultaneous attack upon my character, which has been followed up with a vindictive, fiendish spirit that shows that nothing but the sacrifice of its victim will appease its malice. My acts have been misrepresented, my opinions perverted, my motives impugned, and my character traduced in language as unkind and ungentlemanly as it was unjust and untrue. These outpourings of abuse and slander I have passed in silence, resting upon your intelligence and sense of justice for my vindication, against charges and insinuations, that bore the evidence of malice on their face, and I should not notice them on this occasion, had not my *private* and *moral*, as well as public and political character been assailed in a manner calculated to destroy my standing as a man and a citizen, if permitted to pass unnoticed, and my silence construed into an admission of guilt. The last number of the Sangamo Journal contained an article over the signature of "A Conservative," charging me with a corrupt bargain with a "certain gentleman of Sangamon county," by the terms of which the author asserts, that I *"agreed to have that certain gentleman appointed Register of the Land Office in Springfield, if he would procure for me the nomination of the Peoria Convention as a candidate for Congress."* The writer then proceeds with a long and minute detail of the supposed circumstances of the Peoria nomination, and then adds: "But the nomination was made; and according to *contract*, I presume at this time a correspondence is going on between Washington and this place, in regard to the *regular transfer of the Land Office.*" It will be perceived

[52]

that the writer of the article *conceals* himself behind the mask of a fictitious signature; that he *dare* not subscribe his name to his charges; that he has failed to give the name of the "certain gentleman" with whom the contract is alleged to have been made; and that he mentioned no time or place, or witnesses by whom the truth or falsity of the accusations could be established. I fear no investigation, however strict or rigid; I invite, I challenge it. Conscious of my own innocence, and the rectitude of my conduct, I am desirous that the curtain should be raised, and every act of my life exposed to the searching eye of public scrutiny. I also desire to drag my accusers from their hiding places, to strip off the mask that conceals their names from the public eye, give them an opportunity of maintaining their assertions, or let them cover themselves with infamy, which is the certain reward of the midnight assassin, and foul mouthed slanderer.² With this view, immediately upon the receipt of the paper containing the article alluded to, I addressed the following note to the editor of the Journal, demanding the name of the author.

"Springfield, Jan 26, 1838.

"*S. Francis, Esq.*

"Sir—in your paper of this evening I perceive an article over the signature of "A Conservative," containing statements reflecting upon my character as a man of honor and integrity. Not feeling disposed to rest under the imputation, I demand of you the name of the author of the article alluded to, which you will please communicate to me by the bearer."

To this note a verbal answer was returned by the editor, that "the article alluded to does not contain any thing that *requires* the author's name to be furnished, and that he expected to be treated as the author."

What! Are we to be told that a direct charge of *corrupt bargain and sale* "does not contain *any thing* that requires an author's name to be furnished?" Is the charge of a "regular transfer of a Land Office *according to contract*" to *purchase* a nomination for Congress a mere trivial, unimportant circumstance, "not containing anything that requires an author." Is there nothing dishonest, disgraceful, and degrading in an act of this kind? If my enemies think not, if *their* principles of moral and political honesty can perceive no impropriety, nay terpitude, in such conduct, why do they make the charge against me and urge it as a reason why I should not receive the countenance and suffrage of a free, virtuous, and enlightened people? If there is nothing disreputable in it, as they seem to think, why go to the trouble and expense of writing, publishing, and circulating it? If in *their* estimation it is a *virtuous act*, one in accordance with their notions of honor and integrity, why blazon it forth to the world at the very time when *they* are using every

[53]

exertion to prostrate me personally and politically? If on the contrary they look upon it in the light I do, and every honest man must; if they would view the man, who would be guilty of such conduct, as a disgrace to humanity, upon what principle of honor or justice can they pretend that the charge of such an act "does not contain *any thing that requires* an author's name to be furnished?" Are you required to believe it without an author? Is no name, no witness, no proof necessary? Are you willing to have *your* characters blackened, and prospects blighted by the foul slanders of some dastardly midnight assassin, who makes his deadly thrust in the dark, and screens himself from public indignation, behind the false, fictitious name, "A Conservative?" Or will you require him to throw off his mask, affix his name to the accusations, produce his witnesses, and stand or fall by their testimony? If you would require this in your own case, I know your sense of justice will extend the same equitable rule to mine. I desire the name of the author; I would like to see the face of the cowardly wretch, who has had the hardihood to prefer false charges against me, over a false name, and then sneakingly shrink from the responsibility and infamy that would follow the exposure under the poor, pitiful, comtemptible pretext that his charges "did not *contain any thing* that requires an author's name to be furnished." I dislike to use harsh language or opprobious epithets. It is repugnant to my feelings, contrary to my usual intercourse with my fellow-citizens, and I always scrupulously avoid it, whenever milder terms can be employed to call things by their right names. But a sacred regard for the truth and my character compels me in this instance to pronounce the author of the article alluded to an INFAMOUS, VILLAINOUS LIAR, and a COWARDLY SCOUN-DREL, and if the editor of the Journal is anxious to be "treated as the author," he is at liberty to make the application to himself *personally*. I indignantly repel the charge. I never made a contract, or any arrangement whatever in relation to "the Register's office in Springfield" to procure the Peoria nomination. I have made no promise of that or any other office or patronage in the gift of the Government to any man on earth, and I defy the world to prove the contrary. If elected, I shall go into Congress untrammelled by the corrupt and corrupting shackles of bargains and promises of offices and patronage. My standard of moral and political integrity has not taught me, and I trust in God never will teach me, that such bargains and promises are consistent with moral or political honesty, or that charges of that kind do "not contain any thing that requires an author's name to be furnished." Most of the other statements in the article in question were predicated upon the charge referred to, and do not therefore deserve further notice. The whole article is a tissue of falsehoods and misrepresentations, and in that fact may be found the motive that induced the author to withhold his name. I hope that my opponents will reflect seriously upon the course they are pursuing, will observe its manifest unfairness and injustice, indirect tendency and inevitable consequences, and will in future refrain from such wanton abuse and detraction. The people of this country are too intelligent, honest and virtuous to be led and captivated by slander and falsehood, and those who use them as weapons are certain to injure their own cause more than the object of their attack. Yet it is so disgraceful to all who engage in them, and so unplea[sant] for me to be under the necessity of vindicating my character from the effects of their assaults, that I will always rest until forbearance ceases to be a virtue. If however I am to be attacked, vilified and traduced by a corrupt combination of anonymous slanderers and assassins, my character is dearer to me than life and I am determined to vindicate it at all hazards. I trust that the people that have published their attack will do me the justice to publish this, my defence.

Vandalia *Illinois State Register*, February 23, 1838; from the *Illinois Republican*. George R. Weber was editor of the *Republican*, a Democratic and pro-Douglas newspaper founded in 1835. In 1839, the paper merged with the *Register*. Douglas was a frequent contributor to the columns of the *Republican*, but unfortunately no file of the paper has survived.

[1]The editor of the *Sangamo Journal*, Springfield's Whig organ, was Simeon Francis, a former New York state publisher who arrived in Springfield in 1831. Francis' connection with the paper, afterwards the *Illinois State Journal*, was to continue until 1855.

[2]Two letters signed by "Conservative" had appeared in the *Sangamo Journal* on January 12 and 27 prior to Douglas' reply. Douglas' answer in the *Republican* evoked "An Addendum to Conservative No. 2" on February 3 and a third letter on February 10. All of the letters were scathing attacks on Douglas' nomination and candidacy for Congress. Glenn H. Seymour has speculated on the possibility that Lincoln wrote the second letter and its addendum in " 'Conservative'—Another Lincoln Pseudonym?" *Journal of the Illinois State Historical Society*, XXIX (July, 1936), 135-150. Evidence of Lincoln's authorship, however, is not definite, and hence the letters have not been included in the Roy P. Basler edition of *The Collected Works of Abraham Lincoln*.

To Lewis W. Ross

Dear friend   Springfield March 17th 1838

Your kind favor of the first instant was duly received, and would have drawn from me an earlier reply but for the Press of business in Court, and a mencholly occurence here which has put a large portion of our fellow citizens in mourning. I allude to the murder of Doct J W Early by Henry B Truett,[1] the particulars of which I presume you have learned before this. Truett has been Indicted for Murder & lies in Jail awaiting his trial.

I thank you for your kind assurance of support in the Election, and will endeavor to prove myself worthy of the confidence that me be reposed in me, and ever grateful to my friends for their assistance.[2] In your county I have no personal acquaintance with the people, & will have to rely to a great Extent upon you & other friends to present my pretensions. I shall however take the earliest possible opportunity to visit your county & the Military Tract generally & shall take the liberty of calling on you to introduce me to the people. Your suggestions in relation to Col Kinney[3] & Stuart[4] are worthy of consideration, and meet with my entire approbation. I know of no one better qualified to write the communications than yourself, and your residence on the North side of the River favors the plan. The head that can conceive is certainly best calculated to execute. I therefore leave this matter to you feeling assured that you will perform it with more success than any other person within my acquaintance.

In regard to the Patents for cession Mr. Ross I must inform you that we have a large number of Patents on hand say 10 or 12000, but a list of the *names* of the Patentees is not furnished us. We can only tell when Patents are here by the *number of the Duplicate*. I shall leave here for Jacksonville tomorrow; but if you will write to Mr Eastham[5] giving the numbers of your Duplicates he will inform you whether the Patents are here or not. Give my respects to my friends & accept for yourself the assurances of Esteem of your friend

S. A. DOUGLASS

ALS, Illinois State Historical Library.

[1]Dr. Jacob W. Early, a Methodist preacher in Springfield, was shot and killed by Henry B. Truett during a political argument on March 7. Truett was later defended by the legal firm of Stuart and Lincoln and acquitted.

[2]Douglas refers to his campaign for Congress from Illinois' Third District.

[3]William C. Kinney had served two terms in the state legislature early in the state's history and one term as Lieutenant Governor. In 1830 and 1834 he made unsuccessful bids for the governorship.

[4]John T. Stuart was Douglas' Whig opponent in the race for Congress. A Springfield attorney and law partner of Abraham Lincoln, Stuart had served two terms in the state legislature and had been defeated for Congress by William L. May in 1836. In 1838, he eked out a narrow victory over Douglas.

[5]Marvellous Eastham, a Springfield contractor, succeeded Douglas as Register of the Springfield Land Office in 1839. In 1841, he was appointed County Clerk of Sangamon County.

Autobiographical Sketch, September 1, 1838

I this day commence this memorandum or journal of passing events for the purpose of refreshing my mind in the future upon subjects that might otherwise be forgotten. It may be well to turn my attention to the past as well as the future, and record such facts as are within my recollection or have come to my knowledge, and may be interesting or useful to myself or others hereafter.

I learn from my mother that I was born in the town of Brandon in the County of Rutland and State of Vermont on the 23d day of April, 1813. My father, Stephen A. Douglas, was a graduate of Middlebury College, a physician by profession, and a man very much beloved by all who knew him. I only speak of my father as I have always heard others speak of him, for he died when I was only about two months old, and of course I cannot recollect him. I have often been told that he was holding me in his arms when he departed this world. My mother, who thank God yet lives, was a Miss Sarah Fisk before she was married. My parents had but two children, my sister Sarah A. Douglas (who has since married Julius N. Granger of Manchester Centre, Ontario county, N.Y.) and myself. Upon the death of my father, my mother moved to a small farm left by her father about three miles north of my native village, and resided with her brother Edward Fisk, who was an industrious, economical, clever old bachelor, and wanted some one to keep house for him. This arrangement suited them both as their farms joined, and each was so situated as to need the aid of the other. Here I lived with my mother and uncle upon the farm until I was about fifteen years of age, and then determined to select some other mode of living. I had no great aversion to working on a farm, nor was I much dissatisfied with my good old uncle, but thought him rather a hard master, and unwilling to give me those opportunities of improvement and education which I thought I was entitled to. I had enjoyed the benefits of a common school education three months each year, and had been kept diligently at work the rest of the time. I thought it a hardship that my uncle would have the use of my mother's farm and also the benefit of my labour without any other equivalent than my boarding and clothes. I therefore determined upon leaving my home and my true friends, and see what I could do for myself in the wide world among strangers. My mother remonstrated, warned me of the dangers and temptations to which young men are exposed, and insisted upon my selecting some trade or engaging in some business that would give me a steady home and regular employment. I promised to comply with her wishes, that is, keep good company, or in other words keep out of bad company, avoid all immoral and vicious practices, attend church regularly, and obey the regulations of my employer; in short I promised everything she wanted, if she would consent to my leaving home. Accordingly in the Spring of 1828, being about fifteen years of age, I bid my mother, sister and uncle farewell, and left home for Middlebury, about fourteen miles distant, and engaged to learn the Cabinet making trade with one Nahum Parker. I put on my apron and went to work, sawing table legs from two inch plank, making wash stands, bed stead, &c., &c. I was delighted with the change of home and employment. There was a novelty about it that rendered it peculiarly interesting. My labor furnished exercise for the mind as well as the body. I have never been placed in any situation or been engaged in any business which I enjoyed to so great an extent as the cabinet shop. I then felt contented and happy, and never aspired to any other distinction than that connected with my trade and improvements in the arts. Towards the end of the year I became dissatisfied with my employer in consequence of his insisting upon my performing some menial services in the house. I was willing to do anything connected with the shop but could not consent to perform the duties of a servant in the house. A difficulty soon arose between Mr. Parker and his wife and myself, and resulted in my leaving him and returning home. So much was I attached to the life of a mechanic, I could not content myself at home and soon got a situation in the shop of Deacon Caleb Knowlton, a cabinet maker in Brandon, my native village. I remained with my new employer about a year, and pursued my business strictly, as all the apprentices in the shop were required to do. Whilst I lived with Mr. Parker I formed a taste for reading, particularly political works, by being associated with a number of young men who spent their time nights and Sundays in reading and study. At this time politics ran high in the presidential election between General Jackson and J. Q. Adams. My associate apprentices and myself were warm advocates of Gen. Jackson's claims, whilst our employer was an ardent supporter of Mr. Adams and Mr. Clay. From this moment my politics became fixed, and all subsequent reading, reflection and observation have but confirmed my early attachment to the cause of Democracy.

In the winter of 1829 and 1830 I was taken sick and compelled to return home. My physicians informed me that my physical strength was too feeble to enable me to work at the cabinet business, and that it would be necessary for me to select some other occupation. Finding my health too feeble to work in the shop, I commenced going to school at the Academy in Brandon, under the direction of J. N. Chipman, and continued under his instruction until the fall of 1830, when I removed to Canandaigua, Ontario county, N.Y. My sister had previously married Julius N. Granger, and removed to his residence in Manchester Centre, Ontario County, N.Y., and this year, 1830, my mother married his father; and now the father and mother and only son and only daughter became united in one family where they continue to reside in the enjoyment of peace, plenty and happiness. Upon removing to the State of New York in December, 1830, I became a student in the Academy in Canandaigua under the superintendence of Prof. Henry Howe, where I continued until the latter part of 1832. Whilst connected with the Academy at Canandaigua I devoted myself zealously to my studies, the Greek and Latin languages, mathematics, rhetoric, logic, &c., and made considerable improvement.

About the 1st of January, 1833, I left the Academy and entered the office of Walter & Levi Hubbell as a student at law. I pursued my law studies diligently five days in the week, and the sixth I spent in reviewing my classical studies, until sometime in the month of June in that year. Finding myself in straightened pecuniary circumstances, and knowing my mother's inability to support me through a regular course of law studies, which would continue about four years longer according to the statutes of New York requiring a course of seven years classical and legal study before admission to the bar, I determined upon removing to the western country and relying upon my own efforts for a support henceforth. My mother and relatives remonstrated, urging that I was too young and inexperienced for such an adventure; but finding my resolution fixed and unchangeable, they reluctantly consented, and kindly furnished me with three hundred dollars, the last of my patrimony, with which to pay my expenses. On the 24th of June, 1833 (being 20 years of age) I bid farewell to my friends, and started alone for the "great west," without having any particular place of destination in view. The first night I arrived at Buffalo, and thence took a trip to the Battle Grounds of Chippewa, Niagara, the Falls &c., &c., and returning to Buffalo in a few days, I embarked on a steam boat for Cleveland, Ohio. Arriving in Cleveland I presented a few letters of introduction to some gentlemen of that place which I had received from Messrs. Francis Granger, Mark H. Sibley and other kind friends.[1] By means of these letters I immediately became acquainted with Sherlock J. Andrews, Esq., an accomplished and intelligent gentleman and distinguished lawyer of that city. Being pleased with Cleveland and its prospects for business, and also with the few acquaintances I formed there, I immediately determined upon remaining there. By the statutes of Ohio I was required to pursue the study of law one year within the limits of that State before I could be admitted to practice. For this purpose Mr. Andrews was kind enough to offer me the use of his office and library, which I gladly accepted, and entered upon my studies with increased spirit and zeal. In a very few days however, I found myself prostrate upon my bed with the bilious fever, and was confined until some time in the month of October, about four months. This sickness has often since been, and still continues to be, the subject of the most serious and profound reflection. My condition, the circumstances with which I was surrounded, the doubtful and sometimes hopeless issue, and especially my feelings, thoughts, and meditations, are all now fresh in my mind. I was among entire strangers. During the whole time I never saw a face I had ever seen before; I was so feeble as to be entirely helpless, unable even to turn myself in bed; I was advised by my physicians that there was no reasonable hope of my recovery, and that I ought to be prepared for my final dissolution which was then expected to take place from day to day. I was in the full enjoyment of my senses, perfectly conscious of my condition, and listened patiently and calmly to all they told me, and felt perfectly indifferent as to the result. I felt satisfied with the past and no particular hopes or apprehensions of the future. I thought I was on the dividing line between this world and the next, must continue to exist in the one or the other, was willing to take either, and felt no choice which. In short, during that four months of severe sickness, I enjoyed more peace and contentment of mind, more perfect freedom from all care and trouble, except occasional bodily pain, and more negative happiness than during any other similar period of my life.

That such should have been the state of my mind under such peculiar and trying circumstances, has ever been to me the subject of curiosity, wonder and amazement. I can account for it upon no principle of philosophy or human nature, and now make this private record of the same for the purpose of seeing if future experience and observation shall solve the mystery.

Upon regaining my strength in the month of October so far as to be able to walk, I paid off all my bills occasioned by my sickness or otherwise and found I had about $40.00 left. I then became reckless and adventurous, and determined to leave the place. Accordingly I took passage on a canal boat for Portsmouth on the Ohio River, thence on a steam boat to Cincinnati, thence to Louisville, thence to St. Louis, Mo., remaining in each place a few days, without any particular object in view, and ready to embark in any adventure adapted to my taste and feeling which should present itself.

At St. Louis I soon found my small pittance of money was about exhausted, and that I must immediately engage in some employment there which would defray my expenses, or go to some place not far distant where I could do so. My first effort was to obtain a situation in some law office in the city, where I could write and perform office labor sufficient to pay my expenses, and during the rest of the time pursue my law studies. Here a difficulty presented itself which I had not foreseen and guarded against. I was more than a thousand miles from home, or any person whom I knew or who knew me, and had no letters of introduction. Perceiving this difficulty I felt great delicacy in offering my services. Stern and impending necessity staring me in the face, I resolved at all hazards to make the effort. I first called on Mr. Bates,[2] introduced myself and told him my business and situation. He received and treated me kindly and politely; and informed me that he had nothing for me to do; but would be happy to see me at his office, &c., for all which I tendered him my grateful acknowledgments and retired. After making a similar effort with like success with Mr. Spaulding,[3] I paid my Tavern bill and left the city, going to Jacksonville, Illinois.

At Jacksonville I formed a few acquaintances and attempted to get into business of some kind, say teaching school, clerking, &c., but without success. When I arrived at Jacksonville I had left one dollar and twenty-five cents in money, and finding that would not pay my board more than one day at the tavern, I sold a few school books I had with me for a few dollars, and took up my lodgings at a private house, Mr. Heslip's,[4] whose family I have known and esteemed ever since. One of my first acquaintances at Jacksonville was Murray McConnel, Esq., a lawyer of some reputation, who advised me to go to Pekin on the Illinois river and open a law office. I informed him that I had never practiced law, had not yet procured my license, nor had I any library. He informed me that he would furnish me with a few books, such as I would stand in the most need of immediately, and wait for the pay until I was able to pay him, and did so to the amount of $30.00 worth, which I received and subsequently paid him for. He told me that a license was a matter of no consequence, that I could practice before a justice of the peace without one, and could get one at any time I desired to do so. I concluded to take his advice, and consequently packed up my things and went to Meredosia on the Illinois River to take a steam boat to Pekin. Arriving at the River, I waited one week for a steam boat, and then learned that the only boat which was expected up the river that season had blown up at Alton, and consequently there would be no boat up until the next spring. What was now to be done? After paying my bill at the tavern, I had but fifty cents left. I could find nothing to do there, and had no money to get away with. Something had to be done, and that soon, I enquired as to the prospect of getting a school, and was told by a farmer residing in the country a few miles that he thought that I could obtain one at Exeter, about ten miles distant; and if I would go home with him that night, he would go to Exeter with me the next day. I accepted his invitation, left my trunk at Meredosia, rode behind the farmer on the same horse to his home, and the next day we both went to Exeter. He introduced me to several citizens who were very polite and kind; but did not think a school could be obtained there; but if I would go to Winchester, eight or ten miles further they had no doubt I would succeed in obtaining one. I thought this was rather poor encouragement; but what was to be done? I was out of money, and still too feeble in health to perform any very arduous labor; and must do something to live; for I was too proud to beg. I therefore determined to go to Winchester and make another effort. Accordingly I parted with my friend, the kind hearted, hospitable farmer and taking my cloak in my arm, went to Winchester on foot that night. Arriving in the town, I went to the only tavern in the place, introduced myself to the landlord and told him I wished to stop a few days with him to which he readily assented. The landlord introduced me to the citizens generally, who seemed pleased with the idea of a new school in their little town, and in a few days obtained for me a subscription list of about forty scholars. In the meantime there was, on the second day after my arrival, an administrator's sale, at which all the personal property of a dead man's estate was to be disposed of at auction, and the administrator applied to me to be clerk at the auction, make out the sale bills, draw the notes, &c., which I very cheerfully consented to do, and performed the duty in the best style I knew how, and received five dollars for two days labor therein. About the 1st of December I commenced my school, and closed it about the 1st of March, having during the whole time a goodly number of scholars, and giving as I believe general satisfaction to both scholars and parents. During this period I attended to considerable law business before justices of the peace, and formed an extensive acquaintance with the people in that part of the county. There was considerable political excitement growing out of the veto of the U.S. Bank and the removal of the deposits by Gen. Jackson, or rather the removal of the secretary of the treasury because he would not remove the deposits, and the appointment of Mr. Taney in his place, who did remove them from the vaults of the U.S. Bank. One evening at the Lyceum, Mr. Josiah Lambert, a lawyer of some distinction from Jacksonville,[5] made a speech, denouncing the leading measures of Gen. Jackson's administration, and especially the veto and removal of the deposits. He characterized the first of those acts as arbitrary and tyrannical, and the last as dangerous and unconstitutional. Being a great admirer of Gen. Jackson's public and political character and a warm supporter of the principles of his administration, I could not remain silent when the old hero's character, public and private, was traduced, and his measures misrepresented and denounced. I was then familiar with all the principles, measures and facts involved in the controversy, having been an attentive reader of the debates in Congress and the principal newspapers of the day, and having read also with great interest, the principal works in this country; such as the debates in the convention that formed the Constitution of the United States, and the convention of the several States on the adoption of the Constitution, the Federalist, John Adams' work denominated a defense of the American Constitution, the opinions of Randolph, Hamilton and Jefferson on the Constitutionality of the Bank, and the History of the

Bank as published by Gales & Seaton, Jefferson's Works, &c. I had read all of them and many other political works with great care and interest, and had my political opinions firmly established. I engaged in the debate with a good deal of zeal and warmth, and defended the administration of Gen. Jackson and the cause of the Democratic party in a manner which appeared highly gratifying to my political friends, and which certainly gave me some little reputation as a public speaker; much more than I deserved.

When the first quarter of my school expired I settled my accounts, and finding that I had made enough to pay my expenses, I determined to remove to Jacksonville, the county seat of the same (Morgan) county, and commence the practice of law. In the month of March I applied to the Hon. Samuel D. Lockwood, one of the justices of the Supreme Court, and after a short examination, obtained a license, and immediately opened an office, being then less than twenty-one years of age. During the first week of my residence at Jacksonville the Whig (alias Federal Party) called a county meeting, and made speeches and passed resolutions denouncing the administration in the severest terms, and more especially in relation to the bank and currency question. The next week the Democrats called a meeting, one of the most numerous and spirited I have ever witnessed in that county. It was composed principally of farmers and mechanics, men who are honest in their political sentiments and feel a deep interest in the proper administration of the public affairs, although but few of them are accustomed to public discussion. It so happened that at that time out of twelve members of the bar there was not a Democrat among them. This meeting I attended, and at the earnest solicitation of my political friends, (for personal friends I had not then had time to form) I consented to make a speech. The excitement was intense, and I was rather severe in my remarks upon the opposition; so much so as to excite the bitter hostility of the whole of that party, and of course the warm support of my own party. The next week the Patriot, the organ of the opposition, printed and published by James G. Edwards, Esq., devoted two entire columns of that paper to me and my speech, and continued the same course for two or three successive weeks. The necessary consequence was that I immediately became known to every man in the county, and was placed in such a situation as to be supported by one party and opposed in the other. This notoriety, acquired by accident and founded on no peculiar merit, proved highly serviceable to me in my profession; for within one week thereafter I received for collection demands to the amount of thousands of dollars from persons I had never seen or heard of, and who would not probably have known that such a person as myself was in existence, but for the attacks upon me in the opposition papers. So essential was the service thus rendered me by my opponents that I have sometimes doubted whether I was not morally bound to pay the editor for his abuse according to the usual prices of advertisements. This incident illustrates a principle which it is important for men of the world and especially politicians to bear in mind. How foolish, how impolitic, the indiscriminate abuse of political opponents whose humble condition or insignificance prevents the possibility of injury, and who may be greatly benefited by the notoriety thus acquired. I firmly believe this is one of the frequent and great errors committed by the political editors of the present day. Indeed, I sincerely doubt whether I owe most to the kind and efficient support of my friends, or to the violent, reckless and imprudent opposition of my enemies. Certain I am that without both of these causes united, I never could have succeeded as well as I have done. But I must forbear; for I find that I am philosophizing, which is far from my present purpose.

During the summer of 1834 my time was about equally divided between law and politics, reading and practicing the one and preaching the other. There was a general election pending for Governor, Congressman, and members of the Legislature, in which I felt no ordinary interest and took an active part. I supported the Democratic candidates; William Kinney for Governor against Gen. Joseph Duncan, and Wm. L. May for Congress against Benjamin Mills, and the Democratic ticket for the legislature in my own county. We lost our Governor; elected our Congressman; and a part of our legislative ticket.

At this time John J. Hardin, Esq., (now Gen. Hardin) held the office of state's attorney, under an appointment from Governor Reynolds, which then had two years to run. He had procured this appointment through the aid and influence of Col. James Evans, Col. William Weatherford, Capt. John Wyatt and other leading Democrats, every one of whom he opposed at the next election after the appointment. Capt. Wyatt was the only one of them who succeeded in his election, and was so indignant at Hardin for what he called his ingratitude, that he determined upon removing him from office at all hazards. The opposition having succeeded in electing their Governor, there was no hope from that quarter; and the only resort left was to repeal the law conferring the appointment upon the Governor, and make the office elective by the legislature. At the request of Capt. Wyatt, I wrote the Bill, and on the second day of the session of the Legislature which commenced on the first Monday in December, 1834, he introduced his bill, and also another bill written by myself making the county recorder's election by the people, instead of being appointed by the Governor. I felt no peculiar interest in these bills any further than I thought them correct in principle, and desired to see them pass because my friends warmly supported them. Both the bills were violently opposed by the opposition (alias Federal Party) and advocated by a large majority of the Democrats, and finally passed by a small majority. When sent to the Council of Revision (composed of the Governor and Judges of the Supreme Court) for approval, they were both vetoed; the former as unconstitutional, and the latter because it was inexpedient. Then came a desperate struggle between the friends and opponents of the bills, and especially the states attorney bill. The opposition charged that its only object was to repeal Hardin out of office in order to elect myself in his place, and that the whole movement had its origin in Wyatt's malice and my selfishness and ambition. I will here remark, and most solemnly aver it to be true, that up to the time this charge was made against me, I never had conceived the idea of being a candidate for the office, nor had any friend suggested or hinted to me that I could or ought to receive it. But from that moment forward, the friends of the bill declared that, in the event they passed the bill over the heads of the Council, I should be elected to the office. At this time I did not desire to be a candidate, for I had no reason to suppose I could be elected over so formidable an opponent who had been a long time a resident of the State, had fought in the Black Hawk War, and was well acquainted with the members. My short residence in the State, want of acquaintance, experience in my profession and age, (being only twenty-one years old) I considered insuperable objections. My friends however, thought differently, passed the bill, and elected me on the first ballot by four votes majority.

I will here remark that although I wrote this bill and reaped first fruits under it, and was inclined at that time to think it correct in principle and ought to become a law; yet subsequent experience, observation and reflection have convinced me of my error; and I now believe that all Legislative elections ought to be abolished, and the officers either appointed by the Governor and Senate, or elected by the people. In this remark I do not mean to include clerks of our courts, whose appointments, I am inclined to think, ought to be vested in the judges.

Immediately upon my election as states attorney I procured all the standard works upon criminal law within my reach, such as Archbold, Chitty, Roscoe, McNally, Hale's Pleas of the Crown, &c., &c.; and devoted myself to the study of them with a determination of making myself master of that branch of my profession. My official duties being exclusively within the line of my profession, I now applied myself assiduously to study and practice. How far I succeeded in this, I must leave to others, who are more impartial judges than myself. An amusing circumstance occured in McLean county at the first court after my election as prosecuting attorney. The grand jury had found a large number of indictments for different offences, and I had been engaged all night in writing them, in great haste, in order to discharge the grand jury and enable them to return to their families. After the grand jurors were discharged John T. Stuart, Esq., came into court and moved to quash all the indictments, although he had been employed in but a small number of the cases. He stated his reasons for quashing the indictments, which were that they were presented by the "grand jurors in and for the county of McClean" when in fact there was no such County as "McClean," the true name of the County being "McLean". The manner of making this motion was very pompous and accompanied with some rather contemptuous remarks imputing ignorance to the writer of the indictments. Contrasting my youth and inexperience with the long practice and reputation of the opposing counsel, I considered his conduct extremely ungenerous, and more especially in a county where he was well acquainted with the people and I was an entire stranger. The moment the motion to quash was made and the objection was pointed out, it struck my mind as being fatal to all the indictments, and had it been done in a respectful and courteous manner, I should have made no objection to the indictments being quashed. When the Judge (Stephen T. Logan) asked me if I had anything to say in support of the indictments, I told him I did not consider it necessary as yet to say anything, Mr. Stuart having made the motion and having the affirmative of the question, the burden of proof of course rested upon him. That I presumed the court would not take official notice that I had not spelled the name of the county right until some evidence had been adduced to sustain the motion, and when such evidence should be produced, it would then be time enough for me to rebut such evidence. The court decided that it could not officially take notice of the precise mode of spelling the name of the county, and gave Mr. Stuart time to procure the statute creating and naming the county. My object was now accomplished; knowing there was none of the statutes to be found in the county, and that it would require a good deal of traveling, trouble and expense to procure one, which would sufficiently rebuke the gentleman's insolence; but not doubting that when the statute was produced, it would show that the defect in the indictments was fatal and they ought to be quashed. After a lapse of two days the Statute was procured from an adjoining county, and produced and read to the court by Mr. Stuart, when to his astonishment, and I will say to the astonishment of myself and the whole bar, it appeared that the name of the county in the indictment was right, and that the learned gentleman did not know how to spell the name of the county he had practiced in for years. It turned the joke upon him so completely, and excited so much mirth and humor at his expense, that he could not conceal his chagrin and mortification. The indictments were all sustained by the court, much to my gratification. Some time afterwards I took the pains to compare this printed statute with the enrolled bill in the office of the Secretary of State, and found there was a misprint, the true name of the County being McLean. This small incident, although of no consequence of itself, has been an instructive lesson to me in the practice of law ever since, to-wit: Admit nothing, and require my adversary to prove everything material to the success of his cause. Every lawyer's experience teaches him that many good causes are saved and bad ones gained by a strict observance of this rule. During the time I held the office of states attorney, I conducted many important criminal prosecutions, and as far as I have been able to learn, acquitted myself in a manner satisfactory to my friends and the public generally.

In August, 1836, I was elected to the Legislature from the County of Morgan. The contest was a very spirited one, conducted almost solely upon national politics and party grounds. Each party ran a full ticket and strived to elect the whole ticket. The stump speeches were made, principally by Gen. John J. Hardin on behalf of the Whig ticket, and by myself in support of the Democratic ticket. The contest resulted in the election of five Democrats and one Whig (Gen. Hardin).

On the 1st Monday of December, 1836, I resigned my office of states attorney, and took my seat in the Legislature. It was during this session that Illinois embarked in her mammoth system of internal improvements. Before the election I had announced myself in favor of a general system of internal improvements, and was really anxious to see one of reasonable extent and expense adopted; but never for a moment dreampt of anyone's advocating such a wild and extravagent scheme as the one which was finally adopted.

When I learned the nature and extent of the bill which the Committee on Internal Improvements were maturing, I attempted to arrest it by introducing resolutions by way of instructions (see House Journal of 1836-7, page 36) setting forth the kind and extent of a system I thought ought to be adopted. My resolutions proposed 1st: To finish the Illinois and Michigan canal. 2nd: To construct a railroad from the termination of the canal to the mouth of the Ohio river. 3rd: To make a railroad from the Mississippi river to the Wabash to connect with the Wabash and Erie canal.

I was willing and anxious to make these three works on the faith of the State; but was unwilling to go further. I believed the canal to be an important State and National work, which would be useful to the government and people. I entertained doubts whether the plan of construc-

[67]

tion adopted by the commissioners was the best one that could be pursued, but rather than hazard the success of the work by differences of opinion as to the best manner of doing it, I determined to support and did support the bill which was passed that session. In fact the bill passed that session was a compromise bill written by myself and introduced by Capt. Joseph Napier of Cook county from a committee of which we were both members.

But to return to the internal improvements system; when it was ascertained from my conversation, speeches, and resolution that I would oppose the mammoth bill, its friends procured me to be instructed by my constituents to go for it. It must be remembered that at that day the people were for the system—almost en masse. So strong was the current of popular feeling in its favor that it was hazardous for any politician to oppose it. Under these circumstances it was easy to obtain instructions in favor of a measure so universally popular, and accordingly the friends of the bill got up instructions, which, from my known sentiments in favor of the doctrine of instruction, I did not feel myself at liberty to disobey. I accordingly voted for the bill under these instructions. That vote was the vote of my constituents and not my own. My own sentiments upon this subject are found recorded in the resolutions above referred to. If a limited and reasonable system, such as I proposed, had been adopted, instead of the one which did pass, I have no doubt it would have been entirely completed at this time, would be useful to the State and sustained by the people.

There was another question which excited much interest during that session. Immense numbers of applications were made for charters of all kinds and description; railroads, canals, insurance companies, hotel companies, steam mill companies &c., &c. I first attempted to arrest this whole system of legislation as unjust, impolitic and unwise. Failing in this, I next attempted to cripple it by inserting in each charter a clause "reserving the right to alter, amend or repeal this act whenever the public good shall require it."

Printed in Frank E. Stevens, editor, "Autobiography of Stephen A. Douglas," *Journal of the Illinois State Historical Society*, V (October, 1912), 323-342.

[1]Francis Granger and Mark Sibley were prominent Canandaigua attorneys. Granger was elected to Congress in 1834, eventually serving three terms in the lower house, and in 1841 was appointed Postmaster General by President Harrison. Sibley later served in Congress from 1837 to 1839.

[2]Edward Bates, a member of Congress from Missouri between 1827 and 1829, practiced law in St. Louis and was a member of the Missouri Senate at this time.

[3]Josiah Spalding was an important member of the early St. Louis bar and editor of the *Missouri Republican* for a time.

[4]Joseph Heslep, of Jacksonville, was active in Morgan County Democratic politics.

[5]Douglas meant to write Josiah Lamborn.

To Francis Preston Blair

(Private)

Dear Sir   Springfield Ill Nov 2nd 1838

I have taken the liberty of addressing you without the formality of an introduction, and offer the contents of the Letter itself as my apology for doing so. You may have seen my name before the people of this district as a Candidate for Congress, and that I received a majority of about one hundred votes over my opponent, and that he has received the Certificate of Election by means of *false* returns made by some of the Clerks, and the Governor having refused to count some of the votes actually returned for me.[1] Great interest is felt in the matter here by the Democracy of the Country, as the question was made directly before the people between Democratic & Federal principles and particularly between the *subTreasury* & a *National Bank*. The result is important also in another respect. In case the next Presidential Election should go into the House of Representatives, it is considered doubtful how the vote of this State should be cast if my opponent had a seat. These added to the ordinary causes which are in operation in a heated contest, have created great solicitude as to the result. All of my friends agree as to the propriety of contesting the election, and I have to ask of you the favor to inform me as to the *manner* of making the contest, and the *preliminary* steps necessary to be taken, the *notices* if any to be given &c &c.[2]

Will you also have the kindness to inform me of the political complexsion of the next Congress as indicated by the recent elections. We are in high spirits here, and confident of the complete triumph of Democratic principles throughout the Union. The late crises has had a salutary effect upon the noble cause; has purged the party of all those weather cocks that change from Party to Party as self interest would impel them, and left the Democratic Party in a purer, healther & stronger condition than it has ever been at any former period. Enclosed you will find a five dollar Bill which you will please accept & send me the Globe.

Please communicate with me upon this subject & if I can be of any service to you I shall always be ready & willing. I am so very respectfully your obedient servant

                                                      S. A. Douglass

                                            Stephen A. Douglass
Send him the Semi-Weekly Globe, & charge. You need not send a bill, as I have written to him. The $5 which he enclosed I took to purchase a book on contested elections for him.

                                                      J. C. R.[3]

[69]

ALS, Historical Society of Pennsylvania, Philadelphia. Francis Preston Blair was editor of the Washington *Daily Globe*, the official organ of the Jackson administration, and had been a close confidant of the former President.

[1]Douglas was defeated for Congress by John T. Stuart by the narrow margin of 35 votes, in a total of over 36,-000 cast. Many of Douglas' votes had been thrown out because of technicalities, forming the basis for his decision to contest Stuart's election.

[2]Douglas also wrote Thomas Hart Benton, then a member of the United States Senate, for advice in contesting the election. For Benton's reply, see Benton to Douglas, October 27, 1838, owned by Martin F. Douglas, and reprinted in Frank E. Stevens, "Life of Stephen Arnold Douglas," *Journal of the Illinois State Historical Society*, XVI (October, 1923–January, 1924), 321. Douglas later abandoned the idea of challenging Stuart's election.

[3]John Cook Rives was Blair's partner and financial manager of the *Globe*. The postscript is in Rives's hand.

To John T. Stuart

Springfield, March 4, 1839.

Sir—There seems to have been much difficulty in determining which of us is duly elected to Congress *by the people*, and by some the result is even yet considered doubtful. I understand that you have received a certificate of election, issued after the expiration of the time prescribed by law, whilst I have reason to believe that I have received a majority of the votes. Disdaining myself to accept a seat in Congress except by the will and votes of the majority of those I should represent, I will do you the justice to say that I am unwilling to believe that you would desire it upon any other condition. I cannot believe that you will claim a seat in Congress upon the mere ground that you have been so lucky as to receive a certificate of election, made in violation of law and in opposition to the votes of a majority of the people. I believe, and I think that you will admit the correctness of the position, that a majority of the people should rule, and consequently that the candidate receiving a majority of the votes is entitled to and should obtain the seat. If you entertain any doubt which of us received the majority, I will cheerfully unite with you upon any fair and honorable plan to render that point certain, and at the same time avoid the trouble, excitement, delay and expense of a contested election in Congress. With this view I submit to you the following propositions, and solicit your acceptance of the one you shall think most favorable to your cause and the accomplishment of the object.

1st. I propose that the officers of State, whose duty it is made by law, shall cast up and canvass all the votes in the office of Secretary of State according to the corrected returns, and report which of us has the majority. In the canvass thus to be made I propose that all the votes returned for the name of "Stuart" be counted for you, and all the votes returned for the name of "Douglass" be counted for me, without regard to the christian name or the spelling; or, if *you prefer* it, I will agree that *all* the mispelling on both sides be rejected, and those votes only be counted that are returned for John T. Stuart and Stephen A. Douglass. In case this proposition is accepted by you, we will mutually pledge our honors to abide the decision that may be made in accordance herewith, and yield the seat to the person so declared to have received a majority of the votes.

2d. If you object to the State officers making the examination and decision as above proposed, I propose next that you will select a friend and I will select another and those two shall choose a third, and the three thus chosen shall make the examination and decision aforesaid upon the terms above prescribed, and we will pledge ourselves to abide their report. Under this proposition as in the first, I leave it to your option whether the misspelling shall all be counted or rejected.

By either of these propositions we can ascertain satisfactorily which of us has a majority of the votes returned to the office of Secretary of State. I cannot conceive what objection can be made to either of them, unless you doubt the correctness of the returns made to the Secretary. In that event I will submit the following proposition which will obviate the objection.

3d. I propose that three persons to be chosen in the manner stated in the second proposition, shall visit the Clerk's Offices of each county in the district, examine the Poll Books. Add up the votes and decide which of us has a majority of the votes upon the poll books. In this as in the other propositions, I leave it with you to say, whether all the mispelling shall be counted or all rejected. I submit each of these propositions for your consideration, and upon your acceptance of either of them, I will pledge myself to abide any decision that may be made in conformity therewith. These propositions seem to me fair and reasonable, and well calculated to decide the question, without resorting to a contest in Congress. If, therefore, you really believe you have received a majority of the votes, I presume you will unhesitatingly accept one of them.

But, sir, it is possible that you are laboring under the impression that, although you did not get a majority of the votes at the last election, yet, if the question was again submitted to the people, you could run better next time. If so, I feel disposed to accomodate you in that respect, and do therefore propose, in that event,

4th. That we sign a joint resignation and run the race over again on the first Monday in August next.

I hope you will reflect upon the subject and favor me with your views as soon as your convenience will permit.[1] I shall be in town until Saturday next, and shall expect a definite answer by that time.

This letter together with your answer, is intended for publication. I am, very respectfully, Your obedient servant,

S. A. DOUGLASS

Vandalia *Illinois State Register*, April 5, 1839; from the *Illinois Republican*.
[1]Stuart rejected Douglas' proposals. See below, Douglas to Weber, March 12, 1839.

To George R. Weber

Mr. Weber: [March 12, 1839]

Enclosed I send you a copy of a letter addressed by me to John T. Stuart, Esq. on the 4th inst. in relation to the Congressional election in this district. You will perceive that a definite answer was expected on Saturday last, either accepting or rejecting the propositions contained in my letter. I have received no *written* reply to my letter, but have been *verbally* informed by Mr. Stuart, that he should not accede to any of the propositions made to him by me to terminate the controversy without a contest in Congress, and that he will hereafter give his reasons for declining them.[1] Under these circumstances I feel it my duty to my country, to those kind friends who have sustained me, and to myself, to contest the election in vindication of the right of a majority of the people to rule. You will do me the favor to insert in your paper my letter to Mr. Stuart for the information of those who may feel interested in the subject.

March 12th, 1839.   S. A. DOUGLASS

Vandalia *Illinois State Register*, April 5, 1839; from the *Illinois Republican*.
[1]Stuart wrote to Douglas on March 13, rejecting Douglas' propositions on the ground that their acceptance would be an acknowledgment of doubt concerning the outcome of the election. "I do not consider your various propositions worthy of a more particular reply," Stuart concluded, "as they are all evidently intended for the *Public* and not for me." Stuart's reply was published in the *Register* for April 5.

To Henry B. McClure

Dear Sir,   Springfield July 11th 1839

I have one or two cases in the supreme Court the trial of which it becomes necessary for me to have the following authorities towit—

5 Sergent & Rowels Repts Penn

1st McCords South Carolina Rept

1st Davies Rept

3rd Sergent & Rowles Repts

Wallace Repts

I believe all the above Books are in Jacksonville & may probably be found in McConnel's, Berdon's[1] and your Libraries. If you will do me the favor to collect & send them to me by the bearer, I will take good care of them and see them returned as soon as Court adjourns.

Your compliance with this request will confer an especial favor which I will take great pleasure in reciprocating. I am very respectfully your friend

S. A. Douglass

P.S. Please send also Chapman on Government & Sargent Cont Law if they are to be found. Yours &c.

S. A. D.

ALS, Illinois State Historical Library. Henry B. McClure was a Jacksonville attorney.

[1]James Berdan was a Jacksonville attorney.

To Frederick R. Dutcher

Dear Sir   Springfield Oct 2nd 1839

Mr Roberts has just placed in my hands a letter from you show[ing] a mistake in the Poll Book of your precinct of 3 votes. Every vote is important at this crisis. You have my grateful acknowledgement for the kindness you have already shown. But I must ask of you the favor to carefully add up the votes in each of the other precincts and see if there have been no mistakes in the *addition* of them by the Clerks & Judges. This can all be done at the Clerks Office where you will find all the Poll Books of the county. When you shall have examined all the Poll Books I wish you would get the Clerk of the Co Comis[sioners?] Court to call to his assistance two Justices of the Peace & to make a new return correcting the mistakes. This has been done in many other Counties and will be in all soon. It is important that this should be attended to *immediately* as the time is fast approaching when I must leave for Washington. Please send the names of the illegal voters and also the witnesses by whom they can be proven to be illegal. I am with great respect your friend

S. A. Douglass

ALS, Chicago Historical Society. Frederick R. Dutcher, merchant and Democratic politician in Lee County, had been entrusted by Douglas with the investigation of the Douglas-Stuart election returns in his county.

To Lewis W. Ross

Dear Sir   Springfield Oct 14th 1839

Permit me to introduce to your acquaintance Charles H Lanphier Esq[1] who visits your county for the purpose of examining the Poll Books for Congress with a view to the detection of errors. Any aid you can render him will be gratefully acknowledged by your friend

S. A. Douglass

[73]

ALS, Illinois State Historical Library.
[1]Charles H. Lanphier was at this time employed as a printer on the *Illinois State Register*. The paper was owned by his brother-in-law, William Walters; in 1846, Lanphier assumed the proprietorship upon Walters' death.

To the Editors of the *Illinois State Register*

[February 18, 1840]

Gentlemen:—We have been furnished by the editors of the "Old Hickory,"[1] with a circular and a letter of Mr. Bloodgood,[2] which are of such an extraordinary character, making developments which deeply affect the interests of the people of the United States, that we think they should appear in the columns of the State Register, and every other Democratic paper in the Union. For this purpose we have sent them to many distinguished gentlemen in different parts of the country, in a letter, of which the following is a copy. We hope that you will lay the same before your readers.

S. A. Douglass
E. D. Taylor
V. Hickox
J. R. Diller
of the Democratic Central Committee,   W. Walters[3]
Springfield, Ill., Feb. 18, 1840.

_____

Springfield, Ill., Feb. 17, 1840.

Sir,—Enclosed we send you a copy of the "Old Hickory," containing a Circular and Letter signed S. Dewitt Bloodgood, dated Albany, N.Y. Oct 23rd, 1839. These papers show the causes which produced the nomination of Gen. Harrison, the means by which that nomination was effected and the objects intended to be accomplished by it. That the Letter and Circular are genuine there can be no question. The originals are in our possession with the signature of Mr. Bloodgood in his proper hand writing. If its authenticity is denied we are prepared to prove it genuine. As these papers relate to a subject in which a large portion of the community feel a deep interest, we send them to you with the privilege of using them as you think proper. We are respectfully, your obedient servants,

S. A. Douglass
E. D. Taylor
V. Hickox
J. R. Diller
W. Walters

Democratic State Central Committee of Illinois.

_____

[74]

From Old Hickory.

CONSPIRACY AGAINST THE RIGHTS OF THE PEOPLE OF THE UNITED STATES! A FOUL PLOT DETECTED!

We have been favored by some unknown friend with the following most important document, which clearly discloses the objects and designs of the Opposition in making General Harrison their candidate for the Presidency, as well as the means by which his nomination was procured from the Harrisburg Convention.[4]

It will be borne in mind that the federal party throughout the Union, held up Mr. Clay as their candidate for the Presidency, from the commencement of Mr. Van Buren's administration till after the last August elections. The measures of Mr. Van Buren's administration had been submitted to the good sense and intelligence of the country, and the last summer's elections in the several States showed that they were gloriously and triumphantly sustained. Mr. Clay himself was in the field, actively engaged in electioneering—travelling from State to State —eating public dinners, and making political speeches, when the news of his utter and entire overthrow in the States of Tennessee, Indiana and Ohio, drove him home to Ashland in despair.[5] The fall elections completed the triumph of the great measures of Mr. Van Buren's administration; and by demonstrating that those measures were and would continue to be sustained, it was also shown that Mr. Clay, a high tariff, internal improvements, and a National Bank, would no longer meet with the encouragement and support of the American people. In many parts of the Union, the federalists gave up the contest in despair, and every where it was admitted that Mr. Van Buren had triumphed, and that his success in the next contest was certain. Some of the leading federal papers even went so far as to urge the dismemberment of the party, and the cessation of all hostilities to the present democratic administration.—To the federal party all hope had fled; and it was not by an advocacy of the principles which had ever characterized them that they could ever again expect success. Boldly and openly had they battled for years in support of a protective tariff, a grand system of internal improvements, and a National Bank. Upon these questions they had failed, and with them had fallen their great champion, Mr. Clay.

During the past season, the Abolitionists and Abolition newspapers had shown themselves against Mr. Clay, and had given the most decided manifestations in favor of General Harrison.

To abandon Mr. Clay—to secure the co-operation of the ABOLITIONISTS—and to procure the nomination of General Harrison, to whom the anti-masons and abolitionists were supposed to be attached —was now the object of the federal leaders. To seek this alliance

[75]

openly, they dare not. To proclaim the motive publicly and boldly, would be fatal. But to secure the nomination of Harrison, it was necessary that it should be known all over the Union, that the abolitionists and anti-masons would give him their support.—With this view, the "Central Abolition Committee" at Albany, in New York, got up the following circular, which was directed by Mr. S. Dewitt Bloodgood, a leading abolitionist in Albany, to various leading men of the federal party in all the States in the Union—instructing them to urge their delegates in the Harrisburg Convention to go for Harrison.

One of these circulars was sent to Mr. Simeon Francis, the editor of the Sangamo Journal, supposing, from his station, that he could influence the vote of Illinois. Mr. Francis and the whole federal party of the State, had long been for Clay. And as the vote of this State was cast for Harrison in the Harrisburg Convention, and as all the leading federalists of this State, about that time, became very friendly to General Harrison, we have every reason to believe that it was under the influence of the ABOLITION and ANTI-MASONIC CIRCULAR.

Here is the circular, together with the letter of Mr. Bloodgood:

"Albany, Oct. 23, 1839.

"*To the Editor of the Sangamo Journal.*

"Dear Sir:—I send you (CONFIDENTIALLY) a Circular which is circulating here, and is producing great effect. Mr. Clay cannot possibly get this State, or New England. Our only hope is in Gen. Harrison, who is perfectly unexceptionable, and has no serious opposition to him on any possible ground. The leaders do not feel perhaps as sure of getting paid for their services with him as with other candidates who have impliedly come into their views. But we can make a glorious rally under his banner, and reach the hearts of the people, with his services and virtues. Gen. Scott has been pushed by a few Anti Claymen, but it is all nonsense. I send you a pamphlet which is also circulating here, and which shows that no Jacksonmen or Clintonians can or will support him. The great point now is to have the public voice indicate a preference, or there may be fatal mistakes made at Harrisburg. I am the Chairman of the State Central Committee of Young Men, but do not speak officially. I should like to forward some papers and letters to your delegates but their residence is not mentioned. Will you publish their residence and send me a paper.

Yours truly,
S. DEWITT BLOODGOOD."

(CONFIDENTIAL.)

"Dear Sir,—The peculiar crisis in which the Whig party is placed, and the circumstance of my connection by means of an extensive political correspondence, with many of the purest and most patriotic of our fellow citizens in other States, induce me to address you at this time, in relation to the Presidential question. And first, let me avow myself as the warm, devoted, personal friend of Mr. Clay, and an unqualified admirer of his talents and services. I believe he deserves to be President of the United States, above all our other candidates, and yet with all these admissions I can not but consider his prospect at present a hopeless one. We have lost three years in contests about men, and the tide of victory carrying us no where, except into the eddies formed by opposing sections, or upon the barren beach of useless controversy, seems ebbing to leave us there. The Whig party being an intelligent and intellectual class must necessarily do its own thinking, and with thought comes variety of opinions, and with variety, want of unity and concord. This is our predicament and our danger. If we were united, we should be formidable to the enemies of our country; but alas, we are beaten in detail. Let us apply this fact to the choice of candidates. Mr. Clay's political course, and long conflicts with portions of his fellow citizens, have rendered him liable to warm opposition, personal hatred, and unjust prejudice. Is it the part of sagacious men to venture against such odds? With a majority of the States against us, is it prudent to risk every thing left us? Our party leaders want sagacity, or as I prefer styling it, philosophy. They act as if mankind were always actuated by the best motives, and that the holding up an abstract truth, is the pledge of victory. Not so. Nations, like individuals, often rush blindly to ruin, from passion, prejudice, ambition, and many other causes. It is in vain to oppose their will when they take a particular bias. They who attempt it are sacrificed, and thus history tells us with its monitory page, of the downfall of patriots vainly struggling against their erring countrymen, and finally of the downfall of the masses themselves. This is the law of nature and the will of Providence. Let us also apply this fact to politics. We can not expect *perfection* in the people at large; we can only rely on their general good intentions, sustained by a consciousness, that their own interests individually, are at stake with those of the mass. When they are right in the main, it is as much as we should expect. We can not hope that they will cease to be men in order to please *us*. In this knowledge consists the tact of the administration party. They studiously seek to know the public will, and they follow it long enough to profit by its force and power.—How adroitly they availed themselves of the popularity of Jackson! By bad measures they have lost much of its advantage, and by prosecuting such a scheme as the subtreasury, they will lose more. But still they are strongly entrenched, and we must carry their entrenchments, or be doomed to political slavery. How can this be done? Only by uniting on the man who has

[77]

less opposition to him than another. Superior or splendid talents or exalted claims are not the questions to be considered. What is any man compared to the cause? What have we to do with political rewards when our country is on the brink of ruin?

Herein the friends of Mr. Clay have made a fatal mistake. In their love for him they forget that a battle is to be fought. Enthusiasm will not always overpower superiority of numbers. If it could, Mr. Clay would have been President long ago.

If Mr. Clay runs, he will meet with opposition from old party antagonists, whose heads have grown gray in political iniquity.

The old JACKSON MEN will oppose him.

The ABOLITIONISTS generally, will oppose him.

The violent anti-masons will oppose him.

The Irishmen, who have already denounced him for his attack on O'Connel, will oppose him.

The enemies of the United States Bank will oppose him.

The WESTERN SQUATTERS will oppose him.

The Southern States Rights men will oppose him. (So say several leading papers in Georgia.)

Now, in the name of heaven, shall we run the risk of this opposition, or even of the show of it? Can we go headlong into a fight with these adverse elements actively at work against us? Are we strong enough to venture so much? It seems to me that some men must have taken leave of their senses, to advocate any candidate against whom any portion of this opposition may be brought. Nothing but a strong and decided course on the part of our editorial friends, and an appeal without delay to the good sense of the party will save us from utter ruin.

To whom shall we then look for aid? where is the man sufficiently popular to be our candidate, and one free from these objections?

I answer, we have him, and have had him for three years, and if good policy had prevailed, we would by this time have looked down all opposition.

Among the "people" of this state he is at this moment vastly more popular than any other candidate; and the reasons for it lie deep in the human heart.

Since the reverses in the West, and South and North, men have begun to think, and thinking has produced wonderful changes under our own eyes. Our letters from the western counties assure us that the delegates to the National convention will generally be Harrison men, and such they will be from this vicinity.

The name of Gen. Scott has been brought out here by a few of our leading office holders. It is suspected that it was *at first* merely a scheme to get rid of Mr. Clay, and the implied obligation of his support. As it took a little better than was expected, a few have attempted to press it. But it is the idlest of all attempts, and even now signally fails. Gen. Scott is not known as a whig, and not identified with us. A few ambitious men in New York, and in the army, doubtless hope to advance themselves by advancing him. But leaving all other objections out of view, two circumstances are fatal to him, growing out of a celebrated personal controversy. Gen. Jackson's letter, and that of De Witt Clinton, will shortly make their appearance, by which all hopes of support from any of their friends will be entirely cut off. Read for yourselves from Niles' Register for 1818, and you will judge how much popularity will be left him in this struggle. But I forbear.

I hope you will give this letter your serious attention, and if you agree with me, you will at once throw yourself into the front rank, for the purpose of producing "union and harmony" IN TIME.

Yours with great respect

A friend of Clay, but a greater friend of the Cause."

General Harrison was nominated and is now the federal abolition candidate for the Presidency of the United States. He was nominated for the reasons contained in the above circular. He was nominated, because the "ABOLITIONISTS" would go for him!

Because the "ANTI-MASONS" would go for him!

Because the Western "SQUATTERS" would go for him!

And because, the *"Abolitionists,"* and the *"anti-Masons,"* and the Western *"Squatters"* would "not go for Mr. Clay."

Having secured the nomination of Gen Harrison, and the co-operation and support of the abolitionists and anti-masons, a new hope inspired the federal party—a fresh and vigorous shout was raised. The abolition papers all over the nation, boldly and loudly proclaimed that General Harrison's nomination was produced by the firmness and energy of the abolitionists. Some of these extracts from abolition papers have been already published. The federalists every where seem to be animated with the hope of success; but that hope is founded on the support of the abolitionists. Wherever an abolitionist is found, he is loud and warm in the support of Harrison. There are some three hundred abolitionists, it is said, in the county of Sangamon, every one of whom is for Harrison. We call upon our fellow-citizens in every neighborhood of this county and State, to notice the course of the abolitionists. We defy them to find one anywhere who is not for Harrison. Such is the case all over the nation. Yes! the men who boldly say they would sacrifice their country and its proud and holy institutions, and bathe its fields with the blood of their fellow-citizens to make the negro free, are the men who boast of having made Harrison the federal candidate for the Presidency; and the men who are every where giving him their most zealous support.

The renewed hope and active exertions of the leading federalists, can be attributed to nothing else but their coalition with the abolitionists. —Upon every question of political principle, they have lost ground in the last three years. And their course last fall towards Mr. Clay, demonstrates this; for he was the able champion of all their political principles. Clay is now thrust aside; and under the *dark banner* of ABOLITIONISM, the federalists hope to conquer by secrecy and intrigue. At this very moment, a secret and dangerous organization is going on in every neighborhood of this State; and, it is said, in every State in the Union. In every precinct, poll books are secretly kept by a secret committee, appointed by a secret Central Committee, living at Springfield. In these poll-books every voter's name is taken down, and his vote recorded some nine months before the election. But this secret organization is of a piece with that which made Harrison the candidate for the Presidency. Secret committees are the best possible resort of those who wish the grounds and motives upon which Harrison was nominated, known to all their friends, especially the abolitionists. They could not make them known by stump speeches or thro' the press, for THEY DARE NOT. The union of ABOLITIONISM with FEDERALISM, can best be communicated by SECRET COMMITTEES. But we leave this subject now to resume it hereafter.

Springfield *Illinois State Register,* February 21, 1840.

[1]*Old Hickory* was a Democratic newspaper published in Springfield during the Presidential campaign of 1840. According to its prospectus, first published in the *State Register* on January 25, the paper was edited by "Several Democratic Citizens," but Douglas seems to have played an important role in its publication.

[2]S. Dewitt Bloodgood is identified in an accompanying news item as a former Whig editor in Albany, New York.

[3]Edmund Dick Taylor had represented Sangamon County in the state legislature, both House and Senate, during the early 1830's; Virgil Hickox was a Springfield merchant; Jonathan R. Diller was later to be appointed Postmaster of Springfield.

[4]The "Democratic Whig National Convention" met in December, 1839, in Harrisburg, Pennsylvania, and nominated William Henry Harrison for the Presidency.

[5]Henry Clay, considering himself to be the logical choice for the Whig candidacy in 1840, had made a northern campaign tour the year before. While on the tour, news of Democratic victories in the state elections reached him, and he seems to have had some apprehension that his candidacy was the cause of the Democratic triumph. He was not, however, driven in despair back to his Kentucky home but continued to seek the nomination. It is not true that he had been, up to the state elections, the widespread choice of the party; movements on behalf of Harrison and Winfield Scott were already under way.

Call for Democratic County Convention

[March 26, 1840; Springfield *Illinois State Register*, March 27, 1840. Call for election of precinct delegates to a Sangamon County convention, to be held at Springfield on April 11, for the purpose of nominating candidates for the state legislature and for the county offices. The call was signed by 195 voters of Sangamon County, including Douglas.]

Application for Membership in Masonic Lodge

Springfield April 21st A L. 5840 A D. 1840

To the W. Master, Wardens & brethren of Springfield Lodge No. 26, of Free and Accepted Masons.

The subscriber residing in the City of Springfield State of Illinois of lawful age and by occupation a Lawyer, begs leave to State that unbiassed by friends and uninfluenced by mercenary motives, he freely and voluntarily offers himself as a candidate for the mysteries of Masonry, and that he is prompted to solicit this privilege, by a favourable opinion conceived of the Institution, a desire of knowledge and a sincere wish of being serviceable to his fellow creatures. Should his petition be granted he will cheerfully conform to all the antient established usages & customs of the Fraternity.

Recommended by   S. A. DOUGLASS

   L. S. Cornwell.

   J. S. Roberts[1]

DS-Photostat, Illinois State Historical Library.

[1]Love S. Cornwell, of Springfield, was President of the Young Men's Lyceum. John S. Roberts was Postmaster of Springfield in 1840.

To Robert Allen

[April 23, 1840]

Sir—Your note as President of the late Democratic Convention, informing me of my nomination as a candidate for Representative in our Legislature from this county, is received. I feel grateful to the Democracy of Sangamon, for this evidence of their continued confidence and esteem. Considerations of a private nature however, constrain me to decline the nomination, and leave the field to those whose avocations and private affairs will enable them to devote the requisite portion of their time to the canvass.[1] You will accept my thanks for the very complimentary manner in which you have been pleased to communicate the result of the deliberations of the convention. I am, Sir, very respectfully your fellow citizen,

Springfield, April 23, 1840.   S. A. DOUGLASS

[81]

Springfield *Illinois State Register*, April 24, 1840. Robert Allen was a Springfield merchant.

[1]Douglas was not present at the county convention when he was nominated for the state legislature. At the request of several members of the convention, Jesse B. Thomas, Jr., agreed to fill Douglas' place on the legislative ticket. Douglas was appointed Secretary of State of Illinois by Governor Thomas Carlin on November 30, 1840; Thomas was defeated in his bid for the legislature.

To the Democratic Party of Illinois

[May 13, 1840]

We have received intelligence from our friends in various parts of the State, assuring us that at this busy season of the year, the Democratic farmers cannot, without great inconvenience, leave their farms for a period of time necessary to attend a Convention in Springfield. A very few counties have already appointed delegates, and have shown a disposition to make every sacrifice for the interests of their party and country. In view, however, of the times, and the inconvenience to which democrats will be subjected at this busy season of the year, in leaving their work to attend a convention hundreds of miles from home, we beg leave to suggest to our friends in all parts of the State that it is inexpedient to hold a young men's Convention in June next.[1] The Democratic party is emphatically a sober and reflecting party. It believes not in pomp, parade or show. It leaves such humbuggery to that party whose opinion of the public intelligence is of so low a grade as to lead them to act upon the unworthy principle that "the people are to be led by show, and not moved by sober honest appeals to their judgment." To that party we are willing to yield all the benefits of pompous exhibitions of pictures, log-cabins, canoes and old cider barrels; and for our own cause we trust to the quiet but certain influence of truth and correct principle again to conduct us to victory.
Springfield, May 13th, 1840.

S. A. DOUGLAS

J. R. DILLER

M. K. ANDERSON[2]

WM. WALTERS

V. HICKOX

State Central Committee.

Springfield *Illinois State Register*, May 15, 1840.

[1]The Democrats had scheduled a Young Men's Convention for Springfield in June, 1840, to compete with a similar gathering planned by the Whigs. As the tide began to run stronger in favor of Harrison and as the effectiveness of the political pageantry employed by the Whig campaigners was demonstrated, the Democrats altered their plans.

[2]Moses K. Anderson, a Sangamon County justice of the peace, had been an unsuccessful candidate for state senator in 1836 and for state representative in 1838. He was to fail a third time in his bid for election to the state legislature in 1840.

To the People of Illinois

[June 4, 1840]

A large number of Democrats having casually met on business, in the City of Springfield and having witnessed the transactions of the Federal-Whigs in this State, it has been deemed expedient for the Democrats now here, to meet and express their views on what has transpired under their own observation.

They have for the last three days witnessed a series of intrigues and deception practised by the Federal-Whig party, in their desperate struggle to elevate Gen. Harrison to the Presidency, without regard to the means used, adopting the maxim that "the end justifies the means."

They have heard the arguments, the speeches, and the clap-trap harangues of their leaders, in which neither consistency nor truth were adhered to. They have seen the degrading and unhallowed means which have been adopted to deceive the people and possess themselves of the Government. They desire to speak respectfully, but cannot, in justice to themselves and the occasion, refrain from expressing, in plain and unequivocal terms, the opinions they entertain of their measures and party. By trick and stratagem they are attempting to create a false issue before the people and to defeat by ridicule what they cannot meet by argument. They are diligently engaged, by secret organization and political chicanery, in imposing upon the fears and exciting the credulity of the People. They are employing measures alike degrading, disorganizing and revolutionary in their tendency. They seek to defeat the Democratic candidate by forming an union with the disaffected and disappointed of all parties,—Clay-men, Bank-men, Hartford Convention-men, Anti-masons, Abolitionists, and *old Federalists*, as well as new *Federal-Whigs*, now constitute their leaders. They are practising the most gross hypocrisy—in all their speeches—on their banners and exhibitions they affect to be Democrats, while their acts and their measures, which they have always advocated, prove that they are the old Federalists of the Hartford and Essex junto school.

We therefore, offer, for the consideration of our Democratic friends, the following resolutions as expressive of our views at this time. But while we have herein set down, in terms of disapprobation, what we have lately seen in this place, and have briefly and boldly given our reasons for such opinions, yet, still we wish it distinctly understood by our fellow-citizens of the Democratic party in this State, that whatever we may have said, or whatever resolutions we may adopt, nothing is meant in the spirit of dictation.

We say this, because we know that our whole party is not represented here at this time. What we have said, cannot, and ought not, to be set down to such a spirit as party dictation in any way whatever.

We know that our friends, though distant, feel the same solicitude for the success of an honest cause as we do, and would deem it their duty spontaneously to give warning if they should witness this or any other scene as well calculated as this is to destroy the confidence of the people in the Democratic institutions of the country.

We claim not to be dictators, nor were we regularly planted as sentinels to sound an alarm on the approach of an enemy, but videttes on the outposts, thrown together by chance, not in the pursuit of our foes, but that of business. Hence we have deemed it our duty to inform you, through the forms of a spontaneous meeting, of the things we have seen, and to warn the honest and unsuspecting to beware of *hypocrisy*, *treachery*, and *deceit*.

RESOLUTIONS.

1. *Resolved*, That as citizens of the State of Illinois, we deem it our duty to express upon all proper occasions our opinions on the political movements of the day, and in like manner to declare the principles which govern us in our political action.

2. *Resolved*, That we regard the principles of Democracy as secured to us by the Constitutions of the United States and of this State, the only means of securing the rights of the weak against the encroachments of the strong, and of administering equal-handed justice to the poor as well as the rich, protecting the just rights of all alike.

3. *Resolved*, That in our opinion attempts by politicians to mislead the people by shows and exhibitions instead of argument and reason, is one step to the subversion of the Government of the United States.

4. *Resolved*, that we deprecate the movements now carried on by the political friends of General Harrison, throughout the country, as revolutionary in their tendency, subversive of the rights of the people, and destructive alike of the best interests of all. First, because we do not believe that candidates for the office of President of these United States should, by either silent, cautious, or attempted concealed opinions, induce the support of a portion of the people to be given, in conjunction with that separate, distinct, and fanatical party, called Abolitionists, now in the United States, and to whom all others, of whatever political party they may be, are in good faith, honor, and integrity, opposed; and that we believe that any candidate or party who would in any way whatever yield to the support of such a party as the Abolitionists, is not, in our opinion, entitled to the support of the Democrats of this Union. Second, because, while we appreciate military merit and military services, and give them our hearty approbation, and declare that their authors should receive the reward and the just confidence of their countrymen, it by no means follows that individuals should be ad-

vanced to office exclusively on the ground of their personal courage or military achievements. Third, because, the party now supporting General Harrison for the Presidency is essentially and materially the same that supported both the elder and the younger Adams, and have been opposed to the Administrations of Andrew Jackson and Martin Van Buren; and are the same party who denounced *war, pestilence, and famine upon the country*, sooner than see a military chieftain elected President, solely on the ground of his military services. Fourth, because it is not, in our opinion, expedient to submit either to military rule on the one hand, nor to the control of civil moneyed corporations, or associated bodies of wealth on the other. Fifth, because the people of these United States have long since settled the question of an United States Bank, not only by the election of Gen. Jackson to the Presidency during the pendency of that question before the American people, but also by the election of Martin Van Buren to the same office in 1836—*who declared his uncompromising hostility thereto, before such election*. Sixth, because the party now supporting Gen. Harrison are open and undisguised in the advocacy of a United States Bank, and desire its restoration with all its attendant evils.

5. *Resolved*, That in the pageant we have just witnessed, and its outriders in silks and satins, decorations of gilt buttons with a log cabin stamped thereon worn by the gentry—badges stamped with various devices—and above all, the full-length portrait of Gen. Harrison borne among a deluded crowd, commanding their shouts and huzzas, we are forcibly reminded of that page of history which tells us in words not to be mistaken, of the days of the elder Adams—of the alien and sedition laws, and of standing armies, when his adherents paraded the streets of our cities with their banners and emblems, each individual designated by his black cockade—we are struck with the extraordinary similarity of the same motive and purpose which now animates the same men in principle, as those who warred against the immortal Jefferson—the acknowledged People's friend, the opposer of corporations and associated wealth, and the bold asserter of the Rights of Man.

6. *Resolved*, That we cannot refrain from expressing our deep regret and mortification at the hauling of log cabins in procession through the streets of a flourishing city, and the wild fantastic freaks that were played as if in scorn and reproach of the early settlers of the country, who had no other shelter to protect themselves and families; and that we have heard with surprise and indignation the expression of those who are stockjobbers, brokers, bank stockholders, and various others who would scorn to inhabit a log cabin, and who would treat with derision and contempt an invitation to enter the door of their humble

[85]

but honest occupants—declare that "So it was, that *Jackson* was elected, and that there was no other way of changing the minds of the ignorant, and obtaining political success but by shows and exhibitions."

ADDRESS.

The undersigned, in pursuance of the duty imposed on them, by a numerous meeting of the Democratic party, casually attending, and called together at the seat of the State Government, in consequence of the unparalleled efforts of the Federal Whig Convention, now about to disperse, at the same place, proceed to address their Democratic fellow-citizens, of the various parts of the State; and to beg their earnest attention to a candid exposition of facts and circumstances, which have recently transpired during the sitting of said convention.

Never in the political annals of the country, has there been, it is believed, since the memorable days of the famed reign of terror, so notorious under the Presidency of the elder Adams, such extraordinary spectacles, as are now being exhibited in the United States. The Federal party having for forty years been unable to restore to themselves, the political power which they lost in the great, and to them disastrous battle of 1800, have now resorted to one of the most desperate efforts, of which any political party is capable. Its course is marked not only by its extraordinary disregard of common respect for the moral habits, and offices of life, but the people are treated as though they are the dupes of passion, of vain and ostentatious outward shows, and fit subjects of artifice and deception.

The usual appliances of despotic Governments, so frequently resorted to by the despotic head, to amuse, and turn the people from reflection, and enquiry into the sources and causes of their oppression and misery, have been furnished at this time with no sparing hand, and in proportion to the extent of the great object sought to be obtained (the possession and control of the government) have the means been employed without limitation or measure.

Hundreds of thousands of dollars have been already, and still continue to be expended on such exhibitions, and parades, as are calculated to attract the senses only; lavish expenditures are made in furnishing gaudy banners, with specious devices calculated to allure the eye, and produce false impressions, being false banners, intended for deception. Martial music and the roar of cannon, reverberate through the atmosphere, and then the multitude satiated with stimulants, and fed with costly food, are excited to actions, which in their cooler moments they themselves would readily condemn.

It may be gravely asked, at whose expense have all these means been obtained and furnished?

If from secret sources, then is there danger indeed, in the very fact of that secrecy, that same hidden and mysterious power is secretly and actively at work, to sap the very foundation of the Republic.

On the other hand, assuming their supplies and means to have been drawn from the pockets of known individuals; then it is manifest that this prodigality, profusion, and waste, is but illy to be sustained by those, whose moral and social duties admonish them, against all such useless expenditures of means, which should be scrupulously applied to the support of their families.

There is another fact connected with this wasteful profusion which certainly stamps, with strong marks of inconsistency & want of candor, the declarations of those who affirm, that the depression and derangement of the business pursuits of life, are great and unparalleled, and that the means of obtaining subsistance are so greatly abridged, as to subject the larger masses of community to deprivations heretofore unknown. This lavish expenditure of money for such objects, as we have seen, contradicts the assertion, and shows its utter fallacy. Unless indeed many are disposed to expend their *last shilling* for the objects, and in the efforts of this desperate struggle.

In our own State, we presume the fact will not be controverted that a sum of not less than *one hundred thousand dollars*, has been expended on the occasion of this Convention; *a trifle it will be said in these* HARD TIMES, when the play is for so great a stake. We have been informed, from what we deem good whig authority, and which we are not disposed to dispute, that at the public free Barbacue, given on yesterday, by this universal whig party, six thousand pounds of fresh beef, eighty head of sheep, and hogs, bacon hams by hundreds, with numerous other articles of refreshment, were furnished at an immense cost.

How, and by whom the means have been furnished, to liquidate this great expenditure, as we have intimated already, yet remains a mystery, and probably will so ever continue? We feel no anxiety to unravel the mystery *itself*, and are perfectly content it shall remain shrouded in the bosom of night itself, and whatever pleasure, exhileration and joy, these exhibitions may have produced, we have no disposition, at this time, to abstract from their authors, the full effects they may have produced.—We may however add one just remark, as peculiarly applicable to this party, at this time, and that is, that their rejoicing from some strange fatallity, has always been the precursor of a coming storm, and terrible defeat.

The moral degradation of the human character is not among the least of the evils to be dreaded, from the extraordinary scenes now passing before us, more in the character of a dream than a substantial reality.

[87]

We cannot, however, shut our eyes to what, for the honor of the American character, we had hoped would have been otherwise.

The degradation of the intellect of man is, and always has been, one of the most efficient means of destroying free and representative Governments: and if ever the liberties of the people of this Republic are to be lost, and forever destroyed, it can, alone, be accomplished by such means as those now in progress, where reason and intellect are utterly disregarded, and nothing but the baser passions of our nature appealed to.

For three days has the capital of the State of Illinois exhibited scenes of excesses, unparalleled in the history of its Government. Demoralization has stalked abroad, at noon day, with nothing to arrest, or stay, for even a moment, its fatal course.

Allured by the scenes and glitter of the "pomp and circumstance of glorious war," in feeble imitation, many were attempted to be deluded, amid the sounds of trumpets and the noise of drums, and sought to be made the victims of the artifice of demagogues, with the vain hope that they would bind themselves to the support of a cause and party, who dare avow no political principles, or rule of action, for its guidance; and whose Chief is prohibited the expression of any opinion whatever on questions of public interest, and even debarred an intercourse with many of his fellow-citizens, except under the strict surveillance of a committee of inspection and safety. There is among the many circumstances which have transpired, one which marks, with characters not to be misunderstood, the singular and daring efforts which these men have resorted to for the accomplishment of their objects.

The invitation of, and attendance of, numerous delegates from the city of St. Louis, in Missouri, and the State of Indiana, forms no small portion of the scenes of this Convention. The introduction into our State of influence foreign to it, to operate on and control, if not to actually overcome, the opinions and deliberations of our people, is a spectacle so novel, unprecedented, and repugnant to political and personal propriety, that when first observed its truth was doubted; but the reality was conclusively established; and the efforts of these individuals in their conduct and remarks, were marked by no peculiar delicacy of language or manner. We trust the people of this State will duly appreciate this effort to influence our elections, and scorn with disdain and unmitigated contempt, the peculiar efforts of this foreign band of intermeddling politicians.

We learn that it is attempted to be justified on the ground of returning *work for work;* and that it is but to repay the Whigs of this State the political debt due by their brethren of St. Louis, for a similar political interference, at a meeting in St. Louis, by the Whigs of this State.

[88]

If we are indebted to the Whigs of this State for this *kind* interference, at Springfield, in our elections, by the Whigs of Missouri, we trust that our own people will apply the proper corrective, at the proper time.

To dwell on scenes like these is alike painful and humiliating; and we cannot but deeply regret that a desire to obtain political power should have led any portion of the American people to the use of means which cannot, in our judgment, do otherwise than throw a deep shade on the American name, and degrade the hitherto high character of its citizens in the eyes of the people of other nations.

It was to avoid such consequences as have flowed from the recent Whig Convention at Springfield, and to spare to the members of the Democratic Party the useless expenditure of their money and loss of time, so necessary to be rightfully applied, and economised for the benefit of their families, that the Democratic Young Men's Convention, proposed to be holden on the 8th of June inst. was postponed. The contagion of the examples of our opponents was to be feared, and the pernicious consequences, which it was early foreseen would mark the course of the Whig Convention, and which has, most unfortunately for them we think, actually transpired, sufficiently admonished the Democratic State Central Committee to take the responsibility of its postponement; and in that act we see much to approve. We have escaped errors into which it is possible we might have been precipitated from example, though never to any thing like the same extent; for the Democratic party look to reason, reflection, and intelligence for their guide; and we trust ever will rigidly give its adherence to the dictates of the cool and deliberate judgment of its members. In enforcing its political principles, and maintaining its measures, it has no need, nor can it ever consent, to resort to any of the appliances so freely and generally now used by its opponents; and we are free to confess, that if their cause is to be alone sustained by a resort to such miserable mummery and disgraceful prostitution of mind and character, we cannot hesitate to declare, that a cause which requires the adventitious aid of such desperate and debasing efforts, is unworthy to be upheld, and should be suffered to perish amidst its own corruptions and putridity.

Fellow-citizens, who witnessed the spectacles of the 3d, 4th, and 5th of June, at Springfield, we appeal to your candor to say if you have received any information the Federal Party have afforded you, at or since this gorgeous celebration of *Tippecanoe*, of the principles of the party who now seek to deceive the people, to obtain power and office? Have they told you what measures, to benefit the people, they will propose, and adopt, if so be they succeed to power and office? Have they even, on the score of policy, made any allusion to those great

[89]

democratic principles of Jefferson, Madison, and Jackson, with which Mr. Van Buren is so clearly identified—or in any way whatever shown a devotion to them? No! But rather have they sought to ingratiate into your confidence a man, who was an open advocate of the high-toned Federal measures of John Adams, believing that you are so dull and stupid as to overlook the principles of a man, by being dazzled with the glare of military renown—sinking, *now*, amid the noise of cannon, and of drums, and the shouts of "Hard Cider" and "Tippecanoe" the anathemas of *"war, pestilence, and famine,"* denounced by Mr. Clay on the heads of the American people, for the support of a military chieftain—Gen. Jackson.

But why commingle tender youths in the unmeaning pageant of the day, and teach them, by the delusive scenes and frenzy of the hour, the vices and immoralities of others? Why bring them to witness scenes of boisterous revelry and mirth, and thus inure their tender hearts to scenes of dissipation, which it would well become those whose charge they are, by precept and example, to cause them to shun. About sixty youths were drawn into the procession to swell up the train; and hence we have adverted to this pernicious example, exhibited on this occasion.

The exhibition, in the procession of a full-length portrait of General Harrison, representing him in the full vigor of life, did but forcibly remind us of his present condition, and bring to our minds the extraordinary contrast, of one represented as present on canvass, and he who is now restricted within the limits of a space he dare not pass, and prohibited the exercise of his own volition, and freedom of speech, on all subjects of a political character. We could not repress the natural feelings of indignation which animates every American heart not lost to the consciousness of the necessity of the preservation of the dignity of the human mind and character, when we observed the humiliating spectacle of freemen, bowing amid shouts of joy to the painted image of one who seeks the suffrages of the American people for the highest office within their gift, who is prevented from visiting them in person, because of the danger which would exist, that he would incautiously expose his real opinions on public questions, when thus placed in contact with his fellow-citizens. But one step more was wanting to fill up the measure of degradation and submission. As well might those who pay this adoration to a shadow, imitate the followers of Juggernaut, who having bowed themselves to the painted wooden idols which adorn the temple of worship, of the ignorant and superstitious Hindoo, throw their bodies beneath the wheels of the moving altar, and in their phrenzy submit themselves voluntary victims, to be crushed to death beneath its wheels, as a propitiation to their supposed offended deities.

There may be some who have been deluded into a participation in some of the acts of this Convention. The censurable ones were doubtless not those in which they participated; and we have no doubt that on reflection they will have seen enough to condemn, and never again yield their support to those who have deceived them. To such we say, that we have an entire confidence in the convictions, which we believe will follow their reflections, and that they will have lost none of our confidence, or that of their other Democratic friends.

Notwithstanding all the efforts our opponents have made, at this time, to mislead the public mind, we declare that we have seen nothing to shake our confidence in the justice of the cause we advocate; nor do we apprehend that it is in any way seriously endangered. We believe that the scenes we have been the witnesses of will re-act on its authors, and produce a result essentially different from that anticipated by them.

Fellow-citizens, we appeal alone to your reason for the support of your cause, which we advocate. It is your cool and deliberate judgments we invoke; and if, on a candid re-examination of the principles of the cause and the measures of its action, we believe you approve, and they find with you a free and frank response, then animate yourselves with the convictions which have flown from and are embraced in the answers to the interrogatories you have put to your consciences, that all is right; and in the true, just, and forcible phrase of an honest, plain, and noble heart, "GO AHEAD!"

Not doubting that you readily concur with us, we ask of every member of the Democratic Party to assemble at the county seat of his county on the 4th day of next July, at 12 o'clock, M.—the great and glorious anniversary of our national birth, and then resolve, that he will adhere to, and support those principles contained in the immortal Declaration of Independence, which were achieved by the bravery, exertions, and indomitable perseverance of our forefathers, and cemented by their blood.

That he will live and die a freeman, uncontaminated, and unstained by political heresies, which would wither and blast the fair escutcheon of our national character, and spurn, as freemen should, the corrupting influences of banking corporations and associated wealth.

Our opponents selected for the day and hour of their celebration, the birth day of George III, him from whom our ancestors wrested our liberties from sacrilegious destruction, and bore them aloft amid scenes of blood and carnage,—we select the Fourth of July, not to desecrate it with unhallowed shouts, not of tumult and disorder, but in cool and calm devotion to our country, to renew upon the altar of its liberties, a sacred oath of fidelity to its principles, and the preservation of the Union of these States, against the open or insidious attacks of domestic or foreign assailants, and we trust that on that day, in this State, no one will be found wanting to join with us in a cause so holy and patriotic.

Amid the scenes already described, of revelry and dissipation, of rude and boisterous sounds issuing from the camps of men who play such

"Fantastic tricks before high heaven,
As make the angels weep,"

we have met, unawed by clamor, unmoved by noise and tumult, which rends the very heavens. 'Tis the cause of our common country we have here assembled to support, and like the small but Spartan band which commenced the Revolution of '76, we ask each to pledge to the other, his sacred honor, to stand together, shoulder to shoulder, and breast to breast, amid the storms and tempests which now threatens to break over the land. Let us, like men determined to uphold the liberties of our country, meet the tempest without fear or doubting, in a solid phalanx—let us battle with the arms of our political warfare in our hands, and IF WE FALL, let it be on the LAST RUINS of the CITADEL OF AMERICAN FREEDOM.

Let us entreat you by every consideration of duty and of pride, to devote, at your own firesides, among your neighbors, and at your county seats, (without the acceptance of appliances from others to becloud your judgments and your reason,) some few hours to the service of your country. She has a right to demand it at your hands, and recreant would you prove to the trust confided to you by the founders and fathers of the Revolution, did you not cheerfully and faithfully execute that sacred duty.

To its performance then, and each and every one of you will find in the result of your exertions, that he will be enabled to say, *I was at the great political battle of November, 1840, which protected and preserved the liberties of the American people from violation and destruction.*

Springfield *Illinois State Register*, June 12, 1840. At an informal meeting of Democrats from all parts of Illinois in Springfield on June 4, Douglas was appointed one of a committee of nine to prepare resolutions and an address to the people of Illinois concerning the Presidential campaign then in progress, and especially the campaign techniques adopted by Illinois Whigs. The occasion of the meeting, and the subject of the Resolutions and Address, was a convention in Springfield of young Whigs and old soldiers who had served under William Henry Harrison in the War of 1812. Delegations from all over the state, complete with bands, glee clubs and fireworks, converged on Springfield in early June. On June 3, a formal meeting was held, attended by an estimated 5,000 persons, at which resolutions were passed in support of General Harrison. The following day, the delegations staged a great parade through the streets of Springfield, with marching veterans, log-cabin floats, bands, and 1,500 men carrying signs and mottoes. The convention was climaxed by a barbecue, at which the delegates partook of "plain, substantial, log-cabin fare." Following the demon-stration, Whig leaders expressed satis-faction that the convention had re-sulted in a more firm organization of the party. The Address prepared by the Democrats reflects an extreme an-noyance with the Whigs for their "un-orthodox" campaign techniques.

To Lewis W. Ross

Dear Sir   Springfield June 27th 1840

You will pardon the delay in answering your letter when you hear the causes which produced it. At the time it was received I was just starting on the circuit and then delayed answering until I could deter-mine whether I could attend your court or not. Upon examination how-ever I found that the U.S. Court at this place commenced it[s] session on the same day. I would like to address the people of Fulton before the Election & will yet do so if possible. I am glad to learn that you are on the track this year with fair prospects of success. Every thing is depending on the result this year. Our prospects are brightening evry day. Energy and activity are all that is necessary to gain the victory. Let us not relax our exertions because we feel confident of success. I wish you would write to me what you candidly think will be the result in your county at August and also in November.[1] Our friends here have some fears of the Military Tract. In every other part of the State we are perfectly safe, and if you can only hold your own on the West side of the River Van Buren's Majority will be much greater this year than it was in 1836.[2] I leave tomorrow for Jacksonville. We keep up the fire wherever we go. Your friend

S. A. DOUGLASS

ALS, Illinois State Historical Library.
[1]Douglas has reference to the state and national Presidential elections.
[2]Van Buren carried Illinois in the election of 1840 by a vote of 47,443 to 45,576, a majority of 1,867. Van Buren's majority in 1836 had been 3,219.

To the Speaker of the Senate

[December 18, 1840, Springfield; Copy, Illinois State Archives. A rou-tine letter, written by Douglas in his capacity as Secretary of State (to which office he had been appointed on November 30, 1840), listing the counties from which census returns for 1840 had not yet been re-ceived.]

To the Speaker of the Senate

[December 29, 1840, Springfield; Copy, Illinois State Archives. Submit-ting the census returns for Illinois, with the exception of several coun-ties.]

To the Speaker of the Senate

[December 29, 1840, Springfield; Copy, Illinois State Archives. Transmitting documents pertaining to the sale of Illinois state bonds.]

To the Speaker of the House of Representatives

[December 29, 1840, Springfield; Copy, Illinois State Archives. Transmitting information, in obedience to a House resolution, on the number of copies of the laws passed by the last several legislative sessions necessary for distribution to "public Officers, and for public convenience."]

To the Speaker of the Senate

[December 30, 1840, Springfield; Copy, Illinois State Archives. Transmitting documents relating to the Illinois and Michigan Canal.]

To C. B. Dungan

[January 8, 1841, Springfield; Copy, Illinois State Archives. Transmitting the Governor's refusal to accede to the demand of the Governor of Pennsylvania for the extradition of H. W. Vansyckle.]

To William L. May

Sir   Springfield Jan'y 20th 1841

In compliance with your request of this inst I state to you the facts in relation to the entry of fractional section 29 Township 26 N R 4 west as far as the same have come to my knowledge. According to the best of my recollection sometime in the fall of 1838 Messrs. [...] & Green filed an application at the Land office at Springfield, of which I was Register, for the entry of a small portion of said fractional section, containing 16 acres, alledging that the same was vacant land. I declined permitting the Entry to be made upon the ground that the same land was included in a previous entry by Alfred Sams[1] and afterwards transfered to Messrs Latham and May[2] and the Patents issued to them. Messrs Loose & Green[3] appealed from my decision to the General Land Office at Washington, asking the Department to override my decision and to direct me to permit them (Loose & Green) to enter said 16 acres. The department confirmed my decision, deciding that said 16 acres were included in the previous entry as above stated and paid for as such and were the property of Latham & May. No entry of said 16 acres was ever made by Messrs Loose & Green or any other persons, except as above stated, to my knowledge, and I know of no person having a legal claim to said Land except Latham & May. I have stated the above facts from my recollection of the circumstances as they transpired and presume they will be confirmed by reference to the Books & Plats of the Land Office in this City. Very respectfully yours

S. A. Douglass

ALS, Illinois State Historical Library.
[1]Alfred Sams was a resident of Salt Creek, Sangamon County.
[2]Philip Clayton Latham was a Springfield land speculator. From 1827 to 1835, he had been employed in the Sangamon County Clerk's office.

[3]Jacob Loose was a Springfield merchant. Green's identification is not certain; he might possibly have been James Green, a resident of Sangamon County, or Bowling Green, a New Salem merchant.

To John A. McClernand

Springfield, Jan. 29, 1841.

Sir—I have this moment received your letter of this date informing me, that the Judges of the Supreme Court had denied in a written communication, the truth of certain statements made by yourself in the House some days since, and requesting me to state what I know upon the subject.[1]

I was of council for the aliens in what is called the "alien case;"[2] previous to and during the argument of that case it was expressly agreed that nothing but the *constitutional* question as to the right of aliens to vote, was to be submitted to the court. The case was argued at the last Winter term, and continued till the last June term, to enable the judges to prepare their decisions. At the June term one of the judges notified me that the court was ready to decide the case and appointed the hour for making the decision. The Hon. T. W. Smith, one of the judges of the court, informed me that the decision was to be three against one, Judges Lockwood, Wilson & Brown,[3] being in favor of cutting off the alien votes, and himself dissenting. When the appointed hour arrived for making the decision, the judges appeared upon the bench and laid their papers before them upon their tables as was their custom, when about to deliver opinions. I rose and moved to dismiss the cause in consequence of a defect in the record. One of the judges replied from the bench that "it was agreed that nothing but the *constitutional* question was to be submitted to the court, and the court was then ready to decide." I replied that "that was and still is the agreement, but that the defect in the record was of such a nature that no decision could be made upon it, even on the constitutional question, unless the record was corrected." I then filed the reasons for my motion, and after argument the cause was continued until the present term of the court. During the present term the said T. W. Smith has repeatedly stated to me that if I had not made the motion to dismiss the case in June the entire alien vote would then have been cut off by the decision of the court in June, and that the other three judges had their opinions prepared and in their pockets ready to be delivered, disfranchising the aliens. Similar statements to these have been made, as I am informed, to some twenty or thirty or more individuals, to whom I must refer you for corroborative testimony. I am very respectfully, your obedient servant,

S. A. DOUGLASS

Springfield *Illinois State Register*, February 5, 1841. John A. McClernand of Jacksonville was at this time a member of the state House of Representatives. He was elected to Congress in 1842.

[1]McClernand's letter to Douglas, dated January 29, 1841, was printed in the same issue of the *Illinois State Register*. In it, McClernand wrote:

"I stated the other day, in my place on this floor, while I was debating the Judiciary bill, now pending before the House, that I was informed that certain judges of the Supreme Court prepared a decision in June last, against the right of unnaturalized foreigners to vote in this State; and that this decision was not pronounced at that time because of some defect of the record, which was pointed out at the time; and since that time, to wit: during the present term of the Supreme Court, the judges referred to have pronounced a different decision on another point than the constitutional one.

"This statement has been today contradicted by T. W. Smith, and the other Judges of the Supreme Court.

"Now, sir, I wish you and such other persons as are prepared to speak on this subject, to state all you know about the facts in question.—Immediate attention is invited to the subject of this letter; and the earliest answer practicable."

Answers to McClernand's appeal were not only written by Douglas but also by six other individuals, A. R. Dodge,

Virgil Hickox, J. H. Ralston, John Pearson, Murray McConnel, and James A. McDougall. The judiciary bill referred to by McClernand provided for the appointment of five additional judges to the state Supreme Court, raising the total number to nine. The bill passed both houses of the state legislature and Douglas received one of the additional judgeships.

[2]The "alien case" concerned the right of aliens to vote in state elections. A circuit court decision at Galena ruled earlier that unnaturalized aliens could not vote in Illinois, although the constitution provided the right of suffrage for all free white males, over twenty-one years of age and residents of the state for at least six months. The decision was immediately appealed to the state Supreme Court, where Douglas argued against the lower court's restriction. Because of a technicality, Douglas was able to secure postponement of the case until after the election of 1840. The issue was a crucial one to Douglas and the Democratic party, since the alien vote constituted a sizable portion of the party's support throughout the state. The Whig members of the court became targets for Democratic campaigners in 1840 and Douglas played a leading role in the denunciation of the jurists.

[3]Theophilus Washington Smith, Samuel Drake Lockwood, William Wilson, and Thomas C. Browne were elected to the state Supreme Court under the terms of a judicial reorganization bill passed in 1825.

To B. H. Covey

[February 1, 1841, Springfield; Copy, Illinois State Archives. Asking that a certificate of the fact that bond had been filed be furnished the Secretary of State's office. Covey was County Clerk of McLean County.]

To Thomas Carlin

Department of State
Sir,   Springfield Feb'y 16th 1841
I have the honor to tender you my resignation as Secretary of State, to take effect as soon as your convenience will enable you to appoint my successor.[1] In dissolving the official relations that have existed between us, justice to my own feelings will not permit me to say less, than to express to you my grateful acknowledgements for that kindness, frankness and generous confidence which have characterized your intercourse with me, whilst I have had the honor of an official connection with you. I remain with sentiments of high regard and esteem your friend and fellow citizen

S. A. DOUGLASS

ALS, Watertown Library Association, Watertown, Connecticut. Thomas Carlin had been elected to the governorship in 1838.
[1]Douglas resigned the office of Secretary of State upon his election to the Illinois Supreme Court.

Oath of Office

[March 1, 1841]
I Stephen A. Douglass Justice of the Supreme Court of the State of Illinois do solemnly swear that I will administer justice without respect to persons and do equal right to the poor and the rich without sale or denial promptly without delay conformably to the laws, without favor, affection or partiality to the best of my judgment and abilities. I do further swear that I will truly & faithfully support the Constitution of the United States and of the State of Illinois
sworn & subscribed   S. A. DOUGLASS
before me this 1st day
of March 1841
James W Keyes[1]

ADS, Illinois State Historical Library. All except Keyes's signature is in Douglas' handwriting. Douglas, only twenty-seven years of age, had been elected to one of the five additional Supreme Court judgeships created by the state legislature earlier in 1841.
[1]James W. Keyes, former Postmaster of Springfield, was a justice of the peace.

To James Shields

Dear Sir   Lewiston April 2nd 1841

Enclosed I send you a Letter from Mr Maguire of St Louis[1] containing a certificate of Deposit upon one of the New York Banks which I hope you will find it convenient to arrange according to his Letter of instructions. I hope you have found no difficulty in obtaining the money on the order I left with you for my salary with which to pay Mr Maguire the ballance due him towit $300.00. I have informed Mr Maguire by letter of the arrangement with you to attend to his business & refered him to you.

Business aside, I have a few words to say on the score of friendship. I have entirely cleared the Dockett in this county the first time for seven years, having disposed of between 300 & 400 cases. The members of the Bar and the people generally have received and treated me with great kindness and courtesy, and seem to be entirely satified with the Judicial Change. In this respect [I] have been agreeably disappointed, particularly with the Whigs, from whom I had a right to expect some opposition; but have experienced none. I shall leave here in the morning for Rushville where I shall expect to have the pleasure of receiving a Letter from you. You will excuse my neglect in writing to you and place it on the ground of great pressure of business which could not be postponed.

Present my respects [to] our friends Doyle, Eastham, Tyler,[2] Walters &c &c and tell them that absence strengthens the ties of friendship. I remain truly your friend

S. A. DOUGLASS

ALS, Illinois State Historical Library. James Shields, of Irish birth, had been elected to the state legislature in 1836, and in 1841 held the post of State Auditor. His political career was a full one; he held the offices of Justice of the Illinois Supreme Court and Commissioner of the General Land Office in 1843 and 1845 respectively, and later was elected to United States Senate seats from Illinois, Minnesota, and Missouri.

[1]Possibly John Magwire, a St. Louis merchant.

[2]The Tyler referred to by Douglas may have been John Taylor, a partner in the firm of John Duff and Company, with which Marvellous Eastham was also associated, or it may have been Edmund Dick Taylor.

To Julius N. Granger *et al.*

Dear Brother, Sister, Father & Mother.   Lewiston April 3rd 1841

I have delayed writing to either of you for some months with confident expectation of surprising you by my personal suden appearance among you. This expectation was increased, altho the time of realizing it postponed, by my appoint[ment] of Secretary of State last Fall, which required my personal attention during the Session of the Legislature. It pleased my friends, however, at the close of the Session of the Legislature, to transfer me from the office of Secretary of State to that of Judge of the Supreme Court, the duties of which station will require my personal attention, and blast all my anticipations of enjoying the society of a Mother & Sister, a Father & a Brother, the only persons on earth to whom I feel any peculiar attachments. I assure you that I have been so completely engrossed with the excitements and strifes of partizan conflicts and official stations, that office and honors have lost their charms, and I desire and seek repose and the society of friends. Friends, warm, devoted & disinterested friends, I have, who delight to serve me, and whom I delight to serve, and so much of time and effort have I devoted to these, that I have neglected my duties to my kindred and myself. I have thus far led a life of extraordinary activity, and have endured great efforts of Mind and body, and have yet left a Constitution strong healthy and unimpaired. But this, and whatever of character and of fame I may have acquired are all I have left. I have neglected my pecuniary affairs, am somewhat embarrassed; but by no means discouraged. I have now commenced upon a new theatre, and expect to devote all the energies of my mind to my Judicial duties and my private affairs for at least a few years to come. I know not when I can visit you; my engagements will not now permit it; but I will do so at the earliest opportunity. Altho I shall be absent on duty much of the time, yet my Home will be at Springfield, and [I] desire you to direct your letters there. I remain your affectionate Brother & Son.

S. A. Douglass

ALS, owned by Martin F. Douglas.

To William S. Prentice

Confidential
Dear Sir   Springfield Aug 30th 1841
   I have returned from the Fulton Court & received your letter of the 23rd inst, and drop you a few lines in return. First as to Politics. Things seem to be moving on gloriously. Tyler's veto is a perfect windfall to the Democrats.[1] He has met the question nobly & [is] immortalized by it; yet we should be cautious how we commit ourself in his favor. Indiana is right side up again & from the cause to which you attribute it I am inclined to think. She is Democratic in principle and will never sustain Clay, nor the Whig party when Clay is the candidate. New York, Pennsylvania, & Main[e] will come right this fall, and possibly Maryland. Tennessee has given an assurance that she also is coming back. By next winter the Whigs will again be in a minority in the Union, and that moment their power is gone & their party dissolved. I am glad you

have concluded to run for the Legislature.[2] You ought to begin to make your arrangements immediately & take an early start, not publicly, but let your confidential friends understand it and act accordingly. Let the party in the county be thoroughly organized. The best way to do that, perhaps, would be to call a county meeting to appoint delegates to the State convention in December & then appoint a county corresponding committee, say of five, seven or nine persons men the county sent. Let the county committee appoint sub-committees in each Precinct composed of three men each. In this way you can have the most perfect organization in the whole county & the Whigs need know nothing about it. If you thing it advisable you could have a county convention to nominate a candidate for the Legislature next spring. By producing a perfect organization this fall & becoming well acquainted with the committee men in each Precinct, you can have any man you please nominated for the Legislature & can in all probability elect him. Any man who comes out against the regular nominee will be regarded as a Whig brought to divide the party. These are mere suggestions for your consideration, to act on or not as your judgment shall determine. *This letter must be strictly confidential*, the necessity of which is obvious. I don't know what to say about a called Session of the Legislature, but am inclined to think there will be one. I will let you know as soon as I find out, probably in a few weeks. Let me once more urge you to make a bold push for the Legislature, but am certain you can succeed. Now is your time for many reasons which I can explain to you when I see you. I leave in a few days for the Military Tract. Write me at Quincy. So good buy. Your friend

S. A. DOUGLAS

ALS, Illinois State Historical Library. William S. Prentice, after serving as a clerk in the United States Land Office at Vandalia and working in the State Auditor's office, was clerk of the circuit court in Shelby County. In 1849, at the age of thirty, he became a Methodist preacher.

[1]On August 16, 1841, President John Tyler vetoed a bill to re-create a Bank of the United States.

[2]Prentice was a candidate for election to the state House of Representatives from Shelby County in 1842, but was not successful. He failed a second time in 1844.

To Harry Wilton

(*Confidential*)

My Dear Sir   Lewiston Fulton Co March 27th 1842

I have not had the pleasure of seeing or hearing from you since I saw you at Springfield. Since the adjournment of the Supreme Court I have been holding a Special Term of the Circuit at Quincy, which continued 3 weeks & since that time I have been here, so you will perceive that I have not had much leisure.

It so happens that most of our little towns over here are off the road so that we hardly ever get the news. I don't know whether you are a candidate for the Senate or not but hope you are. I believe all the aspirants would give away to you cheerfully; and am afraide they will not unite cordially upon any other man. Of this however you are the best judge. The prospects of our party in this part of the state are good; probably better than usual. As you were the first to solicit me to become a Candidate for the U.S. Senate, I feel it due to you to inform you that our friend Breese[1] is in the field actively electioneering for himself. He has written to the senator in this county soliciting his support, and I presume has written to each senator & candidate in all the other Democratic Counties to the same effect. This is a pretty strong game & may do mischief if no[t] counteracted. In this circuit it will do no harm. I have not mentioned the subject of my being a candidate to a human being who has not first introduced the subject. Many kind friends have done so, and whether successful or not, I shall ever full [feel] grateful to them.[2] You will be able to inform me what the prospect is in your part of the State? and whether there is any danger of divisions which will result in defeating any members of the Legislature. Please write to me, and give me your views generally. I shall be at Rushville on the 1st Monday, at Mt Sterling on the 2nd, and at Quincy on the 3rd Monday of April & will be at Quincy 2 weeks. If convenient, let me hear from [you] at Quincy. I remain truly your friend

S. A. DOUGLAS

ALS, Chicago Historical Society. Harry Wilton, an early supporter of Douglas, held the post of United States Marshal for Illinois under Presidents Jackson and Van Buren.

[1]Sidney Breese was Associate Justice of the state Supreme Court, having been appointed with Douglas in 1841. Previously, he held the offices of United States District Attorney for Illinois, and circuit judge of the Second Judicial District. Breese was elected to the United States Senate in 1842. Wilton lived in Breese's home town of Carlyle.

[2]Douglas had determined to seek the United States Senate seat of Richard Montgomery Young, whose term was expiring. In Judge Sidney Breese, however, he encountered a formidable opponent. The legislative caucus in December, 1842, was a stormy one, but Breese won the nomination. On the nineteenth ballot, Breese received 56 votes to Douglas' 51. Douglas was only twenty-nine years old when he campaigned for the Senate, and would not be thirty, the constitutional age for Senator, until after March 4, 1843, when the new Senator would take his seat. His youth was probably one factor in his defeat.

To James Semple

[N.d., n.p.; quoted in Frank E. Stevens, "Life of Stephen Arnold Douglas," *Journal of the Illinois State Historical Society*, XVI (October, 1923–January, 1924), 394. According to Stevens, the letter was congratulatory on Semple's appointment to the United States Senate in 1843, to fill the vacancy caused by the death of Samuel McRoberts. "I am glad we will spend the winter in Washington together, and propose that we make a mess of the entire delegation. They are all good fellows and would make pleasant companions." Semple, before his appointment, had been a member of the state legislature, Attorney General of Illinois, Chargé d'Affaires to Colombia, and a Justice of the state Supreme Court. He was an unsuccessful candidate for the United States Senate in 1836. Douglas had been elected to his first term in the national House of Representatives earlier in 1843. By the census of 1840, Illinois increased its representation in the lower house by three Congressmen. The state was redistricted by the legislature in accord with this apportionment early in 1843. In June, a convention in the new Fifth Congressional District nominated Douglas, who was elected after a very active and strenuous campaign against the Whig nominee, Orville H. Browning. Douglas took his seat in the House in December, 1843, when the new Congress met.]

To James M. Porter

[December 28, 1843, House of Representatives; ALS, owned by Ray Trautman, New York, N.Y. Relating to a pension for John Edmonstone, of Fulton County, Illinois. Porter was Secretary of War in John Tyler's cabinet. I am indebted to Mr. Trautman for a description of the contents of this letter.]

To ———

(*Private*)   Washington
Dr Sir,   Jan'y 12th 1844
   I return you my thanks for your very handsome notice of me in your paper of the 4th inst.[1] I had not supposed that so humble a name as my own had attracted the attention of any except my immediate relatives in my native state. But as you have been so kind as to notice me I have thought but just and proper that I should furnish you with the means of correcting some slight errors into which you have been inadvertently lead. I am a native of Brandon as you state, having been born April 23d 1813, and resided there until 1830 when I removed to Canandaigua, Ontario County N.Y. where I studied Law. Ten years ago I removed to the State of Illinois where I have ever since resided. I have held in succession the following offices: State attorney, —member of the Legislature, —Register of the U.S. Land Office; —Secretary of State; and Judge of the Supreme Court. It was in 1838 instead of '39

that I was defeated by 5 votes out of 36,500. votes for Congress. The same District gave a Whig majority of 3,700. in 1840—I have no desire to see my name in the Newspapers; but at the same time feel grateful to those whose kindness has prompted them to give me a passing notice. I send you herewith a copy of my speech on the Bill refunding the fine on Gen'l Jackson[2] & will send you public Documents during the Session. I desire you to consider & treat this letter as *strictly confidential*. My apology for not addressing you by name is to be found in the fact that I have not the good fortune to know your name. Respectfully your obedient servt

S. A. DOUGLASS

ALS, Maine Historical Society, Portland.
  [1]The notice referred to by Douglas appeared in the Woodstock (Vermont) *Spirit of the Age,* January 4, 1844.

  [2]This was Douglas' first speech in the House of Representatives, delivered on January 7, 1844, on behalf of a bill to refund the fine imposed upon General Andrew Jackson at New Orleans in 1815 for contempt of court.

To John Tyler

Washington
March 20th 1844

Sir,

I have the honor herewith to enclose to you a recommendation of James H Spottswood of Springfield Illinois to be purser in the Navy.[1] The recommendation is signed by five of the most distinguished citizens of Springfield, all of whom I believe are recognized as your warm & devoted friends. Mr Spottswood does not reside in my district, but I know him well and also his father Col George W. Spottswood formerly of Virginia, and take great pleasure in recommending his appointment. I have the honor to be very respectfully your obedient servant

S. A. DOUGLASS

ALS, Boston Public Library.
  [1]James H. Spottswood became Acting Postmaster of Springfield in December, 1844. He was not appointed to the office of purser in the Navy.

To Jesse W. Fell

Dr Sir   Washington March 21st 1844

I have been confined to my room by sickness ever since I rec'd your letter & this is my excuse for not answering it sooner. I have endeavored to procure the [. . .] document for you that you desire but am unable to get even a single copy. But a small number were published & these sent off immediately by those who felt an interest in the subject. If any

[103]

documents I think you will find an interest in should be published I will send them to you. Respectfully your friend

S. A. Douglass

Copy, Illinois Historical Survey, University of Illinois, Urbana. Jesse W. Fell was at this time a Bloomington, Illinois, lawyer and real estate agent.

To Silas Reed

Washington
March 21st 1844

Dear Sir,

I have the honor to acknowledge several letters from you most of which arrived during my sickness. I have been confined nearly two months, but am now about well again. I will examine the estimates & Bills for the appropriations connected with your office as soon as I am able to go to the House. It is a matter of importance to my constitutents that the surveys on the Illinois river should be completed & the Plots returned. I have not seen the Report of the Commissioner of the Gen'l Land office & presume it has not yet been printed. I have heard nothing of the contemplated charges against your official conduct & presume they will not be made. I shall be happy to hear from you at all times. Yours respectfully

S. A. Douglass

ALS, Historical Society of Pennsylvania. Silas Reed was Surveyor General of Missouri and Illinois.

To John C. Spencer

[March 22, 1844, Washington; ALS, RG-59, National Archives. Enclosing a letter from John Hendrickson of Columbus, Illinois, inquiring whether the losses sustained by a Baltimore brig under the Berlin and Milan decrees have been repaid to the heirs of the owner. John C. Spencer was Secretary of the Treasury.]

To Ezra Williams *et al.*

Quincy Ill
Oct 7th 1844

Gentlemen

On my return home, after an absence of about two months, I had the honor to receive your invitation to attend a mass meeting of the Democracy of Michigan at Marshall on the 10th ult. I have long wished an opportunity to visit numerous old friends in Michigan, and especially to meet her assembled Democracy, and should most assuredly have done so on the occasion alluded to, had not my absence prevented the reception of the invitation in time. I have the pleasure to inform you however that I was at that time doing battle to the best of my public abilities in other States where greater efforts were necessary, because the result has been by some deemed doubtful.[1] But in Michigan I have been induced to believe there was no doubt of our success in November, and I will add, that I regard the presidential election as already settled, and the only question now to be determined is the extent of our majority. You will accept, Gentlemen, my warmest thanks for your polite invitation, and the expression of my regret that I could not have been with you on the occasion refered to. I have the honor to be very respectfully your obedient servant

S. A. DOUGLASS

ALS, Illinois State Historical Library. Ezra Williams was clerk of the Michigan House of Representatives.

[1]During the campaign of 1844, Douglas spoke on behalf of Polk's candidacy in Tennessee, where he addressed a large ratification meeting in Nashville, and in St. Louis.

To James Dunlap and Joseph Heslep

Quincy, Oct. 7, 1844.

Gentlemen: After an absence of some two months, I have the honor on my return home to receive your kind invitation to attend a mass meeting of the Democracy at Jacksonville on the 3d September last.

I cannot command language sufficiently forcible to express to you my gratitude for the kind and complimentary terms in which your partiality has induced you to speak of my character and my public efforts in the glorious cause in which we are all so heartily engaged. I appreciate this compliment the more highly coming as it does from the citizens of Morgan county, my early friends and supporters, to whom I owe and feel a deeper debt of gratitude than to any other community living. It was my intention to have been with you upon that occasion without the ceremony of a formal invitation, but our political friends in Tennessee, where I happened to be at the time, induced me to remain there and take a part in the glorious and gallant battle in which they were engaged for the redemption of that noble State from the thraldom of Federalism. The struggle is a desperate one, but my confidence in the cause and the intelligence and patriotism of the people, has impressed me with the firm conviction that a brilliant triumph awaits them.

You will be pleased to express to those you represent and accept for yourselves individually the kindest regards and best wishes of your friend,

S. A. DOUGLASS

Springfield *Illinois State Register,* October 18, 1844. James Dunlap and Joseph Heslep were prominent Morgan County Democrats.

To William Walters and George R. Weber

Washington, Feb. 16, 1845.

Gentlemen: I have just received your paper of the 7 inst. containing an editorial article under the title: "JUDGE DOUGLASS IN THE CABINET—THE CLAIMS OF ILLINOIS,"—in which you say that you have seen in many of your exchange papers intimations, that I would be offered a seat in the cabinet of the new President.[1] Feeling an aversion to thrusting myself before the public to correct a newspaper report relating to myself, and especially one so complimentary, I should not have noticed it, but for the zealous manner in which you have advocated my appointment. I presume that there is not the slightest foundation for the report, as I have no reason to believe that President Polk ever contemplated offering me that or any other office. I am content with my present position; and have never on any occasion intimated a desire or willingness to exchange it for another. My own inclinations, as well as a sense of duty to my constituents, have produced in my mind a settled determination not to abandon my seat in Congress for any office within the gift of the Executive.

Grateful to you and the other editors alluded to for your good opinion, and the many unmerited compliments so lavishly bestowed upon me, but regreting that the publication of them has rendered this note alike due to myself and my constituents, I have the honor to be Your friend,

S. A. DOUGLASS

Springfield *Illinois State Register*, March 7, 1845.

[1]Because of the majority given Polk in his race for the Presidency by Illinois, many Democrats in the state felt that Illinois was entitled to a place in Polk's cabinet. Douglas' name was proposed and rumors circulated that he would be given an appointment. No particular post was mentioned in connection with Douglas' name.

To James K. Polk

[February 22, 1845, House of Representatives; LS, RG-59, National Archives. Petition for the appointment of George W. Hopkins, Representative from Virginia, to the office of United States Consul in Liverpool, England. Hopkins, however, served an additional term in Congress, being appointed by Polk Chargé d'Affaires to Portugal in 1847. Signed by twenty-four members of the House of Representatives, including Douglas.]

To James K. Polk

[February 22, 1845, n.p.; LS, RG-59, National Archives. Petition for the appointment of Edmund Burke, Representative from New Hampshire, to the office of Commissioner of Patents. The appointment was made by Polk the following year. Signed by thirty-five members of the House of Representatives, including Douglas.]

To James K. Polk

[February 25, 1845, Washington City; AES, RG-59, National Archives. Letter of John A. McClernand, Representative from Illinois, asking the appointment of Alexander Duncan, outgoing Representative from Ohio, to the post of Minister to Austria, or "some other foreign mission." The request was endorsed by Stephen A. Douglas, John Wentworth, and Robert Smith, all members of the House of Representatives from Illinois. The appointment requested was not made.]

To James K. Polk

[March 7, 1845, Washington City; LS, RG-59, National Archives. Letter of Sidney Breese, Senator from Illinois, urging the appointment of Ebenezer Peck, a former member of the Illinois legislature, to the office of Chargé d'Affaires to Venezuela. The letter was also signed by Stephen A. Douglas and John A. McClernand, Representatives from Illinois.]

To James K. Polk and James Buchanan

Washington City March 7th 1845

To his Excelency James K. Polk President of the United States and the Honorable James Buckhannon Secretary of State

We the undersigned of the Delegation in Congress from the State of Illinois respectfully recommend Murray McConnel Esq[1] of our State and solicit for him the appointment of commissioner to the Sandwich Islands.

We solicit this appointment for the west as being in some degree connected with our intercourse with Oregon Territory, and we do not hesitate to recommend Mr. McConnel knowing that he has been and is a firm friend to the Occupation of that country by the United States. With much respect we are yours &c—

JAMES SEMPLE
JOHN A. MCCLERNAND
S. A. DOUGLASS
J. P. HOGE[2]
ROBERT SMITH
ORLANDO B. FICKLIN[3]

LS, RG-59, National Archives. Buchanan was Secretary of State.

[1] Murray McConnel, a prominent Jacksonville attorney and leader in local Democratic politics, had helped Douglas to get his start in the legal profession when the latter first arrived in Illinois. In 1855, he was appointed, at Douglas' suggestion, Fifth Auditor of the Treasury by President Franklin Pierce. The appointment asked for in this letter was not granted.

[2] Joseph Pendleton Hoge, of Galena, Illinois, served two terms as Representative in Congress from Illinois, from 1843 to 1847.

[3] Orlando B. Ficklin, of Charleston, Illinois, served in Congress from 1843 to 1849 and from 1851 to 1853.

To James K. Polk

Washington
March 8th 1845

Dear Sir,

Pardon me for trespassing upon your time so far as to introduce to your acquaintance my friend Edward F. Hodges Esq of Vermont.[1] Mr H is an applicant for an appointment abroad, say at Sweden, and desires an opportunity of laying before you his testimonials and recommendations. If you can take the time to examine & weigh his claims and qualifications and the propriety of his appointment to that office, his friends feel entirely confident of success. His qualifications are undoubted, his endowments of a high order, his character above reproach or imputation, in short he is a gentleman in whose appointment there would be a propriety, morally, intellectually, politically and in all respects. He is & has been a firm & consistent Democrat always active & laborous in the cause & as his testimonials will show has made great sacrifices of health as well as time & money for the success of our principles.

I have not written this as a mere matter of form or an act of courtesy, but as an act of strict justice feelling well assured that Mr Hodges deserves well at your hands. I do most sincerely hope that his application will be successful, and shall acknowledge the appointment to be a particular favor to me individually as well as to my friend. I have the honor to be your friend

S. A. DOUGLASS

ALS, RG-59, National Archives.

[1] Edward F. Hodges was a Rutland, Vermont, lawyer. The appointment asked for Hodges was not made.

To James K. Polk

[N.d., n.p.; LS, RG-59, National Archives. Petition for the appointment of Edward F. Hodges of Vermont to the office of Chargé d'Affaires at Stockholm, Sweden. Signed by eleven members of the House of

Representatives, including Douglas. The letter is in the hand of Paul Dillingham, Jr., Representative from Vermont.]

To James K. Polk

[March 10, 1845, Washington City; LS, RG-59, National Archives. Petition for the appointment of David L. Gregg, of Will County, Illinois, a member of the state legislature, to the office of United States Attorney for Illinois. Signed by Senators Sidney Breese and James Semple, and by six members of the House of Representatives from Illinois, including Douglas. The petition is in Breese's hand. The appointment was not made.]

To James K. Polk

[March 10, 1845, Washington; ES, RG-59, National Archives. Letter of Illinois Representative Orlando B. Ficklin submitting the recommendation of a large number of the members of the Illinois state legislature for the appointment of Dr. Isaac S. Berry to a South American consulate. The recommendation was endorsed by Illinois' two Senators and six Representatives, including Douglas. Berry, of Fayette County, was a member of the Illinois state legislature from 1844 to 1846.]

To James K. Polk

[March 10, 1845, Washington City; LS, RG-59, National Archives. Recommendation, signed by Illinois' two Senators and six of its Representatives, that Thomas M. Hope be removed from the office of Marshal of Illinois and that he be replaced by Stinson H. Anderson of Jefferson County. Anderson, a former Lieutenant Governor of Illinois, received the appointment.]

To James K. Polk

Washington
March 10th 1845

Dear Sir,

I had intended to join the delegation from Indiana in recommending the appointment of William H English Esq[1] of that State to be Recorder of the General Land Office, but having been deprived of the opportunity at that time, I hope you will pardon me for troubling you with a letter in his behalf. I have some personal acquaintance with Mr English and know him well by reputation & have no hesitation in expressing the firm conviction that he will make an active, attentive, and faithful officer. His appointment would not only be highly gratifying to the peo-

[109]

ple & delegation from his own State, but would be esteemed a favor to us of Illinois, where he has a large number of relatives (principally in my District,) all of whom are men of high character & standing and firm & unwavering Democrats. I do *most sincerely* hope that he may receive the appointment & would esteem it a favor to me, *personally*, as well as to those I have the honor to represent & who take a lively interest in his success. I have the honor to be your friend

S. A. DOUGLASS

ALS, Illinois State Historical Library. A fragment of a letter with the identical wording is in the English Papers, Indiana Historical Society, Indianapolis. [1]William H. English was clerk of the Indiana House of Representatives in 1843 and served as a clerk in the United States Treasury Department from 1844 to 1848. He was elected to Congress later in the 1850's.

To ――――――

[March 11, 1845, n.p.; ALS, Chicago Historical Society. Recommendation for the appointment of Calvin A. Warren to such office "as he, after consultation with his friends, shall ask." The recommendation is signed by six members of the Illinois delegation in the House of Representatives, and is endorsed by Illinois' two Senators. Warren was a Quincy lawyer; no appointment was apparently made.]

To James Buchanan

Washington

Sir,   March 13th 1845

I have made a great number of unsuccessful efforts during the past week to see you for a few moments for the twofold purpose of paying my respects to you and of presenting the claims of a friend for a foreign appointment. I have just returned from your Department, where for the first time I was informed that you were in your room, but the messenger refused to carry in my card, alledging that he was so instructed by yourself. The friend to whom I allude is Ebenezer Peck Esq of Illinois, whose name has been presented by your delegation for the appointment of Charge de Affairs to Venesuala.[1] Mr. Peck is a gentleman of fine talents, great attainments, & accomplished manners. I know of no gentleman in the western country whose qualifications are superior, and whose appointment would do more credit to the administration & afford more satisfaction to our friends. I am informed that the place is now vacant, and of course must be filled soon. I was anxious to have had a personal interview for the purpose of assuring you of the degree of interest we feel in the matter and of our entire conviction of the propriety of the appointment. Despairing of a personal interview, permit me to express to you the anxious hope that the appointment will be confered upon my friend Mr. Peck. I have the honor to be very respectfully your friend & obedient servant.

S. A. DOUGLASS

ALS, RG-59, National Archives.
[1]See above, Douglas to Polk, March 7, 1845.

To James K. Polk

Washington

Dear Sir, March 15th 1845

My old friend Charles Lindsy Esq of Middlebury Vermont has been recommended for U.S. Attorney for the District of Vermont.[1] I have known Mr Lindsy for about sixteen years, and know him to have been a firm, active, and unwavering Democrat during the whole time. He is a distinguished Lawyer, a man of fine talents and unblemished character. I have the fullest confidence in him as a man & a politician, & believe him worthy of the confidence of the government. I have no doubt his appointment would be entirely satisfactory to our friends there, while I assure you it would be regarded as an especial favor by his and your numerous friends. I have the honor to be your friend & obedient servant

S. A. DOUGLASS

ALS, RG-59, National Archives.
[1]Charles Linsley, not Lindsy, of Middlebury, received the appointment and held office as United States Attorney for Vermont from 1845 to 1849.

To Cave Johnson

Washington

My Dear Sir, March 18th 1845

Permit me to trespass upon your time so far as to recommend to you for appointment to some good & proffitable place in your Department W. W. Curran Esq[1] (lately a resident & citizen of the State of Illinois). I have know[n] Mr C for several years, and for some time lived in the same town with him in Illinois. He is & ever has been a firm & unwavering Democrat—his whole life has been devoted to the cause. He sustains an unblemished character for purity and integrity, and is inured to strict & regular business habits. I have no hesitation in saying that Mr. Curran will discharge the trust confided to him with promptness & fidelity. I most sincerely hope that his application will be successful. I have the honor to be your friend

S. A. DOUGLASS

ALS, Illinois State Historical Library. Cave Johnson, formerly a Representative from Tennessee, was Postmaster General in Polk's cabinet.

[1]William W. Curran was editor of the *Illinois State Gazette and Jacksonville News,* in Jacksonville, for a few months in 1837. He was appointed to a clerkship in the General Land Office in 1845.

To James K. Polk

Washington

Sir, April 16th 1845

I trust you will excuse me for trespassing upon your time so far as to say a word in behalf of a friend & colaborer in the Democratic cause last summer. I allude to Gansevort Melleville Esq of New York.[1] He is so well known to you personally as well as to the Democracy of the Union, that I deem it unnecessary to speak of his distinguished abilities or to his services during the last Presidential campaign. I consider him not only eminently qualified but justly entitled to any place, which he will ask of the Administration, and assure you that his appointment to a prominent place of honor & profit would be exceedingly gratifying to those of us whose good fortune it was to canvass the western country with him. I forbear to name any particular office for the reason that I would not like to interfere with the local appointments in the State of New York, but would be pleased to see him appointed to the office for which his friends in that State will present his name. I have the honor to be your friend

S. A. DOUGLASS

P.S. His appointment would be particularly gratifying to the Young Democracy of the country.

ALS, RG-59, National Archives.
[1]Gansevoort Melville, a New York lawyer and brother of Herman Melville, had campaigned for President Polk in 1844. On July 8, 1845, he was appointed secretary for the United States legation in London.

To James K. Polk

Washington

Dear Sir, April 17th 1845

I desired to say a few words to you in behalf of our friend Gen'l Van Antwerp of Mo before I left.[1] He is an old friend as well as political associate, and hence it was unpleasant for me to present a friend in opposition to him for commissioner of the Gen'l Land Office,[2] but that being disposed of much to my gratification, I wish to say to you that I would feel under still greater obligation if you could confer some suitable place upon him. He is man of decided talents, good attainments, and a sound unwavering Democrat. I do not wish to be importunate about this or any other appointment, and shall be entirely satisfied with any determination you shall make, while I express my earnest desire that he should be well provided for.

Gen'l Van Antwerp is well known to our people, and I will refer you to my friend Judge Shields & the western men generally for further information. I have the honor to be your friend

S. A. Douglass

ALS, Library of Congress, Washington, D.C.
[1]Ver Planck Van Antwerp was a resident of Iowa at this time, not Missouri, as indicated by Douglas. Van Antwerp had been Adjutant General of Iowa Territory; editor of the *Iowa Capitol*

Reporter, Iowa's third newspaper; and Receiver at the Fairfield, Iowa, Land Office.
[2]The friend to whom Douglas refers was James Shields, who was appointed Commissioner of the General Land Office in April, 1845.

To ———

[June 10, 1845, n.p. Recommendation for the appointment of James F. Reed to the office of Indian Agent in Oregon, signed by Stephen A. Douglas and Robert Smith, Representatives from Illinois. This letter is listed in Register #30 of Letters Received in the Office of Indian Affairs, RG-75, National Archives, but the original has not been located. Reed, a merchant and cabinetmaker in Sangamon County, later departed for California in 1846 in the famous Donner party.]

To James K. Polk

[June 23, 1845, Chicago; LS, RG-59, National Archives. Recommendation for the appointment of William Scott Brown of Chicago to a consulate in Switzerland. Signed by Thomas Ford, John Wentworth, James Shields, and Stephen A. Douglas. The letter was written by Shields.]

To James K. Polk

[June 24, 1845, Chicago; ALS, RG-59, National Archives. Recommending the appointment of Samuel Hubbel Treat "to some foreign country as *Charge des affairs,*" signed by Thomas Ford, Edmund Dick Taylor, and Stephen A. Douglas. Treat was a member of the Illinois Supreme Court at this time; the appointment sought by Douglas for him was not made.]

To the Editors of the *Illinois State Register*

To the Editors of the State Register: [June 28, 1845]
    On my return from Washington, a friend was kind enough to call my attention to several numbers of your paper, reflecting upon the entire

delegation in Congress from this State, for what you are pleased to call the loss of the western measures of last session. In some of the articles alluded to, I am asked to turn states-evidence against my colleagues, and explain why it was that we failed to secure the passage of the bills for the improvement of the western rivers, the lake harbors, the national road, the western armory, and possibly some other measures which may have escaped my memory at this time, not having your paper before me.[1]

I declined responding to your call for the simple reason that your charges against the delegation were so palpably unjust and so inconsistent with the facts of the case, as shown by the published proceedings, you could not long fail to discover your error, confidently believing that when discovered, it would be promptly corrected. But I must confess my surprise, when I saw in each succeeding number of your paper, a repetition of the charges in language more bold and severe. I could not suppose that you were ignorant of the true state of the facts, as you might have found them published in your exchange papers; and I was unwilling to believe that you were disposed wilfully to distort and misrepresent them. To remove all misapprehension on this subject, and to save you the trouble of again repeating these charges, I will inform you that the delegation did not fail to secure the passage of liberal appropriations for the improvement of the western rivers, nor for the lake harbors, nor the national road. Each of these measures passed both Houses of Congress by large majorities, and was sent to President Tyler in ample time for his approval. It is true that he withheld his signature, and thus defeated these great western measures; but I trust that the Illinois delegation is not to be held responsible for the sins of Mr. Tyler. I am willing to take the responsibility of my own acts, and be judged by my own conduct, but I protest against your right to cast the odium of the defeat of these measures upon the delegation in Congress for the purpose of screening Mr. Tyler from the censure that might attach to his conduct, when the true state of the facts was presented to the people. I condemn no one for differing with me in opinion in regard to these or any measures of public policy, nor do I claim any peculiar credit for myself and those who acted with me in securing their passage. We only did what we conceived to be our duty; but we did suppose that the success which crowned our efforts would shield us from attacks, not only from professed friends, but from all manly opponents. You should remember that these measures have not always been successful—they have not passed as a matter of course—success has always required a strenuous effort, and has then often failed. It is now many years since an appropriation has been made for the national road; and the river and harbor bills have frequently been lost; but I may be permitted to say, without boasting, that they have not failed to pass both Houses of Congress at any session since those whom you now condemn have had the honor to represent the State.

In regard to the western armory, I have but a few words to say. The bill for its establishment at Fort Massac, in this State, passed the House of Representatives at the last session, and once received a majority of the Senate, but was eventually defeated in that body in consequence of local and political jealousies. Yet the Representatives from this State are denounced for the loss of this bill, when we gave it our unanimous support, and by our united efforts succeeded in passing it through the House of which we were members. Even if we had failed in this respect, we would then have been as successful as those who preceded us. The measure never passed either House until the last Congress. I mean no reflection upon our predecessors by this remark, for I am aware of the difficulty in originating and passing a new measure, and I only refer to ours being the first successful effort, for the purpose of showing how unjust are your complaints.

There is yet another subject of complaint to which I will allude—I believe you did not originate it, but contented yourselves with becoming endorser for its author—I refer to the resolution directing the Secretary of the Treasury to withhold any moneys in his hands belonging to any of the States of the Union, when such States were indebted to the United States and refused, or failed to pay. I have not the resolution before me, but this, I believe, is the substance of it.[2] The grand discovery has recently been made, that this resolution authorizes, and was intended to authorize, the Secretary to deprive the State of Illinois of the school fund. With all due respect for your opinion, and for his, for whom you have become the voluntary endorser; I must be permitted to dissent, and assign briefly the reasons why I do so. The evil intended to be remedied by the resolution, as I understand it, was this. One or two States had borrowed from the United States the Smithsonian Bequest, and the monies appropriated for Indian annuities, and had failed to pay the interest, and had thus devolved upon Congress the necessity of making new appropriations for the same objects. The Secretary of the Treasury had taken the responsibility of retaining their proportion of the moneys accruing under, what is called, the distribution bill, and had applied it to the payment of the interest on these loans. The right of the Secretary thus to retain and apply those moneys, without any express law to that effect, being denied, this resolution was for the double purpose of legalizing those acts, and authorizing him to so apply any moneys belonging to States thus situated in future. I never understood that our State was in the predicament to be embraced by the objects of the resolution, for the Secretary had always paid our proportion of the distribution moneys as well as the school fund. But the principle is the same, whether it affects our State or not. Does it apply to the school fund of this or any other State? Does the school fund *belong to the State* in the sense in which that term is ordinarily used, or is it a trust-fund for the proper application of which the State is the trustee merely? The State can dispose of her own money as she pleases—apply it to any purpose she chooses, connected with the public good. Not so with the school fund. That is a sacred fund, secured by an express compact, irrevocable except by common consent, between the people of the State of Illinois and the federal government, and appropriated by the compact itself to a specific object, the State being a mere trustee for the execution of the trust. Can one party to a compact change its terms, without the consent of the other contracting party? The State of Illinois has no right to apply this fund to objects other than those designated in the compact, nor has the government of the United States any authority to withhold it for any cause or on any pretext whatever. Had Congress passed a law to that effect, in so many words, it would have been an indirect violation of the compact, and therefore a nullity. Should we, then, by a forced construction, torture the resolution into a meaning, which its words do not import, and which would not only be unjust and perfidious, but would transcend the legitimate powers of Congress itself? Why should we exhaust our ingenuity in attempts to fix a construction upon this resolution alike repugnant to common sense and to the intentions and motives of those who adopted it. Suppose you succeed in your zealous effort, and by the force of your reasoning, in-duce the Secretary of the Treasury to adopt your construction; what service will you have rendered the State by your triumph? What ad-vantage will you have gained for our people? Will you not then be entitled to the credit of having accomplished what you so ardently profess to deprecate, and so indignantly denounce as a vile robbery of children yet unborn? If your construction shall prevail, which I do not anticipate, I for one, will feel it my duty, and I trust the entire delega-tion from this State, will feel it their's, to protest against it, as a palpable violation of the compact, and demand its immediate revocation. If such an issue should arise, am I to infer that you and those with whom you are acting, will be found arrayed against our own people and in favor of a forced construction of that resolution, which would sacrifice the school fund? The articles in your paper may be quoted in support of that position. For myself I can only say, that so far as my knowledge or belief extends, no member of the House ever conceived that this meas-ure would or could be tortured into an attack on the school fund. The fact that it is alleged to have passed the House without opposition, and that a learned Senator with all his talents and influence tells us that he could not rally but two or three out of fifty-two Senators to oppose it,[3] it would seem to be conclusive upon this point. If it was understood to be an attack upon the school fund in direct violation of the compact with all these States, could not more than two or three have been induced to oppose it? Were there no more just men in both Houses of Congress? Had the dear children no more friends there? Has senatorial eloquence lost its power to awaken a sense of justice in the stony heart, when the rights of millions of unborn infants are wantonly invaded? I must be permitted to believe that there is some mistake about this matter, and that the resolution was intended to mean just what its language, considered with reference to the compact, would import, and nothing more.

I decline to notice the unworthy motives which you assign as the cause of the alleged sins of the delegation. Who would not feel grateful to find one's self advertised as the innocent victim of a heartless conspiracy, of the very existence of which, he had remained in profound and happy ignorance! But I trust that the delegation will be able to act together with quite as much harmony and as little jealousy as might be supposed to exist between the editors of the Register and their brethren of the Press. When we shall fail to do this, and the loss of the western measures shall be the consequence, I presume that the delegation will submit meekly and with a good grace to a new series of lectures from their friends of the Register.[4]

Peoria, June 28th, 1845.   S. A. DOUGLASS

Springfield *Illinois State Register,* July 11, 1845.

[1]In the issue of May 30, 1845, the editor of the *State Register* retracted an earlier allegation, after a conference with Douglas, that the loss of the Illinois measures in Congress had been due to quarrels among the Illinois delegation in the House. He still maintained, however, that the loss of the bills remained unexplained.

[2]The resolution referred to by Douglas provided that "whenever any State shall have been or may be in default for the payment of interest or principal on investment in its stocks or bonds held by the United States in trust, it shall be the duty of the Secretary of the Treasury to retain the whole, or so much thereof as may be necessary, of the per centage to which such State may be entitled of the proceeds of the sales of the public lands within its limits, and apply the same to the payment of said interest or principal, or to the reimbursement of any sums of money expended by the United States for that purpose." The resolution passed the House on February 25 and the Senate on March 1, 1845.

[3]Senator Sidney Breese, in a letter to Governor Ford published in the *State Register,* March 21, 1845, wrote of his opposition to the passage of the resolution.

[4]Douglas' letter was answered in the columns of the *State Register* on July 18, 1845. Although restating the paper's support of Douglas, the editor stood on his former statements and castigated Douglas for supporting the resolution depriving states in default to the United States government of their share of the proceeds from public land sales.

To James K. Polk

Quincy Ills

Dear Sir, Augst 21st 1845

From the late news received from New Orleans and Mexico we are inclined to the opinion that the next mail will bring the news of a declaration of war.[1] In that event I presume that volunteers will be wanted in addition to the regular army. Ferdinand Kennett Esq of St Louis[2] desires a commission as Colonel with authority to raise a rigament for the purpose of marching against Santa Fe—and California. I know Mr Kennett well and have been intimate with him for years. I think him admirably adapted to the service he seeks. He is a gentleman of fine talents, and with a chivalry of character unsurpassed, and possess[es] an intimate knowledge of the habits & character of the Indians Tribes as well as the intervening country. Were I going on such an expedition, I would prefer Mr Kennett for a leader to any gentleman of my acquaintance. If he succeeds in obtaining authority, his intention is, I understand to make up a rigament of mountain-men as they are called in this country—being a peculiar class of men, who have been in the habit of trading to the Rocky Mountains—New Mexico and California, and are perfectly familiar with the country, the Indians tribes, the mode of travel and subsistence. Mr K['s] acquaintance with and influence over that class of men would enable him to raise a rigament without any difficulty. In the event therefore that you shall deem it your duty to authorize the raising of volunteers I do sincerely hope that Mr K may be selected for that service, believing that he would discharge the duty in a manner highly honorable to himself and his government. I have the honor to be your friend

S. A. DOUGLASS

ALS, Illinois State Historical Library.
[1]Following the passage by Congress of the joint resolution inviting Texas to become a state in the Union, Mexico terminated diplomatic relations with the United States. In July, 1845, President Polk ordered Regular Army troops under the command of Zachary Taylor to take up positions along the Nueces River in Texas. Reports carried by American newspapers at this time indicated that Mexico had decided on war with the United States over the Texas annexation.
[2]Ferdinand Kennett was a prominent merchant, banker, and member of the Democratic party in St. Louis. He was elected an officer of the St. Louis Legion following the declaration of war against Mexico in May, 1846.

To Charles H. Lanphier

Quincy

My Dear Sir, Aug 22d 1845

Your favor of the 18th May last [did] not reach me until this week in consequence of my absence from home. I had previously heard that you and Mr Walker[1] were negotiating for the Chicago Advocate,[2] and had expressed the hope that you might succeed with it. I did so not only on account of the friendly regard I have long entertained for you, but for the further reason that I believe you both possess talents that would be very serviceable to the Democratic Cause. I was not aware however that you had concluded the negotiation until the receipt of your letter, and must yet [wonder] whether you are really editing that paper. I cannot permit myself to believe that under your direction that paper would pursue so illiberal and unjust a course towards myself individually. Such a course is certainly inconsistent with the personal & political relations existing between us and the estimate I have formed of your character as well as the sentiments of your letter. I take it for granted therefore that there is some mistake about it, and that you are not the editor & conductor of that paper; and on this supposition I shall direct this letter to you at Springfield instead of Chicago. I shall be pleased to hear from you, and learn your objects and whereabouts. I expected to have had the pleasure of meeting when at Springfield and again at Chicago, but unfortunately I missed you at both places. I remain respectfully your friend

S. A. Douglass

ALS, Illinois State Historical Library.
[1]George Walker, a Springfield lawyer, was deputy clerk of the state Supreme Court until 1847, when he became associated with Charles H. Lanphier in the publication of the *Illinois State Register*.

[2]The *Democrat Advocate and Commercial Advertiser*, published in Chicago from 1844 to 1846. The negotiations of Lanphier and Walker to assume control of the paper apparently were not successful.

To James K. Polk

Quincy Ills

Sir,   August 25th 1845

Last night's mail brought the news that the Mexican government, in anticipation of a declaration of War against this country, was preparing for the invasion of the State of Texas, and that ten thousand Mexicans were on their way and within eight days March of Gen'l Taylor's encampment. It is also stated that a requisition has been made upon the Governor of Louisiana for several Regements of the militia. Relying upon the correctness of this information, I presume that actual hostilities have already commenced. In such an event policy and honor would alike require that the invasion should be promptly repelled, and such chastisement inflicted upon its authors as will teach them to respect our rights in future. I do not think that our government ought to confine its operations to mere defensive warfare. The Northern Provinces of Mexico including California ought to belong to this Republic, and the day is not far distant when such a result will be accomplished. The present is an auspicious time. The declaration of war by Mexico renders such a step necessary and proper; and I hope the administration will resolve upon an expidition against New Mexico and California immediately. Such a movement will meet with the enthusiastic support of the whole west. In the event you shall determine upon this line of policy I would like to receive your authority to raise a Regement of Voluntiers from this State.[1] As I have given Mr. Kennett of Missouri a letter to you recommending him for a similar appointment in that State I do not [wish] to have this application interfere with his appointment. But I presume that both and perhaps more will be necessary, and if consistent with your views of propriety and the public interests I would feel grateful for the commission asked for.[2] I have the honor to be respectfully your obedient servant.

S. A. Douglass

ALS Copy, owned by Martin F. Douglas.

[1] Douglas' assumption that hostilities had begun was erroneous. No authorization was given him to raise a volunteer regiment in Illinois.

[2] Douglas seriously considered for a time volunteering for military service in Mexico, but later changed his mind. For other indications of his military ambitions, see below, Douglas to Hardin, June 16, 1846.

To the President and Council of the Church of Latter Day Saints

Nauvoo, Oct. 1, 1845.

To the first President and Council of the Church at Nauvoo.

Having had a full and free conversation with you this day in reference to your proposed removal from this county, together with the members of your church, we have to request you to submit the facts and intentions stated to us in said conversation to writing; in order that we may lay them before the Governor and people of the State. We hope that by so doing it will have a tendency to allay the excitement at present existing in the public mind.[1] We have the honor to subscribe ourselves, Respectfully, Yours &c.

John J. Hardin
S. A. Douglas
W. B. Warren
J. A. McDougal[2]

Springfield *Illinois State Register*, October 10, 1845. Brigham Young was President of the Church. In the fall of 1845, the resentment against the Mormon settlements in Illinois, about the city of Nauvoo, reached a peak and resulted in mob outbreaks against Mormons and their property. The Mormons retaliated and the Governor, Thomas Ford, sent a militia force under the command of John J. Hardin into the area to restore order.

[1]The reply of Brigham Young to this request, also dated October 1, 1845, appeared in the same issue of the *State Register*. In it, Young reiterated the intention of the Church to move from Illinois and described the preparations that had been made for the removal to that time.

[2]Douglas was asked by Governor Ford to accompany the militia force. In a subsequent letter, he signed himself as "Aid-de-Camp." He was the Congressman in whose district the Mormon settlements were located. John J. Hardin, commander of the militia force and Douglas' political opponent of earlier days, had been elected as a Whig to Congress in 1842, where he served one term. With Hardin and Douglas were James A. McDougall, state Attorney General, and William Barton Warren, clerk of the state Supreme Court and a prominent Whig in local politics. These four men were empowered to act as commissioners in negotiating with the Mormons.

To the President and Council of the Church of Latter Day Saints

Camp Carthage, Oct. 3d, 1845

To the First President and High Council of the Church of Latter Day Saints.

Since our conference with you yesterday, we have arrived at this place, and have held free conversation with the Anti-Mormons of this and the surrounding counties.

We have read to them your statement made to us on the 1st inst. We have informed them that you individually made similar statements to us, with the most solemn protestations of truth, and with every appearance of earnest determination to carry out your expressed intentions in good faith.

In the resolutions which were adopted on yesterday, in this place, by the delegates from nine counties,[1] (the citizens of Hancock being excluded from the meeting,) it was resolved (as we are informed, not having seen a copy of the resolutions) to accept your proposition to remove in the spring.

Since we have made public the statement by you made to us, there seems to be a general acquiescence in it by the citizens of other counties and of this, so far as to agree to restrain and withold all further violence, and that you be permitted to depart in peace next spring.

We are convinced that affairs have reached such a crisis that it has become impossible for your church to remain in this county.

After what has been said and written by yourselves, it will be confidently expected by us and the whole community, that you will remove from the State, with your whole Church in the manner you have agreed in your statement to us.

Should you not do so, we are satisfied, however much we may deprecate violence and bloodshed, that violent measures will be resorted to, to compel your removal; which will result in most disastrous conse-

[121]

quences to yourselves and your opponents, and that the end will be your exclusion from the State.

We think that steps should be taken by you to make it apparent that you are actually preparing to remove in the spring.

By carrying out in good faith, your proposition to remove as submitted to us, we think you should be, and will be permitted to depart peaceably next spring for your destination west of the Rocky Mountains.

For the purpose of maintaining law and order in this county, the Commanding General proposes to leave an armed force in this county, which will be sufficient for that purpose, and which will remain so long as the Governor deems it necessary.

And for the purpose of preventing the use of such force for vexatious or improper objects, we will recommend the Governor of the State to send some competent legal officer to remain here, and have the power of deciding what process shall be executed by said military force.

We recommend to you to place every possible restraint in your power over the members of your church, to prevent them from committing acts of aggression or retaliation on any citizen of the State, as a contrary course may, and most probably will, bring about a collision which will subvert all efforts to maintain the peace in this county; and we purpose making a similar request of your opponents in this and the surrounding counties.

With many wishes that you may find that peace and prosperity in the land of your destination, which you desire, we have the honor to subscribe ourselves, yours, &c.,

JOHN J. HARDIN
W. B. WARREN
S. A. DOUGLASS
J. A. McDOUGAL

Alton (Illinois) *Telegraph,* October 11, 1845.

[1]The counties were Adams, Marquette, Schuyler, Pike, Brown, McDonough, Knox, Warren, and Henderson. Marquette County was formerly the eastern half of Adams County.

To the Anti-Mormon Citizens of Hancock County

Camp Carthage, Oct. 4, 1845.

To the Anti-Mormon Citizens of Hancock and the Surrounding Counties.

We submit for your consideration copies of a correspondence between ourselves and the "Twelve" at Nauvoo. Having witnessed with deep regret the deplorable condition of things which exist in this county, as it regards both the peace and the safety of the community, we have applied our most strenuous efforts to restore confidence and set on foot a permanent settlement of the difficulties which distract this county. We sincerely trust that object is in a fair train of being accomplished.

The Mormons have pledged themselves by word and by writing, to remove from the State. Aside from these pledges, there are reasons which incline us to the opinion that such is their intention. You desire to see them removed. We think, also, that for the preservation of peace and quiet in this county, they had best remove; and we have so advised them. But it is not consistent with a proper sense of justice or humanity, that families of women and children, should be driven from their homes by threats or violence, at this season of the year, to breast the storms of winter, unprotected by the covering of a roof.

Five or six thousand of the Mormons, including the entire Church organization, their prominent men, and all their Church judicatories have pledged themselves to remove next spring; and, judging from appearances, they will do so. The history of their church has shown that wherever their leaders go the members will follow. This is a part of their religious duties. When, therefore, this colony shall have started for a home west of the Rocky Mountains, it will be the best possible evidence that all design removing, and will remove. Many citizens of other counties than Hancock, have resolved to accept the proposition of the Mormons, to remove in the spring; and most or nearly all of those with whom we have had an opportunity of conversing, have expressed themselves satisfied with the agreement of the Mormons to remove as submitted to us, if it is carried out in good faith.

At the solicitation of all parties, and from a conviction of the necessity of the measure, Gen. Hardin has determined to station a portion of his troops in this county, to maintain order, who will continue in the field until the Governor shall order them to be disbanded. We have also recommended to the Governor to appoint an Attorney to act for the State, who shall decide what process the military force shall execute; and thus prevent them from being harrassed by being called out to act on frivolous and improper cases, and at the same time to check and restrain the troops from any improper action.

Order and quiet are again being restored to your county, and men are daily returning to their homes and business, without apprehension of illegal and improper interruption.

These measures, we think, ought to satisfy you. All that some of you might demand, could not be granted consistently with the rights of others. You should be satisfied with attaining that which is practical and probable.

[123]

We beseech you, therefore, to be quiet and orderly—and at the same time warn you not to violate the law. The troops stationed in Hancock will enforce it at all hazards.

Remember: whatever may be the aggression against you, the sympathy of the public may be forfeited. It cannot be denied that the burning of the houses of the Mormons in Hancock county, by which a large number of women and children have been rendered homeless and houseless, in the beginning of the winter, was an act criminal in itself, and disgraceful to its perpetrators.—And it should also be known, that it has led many persons to believe, that, even if the Mormons are as bad as they are represented, they are no worse than those who have burnt their houses.

Whether your case is just or unjust, the acts of these incendiaries have thus lost for you something of the sympathy and good will of your fellow citizens; and a resort to, or persistence in such a course, under existing circumstances, will make you forfeit all the respect and sympathy of the community.

We trust and believe, for this lovely portion of our State, a brighter day is dawning: and we beseech all parties not to seek to hasten its approach by the torch of the incendiary, nor disturb its dawn by the clash of arms. Your fellow citizens,

JOHN J. HARDIN
S. A. DOUGLASS
W. B. WARREN
J. A. McDOUGAL

Alton *Telegraph*, October 11, 1845.

To Thomas Ford

CARTHAGE, Oct. 4, 1845.

His Excellency Thos. Ford, *Governor*,

The undersigned having come to this county under the orders and proclamation of your Excellency, for the purpose of restoring and maintaining the supremacy of the laws, beg leave to submit the following statement for your consideration.

On our arrival in this county, there were several military organizations in different parts of the county; some were anti-Mormon, and some Mormon; the latter acting as a posse under the command of J. B. Backenstos, sheriff of this county.[1] The forces were exceedingly hostile to each other, and any collision between them would have been almost certain to result in open war.

All those families that were burnt out, and a great number of other

Mormon families, have fled from their homes and taken refuge in Nauvoo.

Since the sheriff and his posse obtained the ascendency in the county, very many anti-Mormons have fled from the county, and many of them took their families with them. Numbers of those who have thus left their homes and fled into Nauvoo and from the county, including Mormons and anti-Mormons, are not accused of any crime, but have fled under an apprehension of real danger from the different hostile parties who have been marching and marauding through the county. The lives of a considerable number of individuals of both parties have been threatened to be taken; there seems to be just cause of apprehension that these threats may be carried into effect, in several instances.

There has been a great deal of sickness and suffering among those who have been forced to flee into Nauvoo, as well as amongst those who have left the county.

There are many individuals who reside in the county, belonging to each party, who are accused of being guilty of murder, arson, larceny, and robbery. The friends of those who stand accused, constitute a very large portion of the population of the county.

Although there has not been as much injury and violence actually committed as has been reported, yet the state of feeling of the inhabitants of the county is as fully exasperated as can be well imagined. Under the present state of excitement prevailing throughout the county, we are convinced that if the Mormons or anti-Mormons have the uncontrolled legal ascendency in the county, their opponents will not be safe or free from violence and aggression.

The members of the High Council of Twelve, among the Mormons, and the anti-Mormons, thro' delegates and individuals, have requested that the General in command of the troops should not disband them all, but should leave a portion of his force sufficient to maintain order and quiet. Many individuals have declared they would be glad to live until spring under martial law, enforced by troops who are sent here from other counties by order of the Governor, as they believed it would be the best and perhaps the only way of preserving peace and safety. The citizens of other counties who are familiar with the situation of things in this county, have expressed the request that the troops be left here.

Since the arrival of the troops, and the publication of the address of General Hardin, to the citizens of Hancock, the military organizations of the sheriff's posse and of the anti-Mormons, have been disbanded. Order and quiet have been restored—many persons have returned to their homes, and others say they will bring back their families if the troops remain. All parties express themselves under apprehension of another and more serious outbreak unless a military force is left here in the county.

The Mormons have expressed a determination to remove from the county, and a large number are pledged to leave in the spring.

Under existing circumstances, therefore, the undersigned, would respectfully submit to your Excellency that to maintain peace, quiet, and order, it is necessary that a competent military force should be maintained in this county for some time to come.

General Hardin, therefore, by the advice of the remainder of the undersigned, has determined to leave about one hundred men in this county, under the command of Major W. B. Warren who will keep up that force until it shall be ordered to be disbanded by your Excellency.[2] After a short time the number of troops may be reduced; but until it is certain that there will not be attempts to commit further breaches of the law, we consider this force none too large.

We would further suggest that for the purpose of preventing this force from being harrassed by calls to act as a posse, by all the civil officers of the county, and to act also as a check upon these troops, that some competent lawyer be appointed to act as the attorney of the State, who shall examine and direct in what cases the military force shall assist in the execution of process. We have the honor to subscribe ourselves Yours, respectfully,

JOHN J. HARDIN, Brig. Gen.
W. B. WARREN, B. Major
S. A. DOUGLASS, Aid-de camp
J. A. McDOUGALL, Att'y Gen.

Springfield *Illinois State Register*, October 17, 1845. Thomas Ford was Governor of Illinois from 1842 to 1846.
[1]Jacob B. Backenstos, Sheriff of Hancock County, was a Mormon sympathizer.

[2]The military guard under Major Warren remained in Nauvoo until the following May, 1846, ostensibly to prevent continued depredations by Mormons against the property of non-Mormons.

To John J. Hardin

To Gen'l John J. Hardin   Quincy Oct 10th 1845

In acknowledging the receipt of your note of this date, "expressing to the officers of your staff the entire satisfaction you have felt with each of them during our term of service",[1] I would do injustice to my own feelings if I withheld from you the expression of my gratitude for the complimentary terms in which you have spoken of my conduct as a member of your staff, and my full approbation of the measures adopted and course pursued by you during the campaign. I found you

[126]

ever true to the avowed objects of the expedition—firm, impartial, and inflexible in enforcing the supremacy of the laws—kind and courteous to both officers & men, and prompt in the discharge of the arduous duties devolving upon you as the Commanding General. I felt a peculiar gratification at the perfect unanimity which prevailed in all our consultations, as well in our conferences with the leaders of the church at Nauvoo in arrainging the terms of their voluntary & favorable removal from the State, as in the performance of our official duties. With unfeigned wishes for your happiness & prosperity I remain respectfully yours

S. A. DOUGLAS
Aid de Camp

ALS, owned by Martin F. Douglas.
[1]Hardin's letter to the "Officers composing my staff," October 10, 1845, is owned by Martin F. Douglas.

To Asa Whitney

SIR,   Quincy, Illinois, Oct. 15th, 1845.

I have the honor to acknowledge the receipt of several letters from you, dated at New York, Chicago, Milwaukie, and St. Louis, together with various printed papers, all relating to your project for a Rail Road from Lake Michigan to the Pacific Ocean.[1]

I have no doubt the time will come, when there will be a continuous line of rail roads from the Atlantic to the Pacific. Indeed, several links in the chain are already in operation, and others rapidly progressing to completion. From Portland to Buffalo, via Boston and Albany, the cars have been running for sometime. It is in contemplation to continue this line through Upper Canada, to Detroit, where it will connect with the Central Rail Road of Michigan, across the peninsula, in the direction of Chicago; the greater portion of which is now completed, and in successful operation, and the work rapidly advancing on the balance of the route. Steps have recently been taken to ensure the completion of the New York and Erie road, which will strike the lake at a point near the Pennsylvania line, and connect with the Boston and Portland line, at New York. It is confidently expected that this road will be continued westward, along the southern shore of Lake Erie, and the southern point of Lake Michigan, to Chicago, and thence to the Mississippi. These two rival lines will probably converge to the same point, near the head of Lake Michigan, and be merged in one, during the remainder of their journey westward. In view of these facts, I am unable to comprehend the reasons which induce you to fix your starting point at Milwaukie, and pursue the circuitous route via Fond du Lac, Prairie de Chien, the St. Peters river, and the big bend of the Missouri, instead of the more direct and natural one from Chicago to the south pass of the Rocky mountains, as indicated by the course of those links, in the same great chain of improvement, which have been completed, or are progressing to completion. The places on the lakes, and other points of intersections, should be chosen with reference to extensions eastward as well as westward; otherwise, the harmony of the system will be disturbed, and a great portion of the anticipated advantages lost. It will not do to rely *solely* upon the lakes as links in the chain, for their navigation will be interrupted by ice about four months in the year, and during that time, the connexion with the Atlantic cities destroyed. For these reasons, the route must run around the head of Lake Michigan, or on a line still further south, if we are to secure the advantages of a communication between the Atlantic and Pacific, which may be traversed at all seasons of the year. The route from New York to the Mississippi, at or near St. Louis, by way of Baltimore, is worthy of consideration. This line of rail roads has been in successful operation, for sometime, as far as Cumberland, Md., and Winchester, Va., with the expectation of its speedy extension to the Ohio river, at Wheeling, or Parkersburgh; thence to Cincinnati and St. Louis. It is not impossible that this may be selected as the great route to the Pacific; especially, if the western terminus should be located in California, as some anticipate.

Passing from this branch of the subject, I have carefully examined your plan for the construction of the work, with the anxious desire of finding it well adapted to the end in view, and consistent with the principles which ought to govern so great an enterprise. You ask for a grant of lands to yourself, properly guarded, so as to secure the faithful application of the proceeds to the construction of the road, sixty miles wide, and stretching from Lake Michigan to the Pacific ocean; a distance which you estimate at 2400 miles. This grant would amount to 144,000 square miles, or 92,160,000 acres; a quantity greater than is contained in the entire states of New York, New Jersy, Pennsylvania, and Ohio, collectively. This immense territory, more extensive than England, Ireland, Scotland, and half a dozen of the German states, combined, it is proposed to grant to one individual, and authorise him to dispose of the same, and apply *so much* of the proceeds, as shall be necessary, to the construction of the road, and the balance to inure to his individual benefit. You estimate the cost of the road, at $50,000,000, to which you add $15,000,000, for repairs, making a total expenditure of $65,000,000. To meet this sum, you ask for 92,160,000 acres of land, which, at one dollar and twenty-five cents per acre, (the minimum price at which government sells the public lands,) would make $115,-200,000. Deducting from this sum the $65,000,000, which you estimate as the aggregate cost of contruction and repairs, and you have the snug little sum of $50,200,000, as your individual profits, to compensate you for your time and trouble in superintending the work. I have no data by which to test the accuracy of these estimates, and therefore take them as I find them in your "Address to the People of the United States," without comment. It is certain, however, that a considerable portion of these lands are of an inferior quality—many of them almost valueless; while, on the other hand, the remainder of them are the best wild lands in the world; and stretching along on either side of the proposed road, their value would be greatly enhanced by its construction. But not having the means of forming an estimate of their average value, I shall leave the figures as they appear above, with the round sum of fifty millions of dollars standing to your credit.

I am unable to determine from the memorial, address, and other papers you have done me the honor to send me, to whom the road is to belong, when completed; whether to yourself—to the several States and Territories through which it may pass, or to the government of the United States; but I presume that you do not intend to claim it for yourself, as you seem to rely upon the surplus lands and their proceeds as your reward.—Passing over the difficulty arising out of the uncertainty, whether the improvement, when completed, would belong to the Federal government or to the individual states in which it might lay, I am of the opinion that your scheme is too magnificent—the trust too great—the grant of lands too extensive—and the power over the rights and interests of the people, states, territories, and government, too monstrous to be confided to any citizen, no matter how virtuous, enlightened and patriotic. For these reasons, if there were none other, I should feel constrained, as at present advised, to withhold my support from your plan. Besides, I am not sure that it is feasible. In the first place, I apprehend you would find it difficult to obtain this immense grant of lands from the Congress of the United States; and secondly, to procure the assent of the states and territories through which it would extend, to the establishment of such a tremendous engine of power within their limits. But, passing over these obstacles, and supposing you succeed in surmounting them, yet, I have not implicit faith that you would be able to construct the road. As I understand your plan of operations, you propose first to procure the grant of lands—then to withhold them from sale and settlement for the present—to raise the money to commence the work on the pledge of the lands;—and, as the work progresses, make sales on the line of that part which shall have been completed, to pay the interest on previous loans, and obtain means for continuing operations:—thus advancing, step by step, and making the construction of the road *precede*—not follow—the tide of emigration, and the settlement of the country. This looks very well on paper, and appears plausible at the first view, but I fear you would find a serious practical difficulty in carrying it out. The first effect would be to postpone the peopling of the country—to exclude all inhabitants and improvements from within thirty miles of the route on each side—and to keep the whole line a savage wilderness, until the road shall have been constructed. The result of this policy, on the future destiny of the country west of the mountains, will be too apparent, from a glance at its topography. As you advance to the Rocky Mountains, you will enter the valley of the north branch of the Nebraska,[2] thence pursuing the valley of the Sweet-Water to the South Pass, you will descend the valley of the Columbia to the Ocean. This is the route proposed by you, and may be adopted, although I am inclined to the opinion, that the Bay of San Francisco, in California, would be preferable for the western terminus, if that country could be annexed in time. The line of your road would probably follow the valleys of those streams—your grant of lands, sixty miles wide, would nearly, if not entirely, cover the whole width of those valleys, from hill to hill, and mountain to mountain, (excepting, of course, the tributary streams,) for it is a hilly, mountainous country, with fine valleys upon the water courses. The withholding of all those lands from sale and settlement, until your road shall have been completed, would block up the South Pass, and stop the tide of emigration to Oregon, about as effectually as the British Government, and the Hudson's Bay Company, could desire. This vast tide of American emigration, once stayed—and all future settlements excluded from the South Pass and the valley of the Columbia,—anxiously waiting for you to advance in your rail road car, from Milwaukie via Fond du Lac, Prairie du Chien, the St. Peters, and the big bend of the Missouri, to the South Pass, to bring the lands into market, and give emigrants permission to plant their homes on the banks of the Columbia;—and, in the mean time, Great Britain continuing to pour in the masses of her surplus population—to extend her settlements, and increase the number of her forts;—I greatly fear, that, on your arrival at the summit of the Rocky Mountains, you would find that the treaty of joint occupation had long since ceased, and your eyes would behold a dense and prosperous British colony, possessing and cultivating the whole valley below. While, therefore, I regard your project as objectionable and impracticable, I doubt not the time will come, when we will see a continuous line of rail roads to the Pacific ocean. It will be the work of years, however, and progress gradually, from east to west, keeping up a connected chain of communication, and following the tide of emigration, and the settlement of the country. In addition to the India and China trade, and the vast commerce of the Pacific ocean, which would pass over this route, you must create a further necessity for the road,

by subduing the wilderness, and peopling it with a hardy and industrious population, who would soon have a surplus produce, without the
means of getting it to market, and require, for their own consumption,
immense quantities of goods and merchandize, which they could not
obtain, at reasonable rates, for want of proper facilities of transportation; and that necessity will make the road. Causes are now in active
operation, and have been for several years, which must soon produce
this result. To those vast multitudes, who wish to change their condition, and select new homes, the promised land is westward. Nebraska,
whose name was unknown about one year ago, has now a local habita-
tion upon our maps, and we talk of seeing our friends in California and
Oregon, as familiarly as in New York and New Orleans. When Congress shall do its duty, as I trust it will at the ensuing session, by establishing the territories of Nebraska and Oregon,[3] and fostering a continuous line of settlements from the Mississippi to the Pacific, the tide of
emigration will set in that direction with redoubled force. In the meantime, some decisive measures should be adopted immediately to insure
the completion of this great railroad communication within the period
that the course of events will render necessary. Among these I would
specify the following:

Let the Oregon territory be established, extending from the summit
of the Rocky Mountains to the Pacific.

Let the territory of Nebraska be established, (according to a bill introduced last winter with reference to this very object among others,)
extending from the western borders of Iowa and Missouri to Oregon,
and embracing sufficient country on both sides of the Nebraska or
Platt river to make a good State.

Let the route of the proposed railroad be immediately surveyed and
located from Lake Erie, or the Ohio, to the Pacific.

Let Congress grant to each of the Territories, Iowa, Nebraska and
Oregon, the ALTERNATE SECTIONS of the public lands for a reasonable distance on each side of the line of the road, as was done on
various occasions to Ohio, Indiana, Illinois, Alabama, and the other new
States and Territories, in aid of their public works.

Let grants also be made to those States through which the route may
pass, of public lands lying on either side of the line of the road within
their own limits.

Let all these grants of land be made to those states and territories on
the *express condition* that the proceeds thereof shall be faithfully applied to the construction of the road, and shall be diverted to no other
purpose whatever; and also, on the *further condition,* that the United
States mails, troops, supplies, and munitions of war, shall be forever
transported over said road free of charge.

[131]

Let these states and territories adopt such plan and means for the construction of the road through their respective limits as they shall deem wise and proper, either by making it a state work to be owned and controlled by the State in its corporate capacity, or by incorporating companies, and imposing such conditions and restrictions, and retaining such right of supervision, as each state shall deem necessary and expedient. All legislation, by the territories upon this subject, as long as they remain such, would of course be subject to the supervision of Congress.

This is the synoposis of a plan which will be submitted to Congress, unless you, or others, can point out some insupperable objection to it, or devise a better one. It is simple in principle and detail, and involves no mystery or uncertainty. It does not concentrate, in the hands of a single individual, the public domain and political power, to a fearful extent.

It presents no question of conflict, in power or interest, between the Federal government and individual states and territories, through which the road would pass. It does not involve the question, as to the constitutional power of the Federal government to prosecute a system of internal improvements, within the limits of the several states; for, in this case, it is to be done by the states themselves. Nor is it liable to the objection, that Congress donates the means for making the improvements; for the most ample and liberal compensation is provided in return, by the free transportation of the mails, troops, supplies, and munitions of war. It introduces no new principle into the legislation of Congress or the states; for the practice of making grants of lands to the states, in which the public domain is situated, in aid of their public works, on similar conditions, has long obtained, and may be said to have become a part of the settled policy of the country. You propose, that a grant be made to yourself, of *all* the lands within sixty miles, and that they shall not be disposed of faster than the road shall be completed. I propose a grant of only *alternate sections*, and to vest the title to them in the states and territories in which they lie, and that the *other* alternate sections be thrown open, for settlement; and I will add, that west of the Missouri river, they be donated in tracts of 160 acres, to the actual settler. These provisions will foster and facilitate the settlement of the country. The line of the road being located, the caravans of emigrants would follow its course, from the desire to settle in its vicinity, and avail themselves of the advantages of the appreciation of the land in value, and the facilities it would present for markets. All the vacant lands would immediately be taken up and improved, that were worth improving; and thus, we would soon have a continuous line of settlements, from the Mississippi to the Pacific. Their necessities and interests would alike call for the construction of the road. The making of it depending entirely upon themselves, and their representatives in the legislature, and Congress having supplied the means, by the grant of lands, and they being anxious that those lands should be sold, peopled and taxed,—it is not reasonable to suppose that they would loose much time, in the commencement and prosecution of the work. If there should be any apprehension that the road would not be commenced and finished, within a reasonable period, Congress could impose a limitation on the grant, and provide for a forfeiture and reversion, after its expiration. I have thus given you a synopsis of my views, crude and undigested as they are, upon this great measure; and ask that they be received and considered in the same spirit of frankness and freedom in which they have been advanced. I am wedded to no particular plan, and if the one I have proposed be objectionable, and you, or others feeling an interest in the matter, and deeming it of sufficient importance, will point out the objections, I will be the first to acknowledge and correct them.[4] I have the honor to be, Very respectfully, Your obedient servant,

S. A. DOUGLASS

Atlantic & Pacific Railroad. A Letter from the Hon. S. A. Douglass, to A. Whitney, Esq., N.Y., Quincy, Illinois, [1845].

[1]Asa Whitney, a New York merchant, had formulated his plan for a transcontinental railroad, running from Milwaukee to the mouth of the Columbia River, late in 1844, and had presented it to Congress in the form of a memorial in January, 1845. During the following years, he further elaborated its details, and the plan became the subject of much discussion in state legislatures, public meetings, and railroad conventions. In 1849, he published a final report, *A Project for a Railroad to the Pacific* (New York, 1849), in which he included the reports of Congressional committees which considered his plan, the endorsements of state legislatures and public meetings, and approving letters from private individuals. Although Whitney did much to promote an interest in a Pacific railroad, his plan was not finally successful.

[2]The North Platte River.

[3]In December, 1844, Douglas introduced bills for the organization of Nebraska and Oregon territories, but no action was taken on them during the session.

[4]Whitney answered Douglas' objections in a pamphlet, *Reply to the Honorable S. A. Douglass* (Washington, D.C., 1845). In spite of Douglas' opposition to Whitney's plan, the Illinois state legislature endorsed it and instructed the state's Senators and Representatives to support it in Congress.

To James K. Polk

[November 1, 1845, Quincy, Illinois; ALS, RG-59, National Archives. Recommending the appointment of Josiah McRoberts as Chargé d'Affaires to a foreign post. McRoberts, of Vermilion County and a recent law graduate of Transylvania University, had failed in 1844 in his bid for election to the Illinois state legislature. In 1846, he was elected to the state Senate.]

To William L. Marcy

[December 20, 1845, n.p.; AN, Illinois State Historical Library. Note covering the delivery of the papers of Louis Winkelmaier, of St. Louis, concerning the establishment of a company of sappers, miners, and pontoniers in the United States Army. Marcy was Secretary of War.]

To Edmund Dick Taylor

[N.d., n.p.; summarized in the Springfield *Illinois State Register*, January 23, 1846. In this letter, the original of which has not been located, Douglas assured Taylor that no bargain, compromise, or understanding of any kind whatever had ever been entered into between himself and John A. McClernand, or any other person, with reference to the United States Senate, or any other office. Douglas' statement was the result of the charge made earlier by the *State Register* that he had made a bargain with McClernand in order to secure Douglas' election to the United States Senate. McClernand was at this time a member of the Illinois delegation in the national House of Representatives.]

To Augustus C. French

Washington

My Dear Sir,   Feby 20th 1846

I have just received the result of the deliberations of the State convention, and I need not tell you how much gratification it afforded me to learn that you received the nomination for Governor. As you are aware, I anticipated this auspicious result, still I had my apprehensions, in consequence of the multiplicity of candidates and exasperated feelings engendered by those who delight [in] producing discord and mischief. I rejoice that harmony has been restored to the party—that we have candidates in the field around whom we can rally with pride and satisfaction—and that when victory shall have crowned our efforts, we can rely upon an honest and patriotic administration of the government. Personally you know I feel highly gratified at the choice, and on account of the harmony and success of our party, I regard it as still more important. I cannot claim for myself [any of]¹ merit of this happy result. I can only say that I rejoice over the good others have done. Here the Oregon question is the great measure of the day. The *notice will* be given. Our laws & institutions will be extended over the country—and adequate protection given to our people there.² The news from England today is important and favorable to our interests. The Prospect is that the corn laws will be speedily abolished & the ports thrown open to

[134]

our produce.[3] There is no prospect of war—England cannot fight us at this time—she does not risk such a contest. Please write me often, and give me all the news. Let me know what documents you want & I will furnish them, if in my power. Truly your friend

S. A. Douglass

ALS, University of Chicago Library. Augustus C. French had been a member of the state legislature in the 1830's and held the office of Receiver in the United States Land Office at Palestine, Crawford County. In 1846, he was nominated for the governorship by the Democratic party and was elected by a wide margin over his Whig opponent. He held the office of Governor from 1846 to 1852.

[1]The words "any of" were crossed out by Douglas.

[2]On February 9, 1846, a resolution in favor of giving notice to Great Britain that the Joint Occupation agreement with respect to Oregon would be terminated passed the House of Representatives. The Senate, however, declined to concur in the resolution. A conference committee reported a compromise resolution authorizing the President to give notice of the termination of the treaty at his discretion. Douglas opposed this compromise move.

[3]The Corn Laws, which placed a high duty on grain imported into England, were repealed by the British Parliament in June, 1846.

To Harry Wilton

Ho of Reps
March 8th 1846

My Dear Sir

I have intended to write you somtime, but the pressure of business has prevented. I regret that your friends here were unable to secure your appointment as Register of the Land Office at Vandalia. Your friend Ficklin & myself went to the President in person on two or three different occasions & made a personal appeal in your behalf. The President was anxious to grant our request, but said that as the incumbent was the only relative of one of our Senators in office, and as that senator asked his continuance as a personal favor, and asked no other favor of the administration, he did not see how he could avoid retaining him.[1]

I presume that you have already received this explanation before, but it is due to the long friendship between us that you should receive it from me. You will always find me ready to serve you and with the aid of your friend Ficklin who has shown great solicitude in your behalf, I believe we will be able to succeed, when another opportunity should present. Write me often & let me know what is passing. Your friend

S. A. Douglass

ALS, Chicago Historical Society. Wilton had served as United States Marshal during the administration of Jackson and Van Buren.

[1]Robert K. McLaughlin was Register of the Vandalia Land Office from 1837 to 1849. McLaughlin was rather tenuously related by marriage to Senator James Semple.

To James K. Polk

[March 9, 1846, Washington; ALS, RG-59, National Archives. Recommending Charles Fay for appointment as Consul "for the Rhenish ports & provinces." Fay, a New York importer, went to Aix-la-Chapelle in 1846 to open a commercial house. He was not appointed Consul but was designated a Consular Agent for Westphalia and the Prussian provinces of the Rhine.]

To Robert J. Walker

[April 1, 1846, Washington; ALS, Illinois State Historical Library. Introducing Edmund Roberts, of Springfield, Illinois. Walker was Secretary of the Treasury. Roberts, a member of the Board of Trustees of McKendree College, Lebanon, Illinois, was visiting the Eastern states in the interest of the institution.]

To William L. Marcy

[April 4, 1846, Washington; ALS, RG-49, National Archives. Covering the enclosure of a letter from Paris I. Judy, asking if certain land patents have been issued.]

To Archer G. Herndon

WASHINGTON, April 14, 1846.

My Dear Sir:—I have delayed answering your several letters partly for want of time, and partly because I could not say with any certainty what would be done. But by this morning's 'Union' I see that you have been re-appointed, by and with the advice and consent of the Senate. I claim no credit for this appointment, for it was made without my knowledge. I had not supposed that it would be decided upon by the President for some time to come, and for this reason had never spoken to him or the cabinet on the subject. This statement is due to you, as well as to others to whom you are indebted for the appointment.

We are now engaged in the discussion of the bill to extend the laws over Oregon. The bill will pass in some shape on Thursday. I hope it will pass in a satisfactory shape.

I shall be glad to hear from you often. Your friend,

S. A. DOUGLAS

Printed in Joseph Wallace, "Stephen A. Douglas: Some Old Letters by, and Relating to, the Distinguished Statesman," *Transactions of the Illinois State Historical Society, 1901*, p. 113. Archer G. Herndon, a Springfield merchant and member of the state legislature, was appointed Receiver at the Springfield Land Office in 1842, a position to which he was reappointed by Polk in 1846. He was the father of William H. Herndon.

To James K. Polk

[May 2, 1846, Washington; ALS, Library of Congress. Introducing William Chapman of Oregon, who "desires to have some conversation with you upon that interesting country." Chapman migrated to Oregon in 1843, and returned to the States two years later.]

To John J. Hardin

(*Private*)   Washington
My Dear Sir   May 2d 1846

I owe you many apologies for my apparent neglect in our correspondence. I have been expecting that every succeeding day would enable me to give you some deffinite information in regard to our Mexican affairs. But all yet remains in doubt & uncertainty. We are in a state of quasi war with that country, and are left to conjecture as to what is to be the sequel. The capture of Col Cross (if indeed he is alive) must bring things to a crisis soon.[1] The intentions of the administration in this respect are a profound secret. No one pretends to know what course will be pursued. I have had a confidential conversation with Mr Crittenden[2] in regard to yourself in the event of war, and he wishes me to say to you that he and his friends will join me in any efforts to give you an opportunity to serve your country in the tented field. I was much gratified with your views in regard to the plan of the expidition. I have no doubt of its success in the event government gives its sanction to it, until then all is suspence.

Write to me[3] & I will try & be more punctual in future. I will give you the earliest information of the Mexican news of a hostile character. I see from the papers that Maj Warren is about to disband his troops & return home.[4] I trust in God we are not to have another Civil War. For the credit of our country & the course of humanity, do try to avert it if possible. From all I can learn I believe the Mormons are leaving & intend to leave as fast as possible. Let them leave in peace. My hopes are on you to avert another outbreak. I believe you have the power to do so, if you are willing to make the sacrifice.

Rem[em]ber me kindly to Mrs Hardin & accept assurances of the kindest regards of your friend

S. A. DOUGLASS

ALS, Chicago Historical Society. This letter was in answer to two letters written by Hardin, on February 2 and 5, 1846, in which Hardin discussed matters of policy toward Mexico and Great Britain. In the first letter, Hardin urged that, in the event of war with Mexico, a land expedition be organized to seize California. He outlined the proposed expedition in detail and volunteered his military services. If war should develop with Mexico and Great Britain, he wrote, a similar expedition should be sent against Oregon. The originals of these letters are owned by Martin F. Douglas.

[1] Colonel Trueman Cross was murdered by Mexican bandits near Fort Brown, Texas, on April 10, 1846. His murder, regarded with complacency by the Mexican authorities, caused intense resentment among the American troops. The United States declared war against Mexico on May 13.

[2] John J. Crittenden, of Kentucky, was at this time a member of the United States Senate. He was former Attorney General in the cabinet of President Harrison.

[3] Hardin acknowledged this letter on May 20, 1846, a week after the declaration of war. He urged once again that an expedition be sent against California and suggested that Illinois and Northwestern troops be used in that campaign, since, he assumed, the people of Kentucky, Tennessee, and the Southwest would monopolize the attack on Mexico by the Gulf. The original of this letter is owned by Martin F. Douglas.

[4] William Barton Warren, one of the commissioners to treat with the Mormons, had remained in Nauvoo with a small detachment of militia during the winter of 1845-46.

To John J. Hardin

Ho of Reps
Washington

My Dr Sir   May 15th 1846

You have doubtless heard of the declaration of war against Mexico, and of the law requiring 50,000 men to be raised by the President, if he deems that number necessary. I have just learned that the President has determined to call on Illinois for three Regiments of 900, or 1000 men each making 2700 or 3000 in all. I understand that they are all to be infantry—at least footmen. The officers are to be elected under the laws of the state. I take it for granted therefore that you will have a high command.[1] I don't know who will be your competitors, altho I hear several gentlemen here talking about it. I doubt, whether any of them will return home however for that purpose. Tell Maj Warren that I look to him to sustain the reputation he has so justly acquired at home, where there was less opportuni[tie]s for glory. I feel desireous to see you call arround you our old friends & companions of the last fall campaign. I hope to come down & take a look at you after Congress adjourns. I shall claim to be your Representative during this war. I think I can venture to speak for you on this subject. Write me & let me know your plans & also if I can serve you. Your friend

S. A. DOUGLASS

ALS, Chicago Historical Society.

[1] Hardin was elected Colonel of the First Regiment of Illinois Volunteers on June 30, 1846.

To George Bancroft

[June 2, 1846, Washington; ALS, Chicago Historical Society. Encloses a letter from "Mr Cook one of my much esteemed constituents," and inquires as to Cook's chances "for the appointment he desires." George Bancroft was at this time Secretary of the Navy. Cook had applied for the position of purser in the United States Navy but apparently did not receive the appointment.]

To John J. Hardin

Washington
June 16th 1846

My Dr General

I have the pleasure to acknowledge the receipt of yours of the 2d & 4th ints. I have just had an interview with the Sec of War. He will no[t] consent to let you enrol more than 10 companies in your Regiment—nor will he allow you to mount your men, nor will he send you to Santa Fe or California. He gives many luminous or voluminous reasons for his course in this respect which I will not provoke you by reciting. He assures me however that if any more mounted [men] are needed, they shall be ordered from Illinois, but is very sure that none will be required. You will be ordered to Chihuahua by way of New Orleans, Matagorda Bay and San Antonio in Texas. The latter place will be the point of general rendezvous. From San Antonio you will keep on the high lands to Chihuahua, then towards the interior of Mexico. Mark me! You must not quote me or the War Dept for the information respecting the route & destination, but can use it privately as coming from a *reliable* source.

The bill in regard to the Generals has not yet become a law.[1] Probably it will pass sometime. Taylor will remain in the command of the Army during the war & will probably be the Major General under the new bill. It is said, but I know not up[on] what authority, that Col. Butler of Ky & Col Kearny of the Army will be the Brigadiers.[2] The latter (Col Kearny) is now on his way to Santa Fe & thence to California & will have under his command at least 4 Regiments of mounted men—the 2d Dragoons—two Reg from Mo.—one from Arkansas, and probably one formed at Bents Fort & Santa Fe making 5 Reg in all. This circumstance gives color to the report that he is to be appointed General. I don't know therefore whether it will be prudent or not to present your name.[3] Will consult & determine, when the law is passed. There is much confusion here now, about the Oregon [question]. The question will undoubtedly be settled this week, on terms which I reprobate.[4] You will find the rumors in the papers. You can rely upon them with the exception that the fact is infinitely worse than the rumors. The Secretary of War assures me that all needful arrangements have been made for supplying tents & supplies for the troops—that the officers have been sent to muster them into service & furnish everything needful. I hope to be with you in some capacity. A high privates place will suit me about as well as anything. I would not object however to be *Major* as you persist in keeping up that title for me.[5] Write me soon & tell me where to direct my letters. Your friend

S. A. DOUGLASS

ALS, Chicago Historical Society.

[1]This bill would authorize the President to appoint two major generals and four brigadier generals in addition to the regular number of general officers already provided for. It passed on June 17, 1846.

[2]William Orlando Butler, a member of Congress from Kentucky from 1839 to 1843, and a veteran of the War of 1812, was commissioned a major general of volunteers on June 29, 1846. Stephen Watts Kearney, a career soldier who had served on the western frontier almost continuously since 1819, was appointed brigadier general on June 30, 1846.

[3]In a letter written June 3, 1846, Hardin asked if Douglas thought it advisable to present his name for appointment as a general officer (owned by Martin F. Douglas).

[4]Douglas throughout the discussion of the Oregon question held out for the acquisition of all of Oregon, to 54°40', and opposed the settlement of the boundary along the forty-ninth parallel.

[5]In his June 3 letter, Hardin asked Douglas, "Cant you adjourn Congress and go along with us?" Several of Hardin's letters were addressed to "Major" Douglas, perhaps in reference to Douglas' service with the militia during the Mormon troubles. Douglas for a time considered leaving his seat in Congress for military service.

To James K. Polk

[July 1, 1846, n.p.; ALS, RG-59, National Archives. Recommending Alexander Duncan, former member of Congress from Ohio, for appointment to a foreign mission. Signed, in addition to Douglas, by Illinois Representatives Orlando B. Ficklin, John A. McClernand, and Robert Smith. Duncan was not appointed.]

To John J. Hardin

(*Private*)   Washington
My Dr General,   July 6th 1846

Your several letters were received. I confered with Mr Owen[1] about his brothers appointment as a scientific amateur in the Army. He tells me that the President has no power to make the appointment. I have sent your letter to the President & also one to Liut Maury.[2] I regret that I could no[t] have seen him in person. The requisite number of Quarter Masters, Commissaries, & Surgons have been appointed for all our volunteers. You will find the list in the newspapers. Now in regard to General. You have doubtless heard of the appointment of Shields as Brigadier.[3] The facts are these. Before the passage of the late law giving the power of appointment to the President, he sent a member of his cabinet to the Illinois delegation requesting us to name a Brigadier in commission under the state laws to take the command. In the consultation I proposed your name, but a majority decided to tender it to General Semple, who agreed to accept it.[4] I cheerfully acquiced in the selection & joined in the recommendation. But before any action was heard on this recommendation, a bill was passed giving the power of appointment to the President. As Semple had been recommended for the other place his name was allowed to remain before the President for the appointment. The President declined appointing Semple because he was a member of Congress, and expressed a desire to appoint Shields, if not contrary to the feelings of the delegation. We called another meeting to consult about it, at which a majority decided to recommend a new man leaving Shields in the Land office. Semple & myself (altho willing to see Shields appointed) then proposed your name to be presented to the President, but a majority then expressed themselves for either Dement or Lt Gov Anderson.[5] At this stage of the proceedings we learned that Shields name had already been sent to the Senate while we were consulting. Of course the consultation here ended & Shields was appointed. I give you these facts as they occured for your own satisfaction. I desire them to be strictly confidential as I do not desire to be brought into collision with any of the applicants nor do I desire to bring my colleagues in collision with them. I based my proposal to recommend you upon the ground that I believed you were the best qualified and that the volunteers would elect you if the power had been vested in them. I fin[d] that I have filled up this sheet in dull details. I will write you again soon. The Tariff bill has passed.[6] The Graduation Land bill comes next. Your friend

S. A. DOUGLASS

ALS, Chicago Historical Society.

[1]Probably Robert Dale Owen, son of Robert Owen, the founder of New Harmony, Indiana, and a member of Congress from Indiana. One of Owen's brothers, David Dale Owen, was appointed United States geologist for the Chippewa land district, while another, Richard Owen, became a captain in the sixteenth infantry of the United States Army. Both appointments were made in 1847.

[2]Matthew Fontaine Maury, a renowned oceanographer and professional naval officer, was at this time Superintendent of the Depot of Charts and Instruments of the Navy Department.

[3]James Shields was commissioned Brigadier General of Volunteers on July 1, 1846.

[4]James Semple, who had served under Jackson during the War of 1812, was United States Senator from Illinois from 1843 to 1847. His appointment as brigadier general was not made. At the same time that the members of the Illinois delegation recommended Semple, they proposed that Douglas be appointed brigade major.

[5]John Dement, elected three times to the state legislature, held the office of Receiver of Public Moneys under Presidents Van Buren, Polk, and Pierce. Stinson H. Anderson, former Lieutenant Governor, was appointed United States Marshal for Illinois in 1845.

[6]The Walker Tariff Bill, providing for lower tariff duties, had passed the House of Representatives but was not to become law until July 31, 1846.

To George Manierre

House of Representatives
July 15, 1846

Dear Sir—I am surprised to learn that there exists any misapprehension as to the course of Col. Wentworth in regard to the repeal of the Wisconsin Banking Institutions.[1] When Mr. Martin (the delegate from Wisconsin,)[2] introduced his resolution confirming the repeal of certain charters in Wisconsin, and have the same referred to the committee on Territories, of which I am chairman, Col. Wentworth called on me and urged immediate action on the subject, and expressed great anxiety for its passage, and assigned as a reason for his anxiety that it affected the Wisconsin Marine and Fire Insurance Company, which was banking in Illinois contrary to the laws of our State. He expressed more anxiety for the early passage of the resolution, than any other member of the House. Indeed, he was the only one, except, perhaps, Mr. Dodge, of Iowa,[3] and Martin, of Wisconsin, who spoke to me on the subject. In this case, as when the District Banks were before the House, and all others relating to paper money institutions, to the extent of my knowledge, Mr. Wentworth has been the decided advocate of repeal, and the uncompromising opponent of all paper money. I have the honor to be very respectfully your friend,

S. A. DOUGLASS

Chicago *Democrat*, August 4, 1846. George Manierre, a Chicago lawyer, was alderman of the city from 1846 to 1847.

[1]On May 11, 1846, Douglas introduced into the House of Representatives a bill "disaffirming" all the laws of the territories of Iowa and Wisconsin which granted banking privileges. The bill passed the House in June, 1846, but was tabled in the Senate. John Wentworth, Chicago lawyer and editor of the Chicago *Democrat*, represented Illinois in the House of Representatives from 1843 to 1851, and again from 1853 to 1855 and from 1865 to 1867. Although originally a Democrat, his free-soil convictions caused him to affiliate with the Republican party in the 1850's.

[2]Morgan Lewis Martin was Delegate from Wisconsin Territory from 1845 to 1847.

[3]Augustus Caesar Dodge was Delegate from Iowa Territory from 1840 to December 28, 1846, when Iowa was admitted to the Union as a state.

To Charles H. Lanphier

(*Private*)   Washington
My Dr Sir,   July 20th 1846

I herewith send you a copy of a letter I have just written to the Editors of the Alton Telegraph.[1] As the article in the Telegraph was doubtless intended to have an effect on the election by leaving the impression that I had abandoned my seat in Congress, you will please publish the copy I send you in your next paper so as to give it a general circulation before the election.[2] I see there is some dissatisfaction among the volunteers in regard to the appointment of the Staff officers. The facts are these. The President sent a member of his cabinet to the delegation & requested a list of names for those offices to be made out *that day* as he desired to make the appointments instantly. We had no time to write home, and were compelled to guess at the persons who were desirous of going. I suggested the name of Mr Walters because I had seen in the Register a statement that he had volunteered.[3] We regretted that we were compeled to act in the dark in this way, and did the best we could under the circumstances. Your friend

S. A. DOUGLASS

ALS, Illinois State Historical Library.
[1]See below.
[2]Douglas was a candidate for re-election to Congress in 1846, notwithstanding the fact that he had determined once again to seek election to the

United States Senate.
[3]William Walters, proprietor of the *State Register*, volunteered in June, 1846; he died the following month in St. Louis before the departure of his regiment for Mexico.

To the Editors of the Alton *Telegraph*

Washington, July 20, 1846.

To the Editors of the Alton Telegraph:

I observe from your paper of the 11th inst. (this moment received,) that an erroneous impression prevails respecting a supposed intention on my part, to abandon my seat in Congress, for the purpose of going to Mexico. This error, I presume, arose from the following circumstance. When I heard of so many of my friends volunteering their services, I felt a very strong desire to go with them, and even received letters from home soliciting me to do so. I expressed this feeling to my colleagues, who unanimously concurred in recommending me for a suitable appointment, although not the one indicated by you. It is due to my colleagues to state, however, that some of them intimated a doubt whether I ought to accept it, as it was probable, I might be required to leave Washington before the adjournment of Congress. One night's reflection convinced me that I ought not to vacate my seat in Congress even for a portion of the remnant of the session to accept that or any other appointment. Accordingly, I voluntarily abandoned the idea, and from that moment have not entertained the slightest intention of leaving Washington until the end of the session, and then only to return to my constituents.[1] I trust that those editors in our own State, who have given currency to the report, will see the propriety of making the correction. Respectfully, your obedient servant,

S. A. DOUGLASS

Springfield *Illinois State Register*, July 31, 1846.

[1]Although Douglas had been recommended for a military appointment by

the members of the Illinois delegation in Congress, he could not have received it, since the law required the President to make appointments only from officers already in command of the state militia. Polk persuaded Douglas that he could serve his country more effectively in Congress than in the military establishment.

To Sidney Breese

Quincy
Dear Breese,   Oct 20th 1846
Your note for me at Chicago found me at this place thro the mails. I am gratified to learn that in your opinion there can be no doubt of my election to the U.S. Senate.[1] So far as I can judge this is my opinion also. Indeed I cannot learn that I will have any opposition. In the North I heard much said of your course, especially on the River & Harbor Bill and on Oregon, and all in terms of the warmest commendation. Those are the great Measures of the day in that region as you must have learned while passing thro. I hope to meet you before we leave for Washington. Your friend

S. A. DOUGLAS[2]

ALS, Illinois State Historical Library.
[1] James Semple's term as United States Senator would expire in 1847, and he had already expressed his determination not to seek re-election. Douglas sought election to this Senate seat. In spite of his Senatorial ambitions, Douglas accepted the nomination for a third term in the House of Representatives, defeating his Whig opponent by a 2,700-vote margin.
[2] Douglas dropped the final *s* in his name sometime between July and October, 1846.

To James K. Polk

[November 6, 1846, Springfield, Illinois; ALS, Chicago Historical Society. Recommending the appointment of William Scott Brown, of Chicago, to the office of United States Attorney for Oregon Territory. Although that part of the Oregon country south of the forty-ninth parallel became a part of the United States earlier in 1846, a territorial government for Oregon was not established by Congress until 1848. The appointment asked for by Douglas was not made.]

To Sidney Breese

(*Confidential*)   Springfield
My Dear Sir,   Nov 6th 1846
I have just received your favor of the 29th ult forwarded to me from Quincy. I feel grateful to you for the deep interest you take in my election and hope for an opportunity to show my gratitude by my acts. I remember well what you said to me on that subject four years ago, and now have an opportunity of seeing the noble manner in which you are

redeeming that assurance and of comparing your conduct with the professions of others. This contest will be a good lesson to teach me my real friends. I presume you are right in the supposition that McClernand is a candidate. I have learned the same fact from others on the most reliable authority, but the plan was to keep me and my friends ignorant of the fact until I left the State for Washington. Your enemies are all combined in the same scheme for the purpose of beating you next time by electing a Southern Senator now. I don't think Judge Young is a candidate; but the conspirators intend to coax him into the field if possible, not with the view of his election, but for the purpose of producing confusion & then uniting his friends on McClernand. *I have been put in possession of all the secrets of the plan in detail & the parties to it.* You will be astonished when I lay it before you. It will not do for you to rely upon the general impression that your friends will go for me but should *write especially to each* one, and urge him to it where you cannot see them in person. If my friends are active I will be elected by more than two to one. But they must not be too confident. In regard to the Alton movement, I can only explain it on the supposition that there is a *candidate* there. By the way I was cautioned to that effect when there & but told it was all *conditional*. This may be a part of the general scheme, the object of which you will understand. In regard to our friend Slocumb, you are authorized to write to him as you proposed and also to Dick Murphy.[1] The latter is a devoted friend of mine and I have been of his for years, and I believe the same of the former.

I entrust that matter to you.

I regret my inability to tell you anything about Davis & Harris.[2] I have seen neither of them for a year or two nor have I heard from them. Harris is in Mexico & I fear he will not return this session. He is a particular friend of mine in all things and a very able & good man.

In regard to my election, I hope you will urge all your friends to go for bringing it on the first week of the Session. If you will take the trouble I believe you can get them to do it. Now is the time for prompt action. I have no doubt but all is sound, & all that is necessary is to keep it so. Can't you go down thro the South & See the Morrisons, Daugherty,[3] and all your Southern friends? I will be able to meet you at some point on the Ohio River. Your friend

S. A. DOUGLAS

ALS, Illinois State Historical Library.
[1]Rigdon B. Slocumb was a member of the state legislature from Wayne County. Richard Murphy, of Cook County, had held three terms in the legislature, being elected in 1838, 1840, and 1842.
[2]There were three members of the state legislature named Davis: William P. Davis, of Vermilion County;

Jacob C. Davis, of Hancock County; and Thomas G. C. Davis, representing Pope, Hardin, Johnson, and Massac counties. Thomas Langrell Harris, of Petersburg, Menard County, was elected to the state Senate in 1846, although he was at the time serving with the Fourth Regiment, Illinois Volunteer Infantry, in Mexico. He was subsequently elected to Congress.

[3]John Morrison was a member of the state legislature, representing Randolph and Monroe counties. Joseph Morrison was elected in 1844 to a single term in the state Senate, also representing Randolph and Monroe counties. John Dougherty, of Union County, represented Union, Alexander, and Pulaski counties in the legislature.

To Harry Wilton

Charleston Coles Co
My Dr Sir,   Nov 14th 1846

I had entertained the hope that I would have had the pleasure of meeting you before my return to Congress. Indeed I intended to have visited you at your house, but want of time I fear will prevent. I am now making a tour through the Wabash Counties & by the time I reach the Ohio River, it will be time for me to take a Boat East. You are aware that my name will be presented to the Legislature this winter for the U.S. Senate. It is not my intention to electioneer with you; for I know your feelings too well and have received too many evidences of your friendship to deem that necessary. I only regret that I could not have succeeded better in my efforts at Washington last Session to serve you. If your other friends had stood by you as well and firmly as I did, all would have been made right then. But I trust that another opportunity will yet be presented for you to test the fidelity of your friends, and their disposition to serve you.

In regard to my election this Winter I have been gratified to learn of the firm stand you have taken in my behalf. Indeed I believe you were the first of my friends who ever did me the honor to propose my name for the office. I do not apprehend any serious difficulty about the result. So far as I can now ascertain I have no opponent in the field. I have heard of some rumors of a secret arraingement to bring out a candidate after I leave for Washington; but I cannot credit the idea. The manifest injustice and unfairness of such a movement would ensure its defeat. The Democratic Party always deals fairly with its members, and certainly would not sanction a secret arraingement of that kind. As I will be compelled to be absent I must rely solely on my friends. You will of course be at the Legislature at the opening of the session. Your acquaintance with the members gives you great influence, and will enable you, by its vigorous exercise, to place your friend under still greater obligation to you. Will you do me the favor to speak to the members from your county in my behalf particularly as well as the Southern members generally. I have been told that your members were already for me, but it will do no harm to render it certain. Please write me frequently & let me know all the news, and particularly what I can do for you. Your friend

S. A. Douglas

ALS, Chicago Historical Society.

To Hall Simms

Charleston

My Dear Sir,   Nov 16th 1846

I arrived here today on a visit to the Wabash Counties, yours included among the number; but have received such information as will compel me to proceed South immediately and will deprive me of the pleasure of seeing you. You are aware that my name will be presented to the Legislature this winter as a candidate for the U.S. Senate. My present object is not to electioneer with you; for our long acquaintance and your former friendship would seem to render this unnecessary. Yet I would have been glad to have seen you at your own house & have spent a pleasant evening in talking over old times. I am not aware that I will have any opposition. There have been rumors that Col McClernand will be a candidate, but I have just learned that he will not run. As he has declined I know of no candidate on the track but myself. I have heard some rumors that a secret arraingement had been entered into by a few persons to bring out a candidate after I leave for Washington; but I discredit such reports, for the unfairness of the thing would certainly defeat the success of the scheme. Of course I would dislike to be beaten by such an arraingement as it would greatly impair my standing in the House & before the country. As I must be absent, I must rely solely on the activity and vigilance of my friends. I bear you in grateful remembrance for your friendship for me on former occasions and expect now to be placed under additional obligations to you. I shall be happy to hear from you often, and to render you any service in my power at Washington. Your friend

S. A. Douglas

ALS-Photostat, Illinois State Historical Library. Hall Simms, of Edgar County, was a member of the state legislature.

To Sidney Breese

Lawrenceville

My Dear Breese   Nov 19th 1846

I arrived here yesterday from Springfield by way of Shelby, Coles, Clark, & Crawford, and expected to pursued my route through Clay, Marion, Jefferson, Franklin and Williamson to Shawneetown; but the rail, and bad weather & bad roads have induced me to give up that part of the trip & proceed to the Ohio river by way of Mt Carmel & Evansville. I shall be glad to meet you at Louisville. I presume I will be there when you arrive. Come to the "Louisville Hotel" where I will stop for a day or two.

My prospects in the Wabash region are very flattering I don't think I will loss a vote in this part of the state. I have found your friends warmly for me wherever I have been. This fact speaks for itself & will not be forgotten. I desire to make a suggestion to you in confidence. I have heard it hinted [th]a[t] the friends of a certain gentleman will endeavor to get Resolutions passed through the Legislature this winter approving of the veto of the River & Harbor Bill & of the course of those who voted against the Bill.[1] The object as I understand is to prepare for future operations, and to commit the party now under the impression that it is necessary to vindicate the President. You cannot fail to see the effect of such a Resolution on yourself two years hence.[2] I have felt it my duty to suggest this matter to you in confidence that you may advise your friends how to meet it.

Will you do me the favor to write to the two Morrisons in my behalf Joseph and John from Randolph & Monro? Also to Gregg, Herndon, Coverly, and such other of your friends as you have the most influence with.[3] All of the gentlemen named are warmly for me now, but a letter from you would warm them up a good deal, and they are so devoted to you that no one would ever know that you had done so, except myself. I want to meet you at Louisville & go on with you. Write me by the first mail & direct to that place. Yours

S. A. DOUGLAS

ALS, Illinois State Historical Library.
[1]President Polk vetoed the River and Harbor Bill on August 3, 1846. No such resolutions as those referred to here by Douglas were passed by the Illinois legislature.
[2]Breese's term as United States Sena-

tor would expire on March 3, 1849.
[3]David L. Gregg, of Will County, had been a member of the state legislature from 1842 to 1846; Alfred W. Cavarly, of Greene County, was a member of the state Senate.

To William Martin

Lawrenceville
Nov 19th 1846

My Dear Judge

I have delayed writing you with the expectation of receiving a letter from you. Since we met I have been over a good portion of the State. I find my prospects for the Senate of the most cheering character. I cannot bring myself to doubt my success from the evidences I have had of public sentiment. I am now satisfied that none of the gentlemen spoken of as probable candidates at Alton are really so. I have seen Gov Carlin

& Calhoun,[1] and they assure me they are for me in preference to any one. I understand also from his neighbors in Carrolton that Judge Coverly is openly for me. I regret he was absent when I was there.

I understand that Col McClernand did think of being a candidate at one time; but I have reliable information that [he] has since declined & will not be a candidate under any circumstances. I have good reason to believe also that there will be no opposition to my being a candidate from my own District, but on the contrary they will be warmly for me. Under these circumstances I submit to you whether the state of case does not exist in which you said you would take ground for me. I do really hope you will take this view of the subject. I attach great importance to your position and line of policy, and feel exceedingly anxious to number you among my unconditional supporters. I have no doubt of your friendship for me. I believe you strictly candid and sincere in all the compliments & kind things you said to [me] when we last met, and am solicitous to have your position so defined as to place you in line at the opening of the session with my other friends. You will place me under deep and lasting obligation, and will be authorized to draw largely on my gratitude in return. I have now been a candidate for several months without opposition, and to be beaten under these circumstances, would not only be a defeat, but would be followed by much more serious consequences to myself, and greatly impair my power of usefulness to my party & country. Write me often & let me know all the knews. Very truly your friend

S. A. DOUGLAS

P.S. I leave here tomorrow for the Ohio River & thence direct to Washington.

ALS, Illinois State Historical Library. William Martin, of Madison County, was a member of the lower house of the state legislature.
[1] Thomas Carlin was Governor of Illinois from 1838 to 1842. John Calhoun, of Sangamon County, was a member of the state legislature from 1838 to 1840, and was defeated for the Democratic nomination for governor in 1846.

To John D. Caton

Mount Vernon
Nov 24th 1846

My Dear Sir,

I leave this place for Washington in the morning so as to be in my seat on the first day of the Session. Since I had the pleasure of meeting you at Princeton, I have been over a good portion of the State. From all the indications, I cannot see ground for reasonable doubt of my election to the Senate this winter. I do not suffer myself to be too sanguine however, for I have learned that a candidate is never in so much danger as when he and his friends regard his success as perfectly sure. I have not see[n] Gov Ford—he being in Hancock when I was at Springfield; but I understand that he is not and will not be a candidate. This removes all embarrassment from your free and positive action in my behalf, as you were *kind* enough to assure me that you would support me as against any other candidate. I cannot say what candidates will be in the field, if any, except Dougherty of Union. I have recently understood that Col McClernand had declined, and if so I am not aware that I will have any other opposition. However, I must leave all to the vigilance and activity of my friends, as I will necessarily be absent. Your hearty cooperation with my friends will place me under lasting obligations. I know your influence with a large portion of the members, and will know how to appreciate the value of its exercise.

I shall be happy to hear from you often during the Session, and to learn all the news. Write often, and oblige your friend

S. A. DOUGLAS

ALS, Library of Congress. John D. Caton was Associate Justice of the Illinois Supreme Court.

To James Buchanan

[December 21, 1846, House of Representatives; ALS, RG-59, National Archives. Acknowledging receipt of a package of papers to be sent to "Mr Beck of Peoria Illinois."]

To Robert J. Walker

[January 5, 1847, Senate Chamber; ALS, RG-56, National Archives. Recommending the appointment of George McDuffie Burk to a post in the Treasury Department. Burk had been a clerk in the House of Representatives.]

To Charles H. Lanphier

Washington
My Dear Sir,   Jan'y 9th 1847

Permit me to congratulate you on your election as Public Printer.[1] I need not tell me that your success affords me sincere satisfaction. I only regretted that I was so situated that I could not render you any more active & efficient services than I did. My position however you well understood, and I trust that upon consultation with your friends in different parts of the State, you found I had fully acted up to it. Remember me kindly to your Lady & Mrs Walters & family. Truly your friend

S. A. DOUGLAS

ALS, Illinois State Historical Library.
[1]Lanphier was elected Public Printer by the same legislature which elevated Douglas to the United States Senate. On December 13, 1846, Douglas was elected United States Senator by an easy margin over his Whig opponent, Cyrus Edwards. Douglas retained his seat in the House, however, through the end of the Twenty-ninth Congress, resigning on April 7, 1847.

To James K. Polk

[N.d., n.p.; LS, RG-59, National Archives. Recommendation of the Illinois delegation, including Douglas, for the appointment of Calmes L. Wright to the office of Secretary of Minnesota Territory. The recommendation is also signed by William F. Giles and Thomas Perry, members of Congress from Maryland. Although undated, the manuscript is endorsed, "Transmitted to the President by Sidney Breese, Feb. 23, 1847." Minnesota Territory was not organized until 1849; the appointment asked for was never made. Wright, of St. Clair County, served in the Mexican War as a captain, from June, 1847, to July, 1848, when he was discharged. He died of cholera in 1849.]

To James K. Polk

Sir: Washington, Feby 25th 1847

We respectfully call the attention of the President to the name of the Hon. John A. Bryan of Ohio[1] for some situation abroad, under the government. It is presumed that the character and capacity of Mr. Bryan are too well known to the President to require a single word on that subject. Mr. Bryan has long enjoyed the esteem and confidence of the citizens of his own State, particularly with the democratic party there, by whom he has been twice honored with the second office in their gift.—subsequently, Mr. Bryan occupied two several situations under the government of the United States, of which the President is probably apprised.

Mr. Bryan is a gentleman of fine talents, and is possessed of very distinguished literary attainments. We have a particular desire to see him placed in some similar post to the one he recently held as Charge d'Affaires to Peru, and we feel assured that the President will kindly entertain and consider this our request. We were among the number who very much regretted Mr. Bryan's return from his mission abroad, which we have always supposed was entirely the result of the non action of the Whig senate of 1845, on his nomination,—thus leaving a vacancy in that Mission.

Knowing, as we do, the many deserving qualities of head and heart of the gentleman to whom we have thus freely invited the attention of your Excellency, we have sincerely to hope that he may, through the favorable consideration of the President, be returned to some like situation to that he temporarily occupied in South America during the early part of 1845. With assurances of due consideration and regard, we are, Sir, your ms. obt. Servts.

S. A. Douglas
Robert Smith

LS, RG-59, National Archives.
[1] John A. Bryan, publisher of the Columbus *Ohio State Bulletin*, was State Auditor of Ohio from 1833 to 1839.

To James K. Polk

[March 1, 1847, Washington; LS, Illinois State Historical Library. Recommendation of five members of the Illinois delegation to Congress, including Douglas, for the appointment of Dr. Edward B. Price to the office of Surgeon or Assistant Surgeon of the United States Army. Dr. Price at this time was serving as Surgeon of the Second Regiment, Illinois Volunteers, in Mexico. The recommendation is in Sidney Breese's handwriting.]

To James K. Polk

[N.d., n.p.; LS, RG-59, National Archives. Recommendation of twelve members of Congress, including Douglas, for the appointment of C. Frank Powell, of New York, to the office of Consul of Smyrna and Muscat. The manuscript is endorsed in the margin, "recd. March 5," and on the back, "1847." Powell was appointed Consul for Muscat.]

To Thomas, Cowperthwait and Company

Washington

Gentlemen March 8th 1847

You will accept my thanks for a copy of "Sanderson's Biography of the signers to the declaration of Independence, revised and edited by Robert T Conrad" and recently published by yourselves.[1] I have examined the work with care, and do not hesitate to award it my entire approbation. It deserves a place in every gentleman's library and ought to be brought within the reach of every youth in the land. I take pleasure in commending it to the patronage of the public. I have the honor to be very respectfully your obedient servant

S. A. Douglas

ALS, Historical Society of Pennsylvania. Thomas, Cowperthwait and Company was a Philadelphia publishing firm.

[1]Robert Taylor Conrad was an eminent journalist and dramatist, as well as a judge. His edition of *Sanderson's Biography of the Signers of the Declaration of Independence,* considerably abridged from the original seven-volume edition published twenty years before, appeared in 1847.

To James K. Polk

[May 17, 1847, Quincy, Illinois; ALS, Illinois State Historical Library. Enclosing a letter signed by James Shields, Thomas Langrell Harris, and Edward Dickinson Baker recommending the appointment of Samuel D. Reynolds to a lieutenancy in the Army. Douglas strongly concurred in the recommendation. Shields and Harris, Democratic politicians in Illinois, both held military commissions and were serving in Mexico. Edward Dickinson Baker, a prominent Whig politician and former member of the state legislature, was elected to Congress in 1844, but resigned at the end of 1846 when he was commissioned as Colonel of the Fourth Regiment, Illinois Volunteer Infantry. He, too, was at this time serving in Mexico. Reynolds was a sergeant in the Fourth Regiment.]

To George W. Jones

[June 1, 1847, Quincy, Illinois; ALS, Iowa State Department of History and Archives, Des Moines. Recommending that C. C. Dodge be given a surveying contract. Jones, former Congressional Delegate from both Michigan and Wisconsin territories, was at this time Surveyor General of Wisconsin and Iowa. He was soon to be elected one of the first Senators from the new state of Iowa.]

To P. N. O. Thompson

Quincy

My Dear Sir   June 2nd 1847

I this moment received your letter of the 29th ult. I received one from our friend Trumbull[1] on the same subject several days ago, and have written to the Postmaster Gen'l recommending your appointment. You will undoubtedly receive your commission in time to enter on the discharge of your duties on the first of July or a few days thereafter. Present my respects to Mr Trumbull and all other friends.

Doct Sutphin[2] was here some two weeks ago & he also advised your appointment. Your friend

S. A. DOUGLAS

ALS, Illinois State Historical Library. P. N. O. Thompson, of Pittsfield, Illinois, was clerk of the circuit court for Pike County from 1843 to 1852.

[1]Lyman Trumbull, of Belleville, Illinois, was a former member of the state legislature and Secretary of State of Illinois. He served as a Justice on the state Supreme Court from 1848 to 1853.
[2]Hugh L. Sutphin, of Pike County, was a member of the Illinois Senate from 1846 to 1850.

To James K. Polk

Quincy Ills

Dear Sir,   June 23d 1847

I have just received a letter from an esteemed friend in Springfield informing me that Maj Dunlap[1] of this State had resigned the office of Quarter Master in the volunteer Service, and that Col Robert Allen of Springfield will apply for the vacant place.[2] I have known Col Allen intimately for about fourteen years, and can assure you that Illinois claims, among her patriotic citizens, none more honorable and chivalrious. He possesses in an eminent degree all the qualifications requisite for the station. Brave, intelligent, and accomplished, he possesses business qualifications in a high degree. In short he is just the man for the situation, and I should be exceedingly gratified to learn that you have given him the appointment. I have the honor to remain very respectfully your friend

S. A. DOUGLAS

ALS, Illinois State Historical Library.
[1]Major Alexander Dunlap resigned as Quartermaster on June 14, 1847.
[2]Allen was appointed Quartermaster, with rank of major, on September 9, 1847.

To Charles S. Hempstead and Elihu B. Washburne

Quincy

Gentlemen   Sept 8th 1847

I have the honor to acknowledge the receipt of your letter of the 30th ult asking my opinion as to the true construc[tion] of the act of the last congress relative to the land bounties for Soldiers & volunteers.[1] I regret that I have no copy of the law with me & am therefore unable to give you my opinion as to its true meaning. I am free to say that the benefits of the law ought to extend to the volunteers, who defended Fort Crawford & those engaged in all similar service,[2] and that if the present law will not admit of such a construction, we will try this winter to amend it so that it will do justice to them as well as others. I have no doubt that Congress will make it read that way, whether it now reads so or not. At the time of the passage of the law it is probable that we acted under the supposition that all the volunteers would serve in Mexico & did not anticipate such a case as has since arisen. Respectfully your friend

S. A. DOUGLAS

ALS, Library of Congress. Charles S. Hempstead and Elihu B. Washburne were law partners in Galena, Illinois. Washburne was elected to Congress in 1852, where he served until his appointment as Secretary of State by Ulysses S. Grant in 1869.
[1]A law providing land bounties to veterans of the Mexican War was passed by Congress early in 1847.

[2]Fort Crawford, Wisconsin, on the Mississippi River midway between Prairie du Chien and the mouth of the Wisconsin River, was an important Army post during the Black Hawk Indian War. The law for land bounties to veterans of the Mexican War made no provision for those who had volunteered and served in the Black Hawk War.

To Charles H. Lanphier

(*Private*)   Washington

My Dear Sir,   Dec 7th 1847

I desire to ask a favor of you. You will doubtless recollect that some two years ago Mr Walters published in the Register Editorially an account of the interview between Gen'l Jackson & myself at the Hermitage in 1844 at which he was present in regard to my speech on the remission of Gen'l Jackson's fine.[1] Will you turn to the files of the Register & cut out the article & send it to me, or copy it & send me the manuscript? I want it for a friend. Do me the favor to attend to this & send it by *return mail*. Present my respects to your Lady & Mrs Walters family. Respectfully yours

                                            S. A. DOUGLAS

ALS, Illinois State Historical Library.
[1]A search of the available files of the *Illinois State Register* has failed to locate the editorial referred to by Douglas. Walters, editor of the *Register* at the time, accompanied Douglas when the latter visited Jackson. James Washington Sheahan described the visit and quoted Walters' account, undoubtedly the editorial referred to, in his 1860 campaign biography of Douglas. Sheahan wrote that Walters published his account a few days after his return to Springfield (James Washington Sheahan, *The Life of Stephen A. Douglas* [New York, 1860], pp. 70-71).

To W. W. Corcoran and George W. Riggs

$167   [December 21, 1847]

Pay to Hon A Lincoln on order one hundred & sixty seven dollars— & charge the same to my account.[1]

Washington Dec 21st 1847   S. A. DOUGLAS

ADS, owned by Martin F. Douglas. W. W. Corcoran and George W. Riggs were Washington, D.C., bankers.
[1]Lincoln was acting as an intermediary between Richard Yates and Douglas. In a letter to Yates, on December 10, 1847, Lincoln wrote, "I presented your claim to Douglass this morning; he says it is all right & that he will pay it in a few days. When he shall have done so, you will hear from me at once" (Roy P. Basler, editor, *The Collected Works of Abraham Lincoln* [9 vols., New Brunswick, New Jersey, 1953], I, 419). Yates, a Jacksonville attorney, had been a member of the state legislature from 1842 to 1845.

To Roger Jones

Senate Chamber

Sir,   Jan'y 24th 1848

Will you do me the favor to inform me at your earliest convenience, what number of men Gen'l Taylor had under his command in the Vally of the Rio Grande from the 1st of Sept to the 1st of October 1846 including his command at Monterey, and also exclusive of that force. I have the honor to be very respectfully yours

S. A. DOUGLAS

ALS, Illinois State Historical Library. Brevet Major General Roger Jones was Adjutant General of the United States from 1825 until his death in 1852.

To Sidney Breese

Willards' Hotel

Dear Sir,   Feb'y 12th 1848

Permit me to introduce to your acquaintance Mr Henry G Wheeler, who is engaged in writing a history of the members of the present Congress.[1] I have favorably known Mr Wheeler for several years, and have a high appreciation of his abilities and attainments as well as impartiality for the arduous duty he has undertaken to perform. There are peculiar reasons for his desire to write & publish your biography at an early period, which he will explain to you as he has already stated them to me. Respectfully yours

S. A. DOUGLAS

ALS, John Carter Brown Library, Brown University, Providence, Rhode Island.

[1] Henry G. Wheeler reported Congressional debates for a number of years for various Washington newspapers. His book, published in 1848, was entitled *History of Congress, Bio-graphical and Political: Comprising Memories of Members of the Congress of the United States, Drawn from Authentic Sources; Embracing the Prominent Events of Their Lives, and Their Connection with the Political History of the Times* (2 vols., New York, 1848).

To Samuel Treat

(*Private*)   Washington

My Dear Sir,   Feby 19th 1848

Yours of the 25th ult came to hand some days ago, but my sickness for the last two weeks has prevented an earlier reply. I regret especially that you have determined to retire from the chair Editorial of the Union.[1] I know it is a laborious and even a slavish position. But who can be got to take your place? I know of no one competent to the task, who could be induced to go to your city, if indeed a man could be found equal to the task. There is no one here whom I could recommend to you. I had hoped that you would conclude to make the profession of the quil the business of your life. I know it would be for the interest of your friends to do so—but I do not know that it would be for your own interests. I fear the consequences of your retirement before the Presidential Campaign is over. We have a fearful struggle before us. It will require all our energies and all our strength to win the victory. No one can now tell who will be our candidate. Appearances at present would seem to favor the nomination of Woodbury or *Cass*.[2] I agree with you that Cass made a great mistake in his avowal of opposition to the whole of Mexico. Such an avowal was uncalled for. He will loose many friends & gain none by it. Besides it may prove to have been unwise as an act of patriotism as well as policy. I am not prepared to assume any such possition nor to have the Democratic party committed to any such doctrine. I wish to be left free to act as circumstances and future developments may render necessary. It is now reduced to a certainty that in the event of Cass's nomination, the Barnburners of New York[3] will oppose him & cause the State to be given against him. The same is true as respects Buchanan & Dallas,[4] and it may be true in regard to Woodbury. It is not certain how they would act in regard to the latter—they might go for Woodbury, but I doubt it. My own opinion is that they do not wish to be admitted into the Baltimore convention. Their policy is to be refused admission at Baltimore and to make that refusal the pretext for separating, & supporting Taylor.[5] This will certainly be the case if Clay should be the Whig candidate, and maybe if Taylor should receive the Whig nomination. John Van Buren[6] is known to be a Taylor man against the world. In this state of the Presidential question I should regret exceedingly to have you retire from your present post. I shall at least claim the benefit of your counsels & advice as to the safest course for the party to sail. I have great doubt who ought to be our man. I am not committed to any one, and shall remain uncommitted until the time for action approaches. Let me hear from you frequently. Your friend

S. A. DOUGLAS

ALS, Missouri Historical Society, St. Louis. Samuel Treat was a St. Louis attorney and editor of the St. Louis *Union*, a Democratic party organ. He was a delegate to the Democratic national convention at Baltimore in 1848 and was elected secretary of that body.

[1]In a penciled notation attached to Douglas to Treat, April 26, 1848 (see below), Treat wrote at a later date, "I was editor of the St. Louis Union and determined to quit, but held on to the end of the campaign, when from broken health, I was ordered to Cuba for the winter. On my return in the spring of 1849, I left the editorial life."

[2]Levi Woodbury, of New Hampshire, former member of the United States Senate and Secretary of the Treasury, was at this time Associate Justice of the United States Supreme Court. Lewis Cass was United States Senator from Michigan from 1845 until his nomination for the Presidency by the Democratic party on May 25, 1848.

[3]The Van Buren faction of the Democratic party in New York became known in the 1840's as the "Barn-

burners," as opposed to the more conservative group, the "Hunkers." The Barnburners, moved by a dislike for Cass, had announced their nonsupport of the Democratic ticket if Cass were nominated.

[4]George M. Dallas was Vice-President of the United States under Polk.

[5]Zachary Taylor had been an active candidate for the Presidency since the middle of 1847. He received the Whig nomination at that party's convention in June, 1848.

[6]John Van Buren, "Prince John," was the son of former President Martin Van Buren and a member of the Barnburner faction of the Democratic party in New York state.

To Francis Preston Blair and John Cook Rives

[February 23, 1848, Senate Chamber; ALS, Chicago Historical Society. Asking that 500 copies of Douglas' speech "on the Mexican War & the boundary of the Rio Grande," delivered in the Senate on February 1, 1848, be sent to Charles H. Peaslee, Congressman from New Hampshire.]

To Robert J. Walker

[March 7, 1848, Senate Chamber; ALS, Illinois State Historical Library. Enclosing a letter from George W. Hopkins, Chargé d'Affaires to Portugal.]

To Samuel Treat

(*Private*)   Washington

My Dear Sir,   April 26th 1848

I have pondered well on your letter & am in doubt what to say in reply. The chances seem to tend to the nomination of Gen'l Cass. At least I have but very little doubt but this will be the result in case the majority rule shall be adopted for the government of the convention. In case the two thirds rule should prevail, no man can foresee the result. Cass's friends will probably favor the majority rule. It is not known what course will be pursued by the friends of Woodbury, Polk, Buchanan, Dallas, & others. If they are to be supposed to be governed by their interests with the view of promoting their chances of success, the presumption is that they would favor the two thirds rule. Much, if not the result of the convention, depends upon the decision of this preliminary question in the organization of the convention. There is another question however that must produce serious results not only on the nomination, but the election. I refer to the double set of delegates from New York. If the Barnburners are admitted to their seats, it is understood that they will give the vote of New York unanymously *against* Cass. On the other hand if the Hunkers get their seats, they will go unanymously for Cass. So it is said by the knowing ones here. The first question will be to determine which of these sets of delegates shall be admitted. Some propose to admit both sets & make them agree among themselves how the vote of the State shall be cast. But it is said that the Burners will not agree to this. They will have nothing to do with the Hunkers, nor with the convention, unless the Hunkers are excluded. This vexed question will probably have much to do in controlling the nomination & the election.[1] The Barnburners are understood to be violently against Cass, Woodbury, Buchanan, and probably against Polk. Bob Walker will have some friends in the convention—there is some talk of Gov Shunk of Penn & also of Gov Dodge of Wisconsin.[2] Such is the glorious state of confusion in which the whole subject is now enveloped. No man can even conjecture what is to be [the] result, and very few even know what they will do or advise when the time arrives. I am taking no part in the controversy as yet & shall for the present stand entirely aloof. I do not take this course from policy, but because I do not know what course we ought to pursue. You will be here in time to see & judge for yourself. My advice is not to be in a hurry in coming to a conclusion. I am stopping at Willards Hotel in Washington & hope you will come to the same House. Your friend

S. A. DOUGLAS

ALS, Missouri Historical Society.
[1]The Democratic convention actually offered to admit both the Barnburner and Hunker delegations, and to split New York's vote between them. The Barnburners, not to be conciliated, withdrew, and in the end, neither delegation was admitted.
[2]Francis R. Shunk was Governor of Pennsylvania from 1845 to 1848, when he resigned because of poor health. Henry Dodge was Governor of Wisconsin Territory until Wisconsin's admission to the Union in 1848, whereupon he was elected to the United States Senate. Dodge was nominated for the Vice-Presidency by a Barnburner convention in Utica, New York, but his candidacy was later withdrawn.

To Ebenezer Peck and James A. McDougall

Washington
Gentlemen   May 7th 1848

Permit me to introduce to you Mr C H McCormick of Virginia,[1] who comes to me highly recommended from Gov McDowell[2] of that State as a highly respectable and worthy gentleman. He is the inventor of a machine known as the Virginia Reaper, and wishes to introduce it into use in Illinois.

Any assistance you may render him will be duly acknowledged by your friend

S. A. DOUGLAS

ALS, owned by Roger W. Barrett, Chicago, Illinois. Ebenezer Peck and James A. McDougall were Chicago law partners. Peck was a former member of the state legislature and was clerk of the state Supreme Court from 1841 to 1845. McDougall was Attorney General of Illinois from 1842 to 1846.

[1]Cyrus Hall McCormick moved from Virginia to Chicago in 1847, where he

engaged in the manufacture of grain-cutting machines.

[2]James McDowell, Governor of Virginia from 1842 to 1846, was a member of Congress from 1846 to 1851.

To Lewis Cass

Monticello Miss.
June 13th 1848

My Dear Sir,

You will doubtless be surprised to get a letter from me at this place. A family affliction called me from Washington to N Carolina a few days before the Baltimore convention & the business of my father-in-law['s] estate required my attention here.[1] I first heard of your nomination in N Carolina. I need [not] say that it met with a cordial response in my breast. You know my sentiments, and probably feel more interest in knowing what others say of it. In N Carolina the nominations were received with great enthusiasm. I have travelled over more than half of the state since the convention & saw no Democrat who was not well pleased. The Democrats of that state felt confident of carrying it for you unless Taylor should be nominated by the Whigs. In South Carolina I found an entirely different state of things. Some were pleased—some displeased—and by far the greater number were doubting & hesitating what they would do. I would form no diffinate opinion what the state would do when the trial comes off. I saw several leading men at Columbia & other places who were decidedly for you & who had hopes of carrying the state. At Augusta Ga the Democrats had a ratification meeting the night I got there, & responded to the nomination unanimously & with enthusiasm. I was assured that you would not loose a Democratic vote in Georgia & the Democrats think they can carry the state. I heard the same opinions expressed in the cars & stages & also at Atlanta & Griffin & other places where I stoped. In Alabama the best kind of feeling prevails. The Democrats are well pleased with the nomination & disapprove of the course of Yancy.[2] In Montgomery, where he lives, I was assured that you would not loose a Democratic vote. I was told the same thing on the Steam Boat—in the cars & at Mobile. Even the Whigs concide the state to you by a large majority as against Taylor even. You will perceive by this that I have not yet heard from the Whig Convention. I attended the ratification meeting at New Orleans last week. The meeting was large & enthusiastic. The party are in fine spirits & you would think that they would not have supported any one than yourself. The Democrats claim the state against the world & I think with good reason as to everybody except Taylor. From N Orleans I came up here by private conveyance & saw some voters on the

route. Mississippi is safe for you by a large majority as against Taylor
or any body else. The Democrats are in the best of spirits & the Whigs
give up the contest. And here I must stop my report as my journy is at
an end at the present. There will be a ratifycation meeting here next
Satudy which I shall attend. Write no more letters.[3] The South are satisfied with your views on the slavery question, as well as all others. I
may inflict another prosy letter on you during my journeyings. My respects to your family. Your friend

S. A. DOUGLAS

ALS, William L. Clements Library,
Ann Arbor, Michigan.

[1]Colonel Robert Martin, Douglas'
father-in-law, was a North Carolina
planter. When he died in May, 1848,
he left two plantations, one in North
Carolina and a second on the Pearl
River in Mississippi. It had been Martin's intention to leave the latter to
Douglas, but Douglas dissuaded him
from his purpose. Instead, the Pearl
River holding, with its Negro slaves,
was left to Mrs. Douglas and the Douglas children.

[2]William Lowndes Yancey, former
Congressman from Alabama, was a
delegate to the Democratic convention.
Earlier in the year he had persuaded
the state convention to adopt the "Alabama resolutions," repudiating the Missouri Compromise and maintaining that
the Federal government not only could
not touch slavery in the territories but
was obligated to protect it. In Baltimore, his resolution that "the doctrine
of non-interference with the rights of
property of any portion of this con-
federation, be it in the States or in the
Territories, by any other than the parties interested in them, is the true republican doctrine recognized by this
body" was decisively rejected by the
Democratic convention.

[3]This is probably a reference to Cass's
famous "Nicholson letter," written to
A. O. P. Nicholson on December 24,
1847, in which he declared that slavery
could exist in the territories only
through action by the territorial legislatures.

To James K. Polk

[N.d., n.p.; LS, RG-59, National Archives. Recommendation of the
Illinois delegation in Congress that Orville C. Pratt be appointed to a
judgeship in Oregon Territory. Although undated, the recommendation must have been written sometime before July 22, 1848, since reference is made to it in a letter by Douglas of that date. Pratt, who had
been a member of the 1847 Illinois constitutional convention from Jo
Daviess County, received the appointment.]

To James K. Polk

Senate Chamber

July 22d 1848

Sir,

You will doubtless recollect that I joined with my colleagues of the
Illinois Delegation sometime since in recommending the appointment
of a citizen of Illinois as one of the Judges in Oregon.[1] I do not wish
that this my recommendation of the Hon J. Quinn Thorton[2] should be

deemed as waiving or weakening in the least degree that recommendation, which is hereby renewed. I have known Judge Thornton intimately for several years & lived in the same town with him in the west before his removal to Oregon. I do no more than strict justice when I say that he always maintained an unblemished & spotless character as a gentleman of high honor & integrity. He is a thorough schollar & well read Lawyer. I have received many letters from citizens of Oregon speaking in the highest terms of Judge Thornton as a citizen of & a Judge in that country & warmly recommending his appointment as one of the United States Judges under the Territorial Bill. The fact that he is a resident of that Territory—that he has discharged the duties of Chief Justice there to the satisfaction of the inhabitants—and that he has endured all the toils, expenses, and perils of emigrating to the country and of returning here for the purpose of rendering service to the people, ought in my humble judgement to give him peculiar claims upon the government. In view of all the circumstances I should be exceedingly gratified if your Excellency should conceive that the public interest would be promoted by his appointment. Your favorable attention to this letter will be gratefully acknowledged by your friend & obedent servant

S. A. DOUGLAS

ALS, RG-59, National Archives.
[1]See above, recommendation of the Illinois delegation for the appointment of Orville C. Pratt.
[2]Jesse Quinn Thornton, formerly a lawyer and newspaper publisher in Missouri, had moved to Quincy, Illinois, in 1841, thence to Oregon in 1846. In Oregon, he became the chief justice of the provisional government which functioned prior to the organization of Oregon Territory. He was not appointed to the position mentioned by Douglas.

To James K. Polk

[July 26, 1848, Washington; LS, RG-59, National Archives. Recommendation that Captain James D. Blair be appointed to the office of Secretary or one of the judges for California, "should the bill for the establishment of a territorial government in California become a law." The recommendation is signed by twelve members of the Senate and House of Representatives, including Douglas. No territorial government was provided for California, that area being admitted to the Union directly as a state in 1850. Blair, a native of Kentucky, was a captain in the infantry from 1847 to 1848.]

To James K. Polk

[N.d., n.p.; LS, RG-59, National Archives. Recommendation that William P. Bryant, of Rockville, Indiana, be appointed Chief Justice of

Oregon Territory. The recommendation is signed by ten members of Congress, including Douglas, and is in the hand of Senator Edward A. Hannegan of Indiana. Although undated, the recommendation, endorsed "1848," presumably was written sometime before August 14, the date on which Polk signed the bill creating Oregon Territory. Bryant, a Rockville lawyer and former member of the Indiana state legislature, received the appointment as first Chief Justice of the Supreme Court of Oregon Territory.]

To James Morse

Washington
August 19th 1848

Dear Sir,

In reply to your letter of the 8th inst I take pleasure in stating that you had an active agency in passing the Mail Steamer Bill by the last Congress.[1] Altho not a member of the House, the friends of the Bill consulted you oftener than any other person, and, in my opinion, derived more assistance from your exertions than from any one else. The passage of the Bill on the last night of the Session was the result of a well devised & skillfully executed movement, which probably would not have been attempted but for yourself. By this statement I do not intend to detract in the slightest degree from the credit due those members of the House to whom the country has awarded the merit of establishing the Mail Steamer System. The united & energetic exertions of all were necessary to success. But to you more than any man who had not a vote to give ought the merit to be awarded. Respectfully your friend

S. A. DOUGLAS

ALS, Illinois State Historical Library. James Morse was a resident of Stamford, Connecticut.
[1]The "Mail Steamer Bill" to which Douglas refers was passed on July 21, 1848, and provided subsidies to several steamship lines for carrying the United States mails.

To Robert Smith

Rockingham Co., N.C., Sep. 20, '48.

My Dear Sir: When we parted at Washington I intended to have been home before this or about this time. You may recollect that I was very unwell when you last saw me, and that it was thought imprudent for me to start at that time. The next day I was attacked with an ague chill in the cars, and I was detained some time at Richmond, with a slight attack of bilious fever. Having managed to join my family here,[1] I thought I was well enough to return, and, accordingly, all my arrangements were made even to the packing of my trunks; but I was again attacked with the fever and ague, from which I have not yet recovered. I, however, hope that I will be able to start home in a few days. I shall go by the northern route, and land at Chicago, thence by Springfield and Jacksonville to Quincy. I expect to be also at Alton. Remember me to my friends, and tell them I will certainly be with them at the election in November, if I am able to travel. I remain truly your friend,

S. A. DOUGLASS

Springfield *Illinois State Register,* November 3, 1848.
[1]The family of Douglas' wife, Martha Martin Douglas, resided in Rockingham County, North Carolina.

To William L. Marcy

[December 28, 1848, "Com: Room on Territories of Senate"; LS, RG-75, National Archives. Forwarding the petition of John P. Duval, former Secretary of Florida Territory, for compensation for having served as Acting Governor and Acting Superintendent of Indian Affairs during the absence of the Governor, and requesting information on the rate of compensation due territorial secretaries in such instances. Duval was Secretary of Florida Territory from 1837 to 1839.]

To William L. Marcy

[January 22, 1849, Senate Chamber; LS, RG-75, National Archives. Request by Douglas, as Chairman of the Committee on Territories, for further information regarding John P. Duval's role during the Seminole Indian War in Florida in 1838 and his services in removing the Apalachicola Indians during the same year, to be used in deciding Duval's claim for compensation. See above, December 28, 1848.]

To Mrs. Richard Montgomery Young

[February 5, 1849]
Senator Douglas presents his compliments to Mrs Young and will be happy to take her & her daughter to Mr R. J. Walkers tonight, if convenient and agreeable to her.
Feby 5th 1849
P.S. I will call with a carriage at 9 oclock.

S. A. D.

ANS, Boston Public Library.

To Robert J. Walker

Senate Chamber

My Dear Sir,   Feby 21st 1849

My friend Mr William S Prentice, whom you were kind enough to say you would appoint to examine the Land offices in Illinois, desires to start home in a day or two. You will therefore excuse me for reminding you of the appointment and for soliciting it at as early a day as convenient to you.[1] I shall ever feel gratefully very grateful to you for this make [mark?] of your kindness.

S. A. DOUGLAS

ALS, Houghton Library, Harvard University, Cambridge, Massachusetts.
[1]Walker made the appointment discussed in this letter.

To William L. Marcy

Senate Chamber

Sir,   March 3d 1849

In looking over the list of Brevets, we do not find the name of Major David Hunter, Paymaster, who has been a long time in the service & has always performed his duties with great ability & fidelity—both in the enemy's country & at Home.[1] He served on Gen'l Wools[2] line until it joined Gen'l Taylor and then with the latter until the close of the War. We take it for granted that his name was omitted by mistake, and would respectfully ask that it may be sent in today, if the Department shall concur with us as respects his meritorious services. We have known Major Hunter long and intimately & feel a lively interest that justice may be done him. We have the honor to be your obed servt

S. A. DOUGLAS
JEFFER. DAVIS

ALS, RG-107, National Archives.
[1]David Hunter, an 1822 West Point graduate, was appointed major and paymaster in 1842. He did not receive a brevet appointment following the Mexican War.

[2]John E. Wool was brevetted major general after the battle of Buena Vista; following the war he was appointed to the command of the Eastern Military District.

To ———

[N.d., n.p.; ANS, RG-59, National Archives. Recommendation for the appointment of Onias C. Skinner, of Quincy, Illinois, to the office of Associate Justice in Minnesota Territory. The recommendation is undated, but the Territory of Minnesota was formally organized on March 3, 1849, and possibly the note was written just prior to or just after that date. It is signed by Stephen A. Douglas, Robert Smith, and Thomas J. Turner, the last two being members of the House of Representatives from Illinois. Skinner was a member of the Illinois state legislature at this time. He was not appointed.]

To John M. Clayton

Washington
March 9th, 1849.

Sirs:

Col. Wm. B. Warren[1] of Illinois, who will hand you this letter, will I understand become an applicant for the office of Survet General in one of the Western States. I have known him for many years and have no hesitation in saying that I regard him well qualified for the station. His education, habits of life and business capacity are well adapted to the discharge of the duties of such an office. If changes in those offices are to be made, I know of no greater man, differing with me in politics, whose appointment would afford me so much pleasure and I believe also it would be gratifying to the people of Illinois generally. He has many devoted friends in the ranks of the Democratic party, growing out of his service to the country in the Mexican war.

I do not wish to be understood as advising even by implications any removals to be made; but in the event that changes shall take place, the appointment of Col. Warren would be decidedly acceptable. I have the honor to be very respectfully, your obedient servant,

S. A. DOUGLAS

Printed in Erwin J. Urch, "The Public Career of William Barton Warren," *Journal of the Illinois State Historical Society*, XXI (April, 1928), 108. The original of this letter has not been located. John M. Clayton, former United States Senator from Delaware, had been appointed Secretary of State by President Zachary Taylor.

[1]Warren was prominent in Whig circles in Illinois. Since participating with the militia in the Mormon difficulties in 1845-46, he had served as an officer with the Illinois volunteers in the Mexican War. He was not appointed to the office discussed by Douglas.

To John M. Clayton

[March 27, 1849]

The foregoing paper has been presented to me with the request that I will state what I know of the respectability of the signers. I know most of them by reputation & know them to be gentlemen of the first respectability and in all respects worthy of entire confidence. They include the leading & most influential names of the two great political parties in the portion of the State where they live. The Hon. Elias S. Dennis[1] I have had the pleasure of knowing intimately for many years. He is a gentleman of the highest respectability—a Democrat in politics and has been a Representative and Senator in the Illinois Legislature for many years. He has also filled many other important offices, and his statements should be taken with implicit confidence & be considered conclusive upon any subject he may give his testimony. I have the honor to be very Respectfully your obedient servt.

S. A. Douglas

AES, RG-59, National Archives. The endorsement appeared on a letter to Clayton, March 27, 1849, signed by sixteen men, "principally Whigs of the most, uncompromising kind and others democrats." The signers recommended the appointment of Benjamin Bond to the office of United States Marshal. Bond, of Clinton County and a former member of the Illinois state legislature, was described in the letter as "one who has thro a long series of years battled as manfully & successfully for Whig principles as any man in Illinois." Bond, however, was not appointed to the office.

[1] Elias S. Dennis was one of the signers of the recommendation.

To Augustus C. French

Chicago

My Dear Sir, May 16th 1849

I have the honor to receive your letter of the 9th inst, intimating doubts in your mind as to your constitutional power to appoint a Senator in the place of Gen'l Shields,[1] and asking my opinion; first as to your power under the constitution, and secondly, what view the U.S. Senate would take of it. The kindness, frankness, and confidence, which you have ever manifested towards me, entitle you to the most unreserved expression of my opinions. Yet, however clear my own mind may be upon the subject, I advance my opinion with great diffidence & deffrance in view of the intimation that it may come in conflict with the inclination of your own thoughts. I have frequently and, very freely in private conversation, expressed the decided & undoubting opinion that the vacancy occasioned by the resignation of Gen'l Shields is one which may be properly and rightfully filled by executive appointment, and that the Senate of the United States would take the same view of the subject whenever it should be presented to that body for its decision. Of course the confined limits of a private letter will not permit me to adduce the argument upon which this proposition is predicated. I may venture, however, to suggest that by the constitution of the United States the power to elect Senators is vested in the Legislature of the State and the right to determine the validity of the election so made is lodged solely in the Senate of the United States—that when the Legislature shall have effected an election and have officially announced the result, its duty is complete and its power exhausted until the Senate shall have determined the validity of that election. The election must be deemed valid until decided invalid, and the person elected entitled to exercise the functions and enjoy the rights & privileges of the office, as was held in the case of Gen'l Shields, until vacated by the decision of the Senate. The vacancy therefore resulted from the decision of the Senate declaring Gen'l Shields ineligible, and took effect from that date; for, prior to that time and coming down to that instant, he as well as I and every other Senator, had taken the oath of office, had been assigned a Seat in the body, had voted upon each question as it arose, had been elected to serve upon the various committees, and had exercised & enjoyed all the rights & privileges of a Senator, and all this too under the sanction and by authority of an express vote of the Senate. But from the instant of time when the decision of the Senate was announced establishing his ineligibility, his rights & functions as Senator ceased and a vacancy happened, which, the constitution of the United States says may be filled by the Executive, the legislature not being in Session. It is probable that the resolution of the Senate declaring the election of Gen'l Shields void, instead of voidable, had done much to produce the impression that in the opinion of the Senate it was not such a vacancy as could be filled by executive appointment. I objected to the form of that resolution upon the ground that it might be construed to contain such an implication. But it is due to many of those who voted for it to say that they expressly disapproved such a construction. Several of them made able arguments to prove that under the constitution of the United States it was such a vacancy as could be filled by executive appointment consistently with that resolution. The view which they took of the subject was this: that the theory & policy of the constitution of the United States required that each State should always have a full representation in the Senate—that while the power of electing Senators was vested exclusively in the Legislature, yet in order to guard effectively against the possibility of leaving a State without a full representation in the Senate, the constitution had provided that "if *vacancies happen by resignation or otherwise during the recess of the Legislature of any State*, the executive thereof may make temporary appointments until the next meeting of the Legislature, which shall then fill such vacancies." The language of the constitution was supposed to be sufficiently broad & comprehensive to include every description of vacancy which might occur during the recess of the Legislature, no matter how or from what cause it might arise, whether from death, removal, failure to elect, illegal election, resignation, or otherwise; and as it was manifestly the design of the framers of the constitution to provide for vacancies from these and all other causes in order to insure a full delegation from each State, it was contended that such a construction should be given to that instrument as would accomplish the objects in view. If this view of the subject be correct it is entirely immaterial whether the vacancy happened on the 4th day of March by the expiration of the term of Senator Breese or on the 14th day of March by the decision of the Senate that Genl Shields was ineligible. In either event it was a vacancy happening "by resignation or otherwise during the recess of the Legislature" and, therefore, by the very letter as well as spirit of the constitution, competant to be filled by executive appointment.[2]

Whether the public interests require a special session for other causes than the election of a Senator, or whether it is wise and proper to convene the Legislature for this reason alone are not questions embraced within your enquiry and in regard to which you and others have much better opportunities than I of judging. I have the honor to be very truly your friend and most obedient servant

S. A. Douglas

ALS, Illinois State Historical Library. This letter was also printed in the Springfield *Illinois State Register*, August 30, 1849.

[1]James Shields was elected to the United States Senate by the Illinois state legislature for the term commencing on March 4, 1849. He served from March 6 to March 15, when the Senate declared his election void on the ground that he had not been a citizen of the United States sufficiently long to qualify for a Senate seat. In 1846, he was commissioned Brigadier General of Volunteers, and the following year was brevetted major general for gallant and meritorious conduct at the Battle of Cerro Gordo.

[2]Governor French made no appointment. Shields was again elected to the Senate in October, 1849, and served until the expiration of his term in 1855.

To Augustus C. French

(*Private*)   Chicago
My Dear Sir,   May 17th 1849

I herewith send you a letter in answer to yours of the 9th inst in regard to your right to appoint a Senator. You are entirely at liberty to make such use of it as you may desire. I expressed the same opinions so often & to so many different persons that I can have no motive for making it confidential. I have no desire for its publication, nor have I any objection to it if you shall wish to make it public. I have several letters on hand from others from different parts of the State propounding the same questions which I may find it convenient to answer by sending a copy of the one to you or by imbracing the same views in an original letter. I shall be in Springfield in the course of a month or six weeks when I will have the pleasure of paying my respects to you in person. I have the honor to remain very truly your friend

S. A. Douglas

ALS, Illinois State Historical Library.

To John M. Clayton

Chicago Ills

My Dear Sir,   May 23d 1849

I take the liberty of presenting to you my friend Gen'l J A McDougall of this city who is about to proceed to the valley of the Gila in California.[1] He is a lawyer of learning & eminence—has filled several high official stations in this State and among them that of Attorney General, and is a man of the strictest honor & integrity. He desires no office—and asks no favors which every American citizen, who is about to migrate to that country, may not claim of his government. He wishes to ascertain the policy of the government in respect to that country in regard to intercourse with the Indians—the protection to be afforded to settlers—and especially the supply of arms which it is understood will be furnished. Permit me to ask that you will confer with him freely, as my especial & particular friend, and introduce him to such other members of the Administration as he may find it necessary to consult, and finally to render him all the assistance in your power, consistant with your official position. I have the honor to be very truly your friend & obedient servant

S. A. DOUGLAS

ALS, Library of Congress.

[1]James A. McDougall emigrated to California in 1849, where he served as Attorney General from 1850 to 1851. He was elected to Congress in 1852 for one term and served in the United States Senate from 1861 to 1867.

To Adelaide Granger

Chicago Ills

My Dear Neice   May 30th 1849

I am greatly obliged to you for your nice letter. You must continue to write to me often & give me all the news. I am sorry to hear that Grand-ma is not so well.[1] I hope she will be well enough to go to Vermont this Summer. Tell her there is no danger of the cholera if she will only take Doct Bird's Sulpher Pills, the account of which you will find in the paper I herewith send you. Tell grandma that Moffats Pills do not compare with them. These Pills are nothing but sulpher & charcoal —3 parts sulpher & one part charcoal. And yet they have cured every case of cholera where they have been given. Not a single death of cholera has occured since this discovery was made a few days ago. We have all got our Pocketts full of sulpher Pills, and care no more for the cholera than we do for the Itch; for it will cure the cholera in an hour, & it takes all winter sometimes to cure the Itch. Doct Bird lives in this city & boards at the same House with me.[2] He discovered this remedy by a series of chemical experiments upon the air, by which he ascertained that there was a certain amount of *poison* in the atmosphere & that this poison produced cholera, and that sulpher was an *antidote* for this poison. If this theory be true, as we all think it is, your sulpher water at the Springs will prevent any one from taking the cholera who drinks it freely. (Don't tell the Landlord down at the Springs about this, if you do he will publish it in the news papers,) and then the whole world will be sure to go to the Springs. You would have people enough there in a short time to drink the little stinking creek dry, and then what would you do for sulpher water. Tell Grand Pa that he must not rely upon the water, but must send to the store and get some sulpher & mix it with charcoal & make some of the real anti-cholera Pills, and take one every day, and more if he has the diarrhea or the Itch.

Give me love to all & write to me often. I have not heard from your Aunt Martha for sometime; but she & the little Boy were very well when I last heard from them.[3] Good buy my Neice, Your affectionate Uncle

S. A. Douglas

ALS, owned by H. F. Sherwood. Adelaide Granger was the twelve-year-old daughter of Douglas' sister Sarah and Julius N. Granger, of Clifton Springs, near Canandaigua, New York.

[1]"Grand-ma" was Douglas' mother, Mrs. Gehazi Granger. She died in 1869, surviving Douglas by eight years.

[2]Dr. J. Herman Bird was one of the founders of the Chicago Medical Society in 1850. A cholera epidemic hit Chicago and other parts of the West between the years 1848 and 1850; its most devastating effects were felt in 1849.

[3]"Aunt Martha" was Douglas' wife, Martha Martin Douglas, who was visiting with her family in North Carolina at this time. The "little Boy" was Douglas' son, Robert Martin, born in 1849.

To Adelaide Granger

Chicago Ills
July 28th 1849

My Dear Neice

I have just received your welcome letter. It has afforded me great satisfaction—especially to learn that you had a pleasant trip to Vermont and that Mother had returned with improved health. My own health is good—in fact I have never enjoyed better health than I do now. I take a sulpher Pill a day & believe that a perfect protection against cholera. The epidemic is abateing through the entire West & we hope it will wholly disappear very soon. Your Aunt Martha was well the last time I heard from her and so was the baby. She does not write as often & regularly as I could desire; but promises to do better in future. Give my love to all & write often. Your affectionate Uncle

S. A. Douglas

ALS, Illinois State Historical Library.

To Charles H. Lanphier and George Walker

Chicago, August 13th, 1849.

Gentlemen: I have observed in several papers, all of which, I believe, are disposed to do entire justice, a controversy in regard to my opinions respecting the constitutional right of the governor to fill the vacancy now existing in the Senate of the United States from this state.

It is needless for me to say that these statements on both sides are without my sanction or authority. I have *volunteered* no opinions upon the subject, and have furnished none for publication, not because I have any motive for concealment, but from a sense of obvious propriety, in view of the fact that the constitution had devolved the decision of this question, in the first instance, upon the Governor alone, to be determined according to his convictions of duty, and not in obedience to the opinions of others. But since my opinions have become the subject of discussion and controversy in the newspapers of my own political faith, and especially since I have been claimed as the advocate of both sides of the question, I trust I may be excused for saying so much as may be necessary to my own vindication.[1] When this subject was under consideration in the United States Senate upon a resolution declaring the election of Gen. Shields *void*, my opinions were very freely and fully expressed.

I then endeavored to maintain by argument the following propositions: That the election of Gen. Shields was not *void*, but *voidable* only; that the vacancy would be one, which, under the constitution of the United States, could be filled rightfully and properly by executive appointment; and that the resolution, in the form in which it then existed, ought not to be adopted, because, in my opinion, it contained an implication that the governor would not possess the power to fill the vacancy. How far I succeeded in maintaining these propositions by argument, I leave to others to determine. The resolution passed however in opposition to my vote, but not without an express disclaimer on the part of many of its supporters, that it ought to be construed to deny the right of the governor to fill the vacancy.

Some time after I returned home, I received a letter from the governor, dated the 9th of May, asking my opinion upon two questions: First, whether he possessed the constitutional right to make the appointment; and second, whether, if he should make an appointment, the Senate would recognize its validity. It is due to the governor to say that in his letter he intimated serious doubts on both propositions. In a letter dated the 16th of May, I answered each of these questions in the affirmative, and briefly gave the reasons for my opinion. It is unnecessary to repeat the arguments in support of these propositions. They will be found in full in the reports of the discussion in the Senate to which I have referred.

In my speeches in the Senate, I have contended that the vacancy was such a one as the constitution of the United States, in so many words, authorized the governor to fill. Having seen no reason to change my mind upon the subject, I had no hesitation in expressing the same opinion to the governor, when called upon for that purpose. It is true, that my construction of the resolution which passed the Senate, implied a denial of the governor's right to appoint, and for that reason I voted against it. But it is also true, that many of those who supported it denied the correctness of this construction, and contended that under the constitution of the United States the governor was clearly authorized to fill the vacancy consistently with that resolution. The speeches of Senators Badger and Dawson[2] on the last day of the discussion will furnish you the course of argument in support of this view of the subject. Thus it will be perceived that the resolution declaring the election void cannot be considered as a decision against the right of the Governor to appoint, although it was opposed by many of us upon the ground that such a construction might be placed upon it. I thought then, and now think, that its language tolerates this construction, and authorizes the public to infer that such was the sense of the Senate. But supposing this construction to be correct, notwithstanding the disclaimers and arguments of its supporters to the contrary, nothing can be clearer than that a mere resolution of the Senate could not deprive the governor of a power conferred upon him by the constitution. Entertaining these views, I returned an affirmative answer to each of the governor's interrogatories, in a letter, a copy of which I herewith enclose to you. About that time in answering the letters of two or three friends, I mentioned the fact that I had expressed these opinions to the governor. A few weeks afterwards, I saw in the newspapers a well written and able letter from the governor to Mr. Manly,[3] in which he arrived at the conclusion that he did not possess the power to make the appointment. From the date of the publication of that letter, I have taken it for granted that there would be an extra session of the legislature. I have used no means to procure or prevent one. In my letter to the governor, all I said upon that subject is contained in the concluding paragraph as follows:

"Whether the public interests require a special session for other causes than the election of a Senator, or whether it is wise and proper to convene the legislature for this reason alone, are not questions embraced within your enquiries, and in regard to which you and others have much better opportunities than I of judging."

I was willing to leave the decision of that question where the constitution placed it—in the hands of the governor, with the most implicit confidence in his integrity, patriotism and discretion.

Regretting the occurrences which render this explanation necessary, I have the honor to remain, very truly, your friend and obedient servant,

S. A. Douglas

Springfield *Illinois State Register,* August 30, 1849.

[1]The *State Register,* in response to statements that Douglas believed the Governor possessed the power to appoint a successor to Shields, had denied that this was Douglas' position. The editors based their denial, they wrote, on Douglas' remarks in the United States Senate while the resolution dealing with Shields's eligibility was pending. Although Douglas set the matter straight in this letter, the editors continued to argue the opposite point of view, that the Governor did not have the power to select Shields's successor.

[2]George E. Badger of North Carolina and William C. Dawson of Georgia.

[3]Uri Manly, of Marshall County, had been a former member of the state legislature. French's letter to Manly, dated June 8, 1849, was printed in the Springfield *Illinois State Register,* June 21, 1849.

To Augustus C. French

Chicago
My Dear Sir,   Aug 24th 1849

Your letter of the 20th inst was received by this morning's mail. With the most anxious desire to conform to your wishes I have carefully considered your suggestion that I should withdraw the authority I have given for the publication of my letter to you of the 16th of May last in regard to your right to make a Senatorial appointment. I regret the necessity which seems to demand its publication. But I do not see how the clammors of the newspaper Press for the publication are to be satisfied or my own vindication against the charge of being on both sides of the question is to be complete without the publication.[1] The very point at issue is whether I have written such a letter, and, if so, what are its contents. The papers on one side assert the affirmative of the proposition, to which the others give a direct denial and demand the proof, and at the same time state that nothing but the publication of the letter itself will be satisfactory proof. It is clear therefore that anything short of the publication of the letter itself would be considered as a mere evasion, falling far short of my own vindication or of satisfying public curiosity. On the other hand let me ask what possible objection can there be, under existing circumstances, to its publication? Who is there, except its author, under the wide panoply of heaven that can be injured by it? Certainly not you, for you are in nowise responsible for its contents. Nor can its publication put you in a false position, for it will show that your opinions have been all the time uniform and consistent—that your opinions then were what they now are and what you have since published them to the world to be. It cannot place me in a false position, for it will show that my opinions then were what they now are and what I proclaimed them in the Senate to be. Where then is the harm? The only objection I see stated in your letter is that the publication will actually show that you and I conscientiously differed in opinion as to the true construction of one line in the constitution of the United States. Well, I regret that we should differ even thus much. But the fact unfortunately appears. It was made to appear by the publication of your letter to Mr Manly in opposition to my speeches in the Senate and to my letter to you. The fact of the controriety of opinion upon the subject is, therefore, already before the public. This fact is not to be changed either by the publication or suppression of my letter, nor ought our personal & political relations to be in the slightest degree modified by it. The only object of the publication is to vindicate myself from the charge of occupying the mortifying & disreputable position of being on both sides. This is a duty I owe to myself & friends. How my vindication can injure or embarrass you I do not perceive. I have discharged my duty according to my own convictions of right, and you no doubt have and will do the same. Each of us will have the approval of our own consciences and with this we ought to be content. I have not presumed to express any opinion as to what you *ought to do*. I have only expressed my opinion, at your request, as to what you have the *right to do*. In my opinion you have the right either to appoint a Senator or to convene the Legislature, and that is a question for you alone to decide which you ought to do. Whatever course you may adopt in this respect will be entirely agreeable to me, and, I believe, will give no offense to the people so far as my information extends. My feeble health has deprived me of the privilige of visiting other portions of the State and hence I know but little of public opinion in regard to an extra Session. There is another reason which seems to render the publication necessary. You say that before you received my letter you were under the impression that I thought you had no power to appoint a Senator and that you had so expressed yourself to our friends. While you were expressing these opinions privately the papers favorable to your construction publicly claimed me as agreeing with you and them. They have persevered in this course up to this day, and now, if I, after remaining silent more than three months, should publish my present opinions without disclosing the fact that you had been all the time notified of them, they and the public might be justified in the conclusion that I had treated you unfairly in leaving you to infer from my silence that I agreed with you in opinion when in fact I differed with you in *toto* in regard to the question. It would be doing me great injustice to allow the public to suppose that

[175]

I was capable of misleading you either by expressing my opinions to you or by withholding them from you until you had acted and then of coming out against your action. I should also have deemed it proper for me to have written to those Editors who were laboring under the same error had I not relied upon you to make the correction inasmuch as they were acting in support of your views.

I do not precisely understand the point of your allusion to the Rail Road excitements in the South,[2] the extent and nature of which you tell me I am not aware of; nor do I perceive what that excitement has to do with my opinions concerning your right to appoint a Senator. You are right in assuming that I do not understand the nature and extent of that excitement, and because I did not understand it I have formed & expressed no opinions about it. That is a question of purely state policy to be decided by the Legislature, and whatever the representatives of the people do I presume all good citizens will be disposed cheerfully to acquiesce in. Certainly I shall for one. Now I must bring this letter to a close. My strength will not enable me to say more, for I have been confined to my room and a good portion of the time to my bed for three weeks. The subject to which I refered as worthy to be named in your proclamation for a called Session, as you have decided to call one, is the "improvement of the navigation of the Illinois River by Locks & Dams or otherwise as a part of the Illinois & Michigan Canal."[3] I will send you a communication upon this subject in a few days.[4] I commenced it sometime ago, but business & sickness have prevented its completion. I shall be in Springfield as soon as my health will admit. I remain very truly your friend

S. A. DOUGLAS

ALS, Illinois State Historical Library.

[1]Douglas' letter to French of May 16, 1849, was published in the Springfield *Illinois State Register* on August 30.

[2]French's allusion was probably to the desire expressed in the southern part of Illinois for a cross-state railroad that would connect that area with St. Louis and Cincinnati. The supporters of this plan favored the idea of a special session in the hope that they might achieve legislative approval of it. French was sympathetic to their position. The plan for an east-west rail connection ran directly counter to the alternative proposal for a north-south railroad that would tie southern Illinois to the cities of the north.

[3]Governor French called a special session of the legislature to meet on October 22 for the purpose of electing a United States Senator and of dealing with the question of internal improvements.

[4]No such communication as that described by Douglas has been located.

To Charles H. Lanphier

Chicago

My Dear Sir,
August 24th 1849

I have just finished a long letter to the Governor in explanation of my reasons for insisting upon the publication of my letter and communication as it [was] first prepared. I desire that you & Mr Walker should be in possession of all the facts and fully understand my motives. With this view I had intended to write you at length today, but my strength fails me and I will not be able to do so. I wish therefore that you and Mr Walker would call upon the Governor and read my letter to him the same as if it had been written to you. You will perceive that I could not have complied with the Governor's request without subjecting my own motives & character to injurious imputations. I had supposed that you had read my letter to the Governor of the 16th of May at the time it was received and being under that impression I have been surprised at the course of the Register. I came to this conclusion from the fact that [I] was informed upon good authority that the Governor was the author of several of the articles in the Register referring to my speeches in the Senate. From this I felt authorized to infer that he would show you all the information he had on the subject. I now infer that he considered it his duty to treat my letter as confidential & not let any one know of its existance. This view of the subject explains evrything between us. I shall be down South as soon as my health will admit. I am now improving. I remain very truly your friend

S. A. DOUGLAS

ALS, Illinois State Historical Library.

To [George W. Crawford]

Senate Chamber
Sir,   Dec 15th 1849
    I have the honor to enclose to you herewith a letter from my relative Judge Warner of New York, who was a Brother of the late Capt Wm H Warner of the United States Army, who was recently murdered in California while in the discharge of his official duty.[1] I think his request is reasonable. He only asks that when you find it necessary to appoint a bearer of dispatches, you will give him the preferance in order to enable him to bring back the remains of his deceased Brother.

    Permit me to ask your favorable consideration of this ap[pointment].

AL, RG-107, National Archives. The bottom portion of the letter, including the signature and the name of the addressee, has been torn off. The letter is endorsed by the War Department, so it is presumed that Douglas directed it to the Secretary of War, George W. Crawford. Crawford had been Governor of Georgia before his appointment to the War Department by President Taylor.

[1]Horatio Gates Warner was a county judge in Madison County, New York, before he moved to Rochester in 1840, where he became a newspaper editor. His brother, Captain William H. Warner of the Topographical Engineers, was ambushed and killed by Indians near Goose Lake, California, in September, 1849. Warner and Douglas were distant cousins; their grandfathers were brothers.

To Augustus C. French

Dear Sir,   Washington Dec 27th 1849

I have been requested by the Hon John A Rockwell of Conn[1] on be-half of the Cairo City & Canal Company[2] to forward to you the en-closed paper, being a release to the State of Illinois by said company of the charter of the Great Western & Central Rail Road Companies[3] & all acts & parts of acts supplemental or amendatory thereof & all the rights & privileges granted by them or either of them as fully as if those acts had never been passed by our Legislature.[4] The circum-stances under which this release was executed so far as the facts have come to my knowledge are as follows. Sometime ago Mr G W Billings[5] as agent of said company placed in my hands a letter written by Mr. D. B. Holbrook to your excellency in which he enclosed to you what purported to be a Release or rather a promise to release to the State those charters upon certain conditions hereafter to be performed. Mr Billings at the same time placed in my hands a copy of said Release or Promise to release executed in Duplicate and bearing date the 15th of this month, for the purpose of satisfying me that the interests of Illinois would not be sacrificed in the manner & to the extent I had appre-hended in my speeches at Chicago & Springfield last October,[6] and for the further purpose of enabling me to obviate the well known & in-superable objections of Congress to making grants of land to or for the benifit of private corporations. Mr Holbrook's letter to you, of which a copy was also furnished me, confirmed this view of the subject as to the motives for executing the release. I informed Messrs Billings & Rockwell who represented the interests of the Cairo City & Canal Company in this affair that I was invested with no authority to speak & act for the people and State of Illinois in this matter and had no other interest in it or right pertaining to it than that which was common to evry citizen of our State who felt a deep interest in her prosperity & welfare. But that I was entirely willing to express to them my opinions upon the subject as a private individual. I then informed them that I did not regard the paper, executed in Duplicate on the 15th of Decem-ber and purporting to be a Release or promise to release the rights under the Rail Road charters granted by our legislature, as being valid & binding in law upon the Cairo City & Canal Company. It was executed by D B Holbrook as President & on behalf and under the corporate seal of the Cairo City & Canal Co, but without the sanction & authority of the stock holders or even the Board of Directors. That the President possessed no power to act for the company except under the authority & by the direction of the Board of Directors, and then only in pursuance and in the exercise of the powers granted by the charter. That neither he nor the Directors could deprive the Stockholders of their rights by surrendering up their charter without their consent. That the paper was worthless therefore so far as it purported to surrender the rights of the company or to restore those of our state. This paper however poss[ess]ed one merit. It furnished the evidence that the company were willing to execute a valid release in due form when called upon to do so. I also took the liberty of pointing out some objections to the terms & conditions of the release. For instance, one of the conditions was that "in case Congress shall at its present session donate to the State of Illinois or give a preemption to lands for [the] purpose of aiding in the construction of a rail Road from Cairo to Chicago that the Cairo City & Canal Co shall & will authorize the Governor of Illinois to offer said land to the Bond holders of the State debt, on condition that said bondholders will agree to receive said lands and make the proposed road from Cairo to Chicago" &c &c. The first objection I urged to this clause was that the Release was to be void unless Congress made the grant at the present session. This however was of minor importance compared to the next. It recognizes the title to the lands, the moment Congress makes the grant, as being vested in the Cairo City & Canal Co, and gives the promise of the company that it will permit the Governor to offer the lands to the Bondholders on condition that they would receive them & make the road. Suppose that the Bondholders should refuse to receive the lands & make the road! In that event the release would be void, and the charter, & the Road, and the lands granted would all remain the property of the company. Is it unreasonably to suppose that such might be the case when an understanding between the Bondholders & the Company would enable them to get all the lands & devide them among themselves & still retain all their chartered privileges. Without imputing any such design to any of the parties concerned I frankly told the agents of the Cairo Company that no arraingement could receive my approval by which our State could possibly be deprived of any of the benefits & advantages which might result from a grant of lands by Congress in aid of Rail Roads in the State. To enable us to protect the rights of our State in this respect as well as to give us the slightest chance to secure the grant of land from Congress I told them that the Cairo City & Canal Co ought to execute to the State of Illinois a full & complete release & surrender of the charter of the Great Western Rail Road Co. and of all acts & parts of acts supplemental or amend[at]ory thereof or relating to the Central Rail Road together with all the rights & privileges granted by all or any of said acts as fully & completely as if they had never been passed by the Legislature, leaving the State through its Legislature to make such disposition of the lands & such arraingements for the construction of the Road with the Bondholders or others as the people of Illinois should deem best. I also expressed to them the opinion that in order to make such a release valid & binding upon the Company it would be necessary to call a meeting of the Stockholders in pursuance of the charter and that they should pass a resolution authorizing & directing the President & Directors of the Company to execute the release and that the instrument should recite the authority in obedience to which it was made. Of course I did not pretend to possess any authority to impose these or any other terms upon the Company nor to give the assurance that they would meet with the approbation of yourself or the legislature or the people of Illinois. On the contrary I expressly informed them that I had no authority to act in the premises. It is proper however to state that I did inform them that my action would be modified in a great measure by the execution of such a release; that I was about to introduce a Bill for a grant of land for Rail Road from Lake Michigan to the Ohio River upon such line and to terminate at such point as the Legislature should prescribe;[7] that my object in this would be to secure the benefits of the grant to the State and at the same time keep them out of the hands of the Cairo City & Canal Co, unless the Legislature should hereafter choose to convey them to the Company; but that if the Company should determine to execute such a Release in due form so as to protect the rights & interests of the State in this respect I should provide for the grant on the line of the Central Rail Road with the Southern terminus at Cairo as now provided by law. Messrs Rockwell & Billings on the part of the company expressed their entire concurence in the reasonableness of these views and added their belief that the company would unhesitatingly execute the release in the form suggested as a measure beneficial to the interests of the State & Company both & essential to the securing of a grant of land from Congress. Thus the matter stood until yesterday when I received the release which I herewith enclose, executed in Duplicate, one copy of which I was requested to retain to be used if necessary in Congress and the other to forward to you as the executive of the State. I entertain the hope that this will remove many if not all of the obstacles in the way of securing the grant of land and making the Central Rail Road. I am assured that they have the prospect of making a favorable contract for the iron for the whole work and of commencing operations during the present season. I should repose implicit confidence in these assurances now if we had not been so often duped & disappointed before. But as the principal interest & control of the company is said to have passed into new hands it is possible that we are now authorized to hope that something is about to be accomplished. With this dessultory explanation of this transaction so far as I have any knowledge of it I enclose the Release to you as the Executive of the State. I have the honor to be very respectfully your friend & obedient servant

S. A. DOUGLAS

ALS Copy, owned by Martin F. Douglas.

[1] John A. Rockwell served as a Whig member of Congress from Connecticut from 1845 to 1849. Following his defeat for re-election, he assumed a law practice in Washington, D.C.

[2] The Cairo City and Canal Company was incorporated by the Illinois state legislature in 1837. The company was given the right to own and operate banks, manufacturing establishments, stores, hotels, and other enterprises. Following its incorporation, the company acquired several thousand acres of land at the junction of the Ohio and Mississippi rivers on which the city of Cairo was laid out. The dominant figure in the company was Darius B. Holbrook.

[3] In 1843, the Illinois legislature chartered the Great Western Railway Company, to be controlled by the officers of the Cairo City and Canal Company, with authority to construct and operate a railroad from Cairo to the Illinois and Michigan Canal. The Central Railroad Company was incorporated by the legislature in 1836 to build and operate a railroad from the Ohio River to Galena, with a branch line to Belleville. Sidney Breese, later United States Senator from Illinois, played a strong and active role in the creation of this company. To assist him in developing a central railroad, Breese chose Darius Holbrook, described as "a shrewd Boston Yankee." Holbrook, who later controlled both the Cairo Company and the Great Western, was Treasurer of the Central Railroad Company. The Great Western Railway Company was actually the central railroad project under a new name.

[4] After two years of inactivity by the company, the charter of the Great Western Railway Company was repealed by the legislature in 1845. In 1849, as the prospects for the construction of a central railroad brightened, the company was rechartered. While Congress debated Douglas' proposal for a land grant to aid in the central railroad, Holbrook induced the legislature to pass a resolution transferring to the Cairo City and Canal Company any lands granted to the state. Douglas became convinced that no land grant would be approved by Congress as long as Holbrook had this claim on the state, and he insisted that the state be released from the obligation.

[5] George W. Billings, of New York, also acted as the agent of a group of New York capitalists with whom Douglas was negotiating for carrying out the central railroad project. The group included Morris Ketchum, New York banker and locomotive manufacturer, reputed to be one of the ablest financiers in the country; George Griswold, New York merchant and shipowner; and Robert Schuyler, President of the New York and New Haven Railroad, and soon to become the first President of the Illinois Central Railroad.

[6] Douglas spoke in Chicago on October 4 to a meeting that had been called to appoint a delegation to the St. Louis railroad convention, held later in the month. His Springfield speech was delivered on October 23 in the Hall of Representatives.

[7] Douglas introduced his bill on January 3, 1850. For a discussion of Douglas' efforts to secure a land grant to aid in the central railroad, see below, Douglas to Breese, January 5, 1851.

To Asbury Dickens

My Dear Sir   [1849-52]

I had intended to have spoken to you in behalf of a colored man who has been waiting on me this winter. He desires to be employed as an additional Laboror & I am very anxious that he should get it. He is one of the best servants I ever knew. His name is Wallace & is know[n] to Gov. Whitcomb[1] & many other Senators who take an interest in him. I write from Bed as I can not move. Regards

S. A. DOUGLAS

ALS, owned by John Carlon, Rankin, Illinois. This letter was not dated, but since Senator James Whitcomb, mentioned in the letter, held his Senate seat from March 4, 1849, until his death on October 4, 1852, the letter must have been written between those dates. Asbury Dickens, of North Carolina, was first elected Secretary of the Senate on December 12, 1836, and held that office until March, 1861.

[1] James Whitcomb, with whom Douglas corresponded frequently when the former was Commissioner of the General Land Office, was Governor of Indiana from 1843 to 1849, and Senator from 1849 until his death in 1852.

To Charles H. Lanphier and George Walker

(*Private*)

Gentlemen   Washington Jan'y 7th 1850

Above you will find a slip I have cut from the "*Republic*" of this city of the 4th inst.[1] It is important as showing the position of Gen'l Shields upon the slavery-question. It seems that tho General Shields has written to Gen'l Quitman (Gov of Mississippi)[2] that it [is] "*a vile slander of his enemies*" to charge him with favoring the Proviso.[3] This charge must attach to Wentworth & the free soilers up north. How will they relish this? I only regret that Gen'l Quitman did not publish the whole of Gen'l Shields' letter. It is but fair that the people of Illinois should know the sentiments of their Senators upon this exciting subject. It is true that Gen'l Shields told me at St Louis that he agreed with me fully upon this question as my views were expressed in my speech at Springfield.[4] But the people do not know it. At the North he is understood one way & at the South the other. This letter to Gen'l Quitman fixes his position on the platform we all stand upon.

My impression is that we will all be together in favor of the admission of California as a State. I started the proposition at the beginning of last Session & then predicted that the people would decide against slavery if left to settle the question for themselves. The result has verified the prediction. Gen'l Cass expressed the same opinion I believe in his Nicholson Letter[5] & the whole Democratic Party of the North took the same ground. The free-soilers declared that slavery would go there unless, Congress prohibited it. The result has shown that we were right & they wrong. They now have to come to the support of our measure. Gen'l Cass will take strong ground in favor of the State admission of California & the Whigs & abolitions will be com-

[182]

pelled to follow suit. The people should not be allowed to forget these things. I am glad to see that you frequently remind the people of them.

Burn this hasty scrawl for I am ashamed of the resulting manner in which it is written. I remain very truly yours

S. A. DOUGLAS

[*Clipping attached to letter*]

GEN. SHIELDS ON THE WILMOT PROVISO.—The Vicksburg (Miss.) *Whig* announces, upon the authority of Gen. Quitman, Governor elect of Mississippi, that Gen. Shields is not a Free-Soiler, or in favor of the Wilmot proviso. In a letter to Gen. Quitman the Illinois Senator says, to charge him with proviso views *"is a vile slander of his enemies."*

Memphis Eagle.

We never made any such announcement. Gen. Quitman must have an enormous bump of credulity if he can believe what Shields is made to say in the above extract, since the recent canvass for Senator in Illinois, during which he pledged himself fully to the Free-Soil platform for the sake of obtaining Free-Soil votes.—*Vicksburg Whig.*

ALS, Illinois State Historical Library.

[1] The clipping, from the Washington *Republic*, January 4, 1850, was pasted at the top of the page; it is printed following this letter.

[2] John A. Quitman, after a long career in Mississippi state politics, was Governor of the state in 1850 and 1851. He had served in the Mexican War as a major general in the Regular Army.

[3] The Wilmot Proviso, which would prohibit slavery in all territory acquired from Mexico as a result of the Mexican War, was first introduced in the summer of 1846. Although it was not successful, it remained the subject of bit-ter controversy during the succeeding years.

[4] Douglas delivered a speech on the Wilmot Proviso in the Hall of Representatives at Springfield on October 23, 1849.

[5] Lewis Cass, in his letter to A. O. P. Nicholson, December 24, 1847, gave the first full expression to what later became known as popular sovereignty. With a view to defining his position for the forthcoming Presidential election of 1848, Cass declared that the question of slavery in the territories could only be decided by the territorial legislatures.

To William S. Prentice

My Dear Sir,   Washington Jan'y 16th 1850

Our friend Mr Young[1] informed me a few days since that he had received a letter from you in relation to the settlement of your accounts at the Treasury. I then explained the matter to him as I did to you in my letter of the 28th of December, which you have doubtless received sometime since. While at the Department today I called the attention of the secretary to the subject again & he furnished me the report of the clerk upon which his letter to you was predicated. As this report is more full than the secretary's letter, I send it also. I hope to receive the copy of your report soon so that I may have the matter closed. I shall be happy to hear from you often, and especially in the line of your new vocation.[2] My own mind has undergone material changes upon the nature & importance of our religious duties since I last saw you. Most heartily do I wish you success in your mission. You have my prayers for your success & may I venture to ask yours for my salvation. I remain very truly your friend

S. A. DOUGLAS

ALS, Illinois State Historical Library.

[1]Richard Montgomery Young, former Commissioner of the General Land Office, was elected clerk of the House of Representatives on April 17, 1850.

[2]In 1849, Prentice was licensed as a Methodist preacher.

To the Editors of the Chicago *Tribune*

Washington, Jan. 29, 1850.

Gentlemen:—I seldom correct the errors into which the press frequently fall, touching my political course, trusting to the people to do me justice in all cases where the sources of information are equally open to all. But I observe in a late number of your paper, an article censuring my course in the caucus, which assembled to arrange the senate committees, and charging me with having been actively instrumental in excluding Col. Benton from his former position as chairman of the committee on foreign relations, *on account of his opinions upon the slavery question.*[1] I know not who your correspondents are, upon whose authority this statement is made, nor is it material, as the caucus was held with closed doors, and the votes and speeches of each senator could have been witnessed only by the senators present. It is due to myself and my constituents, that I should make a brief statement of the facts, so far as they relate to my action, although I feel great delicacy in doing so, inasmuch as the caucus, as is usual in such cases, was held with closed doors. But as most of our proceedings have already found their way into the newspapers, and there can be no motive or desire for concealment, I will make the statement:

I was not present when the proposition was made to drop the name of Col. Benton from the committee on foreign relations, but entered the room during the discussion upon that question.—Inferring from what I heard upon the occasion, that some were in favor of excluding Col. Benton from the committee, on account of his speeches on the slavery question during the last season, I arose for the purpose of expressing my opinions upon the propriety of such a course. I insisted that the caucus had nothing to do with this local controversy in the state of Missouri—that the parties to it have appealed to their own constituents for a verdict of approval, each in his own favor against the other, and that it was unwise and improper for us to interfere one way or the other. I stated that my opinions upon this vexed question, were well known to all present, and remained unchanged, and that I must be permitted to act according to my own sense of duty, and settle the matter with my own constituents, leaving each other senator to do the same thing.

I desired to know whether Col. Benton was to be excluded merely because he believed that congress possessed the power to legislate upon the subject of slavery in the territories, when opposed to the exercise of the power. If so, the same rule would exclude me, and, indeed, every gentleman present who was a senator in August, 1848—that we had all, at some time and in some form, by way of compromise, or otherwise, voted for bills which affirmed the right of congress to legislate upon the subject of slavery in the territories, although most of us, like Col. Benton, thought it inexpedient and unwise to exercise the power.

If Col. Benton was to be excluded on this ground the rule must be extended to all others, and hence a democratic caucus would find itself in the same predicament of prescribing a test of faith, according to which no one of us would be competent to serve on committees as democrats. I also referred to the fact that the senator already selected, on my motion, as chairman of the committee on commerce, and the nominee for the chairman of the committee on public lands,[2] were known to be in favor of prohibiting slavery in the territories, and that many other senators entertaining similar opinions upon this subject, have already been assigned prominent positions upon the various committees; that, in fact, the whole list of committees have been formed without reference to the opinions of the persons composing them on the slavery question. Under these circumstances, I asserted that if Col. Benton was made an exception to the rule which was applied to other democratic senators, the blow aimed at him would assuredly recoil on the heads of those who gave it, and protested against the adoption of any rule which would make the slavery question a test of faith in the democratic party. This is the substance of what I said on that occasion. It is proper to remark that those who urged the exclusion of Col. Benton, denied that they did so because of his opinions on the slavery question; but insisted that he was agitating that question in Missouri unnecessarily, and in a manner calculated to destroy the democratic party, and therefore he should not be placed upon the committee as a democrat, having shown himself hostile to the unity and success of the party.

Subsequently it was proposed to place me upon the committee on Foreign Relations, instead of Col. Benton, to which I positively objected, adding, at the same time, that under other circumstances, I would prefer serving on that committee to any other in the Senate, yet I could not accept it to the exclusion of Col. Benton or any other senator, who had a prior and higher right to the place. The vote being taken, it was announced by the chair that I had received a majority; although I had voted for Col Benton. I therefore rose again and announced to the caucus, that although under other circumstances I would prefer a place on that committee to any other in the Senate, yet I could not consent to accept it, when my acceptance would exclude Col. B. from it. At a subsequent meeting of the caucus Col. Benton was placed upon the committee, although not as chairman, as I had desired. The reason assigned for leaving him off as chairman was, that he had made a formal request through a personal and political friend, that he should not be made chairman of any committee. Although he subsequently withdrew that request, the caucus having in the meantime selected another gentleman for chairman, was unwilling to make the change, and therefore assigned him a place as a member of the committee. From this statement you can judge how much credit is due to charges of your correspondent, that I acted a prominent part in excluding Col. Benton from the chairmanship of the committee of Foreign Relations. Had this transaction taken place with open doors, I should not have noticed the misrepresentions of your correspondent.

In conclusion, it is due to you, Messrs editors, that I acquit you of any intention to do me injustice. I am, very respectfully, Your obedient servant,

S. A. Douglas

Springfield *Illinois State Register*, February 14, 1850.

[1]Thomas Hart Benton was the senior member of the Senate Foreign Relations Committee during the Thirtieth Congress and hence next in line for the chairmanship. In December, 1849, following the opening of the Thirty-first Congress, however, he was passed over by the Democratic caucus in favor of Senator William R. King of Alabama.

[2]The chairmen of the Commerce and Public Lands committees were Senators Hannibal Hamlin of Maine and Alpheus Felch of Michigan, respectively.

To George W. Crawford

[February 14, 1850, Senate Chamber; ALS, RG-94, National Archives. Requests Secretary of War Crawford to approve the application of Peleg Green for a discharge from the Regular Army, "on account of his former services & his present age." The letter was endorsed by the War Department, "Peleg Green a private Compy. A 1st Infy Enlisted 6th Novr 46, for 5 years, and *Died* 17 Octr 49, at Eagle Pass, Texas."]

To James H. Woodworth

Washington, March 5, 1850.

My Dear Sir: I have just received a Chicago paper containing the proceedings of a meeting held on the 21st ult., 'to express their opinions against the extension of slavery,' over which you had the honor to preside.[1] I have read the proceedings carefully, and may truly add, with interest and instruction. From the names attached to the call, and those who appear to have participated in the proceedings, I infer that the meeting must have embraced a large portion of the intelligence and moral worth of the city. It is natural that I should feel a lively and abiding interest in the proceedings of a meeting thus constituted, all being my constituents, and many, my most cherished personal friends. I will add, that I have been enlightened by one of the resolutions, as I have no doubt the United States Senate will be, when it shall be presented to that body. I refer to the following resolution, that being the only one that refers to me specially, and in terms which do not apply equally to my colleagues in the two houses of congress.

"Resolved, that the proposition recently presented by Hon. S. A. Douglas to the senate of the U. States, for the creation of a new state, out of, as yet, the unsettled portions of the territory of Texas, to be admitted into the Union concurrently with California, and also to provide territorial governments for New Mexico and Deseret, which shall leave them open to the introduction of slavery as the basis of a "compromise" with the slave states, is subversive of the true principles of the constitution, and a violation of the wishes and feelings of the people, of this state and the instructions of the legislature, whose expressed will, it is his duty to obey or resign."[2]

I was not aware until I saw the important fact published in the Chicago papers, and now solemnly affirmed in this resolution, that I had introduced into the senate, or even given notice of the introduction of any bill upon the subject referred to—much less one of the character described in the resolution. I was aware that Gen. Foote of Mississippi[3] had introduced such a bill in the early part of the session, and by a vote of the senate was referred to the committee on Territories, of which I am so unfortunate as to be chairman. I am also aware that Col. Benton had introduced a bill for the "creation of a new state, out of, as yet, the unsettled portions of Texas," to use the emphatic language of the resolution, and that this bill was also referred to the committee on Territories.—These facts were known to me and to the senate.—They have been the subject of conversation and consultation, but it happens that the committee on Territories have never come to any conclusion on either of them, nor have they made any report upon the subject.

The facts set forth in the resolution, therefore, will be interesting to the senate when presented to that body, and it may be deemed of sufficient importance to have the journal of the senate corrected, so as to conform to the facts set forth in the resolution.

To be serious about the matter, it has been to me a subject of curiosity and conjecture how a certain description of information concerning myself finds its way into the daily papers of Chicago, before it has any existence elsewhere; and that other measures in which the people may be supposed to have some interest, are known and published everywhere else, except Chicago. In the first class of cases may be noticed the proceedings of the secret caucuses of senators, in which it is represented that I had taken active part in excluding Col. Benton from the committees on account of his slavery notions; and now follows Senator Douglas' compromise for a new slave state in Texas, slave territory in Deseret, New Mexico, &c.

While those things are paraded day after day in all the daily papers, it seems never to have been ascertained by any paper, that I have introduced a bill to secure the Free Navigation of the St. Lawrence, and have high hopes of its passage, and only one of our daily papers, so far as I have noticed, has ever informed its readers that I had brought bills for a grant of land to the Central Railroad, and for the continuation of the Chicago and Galena Railroad, with a railroad bridge across the Mississippi at Dubuque, to the Red River of the north, or for a grant of about 200,000 acres of land for the purpose of making a geological survey of our state. These bills do not seem to have been of sufficient importance to require a passing notice, nor does the bill to grant 160 acres of land to actual settlers who shall reside thereon and cultivate a portion thereof, for the period of four years.

But a studied suppression of all I say and do upon the slavery questions and the constant publication of what I have neither said nor done, seems to be the daily announcement in which the city press indulges, so far as as I am concerned. I have determined from the beginning of this session that if this course was continued towards me, it should not be my fault, and consequently have sent regularly to each of the daily papers of Chicago copies of all the bills and reports of every description which I have introduced this session.

You are at liberty to hand this letter over to any of the editors in Chicago who you think will publish it. Perhaps the Tribune will do so, for I am free to say, that that paper has shown more disposition to deal fairly with me, than any other paper in the city.

In conclusion, I will remark that I entertain no sentiment of unkindness towards any gentleman on account of the resolution. I am aware that the meeting was deceived and imposed upon by those whose business it has been to misrepresent my acts for the last two years. I have the honor to remain, very truly, your friend,

S. A. DOUGLAS

Springfield *Illinois State Register*, March 28, 1850. James H. Woodworth, former member of the state legislature, was Democratic Mayor of Chicago for two terms. In 1854 he was elected to Congress as a Republican.

[1]The effort to discover a solution to the problem of slavery in the newly acquired Mexican cession and to reach a compromise between the slave and free states on this and other issues occupied much of the attention of Congress during the session of 1849-50. Meetings were held in many Illinois communities endorsing these compromise attempts or condemning them in favor of the Wilmot Proviso, which would exclude slavery forever from this new area. Mayor Woodworth pre-

sided over a "nonpartisan" free-soil meeting at the Chicago city hall on February 21, 1850. Resolutions were adopted opposing any compromise that would allow the further extension of slavery, and supporting the Wilmot Proviso. From the tone of the meeting, many observers concluded that it was the work primarily of Douglas' opponents.

[2]The Illinois state legislature passed resolutions on January 3, 1849, endorsing the Wilmot Proviso and instructing the Illinois delegation in Congress to support it. The resolutions were rescinded in 1851.

[3]Henry Stuart Foote, Senator from Mississippi.

To George W. Crawford

Senate Chamber
Sir,   March 8th 1850

In accordance with a memorial of the Legislature of the Territory of Minnesota I have introduced a Bill, which is now pending before the Committee on Territories, for reducing the limits of the Military Reservation at Fort Snelling & to protect the rights of the settlers thereon.[1] I have since understood that a mi[li]tary order had been issued for the sale of those lands. Permit me respectfully to suggest to you the propriety of giving Congress an opportunity of doing justice to the settlers on the lands by law before their farms & improvements are sold from under them.[2] I have the honor to be very respectfully your obedient servt

S. A. DOUGLAS

ALS, RG-94, National Archives.

[1]Douglas' bill, "An Act to reduce and define the boundaries of the military reserve at St. Peter's river, in the Territory of Minnesota, and to secure the

rights of the actual settlers thereon," was introduced on March 1, 1850.

[2]The letter is endorsed by Crawford, "Order of sale to be suspended as requested."

To Charles H. Lanphier

(*Confidential*)   Washington
Dear Sir,   August 3d 1850

I herewith send you a manuscript in strict confidence. If you deem it wise & prudent you can modify it to suit you & copy it & publish it editorially. I leave it entirely to your dicression, but to be shown to no one else. I desire you to destroy this copy in my hand writing. You have doubtless seen the article in the Quincy Whig to which I refer.[1] It will undoubtedly by published in all Whig & abolition papers in the state. You can rely implicitly upon the law of the case as stated in the article I send, can find the laws of Mississippi to the same effect [in] the office of Secy of State. I believe the article was got up in Springfield or by Baker here & sent to Bledsoe who formerly edited the Journal & now is a professor in a college in Miss.[2] I am not certain on this point so it will not do to charge it direct. It is true that my wife does own about 150 negroes in Miss & a cotton plantation. My father-in-law in his lifetime offered them to me & I refused to accept them. *This fact is stated in his will*, but I do not wish it brought before the public as the public have no business with my private affairs, and besides everybody would see that the information must have come from me. My wife has no negroes except those in Miss. We have other property in North Carolina, but no negroes. It is our intention however to remove all our property to Illinois as soon as possible. I put these facts in your possession & trust entirely to your discretion.

I will close this letter here & write you another by this mail about politics.[3] Your friend

S. A. DOUGLAS

The Quincy Whig & other Whig papers are publishing an article purporting to be copied from a Mississippi paper abusing Judge Douglas as the owner of 100 slaves and at the same time accusing him of being a Wilmot Freesoiler. That the article originated in this state, & was sent to Mississippi for publication in order that it might be republished here we shall not question nor take the trouble to prove. The paternity of the article, the malice that prompted it, and the misrepresentations it contains are too obvious to require particular notice. If it had been written by a Mississippian he would have known that the statement in regard to the ownership of the Negroes was totally untrue. No one will pretend that Judge Douglas has any other property in Mississippi than that which was acquired in the right of his wife by inheritance upon the death of her father, and any one who will take the trouble to examine the Statutes of that State in the Secretarys office in this city will find that by the laws of Mississippi all the property of a married woman, whether acquired by will, gift, or otherwise, becomes her separate & exclusive estate & is not subject to the control or disposal of her husband nor subject to his debts. We do not pretend to know whether the father of Mrs Douglas at the time of his death owned slaves in Mississippi or not. We have heard the statement made by the Whigs but have not deemed it of sufficient importance to inquire into its truth. If it should turn out so in no event could Judge Douglas become the owner or have the disposal of or be responsible for them. The laws of the State forbid it, and also forbid slaves under such circumstances from being removed without or emancipated within the limits of the State. But our chief object in refering to the article in question was to correct a gross misrepresentation in regard to Judge Douglas's opinions upon the slavery question. He is charged with pretending to be a Free-Soiler & a Wilmot Proviso man. There is not a man in the [country?] who does not know this charge to be utterly false. He always voted against the Wilmot Proviso from the time it was first introduced in the House until it was finally killed in the Senate by the ratification of the treaty. He has always advocated the right of the people in each State and Territory to decide the slavery question for themselves. When he voted for the prohibition of slavery in the territorial Bills this Session he declared that he did so in obedience to instructions & that the vote was the vote of those who gave the instructions and not his own. His opinions & principles have been uniform & consistent upon this question. The Whigs combined with the Free-Soilers to pass the instructions and now denounce him for yielding obedience according to the usages & principles of the Democratic Party.

ALS, Illinois State Historical Library.
[1] The Quincy *Whig*, July 23, 1850, reprinted an article from the Jackson *Mississippian*, entitled "Hon. S. A. Douglass the Owner of Slaves."
[2] Albert Taylor Bledsoe was a professor of mathematics at the University of Mississippi. He was formerly a resident of Springfield, Illinois.
[3] See below, Douglas to Lanphier and Walker, August 3, 1850.

To Charles H. Lanphier and George Walker

(*Private*)   Washington
Dr Sirs   Aug 3d 1850
     You have doubtless heard of the defeat of the Compromise of the Committee of thirteen. I regrett it very much, altho I must say that I never had very strong hopes of its passage. By combining the measures into one Bill the Committee united the opponents of each measure instead of securing the friends of each.[1] I have thought from the beginning that they made a mistake in this respect. I declined being a member of the committee of 13 for this reason & for the same reason opposed the appointment of the committee. It was as well known before the committee were appointed what they were to do as after they reported. I had previously written & Reported as chairman of the Com on Territories two Bills—one for the admission of California & the other providing territorial Governments for Utah & New Mexico also providing for the settlement of the Texas Boundary. Before I reported

these Bills I consulted Mr Clay & Gen'l Cass whether I should put them in one or separate Bills. They both advised me to keep them separate & both expressed the same opinions in debate about that time. I took their advice & reported the measures in two Bills instead of one. About two weeks afterwards they changed their minds & concluded to appoint a committee for the purpose of uniting them. I opposed the movement as unwise & unnecessary, as they declared they did not intend to change any feature in my Bills. The Committee was appointed & took my two printed Bills & put a wafer between & Reported them back without changing or writing a single word, except one line. The one line inserted prohibited the Territorial Legislatures from Legislating upon the subject of slavery. This amendment was voted in by the Com in opposition to the wishes of Gen'l Cass & Mr Clay, and they gave notice that they should move to strike it out in the Senate & it was stricken out. So you see that the diference between Mr Clay's Compromise Bill & my two Bills was a wafer, & that he did not write one word of it & that I did write every word. After a majority of the Senate decided that they would act upon the measures jointly instead of separately I gave the Bill of Mr Clay my active & unwavering support down to its final defeat. The same remark is true of my colleage Gen'l Shields, and it is also proper to remark that all our Representatives, except Baker[2] & Wentworth were anxious for the passage of the Bill & were ready to support it if it passed the Senate. It is true Col McClernand at one time thought that he could get up a better one, but soon gave it up. His Bill was substantially the same as Mr Clays, differing a little in the details.[3] The Compromise Bill was defeated by a union between the Free Soils & disun[ion]ists & the administration of Gen'l Taylor. All the power & patronage of the Govt was brought to bear against us, & at last the allied forces were able to beat us. The Utah Bill has passed the Senate in the precise words in which I wrote it.[4] We are now ingaged on my California Bill & I trust you will hear of its passage through the Senate before you receive this. We shall then take up a Bill for the Texas Boundary which Mr Pearce of Md[5] & myself are now preparing & he will introduce on Monday next. We shall then take up the Bill for New Mexico & pass it just as I reported it four months ago. Thus will all the Bills pass the Senate & I believe the House also.[6] When they are all passed you see they will be collectively Mr Clays compromise, & separately the Bills Reported by the committee on Territories four months ago. Col Benton has done much to delay action & to defeat all the measures. In my opinion no justification—no excuse can be made for his conduct.[7] On the other hand I must say that if Mr Clays name had not been associated with the Bills they would have passed long ago. The administration were jealous of him & hated

[192]

him & the some democrats were weak enough to fear that the success of his Bill would make him President. But let it always be said of old Hal that he fought a glorious & a patriotic battle. No man was ever governed by higher & purer motives. The same remark is true of Gen'l Cass. Many of our friends talk hard of Buchanan. It is supposed that he encouraged the nullifiers & disunionists to oppose the measure out of jealousy of Gen'l Cass.[8] I hope this will turn out not to be true. I have now given you a pretty full history of the compromise—of its rise and fall. We have great confidance that we will yet be able to settle the whole difficulty before we adjourn. Excuse this long epistle. Your friend

S. A. DOUGLAS

ALS, Illinois State Historical Library.

[1]The Committee of Thirteen had been formed by the United States Senate early in 1850 to receive and consider all proposals and resolutions designed to compromise the issue of the extension of slavery to the territories acquired from Mexico. Henry Clay was appointed chairman of the committee. On May 8, 1850, Clay presented the committee's recommendations, one of which was a bill combining Douglas' earlier measures for the admission of California as a free state and the organization of Utah and New Mexico territories, with one for the adjustment of the Texas boundary. Two other bills, for a fugitive slave act and for the abolition of the slave trade in the District of Columbia, were also proposed by the committee. Debate over the committee's recommendations waxed hot until July 31, when the California and territorial proposal, known familiarly as the "omnibus" bill, was defeated.

[2]Edward Dickinson Baker, Whig Representative from Illinois, had been elected a second time in 1848 and served a single term. In 1851, he moved to California.

[3]John A. McClernand had acted as Douglas' counterpart in the House of Representatives. In February, McClernand proposed that he sponsor bills for the organization of Utah and New Mexico territories on the basis of popular sovereignty, assuming that California should be admitted as a free state. It was understood at the time that

Douglas would follow a similar course in the Senate. Protracted debate in the House over the admission of California, however, prevented McClernand from realizing his objective.

[4]The "omnibus" bill was defeated on July 31 by striking out all its sections except those which provided for the organization of Utah Territory. On August 1, the Utah bill passed the Senate.

[5]James A. Pearce, Whig Senator from Maryland. The Texas boundary question was related to the organization of New Mexico Territory, since that territory, as envisioned, would include within its boundaries an area claimed by Texas. In the final result, Texas was compensated for its loss of area by the assumption of the Texas debt by the national government.

[6]Douglas' forecast was accurate. By the middle of September, the compromise bills had been passed, largely due to Douglas' direction. The compromise acts, known as the Compromise of 1850, admitted California as a free state, organized Utah and New Mexico territories on the basis of popular sovereignty, adjusted the Texas boundary, abolished the slave trade in the District of Columbia, and provided a new and more stringent fugitive slave law.

[7]Benton had opposed Clay's "omnibus" bill and favored a separate bill to admit California as a free state.

[8]Buchanan supported the compromise measures, however.

To George Walker and Charles H. Lanphier

Private   Senate U.S.

Messers Walker & Lanphier.   Sept 5th 1850

I send you a copy of the Globe containing the debate on the Bounty land Bill which passed the Ho of Reps some days ago.[1] In the shape in which the Bill passed the House of Reps none of the volunteers from our State in the Black Hawk war & various other Indian wars would have received any land. They would all have been excluded by the limit of *three* months service instead of *one* month. My first amendment which was adopted gives 40 acres of land to all of those soldiers & volunteers.[2] The Bill will undoubtedly pass in its present shape. You will find the passages marked in the paper which will explain the whole matter.

The Ho of Reps yesterday Killed off the Texas boundary Bill by 46 Majority, but the Bill will come to life today again. They will reconsider, & probably adopt Boyd's[3] amendment & then pass the Bill. Boyd's amendment is a literal copy of my Bill for New Mexico as it passed the Senate. He got me to prepare it for him as he was not so familiar with the subject. I sent you a day or two ago a paper containing some remarks of mine made in June last which I do not recollect to have seen published in any Illinois paper. I allude to the few remarks in which I declared my firm adhearance to *non-intervention* on the slavery question and that any vote which I had or might give inconsistent with that principle *was not my vote*, but *the vote of those who gave the instructions*.[4] I desire the people to know that I made this declaration at the time I gave the vote & repeated it afterwards. Please publish those remarks as they are very brief. I remain very truly your friend

S. A. DOUGLAS

ALS, Illinois State Historical Library.

[1] The Bounty Land Bill, providing for veterans of the War of 1812 and the various Indian wars that followed, passed the House of Representatives on June 24, 1850.

[2] Douglas' amendment was adopted by the Senate on September 2.

[3] Representative Linn Boyd of Kentucky.

[4] Douglas' "Remarks in Reply to Senators Bell and Dawson on Mr. Bradbury's Resolution, June 4, 1850" were published in pamphlet form. Bradbury's resolution would require President Taylor to give Congress his reasons for the removal of any officeholders since March 4, 1849. John Bell, of Tennessee, and William C. Dawson, of Georgia, opposed the resolution in the Senate, the latter making a personal attack on Douglas in the course of his debate.

To Daniel Webster

[September 7, 1850, Senate Chamber; ALS, RG-59, National Archives. Requesting papers relating to the case of Anthony Ten Eyck, United

States Commissioner to the Sandwich Islands. Douglas wrote as a member of the Senate Committee on Foreign Relations. Webster was Secretary of State. Ten Eyck, a Detroit, Michigan, lawyer, was Commissioner to the Sandwich Islands from 1841 to 1843. On September 27, 1850, a bill was introduced in Congress to grant Ten Eyck over $5,000 for his services in Hawaii.]

To W. W. Corcoran

(*Private*)   Senate Chamber
My Dear Sir,   Sept 10th 1850
 I think the time has arrived for purchasing those Illinois Bonds according to the understanding between us. I fix no limit to the amount, for I am satisfied that it is a good investment, and consequently desire as many as you are willing to purchase & hold for me. I remain very truly your friend

S. A. DOUGLAS

ALS, Library of Congress.

To Ebenezer Peck

Senate U.S.
My Dear Sir,   Sept 14th 1850
 I have the pleasure herewith to forward the letter of appointment of Charles[1] as a midshipman in the Navy. You will observe that it will be necessary for him to report himself at Annapolis Md on the 1st day of Oct or within five days thereafter. This is a short notice, but I trust that he will be able to comply with it. I regret the delay in making this appointment, but I could not get it sooner, & had some difficulty in getting it [at] all. I remain very truly your obt servt

S. A. DOUGLAS

ALS, owned by Charles F. Peck, South Windham, Vermont.
[1]Charles Peck was the son of Ebenezer Peck.

To Asbury Dickens

Thursday Sept 26th 1850
Mr Dickens will please send me fifty dollars by my Servant Johnson & I will sign the Recipt for it as soon as I am able to leave my Bed.

S. A. DOUGLAS

ALS, owned by Martin F. Douglas.

To Howell Cobb

Washington
Sept 28th 1850

My Dear Sir,

Permit me to introduce to you Doct Duane A Holden of Ontario County N.Y. He is about to remove to your State with the view of practicing his profession. He has been the family phician of some of my nearest relatives in New York and they have recommended him to me as a gentleman and phicician of high standing, and a man of strict honor and in all respects worthy of confidence. I do not hesitate therefore to commend him to you and to all other friends of mine he may happen to meet and to ask for him your kind affairs and attention.

Any attentions shown him will be thankfully received by him gratefully acknowledged by your friend & obedient

S. A. Douglas

To Hon Howell Cobb and such other friends as this may be presented

ALS, William L. Clements Library. Howell Cobb, Representative from Georgia, was Speaker of the House of Representatives.

To Charles H. Lanphier

Washington
Oct 2d 1850

My Dear Sir,

I was confined to my bed when your letter was received together with Walkers & have been ever since. My general health is good but I have suffered much with a very bad *Abcess* in the hip which I have had cut open to the depth of an inch & a half. It is now getting well. Altho I cannot sit up I shall start home tomorrow & hope to be in Illinois before the middle of the month. You have already heard of the passage of the Central Rail Road Bill.[1] Had you not better call on the Governor & get the release of the Cairo City Co of all their chartered rights & publish it? Holbrook will try to get the Legislature not to accept the release with the hope of getting all the lands granted by Congress for his own proffit. He told me so a few days ago. Those lands should all be applied to the payment of the State debt after making the Road. The Lands will make the Road & pay the State debt both. Every candidate for the Legislature should be made to *pledge* himself before election to go for accepting the release so as to secure the lands to the State. The character of the State depends upon it. It would *disgrace* the whole delegation in Congress to have Holbrook cheat the State out of those bonds. We *pledged* ourselves to both Houses of Congress that the lands would go to the State & not to the Holbrook Company. I have furnished copies of the Release for publication in New

[196]

York & at Home. Everything now depends upon the action of our Legislature.[2]

I will be in Springfield as soon as possible. Your friend

S. A. DOUGLAS

ALS, Illinois State Historical Library.

[1] The Illinois Central Railroad Bill passed the House on September 17, 1850, and became law on September 20. The act provided for a grant of land to Illinois to aid in the construction of the railroad. The route, as finally agreed upon, was from the Ohio River to the Illinois and Michigan Canal, with branches to Chicago and through Galena to Dunleith, opposite Dubuque, Iowa. An amendment to the act provided for the continuation of the railroad from the mouth of the Ohio to the Gulf of Mexico at Mobile, Alabama, and similar grants of land were made to Alabama and Mississippi for this purpose.

[2] On February 17, 1851, a bill of the Illinois legislature accepting Holbrook's release was signed into law.

To the Citizens of Chicago

[October, 1850]

It would afford us sincere pleasure to meet you at the festive board, and there, in the freedom of social intercourse, discuss the measures of the late session of congress, and particularly those having an immediate bearing upon the prosperity and welfare of our state. But we regret that the short time allowed us for visiting our constituents, and our private engagements consequent upon our long absence from home, will compel us to forego this gratification. This manifestation, however, of partiality and regard from so numerous and influential a body of our constituents of both political parties, is peculiarly gratifying to our feelings. But it would be unjust to our colleagues of the house of representatives, one and all, to accept and appropriate this work of distinction—exclusively to our selves. To them is due, so far as our state is concerned, the entire credit of the passage of the measures in the house, to which you refer.

Their talents, energy, and unanimity, and their influence with their fellow members from other states, operated to insure success. Whatever merit, therefore, your partiality may award to us for our efforts in the senate, equal merit at least, is justly due to them for their efforts in the house.—Our state has been peculiarly fortunate in having obtained such a munificent grant of land during such an arduous and exciting session.

This grant, if judiciously managed, will not only insure the speedy completion of one of the most gigantic enterprises of the age—a direct line of communication from Mobile on the Gulf of Mexico to Chicago on the northern lakes, and Galena on the Upper Mississippi—but will enable our state to fulfil its obligations and extinguish its debt without being compelled to resort to onerous and oppressive taxation. This grant has been made to our state in a spirit of liberality, for the use and benefit of the people, and is specially dedicated to a specific object. Congress has reposed a generous confidence in our legislature to enforce the faithful execution of this trust, and we are sure this confidence is not destined to be abused.

Springfield *Illinois State Register*, October 24, 1850. Only an extract of the complete letter, written by both Douglas and Shields, was printed in the *Register*. When Douglas and Shields returned to Illinois from Congress, after having secured the passage of the Illinois Central Railroad Act, they were invited to celebrate the occasion by many public groups. This extract was from their reply to one such invitation.

To Sidney Breese

MY DEAR SIR: WASHINGTON, *January* 5, 1851.
   I have been amused, interested, and instructed, by the perusal of your letter of the 13th ultimo, to the editors of the *State Register*, in relation to the grant of lands for the Central railroad.[1] You seem to be apprehensive that *"these fellows who are making such an ado about it now, and have been whipped into its support,"* will have the presumption to call in question your title to the sole credit of the passage of the grant of land by Congress at the last session. I trust I will be able to convince you that your fears upon this subject are entirely groundless. Whatever injustice may have been done you in this respect, I am sure was wholly unintentional. It is true that, when the people of Chicago tendered to General Shields and myself, upon our return home last fall, a public dinner, for our supposed agency and services in obtaining that grant, we, in our letter declining the honor, awarded the principal merit to our colleagues of the House of Representatives, where the final battle was fought, and mentioned each of them by name, as the persons to whom the chief credit was due. I assure you, that had we been aware of the facts, as modestly stated in your letter, that you originated the project in 1835—that you had devoted more than fifteen years of your life to its accomplishment—that you had passed three different bills in the Senate in aid of its construction—that the arguments contained in your reports had silenced all opposition, and rendered its passage easy—that you claimed for yourself the exclusive credit, and seriously doubted whether either of the Senators or Representatives from our State was in favor of the passage of the bill, we should not have committed so great a blunder as to have attributed any portion of the merit to our colleagues in the other house.[2] In order to relieve your mind from all injurious suspicions, and to satisfy you that I have not intentionally done you injustice, I feel it my duty to go somewhat in detail into the history of the measure, and ex-

plain the reasons for supposing that others, as well as yourself, had sincerely desired the passage of the bill of last session, and really have contributed, in some degree, to its success. We entered Congress together in December, 1843; you a Senator and I a member of the House. On the 27th of that month, you presented a memorial of the "Great Western Railway Company," praying the right of a pre-emption for Mr. Holbrook and his associates, to a portion of the public lands over which this contemplated road was proposed to be run. This memorial, on your motion, was referred to the committee on public lands, and on the 23d of February, 1844, Mr. Woodbridge, of Michigan,[3] as a member of that committee, reported a bill in pursuance of the prayer of the memorial, "to grant to the Great Western Railroad Company the right of way through the public lands of the United States, and for other purposes." This bill, if my recollection serves me right, was prepared by yourself, and shown to me before it was reported from the committee. You urged Col. McClernand and myself, and, I presume, other members of the delegation, to give it our countenance and support, which we declined to do, and gave you our reasons. We insisted, in the first place, that whatever grant was made for railroads in our State, should be conferred upon the State of Illinois, and not upon an irresponsible private corporation. We had no faith in Mr. Holbrook and his associates—none in their ability to make the road—nor in their purpose to make a serious effort for its construction. We believed the object was to enable Mr. Holbrook and his associates to sell their charter, with the preëmption attached, for a large amount in Europe, where their value, or rather their worthlessness, was unknown, and then abandon the whole concern. We urged, that the effect of the measure would be to suspend the land sales, and consequently prevent the settlement of the country for the period of ten years, without the slightest hope of securing the construction of the road, at the same time that it would deprive us of any chance of procuring a grant of land to the State to aid in the construction of that important work. For these reasons, and perhaps others, which have now escaped my recollection, we endeavored to impress upon you the inutility of such a scheme, and suggested the alternative of introducing into the Senate a bill making a donation of land to the State to aid in the construction of the Central railroad. You declined the suggestion, however, and persevered in pressing your bill for the benefit of the Holbrook company through the Senate, upon the ground that a preëmption right to the company would answer all the purposes as well as a grant to the State, and that there was not the least reason to hope that such a donation could be obtained.

At the next session, to wit, on the 12th of December, 1844, you introduced the same bill, or one similar to it in its provisions, with the exception, that you inserted the words "the State of Illinois," instead of the Holbrook company, as the party to which the preëmption right was to be given. You were kind enough to inform me that you had made this alteration in deference to my opinion, and to avoid the objection to making grants to private corporations. This bill, on your motion, was referred to the committee on public lands; and on the 23d of January, 1845, was reported back by Mr. Woodbridge, with an amendment. I cannot recollect, nor can I learn from the journal, that you ever moved to take up the bill for action, or attempted to pass it.

At the next session, to wit, on the 15th January, 1846, you introduced a bill to grant to the State of Illinois certain alternate sections of the public lands, to aid in the construction of the Northern, Cross, and Central railroads in said State. This bill was referred to the committee on public lands, of which you had become chairman, and on the 24th February was reported back by you, with certain amendments, and accompanied by a special report. I suppose that this is one of the reports to which you refer in your letter, when you say, "it was the argument contained in my [your][4] reports on it that silenced all opposition, and made its passage easy." I add my testimony to your own, in respect to the ability of your report, and the soundness of your arguments, and am sure they must have had the effect to silence all opposition; and I only regret that after you had "made its passage easy," you should have allowed it to sleep in silence the sleep of death, without ever moving to take it up or asking the Senate to vote upon it. I have carefully examined the journals and minutes, in connexion with one of the officers of the Senate, and find that the record sustains my recollections that you never moved to take up that bill from the day you first reported it.

At the next session, to wit, on the 17th December, 1846, you introduced a bill for the right of way and a pre-emption right, omitting the donations to the State to aid in making the road. This bill was also referred to the committee of public lands, and on the fourth of January reported back, with an amendment, accompanied by a report from yourself. It does not appear, however, that it was ever acted upon by the Senate, much less passed, notwithstanding your report "silenced all opposition, and rendered its passage easy."

I do not regard the failure to urge the passage of this bill a very great misfortune, however, inasmuch as it would only have allowed the State to enter the lands at one dollar and a quarter per acre, upon the further condition that we would make a railroad through them.

I have now brought down the history of this question to the period when I became your colleague in the Senate. Although you had introduced several bills at different times, you had never seriously urged the passage of but one, and that was a bill to grant a pre-emption right to the Holbrook Company instead of a donation to the State. The difference between us at this time was precisely the same it had been during the preceding four years. You were the champion of the policy of granting pre-emption rights for the benefit of a private company, and I was the advocate of alternate sections to the State to aid in the construction of the roads. During the summer of 1847, after I had been elected to the Senate, but before the time had arrived for taking my seat, I travelled over a considerable portion of the State; and, wherever I went, I told my friends that I should insist upon a *donation* instead of a pre-emption, and that the grant should be made to *the State* in lieu of the Holbrook Company. You can learn, if you will take the trouble to inquire of the Hon. Thomas Dwyer, who is now a member of legislature with you,[5] that, in the month of September of that year, I urged him, and many other citizens of Chicago, to hold public meetings and send on memorials in favor of a donation of land to the State to aid in the construction of a central railroad, and in favor of one terminus at Chicago. It was necessary that the road should connect with the Lakes, in order to impart nationality to the project, and secure northern and eastern votes. The old line from Galena to Cairo,[6] parallel to the Mississippi, with both termini resting upon that stream, was regarded by our eastern friends as purely sectional, calculated to throw the whole trade upon the Gulf of Mexico at the expense of the cities on the Lakes and the Atlantic seaboard.

By making an additional terminus at Chicago, it would connect the lower Mississippi with the Lakes, the St. Lawrence with the Gulf of Mexico, and the upper Mississippi valley with both. I urged these considerations wherever I went, not doubting that I should convince you of their force when we should meet at the Capitol. When we arrived in this city, I had an interview with you upon the subject, before the two Houses organized, and explained my views to you in full. You treated me and my opinions with kindness and frankness, but at the same time insisted that your old plan of a pre-emption right was advisable, under all the circumstances, in preference to a grant of lands to the State. It is but just to you to say, that I did not understand you as being opposed to a grant of lands to our State, but you had no faith in the possibility of accomplishing it, and therefore thought it idle to make the effort. You were also kind enough to show me a bill which you had already prepared for a pre-emption right, and to read me a very elaborate report which you had written in vacation in behalf of your bill. I still urged you to modify your bill and change your report, so as to make it correspond with the bill as modified. I assured you that

I had no desire to take the lead in the matter, nor even have my name connected with it. That inasmuch as I was elected for six years, and your re-election would come off at the end of two years, I was anxious that you should become the author of the measure, and take full credit for its success; but I could not consent to go into a struggle where success would be defeat, and the attainment of it would be of no manner of service to our constituents.

You will, doubtless, recollect that we had several other interviews upon the subject, between that time and the 20th of the month, in which the same points were discussed, and the arguments *pro* and *con* recapitulated, without being able to harmonize our conflicting opinions, and it was finally agreed that each should pursue his own course. At length, on the 20th of December, ('47,) you introduced your old pre-emption bill, and had it referred to the committee on public lands. Subsequently, Messrs. E. B. Washburn and O. C. Pratt,[7] of Galena, called to see me at my rooms, at Willard's Hotel, and I explained to them the points of difference between us. They will do me the justice to say, if they recollect the conversation, that I spoke of you in terms of kindness and respect, and regretted our inability to harmonize our action upon this question, as a misfortune which I was anxious to avoid. I showed them at the same time a memorial which I had just received from Chicago, in favor of a grant to the State, with a letter from J. Butterfield, esq.,[8] informing me that active steps had been taken to procure petitions from all parts of the State in support of the application. Those gentlemen were delighted with the movement, and seemed amazed that you should give any other the preference, especially in direct opposition to the instructions of our legislature, which you had presented to the United States Senate on the 22d of February previous.[9] They told me that they would call upon you next morning, before the Senate met, and urge you to give your support to this plan, for the good of the State, in preference to a pre-emption, for the benefit of the Holbrook Company. I authorized them to say to you that if you would yet change your bill, in this respect, I would not introduce my own, but would support yours, and thus enable you to reap the whole credit of the measure. I still had hope that you would modify your bill and views, in this respect, and enable us to act together for the good of our constituents. On the next day, (January 20), about 12 o'clock, when the Senate was just assembling, I approached you at your desk, under the impression that Messrs. Washburn and Pratt had had their interview with you, and again asked you to change your bill into a donation to the State, which you promptly, but in a kind and respectful manner, refused to do. I then went to my own seat, and, in a few minutes, introduced my bill, for a grant of land to the State, which was then read a first and second time, and, on my motion, referred to the committee on public lands; and, on the 24th day of January, was reported back without amendment; and on the 29th day of April, on my motion, was taken up, and by order of the Senate made the special order for Wednesday, the 3d of May; and on the 4th of May, ('48) on my motion, was considered in the committee of the whole, read a third time, passed the Senate by a large majority, and sent to the House for their concurrence. It must not be inferred from these facts taken from the record that you were opposed to the bill. Such an inference would be as unjust as it is unfounded. I recollect distinctly, a few minutes after I introduced the bill, of seeing you in animated conversation with Messrs. Pratt and Washburn, and that you came directly from them to me, and expressed the regret that I had introduced the bill, and said that you were willing to change your own to suit my wishes. I told you that it was now too late to do that, but as my bill had been referred to the committee on public lands, of which you were chairman, you could take the report which you had prepared in behalf of your pre-emption bill, strike out the words "pre-emption rights," wherever they appeared, and insert the words "grant of lands to the State" in their place, and with a few other slight amendments, the report would fit my bill as well as yours. You agreed to this suggestion, and, for the time being, abandoned your pre-emption scheme, and on the 21st of January you reported back my bill, without amendment, accompanied with your report, so modified as to suit its provisions. Fourteen days afterwards, to wit, on the 7th Feb., you, as chairman of the same committee, reported favorably upon your pre-emption bill, and placed it upon the calendar in competition with my bill for the grant of lands.

I complained of this as being calculated to defeat the donation to the State; that we could hardly expect Congress to make our State a donation of lands while one of our Senators was urging the passage of a bill to compel the State to pay one dollar and twenty-five cents per acre for them. You disavowed all desire or purpose to defeat my bill, and declared that your only object in reporting your own was to get it upon the calendar, where it could be taken up and passed, after mine had been voted down. I at once acquitted you of any intention or purpose to defeat a grant of land to the State, but attempted to convince you that the pressing of a bill by you, which required the State to pay the full price of the lands, must inevitably defeat the passage of a bill to grant the lands to the State without payment; and even if you succeeded in passing your bill, it could be of no service to us, as the State possessed the right, and had unfortunately exercised it, of entering a large amount of public lands without any such law. You thereupon agreed to let your bill sleep until mine had been voted upon, and luckily the passage of mine, on the 4th of May, rendered yours obsolete. The great battle was yet to be fought in the House of Representatives, and there, be it said to the honor of our Representatives, one and all, that each nobly performed his whole duty, although near the close of the session the bill was laid upon the table by one or two majority, and could not be taken up again except by two-thirds vote.

This vote in the House of Representatives was regarded as decisive of the fate of the bill, and seemed to render it necessary to originate a new bill in the Senate, and send it down to the House. Accordingly, early in the next session, to wit, on the 18th of December, 1848, I again introduced my bill to the Senate, and had it referred to the committee on public lands, and you promptly reported it back without amendment.

In the mean time our colleagues in the House had succeeded in taking my former bill from the table, and having it again reinstated upon the calendar, to be acted upon in its order. This circumstance rendered the Senate bill unnecessary, and hence it was never called up for action. During this session, after you had been disappointed in your hopes of re-election, you came to me and appealed to my courtesy to aid you in passing your old pre-emption bill, and stated many reasons, personal to yourself, why it was very important that it should pass. I hardly knew how to resist your appeals to my sympathies and courtesy, and was prepared to yield everything which could be done consistently with my duty to our State.

But the conviction was irresistibly fixed upon my mind that the passage of your pre-emption bill would inevitably defeat a grant of land to the State forever, and would destroy all hope of the speedy completion of the Central railroad. I expressed these opinions to you frankly, as my reasons for denying your request. You then appealed to me to allow your bill to pass the Senate, with the understanding that it should not pass the House of Representatives; and you stated your reasons for this request. I told you that I would yield to this, provided I could first be satisfied there was no danger of the bill passing the House. I then consulted Judge Collamer,[10] the late Postmaster General, who was the chairman of the committee on public lands, whether it would be approved by his committee, and allowed to pass the House if it came down from the Senate. He informed me that in no event could it pass the House; and, being fully satisfied upon this point by him and others, I informed you of the fact, and consented to the passage of your bill through the Senate. Accordingly, on the 31st of January, 1849, your pre-emption bill was taken up on your motion, considered in the committee of the whole, and passed the Senate. Here your official connexion with the subject ceased. You retired to private life, and whatever you may have done since to secure a grant of land to the State is unknown to me. Neither of the bills alluded to passed the House of Representatives that session, and hence it was necessary to begin anew at the opening of the next session. In order to secure perfect harmony among our delegation, and to pay all proper respects to the opinions of each, I consulted them all before I introduced the bill.

We became satisfied that it was necessary to bring forward the Central railroad in a bill by itself, disconnected with all cross roads, in order to ensure success. This being agreed upon, the bill was prepared by Col. McClernand and myself, jointly, and two copies made, with the understanding that he was to introduce one into the House and I the other in the Senate. On the 3d day of January, 1850, I introduced the bill into the Senate, and had it referred to the committee on public lands. On the 12th of February, General Shields, from that committee, reported it back, with various amendments, combined in a form of a substitute. During the whole struggle he and I acted together cordially, consulting on all points, and harmonizing in all our views in reference to it. Of course it passed and went to the House of Representatives. There the great battle was fought, in which every member of our delegation acted a conspicuous and efficient part. The bill passed, and the State now has the means of completing the Central railroad. I do not deem it very important to stop and inquire what individual is entitled to the merit of the measure. I will relinquish to you or any one else, who will ensure the speedy completion of the work in the best manner, all claim to any share in the glory.

I will furnish you a quit claim deed, and permit you to fill up the blanks and insert the name of the grantee. I only claim to have done my duty, and I believe such and all of my colleagues in both Houses did theirs. We may have erred sometimes as to the best mode of proceeding, and the means by which the end was to be accomplished; but I do not concur with you, and doubt whether they will, in the very amiable sentiment expressed in your letter, "that they are not for it now, and do not desire to have it made, because I (you) got the credit of it." It may be true, as you state, "that these fellows who are making such an ado about it *now* have been *whipped* into its support;" but I have serious doubts whether the impartial public after examining the record to which I have referred, will come to the conclusion that the remark is applicable to any of the *present* delegation in Congress.

In conclusion, my dear sir, I trust that the facts to which I have referred will not fail to satisfy your mind, that in my Chicago letter, and in other remarks I may have made complimentary to my colleagues, in which you were not alluded to, I did not intend to depreciate the value of your services, nor deprive you of any of the credit to which you may be entitled, for the grant of lands made by Congress to our State last session, in aid of the Central railroad. I have the honor to remain, very respectfully, your fellow-citizen and obedient servant,

S. A. Douglas

Printed in *Letters of Senator Douglas, Defending Himself and Colleagues Against the Attacks of Judge Breese in Connexion with the Grant of Land by Congress for the Central Railroad* (Washington, D.C., 1851). The letter was also published in the Springfield *Illinois State Register,* January 24, 1851.

[1]Breese's letter, written December 23, 1850, was published in the *Daily Register,* December 28, 1850. In it, Breese maintained that he had originated the central railroad scheme and demanded that he be given just credit for it.

[2]Breese's interest in a central railroad had indeed been a long one. In 1835, Breese formed a partnership that raised money for the purchase of a large tract of land at the junction of the Ohio and Mississippi rivers. To assist in the development of this land and to realize his plan for a central railroad, Breese turned to Darius B. Holbrook. In January, 1836, the Illinois legislature chartered the Central Railroad Company. Alexander Jenkins, one of Breese's partners and Lieutenant Governor of Illinois, became the president of the company and Holbrook the treasurer. The leading spirit in the organization, however, was Breese. The project was later included in the Internal Improvement Act of 1837; when the internal improvement scheme collapsed, the central railroad project collapsed with it, but Breese kept his interest alive. He renewed his efforts following his election to the United States Senate in 1843.

[3]William Woodbridge, Senator from Michigan from 1841 to 1847.

[4]The brackets were supplied by Douglas.

[5]Thomas Dyer, of Chicago, served in the lower house of the state legislature from 1851 to 1852. Breese was elected to the state House of Representatives following his defeat for re-election to the United States Senate in 1849.

[6]The route proposed by Breese in his original scheme for a central railroad, and provided in the charter of the Central Railroad Company in 1836.

[7]Elihu B. Washburne and Orville C. Pratt.

[8]Justin Butterfield, a Chicago lawyer and an active promoter of the Illinois Central Railroad, had been an associate director of the Great Western Railway after its recharter in 1849. He later was appointed Commissioner of the General Land Office.

[9]The Illinois legislature had instructed the state's Congressional delegation to seek a Federal land grant to aid in the construction of the Northern Cross and Central Railroad projects.

[10]Jacob Collamer was Representative from Vermont from 1843 to 1849; Postmaster General in the cabinet of Zachary Taylor from 1849 to 1850; and Senator from Vermont from 1855 to 1865.

To Thomas Settle

Washington

My Dear Uncle   Jan'y 16th 1851

I am very grateful to you for your kind letter of the 10th inst, which was received last night. It was the first news I had received from my family for sometime, and has quieted all uneasiness in respect to their health.[1] I had ceased to write for two or three weeks under the impression that they would have left for Raleigh before a letter would reach them, and their failure to write lead me to apprehend that some

[206]

of the family were ill & that they hesitated to alarm me by communicating the fact. Tonight I have just received a letter from Martha explaining all, and another from Doct James informing me that Martin[2] has entirely recovered from the swelling in the glands of his neck which gave Martha & Mother so much uneasiness. I shall hope therefore to meet them soon, and language cannot express the gratitude I shall feel if you will aid them in making the necessary arraingements for the trip. It is no small undertaking for them, and really requires courage on their part to attempt it, unaided by any one. I need not say to you as a husband & a father how anxious I am to have my family with me and how slowly the time passes while waiting for the letter which shall fix the day for me to meet them.

But I will not bore you longer & you will excuse me for dwelling so much upon a subject which I ought to remember others cannot feel the same interest in as myself.

You will have observed by the papers that the proceedings of congress are dull & quiet. There is very little attempt at agitation & excitement upon the vexed question of slavery. All seem to have exhausted their energies last Session and still need rest. For one I came here prepared to strive hard, if necessary, to do nothing this Session, and I think we will certainly succeed so far as slavery is concerned. If we can get a direct vote on the Repeal of the Fugitive Bill, I am sure that a majority of the northern men will vote to sustain the law.[3] You may rely upon it that law will never be repealed or rendered less efficient in our day. It will be executed at the north with the same fidelity that the several states execute their own local laws. Public opinion is becoming sound & enlightened upon this question and the abolitionists are already reduced to a state of despair. The whole compromise will be adhered to and the Union preserved so far as it depends upon the north. The signs that come to us from the south are all favorable with the exception of South Carolina, and I have faith that she will acquiesce when she finds that she stands alone among her Southern sisters.[4] The friends of the constitution & the Union have much to do at the north to arouse the people to a ful sense of their duty, but the north has men who are able & willing to perform that duty at any sacrifice of time or place. It is important that the Southern states should refrain from all retaliating legislation until we have had a fair trial of strengh in the free states. I send you a revised copy of my Chicago speech.[5] Two new editions have recently been published here & fifty thousand copies subscribed for to be circulated among the people. The Union Committee for the city of New York have sent an order today for five thousand additional copies & new orders of the kind are received each day. I will not disguise from you that I feel this delicate compliment very sensibley. I shall be happy to hear from you often & upon all subjects. Present my kind regards to each member of your family and belive me very truly your friend & nephew

S. A. DOUGLAS

ALS, Southern Historical Collection, University of North Carolina Library, Chapel Hill. Thomas Settle, of Reidsville, North Carolina, and a former member of Congress from North Carolina, was the uncle of Douglas' wife.

[1]Douglas' family was visiting in North Carolina at this time.

[2]Douglas is probably referring to his son, Robert Martin Douglas. Dr. William H. James was the physician attending the family.

[3]A bill to repeal the Fugitive Slave Act of 1850 passed the House of Representatives in September, 1850, but it seems never to have been brought to a vote in the Senate.

[4]Southern extremists in South Carolina had opposed the Compromise of 1850 almost from the day it passed. The idea of secession was debated in the state legislature during the winter of 1850-51, but was finally rejected in favor of an all-Southern convention, a disappointing defeat for the secession spokesmen.

[5]Douglas' speech was delivered at the city hall in Chicago on October 23, 1850, and dealt with the Compromise of 1850. It was published as *Speech of Hon. Stephen A. Douglas, on the "Measures of Adjustment," Delivered in the City Hall, Chicago, Oct. 23, 1850* (Chicago, 1850).

To William Pickering

Hon. Mr. Pickering: Washington, Jan 25, 1851.

Your railroad bill, [Alton, Mt. Carmel and New Albany][1] passed the senate to day.

S. A. DOUGLASS

Springfield *Daily Register,* January 28, 1851. William Pickering, of Edwards County, was a member of the lower house of the Illinois legislature. In 1849, he purchased a graded roadbed running from Alton to Mt. Carmel (the proposed Illinois Southern Cross Railroad of 1837) from the legislature for $300.

[1]The brackets appear in the original newspaper version. On January 25, 1851, the Senate passed "A bill granting land to the States of Louisiana, Mississippi, Indiana, and Illinois, for the construction of certain railroads therein mentioned."

To Sidney Breese

SIR: WASHINGTON, *February* 22, 1851.

Notwithstanding my repugnance to every description of personal controversy, I feel constrained to notice a few points in your letter of the 25th ultimo, addressed to me through the columns of the State Register.[1] You have evidently become conscious that some apology was due to the public for your strange and unprovoked attacks upon my colleagues and myself, in our absence, in reference to the grant of land by Congress to our State last session. By way of excuse for the injustice you have done us, you urge that, in my speeches and letters upon the subject, I have attempted to deprive you of all credit for any

Stephen A. Douglas in 1860, photographed by Mathew Brady.

Adele Cutts Douglas, after her marriage to Douglas in 1856 at the age of twenty-one.

Martha Denny Martin, whom Douglas married in 1847 and who died in January, 1853.

Douglas around 1845, from a steel engraving of a daguerreotype made by Mathew Brady.

Douglas during the 1860 Presidential campaign.

Letter of Douglas to Charles H. Lanphier, August 25, 1854, from the collection of the Illinois State Historical Library. The text is on p. 327.

Douglas in 1860 or 1861.

*Probably the last photograph taken of Douglas before his death,
June 3, 1861.*

The Douglas home in Chicago, photographed in 1907.

participation in the matter. What speeches and letters do you refer to? I am not aware that I have ever made a speech upon the grant of land for the Central railroad since the bill passed. When in Springfield, last November, the newspapers of that city announced that I would address the people the next night upon that subject; but I was deprived of the opportunity of doing so by indisposition, and, consequently, made no speech. You must have been endowed with a genius not only prophetic but romantic, to be able to divine what I would have said in the event I had spoken; and then, assuming the speech to have been made, to construe it into a depreciation of your public services. But how is it with the letters, which you assume that I have written, prejudicial to your claims? I am not conscious of having written but one letter, in which the grant of land for the Central railroad was alluded to, and that was a joint letter of General Shields and myself, declining a public dinner tendered to us by the people of Chicago, for our services during the last session of Congress in procuring the passage of measures favorable to the local interest of our State. The invitation was in terms confined to measures passed at the last session, and of course our reply did not extend beyond that period. We made no allusion to you, for the reason that you were not a member of that Congress. We did allude to our colleagues of the House, and attribute the chief credit to them, because, in the House of Representatives the great battle was fought. Your statement, therefore, that in my speeches and letters I have attempted to deprive you of any credit to which you may be entitled, is shown to be entirely without foundation. I have made no attack upon you, preferred no charge against you, made no allusion or reference to you, in any speech or letter of mine, prior to the publication of your three letters against my colleagues and myself. I have claimed no merit, no credit for myself, in connexion with the grant of land. I have only done what I conceived to be my duty, and was content to remain silent and leave the people to award credit where credit was due, without thrusting myself before them with the declaration that "I am the father of the Central railroad—that I originated it in 1835, and have devoted fifteen years to its accomplishment—that I passed three different bills through the Senate for its construction— that the arguments in *my* reports silenced all opposition and rendered its passage easy, and that all my colleagues were opposed or indifferent to the measure." I made no such pretensions, for the reason that truth and self-respect forbid it in me, as they should have done in any other man who was ever honored with a seat in the Senate of the United States.

In your last letter, reviewing and presenting to the public all your services in behalf of the Central railroad, you conclusively establish two facts, neither of which was ever denied, and which I trust no one will hereafter dispute.

1st. That in the year 1835 you did actually write a letter to John Y. Sawyer in favor of the Central railroad.[2]

2d. That during your Senatorial term you attempted, without success, to procure a pre-emption right to D. B. Holbrook and his associates, instead of a grant of land to the State of Illinois, to aid in the construction of the road.

Upon these two facts, according to your own showing, depend all your claims to be considered the father of the road and the author of the grant of land by Congress at its last session.

The fact that you wrote the letter has never been questioned; that you have rendered any other aid (except the unsuccessful attempt to secure the pre-emption to Holbrook) you do not now pretend. Others labored for it in the legislature, and voted for the bill under which the work was originally commenced, and one million of dollars expended in its construction. Of these you were unfortunate enough in your letter to prove that I was one; and you might have added that several of my colleagues, whom you now charge with being opposed to the road, were also members of that legislature, and voted for it. We were entitled to no credit for our support of the measure then, any more than for the grant of land last session, for, as you justly remark, the people were all for it, and we only carried out the wishes of our constituents. And yet, according to your statement, I voted for it and you wrote a letter in favor of it; and from these facts your logical mind draws the inference that I was opposed to it, and you were the father of it. I shall not attempt a reply to this argument. I admit you wrote the letter. I read it at the time, and have perused it again in your letter to me. The first sentence is so pertinent to our present inquiry that I cannot forego the pleasure of quoting it for your especial benefit. It is as follows:

VANDALIA, *October 16th,* 1835.

JOHN Y. SAWYER, esq.,

DEAR SIR: Having some leisure from the labors of my circuit, I am induced to devote a portion of it in giving to the public a plan, the outline of which *was suggested to me by an intelligent friend in Bond county,* a few days since, by which the north may get their long wished for canal, and the southern and interior counties a channel of communication quite as essential to their prosperity.

Thus it appears that you kindly consented to call the attention of the public to "A PLAN, THE OUTLINE OF WHICH WAS SUGGESTED TO [YOU][3] BY AN INTELLIGENT FRIEND IN BOND COUNTY, A FEW DAYS SINCE."[4] How is this? The father of the

Central railroad, with a christian meekness worthy of all praise, kindly consents to be the reputed parent of a hopeful son begotten for him by an intelligent friend in a neighboring county! I forbear pushing this inquiry further. It involves a question of morals too nice—of domestic relations too delicate—for me to venture to expose to the public gaze! Inasmuch, however, as you have furnished me, with becoming gravity, the epitaph which you desire engraved upon your tomb, when called upon to pay the last debt of nature, you will allow me to suggest that such an inscription is a solemn and sacred thing, and truth its essential ingredient. Would it not be well, therefore, to make a slight modification, so as to correspond with the facts as stated in your letter to Mr. Sawyer, which would make it read thus, in your letter to me:

"It has been the highest object of my ambition to accomplish the Central railroad, and when my last resting place shall be marked by the cold marble, which gratitude or affection may erect, I desire for it no other inscription than this: HE, WHO SLEEPS BENEATH THIS, VOLUNTARILY CONSENTED TO BECOME THE PUTATIVE FATHER OF A LOVELY CHILD, CALLED THE CENTRAL RAILROAD, AND BEGOTTEN FOR HIM BY AN INTELLIGENT FRIEND IN THE COUNTY OF BOND!"

So it appears that you had just about as much to do with originating the measure as one of our phonographic reporters in the Senate had with the authorship of Clay's speeches on the Compromise, which he reported and prepared for the press. For the eight years succeeding the date of your letter to Mr. Sawyer, to wit, from the winter of 1835-'6, until the session of 1843-'4, you do not claim to have made the slightest effort in behalf of the road.

I presume that your inaction, not to say indifference, during the whole of this period, is to be accounted for by the fact that every citizen of the State was in favor of the measure, and hence no special effort was required from any of its friends.

We have now reached that point of time when, in Dec., 1843, you made your first attempt to secure a pre-emption to Holbrook and his partners. Since the fact has been established by your own testimony, that the Central railroad was originated by an "intelligent friend in Bond county," it may be inferred that you rest your claims to be considered the "father" of the measure upon the assumption that you were the first to bring forward the proposition for a pre-emption to the company. I have no interest or desire to deprive you of the exclusive credit of originating that scheme; nor should I have called your claim in question, had you not stated the fact in your last letter, that Gov. Casey,[5] while a member of Congress from our State, and as a member of the committee of public lands, several years before either of us was elected to the Senate, made a very able and favorable report for the right of way and a pre-emption, which was extensively read and circulated." He having failed in his effort, you followed in his footsteps, and renewed the proposition with a like result. Whether this unsuccessful effort to carry a measure which Gov. Casey originated, makes you the father of the Central railroad, I leave others to determine.

You now accuse me, in connexion with Mr. Butterfield and other citizens of Chicago, whom you allege to have acted under my advice, of having "set on foot a great movement in 1847, *to disturb your plans*," by insisting upon a grant of land to the State, instead of a pre-emption for the benefit of the Holbrook Company, and making one terminus of the road upon the lakes, which was deemed essential in order to impart nationality to the scheme, and to secure northern and eastern votes for the measure. I shall interpose no denial, no attempt, to refute the charge. The facts set forth in my letter to you sustain the truth of the material allegation for which you have arraigned me before my constituents in my absence. I rejoice that we have been able at length to agree in reference to the real point at issue between us; that your "plans," which I am accused of having "disturbed," did not contemplate a grant of land to the State of Illinois—that your "plans" did not contemplate a terminus at Chicago, which would connect the whole line of lakes with the Mississippi—the St. Lawrence with the Gulf of Mexico; which would commend the measure to Congress as a great national work, and secure votes from all portions of the Union: that your "plans," which I am accused of having "disturbed," only contemplated a pre-emption for the benefit of Mr. Holbrook and his partners, in which the State was to have no interest, and about which there was not even an odor of nationality to commend it to the favorable consideration of Congress; a "plan" which contemplated a stupendous private speculation, by enabling the Cairo Company to sell their chartered privileges in England for a large amount of money, and then abandon the concern without making the road.

I do not deny the truth of your charge that I did "disturb" your "plans" in this respect, by insisting that the grant should be made to the State of Illinois, and that one terminus of the road should be upon the northern lakes, for the reasons which I avowed at the time, and have never wished to conceal. I will not waste time, nor offend against the common sense of my constituents, by a formal reply to that portion of your letter which attempts to show that a pre-emption would have been better and more effectual than a grant. I can well conceive that it might have been better for Mr. Holbrook and his partners, and more effectual for their schemes of speculation, for *them* to have had a pre-emption than for *the State* to have had a grant; but I apprehend that

[212]

you will find it difficult to convince any one citizen of Illinois, who was not a partner in the speculation, that it was better for the State not to have the lands than to have them, or to be required to pay a dollar and a quarter an acre for them, instead of receiving them for nothing under the act of last session. The declaration in your last letter, that *"in the passage of the present law I had no share, nor have I claimed any,"* has taken me, as I doubt not it did the public, entirely by surprise. If the letters, published by you just before the meeting of the legislature, had been understood as placing you in the position which you now assume, disclaiming all credit or responsibility for the grant of land to the State, and for the branch road through the eastern counties to Chicago, and predicating your claims exclusively upon the superior merits of your old pre-emption scheme for the benefit of the Holbrook Company, I should have been content to have remained silent, and let the people judge between us. It was this Chicago branch, (which you now repudiate,) connecting the main road with the various lines, in progress of construction, from Philadelphia, New York, Boston, and Portland, as well as the great chain of lakes and the St. Lawrence, which secured the votes we obtained from Pennsylvania, New York, and New England.

When you speak of the service rendered us by Mr. Holbrook in securing the grant, you should have told in what it consisted. He did render an essential service, and it consisted in absenting himself from the District of Columbia during the whole struggle, and in the execution of a release, surrendering all his chartered rights and interest in the road to the State, *so as to enable us to cut loose from the odium which attached to his name and his operations.* I felt grateful for this service, for without it the bill could never have passed. I was under the necessity of giving the positive and solemn assurance to the Senate, as the debates will show, that such a release had been executed, and that he no longer had any interest in, or connexion with, the road, before the bill could stand the slightest chance of passing that body; and my colleagues of the House will inform you that they were compelled to give the same assurance, over and over again, to their brother members, before their votes could be obtained for the measure. I felt kindly to-[ward] Mr. Holbrook for having thus surrendered his charters, and withdrawn himself from the scene of action, and remaining in New York an idle spectator, for the purpose of enabling us to secure the grant of land to the State; and this good feeling would have continued, had he not subsequently attempted to resume his charters, seize upon the grant of land, and despoil the State of all she had received, and dishonor the delegation by falsifying the pledges which had been given to induce Congress to pass the bill. The causes and objects of attacks upon my colleagues and myself, by you and Mr. Holbrook, are well understood. We happen to know who wrote, and whose money paid for, the articles published in the New York and Philadelphia papers, traducing General Shields and myself, and lauding you in terms which would put to blush the letters published over your own signature.

I shall make no reply to your charge that my colleagues and myself, during the six years you were in the Senate, were opposed to the Central railroad, or indifferent to its success. The records of Congress speak for themselves upon this subject, and are quite as authentic and truthful in their statements, as your letters to the public arraigning the conduct and impugning the motives of every man who was associated with you in the public service. You tax the credulity of the people of Illinois too heavily, when you call upon them to believe that James Semple, John J. Hardin, Robert Smith, J. A. McClernand, O. B. Ficklin, and *"perhaps* Mr. Hoge and Col. Baker," were opposed to an improvement so intimately identified with the prosperity, happiness, and glory of our State; and the idea becomes no less ludicrous than amusing, when you intimate that this alleged opposition had its origin in jealousy of your distinguished position in the Senate and before the country.

In conclusion, I may be permitted to remark, that I fully understand the cause and the point of time when you and Mr. Holbrook suddenly turned your applause of my conduct in connexion with the Central railroad into bitter denunciation and misrepresentation. One of the causes I have already alluded to; the other I forbear to mention, as it has no immediate connexion with this subject. It may be fairly assumed that the time was not many weeks after the death of General Taylor, when the telegraph had announced that your "friends," Mr. Corwin, Mr. Pierce, Mr. Crittenden, and Mr. Webster, were associated with President Fillmore in his Cabinet.[6] If I did not comply with your wishes in the one case, I assure you that my refusal was not prompted by any unwillingness to promote your interests, whenever I could do so with propriety; and in the other, you and Mr. Holbrook both mistake my motive for maintaining the rights of our State in preference to the interests of private individuals. But enough of this. Your letters have produced no unkind emotions in my bosom, and I therefore heartily respond to the concluding sentiment in your last epistle—"let there be no strife between us." I have the honor to remain, very respectfully, your obedient servant,

S. A. Douglas

Printed in *Letters of Senator Douglas, Defending Himself and Colleagues Against the Attacks of Judge Breese in* *Connexion with the Grant of Land by Congress for the Central Railroad* (Washington, D.C., 1851). The letter was also published in the Springfield *Illinois State Register*, March 13, 1851.

[1]Breese's letter to Douglas was printed in the *State Register*, February 6, 1851.

[2]John York Sawyer was at that time editor of the Vandalia *Illinois Advocate and State Register*. Breese's letter was printed in the issue of October 21, 1835.

[3]The brackets were supplied by Douglas in the original.

[4]Breese's friend in Bond County was William S. Wait, an early railroad promoter in Illinois.

[5]Zadoc Casey, elected Lieutenant Governor of Illinois in 1830, served in Congress from 1833 to 1843.

[6]Thomas Corwin, of Ohio, was appointed Secretary of the Treasury; John J. Crittenden, of Kentucky, Attorney General; Daniel Webster, of Massachusetts, Secretary of State. James A. Pearce, Congressman and Senator from Maryland, was probably the "Pierce" referred to by Douglas, but he was not appointed to a cabinet post by Fillmore.

To Zadoc W. McKnew

[February 28, 1851, Washington; AES, Library of Congress. Endorsement on Daniel S. Dickinson to Zadoc W. McKnew, February 28, 1851, "cordially" uniting with Dickinson "in all that he has said in behalf of Mr McKnew." Dickinson, formerly Lieutenant Governor of New York and United States Senator from 1844 to 1851, wrote a testimonial in McKnew's behalf, declaring him to be an "accommadating business man and a gentleman of frank & manly deportment." McKnew later became a clerk in the War Department. Douglas' endorsement was one of several by members of Congress.]

To George Nicholas Sanders

Washington

My Dear Sir,   April 11th 1851

I am greatly indebted to you for your several letters at Raleigh & at this place. You will possibly have observed that Public Dinners were tendered me in N Carolina & Virginia, which I declined. I might have been induced to have accepted one in the course of my trip home, if I could have done so without giving offense to those whose invitations I would be compelled to decline. You may well imagine therefore that I was gratified on the receipt of your first letter to find that your judgement approved the course which I had marked out for myself. Last night I received your last letter advising me to accept the New York invitation & giving very plausible reasons for your opinion. I have great confidence in your judgment & discretion, and you are well aware that I would be glad to find my views coinciding with yours. But I ask you to reflect that if I should accept the New York invitation & others after declining those at the South would it not give plausible grounds of offense? And if I had accepted all, would it not [have] given my trip all

[215]

the appearances of an electioneering tour? Several of my Virginia friends are now here & they all say that I must not accept any invitations after having declined theirs.

My judgment & feelings unite in telling me that I should accept note [none] & content myself with meeting my friends in the private & social circle.

I shall send a public letter in reply to the N.Y. invitation in a day or two & expect to arrive in New York late next week.[1] I have written my friend West[2] to this effect & I trust that this course will meet the approval of all our friends. I remain very truly your friend

S. A. Douglas

P.S. I regret Mr Webster is absent as I was desireous of seeing him in regard to the matter referred to in the papers which I have.

ALS, Watertown Library Association. George Nicholas Sanders, originally of Kentucky, was a prominent political lobbyist and business agent during the 1840's. In the spring of 1851, he met Douglas and subsequently became a strong supporter of Douglas for the Presidency in 1852. Later in 1851, he purchased the *Democratic Review* and converted it into a pro-Douglas organ.

This is the first of several letters in which Douglas sought to organize support for his candidacy for the Democratic Presidential nomination in 1852.
[1]See below, May 3, 1851.
[2]Edward C. West was a New York attorney and one of those who extended the invitation to Douglas to speak in New York city.

To Francis B. Cutting *et al.*

New York, May 3, 1851.

Gentlemen—I have the honor to acknowledge the receipt of your kind invitation, in the name, and on behalf, of the democratic republican electors of the city of New York, to partake of a public dinner at such time as may suit my convenience.

I need not assure you that this testimonial of your respect and confidence is exceedingly grateful to my feelings, and derives increased value and importance from the consideration that it is intended as a manifestation of your approbation of my course as a member of the democratic party and a senator in the congress of the United States. You do me no more than justice, gentlemen, when you say that my public career has been marked by fidelity and devotion to the principles and measures of that great party, whose triumphs are identified with the most glorious achievements in our national history; and whose ascendancy we believe to be essential to the purity and perpetuity of our republican institutions. Fidelity to the cause is the paramount duty of every democrat who believes that our principles are identified with the peace, glory, and prosperity of the whole country. In view of the long list of older and abler members of our party whose patriotic services have entitled them to the gratitude of their country, to be elected as worthy of this distinguished compliment by my political friends in this city, has excited in my bosom these grateful emotions, which I can find no language adequate to express. The only mode in which I can hope to repay your kindness, will be found in my constant and preserving endeavors to merit your confidence, and realize in the future that which your partiality has so generously awarded me in advance.

At no period in the history of the country has the democratic party had brighter prospects, and higher and nobler objects to stimulate our patriotism and call forth all our energies, than is now presented to our view. The necessity for confining the federal government clearly within the limits of its legitimate functions—for preserving the rights of the states in their original purity and vigor—for maintaining the supremacy of the laws—and for a strict observance of every provision of our constitutions—state and national—has never been rendered more manifest than by our recent experience. We have, gentlemen, important duties and high responsibilities devolving upon us, which demand the immediate organization, union, and the consequent success of the democratic party.

It would afford me sincere pleasure to meet the democratic republican electors of New York around the festive board, and there cultivate those kind, social relations which ought to exist between brethren of the same faith. But having remained in your city much longer than I anticipated, and partaken freely of your generous hospitality, bountifully extended, I do not feel at liberty to protract my visit longer, my public duties have already kept me from my home nearly all the time for the last two years. I leave the city, for the west, this afternoon, and therefore will not be able to accept your kind invitation.[1] I have the honor to be, very truly, your friend and obedient servant,

S. A. DOUGLAS

Messrs. F. B. Cutting, Isaac Townsend, S. Livingston, E. B. Hart, Charles A. Secor, Edward C. West, Henry Nicoll, and others.[2]

Springfield *Illinois State Register*, May 22, 1851. This letter was written in reply to an invitation from 600 New York Democrats to attend a public dinner honoring "your great services to your party and to your country, during the past two years." The letter of invitation was printed in the same issue of the *State Register* as Douglas' reply. Douglas had stopped in New York on his way west following the adjournment of Congress. Francis B. Cutting, a New York city lawyer and former member of the New York legislature, was elected to Congress in 1852.

[1]Douglas, however, did not leave New York until several days later. See below, May 6, 1851.

[2]Isaac Townsend, New York merchant; Anson Livingston, attorney; Emmanuel B. Hart, member of Congress from 1851 to 1853; Charles A. Secor, ship handler; Henry Nicoll, member of Congress from 1847 to 1849.

To Lewis F. Coryell

New York
My Dear Sir,   May 6th 1851

Your letter has just reached me as I was packing my trunk to start home. I leave today for Chicago. I enclose a letter to my friend Judge Young[1] which I hope may be of service to you. It will always give me pleasure to be of use to you or your friends. I remain very truly your friend

S. A. DOUGLAS

ALS, Historical Society of Pennsylvania. Coryell was possibly Lewis S. Coryell of Pennsylvania, who, in the 1840's, held an interest in the Washington *Union*.

[1] Richard Montgomery Young, clerk of the House of Representatives from April 17, 1850, to March 4, 1851, practiced law in Washington, D.C., thereafter.

To Robert M. T. Hunter

(*Confidential*)   New York
My Dr Sir,   May 6th 1851

I move towards home slowly. Everything looks well—much better than either of us had a right to expect. In this state I think both divisions of the party will come together upon the basis of *entire silence on the slavery question* and support "the Tickett."[1] This is the opinion of our best informed friends. I have declined the Public Dinner tendered me. Mr Sanders will send you the correspondence when published, as I leave for Chicago today. I have seen the invitation for a Public Dinner to you. All the great business Houses have signed it and a better list of names cannot be selected in this city. Our friends are anxious that you should accept and will urge you to do so. My opinion however is that you should decline it in a well considered & judicious letter, but at the same time notify them that you intend to visit the city in a quiet way during the hot weather & perhaps some of the northern watering places when you will be pleased to meet them in the social circle &c &c. I think you should come here this summer & remain some time, but I doubt the policy of a public demonstration. All looks exceedingly well in N Carolina. Of Virginia you can judge better than I can, altho I believe the compromise men will cheerfully unite on you for the sake of harmony. At least many of them told me they would do so. Write me at Chicago, freely but confidentially, and I shall read your letters & *instantly burn* them. Very truly your friend

S. A. DOUGLAS

P.S. Our friend George S will keep you advised of all movements here. Entire confidence can be placed in his discretion. He is invaluable to us & will remain here as the point where he can do most. Your letter of invitation would have been sent before, but for my presence here. It was thought prudent to wait until I leave the city.

ALS, Alderman Library, University of Virginia, Charlottesville. Robert M. T. Hunter, of Virginia, was a member of Congress from 1837 to 1843 and from 1845 to 1847, and served as Speaker of the House of Representatives during the Twenty-sixth Congress. He was United States Senator from Virginia from 1847 to 1861.
[1]"The Tickett" was Douglas' slate for the Presidency in 1852: himself for President and Hunter for Vice-President.

To George Nicholas Sanders

Manchester Centre N Y

My Dear Sir,   May 18th 1851

On my return last night from the Erie Rail Road Celebration[1] I received your letter, without date, but mailed the 12th inst. I have written to the Governor of Ills urging the appointment of Mr [...][2] as a personal favor to myself & have no doubt it will be done if the appointments are not already made. I wish you would ask our friend Hart[3] to enquire of the Tailor who made the suit of cloths for me whether he has received his pay. I directed the Bill to be paid at the Astor House as many other Bills were paid, when the things were delivered. Upon looking over my Bill at the Astor Ho I do not find the item for the cloths nor do I recollect having paid it to any one else. I did not think of it until since I arrived here. Tell Hart if it is not paid to let me know at Chicago & I will instantly send the money.[4] I start for Chicago tomorrow & will be there in two days.

We had a great time at Dunkirk & at Buffalo. You will see the account in the News Papers. Send me the Herald at Chicago containing the account as I wish to see what it says & also the other papers. I have not yet seen the Letters in regard to the public Dinners published, but understand they have been copied into the Union.

Things look well wherever I have been. Both sections of the Party treat me kindly. The Editor of the Courier at Buffalo (the Cass Paper) told me he was against the General & for me.[5]

Write me often. Give me respects to our friends West & Hart. Your friend

S. A. Douglas

P.S. Mrs Douglas likes Ruth (her Nurse) very much & is delighted with the change. We are much indebted to you for this kindness. Mrs D sends her kind regards to you & Miss Reid in which I join with great pleasure.

ALS, Watertown Library Association.
[1]On May 14, 1851, over 300 prominent figures, including President Mil- lard Fillmore, Daniel Webster, John J. Crittenden, and others, gathered at Dunkirk, New York, to celebrate the

opening of the New York and Erie Railroad.

²The name is illegible. It might possibly be that of John J. Cisco, of New York city.

³Emmanuel B. Hart.

⁴Douglas' tailor bill, due John G. Wyman and Company and dated August 18, 1851, totaled $175.50, for a black frock, dress coat, plaid silk vest, doeskin pants, striped Valencia vest, and shirts. The original bill is owned by Martin F. Douglas.

⁵William A. Seaver was editor of the Buffalo *Courier*.

To Thomas Allen

Chicago

Dear Sir,   June 5th 1851

Permit me to introduce to you my friend the Hon J A Rockwell of Conn. He visits St Louis on business with your Pacific Rail Road. I have known him intimately for several years. He was for sometime a distinguished member of Congress; and since his retirement has placed the State of Illinois under deep obligation for the efficient aid he rendered in procuring the grant of land for our Central Rail Road. He is a thorough man of business & a gentleman of strict honor & integrity & as such I commend him to you. I have the honor to be very truly your friend

S. A. Douglas

ALS, Henry E. Huntington Library, San Marino, California. Thomas Allen, a St. Louis lawyer, had strong railroad interests. In 1849, he secured a charter for the Pacific Railroad Company, later the Missouri Pacific, and became its president. In 1850, he was elected to the Missouri Senate.

To John O'Fallon

Chicago

My Dear Sir,   June 5th 1851

Permit me to make you acquainted with my friend the Hon J A Rockwell of Conn, who informs me that he visits your city on business connected with your Pacific Rail Road. I have known him well for several years as a gentleman of strict honor & integrity & a distinguished member of Congress. He placed our state under deep obligation by the efficient aid he rendered in procuring the grant of land for our Central Rail Road. I sincerely hope you will have better success in your application next session than you did last.[1] I have the honor to be very truly your friend

S. A. Douglas

ALS, Henry E. Huntington Library. John O'Fallon, St. Louis merchant and philanthropist, was President of the Mississippi and Ohio Railroad and of the Northern Missouri Railroad.

[1]In 1850, a bill was introduced in the United States Senate granting land to Missouri for the Pacific Railroad, from St. Louis to the western border of the state. The bill passed the Senate but did not return from the printer in time to pass the House of Representatives prior to adjournment.

To the Citizens of Chicago

Chicago, June 19, 1851.

Gentlemen:—I have the honor to acknowledge the receipt of your letter requesting my opinion in respect to the right of the Central Railroad Company, under the charter from the Legislature of this state and the grant of land by the congress of the United states, to run the Chicago branch of said road to the state line, in order to form a connection with the Michigan Central Railroad and thence to Chicago, instead of a direct line between the termini of said branch. Your letter reached me at Ottawa, where I was in attendance upon the supreme court, and my professional engagements have deprived me of the opportunity of examining the question propounded until to-day. The Central Railroad company, like all other private corporations, possesses all the powers conferred by the charter, and none other. Whatever powers and rights are not conferred, are withheld and reserved to the state. Those who suppose that a railroad company may run their line of road anywhere and everywhere not prohibited by their charter, greatly deceive themselves. The question is not what restrictions and prohibitions are imposed; but upon what line does the charter authorize them to locate the road? The third clause of the 15th section of the charter answers this question.

"*Third,* That said company shall proceed to locate, survey, and lay out, construct and complete said road and branches, through the entire length thereof—the main trunk thereof or central line, to run from the city of Cairo to the southern termination of the Illinois and Michigan canal, passing not more than five miles from the northeast corner of township twenty-one north, range two east of the third principal meridian, and no where departing more than seventeen miles from a straight line between said city of Cairo and said southern termination of said canal; with a branch running from the last mentioned point, upon the most eligible route to the city of Galena; thence to a point on the Mississippi river, opposite the city of Dubuque, in the state of Iowa; with a branch also diverging from the main track at a point not north of the parallel of thirty-nine and a half degrees north latitude, and running on the most eligible route into the city of Chicago on Lake Michigan."

The main line is to run from Cairo to the southern terminus of the canal, passing within five miles of a specified point, with the limitation that it shall not diverge more than seventeen miles from a direct line between the termini of the road. As the point named is twelve miles east of the direct line, the company is allowed a diversion of only ten miles —five each side of the specified point within which the line of the road should be located. The Chicago branch is to diverge from the main trunk south of the parallel of 39 degrees 30 minutes north latitude, "*and run on the most eligible route into the city of Chicago, on Lake Michigan.*" The termini of this branch being fixed—the one the diverging point from the main trunk, and the other at the city of Chicago—the line is required to pursue "*the most eligible route*" between these points. This is the line of travel covered by the charter and over which the road is authorized to be constructed. I do not insist that they are bound to follow a straight line, regardless of the nature of the country and of the natural obstacles that might interpose. If an impassable mountain intervenes—or a lake or any other formidable object is encountered, they may pass around it in order to secure better ground, but they must return and pursue the general direction indicated in the charter. In other words, the road must run as near a direct line between the points specified in the charter as the nature of the country and the convenience of the public *on that line of travel* will permit. They must follow "the most eligible route" between the points fixed in the charter; but they cannot run in a different direction for the purpose of making the road upon another line of travel and conducting its business to a different terminus than the one prescribed by the act of incorporation. Chicago is about six miles west of the Indiana line, and the general course of this branch road is a south-west direction to its intersection with the main trunk. The question now arises, whether the company has a right to run a southeast course from Chicago until they intersect the state line for the purpose of effecting a junction with the central road of Michigan or any other road, and thence by an angle in a southwest direction until it intersects the main line of the Central Railroad of Illinois. It is evident that the proposed route would run upon lines of travel entirely separate and distinct from the one authorized by the charter.

The road provided for in the charter was to run from Chicago to Cairo, and thence to Mobile, in the state of Alabama, and the act of congress making the grant of land for its construction, is entitled, "THE CHICAGO AND MOBILE RAILROAD." The line proposed pursues the only possible railroad route from Chicago to New York until it intersects the state line of Indiana, and then turns and runs a southwest direction, forming an extension of the Michigan Central Railroad from Detroit in the direction of St. Louis, leaving Chicago some twenty or thirty miles north of the route—in my opinion such a departure from the most eligible route provided for in the charter would be wholly unauthorized by the act incorporating the Illinois Central Railroad company. There is another view of the question which confirms me in this opinion. The act was passed for the purpose of carrying into effect the provisions of an act of congress entitled, *"An act granting the right of way and making a grant of land to the state of Illinois, Mississippi and Alabama, in aid of the construction of a railroad from Chicago to Mobile,"* passed September 20, 1850. The charter transfers to the Central Railroad company all the lands which the state of Illinois received from the United States in pursuance of that act of congress, and imposes upon the company all the obligations which our state assumed in consideration of that grant of land, which obligations the company pledged themselves by the acceptance of the charter faithfully to perform.

The act of congress grants the state of Illinois a quantity of land equal to the alternate section for six miles on each side of said road and branches, and at the same time increases the price of the other alternate sections to two dollars and fifty cents per acre, so that the United States would receive for the remaining half of the lands as much as they would for the whole. It was the enhancement of the value of the public lands upon each side of the road that constituted the inducement to get the grant. It was upon this principle that the measure was successfully vindicated and sustained by its friends. The lands had been in market upon an average of twenty odd years, at one dollar and a quarter per acre, and had failed to find purchasers; not because the lands were not rich and fertile, but in consequence of their remoteness from markets, and the absence of timber. The railroad would supply both of these deficiencies, and thus render desirable that which was before comparatively valueless. Acting upon the wise policy which would govern a large landed proprietor in contributing a portion of his estate to improve and enhance the value of the residue, congress made this munificent grant upon condition that our state should make the road from the termination of the canal to Cairo, with a branch to Chicago, and another to Galena and Dubuque, and upon the further condition that the price of the remaining alternate sections should be doubled, so that the U.S. would receive for one half all that they demanded for the whole. How is this last condition to be complied with, if the road is to be established on the state line? The grant is made to the state of Illinois. All the lands granted lay within the limits of the state. They are to extend in alternate sections for six miles on each side of the road, and where any portion of them have been previously sold, others are to be selected to make up the deficiency, within fifteen miles of the line of the road. Is it not incontrovertible, therefore, that the road cannot approach within six miles of the state line, and probably a greater distance, without violating the grant? The operation of the act of congress is limited to Illinois, and cannot be construed to double the price of lands in Indiana. By locating the road on or near the state line, the public lands on each side of the road would remain in market at one dollar and twenty-five cents per acre, and liable to be entered with Mexican bounty land warrants at a great depreciation upon that price while deficiency in the quantity of lands granted to the state and transferred to the company, would be made up by selection within fifteen miles of other portions of the line. Such a location would be an ingenious device by which the company could extend the length of the road, and thereby increase the amount of land granted by congress, at the same time that it would diminish the advantages to accrue to the United States growing out of the enhancement of the value of the remaining lands. Are the people of Illinois prepared to sanction such a gross breach of faith in return for the generous and enlightened policy pursued by congress towards us in making the grant? The United States have dealt fairly and generously towards us—shall we be guilty of trickery and injustice to them? I think it should be a point of honor, sound and unalterable, on the part of every Illinoisan, to carry out in good faith every provision of the grant according to its letter and spirit.

The United States have other important interests connected with the construction of this road and branches aside from the enhancement of the value of the public lands. The act of congress provides that the said road and branches shall be free to the United States for the transportation of troops and public property forever; also that the United States mails shall always be carried on the same under the direction of the post office department.—These were important considerations, and may be in the course of time of incalculable advantage to the government. We all know the difficulties and disputes which constantly arise between the post office department and the various lines of railroads in regard to the transportation to the mails. The companies demand enormous prices, and upon the refusal of the department to accede to their unreasonable demands, they throw the mail bags out of the cars, and produce confusion in the whole mail service of the country. This evil is effectually guarded against by the act of congress making the grant of land, which provides that the mails shall always be carried on said road and branches, under the direction of the post office department, at a reasonable rate of compensation, and in the event that the department shall be unable to agree with the state or company upon the price, the matter in dispute is to be referred to congress whose decision is to be final. The provision in regard to the transportation of troops and other public property may become still more important in the event of war. In this point of view it was of incalculable importance to have a direct line of railroad from the Gulf of Mexico to the great chain of northern lakes, and hence you find that the act of congress, making the grant, is entitled an act 'to aid in the construction of a railroad from Chicago *to Mobile.'* The United States not only stipulate for a railroad connection between the lakes and the Gulf of Mexico, but they designate the points of connection—make that stipulation a condition to the grant. It will not do to say that other and entirely different points of connections as the termini of the road would subserve the interest of the government just as well. Congress has decided the question and designated the points—the United States have a right to impose that condition, and the state of Illinois has accepted the land and pledged its honor for the faithful performance of all terms and conditions of the grant. But in point of fact these termini were not selected at random or by accident —they were chosen because they afford the most safe and convenient harbors for vessels of a large size at the two extremes of the most direct and eligible route between the lakes and the Gulf. These termini being unalterably established by a solemn compact between the state of Illinois and the government of the United States, and it being manifestly the intention of the parties that the road should run upon the most direct and eligible route between these points, the question recurs whether the Illinois Central railroad company have legal authority to divert the road from the course marked out in their charter and the act of congress, for the purpose of constructing the road on a different line of travel and conducting the business of the road to a different terminus?

In my opinion the company possesses no such authority. Their charter contains no provision which authorizes such a construction, and I apprehend it would not have been competent for the Illinois legislature to have conferred the privilege without a violation of the act of congress and a consequent forfeiture of the grant of land.

In view of this state of fact I respectfully suggest to you whether it is not probable that you have been misinformed in respect to the intention of the Illinois Central railroad company? It will require clear and explicit evidence to convince the public that a body of gentlemen so distinguished for their intelligence and sagacity would for a moment have entertained the idea of hazarding millions of property—their chartered rights—and perhaps their reputation, in a matter promising so little and perilling so much. The company cannot fail to make millions out of their contract with the state provided they pursue it with wisdom and perform all their obligations with fidelity. With the state of Illinois it should be a point of sacred honor to see that the United States realize all the advantages which constituted the moving considerations for the grant so far as those advantages depend upon fidelity on our part. The state of Illinois is responsible to the United States, and the company to the state. The acts of the company therefore become the acts of the state so far as they injuriously affect the interests of the

United States. I doubt not that the company will find it their interest and their pleasure strictly to comply with their charter and the act of congress according to the spirit and the letter, and then it will become the sacred duty, and I may add the pride and pleasure, of the state to guard and protect the company in the full enjoyments of all their rights and privileges under the act of incorporation. Assuming that the company are not responsible for the rumors which are afloat in respect to the contemplated violation of their charter and of the grant of lands, I have deemed it advisable to give you my opinion in the form of a letter instead of an address to a mass meeting of the citizens, as you propose.[1]

With many thanks for the kind terms in which you have been pleased to speak of my public conduct, I have the honor to remain, very respectfully, your fellow citizen.

S. A. DOUGLAS

Springfield *Illinois State Register*, June 26, 1851. This letter was written in reply to one from a group of Chicagoans who feared that their city would not be served by the Illinois Central Railroad and who sought Douglas' opinion on this matter.

[1] As finally constructed, the Michigan Central joined the Illinois Central near the western shore of Lake Calumet, from which point the Illinois Central agreed to take the Michigan Central into Chicago on its tracks.

To William J. Brown

(*Confidential*)   Chicago
My Dear Sir,   June 21st 1851

I have this moment read your letter of the 16th and avail myself of the proffer to open a confidential correspondence in regard to the Presidency. I am grateful to you for your friendship & the manner in which you have shown it. I went to Washington last Session under the impression that Gen'l Cass was to be our candidate & I was anxious that he should be our next President. I thought it due to him & I hold that the Democracy should never desert their best & most reliable friends. When my name was first brought before the public I discouraged it & avowed my prefference for the General. But recent events indicate a determination on the part of other states to bring out new men, & the movement in my behalf having become so much more respectable & general than I anticipated I have concluded to allow things to take their course & to occupy any position my friends may assign me consistent with the harmony & success of our Party. I have noticed with pride & pleasure the course you have taken. I shall never forget it. Notwithstanding your embarrassment in consequence of the nomination of Gen'l Lane[1] in your state, yet you can do more for me than any man in the country. Your intimate acquaintance with all the public men of the

[226]

country & your knowledge of the true state of Parties in each state gives you peculiar advantages. I will avail myself from time to time of your offer to adopt any suggestions I may make in regard to the mode of conducting the campaign, but in the meantime I have so much confidence in your judgment and descretion that I shall rely to a great extent upon your advice. I agree with you that my name should not be brought too promenently before the public at this time. More can be done by private correspondence with our friends in other states than by any other mode. Particular attention should be paid to the Southern states as there will be a great effort to unite the entire South upon Mr Buchanan. I have many friends in the South who think I would be stronger than *him* in their section, but they are waiting for a movement from my own State & the West generally. A Letter from you to Gov Reid of N.C. (at Raleigh)[2] would do much good by way of encouragement, and also to our friend Gen'l A. A. Chapman of Virginia[3] (now at Richmond attending the constitutional convention). They are both warmly for me, but letters from you would give them great encouragement. Also to some of our friends in Ky, Tenn. & other Southern states.

I have recently received many letters from Ohio confirming what you State in regard to that State. In New York I believe it is general[ly] conceded that I could carry that State if nominated. It is alledged that both divisions of the Party would unite on me there & would be able to give me the State. I had a frank & very friendly conversation with our friend Gen'l Cass upon the subject a few weeks ago, & find him well disposed, and he assured me that he viewed the movement in my favor with pleasure & approbation. I have recently received several letters from Pennsylvania expressing the opinion that my name would unite the Party in that state better than any other, after Mr Buchanan & Gen'l Cass shall have destroyed each others chances.

Well I have filled my sheet & must close. Your friend

S. A. Douglas

Write me often & I will do the same by you. Give me the benefit of your advice upon all points that arise. Mrs D joins me in sending our best wishes to Mrs Brown.

ALS, owned by Mrs. Emmett S. Huggins, Indianapolis, Indiana. William J. Brown was a member of Congress from Indiana from 1843 to 1845 and again from 1849 to 1851. During the administration of President Polk he held the post of Second Assistant Postmaster General. From 1850 to 1855, he was editor of the Indianapolis *Sentinel*.

[1]Joseph Lane, long-time member of the Indiana state legislature, served as Governor of Oregon Territory from 1848 to 1850, and as Delegate from Oregon Territory from 1851 to 1859.

His name was presented by Indiana Democrats as a favorite son candidate for the 1852 Presidential nomination.

[2]David S. Reid had been a member of Congress from North Carolina from 1843 to 1847 and was elected Governor of North Carolina in 1850 and in 1852.

He was a nephew of Thomas Settle and a cousin of Douglas' wife.

[3]Augustus Alexandria Chapman had been a member of Congress from Virginia from 1843 to 1847. Brown, Reid, and Chapman had all entered Congress with Douglas in 1843.

To Augustus C. French

[June 29, 1851, Chicago; LS, Illinois State Archives. Asking that General John J. Viele be reappointed as commissioner to take the acknowledgment of deeds in Troy, New York, for the state of Illinois.]

To George Nicholas Sanders

Confidential   Chicago
My Dear Sir,   July 12th 1851

I presume you have returned to N York by this time & will therefore receive my letter. I am greatly indebted to you for your several letters. I like your letters, for you do not flatter me, but write just what you think. I proffit more by your letters than any I receive. By this you must not infer that I adopt all your views, for I am not yet fully convinced that you do not know how to make a mistake in politics. In regard to your views & paper upon Rivers & Harbors I will write you in a few days. I am not prepared to coincide with you entirely.

All the news I get in regard to politics are favorable; but this is a matter of course, for none but friends write to me. Probably all the others have equally as good grounds for thinking that their prospects are now bright and brightening every day. All the Papers in state (Democratic I mean) are out for me and nearly all have my name at the head of their columns. This has been done without any agency of mine. There are strong indications that most of the other Western States are prepared to take the same course. I know but little of what is going on in the South & East.

I have received an invitation to attend the Dinner to Bishop Hughs;[1] but I regret that I will be unable to do so. I would like to be present on that occasion, for I entertain a very high admiration for the character of the Arch Bishop, and would take pleasure by testifying it by my presence if I had the opportunity. My family are unwell at this time & I cannot leave them. I expect to come East in about four weeks. Will stop a while at Cleveland, Niagara, Saratoga, &c &c.[2] Of course I will meet you in my travels. Present my respects to your family. I remain very truly your friend

S. A. DOUGLAS

[228]

ALS, Watertown Library Association.
[1]John Joseph Hughes, Roman Catholic Bishop of New York, was elevated to Archbishop by Pope Pius IX in April, 1851. The dinner to which Douglas was invited was to celebrate Archbishop Hughes's return from Europe.

[2]Douglas journeyed to Middlebury, Vermont, in August, 1851, where he was granted an honorary Doctor of Laws degree by Middlebury College. The trip enabled him to discuss his candidacy for the Presidential nomination with political leaders in the East.

To ———

Chicago Ills
July 17th 1851

Gentlemen

I have the honor to acknowledge the receipt of your polite invitation to attend a Public Dinner to be given at the Astor House New York on Monday the 21st inst, in honor of the return of the most Rev. Arch Bishop Hughes to America from his late visit to Europe.

It would afford me sincere gratification to testify, by my presence & participation in the festivities of the occasion, my high admiration of the character, piety, virtues, and eminent intellectual endowments of the Arch Bishop and to welcome him back to our own happy home as the appropriate theatre of his duties and usefulness. But, in consequence of my almost constant absence from home for several years on public duty, my private affairs demand my immediate attention, and will not allow of my visiting your city at so early a day as that fixed for your festival. With many thanks for the honor confered by your invitation and for the kind terms in which it is clothed, I have the honor to be very truly your friend & obedient servant.

S. A. DOUGLAS

ALS, owned by Martin F. Douglas.

To ———

Detroit
July 27th 1851

My Dear Sir,

I am this far on my way East. My family have been sick & the Doctor has notified me that I must go to the Sea Shore for their health. They are now doing very well altho Mrs. D could hardly stand on her feet when we started two days ago. We are staying at the House of Gen'l Cass by his special invitation. The old General is all right & seems to understand things well & is perfectly reconciled to them. I shall stop at Cleveland two or three days to visit a relative & some friends & arrive at Buffalo about next Friday, & then go to the Falls to stay about a week.

AL, owned by Martin F. Douglas.

To Lewis Cass

My Dear General

Saratoga N.Y.
Aug 13th 1851

Permit me to introduce to you our mutual friend Ebenezer Peck Esq of Chicago, who will pay his respects to you on his way Home. You will find Mr Peck an intelligent & accomplished gentleman, a good Lawyer & a sound Democrat. He controls the political course of the Chicago Dem Argus, the Paper being owned & edited by his son,[1] who, altho a very intelligent & smart young man, places great confidence in the opinions & advice of his father in the management of his paper. You can rely upon Mr P as a frank, open hearted, & honorable man. I have the honor to be remain very truly your friend

S. A. DOUGLAS

ALS, William L. Clements Library.
[1]The *Democratic Argus*, published in Chicago beginning in 1850, was owned by B. F. Seaton and W. W. Peck.

To Richard James Arnold

My Dear Sir,

Newport
Aug 30th 1851

I regret that we did not receive your card & that of Mrs Arnold in time for us to return it & cultivate a better acquaintance. We were not aware that you & your Lady had called upon us until this moment, after we had packed our trunks to leave tonight. The fault was with the Clerk of the House who threw the card in the general Basket instead of my Box or of sending it to our Rooms.

We will be happy to see you when you may visit Washington. Yours in haste

S. A. DOUGLAS

P.S. Please make the same apology for us to Mr & Mrs S G Arnold.[1]

ALS, Illinois State Historical Library. Richard James Arnold was a Providence, Rhode Island, attorney.
[1]Samuel Greene Arnold, Rhode Island attorney and historian, was elected Lieutenant Governor of the state in 1852. He was the son-in-law of Richard James Arnold.

To George Roberts

(*Private*)
My Dear Sir,

Astor House
New York
Sept 8th 1851

During the severe illness of my family and just as I was leaving Chicago I received your letter expressing your preferences for me for the Presidency & tendering your support provided I would give the countenance and patronage of the administration to your paper and provide for your friends in the distribution of places. I have failed to answer you upon these points with the expectation of meeting you, having heard that you were to be at various places which I intended to visit. Our friend Parson's assured me that I would meet you at Newport or I should have written you from that place. I must say to you in all candor that I have not allowed myself to give the slightest promise or intimation to any man living of any personal advantage to be derived from my administration in the event of my election. I have refused such intimations in cases where there was danger of disturbing old personal relations & friendships, and I place the refusal upon a principle from which I can in no instance depart. I have as strong attachments to friends as any man and am as likely to remember their services to me with gratitude; but in the performance of public trusts favors to friends must be consistent with or subordinate to the public interests; and of this I must be allowed to judge from time to time as it becomes my duty to act.

I have thought it due to the friendship which has so long existed between us that I should make this distinct avowal of my principles of action. I am sure that upon reflection you will approve my course in this respect, for he who would make promises to one man upon condition of support, I should be apprehensive would make different & inconsistent promises to other persons upon like conditions.

In regard to the Presidency I will say that I do not consider myself a candidate in the field canvassing for support. I am young & can afford to wait & am not anxious therefore about the present. We have many distinguished statesmen in this country who have rendered good service and deserve much of our party & the country, and whose age will not allow them to wait. They can afford to hazard everything upon the cast of a die because they have no future before them. If any one of them shall be selected I shall go into the canvass cordially & with all the energy of my nature to ensure his success. These are my views & feelings. The relations between us entitle you to know them. I should have been glad to have met you but I have not the time to visit Boston. I remain very truly your friend

S. A. Douglas

ALS, Illinois State Historical Library. George Roberts was editor of the Boston *Times* from 1836 to 1857, when he moved to New York.

To George Nicholas Sanders

Batavia N Y

Dear Sir, Sept. 22d 1851

All went off well at Rochester,[1] and I leave today for the Ohio State Fare at Columbus which takes place this week. I see the Herald publishes my address & perhaps the Union & Richmond Enquirer and other papers further South might be induced to do so, especially the N. O. Delta. I will return to New York next week. Yours truly

S. A. DOUGLAS

ALS, Lincoln College, Lincoln, Illinois. ¹Douglas had just spoken to the fair of the New York State Agricultural Society at Rochester, New York. His speech was published as *Address of the*

Hon. Stephen A. Douglas at the Annual Fair of the New-York State Agricultural Society, Held at Rochester, Sept., 1851 (Albany, New York, 1851).

To George D'Almaine

Washington
Oct 26th '51

My Dear Sir

I have this moment received your kind letter. I desire you to be sure & take the Portraits of my Mother & Sister. They reside in Ontario Co N.Y. seven miles east of Canandaigua on the Rail Road to Albany. Clifton is the Depot nearest to their residence & where you will leave the Cars. They reside within one mile & a half of Clifton. When you arrive at Clifton get the Landlord to take you to Julius N. Grangers Esq's who is my Brother in-Law. You will find my Mother & Sister both there at the same House. I wish you to take both their Portraits & bring them with you to Washington. I will attend to the Committee Room for you. I am glad you have got a good likeness of Gen'l Cass. I shall prize it very highly. He is a noble patriot and a model of a man. Present my kind regards to the General & his family when you go to take leave of him, and express my thanks to him for having done me the favor to permit his Portrait to be taken for me. I remain very truly your friend

S. A. DOUGLAS

ALS, owned by Paul W. Kieser, Toledo, Ohio. George D'Almaine, a portrait painter who emigrated from England in the late 1840's, worked chiefly in Baltimore, Maryland.

To Samuel Treat

(*Confidential*)
My Dear Sir,

Washington
Dec 15th 1851

I received your favor of the 23th ult on my return to this city the first week of the Session, but I have delayed my answer until the question of the Secretaryship was deffinitely answered. The result shows that you were right in not coming on. Who could have thought that a Democratic Senate would have decided not to go into and election & thus keep the old fogies in office for life.¹ Yet such was the fact. We were confident that we had the strength, and were not undeceived until we got into caucus. Your election would have been of incalculable service to our Party and I had personal reasons very strong for desiring your presence here this winter. But you acted right as the result shows.

I agree entire in your views in regard to the Butler movement.[2] It will require all our energies to defeat it. Their plan is extensive & being executed with vigor. They are bring[ing] out local candiates in each state with the view of getting the control of a majority of the delegates & then combining their strength. This explains the Marcy movement in N Y & the Allen movement in Ohio, & the Pierce movement in N.H.[3] Yet the friends of Cass & Buchanan do not seem to understand it. I think we will be able to defeat the scheme, but it will require all our vigilance. What will Missouri do? And when will you move off in the election of delegates. All that is necessary now to enable me to succeed is to show that the West is ready to unite on me. It becomes important therefore that Missouri & Iowa should speak out. Let me hear from you often & tell me precisely how things stand. I remain very truly your friend

S. A. DOUGLAS

ALS, Missouri Historical Society.
[1]Douglas had hoped to secure the election of Treat as Secretary of the Senate. Instead, Asbury Dickens, who had held the post since 1836, was re-elected.
[2]William Orlando Butler, former Representative from Kentucky and a veteran of both the War of 1812 and the Mexican War, had been the Democratic candidate for Vice-President in 1848.

[3]William L. Marcy served briefly as Senator from New York between 1831 and 1833, and held the post of Secretary of War in the cabinet of President Polk; William Allen of Ohio served in the House of Representatives for one term and in the Senate from 1837 to 1849; Franklin Pierce represented New Hampshire in the lower house of Congress from 1833 to 1837 and in the Senate from 1837 to 1842.

To Edward C. West

[December 28, 1851, Washington; ALS. This letter was sold by the Anderson Galleries, New York, in November, 1916. The letter has not been located.]

To George Nicholas Sanders

Confidential   Washington
My Dear Sir,   Dec 28th 1851

Many thanks for your kind letters. I have seen your friend Croswell[1] today & find all right. In regard to the Review I am at a loss what to say. I would gladly let you have the money, but I don't know where to get [it]. I have already borrowed so much that I don't know where to apply. The cost of fitting up my House is not all settled & [I] really don't

[233]

know what to do. I will try and raise it however if absolutely necessary. Write at once & let me know. I appreciate the service you are rendering me & the importance of the movement, and will do all in my power.

When will you be here? Your presence is much needed. What is the matter of the Herald. It is very hostile every day—more so to me than to any one else.

Write soon. My kind regards to your family

S. A. Douglas

ALS, Illinois State Historical Library.

[1] Edwin Croswell was editor of the Albany (New York) *Democratic Argus* and prominent in New York Democratic politics as a member of the anti-Marcy faction.

To Charles M. Conrad

[December 29, 1851, Senate, U.S.; ALS, RG-107, National Archives. Requests a copy of the report of Colonel Francis Lee, commandant at Fort Snelling, in reference to the reduction of the military reservation at that point. Charles M. Conrad, of Louisiana, was Secretary of War in the cabinet of President Fillmore.]

To William H. English

(*Confidential*) Washington
My Dear Sir, Dec 29th 1851

I had the honor to receive your kind letter some two weeks ago, but the pressures of constant engagements has prevented an earlier reply. I need not assure you that I feel grateful for your efforts in my behalf and that I am also gratified at the prospect that Indiana will be found with Illinois when the day of trial arrives. Of course I would not wish my name brought in collision with Gen'l Lane in your state, and I entirely agree with you that it would be better, if the General continues on the track, for you to instruct for him as the first & myself as the second choice of the state. If you can accomplish this, of which you seem confident, it will do equally as well to instruct for me in the first instance. Let me hear from you often & tell me how things stand. Your friend

S. A. Douglas

ALS, William Henry Smith Memorial Library, Indiana Historical Society. William H. English, a clerk in the United States Treasury Department from 1844 to 1848, was at this time Speaker of the Indiana House of Representatives. He was later elected to the national Congress, serving from 1853 to 1861.

To Charles H. Lanphier

(*Confidential*)   Washington
My Dear Sir,   Dec 30th 1851

I have had your letter under advisement for several days & have taken
the advice of most of our delegation in respect to that part of it which
relates to the Bank question.[1] Gen'l Shields and indeed all that I have
seen are clearly & decidedly of the opinion that it would be unwise for
the State officers to refuse to carry the Banking Law into effect. I agree
with them in this conclusion. However obnoxious the Banking law
may be to us & much as we might desire to defeat its adoption by the
people, we are decidedly of the opinion that it will carry as often as it
may be submitted to the people. The Whigs as a party will support it
from partizan considerations & a portion of the Democrats will support
in accordance with what they suppose to be their interests and the supposed public necessities. Thus a combination can always be formed to
carry the measure & we as good democrats are forced to submit to the
will of the people when expressed according to the forms of the constitution. To carry the question into the next general election would
enable the combination to carry not only that measure, but the Legislature & state Government. Under these circumstances I unite with my
colleagues in advising that the law be allowed to take its course.

In regard to the Presidency I will say a few words. Things look well
& the prospect is brightening every day. All that is necessary now to
ensure success is that the north West should unite & speak out. It would
be well that the delegates should be elected from Illinois as soon as convenient and that the convention should express its preference in clear &
unequivocal terms. It is important also that some movements should be
made in Missouri & Iowa soon. Perhaps you & our friends at Springfield
may be able to exert some influence upon the subject.

Write me often & keep my well posted up in affairs. Your friend
                                                     S. A. DOUGLAS

ALS, Illinois State Historical Library.
[1]An act establishing a complete, general system of banking in Illinois was passed
by the state legislature, over the Governor's veto, on February 15, 1851.

To Charles M. Conrad

[January 20, 1852, Senate Chamber, Washington; ALS, RG-107, National Archives. Acknowledges receipt of the report of Colonel Francis Lee in reference to the reduction of Fort Snelling (see above,
Douglas to Conrad, December 29, 1851), and inquires whether the
War Department concurs in the views of Colonel Lee.]

To George Walker and Charles H. Lanphier

(*Confidential*)   Senate U.S.
My Dear Sirs   Jan'y 21st 1852

You will excuse the neglect in keeping you advised of the state of things. Ficklin,[1] who is present, says the will write you often & keep you posted up. My opinion is that all of the Illinois papers should refrain from any attack upon any candidate, at the same time that they stand firm & steadfast in their first choice.

Prospects heighten every day. Your—

S. A. DOUGLAS

ALS, Illinois State Historical Library.
[1]Orlando B. Ficklin, member of Congress from 1843 to 1849, was elected again in 1850 and served one additional term from 1851 to 1853.

To [the Commissioner of Indian Affairs?]

[January 23, 1852, n.p. Asks for authenticated copies of the Pottawatomie Indian treaties. This letter is listed in Register #40 of Letters Received in the Office of Indian Affairs, RG-75, National Archives, but the original has not been located.]

To Ebenezer Peck

[February, 1852]

Prospects look well and are improving every day. If two or three western states will speak out in my favor the battle is over. Can anything be done in Iowa & Missouri? That is very important. If some one could go to Iowa, I think the Convention in that state would instruct for me. In regard to our State I will say a word. Other states are appointing a large number of delegates to the convention. Tenn. 46, Texas about 50, Miss 50 Ala 30 or 40 &c, ought not our State to do the same thing so as to ensure the attendance of most of our leading active politicians at Baltimore? Five could be appointed from each Congressional District and twenty at large making 55 from the State. In other words let every good democrat come, with instructions that the majority of the delegates present must rule in casting the vote of the State. This large number would exert a great moral influence on the other delegates. I make this suggestion in confidence for the consideration of our friends. I would also suggest the propriety, of adding the congressional delegation for the same reason. I merely suggest this as an offset to the action of other States to put us on an equality with them. . . . I received a letter to day from George[1] for which thank him for me.

[236]

This is an extract from a letter written by Douglas to Ebenezer Peck,
and quoted by Peck in a letter to
Charles H. Lanphier, February 25,
1852, Chicago (Illinois State Historical
Library). The original Douglas letter
has not been located.

¹George Walker, a partner with Lanphier in the *Illinois State Register*.

To Caleb Cushing

(Confidential)   Washington
My Dear Sir,   Feb'y 4th 1852

Accept my sincere thanks for your kind letter, and for the favorable
opinions you entertain of my public course. I agree with you fully in
the criticisms you make upon the tone & spirit of the articles in the last
number of the Dem Review. Our friend Sanders is a noble fellow and
a man of remarkable vigor of intellect, but I fear he lacks the requisite
prudence to conduct the Review safely at the present time. The last
number has given me much uneasiness for the very reasons stated in
your letter.¹ In my opinion the Review should make no attack upon
any Democrat—much less upon Democratic candidates for the Presidency, nor should any of my known active friends make any such attacks. I have repeatedly expressed these opinions & pressed them upon
our friend Sanders as my earnest wishes. But it seems that my wishes
in this respect are disregarded by him, altho he is my devoted friend &
is governed by what he deems good policy to promote my interests. I
question both the policy & propriety of the assaults he is making.
Again, while I am a radical & progressive democrat, I fear the Review
goes too far in that direction—especially in regard to European affairs.
I cannot see my way clear to go beyond the rule laid down in my
speeches in the Senate & at the Banquet to which you have refered in
such kind terms of approbation.² The article under the title of *"the
Usurper"* is exceedingly objectionable—indeed its profane allusions to
our Saviour & to religion are shocking to any moral & religious man.³ I
had not read that article until I received your letter & have had time
now only to read the passages refered to by you. But I have read
enough to condemn the spirit & style of the article and to be amazed
that it should have found its way into the Review. No party can or
ought to be sustained which offends against the moral sense of the religious community. I do not deem it necessary or advisable that political periodicals should discuss religious subjects, but whenever the subject of religion is referred to, it should be done in terms of reverence
appropriate to the subject. I have thus expressed my opinions with freedom & candor. It is thus I always deal with my friends & I am gratified
to see that your letter is written in the same spirit. I am glad that you
have consented to become a contributor to the Review. In your hands

[237]

the interests of the Democratic Party are safe, and I have no apprehensions that you will make any of the mistakes to which I have alluded.

Repeating my obligations to you for consulting me upon these points, I must ask of you the favor to write me frequently & give me the benefit of your advice & counsel in the present position of our political affairs. I have often wished that you were here where I could consult you from day to day, and I had thought seriously of writing to you to come to Washington. Write often & freely. Excuse this hasty scrawl. I remain very truly your friend

S. A. DOUGLAS

ALS, Library of Congress. Caleb Cushing represented Massachusetts in the House of Representatives from 1835 to 1843, when he was appointed Minister to China. At the time of this letter, he was Mayor of Newburyport. In 1853, President Franklin Pierce appointed him Attorney General of the United States.

[1]In the January, 1852, number of the *Democratic Review*, Sanders announced, in an article entitled "Eighteen-fifty-two and the Presidency," that the Democratic party must turn to the "young blood" and "young ideas" of the new generation of political leaders, and repudiate the "statesmen of a previous generation, with their personal antipathies and their personal claims." Although Sanders mentioned no names, it was well known that he was backing Douglas' candidacy for the Presidency. Cushing wrote Douglas on February 1, 1852, of his doubts of the wisdom of Sanders' course in the January number of the magazine (Library of Congress).

[2]Cushing, referring to Sanders' well-known sympathy with the liberal revolutionary movements in Europe, had written, "Is it safe to go for the *Reds*, in such terms of startling reprobation of all who are not Reds, as in some phrases of the first and in the general spirit as well as language of the third

and other articles?" Douglas refers to his remarks in the Senate on the occasion of the visit to the United States of Louis Kossuth, the Hungarian revolutionary leader, and to his statements at a banquet given for Kossuth on January 7, 1852, by members of Congress. Douglas had said in his Senate speech, "I hold that the principle laid down by Governor Kossuth as the basis of his action—that each State has a right to dispose of her own destiny, and regulate her internal affairs in her own way, without the intervention of any foreign power—is an axiom in the laws of nations which every State ought to recognize and respect."

[3]The article, "The Usurper," was subtitled "Being a French romance recently produced in Paris, to the great amusement of everybody, and the death of a few thousand of the lookers-on; and now for the first time condensed into seven short chapters; by an old hand." It was an indictment of Louis Napoleon, the "usurper" referred to in the title. Cushing had feared that some of the allusions made in the article would offend the Catholics in the United States, who, he wrote, "are already too prone to go for Scott." General Winfield Scott was the leading contender for the Whig nomination for the Presidency.

To Mark W. Delahay

[February 10, 1852, Senate Chamber; LS. This letter has not been located. It is described in *A Catalogue of Lincolniana*, Thomas F. Madigan, New York, p. 43, #92, and in Catalog 28, Charles Hamilton Autographs, Inc., New York, p. 7, #44. According to the descriptions, the letter read in part: "Yours of the 15th Dec. last making reference to a 'class of people who were in the Black Hawk or Indian War of 1831' has been received. Without a more definite statement of the case than appears to have been expressed in your letter, it is scarcely possible to make any satisfactory effort in the matter." Douglas also asked that Delahay set forth "the points in which they differ from those who have received the benefits of Bounty-land Act of 1850." Mark Delahay, a former newspaper editor in Naples and Virginia, Illinois, moved to Kansas Territory in 1855, where he became editor of the Leavenworth *Kansas Territorial Register*.]

To George Nicholas Sanders

(*Confidential*)   Washington
My Dear Sir,   Feby 10th 1852
    You will pardon me for again expressing to you the uneasiness felt by all my friends here at the course of the Democrat Review.[1] We know your friendship for me & your desire to serve me; and it is because the public know your feelings in this respect, that your course is calculated to do so much injury. The friends of other candidates will hold me responsible for the assaults made by you upon their favorites. It is no answer to say that I am not responsible. You know & I know that my voice in this respect has been disregarded, and yet they will not believe it. I repeat that it is both inpolitic & unjust to make assaults upon any good Democrat. The man whose active friends will try to advance his interests by assaulting others is sure to be defeated. You know this has been my opinion from the beginning. Every day confirms me in its correctness. I have just been informed that you refused to admit the Biography of Gov Marcy into the Review when requested by his friends. If the refusal was intended to serve me & that fact be so understood by his friends I assure you it will injure me tenfold more than it will him. The Review ought to be impartial as between good Democrats and should be conducted solely with reference to the good of the cause. I speak thus plainly at the hazard of giving offense, for I am deeply impresed with the truth of what I say. You may tell me in reply as you have done on a former occasion that you are a free man and have a right to do as you please, and that I had better mind my own business. This is all very true & would do very well if nobody was to be effected by your acts but yourself. But when your active support of me leaves the world to suppose that I instigate these assaults, I submit to you whether my appeals to you to desist ought not to be respected.
    I have expressed myself freely to our friend West upon this subject

& requested him to see you & explain my views to you as I have now stated them. Excuse the freedom with which I write, for I assure you that I appreciate your friendship for me & shall always remember it with gratitude. Yours truly

S. A. DOUGLAS

ALS, Illinois State Historical Library.
[1]In his letters to Douglas, Sanders previewed his future course of action. On February 3, 1852, he wrote, "I shall make an attack on Genl Butler more terrific than was ever made against mortal man before. I'll finish him . . . dont be scared it will not be thunder, but it shall be an earthquake" (Douglas Papers, University of Chicago Library). A few days later, on February 9, he wrote, "Dont be scared. I hope to turn the tables on all our enemies I have the subject in the precise position I want it . . . I shall endeavor to take my full share of the responsibility of the contest off your shoulders. The Democratic Review will be out this week and you may prepare yourself to see the greatest political paper ever issued" (*ibid.*). The February issue of the *Review* carried a scathing attack on William Orlando Butler, of Kentucky, as a man without convictions. Butler's friends were angered by Sanders' statements; early in March, John C. Breckinridge denounced Douglas in the House of Representatives as responsible for the course of the magazine. Undaunted, Sanders carried his assaults against the "old fogies" in the party even further in subsequent issues. When Douglas' attitude toward his course became known, Sanders wrote, "Politicians are all cowards and you are at the head of the list. I am sick" (February 11, 1852, *ibid.*). Sanders' ill-advised statements turned many of the party leaders against Douglas, and contributed a great deal to Douglas' defeat for the Presidential nomination.

<h1 align="center">To William A. Seaver</h1>

(Private) Washington

My Dear Sir, Feby 10th 1852

I am greatly obliged for your kind letter. I regret I could [not] have seen you at my House before you left this city. I had intended to have you and some other friends to spend an evening & Mrs Douglas was much disappointed when she found that she was deprived of the pleasure of your company. We have nothing new here in the political line. Things look about as they did when you were here except that a bad state of feeling is getting up between the two divisions of our party in the South. Ala has made a demonstration for a Union Party & we fear that Geo will follow suit.[1] A third party organization would be disastrious & double sets of delegates to the convention almost as bad. I regret the impudent & reckless course of the Democratic Review. Our friend George means well, but he has made a fatal mistake. I am in hopes he will improve in his next No. If not he will ruin the Review & greatly injure those he intends to benefit.

Let me hear from you often. Give my best respects to your good Lady. I remain very truly yours

S. A. DOUGLAS

ALS, Illinois State Historical Library. ¹The Democratic party in Alabama had split into two factions: a radical group which opposed the Compromise of 1850, led by William Lowndes Yancey; and a "union" group, consisting of those Democrats who acquiesced in the Compromise measures. Both groups presented candidates in the Congressional elections of 1851, although the "union" tickets experienced the greater success. In Georgia, a similar split had taken place.

To W. W. Corcoran

Washington
My Dear Sir,   Feby 18th 1852

Permit me to introduce to you my friend Mr George D'Almaine, an artist of decided genius & high merit who has taken the Portraits of the members of my family. Mr D'Almaine is a gentleman of high tone & in all respects worthy of confidence. Your friend

S. A. DOUGLAS

ALS, Library of Congress.

To Augustus C. French

[February 25, 1852, Senate Chamber, U.S.; LS, Illinois State Archives. Recommendation, signed by Douglas and Iowa's Senators, George W. Jones and Augustus Caesar Dodge, that Hugh W. Sample, of Keokuk, Iowa, be appointed commissioner to take acknowledgments of deeds for Illinois in Iowa.]

To the Editor of the Washington *Union*

[March 19, 1852]

Houston & Douglas

In yesterday's Union we published an article over the Signature of San Jacinto in vindication of Gen'l Sam Houston as a candidate for the Presidency.¹ So far as the article was a defence of the distinguished Senator from Texas against the assaults or insinuations of his enemies, it meets with our entire approbation, and comes within our rule of neutrality as between Democratic aspirants for the Presidency. But upon a more careful perusal of the article we are apprehensive that the publication of the record of votes from the Journals of the Senate, without explanation, was calculated to convey an erronous and injurious impression in regard to other distinguished Democrats who are no less deserving the confidence & support of the party. For instance, Judge Douglas is represented as having voted for various propositions to prohibit slavery in the territories of the United States, while it is well known to the country that no member of either House of Congress was more bold & inflexible in his opposition to the Wilmot Proviso

[241]

than the distinguished Senator from Illinois. He has always opposed the slavery aggetation in Congress. He brought forward the Missouri Compromise as a part of the Bill for the annexation of Texas. He advocated the same measure as a substitute for the Wilmot Proviso in 1846-&'47, and voted against the two & t[h]ree million Bills[2] because they contained the Proviso. He voted against the Proviso in the Senate in 1848, when proposed as an amendment to the treaty of Peace with Mexico. He voted for the Clayton Bill[3] in the Senate the same Session and after its defeat in the House of Representatives, by the votes of a few Southern Whigs, he brought forward the Missouri Compromise which was adopted in the Senate on his motion, but defeated in the House of Representatives. All these measures having failed he wrote most of the Bills & supported & defended all the measures of the compromise which has hapily done so much to give peace & quiet to the country. What man in the nation can show a clearer record than this? But we now come to the votes cited by San Jacinto, and presuming that they are correctly quoted from the record, we dispose of them all by calling the attention of our readers to the fact that each and all of those votes were given under the express instructions of the Legislature of Illinois—that Judge Douglas was well known to disapprove of them at the time—that he entered his protest against those votes before & after they were recorded, and declared that he should never hold himself responsible for them. These facts all appear from the debates in the Senate, and particular in his famous speech before the infuriated populace of Chicago in defense of the fugitive Slave law, and in his speech in the Senate in December last on Foote's resolution.[4] We subjoin extracts from two of these speeches. In his Chicago Speech, in speaking of the Compromise, he says:[5]

Here we find that Judge Douglas immediately upon his return home from the Session when these votes were given, told his constituents— *"those were your votes—not mine. I entered my protest against [them] at the time—before and after they were recorded—and shall never hold myself responsible for them!* We will now close this article with the following extract from his speech this Session on Footes resolution, renewing our purpose of maintaining strict neutrality between all the Democratic candidates:[6]

This speech was immediately printed, and circulated all over the State. I at the time travelled over a good portion of the State, and made many speeches of the same tenor, the last of which was made in the capital of our State. A few weeks afterwards, the legislature assembled, and one of their first acts was to repeal the resolutions of instructions to which I have referred, and to pass resolutions approving of the course of my colleague and myself on the compromise measures, by a vote of three or four to one. From that day Illinois has stood firm and unwavering in support of the compromise measures and of all the compromises of the Constitution.

Now, Mr. President, I have done with these explanations, and I trust forever. If I have said anything which savors of egotism, I know the Senate will pardon me, and at the same time sympathize in the necessity which has imposed it upon me. If I had omitted all that was personal to myself, my defence would have been incomplete and unsatisfactory. I could not have done less and have done justice to myself and to those who are connected with me. In view of all the facts, I submit the question whether the charge or insinuation that I was at any time favorable to the Wilmot proviso was and is not grossly ungenerous and unjust. I am willing to be held responsible for all my acts; but I wish to be judged by my acts and not by malicious misrepresentations of them. I do not claim to be infallible. I may have committed many errors, and doubtless have; but when I am convinced of them, I will acknowledge them like a man, and promptly correct them. I wish to avoid no responsibility. I do not belong to that school of politicians.

In taking leave of this subject, I wish to state that I have determined never to make another speech upon the slavery question; and I will now add the hope that the necessity for it will never exist. I am heartily tired of the controversy, and I know the country is disgusted with it. In regard to the resolutions of the Senator from Mississippi, I will be pardoned for saying that I much doubt the wisdom and expediency of their introduction. The whole country is acquiescing in the compromise measures—everywhere, North and South. Nobody proposes to repeal or disturb them. True, everybody was not for them originally, nor would they be so now were it an open or original question. But since they have been adopted, and time has been given for a little cool reflection, everybody seems to be disposed to treat them as a final settlement of an unprofitable controversy. So long as our opponents do not agitate for repeal or modification, why should we agitate for any purpose? We claim that the Compromise is a final settlement. Is a final settlement open to discussion, and agitation, and controversy, by its friends? What manner of settlement is that which does not settle the difficulty and quiet the dispute?

ADf, owned by Martin F. Douglas. The draft is endorsed "Copy of Article for Union Mch 19th 52." The article was printed with some minor editorial alterations, as a letter to the editor, signed by "A Western Man," in the Washington *Union*, March 23, 1852.

[1]"Gen. Sam Houston and the Presidency," signed by "San Jacinto," Washington *Union*, March 20, 1852.
[2]These were appropriation bills for the Mexican War. The "two million" bill was proposed in the summer of 1846. It passed the House with the Wil-

mot Proviso attached to it, but the Senate adjourned without taking action on it. The "three million" bill was introduced early in 1847; once again the Proviso was attached to it by the House. The Senate, however, defeated the bill; it finally became law without the Proviso.

³The so-called "Clayton Compromise," introduced in July, 1848, proposed to solve the dispute over slavery in the Mexican cession and at the same time provide a government for Oregon. Oregon was to be organized as a territory, retaining the antislavery provisions of its provisional government; California and New Mexico were to be organized as territories, but they were prohibited from acting on the slavery question; and finally, all disputes respecting slavery in the territories were to be referred to the territorial courts, with appeal to the United States Supreme Court.

⁴Henry Stuart Foote, Senator from Mississippi, introduced a resolution early in December, 1851, declaring the Compromise of 1850 to be a final settlement of the slavery question. Douglas responded three weeks later, on December 23, with a speech recognizing the finality of the Compromise and insisting that the slavery question must be banished from politics.

⁵No extracts from Douglas' Chicago speech were included in the draft. They were supplied, however, in the printed version.

⁶The following portion of Douglas' Senate speech was clipped from the published report and attached to the draft.

To Walter S. Gurnee

[March 20, 1852]

No arraingement has been made with the Illinois Central Rail Road Company except the one at New York last fall, upon which I have confidently relied to prevent the cut-off. I write in full today.¹
20 Mch 52²   S. A. DOUGLAS

ALS Copy, owned by Martin F. Douglas. Walter S. Gurnee was Mayor of Chicago. On March 19, Gurnee had telegraphed Douglas: "Has a satisfactory arrangement been made with Illinois and central about cut off. The Michigan central have one thousand men at work in this state forming a junction sixteen miles out. What ought we to do? Meetings have been held and our citizens are highly indignant" (owned by Martin F. Douglas).

¹See below.
²The date is not in Douglas' hand.

To Walter S. Gurnee

Mch 20, 1852

I am surprised at the information communicated by yr letter & telegraph that the Michigan Central R. R are making a connection with the Illinois C. R. R by means of what is known as the "cut-off". I am not aware that we have any right to complain of the conduct of the Michigan R. in this respect for they have never recd. a charter from our state & have made no stipulation with us upon the subject, so far as I am informed, & it is natural for them to wish to get to Chicago by any means in their power. Their legal right to make this cut off is a different question & one upon which I can form no opinion for I do not know upon what ground they predicate their right.

[244]

But the main point in the controversy is as to the action of the I. C. R. R. Co. It is not reasonable to suppose that the M. C. R. R. Co will make the cut-off unless they have assurances from the I. C. R R Co that they might unite with them & use their Road to our city. I should regard any such understanding or connection of the two Roads a gross violation of faith on the part of the I. C. R. R. Co. The basis of yr arrangements with that Co. at N.Y. last fall was the distinct & unequivocal declaration on their part that they abandoned all idea and intention of the cut off & that they wd. run their Road directly to Chicago & have the M. Co. to join them at Chicago or on the Lake shore near the city line. This point being settled as the basis of the arrangement the line was agreed upon to run on the W. side of Calumet lake & not to approach within four & a half miles of the state line. But for this express stipulation not to make the cut off I know that you wd. never have made the arrangement & cirtainly I wd. never have sanctioned it, for what difference was it to us or to the people of Chicago whether the cut off was at the state line or 4½ miles W. of it, if it wd. be made at all? Why was I sent for by telegraph by Mr. Griswold[1] & yrself to come fm Washn. to N.Y. to arrange the terms of the agreement unless it was upon the condition that the cut off was not to be made for I had assured them a few days previous that I could not & wd. not assent to any other terms? But why shd. I argue the questn. for there is no possibility of our being mistaken as to the terms, meaning & understanding of the parties to the arrangement in N.Y. Relying upon that arrangement, I aided them in preventing the reopening of the question as to the confirmation of their grant of lands & told their Attr. Col Bissell[2] at the time that I did so on the sole condition of their observing good faith in regard to not making the cut off & he then read me extracts of a letter from Mr. Schuyler[3] which satisfied me that the understanding was to be carried out in good faith. My support in aid of the confirmation of the grant was procured therefore upon the express consideration that the cut off was not to be made & I informed Col. B. & Mr. Butterfield[4] at the time that I wd. prefer having the Road run within 4½ miles of the state line & rely upon the word & honor of the gentlemen composing the Company, than to have the line moved one mile & a half further W. & thereby release them from the obligation to carry out the arrangement made with you in N.Y. Under these circumstances I am yet unwilling to believe that the company are going to act in bad faith with us.[5]

But we will soon know the facts when I will write you again. Yr frd.

S. A. D.

Copy, owned by Martin F. Douglas.

[1]George Griswold, one of the backers of the Illinois Central Railroad.

[2]William H. Bissell was solicitor for the Illinois Central. Bissell was also at this time a member of Congress, from Illinois, where he served from 1849 to 1855. In 1856, he was elected Governor of Illinois.

[3]Robert Schuyler was President of the Illinois Central Railroad.

[4]Justin Butterfield had died on March 5, 1852.

[5]For an earlier letter on the Michigan Central connection, see above, Douglas to the Citizens of Chicago, June 19, 1851, especially n1.

To George Nicholas Sanders

(*Confidential*)   Washington

My Dear Sir,   April 15th 1852

Mr Croswell has delivered your message to me. From it I fear you have determined to keep up your assaults upon Gen'l Cass & other candidates for the presidency. I need not repeat to you how much I have regretted those assaults, and how much injury they have done me. True it was unjust to hold me responsible for them, inasmuch as it is well known that I always disapproved of them, yet the human mind is so constituted that in high political excitements the public will hold each candidate responsible for the acts of his friends. The public will not allow me to be an exception to this rule. I am held responsible for your attacks upon others to a considerable extent & hence many of their friends have become my bitter & determined enemys solely on account of the course of the Review. If you cease now and make no more attacks upon anybody and especially none on Gen'l Cass, possibly I may yet regain my lost position. If those attacks are repeated my chances are utterly hopeless, and I may be compelled to retire from the field and throw my influence in favor of one of those whom the Review strives to crush. Do not mistake my motives. I write you as a friend—I preserve my entire composure & equinimity—but I write as a friend who has been deeply injured & wounded by his friends in opposition to his remonstrances. It is impossible to convince me or my friends that I am mistaken as to the propriety or effect of the course of the Review. I have all the time felt and now I know that my position has been injured & prospects blighted by this course which represents me as an Ishmaelite with my hand against everybody and inviting everybodys hand to be against me. Besides the position is revolting to my feelings. I am not oversensitive, but I am not willing to be made to appear in a point of view against which my own sense of propriety & self-respect revolts. I speak plainly, but in no spirit of unkindness. I appeal to you to desist, and save my feelings & that of my friends. If not you may drive me to a position, which none but an enemy would desire me to occupy, and which I know you would regret. I therefore again request you to make no more attacks upon anybody; but if you must assail others, also assail me with them, and at the same time select somebody else as your candidate and bend all your energies to elect him. With feelings of kindness I remain very truly your friend

S. A. DOUGLAS

ALS, Illinois State Historical Library.

To Daniel Webster

[May 5, 1852, Washington; LS, RG-59, National Archives. Requesting Webster, Secretary of State, to send a copy of "Storys edition of the laws of the United States" to Governor French of Illinois. The request was signed by Douglas and Shields, Illinois' Senators, and by Orlando B. Ficklin, Willis Allen, Thompson Campbell, and R. S. Molony, Illinois members of the House of Representatives.]

To Samuel Strong

My Dear Sir,   [May 13, 1852]
   Patrick Moroney, the bearer of this note is the man of whom I spoke to you the other day for employment on the Capitol. He has been in my employment for the last two months and is one of the most faithful & industrous men I ever knew. I feel an interest in his success and shall feel grateful to you for giving him employment.
May 13th 1852   S. A. DOUGLAS

ALS, Lincoln National Life Foundation, Fort Wayne, Indiana. Samuel Strong, a Washington, D.C., builder, was Superintendent of the Capitol.

To Robert G. Scott

Washington, D.C., May 22, 1852.
   Sir—I have the honor to acknowledge the receipt of your letter of the 17th instant, and take pleasure in responding directly to your interrogatories; especially as my answer will only require a reiteration of my well matured opinions, which have repeatedly been expressed in my place in the Senate and in the House of Representatives, and to my constituents at home.
   While the series of measures known as the Compromise was supported and opposed by democrats and whigs indiscriminately, and, therefore, could not justly be claimed as party measures, yet I deemed it my duty, under the circumstances, to give them in the Senate, a cordial and unwavering support; and immediately upon my return home, when assailed by my constituents, I defended and vindicated

the provisions of each and all of those acts, and especially insisted upon the faithful execution of the law for the reclamation of fugitives from labor. My opinions upon these questions have undergone no change, and I shall deem it my duty, in whatever official position I may be placed, to exert all legal and constitutional authority to enforce the honest execution of those, as well as all other acts passed in pursuance of the constitution. Inasmuch as the constitution of the United States provides that "no person held to service or labor in one State under the laws thereof, escaping into another, shall, in consequence of any law or regulation therein, be discharged from such service or labor, but shall be delivered up on the claim of the party to whom such service or labor may be due," it became the imperative duty of Congress to pass all laws necessary to carry that provision into effect; and no act calculated to render that provision of the constitution inoperative, or to destroy or diminish the force of the existing laws for its fulfillment, or to impair or obstruct the rights of the citizens of any State under it, can ever receive my approval.

According to the construction I have been inclined to place upon your letter, the foregoing furnishes a full and complete answer to all your interrogatories; but the clause in which you inquire whether I would "discountenance, by every proper means, all attempts to disturb or change the provisions of that law whereby those provisions might be made less effectual," may probably be construed to imply that the Executive would be expected to influence or restrain the action of Congress by other means than those enjoined by the constitution. Lest my answer may not be deemed full on this point, it is due to candor to state that I should not feel at liberty, in any event, to use the patronage of the government for the purpose of influencing the legislative action upon that or any other subject, but would leave to Congress the independent exercise of its constitutional functions, and reserve to the Executive the full measure of responsibility attaching to his approval or disapproval of all acts passed by Congress. I have the honor to be, very respectfully, your obedient servant,

S. A. DOUGLAS

New York *Herald*, May 30, 1852. On May 17, 1852, Robert G. Scott, editor of the Richmond *Enquirer*, addressed a letter to fifteen men whom he considered to be Presidential possibilities in which he asked three questions concerning the Fugitive Slave Act: 1. Would you do everything in your power to sustain the Compromise and the Fugitive Slave Law? 2. Would you do all you could to prevent change in the Fugitive Slave Law to make it less effective? 3. Would you veto a law impairing the Fugitive Slave Law? The answers of all save Franklin Pierce and William Orlando Butler were printed in the *Herald* on May 30.

To David L. Yulee

(*Confidential*)
My Dear Sir,   [May, 1852]
    The first paragraph of your letter has been noted & will be attended to if opportunity presents. I wish to call your attention to one point. Gen'l *Butler was interrogated by Mr Scott of Richmond two days before the rest of us & has not answered.* I know this fact because I saw it stated in a letter from Scott to Father Ritchie.[1] Now the point is this. The Whigs are already charging that some candidate *from the South* will be taken up who *has not answered on the Fugitive Law!* That the Interrogations were a snare to ketch & kill off all *Northern Men,* and then abandon them. You see what trem[end]ous effect this would have against the nominee if such should happen to be the result & such a reason for it should gain credence at the North? In haste—all in the hands of my friend.

                                     S. A. DOUGLAS

ALS, Library of Florida History, University of Florida, Gainesville. This letter is undated, but it was probably written just prior to the opening of the Democratic convention in Baltimore on June 1. David L. Yulee, an early resident of Florida and former Delegate in Congress from Florida Territory, served in the United States Senate between 1845 and 1851, and again from 1855 to 1861. An ardent supporter of Douglas' candidacy for the Presidential nomination, Yulee was present at the convention as a member of the Florida delegation.

[1]Thomas Ritchie was editor of the Washington *Union.* By May 30, two days before the opening of the convention, two of the seventeen individuals to whom Scott had addressed his inquiry had failed to answer. They were Butler and Pierce.

To [David L. Yulee]

                                     [May, 1852]
                                     Washington
Col Richardson[1] will hand you this. Our friend Soulé[2] don't want to be on our private committee. He is with us & will consult with you on all things. See him often. He will do great service. Yours

                                        S. A. D.

ALS, Library of Florida History. This letter was probably written just before the Baltimore convention opened its deliberations.

[1]William A. Richardson, of Quincy, was Douglas' successor in the House of Representatives, when the latter was elected to the Senate. Richardson served in the lower house of Congress from 1847 to 1856. In 1852 he was the leader of the Illinois delegation and of the Douglas supporters at the Baltimore convention.

[2]Pierre Soulé, a supporter of Douglas' candidacy, was a Senator from Louisiana.

To David L. Yulee

My Dr Sir,   [June 1, 1852]

I have just heard that our friend Gen'l Sanders[1] is the temporary President of the Convention. You know my views of this, as we talked it over. This is all the news I have received from the Convention. Tell all our friends to keep cool—& not to become restive—or brag or bet on the result, and to do nothing to irritate anybody & to speak well of everybody. This caution will be necessary to many of my ardent young friends. I have full faith that the case will be managed well and leave all to the discretion of my friends. Write me everyday. Your friend

S. A. DOUGLAS

ALS, Library of Florida History. The letter is undated, but it was probably written on the day the convention opened.

[1]Romulus M. Saunders, of North Carolina, was a member of the House of Representatives from 1821 to 1827 and from 1841 to 1845.

To David L. Yulee

My Dear Sir,   Wednesday June 2d

I hear no other rumors than those stated yesterday. I do not allow myself to be either elated or depressed. I trust all to my friends who are on the ground and shall feel that whatever you may do is right, no matter what may be the result. How is the Indiana matter?[1] Don't forget B[uchanan]. Let me year from you each mail, if but one line. Your friend

S. A. DOUGLAS

P.S. There is rumor here that Alabama will not support me in any event. I do not credit it as I can imagine no sufficient cause. How is this?[2]

ALS, Library of Florida History.

[1]The Indiana delegation was instructed for Joseph Lane, a favorite son candidate, and intended to use Lane until the winner should appear. After the thirtieth ballot, when Douglas reached his peak of strength, Indiana switched to Cass.

[2]Alabama did not support Douglas, but cast its vote for Buchanan until the thirty-sixth ballot, when the delegation switched to Marcy.

To David L. Yulee

My Dear Sir,   June 3d 11 0 clock *AM*

Your letter is the most satisfactory of any I have received. You will have se[e]n my letter written in the night before you get this several persons called on me and were positive as to the facts therein stated. It was probably a ruse of the Cass-men.[1] It will do no harm. Let my friends fight the battle acording to their own judgment is my policy. You are on the ground & understand the whole field,—I can get but a glimpse here & there and cannot rely upon what I do get. As to B. he is supposed to be for Butler—*Look out for that*. I am glad Soulé[2] is on the Committee of Resolutions. That is important. He will be a host when the fight comes off. I shall not be dispirited or elated at the first or any subsequent Ballot. The Cass men regard—*Ky—Ind—Dick*[inson] of N Y, as having played false.[3] *This I Know*. It will be important to note this fact & act on it. I repeat that to me the case looks well—& the policy seems to be to have our friends make no alliances, but hold on—be firm—but quiet—and await the result. This is on[ly] a suggestion. But the whole case is in the hands of my friends. Yours truly

S. A. DOUGLAS

ALS, Library of Florida History.
[1] Douglas apparently wrote a letter to Yulee late on the night of June 2 which has not been located. The "ruse of the Cass-men" refers to Yulee's report to Douglas, June 3, 1852, that "it is very likely Genl Cass will receive advices *tonight* that may lead to his sending authority to be withdrawn" (owned by Martin F. Douglas). Yulee advised Douglas, in the light of this development, to reconcile himself with Cass in order that his candidacy might receive Cass's endorsement. The Buchanan men, Yulee continued, were hoping to rally Cass's supporters to their candidate.
[2] Soulé argued strongly and successfully from the floor of the convention against the proposal that a platform be

agreed upon before the nomination of the Presidential candidate. The proposal was supported largely by those opposed to an endorsement of the Compromise of 1850. The decision of the convention to proceed with the nominations before a platform had been drawn up was a victory for the Cass, Douglas, and Marcy forces against the Southern-rights group.
[3] On the question of whether the convention should frame a platform before nominating the candidates, the Kentucky and Indiana delegations, and the Cass minority of the New York delegation (led by Daniel S. Dickinson), did not follow the other Cass delegations but cast their votes with the Southern-rights group.

To David L. Yulee

(*Confidential*)
My Dear Sir,   June 4th 9 P. M.

I have rec'd no letters to night, and do not know what view our friends at Bal[timore] take of the 33 Ballot.[1] I do not look upon [it] as at all alarming however. When Cass, fails again as I presume he must, it is not improbable that we will get our forces & come to the same position that we occupied before. Of this however my friends on the ground are the best judges. I trust all to my friends & am satisfied that the case will be well managed as it has been heretofore. Your friend

S. A. DOUGLAS

P.S. I have this moment rec'd a Telagraph from a Cass-man stating that Penn—Virginia—and New York are attempting to make a union on Butler & calling on me to save Gen'l Cass & preserve myself for '56. Of course I shall return no answer—make no arraingements and leave my case to my friends from the *North—South—East—& West* all to consult & determine. I see no reason for alarm on the part of my friends, and remain in good spirits.

This letter is intended for our confidential friends. Yours

S. A. D.

ALS, Library of Florida History.

[1]The thirty-third ballot was the last ballot taken on June 4. Douglas had reached his peak of strength on the thirtieth and thirty-first ballots, receiving 92 votes, a plurality of the convention. In an obvious move to head off Douglas, his enemies turned once again to Cass. From 27 votes on the twenty-ninth ballot, Cass jumped to 98 on the thirty-second, while Douglas' support slumped. The thirty-third, which closed the day, revealed 123 votes for Cass, 72 for Buchanan, and only 60 for Douglas.

To David L. Yulee

(*Confidential*)

My Dear Sir,   June 5th 8½ A M

I am glad to learn from Mr Arnold[1] that you are all in good spirits, and prepared to hold on firmly, and come in on the last turn. Rest assured of one thing, and that is that I shall make no arraingements & do no act here that will embarrass or affect the actions of our friends in Bal[timore]. My friends have done noble & I leave all in your hands. Your friend

S. A. DOUGLAS

ALS, Library of Florida History.

[1]Richard D. Arnold, a physician and Mayor of Savannah, was a delegate to the Democratic convention from Georgia.

To [William A. Richardson]

Washington, *June* 5, 1852.

I congratulate the Democratic party on the fortunate result of the nomination, and Illinois will give Franklin Pierce a larger majority than any other State in the Union.

STEPHEN A. DOUGLAS

Printed in *Proceedings of the Democratic National Convention, Held at Baltimore, June, 1852* (reported and published by William Hincks and F. H. Smith, Washington, D.C., 1852), p. 40. Douglas' telegram was read by Richardson to the convention during the afternoon session of June 5. On the morning of that day, on the forty-ninth ballot, Franklin Pierce received the Democratic Presidential nomination.

[252]

To George Foster Shepley *et al.*

Washington

Gentlemen,   June 26th 1852

You will accept my grateful acknowledgements for your flattering invitation to attend the Great Ratification meeting and address the Democracy of Maine at Portland on the 5th of July. It would afford me sincere gratification to mingle with the sterling Democracy of your state on so interesting an occasion; and especial[ly] to contribute, to the extent of my feeble efforts, to swell the tide of enthusiasm which now pervades the whole Union in behalf of the nominees of the Democratic Baltimore convention. *With such a Tickett and such a Platform,*[1] *defeat is impossible, and success inevitable.* I regret that the acceptance of a previous invitation for a similar meeting on the same day will deprive me of the pleasure of attending your Ratification meeting. I have the honor to be very truly your obt sevt

S. A. DOUGLAS

ALS, Historical Society of Pennsylvania. George Foster Shepley, of Portland, Maine, was former United States Attorney for Maine.

[1] The nominees of the Democratic party in 1852 were Franklin Pierce, of New Hampshire, for President, and William R. King, of Alabama, for Vice-President. The Democratic platform contained the usual recital of principles, promised adherence to the Compromise of 1850, and opposed any efforts to renew the slavery agitation.

To Franklin Pierce

Senate U.S.

My Dear Sir,   July 7th 1852

Permit me to introduce to you my friend Major Loring of California.[1] You will find him an intelligent and accomplished gentleman in all respects worthy of your confidence.

He is a good Democrat & was a Delegate to the Dem Baltimore convention. I have the honor to be very truly your friend

S. A. DOUGLAS

ALS, New Hampshire Historical Society, Concord.

[1] Possibly Charles B. Loring, who was appointed Receiver of Public Moneys at Benicia, California, in 1853.

To Samuel Strong

Washington

My Dr Sir,   July 8th 1852

Patrick Nester who has been warmly recommended to me desires work on the capitol as a laborer. I believe him to be in all respects deserving, and I should be grateful if you can give him employment. Respectfully your friend

S. A. DOUGLAS

ALS, Chicago Historical Society.

To Arthur W. Austin

Washington
July 17th 1852.

Dr Sir,

I have postponed an answer to your invitation to attend a mass meeting and address the Democracy in behalf of Pierce & King and our glorious cause at Dedham on the 20th inst, with the hope of being able to so arrainge my public duties as to enable me to comply with your request. It would have been exceedingly gratifying to me to have been with you on that interesting occasion and to have contributed to the extent of my humble abilities to swell that wave of popular enthusiasm in behalf of our tickett and principles which is now overwhelming our political opponents.

I regret that my public duties will not allow me to leave the Senate at this time. Accept my thanks for the flattering terms in which you have communicated the invitation on behalf of the Committee. I have the honor to be very truly your obedient servant

S. A. DOUGLAS

ALS, Lincoln Memorial University, Harrogate, Tennessee. Arthur W. Austin was chairman of a committee of Dedham, Massachusetts, citizens to invite Douglas to speak there on behalf of the Democratic Presidential ticket.

To Millard Fillmore

To the President of the U States   [August 27, 1852]

We are personally acquainted with the Revd Wm D R Trotter of Illinois.[1] He is a methodist Preacher of more than ordinary talents. He has attained considerable distinction. His conduct is that of a sincere & devout Christian. He is about forty five years of age. Many years active employment as a preacher has made it necessary in his opinion as we are informed that he should retire at least for a time from the pulpit to recruit his health. He desires a consulship or some employment under the Government in a warm climate & we recommend him to the consideration of the President for the first consular vacancy within or near the tropics which he will accept.

Augt 27th 1852

J. R. UNDERWOOD[2]
S. A. DOUGLAS

LS, RG-59, National Archives.
[1]William David Rice Trotter, a Methodist minister, was former editor of the

St. Louis *Central Christian Advocate* and was connected with the Methodist Female Academy at Jacksonville. Ac-

[254]

cording to an endorsement on this letter, Trotter was appointed Commercial
Agent at Aux Cayes, Santo Domingo.
  ²Joseph R. Underwood, a Whig, had

been a Representative from Kentucky
from 1835 to 1843 and served in the
United States Senate from 1847 to 1853.

To Parmenas Taylor Turnley

SIR,   Washington, November 30th, 1852.

    Yours of October 30th ult. has been read,¹ and I avail myself of the
first leisure moment to reply. I feel, as you do, full of apprehension
concerning our political relations; and I know that my heart inclines to
do all I can to avert the evils threatened. But what can be done? This is
the question. If we had only to meet ordinary difficulties it were easy;
but we have to meet extraordinary ones. If we only had to provide for
our political necessities, with all hearts disposed to acquiesce in "well
enough," then could we readily see our way clear; but, as it is, a large
portion have their hearts turned to revolution, no matter what may be
the patriot's action. I have already tried my utmost to have the old compromise line of 1820 extended, first to the Rio Grande, then to the Pacific; but it was voted down by the very party who opposed strongest
its first adoption in 1821! This, you will say, is extraordinary. I say so,
too; but it is true, and only proves how perverse, how wicked the
hearts of some among us are! My plan now is to bring forward a Bill to
repeal altogether that compromise. This is what you suggest. I have
tried the extension of it, and have failed. I am now for its repeal. It was
a compromise of principle in the Constitution in the first place, which
was wrong; yet it was acquiesced in, and for that reason I was willing
to continue it. But I am met in my efforts by the most violent opposition from Northern fanatics; so I will try to remove altogether the
question, and we will thus very soon be able to give form and character
to the extensive domain you refer to. It is large enough for three or
four territories, and we will certainly make two, or perhaps three, out
of it in the first place.

    I received your previous letter on the subject of Commercial Power
versus Agricultural Extension, and I am quite of your opinion.² I do not
believe that those people who are so loud in their opposition to slavery
are honest. I do not believe that they really dislike slavery *per se*. On
the contrary, I am frank to confess that they appear to me more and
more every day as the covert, sly enemies to white men's liberties, far
more than they are friends to negro's freedom. The misfortune is, too
few among us thus closely watch their designs; and the danger is, they
will get power, under false pretences, when it will be too late to prevent the ruin they have fully meditated on the country. I do not find
all of these elements of destruction from the North! I find some of the

[255]

most cunning, subtle, and treacherous of them to be from the so-called Slave States originally. These men are more to be watched than all others, because they are false as hell, and have their hands ready to receive their price! Illinois has several of this class; so has Missouri, and Kentucky.

My efforts have always been, and will continue to be, for the best. I have no guide but my heart and my judgment. I had rather be the means of averting the dreadful calamities we both see and dread, than to hold all the offices under Government. Any honest man can perform the duties of office; but it takes also sagacity, effort, courage, and faith, to meet the enemies of popular Government. By this I mean the enemies to our plain Constitutional Government. You justly remark that we have no Government outside of the Constitution; and if that durst be violated with impunity, and persisted in, then are all parties who come together under it absolved from further adherence to the Government. As to how far such violations should be borne before a withdrawal by States, I cannot say. This will of necessity depend on the feelings of those who suffer by the breach of faith. I could hope, however, (and I feel sure such will be the action), that a call for a general Convention of all the States will precede any hasty action by separate States. This would rouse the latent patriotism in the North to strangle at once the enemies to Constitutional Government, who have been permitted to grow and increase unmolested the last half-century.

The South is certainly becomeing very weary of abolition flings at their States and their domestic relations. Still, I have confidence in their patriotism to suffer it still longer; for I do believe the Southern people, rich and poor, are the most devoted people to Constitutional Government on earth.[3] Very truly yours,

S. A. DOUGLASS

Printed in Cinderella L. Turnley, compiler, *Private Letters of Parmenas Taylor Turnley (Together with Some Letters of His Father and Grandfather) on the Character of the Constitutional Government of the United States, and the Antagonism of Puritans to Christianity, &c.* (London, 1863), pp. 104-106. Parmenas Taylor Turnley, a resident of Dandridge, Tennessee, was at this time a first lieutenant in the United States Army, stationed in Chicago on recruiting service. He graduated from West Point in 1846. George Fort Milton, *Eve of Conflict: Stephen A. Douglas and the Needless War* (Boston, 1934), p. 108, has expressed grave doubts as to the authenticity of this letter, on two grounds: (1) his failure, after an extensive search, to locate the original of this letter; and (2) his doubt that Douglas had determined upon the repeal of the Missouri Compromise as early as 1852, as stated in this letter. A search of Turnley's autobiography, *Reminiscences of Parmenas Taylor Turnley* (Chicago, n.d.), has failed to reveal any clues regarding his correspondence with Douglas. Several letters written by Turnley to Douglas in October and November, 1858, while Turnley was serving with the Army in Salt Lake City, have been located in the Douglas collection at the University of Chicago Library, but they likewise fail to cast any light on this earlier Douglas letter. The spelling of Douglas' name in the signature line with a double *s* might add credence to Milton's conclusion if it were not that this spelling continued to be used by many of Douglas' contemporaries long after the final *s* had been dropped. It is possible that the letter is erroneously dated; a more likely date would be 1853, although a comparison of the Turnley letter with one written by Douglas on December 17, 1853, to J. H. Crane, D. M. Johnson, and L. J. Eastin (see below) would seem to cast additional doubts on the authenticity of the former. However, negative evidence of this sort does not constitute sufficient proof of the letter's fraudulent character to justify its omission from this collection. Douglas' letter was printed (and apparently accepted as genuine) in David Rankin Barbee, editor, "Letters on the Issues of 1850-1865," *Tyler's Quarterly Historical and Genealogical Magazine*, XIV (October, 1932), 99-101.

[1]Turnley's letter to Douglas, October 30, 1852, was also printed in Cinderella L. Turnley's compilation, pp. 123-125. In his letter, Turnley urged the necessity of organizing the territory west of the Missouri River, and suggested that either the Compromise of 1850 be extended over this territory or the Missouri Compromise of 1820 be applied to the entire West (including Utah and New Mexico). "Should fanaticism and wickedness refuse to apply the law of 1850, refuse to extend the old line of 1820," Turnley wrote, "then why not repeal it altogether? It must either be acquiesced in, and thus extended, or it must be repealed: the former is good in practice, the latter good in principle: hence, I think either, if agreed to, will suffice—at least, for a time; but, with the present damnable spirit of Radicalism, I don't look for peace very long."

[2]This letter has not been located.

[3]A row of asterisks following the last paragraph would seem to indicate that portions of Douglas' letter were omitted by the compiler.

To Charles H. Lanphier

(*Confidential*)   Washington
My Dear Sir,   Dec 3d 1852

I am greatly obliged for your kind letter. I think you are right as to the feelings of the clique at St Louis. Their purpose has been clear to me for sometime, but I have deemed it best not to seem to be aware of their real objects.[1] Benton is not particularly hostile to me. He hates everybody and only regrets that every leading Democrat in America cannot be prostrated at once. There has never been a personal difficulty betwen him and me. My only crime consists in having attracted some portion of public attention & popular favor, and he deems this an invasion of his rights. His hostility to Cass—Buchanan—and Marcy is open & undisguised. Indeed he compliments me when comparing us together. Yet his vanity is wounded by the course of things in the country—and especially in the West. One thing you may rest assured of I think. He will not attack me by name—certainly he will bring no charges against me. In regard to his boasted reforms, which he is going to present in the Ho of Reps, it looks a little curious that he did not bring them forward in the Senate during his 30 years served there.[2] Why did he not then make war upon the Steam Lines. They were all established while he was in the Senate. If I recollect right Collins Line to Liverpool, and Law's Line to Chagres—and Aspenwall's line from Panama to California & Oregon were all adopted in one Bill,[3] which did not pass the Ho of Reps until after 10 oclock at night on the last night of the Session and was then sent to the Senate for the first time and there read three times and passed on the same night. To do this, it required unanimous consent. Col Benton was present & could have defeated all the lines at once if he had only said *"I object."* This was before I was a member of the Senate (1846-7) but I recollect the facts distinctly. Benton was the author of the Bill for the benefit of the Panama Rail road which I supported, but did not become a law.[4] What pretext has he therefore to abuse the Steam Lines & the Istmus Routes? Yet he talks about Plunder measures in that connection. Besides he says in his late Jackson Speech that he is *not opposed to the Lines to California & Oregon.* His assault upon Congress for the additional allowance to the Collins line last Session does not reach me. It hits Cass, Shields & many others who voted for it, but I voted against it. This is the only steam measure which has become a law since Benton left the Senate. I repeat why did he not show his opposition to these measures when it might have availed something. Nearly all his charges against congress are *confessions against himself.* I do not advise any assault on him, but these things should be borne in mind in the event it becomes necessary in self-defense to use them. You will ex[er]cise your own judgement about replying to the St Louis Democrat, and assume the offensive whenever you think propriety & self respect requires it. I shall hold myself ready to meet the issue when forced on me, and shall not evade it or shrink from it. I like your suggestion as to appointments to office. I shall act on the rule of giving the offices to those who fight the battles. The party has been demoralized & weak[en]ed by requiring one set of men to spend the money & time & do the work while the offices were awarded to a set of droans. This shall no longer be the case with my consent. What do you say to Diller as Pension Agent & Curran for PMaster?[5] Who for the two *land* offices? Do you want anything besides the Patronage for your Paper? and if so what? Who ought to be Marshall & District Attorney? Answer me directly & frankly on all these points. Your answer will be *confidential* and you must treat these suggestions *as strictly so.*

Will I have any opposition for the Senate, and if so who will it be? Let me know everything as it transpires. Send me your Paper. I was surprised the other day to find that you did not exchange with the Union. I had the Register put on the Union exchange list. You will see an article in regard to our Elections, the facts for which I furnished. I have written to Diller, giving general authority to him, yourself & Curran to give a suitable entertainment in the event of my Reelection.[6] Arrainge the affair according to your taste & views of propriety, and draw on me for the expense. I should have associated with you Judge Treat, Hickox,[7] and some others, but I did not wish to trouble them with it. It will be courteous to advise with them, but you three must be the *workies*.

Write me often & do not expect answers to all your letters. Your friend

S. A. DOUGLAS

ALS, Illinois State Historical Library.

[1] The "St. Louis clique" may have been the group, including B. Gratz Brown and Francis Preston Blair, that supported Thomas Hart Benton in his successful campaign for Congress in 1852. In the course of the campaign, Benton made some uncomplimentary allusions to Douglas.

[2] Benton's "boasted reforms" referred at least in part to his opposition to government subsidies to steamship lines.

[3] Edward Knight Collins' Dramatic Line (founded in 1836), George Law's United States Mail Steamship Company (founded in 1847), and William H. Aspinwall's Pacific Mail Steamship Company (founded in 1848) all received government subsidies as a result of legislation passed early in March, 1845. In August, 1852, the amount of subsidy for each line was increased.

[4] In 1848, William H. Aspinwall and John L. Stephens secured a charter from the government of New Granada for the operation of a Panama railroad. On December 14, 1848, Benton, as chairman of the committee on military affairs, reported a bill to contract with the Panama Railroad to carry troops and supplies.

[5] Isaac Roland Diller was clerk of the state House of Representatives. In 1853, he was appointed Deputy Postmaster of Springfield. Isaac B. Curran was a Springfield merchant and real estate agent.

[6] Douglas was re-elected to his second term as United States Senator with ease, receiving 75 out of the 95 votes cast on the joint ballot of the legislature.

[7] Virgil Hickox, Springfield merchant, had been active in the state Democratic organization for many years.

To Edward C. West

Senate U.S.

My Dr Sir,   Feby 25th 1853.

I herewith send you a Deed in Duplicate for the right of way through my land to the Illinois Central Rail Road Co.[1] which has its office in Wall street. The deed contains mutual covenants and therefore must be signed in Duplicate & executed by both Parties. Please deliver the Deeds for execution & forward to me the one executed by the Company, and also receive & send me a check for the ballance of the money now due, which is a little less than six thousand dollars. Your friend

S. A. DOUGLAS

ALS, Illinois Central Archives, Newberry Library, Chicago.

[1] Douglas sold a little over sixteen acres of his lake-front property in Chicago to the Illinois Central Railroad for use as a right of way.

[259]

To William L. Marcy

[N.d., n.p.; ALS, RG-59, National Archives. Recommending the appointment of Charles L. Denman, of California, to the post of United States Consul at Acapulco, Mexico. Marcy was appointed Secretary of State by President Franklin Pierce; consequently, this and the following undated letters were probably written on or soon after March 4, 1853. Denman received the appointment as Consul at Acapulco, and held that post until 1858.]

To Franklin Pierce

[N.d., n.p.; ALS, RG-59, National Archives. Recommending the appointment of the "Hon Mr Gilmore" to "one of the first Class Consulates on the Pacific Coast." Gilmore was probably Alfred Gilmore, member of Congress from Pennsylvania from 1849 to 1853. He was not a candidate for re-election in 1852. The appointment proposed by Douglas was not made.]

To Franklin Pierce

[N.d., n.p.; LS, RG-59, National Archives. Recommending the appointment of Edward C. Marshall to the office of Commissioner to China. The recommendation was signed by fourteen members of the Senate and House of Representatives, in addition to Douglas. Marshall had been a member of the House of Representatives from California between 1851 and 1853. The appointment asked for in this letter was not made.]

To Franklin Pierce

My Dear Sir,   [March, 1853]
  I desire to call your attention to the claims of Mr. Thomas Devlen Reily for a foreign appointment.[1] He is one of the ablest political writers of the age and admirably qualified for any position for which he will apply. He has devoted his life to the cause of liberal principles & progressive ideas, and his appointment would be esteemed a compliment to a large class of our people who sympathise with the efforts in behalf of free institutions throughout the world. I commend his application to your favorable consideration with the earnest desire that it may prove successful. Very truly your friend

S. A. DOUGLAS

ALS, RG-59, National Archives.
  [1]Thomas Devin Reilly, of New York, was a frequent contributor of political articles to the *Democratic Review*. He was not appointed to the office suggested by Douglas.

To Franklin Pierce

Dr Sir,   [March, 1853]

I understand that the friends of S M Johnson of the Detroit free Press Mich,[1] are about to present his name for one of the first class consulates. I desire to say that I known him well & believe him eminently qualified. For a position to one of the Spanish American states or Ports he has peculiar qualifications in consequence of his familiarity with their language, laws and institutions, and his experience in that class of duties would render him a useful officer at any point. I need not say that he is a sound & reliable democrat, an accomplished gentleman, & a man of strict honor & integrity. His success would be very gratifying to me & I cordially recommend him for any position where I have not made a specific recommendation. Very truly your friend

S. A. DOUGLAS

ALS, RG-59, National Archives.

[1]Simeon M. Johnson had been United States Consul at Matanzas, Cuba, from 1845 to 1850. He later became an editorial writer for the Washington *Union* and, following the replacement of that paper by the *Constitution*, held the consulate at Le Havre, France, for a brief time.

To Franklin Pierce

Senate U.S.

Dear Sir,   March 4th 1853—

Having understood that the name of John M. Daniel Esq of the Richmond Examiner[1] will be presented to you for appointment as charges de' Affair or Minister Resident to Belgium or some one of the other European Powers, I desire to say to you that I know him well and intimately as a man of strict honor, high intellectual qualities, extensive literary attainments, sound political faith and an accomplished gentleman. In short he is admirably qualified for the station while no man in the country, on account of partizan service, has stronger claims upon the favor & support of a Democratic Administration. I cordially unite with his friends in his own State in recommending his appointment and sincerely hope that the application may be successful. I have the honor to be very truly your friend

S. A. DOUGLAS

ALS, RG-59, National Archives.

[1]John Moncure Daniel was editor of the Richmond *Examiner*. In August, 1853, he was appointed United States Minister to Sardinia, a post he held until 1861.

To [Franklin Pierce?]

[March 5, 1853, n.p.; LS, RG-59, National Archives. Recommending the appointment of Eli B. Ames, of Illinois, to the post of Chargé d'Af-

[261]

faires to some foreign government. The recommendation was written by James Shields and signed by Shields, Douglas, and six other members of the Illinois delegation in Congress. Ames was appointed United States Consul at Hamburg in 1856 and continued in that office until 1858.]

To ———

[March 7, 1853, n.p.; NS, RG-59, National Archives. Memorandum, recording the action of the Illinois delegation in Congress in unanimously recommending David L. Gregg to the post of Chargé d'Affaires at Turin. Signed by Douglas and eight other members of the delegation. The recommendation was endorsed, "Appointed, during recess, 7 July 1853." Gregg, a former member of the state legislature and Secretary of State of Illinois from 1850 to 1853, was appointed Commissioner to the Sandwich Islands in July, 1853, holding that post until 1858.]

To Franklin Pierce

[March 7, 1853, Senate, U.S.; ALS, RG-59, National Archives. Recommending the appointment of Caleb Jones, of Richmond, Virginia, to the office of General Appraiser of Merchandise. Jones was appointed United States Consul at Foo Chow, China, in 1856.]

To Franklin Pierce

[March 7, 1853, Senate, U.S.; ALS, RG-59, National Archives. Concurring in the recommendation of Isaac I. Stevens to the office of Governor of Washington Territory. Stevens, a major in the United States Army Engineers and a veteran of the Mexican War, had campaigned actively for Pierce in 1852. He was appointed to the governorship of the newly created territory.]

To Franklin Pierce

[March 7, 1853, Washington; ALS, RG-59, National Archives. Concurring in the recommendation of William B. Phillips to the post of United States Consul in Paris. Phillips, a former editor of the Alexandria (Virginia) *Age,* had spent much time in France. Since 1851, he resided in Washington, D.C., writing occasionally for the Washington *Union.* The appointment was not made.]

To James C. Dobbin

[March 8, 1853, Senate, U.S.; ALS, RG-59, National Archives. Recommending the appointment of William G. Dunbar, of Virginia, to a pursership in the United States Navy. Dobbin, formerly a Representative from North Carolina, was appointed Secretary of the Navy by President Pierce. Dunbar's appointment was not made.]

To Franklin Pierce

[March 8, 1853, Senate, U.S.; ALS, RG-59, National Archives. Recommending Frederick P. Stanton, of Tennessee, for Minister to Central America. Stanton was at this time serving his fifth term as a member of the House of Representatives from Tennessee. The appointment asked by Douglas was not made.]

To Franklin Pierce

[March 8, 1853, Senate, U.S.; ALS, RG-59, National Archives. Recommending the appointment of William A. Stone, of Mississippi, to the post of United States Consul at Rio de Janeiro. Stone was a Holmesville, Mississippi, attorney. He was not appointed.]

To Franklin Pierce

[March 8, 1853, Washington; LS, RG-59, National Archives. Recommending the appointment of Elisha Peyre Ferry, of Illinois, to the office of United States Consul in Marseilles, France. The recommendation was signed by Senators Douglas and Shields, Governor Joel A. Matteson, former Representatives Orlando B. Ficklin and R. S. Molony, Representatives Willis Allen and James C. Allen, and former Senator Alpheus Felch of Michigan. Ferry, a Waukegan lawyer, was a Democratic Presidential elector in 1852. He was not appointed to the consulate at Marseilles, but, after the Civil War, received appointment, as a Republican, as Surveyor General and later Governor of Washington Territory. In 1889 he became the first Governor of Washington state.]

To Franklin Pierce

[March 8, 1853, Senate, U.S.; ALS, RG-59, National Archives. Recommending the appointment of Frederick W. Horn, of Wisconsin, to the post of Chargé d'Affaires in "one of the northern States of Europe." Horn, of Cedarburg, Wisconsin, was a member of the state legislature and a well-known Democratic leader in Wisconsin. The appointment was not made.]

To Franklin Pierce

[N.d., n.p.; LS, RG-59, National Archives. Recommendation for the appointment of Frederick W. Horn of Wisconsin to the post of Chargé d'Affaires in either Sweden or Denmark. The recommendation was signed by ten members of Congress, including Douglas.]

To Franklin Pierce

[March 9, 1853, Senate, U.S.; ALS, RG-59, National Archives. Recommending the appointment of T. Hart Hyatt, of New York, formerly Consul at Belfast and Tangiers, to the post of United States Consul General in Egypt. The recommendation was endorsed "Mission to Sardinia," but Hyatt was appointed instead Consul at Amoy, China, a post he retained until 1861.]

To Franklin Pierce

[March 9, 1853, Washington; ALS, RG-59, National Archives. Recommending Duncan K. McRae, of Wilmington, North Carolina, for appointment as minister to "one of the South American Republics." The recommendation was endorsed "Minister to Chile." McRae had earlier written Douglas, January 1, 1853, thanking Douglas for his offer to assist him in any application he might make (University of Chicago Library). In 1854, McRae was appointed Consul at Paris. The same year he acted as secretary at the Ostend Conference and carried, as a special messenger, the Ostend Manifesto to Washington.]

To Franklin Pierce

[March 10, 1853, Senate, U.S.; ALS, RG-59, National Archives. Recommending Dr. Robert P. Hunt, of Kentucky, for appointment as Chargé d'Affaires or minister to "one of the European powers." The appointment was not made.]

To Franklin Pierce

[March 15, 1853, Washington; LS, RG-59, National Archives. Recommending the appointment of Eli B. Ames to the post of United States Consul at Tangiers. The recommendation was written and also signed by James Shields.]

To Franklin Pierce

[March 15, 1853, Senate, U.S.; ALS, RG-59, National Archives. Recommending the appointment of George L. Thurber, of Illinois, to the post of United States Consul at Palermo. The recommendation was concurred in by Alexander W. Buel, former member of Congress from Michigan. The appointment was not made.]

To Franklin Pierce

My Dear Sir,   Washington March 16th, 1853

I have just received a letter from our Minister to Spain,[1] the contents of which he desires me to make known to you. I deem it most appropriate and satisfactory to communicate the letter itself, which I herewith send. I received early in the winter the letter to which he refers, and forgot it in the midst of affliction and duties.

I am sure that the tone and spirit of the letter will meet your commendation as it is in Keeping with the character of its author. I remain very truly your friend

(Signed) S. A. Douglas

Copy, RG-59, National Archives.
[1]Daniel Moreau Barringer, of North Carolina, was United States Minister to Spain. He resigned in 1853 in protest over Spanish interference with American shipping in Havana, Cuba.

To Franklin Pierce

[March 16, 1853, n.p.; AES, RG-59, National Archives. Endorsement on M. M. Dimmick to Franklin Pierce, March 13, 1853, Washington, recommending the appointment of Alexander W. Buel to the post of Minister to Berlin. Dimmick was Representative from Pennsylvania from 1849 to 1853. Buel's appointment was not made.]

To William L. Marcy

[March 24, 1853, Washington City; ALS, RG-59, National Archives. Recommending Benjamin F. Smith for the post of United States Consul in Melbourne, Australia. Smith was a Cleveland, Ohio, merchant. The appointment was not made.]

To Franklin Pierce

[March 28, 1853, Senate; ALS, RG-59, National Archives. Recommending General James Keenan, of Pennsylvania, for appointment to the post of United States Consul in Glasgow, Scotland. Keenan was appointed, in 1854, Consul for Hong Kong.]

To Franklin Pierce

[March 30, 1853, Senate U.S.; ALS, RG-59, National Archives. Recommending Sanders W. Johnston, of Ohio, for appointment as United States Consul at Panama. Johnston did not receive the consulate, but was later appointed an Associate Justice on the Kansas territorial Supreme Court.]

To Caleb Cushing

[N.d., n.p.; ALS, Library of Congress. Introducing Colonel French, of Virginia, to Caleb Cushing, newly appointed Attorney General in President Pierce's cabinet. The letter is endorsed, "April, 1853." Colonel French was probably S. Bassett French of Whitby, near Richmond, Virginia.]

To Franklin Pierce

[April 4, 1853, Washington City; AES, RG-59, National Archives. Endorsement by Douglas on a recommendation for the appointment of Ansel W. Sweet to the post of Chargé d'Affaires in Guatemala. The recommendation was written by A. H. Clark, surveyor of the port of San Pedro, California, and others. Sweet was a California lawyer. The appointment was not made.]

To Franklin Pierce

[April 7, 1853, Senate Chamber; LS, RG-59, National Archives. Recommending the appointment of Edward B. Buchanan, of Maryland, to the secretaryship of some legation in Europe. The recommendation was signed, in addition to Douglas, by Hannibal Hamlin, Senator from Maine, and Isaac Toucey, Senator from Connecticut, and was written by Hamlin. Buchanan was appointed United States Consul at Rochelle, France, in 1854.]

To Franklin Pierce

[May 12, 1853, New York; ALS, RG-59, National Archives. Recommending Wright Hawkes, a New York city lawyer, for a foreign appointment. No appointment was made.]

To David S. Reid

My Dear Sir, May 14th 1853

I herewith send you a Receipt of the express company for a Boxes containing a Tea set of China for your mother. I have had the Box directed to you for greater safety. It contains or ought to contain a full set of forty five Pieces as per memorandum which I enclose. I sail for Europe today to be gone about two months. Soon after my return you may expect to see me with the two Boys—say about the first of Sept. Your friend

S. A. Douglas

ALS, owned by Martin F. Douglas. Douglas' wife had died on January 23, 1853.

To [Charles H. Lanphier]

Private

My Dr friend, Washington Nov 11th 53

Why don't you send me the Register? I have not seen a copy for more than six months. I am certainly a subscriber to it, altho I may never have paid my subscription. Send me the Register that I may see what you are doing & saying. I know all is right & that the paper takes the right course, yet I want to read it so much the more on that account. I have a few words to say personal to myself. I see many of the newspapers are holding me up as a candidate for the next Presidency. I do not wish to occupy that position. I do not think I will be willing to have my name used. I think such a state of things will exist that I shall not desire the nomination. Yet I do not intend to do any act which will deprive me of the control of my own actions. I shall remain entirely uncommitted & hold myself at liberty to do whatever my duty to my principles & my friends may require when the time for action arrives. Our first duty is to the cause—the fate of individual politicians is of minor consequence. The party is in a distracted condition & it requires all our wisdom, freedom & energy to consolidate its power and perpetuate its principles. Let us leave the Presidency out of view for at least two years to come.

I deem it due to you as my old & confidential friend to say thus much that you may understand my position. The administration has made some mistakes—indeed many mistakes in its appointments, yet I have no personal grievances to complain of. I did not expect to be pleased with the great body of the appointments & have not been disappointed. Yet I shall not judge the administration by its appointments. If it stands firmly by the faith—if it is sound & faithful in its principles & measures, it will receive my hearty & energetic support.

I still have faith that it will prove itself worthy of our support. It has difficulties ahead, but it must meet them boldly and fairly. There is a surplus Revenue which must be disposed off & the Tariff reduced to a legitimate Revenue standard. It will not do to allow the surplus to accumulate in the Treasury & thus create a pecuniary revulsion that would overwhelm the business arrangements & financial affairs of the country. The River & Harbor question must be met & decided. Now, in my opinion is the time to put those great interests on a more substantial & secure basis by a will devised system of Tonnage duties. I do not know what the administration will do on this question, but I hope they will have the courage to do what we all feel to be right. The Pacific Rail Road will also be a disturbing element. It will never do to commence making Rail Roads by the federal government under any pretext of necessity. We can grant alternate sections of land as we did for the Central Road, but not a dollar from the National Treasury. These are the main questions & my opinions are foreshadowed as you are entitled to know them. Let me hear from you often & freely. Very truly your friend

S. A. DOUGLAS

ALS, Illinois State Historical Library. This letter has been printed in P. Orman Ray, *The Repeal of the Missouri Compromise, Its Origin and Authorship* (Cleveland, Ohio, 1909), pp. 185-186.

To J. H. Crane, D. M. Johnson, and L. J. Eastin

Washington, December 17, 1853

Your letter of the 15 inst,[1] inviting me, on behalf of the citizens of Buchanan County, friendly to the immediate organization and settlement of the Territory of Nebraska, to address a Convention favorable to that important object on the 9th of January, next, is this moment received.

Believing that I will be able to promote the objects of the Convention more efficiently by remaining at my post and, as chairman of the Territorial committee, reporting and pushing forward, the Bill for the organization of Nebraska, I will avail myself of the alternative presented in your kind letter of invitation, and furnish a brief "statement of my views, to be laid before the convention."

It is unnecessary for me to inform you, who have so long, and so anxiously watched the slow development and progress of this important measure, that I am, and have been, at all times since I had the honor to hold a seat in either House of Congress, the warm and zealous advocate of the immediate organization and settlement of that Territory. Ten years ago, during the first session I was a member of the

[268]

House of Representatives, I wrote and introduced a bill for the establishment of the Territory of Nebraska, which so far as I am advised was the first proposition ever made in either House of Congress to create a territory on the West bank of the Missouri river.[2] That bill gave a beautiful and euphonious name to a great river and the country drained by it, by reversing[3] the aboriginal word "Nebraska" and substituting it for the modern and insignificant word Platte by which the river and adjacent country were at that time generally known. From that day I have never ceased my efforts on any occasion, when there was the least hope of success, for the organization of the Territory, and have scarcely allowed a Congress to pass without bringing forward the Bill in one House or the other. Indeed I am not aware that prior to the last Congress, any other member of the Senate ever felt interest enough in it to bring forward a Bill, or even to speak in its favor when introduced by myself.

I am induced to call your attention to these facts in consequence of having been furnished with a copy of a newspaper published in your State, in which I am charged with hostility to the measure. My reasons for originating the measure, and bringing it forward during my first session in Congress, and renewed it so often since even when the indications of support furnished very light hopes of success, may be briefly stated. It seemed to have been the settled policy of the government for many years, to collect the various Indian tribes in the different States and organized Territories, and to plant them permanently on the western borders of Arkansas, Missouri and Iowa under treaties guaranteeing to them perpetual occupancy, *with an express condition that they should never be incorporated within the limits of territory or state of the Union.* This policy evidently contemplated the creation of a perpetual and savage barrier to the further progress of emigration, settlement and civilization in that direction. Texas not having been annexed, and being, at that time a foreign country, this barbarian wall against the extension of our institutions, and the admission of new states, could not start from the Gulf of Mexico, and consequently the work was commenced at Red river, and carried northward with the obvious purpose of continuing it to the British Possessions. It had already penetrated into the Nebraska country, and the war department in pursuance of what was then considered a settled policy, was making its arrangements to locate immediately several other Indian Tribes on the Western borders of Missouri and Iowa with similar guarantees of perpetuity. It was obvious to the plainest understanding that if this policy should be carried out and the treaty stipulations observed in good faith it was worse than folly to wrangle with Great Britain about our right to the whole or any part of Oregon—

much less to cherish the vain hope of ever making this an Ocean-bound Republic. This Indian Barrier was to have been a colossal monument to the God terminus saying to christianity, civilization and Democracy "thus far mayest thou go, and *no* farther." It was under these circumstances, and with a direct view of arresting the further progress of this savage barrier to the extension of our institutions, and to authorize and encourage a continuous line of settlements to the Pacific Ocean, that I introduced the first Bill to create the Territory of Nebraska at the session of 1853-4.[4] The mere introduction of the Bill with a request of the Secretary of War to suspend further steps for the location of Indians within the limits of the proposed Territory until Congress should act upon the measure had the desired effect, so far as to prevent the permanent location of any more Indians on the frontier during the pendancy of the Bill before Congress, and from that day to this I have taken care always to have a Bill pending when Indians were about to be located in that quarter. Thus the policy of a perpetual Indian barrier has been suspended, if not entirely abandoned, for the last ten years, and since the acquisition of California, and the establishment of Territorial governments for Oregon and Washington the Idea of arresting our progress in that direction, has become so ludicrous that we are amazed, that wise and patriotic statesmen ever cherished the thought.

But, while the mischief has been prevented by prescribing limits to the onward march of an unwise policy, yet there are great national interests involved in the question which demand prompt patience, and affirmative action. To the States of Missouri and Iowa, the organization of the Territory of Nebraska is an important and desirable local measure; to the interests of the Republic it is a national necessity. How are we to develope, cherish and protect our immense interests and possessions on the Pacific, with a vast wilderness fifteen hundred miles in breadth, filled with hostile savages, and cutting off all direct communication. The Indian barrier must be removed. The tide of emigration and civilization must be permitted to roll onward until it rushes through the passes of the mountains, and spreads over the plains, and mingles with the waters of the Pacific. Continuous lines of settlements with civil, political and religious institutions all under the protection of law, are imperiously demanded by the highest national considerations. These are essential, but they are not sufficient. No man can keep up with the spirit of this age who travels on anything slower than the locomotive, and fails to receive intelligence by lightning. We must therefore have Rail Roads and Telegraphs from the Atlantic to the Pacific, through our own territory. Not one line only, but many lines, for the valley of the Mississippi will require as many Rail Roads to the Pacific as to the Atlantic, and will not venture to limit the number. The removal of the Indian barrier and the extension of the laws of the United States in the form of Territorial governments are the first steps toward the accomplishment of each and all of those objects. When I proposed ten years ago to organize the territory of Nebraska, I did not intend to stop at that point. I proposed immediately to establish a line of military posts to protect the settler and the emigrant and to provide for the construction of bridges and making roads by granting a portion of the public lands for that purpose. In 1854,[5] I published a pamphlet in which I proposed, so soon as the territory should be established to make out the line of a rail road to the mouth of the Columbia River, "or to the Bay of San Francisco in the event California should be annexed in time," and then to have the public lands, on each side of the line surveyed into quarter sections, and to set apart the alternate tracts to the actual settler. The object of all these measures was to form a line of continuous settlements from the Mississippi to the Pacific, with a view of securing and enlarging our interests on that coast. The Mexican war operated adversely to the success of these measures, all the revenues in the Treasury were needed for military operations and there was an unwillingness to make any liberal and extensive disposition of the public domain, while we were making loans predicated, in part, upon that fund. The slavery agitation which followed the acquisition of California and New Mexico, also had an injurious effect by diverting public attention from the importance of our old territory and concentrating the hopes and anxieties of all upon our new possessions. Last session the Bill passed the House of Representatives, but was lost in the Senate for want of time, it being a short session. I have a firm confidence that none of these causes can defeat the organization of the Territory this session. It is to be hoped that the necessity and importance of the measure are manifest to the whole country, and that so far as the slavery question is concerned, all will be willing to sanction and affirm the principle established by the Compromise measures of 1850.

You will do me the favor, Gentlemen to communicate this hasty sketch of my views to the convention, and assure the Delegates of my zealous efforts, and hearty cooperation in the great work which brings them together. I have the honor to be, with respect your obedient servant.

STEPHEN A. DOUGLAS

St. Joseph (Missouri) *Gazette*, March 15, 1854. This letter was discovered, edited, and published by James C. Malin, "The Motives of Stephen A. Douglas in the Organization of Nebraska Territory: A Letter Dated December 17, 1853," *Kansas Historical Quarterly*, XIX (November, 1951), 321-

353. Crane, Johnson, and Eastin composed a special committee, charged with inviting Douglas to address a convention in St. Joseph, Missouri, on behalf of the organization of Nebraska Territory. Lucien J. Eastin was editor of the St. Joseph *Gazette*.

[1]According to Malin, the letter of invitation could not have been dated December 15, if Douglas' answer was written on December 17. He has suggested that the invitation was probably dated December 3, the date on which the invitation was authorized by a mass meeting.

[2]On December 17, 1844, during his first term in the House of Representatives, Douglas introduced a bill to establish the Territory of Nebraska.

[3]Malin has suggested that the word "reversing" was a typographical error for "reviving."

[4]This date should read 1843-4.

[5]Not 1854, but 1845. See above, Douglas to Whitney, October 15, 1845.

To Joel A. Matteson

WASHINGTON, *January* 2, 1854.

SIR: I learn from the public press that you have under consideration the proposition to convene the legislature in special session. In the event such a step shall be demanded by the public voice and necessities, I desire to invite your attention to a subject of great interest to our people, which may require legislative action. I refer to the establishment of some efficient and permanent system for river and harbor improvements. Those portions of the Union most deeply interested in internal navigation naturally feel that their interests have been neglected, if not paralized, by an uncertain, vascillating, and partial policy. Those who reside upon the banks of the Mississippi, or on the shores of the great northern Lakes, and whose lives and property are frequently exposed to the mercy of the elements for want of harbors of refuge and means of safety, have never been able to comprehend the force of that distinction between fresh and salt water, which affirms the power and duty of Congress, under the Constitution, to provide security to navigation so far as the tide ebbs and flows, and denies the existence of the right beyond the tidal mark. Our lawyers may have read in English books that, by the common laws, all waters were deemed navigable so far as the tide extended and no further; but they should also have learned from the same authority that the law was founded upon reason, and where the reason failed the rule ceased to exist. In England, where they have neither lake nor river, nor other water which is, in fact, navigable, except where the tide rolls its briney wave, it was natural that the law should conform to the fact, and establish that as a rule which the experience of all men proved to be founded in truth and reason. But it may well be questioned whether, if the common law had originated on the shores of Lake Michigan—a vast inland sea with an average depth of six hundred feet—it would have been deemed "not navigable," merely because the tide did not flow, and the water was fresh and well adapted to the uses and necessities of man. We therefore feel authorized to repudiate, as unreasonable and unjust, all injuries, discriminations, predicated upon salt water and tidal arguments, and to insist that if the power of Congress to protect navigation has any existence in the Constitution, it reaches every portion of this Union where the water is in fact navigable, and only ceases where the fact fails to exist. This power has been affirmed in some form and exercised to a greater or less extent by each successive Congress, and every administration since the adoption of the Federal Constitution. All acts of Congress providing for the erection of light-houses, the planting of buoys, the construction of piers, the removal of snags, the dredging of channels, the inspection of steamboat boilers, the carrying of life boats, in short, all enactments for the security of navigation and the safety of life and property within our navigable waters, assert the existence of this power and the propriety of its exercise in some form.

The great and growing interest of navigation is too important to be overlooked or disregarded. Mere negative action will not answer. The irregular and vascillating policy, which has marked our legislation upon this subject, is ruinous. Whenever appropriations have been proposed for river and harbor improvements, and especially on the northern lakes and the western rivers, there has usually been a death struggle, and a doubtful issue. We have generally succeeded with an appropriation once in four or five years; in other words, we have, upon an average, been beaten about four times out of five in one house of Congress or the other, or both, or by the presidential veto. When we did succeed, a large portion of the appropriation was expended in providing dredging machines and snag boats and other necessary machinery and implements; and by the time the work was fairly begun, the appropriation was exhausted, and further operations suspended. Failing to procure an additional appropriation at the next session, and perhaps for two, three, or four sucessive sessions, the administration has construed the refusal of Congress to provide the funds for the prosecution of the works into an abandonment of the system, and has accordingly deemed it a duty to sell, at public auction, the dredging machines and snag boats, implements and materials on hand for whatever they would bring. Soon the country was again startled by the frightful accounts of wrecks and explosions, fires and snags upon the rivers, the lakes, and the seacoast. The responsibility of these appalling sacrifices of life and property were charged upon those who defeated the appropriations for the prosecution of the works. Sympathy was excited, and a concerted plan of agitation and organization formed by the interested sections and parties to bring their combined influence to bear upon Congress in favor of the re-establishment of the system on an enlarged scale, sufficiently comprehensive to embrace the local interests and influences in a majority of the congressional districts of the Union. A legislative omnibus was formed, in which all sorts of works were crowded together, good and bad, wise and foolish, national and local, all crammed into one bill, and forced through Congress by the power of an organized majority, after the fearful and exhausting struggle of a night session. The bill would receive the votes of a majority in each house, not because any one Senator or Representative approved all the items contained in it, but for the reason that humanity, as well as the stern demands of an injured and suffering constituency, required that they should make every needful sacrifice of money to diminish the terrible loss of human life by the perils of navigation. The result was a simple re-enactment of the former scenes. Machinery, implements, and materials purchased, the works recommenced—the money exhausted—subsequent appropriations withheld—and the operations suspended, without completing the improvements, or contributing materially to the safety of navigation. Indeed, it may be well questioned whether, as a general rule, the money has been wisely and economically applied, and in many cases whether the expenditure has been productive of any useful results, beyond the mere distribution of so much money among contractors, laborers, and superintendents in the favored localities; and in others, whether it has not been of positive detriment to the navigating interest.

Far be it from my purpose to call in question the integrity, science, or skill of those whose professional duty it was to devise the plan and superintend the construction of the works. But I do insist that from the nature of their profession and their habits of life they could not be expected to possess that local knowledge—that knowledge of currents and tides—the effects of storms, floods, and ice, always different and ever changing—in each locality of this widely-extended country, which is essential in determining upon the proper site and plan for an improvement to the navigation. Without depreciating the value of science, or disregarding its precepts, I have no hesitation in saying that the opinion of an intelligent captain or pilot, who, for a long series of years, has sailed out of and into a given port in fair weather and foul, and who had carefully and daily watched the changes produced in the channel by the currents and storms, wrecks and other obstructions, would inspire me with more confidence than that of the most eminent professional gentlemen, whose knowledge and science in the line of his profession were only equalled by his profound ignorance of all those local and practical questions which ought to determine the site and plan of the proposed improvment. To me, therefore, it is no longer a matter of surprise that errors and blunders occur in the mode of constructing the works, and failures and extravagance everywhere appear in the expenditure of the money. These evils seem to be inherent in the system; at least, they have thus far proven unavoidable, and have become so palpable and notorious that it is worse than folly to close our eyes to their existence.

In addition to these facts it should be borne in mind that a large and intelligent portion of the American people, comprising, perhaps, a majority of the Democratic party, are in the habit of considering these works as constituting a general system of internal improvements by the Federal Government, and therefore in violation of the creed of the Democratic party and of the Constitution of the United States. These two-fold objections—the one denying the constitutional power and the other the expediency of appropriations from the national treasury —seem to acquire additional strength and force in proportion as the importance of the subject is enhanced, and the necessity for more numerous and extensive improvements is created by the extension of our territory, the expansion of our settlements, and the development of the resources of the country. As a friend to the navigating interest, and especially identified by all the ties of affection, gratitude, and interest with that section of the Republic which is the most deeply interested in internal navigation, I see no hope for any more favorable results from national appropriations than we have heretofore realized. If then we are to judge the system by its results, taking the past as a fair indication of what might reasonably be expected in the future, those of us who have struggled hardest to render it efficient and useful, are competent to confess that it has proven a miserable failure. It is even worse than a failure, because, while it has failed to accomplish the desired objects, it has had the effect to prevent local and private enterprise from making the improvements under State authority, by holding out the expectation that the Federal Government was about to make them.

By way of illustration, let us suppose that twenty-five years ago, when we first began to talk about the construction of railroads in this country, the Federal Government had assumed to itself jurisdiction of all works of that description to the exclusion of State authority and individual enterprise. In that event, does any one believe we would now have in the United States fourteen thousand miles of railroad completed, and fifteen thousand miles in addition under contract. Is it to be presumed, that if our own State had prostrated itself in humble supplication at the feet of the Federal Government, and, with folded arms, had waited for appropriations from the national treasury, instead of exerting State authority, and stimulating and combining individual enterprise, we should now have in Illinois three thousand miles of railroad in process of construction? Let the history of internal improvements by the Federal Government be fairly written, and it will furnish conclusive answers to these interrogatories. For more than a quarter of a century the energies of the national government, together with all the spare funds in the treasury, were directed to the construction of a McAdamized road from Cumberland, in the State of Maryland, to Jefferson city, in the State of Missouri, without being able to complete one-third of the work. If the Government were unable to make three hundred miles of turnpike road in twenty-five years, how long would it take to construct a railroad to the Pacific ocean, and to make all the harbor and river improvements necessary to protect our widely extended and rapidly increasing commerce on a seacoast so extensive, that in forty years we have not been able to complete even the survey of one-half of it, and on a lake and river navigation more than four times as extensive as that seacoast? These questions are worthy of the serious consideration of those who think that improvements should be made for the benefit of the present generation as well as for our remote posterity; for I am not aware that the Federal Government ever completed any work of internal improvement commenced under its auspices.

The operations of the Government have not been sufficiently rapid to keep pace with the spirit of the age. The Cumberland road, when commenced, may have been well adapted to the purposes for which it was designed; but after the lapse of a quarter of a century, and before any considerable portion of it could be finished, the whole was superseded and rendered useless by the introduction of the railroad system. One reason, and perhaps the principal cause, of the slow progress of all Government improvements, consists in the fact that the appropriation for any one object is usually too small to be of material service. It may be sufficient for the commencement of the work, but before it can be completed, or even so far advanced as to withstand the effects of storms, and floods, and the elements, the appropriation is exhausted, and a large portion of the work swept away before funds can be obtained for finishing it or even protecting that which has been done. The ruinous consequences of these small appropriations are well understood and seriously deprecated, but they arise from the necessity of the case, and constitute some of the evils inseperable from the policy. All experience proves that the numberless items of a river and harbor or internal improvement bill cannot pass, each by itself, and upon its own merits, and that the friends of particular works will not allow appropriations to be made for the completion of others which are supposed to be of paramount importance, unless theirs are embraced in the same bill. Each member seems to think the work in his own district to be of the sternest necessity and highest importance, and hence feels constrained to give his own the preference, or to defeat any bill which does not include it. The result is a legislative omnibus, in which all manner of objects are crowded together indiscriminately; and as there never is and never can be money enough in the treasury to make adequate appropriations for the whole, and as the bill cannot pass unless each has something, of course the amount for each item must be reduced so low as to make it of little or no service, and thus render the whole bill almost a total loss. In this manner a large portion of our people have been kept in a state of suspense and anxiety for more than half a century with their hopes always excited and their expectations never realized.

I repeat that the policy heretofore pursued has proven worse than a failure. If we expect to provide facilities and securities for our navigating interests, we must adopt a system commensurate with our wants —one which will be just and equal in its operations upon lake, river, and ocean wherever the water is navigable, fresh or salt, tide or no tide—a system which will not depend for its success upon the dubious and fluctuating issues of political campaigns and congressional combinations—one which will be certain, uniform, and unvarying in its results. I know of no system better calculated to accomplish these objects than that which commanded the approbation of the founders of the Republic, was successively adopted on various occasions since that period, and directly referred to in the message of the President. It is evidently the system contemplated by the framers of the Constitution when they incorporated into that instrument the clause in relation to tonnage duties by the States with the assent of Congress. The debates show that this provision was inserted for the express purpose of enabling the States to levy duties of tonnage to make harbor and other improvements for the benefit of navigation. It was objected that the power to regulate commerce having already been vested exclusively in Congress, the jurisdiction of the States over harbor and river improvements, without the consent or supervision of the Federal Government, might be so exercised as to conflict with the congressional regulations in respect to commerce. In order to avoid this objection, and at the same time reserve to the States the power of making the necessary improvements, consistent with such rules as should be prescribed by Congress for the regulation of commerce, the provision was modified and adopted in the form in which we now find it in the Constitution, to wit: *"no State shall lay duties of tonnage except by the consent of Congress."* It is evident from the debates that the framers of the Constitution looked to tonnage duties as the source from which funds were to be derived for improvements in navigation. The only diversity of opinion among them arose upon the point, whether those duties should be levied and the works constructed by the Federal Government or under state authority. These doubts were solved by the clause quoted, providing, in effect, that while the power was reserved to the States, it should not be exercised, except by the consent of Congress, in order that the local legislation for the improvement of navigation might not conflict with the general enactment for the regulation of commerce. Yet the first Congress, which assembled under the Constitution, commenced that series of contradictory and partial enactments which has continued to the present time, and proven the fruitful source of conflict and dissention.

The first of these acts provided that all expenses for the support of lighthouses, beacons, buoys, and public piers, should be paid out of the national treasury, on the condition that the States in which the same should be situated respectively, should cede to the United States the said works, "together with the lands and tenements thereunto belonging, and together with the jurisdiction of the same." A few months afterwards the same Congress passed an act consenting that the States of Rhode Island, Maryland, and Georgia, might levy tonnage duties for the purpose of improving certain harbors and rivers within their respective limits. This contradictory legislation upon a subject of great national importance, although commenced by the first Congress, and frequently suspended and renewed at uncertain and irregular periods, seems never to have been entirely abandoned. While appropriations from the national treasury have been partial and irregular—sometimes granted and at others withheld—stimulating hopes only to be succeeded by disappointments, tonnage duties have also been collected by the consent of Congress, at various times and for limited periods, in Pennsylvania, Maryland, Virginia, North Carolina, South Carolina, Georgia, Alabama, Massachusetts, Rhode Island, and perhaps other States. Indeed there has never been a time, since the Declaration of Independence, when tonnage duties have not been collected under State authority for the improvement of rivers or harbors or both. The last act giving the consent of Congress to the collection of these duties, was passed for the benefit of the port of Baltimore in 1850, and will not expire until 1861.

Thus it will be seen that the proposition to pass a general law giving the consent of Congress to the imposition of tonnage duties according to a uniform rule, and upon equal terms in all the States and territories of the Union, does not contemplate the introduction of a new principle into our legislation upon this subject. It only proposes to convert a partial and fluctuating policy into a permanent and efficient system.

If this proposition should receive the sanction of Congress, and be carried into successful operation by the States, it would withdraw river and harbor improvements from the perils of the political arena, and commit them to the fostering care of the local authorities, with a steady and unceasing source of revenue for their prosecution. The system would be plain, direct, and simple, in respect to harbor improvements. Each town and city would have charge of the improvements in its own harbor, and would be authorized to tax its own commerce to the extent necessary for its construction. The money could be applied to no other object than the improvement of the harbor; and no higher duties could be levied than were necessary for that purpose. There would seem to be no danger of the power being abused, for in addition to the restrictions, limitations, and conditions, which should be embraced in the laws confering the consent of Congress, self-interest will furnish adequate and ample assurances and motives for the faithful execution of the trusts. If any town, whose harbor needs improvement, should fail to impose the duties and make the necessary works, such neglect would inevitably tend to drive the commerce to some rival port, which would use all the means in its power to render its harbor safe and commodious, and afford all necessary protection and facilities to navigation and trade. If, on the other hand, any place should attempt to impose higher duties than will be absolutely necessary for the contruction of the requisite improvements, this line of policy, to the extent of the excess, would have the same deleterious effects upon its prosperity. The same injurious influences would result from errors and blunders in the plan of the work, or from extravagance and corruption in the expenditure of the money. Hence each locality, and every citizen and person interested therein, would have a direct and personal interest in the adoption of a wise plan, and in securing strict economy and entire fidelity in the expenditure of the money. While upon the rivers the plan of operations would not be so direct and simple as in the improvement of harbors, yet even there it is not perceived that any serious inconvenience or obstacle would arise to the success of the system. It would be necessary that the law, which shall grant the consent of Congress to the imposition of the duties, shall also give a like consent in conformity with the same provision of the Constitution, that where the river to be improved, shall form the boundary of, or be situated in, two or more States, such States may enter into compact with each other, by which they may, under their joint authority, levy the duties and improve the navigation.

In this manner Pennsylvania, Delaware, and New Jersey could

enter into a compact for the improvement of the Delaware river, by which each would appoint one commissioner, and the three commissioners constitute a board, which would levy the duties, prescribe the mode of their collection, devise the plan of the improvement, and superintend the expenditure of the money. The six States bordering on the Ohio river, in like manner, could each appoint a commissioner, and the six constitute a board for the improvement of the navigation of that river from Pittsburg to the Mississippi. The same plan could be applied to the Mississippi, by which the nine States bordering upon that stream could each appoint one commissioner, and the nine form a board for the removal of snags and other obstructions in the channel from the Falls of St. Anthony to the Gulf of Mexico. There seems to be no difficulty, therefore, in the execution of the plan where the water course lies in two or more States, or forms the boundary thereof in whole or in part; and where the river is entirely within the limits of any one State, like the Illinois or Alabama, it may be improved in such manner as the legislature may prescribe, subject only to such conditions and limitations as may be contained in the act of Congress giving its consent. All the necessities and difficulties upon this subject seem to have been foreseen and provided for in the same clause of the Constitution, wherein it is declared, in effect, that, with the consent of Congress, tonnage duties may be levied for the improvement of rivers and harbors, and that the several States may enter into compacts with each other for that purpose whenever it shall become necessary, subject only to such rules as Congress shall prescribe for the regulation of commerce.

It only remains for me to notice some of the objections which have been urged to this system. It has been said that tonnage duties are taxes upon the commerce of the country, which must be paid in the end by the consumers of the articles bearing the burden. I do not feel disposed to question the soundness of this proposition. I presume the same is true of all the duties, tolls, and charges upon all public works— whether constructed by government or individuals. The State of New York derives a revenue of more than two millions of dollars a year from her canals. Of course this is a tax upon the commerce of the country, and is borne by those who are interested in and benefitted by it. This tax is a blessing or a burden, dependent upon the fact whether it has the effect to diminish or increase the cost of transportation. If we could not have enjoyed the benefit of the canal without the payment of the tolls, and if, by its construction and the payment, the cost of transportation has been reduced to one-tenth the sum which we would have been compelled to have paid without it, who would not be willing to make a still further contribution to the security and facilities of navigation, if thereby the price of freights are to be reduced in a still greater ratio. The tolls upon our own canal are a tax upon commerce, yet we cheerfully submit to the payment for the reason that they were indispensible to the construction of a great work, which has had the effect to reduce the cost of transportation between the Lakes and the Mississippi, far below what it would have been if the canal had not been made. All the charges on the fourteen thousand miles of railroad now in operation in the different States of this Union, are just so many taxes upon commerce and travel, yet we do not repudiate the whole railroad system on that account, nor object to the payment of such reasonable charges as are necessary to defray the expenses of constructing and operating them. But it may be said that if all the railroads and canals were built with funds from the national treasury, and were then thrown open to the uses of commerce and travel free of charge, the rates of transportation would be less than they now are. It may be that the rates of transportation would be less, but would our taxes be reduced thereby? No matter who is entrusted with the construction of the works, somebody must foot the bill. If the Federal Government undertake to make railroads and canals, and river and harbor improvements, somebody must pay the expenses. In order to meet this enlarged expenditure, it would be necessary to augment the revenue by increased taxes upon the commerce of the country. The whole volume of revenue which now fills and overflows the national treasury, with the exception of the small item resulting from the sales of public lands, is derived from a system of taxes imposed upon commerce and collected through the machinery of the custom-houses. No matter, therefore, whether these works are made by the Federal Government, or by stimulating and combining local and individual enterprise under State authority: in any event they remain a tax upon commerce to the extent of the expenditure.

That system which will insure the construction of the improvements upon the best plan and at the smallest cost will prove the least oppressive to the tax-payer and the most useful to commerce. It requires no argument to prove—for every day's experience teaches us—that public works of every description can be made at a much smaller cost by private enterprise, or by the local authorities directly interested in the improvement, than when constructed by the Federal Government. Hence, inasmuch as the expenses of constructing river and harbor improvements must, under either plan, be defrayed by a tax upon commerce in the first instance, and finally upon the whole people interested in that commerce, I am of the opinion that the burdens would be less under the system referred to in the message than by appropriations from the Federal treasury.[1] Those who seem not to have understood the difference have attempted to excite prejudice against this plan for the improvement of navigations by comparing it to the burdens imposed upon the navigation of the Rhine, the Elb, the Oder, and other rivers running through the German States. The people residing upon those rivers did not complain that they were required to pay duties for the improvement of their navigation. Such was not the fact. No duties were imposed for any such purpose. No improvements in the navigation were ever made or contemplated by those who exacted the tolls. Taxes were extorted from the navigating interest by the petty sovereigns through whose dominions the rivers run, for the purpose of defraying the expenses of the pomp, and ceremonies, and follies of vicious and corrupt courts. The complaint was, that grievous and unnecessary burdens were imposed on navigation without expending any portion of the money for its protection and improvement. Their complaints were just. They should have protested, if they had lived under a government where the voice of the people could be heard, against the payment of any more or higher tolls than were necessary for the improvement of the navigation, and have insisted that the funds collected should be applied to that purpose and none other. In short, a plan similar to the one now proposed would have been a full and complete redress of all their grievances upon this subject.

In conclusion, I will state that my object in addressing you this communication is to invite your especial attention to so much of the President's message as relates to river and harbor improvements, with the view that when the legislature shall assemble, either in special or general session, the subject may be distinctly submitted to their consideration for such action as the great interests of commerce may demand. I have the honor to be, very respectfully, your friend and fellow-citizen,

S. A. DOUGLAS

River and Harbor Improvements. Letter of Senator Douglas to Governor Matteson of Illinois (n.p., n.d.). An original draft of the letter is owned by Martin F. Douglas. The text followed here is that of the printed version. Joel A. Matteson, of Joliet, Illinois, was a member of the state legislature in the 1840's and held the governorship from 1853 to 1857.

[1]President Pierce, in his message to Congress on December 5, 1853, proposed that internal improvements of a local character be provided for by the localities involved, rather than by appropriations from the general government. He suggested, however, that, "in all cases where constructions are to be erected by the General Government, the right of soil" should first be obtained. This would obviate all jurisdictional disputes between the state and national governments concerning the right of the nation to protect and preserve its constructions.

To [the Librarian of Congress]

[January 20, 1854, n.p.; ANS, Illinois State Historical Library. Requesting the Librarian of Congress to allow the clerk of the Senate Committee on Territories to withdraw books from the Library of Congress in Douglas' name.]

To Franklin Pierce

[January 28, 1854, n.p.; ALS, RG-59, National Archives. Recommending the appointment of Charles Eames to a diplomatic post in Venezuela. Douglas' recommendation was endorsed by Senator David Rice Atchison of Missouri. Eames, former Commissioner to the Sandwich Islands and editor of the Washington *Union*, was appointed Minister to Venezuela, a position he held from 1854 to 1858.]

To Charles H. Lanphier

(Private)   Washington
My Dear Sir,   Feby 13th 1854
   I have been told that a Plot has been formed between the Whigs, Abolitionists, & some disappointed office-seekers, professing to be Democrats to endeavor to get our Legislature to instruct me on the Nebraska Bill & Tonnage Duties.[1] Of course I have no apprehension that the scheme can succeed. Nor would it alter or change my course it the plan could be executed. In the first place the Legislature is prohibited by the Constitution from acting on any subject at a Special Session not enumerated in the Proclamation. In view of this provision I wrote to the Governor some days ago that I did not expect him to submit the subject to the Legislature in asmuch as my letter did not reach him until after the date of his Proclamation.[2] The Governor will doubtless give you a copy of the Letter if you deem it advisable to publish it. The object of the Whigs & Abolitionists is apparent. They wish to divide the Democratic Party, & thus elect a Whig Senator.[3] Their only chance of success consists in our divisions. The Democratic Party is committed in the most solemn manner to the principle of Congressional non-interference with slavery in the States & Territories. The administration is committed to the Nebraska Bill & will stand by it at all hazards. The only way to avoid a division of the party is to sustain our principles. The vote for the Bill in the Senate will be about three to one—or about 45 to 15 or 17 if there is a full senate.[4] The principle of this Bill will form the test of Parties, & the only alternative is either to stand with the Democracy or to rally under Seward, John Van Buren & co. I have been exceedingly gratified to see the

course the Register has pursued. So far as I know all the Democratic papers of the state are following your lead, so far as they have spoken upon the subject. I forbear to mention the names of the leaders said to be engaged in the plot to which I allude for the reason that if the rumor be true you will have better means of ascertaining the fact than I have. I should like to know whether the confederates get any aid or countenance from Washington, and if so from whom. We shall pass the Nebraska Bill in both Houses by decisive majorities & the party will then be stronger than ever, for it will be united upon principle. Write to me often & give me all the news. Your friend

S. A. DOUGLAS

ALS, Illinois State Historical Library.

[1] The Nebraska bill had been reported by Douglas from his Committee on Territories on January 4, 1854, and by the end of January had been shaped in its final form; the bill provided for the creation of two territories, Kansas and Nebraska, and for the repeal of the Missouri Compromise. The latter, allowing the people of the new territories to determine the slavery question for themselves, resulted in a storm of protest throughout the North. Early in February, the Illinois legislature endorsed Douglas' course on the bill. No bill providing general tonnage duties was pending before the Senate during this session.

[2] Governor Matteson's proclamation calling the state legislature into special session was dated January 9, 1854.

[3] Senator James Shields's term would expire in 1854, necessitating a Senatorial election in the legislature early in 1855.

[4] The Kansas-Nebraska Bill passed the Senate on March 4, 1854, by a vote of 37 to 14.

To the Editor of the Concord (New Hampshire)
State Capitol Reporter

SIR: WASHINGTON, *February* 16, 1854.

I am under obligation to you for your paper which has come to hand regularly from the commencement of the session. I saw with pleasure that you took a bold stand in favor of the Nebraska bill, and spoke in favorable terms of my speech in its support. In this you did no more than what might have been reasonably expected from a sound democratic paper. The bill rests upon, and proposes to carry into effect, the great fundamental principle of self-government upon which our republican institutions are predicated. It does not propose to legislate slavery into the Territories, nor out of the Territories. It does not propose to establish institutions for the people, nor to deprive them of the right of determining for themselves what kind of domestic institutions they may have. It presupposes that the people of the Territories are as intelligent, as wise, as patriotic, as conscientious as their brethren and kindred whom they left behind them in the States, and as they were before they emigrated to the Territories. By creating a territorial government we acknowledge that the people of the Territory ought to be erected into a distinct political organization. By giving them a territorial legislature, we acknowledge their capacity to legislate for themselves. Now, let it be borne in mind that every abolitionist and freesoiler, who opposes the Nebraska bill, avows his willingness to support it, provided that slavery shall be forever prohibited therein. The objection, therefore, does not consist in a denial of the necessity for a territorial government, nor of the capacity of the people to govern themselves, so far as white men are concerned. They are willing to allow the people to legislate for themselves in relation to husband and wife, parent and child, master and servant, and guardian and ward, so far as white persons are to be affected; but seem to think that it requires a higher degree of civilization and refinement to legislate for the negro race than can reasonably be expected the people of a Territory to possess. Is this position well founded? Does it require any greater capacity or keener sense of moral rectitude to legislate for the black man than for the white man? Not being able to appreciate the force of this theory on the part of the abolitionists, I propose, by the express terms of the Nebraska bill, to leave the people of the Territories "perfectly free to form and regulate their domestic institutions in their own way, subject only to the Constitution of the United States."

While I have understood you to support these principles, and to defend the Nebraska bill upon these grounds in former numbers of your paper, I have observed with regret and amazement a leading article in your paper of the 14th instant, this moment received, in which the whole object, meaning, principles, provisions, and legal effect of the bill are so grossly and wickedly perverted and misrepresented, as to leave no doubt that the article was prepared by a deadly enemy, under the hypocritical guise of friendship, for the purpose of furnishing "aid and comfort" to the northern whigs and abolitionists in their warfare upon this great measure of pacification and the Democratic party in New Hampshire and throughout the Union, and especially upon that great fundamental principle which declares that every people capable of self-government ought to be permitted to regulate their domestic concerns in their own way. It is but justice to you to remark, that the article in question, although appearing under the editorial head, has the sign at the end of it which would indicate that it was not written by the editor, but was furnished as a communication. Trusting that such may be the case, and that you will promptly vindicate yourself by exposing the fraud and its author, I will quote a single paragraph as a specimen of the whole article, which contains incontestible proof that the writer is an enemy to the bill, and to the great principle involved in it, and to its friends, and

[285]

that he has assumed the garb of friendship in order to destroy, by fatal admissions, perversions, and misrepresentations, what he could not accomplish by direct opposition over his own signature:

"The Nebraska bill, if it shall pass both houses of Congress and become a law, repeals the Missouri Compromise. And what will be the effect of such repeal? *Unquestionably to revive and re-establish slavery over that whole region.* When Louisiana was ceded to the United States the law of slavery existed over that whole vast territory. It required no law to establish the institution—it then existed in fact and by law. And out of that territory already three slave States have been carved, and admitted into the Union, viz., Louisiana, Arkansas, and Missouri. When they came into the possession of the Union as Territories, slavery had been planted and was flourishing upon their soil; and the whole territory of Louisiana was under the dominion of the law which established and legalized the institution. Therefore, when those States came into the Union, the people did not have to establish and ordain slavery. The Missouri compromise *repealed and excluded* the institution above the line of 36°30′. *The repeal of that Compromise revives and re-establishes slavery in all the remaining territory of the Louisiana purchase.* Therefore, the law which permits slavery will be revived, and slavery will exist in Nebraska and Kansas the very moment the Nebraska bill receives the sanction of the President. This is the only deduction which can be logically drawn from the premises.

"The proposition, therefore, which northern men are to look fully in the face, and to meet without the possibility of evasion, is this: *Shall slavery be revived and re-established in Nebraska and Kansas?* And, as a necessary consequence, shall the slave States regain that political preponderance in the Senate of the United States which they have lost by the more rapid multiplication, of late, of free States? These are the propositions which northern men must meet, and which they cannot now dodge or evade."

Now, Mr. Editor, you must bear in mind that the italics are yours and not mine. When a newspaper writer italicises particular passages in an article, he has an object in doing so. We all know that the object is to invite the attention of the reader especially to passages thus designated. What are the passages thus italicised? The first is, that the effect of the Nebraska bill will be "UNQUESTIONABLY TO RE-VIVE AND RE-ESTABLISH SLAVERY OVER THAT WHOLE REGION!" The second is, that "THE REPEAL OF THE MISSOURI COMPROMISE REVIVES AND RE-ESTABLISHES SLAVERY IN ALL THE REMAINING TERRITORY OF THE LOUISIANA PURCHASE."

[286]

The third is, that the whole question involved in the passage of the Nebraska bill is: "SHALL SLAVERY BE REVIVED AND RE-ESTABLISHED IN NEBRASKA AND KANSAS?"

Now, Mr. Editor, did you not know, when you read the "proof" of this article, that each of these passages, thus italicised, contains a wicked and unpardonable slander against every friend and supporter of the bill, whether he be a northern or a southern man? Do you not know that the southern men deny the constitutional power of Congress to "establish slavery in the Territories?" Yet in the teeth of this undeniable fact, which is well known to every man, woman, and child who has ever read a newspaper, your paper represents these gentlemen as proposing to violate not only the Constitution, but their own oaths, by voting to "*establish*" slavery in Nebraska and Kansas? After attempting to fix this brand of infamy on the brow of more than two-thirds of the members of the United States Senate, the writer of the article in question proceeds to show the kindness of his heart and the purity of his motives, by assuring your readers that he is no better than those whom he assails, and therefore he approves the act and advises its consummation.

Three times in the short paragraph I have quoted has the writer of that article repeated the statement that it was not only the legal effect, but the object of the Nebraska bill, to "revive and establish" slavery in those Territories.

Now, sir, if you be a true friend of the bill, as your paper professes, you will correct these misrepresentations, and vindicate the measure, and the motives and conduct of its supporters, by publishing the bill itself, and especially that portion which relates to the act of 1820, and which your paper represents as being designed to establish slavery in the Territories. For fear that you may not have a copy of the bill, I will transcribe so much as bears upon this point, with the request that during the pendency of this discussion you will keep it standing in your paper under the editorial head, in as conspicuous a place and italicised in the same manner in which the misrepresentation was published. I quote from the 14th section of the bill:

"That the Constitution and laws of the United States, which are not locally inapplicable, shall have the same force and effect within the said Territory of Nebraska as elsewhere within the United States, except the eighth section of the act preparatory to the admission of Missouri into the Union, approved March 6, 1820, which being inconsistent with the *principle of NON-INTERVENTION BY CONGRESS with slavery in the States and Territories as recognised by the legislation of 1850,* (commonly called the Compromise Measure) is hereby declared inoperative and void, IT BEING THE TRUE

INTENT AND MEANING *of this act* NOT *to legislate slavery into any Territory or State,* NOR *to exclude it therefrom, but to leave the people thereof perfectly* FREE TO FORM AND REGULATE THEIR DOMESTIC INSTITUTIONS IN THEIR OWN WAY, SUBJECT ONLY *to the Constitution of the United States.*" Now, sir, inasmuch as you are the editor of a democratic paper, and claim to be the friend of the bill, you will excuse me for repeating the suggestion that you keep this clause standing under the editorial head as a notice to your readers, that whoever shall hereafter say that the object of the bill is to "revive or establish slavery" in the Territories may be branded as he deserves, as a falsifier of the record, and a calumniator of those whom he professes to cherish as friends.

The bill provides in words as specific and unequivocal as our language affords, that the *true intent and meaning* of the act is NOT to legislate slavery into any Territory or State. The bill, therefore, does not introduce slavery; does not revive it; does not establish it; does not contain any clause designed to produce that result, or which by any possible construction can have that legal effect.

"Non-intervention by Congress with slavery in the States and Territories" is expressly declared to be the principle upon which the bill is constructed. The great fundamental principle of self-government, which authorizes the people to regulate their own domestic concerns, as recognized in the Compromise measure of 1850, and affirmed by the Democratic national convention, and reaffirmed by the Whig convention at Baltimore, is declared in this bill to be the rule of action in the formation of territorial governments. The two great political parties of the country are solemnly pledged to a strict adherence to this principle as a final settlement of the slavery agitation. How can that settlement be final, unless the principle be preserved and carried out in all new territorial organizations?

But the professed friend of the measure in the article referred to follows the lead of his abolition confederates in this city, and declares that this bill opens that whole country to slavery! Why do they not state the matter truly, and say that it opens the country to *freedom* by leaving the people *perfectly free* to do as they please? Is it true, as these professed advocates of freedom would wish to make the world believe, that the people of northern latitudes are so adverse to free institutions, and so much in love with slavery, that it is necessary to have Congress appointed their guardian in order to preserve that freedom of which they boast so much? Were not the people of New Hampshire left free to decide this question for themselves? Did not all the New England States become free States under the operation of the principle upon which the Nebraska bill is predicated? If this be so—and every child knows that it is true—by what authority are we told that a country lying between the same parallels of latitude which embrace all of the New England States, is to be doomed to slavery if we intrust them with the same rights, privileges, and immunities which the Constitution guarantees to the people of New England? Are the sons of New England any less capable of judging for themselves when they emigrate to Minnesoto, Nebraska, or Kansas, than they were before they ever passed beyond that circle which circumscribed their vision with their native valleys? Is it wise to violate the great principle of self-government, which lies at the foundation of all free institutions, by constituting ourselves the officious guardians of a people we do not know, and of a country we never saw? May we not safely leave them to form and regulate their domestic institutions in the same manner, and by virtue of the same principle which enabled New York, New Jersey, and Pennsylvania to exclude slavery from their limits and establish free institutions for themselves?

But, sir, I fear I have already made this letter too long. If so, my apology therefore is to be found in the great importance of the subject, and my earnest desire that no honest mind be misled with regard to the provisions of the bill or the principles involved in it. Every intelligent man knows that it is a matter of no practical importance, so far as the question of slavery is concerned. The cry of the extension of slavery has been raised for mere party purposes by the abolition confederates and disappointed office-seekers. All candid men who understand the subject admit that the laws of climate, and production, and of physical geography, (to use the language of one of New England's greatest statesmen,) have excluded slavery from that country. This was admitted by Mr. Everett in his speech against the bill, and because slavery could not go there, he appealed to southern Senators not to insist upon applying the provisions of the Utah bill to Nebraska, when they would derive no advantages from it. The same admission and appeal were made by Mr. Smith, of Connecticut, in his speech against the bill. To-day Mr. Badger, of North Carolina, replied to these appeals by the distinct declaration that he and his southern friends did not expect that slavery would go there; that the climate and productions were not adapted to slave labor; but they insisted upon it as a matter of principle, and of principle alone. In short, all candid and intelligent men make the same admission, and present the naked question as a matter of principle, whether the people shall be allowed to regulate their domestic concerns in their own way or not. In conclusion, I may be permitted to add, that the Democratic party, as well as the country, have a deep

[289]

interest in this matter. Is our party to be again divided and rent asunder upon this vexed question of slavery?

Everything in the past history of the democracy of New Hampshire gives confidence and assurance to their patriotic brethren throughout the Union in a crisis like the present. I believe I know enough of the intelligence, consistency, and firmness of her people, to warrant the belief that while her favorite and honored son stands, as he has stood and now stands, firmly at the helm of the ship of state, calmly facing the threatening danger, regardless of all personal consequences, her noble people at home will sustain themselves and him against the attacks of open foes and the insidious assaults of pretended friends.

You will do me the justice to publish this in your next number. I have the honor to be, very respectfully, your obedient servant,

S. A. DOUGLAS

Letter of Senator Douglas, in Reply to the Editor of the State Capitol Reporter, Concord, N.H. (Washington, D.C., 1854).

To Edward Coles

Washington, *February* 18, 1854.

SIR: A valued friend has had the kindness to call my attention to a communication directed to me in this morning's *National Intelligencer*, in which you assume the responsibility of arraigning me, in terms neither kind nor respectful, for an alleged misrepresentation of the fundamental laws and territorial history of my own State.[1]

As an excuse for your attempt to provoke a controversy by making yourself a voluntary witness against the correctness of some of the facts stated in my speech on the Nebraska bill, you say:

"I hope that my personal relations to that State will excuse my calling your attention in a brief manner to a few of the erroneous assertions to which I allude."

Of course your "personal relations" to the State of Illinois will furnish an ample excuse for pointing out "a few of the erroneous assertions." In order that the public curiosity may be gratified by knowing how distinguished a personage the witness is, I will state that you were once Governor of Illinois under peculiar circumstances, and that you abandoned the State so soon as it was ascertained that the inducements which took you there could no longer be made available. Your avowed object is to vindicate "the truth of history," and do "justice to the conduct and character of Illinois."

How far such a motive is consistent with the whole tenor of your communication, and to what extent you have succeeded in accomplishing so laudable a purpose, I shall leave the public to determine, after calling attention to a few facts pertinent to the issue you have made. Referring to my speech, you use the following language:

"No act, you say, *had ever been passed by Congress to prohibit slavery in any of our new territories,* and, if attempted, it would have been null and void, as well from the want of power in Congress to pass it as from a determination of the people to establish and protect slavery in defiance of Congressional enactments. If this had been known, how much time and excitement would have been saved!"

After attributing this statement to me, you proceed to vindicate the "truth of history" by showing that slavery had been prohibited in the territory northwest of the Ohio river by the ordinance of 1787. Having rescued this important historical fact from that oblivion to which you suppose it had been consigned, you seem to congratulate yourself upon the great achievement with as much complacency as if you had not misquoted my speech, and attribute to me a statement which I had never made, in order to get an opportunity of proving that which some of us may have heard before. In order to give you an opportunity to vindicate the truth of history from the "erroneous assertions" in your own communication, I will invite your attention to what I did say in that part of my speech from which you profess to have derived your authority for the above statement:

"Let me ask you, where have you succeeded in excluding slavery by an act of Congress from one inch of the American soil? You may tell me that you did it in the northwest territory by the ordinance of 1787. I will show you by the history of the country that you did not accomplish any such thing. *You prohibited slavery there by law, but you did not exclude it in fact.* Illinois was a part of the northwest territory. With the exception of a few French and white settlements, it was a vast wilderness, filled with hostile savages, when the ordinance of 1787 was adopted. Yet, sir, when Illinois was organized into a territorial government, it established and protected slavery, and maintained it in spite of your ordinance, and in defiance of its express prohibition."

I cheerfully forgive you for this "erroneous assertion," for without it you would not have had the opportunity of making known to the present generation the important fact, that slavery was prohibited by the ordinance of 1787 in the northwest territory.

The next "erroneous assertion" for which you desire to be excused for calling my attention is, that slavery actually existed in the territory, and was recognized in defiance of the ordinance of 1787. You admit, however, that a few slaves were introduced into the territory, under the laws of Virginia, before the ordinance of 1787, and that they were held and treated as slaves, not only during the entire period of the territorial government, but after the State was admitted into the Union.

This fact proves the truth of what you are pleased to call my "erroneous assertions," so far as they relate to the existence of slavery in the territory under the ordinance and in defiance of its prohibition. But you suggest that the failure (of the ordinance to abolish and exclude the existence of slavery) "might have arisen from the ignorance of the French slaves of their rights under the ordinance, or from their fear of punishment from their masters if they claimed them; or it may have been from prejudice and interest in the officers whose business it was to see justice done them. *Whatever was the cause, it was local in character, and not attributable to Congress.*"

Here the substantial fact is distinctly admitted. It is admitted that slavery did exist in the Territory, and even after it became a State; that its existence was perpetuated by local causes, and in disregard of the ordinance and without the sanction and in opposition to the authority of Congress. I do not perceive that your excuses and conjectures change the result. I am not aware that French slaves were any more ignorant of their rights under the ordinance than any other slaves, or that they were any more afraid of their masters, or that the officers were governed by interest or prejudice in that Territory more than elsewhere. Upon this latter point, however, I am inclined to yield full credit to your testimony, inasmuch as you were an office-holder during the whole period of your residence in the State, and while governor, were especially charged by the constitution and your oath to see the laws faithfully executed. Be the cause what it may, the statement in my speech, which you have presumed to pronounce an "erroneous assertion," is now established and admitted, to wit: that while Congress prohibited slavery there *by law*, it did not exclude it *in fact*. But, sir, perhaps you will now be disposed to change the issue, and say that when you arraigned me before the public upon the charge of having misstated the facts and violated the truth of history, and made yourself the voluntary witness to prove the charge, in consequence of your "personal relations to the State of Illinois," you meant only to deny the truth of the other statement in the same paragraph, to wit: that the Territorial Government introduced and protected slavery, and maintained it in spite of the ordinance and in defiance of its express prohibition. If this be the material allegation in your bill of indictment against me, I will proceed to the trial of the issue upon the record. In accordance with the provision of the "act to divide the territory of the United States northwest of the Ohio into two separate governments," approved May 7, 1800, that district of country now embraced within the limits of the States of Indiana, Illinois, and Wisconsin, was erected into a distinct political organization, under the name of the Indiana Territory, and continued to be thus governed until the further division of the Territory, in 1809, and the establishment of the Territory of Illinois. By reference to the laws of Indiana for the year 1807, at page 423, you will find "an act concerning the introduction of negroes and mulattoes into this Territory," signed Jesse B. Thomas, Speaker of the House of Representatives, B. Chambers, President of the Council, and approved September 17, 1807, by William Henry Harrison, Governor of the Territory. Bearing in mind that the Territory for which this law was enacted embraced Illinois as well as Indiana and Wisconsin, and some other portions of the old northwest Territory, I invite your special attention to some of the provisions of the act:

SEC. 1.—It shall and may be lawful for any person being the *owner* or possessor of any negroes or mulattoes of and above the age of fifteen years, and *owing service and labor as slaves* in any of the States or Territories of the United States, or for any citizen of the said States or Territories *purchasing the same*, to bring the said negroes or mulattoes into this Territory.

The second section provides that within thirty days after bringing the slaves into the Territory, the master or owner shall take them before the clerk of the court, and have an agreement or indenture entered of record between the master and his slave, specifying the time which the slave should be compelled to serve his master, which term was usually fixed at ninety-nine years.

The third section provides that in the event the slave should refuse to enter into such agreement or indenture, it should be lawful for the master, within sixty days, to remove such slaves to any State or Territory where he could hold his slave as property without complying with such conditions.

The thirteenth section is as follows: "The children born in this Territory of a parent of color, owing service or labor by indenture, according to law, shall serve the master or mistress of such parent, the male until the age of thirty, and the female until the age of twenty-eight years."

From these provisions it is manifest that the object of the enactment was to introduce, maintain, and protect slavery in the Territory, in defiance of the ordinance of 1787. The other sections of this act are too voluminous to be set out in this communication, but by reference to them it will be seen that they are all in harmony and keeping with that object. This act not only introduced slavery into the Territory, but made it hereditary by imposing upon the children, born in the Territory under the ordinance, the obligation to serve the owners of their parents, even without contract or indenture, until thirty years of age, if males, and twenty-eight years, if females.

[293]

But this is not the only act upon the subject. By reference to the same volume of laws, you will find on page 340 "an act concerning servants." The first section provides that negroes and servants coming into the Territory under contract of service, shall be compelled to perform such contract specifically during the time thereof. In this act, also, there is no limit to the time of the service; but I am informed that it was usual to fix the period beyond the ordinary term of human life.

The second section made it the duty of the master to provide the servant with food, clothing, &c.

The third section pointed out the mode in which the master might sell his servant by an assignment of the indenture.

The fourth section provided the mode of correcting the servant by "stripes" when lazy, disorderly, or guilty of misbehavior to his master.

The fifth section provides for redressing the grievances of the servant when ill-used by his master.

The eighth section imposes penalties upon the "master or owner for putting away any lame or sick servant under pretence of freedom," &c.

The 9th section is as follows: *No negro, mulatto, or Indian,* shall at any time *purchase* any *servant* OTHER *than of their own complexion;* and if any of the persons aforesaid shall nevertheless presume to *purchase a white* servant, such servant shall immediately become *free,* and shall be so held, deemed, and taken."

The 10th section imposes penalties upon any person who shall trade with a servant "without the consent of his master or owner."

The 11th section is as follows: "In all cases of penal laws where FREE persons are punishable by fine, *servants shall be punished by* WHIPPING, AFTER THE RATE OF TWENTY LASHES FOR EVERY EIGHT DOLLARS: so that no servant shall receive more than forty lashes at any one time, unless such offender can procure some person to pay the fine."

The 13th section is as follows: "If any slave or servant shall be found at the distance of ten miles from the tenement of his or her master, or the person with whom he or she lives, without a pass or some letter or token whereby it may appear that he or she is proceeding by authority from his or her master, employer, or overseer, it shall and may be lawful for any person to apprehend and carry him or her before a justice of the peace, to be by his order punished with stripes, not exceeding thirty-five, at his discretion."

Section 14th is as follows: "If any *slave* or servant shall presume to come and be upon the plantation or at the dwelling-house of any person whatsoever, without leave from his or her *owner,* not being sent upon lawful business, it shall be lawful for the owner of such plantation or dwelling-house to give or order such *slave or servant* ten lashes on his or her bare back."

The 15th section provides that any *slave* or "*slaves,* servant or servants," who "shall be guilty of unlawful assemblies, seditious speeches," &c., "shall be punished with stripes, at the discretion of a justice of the peace, not exceeding thirty-nine."

The 16th section imposes a penalty of one hundred dollars "for harboring any servant or *slave* of color," and a fine of five hundred dollars "for assisting any servant or SLAVE to abscond from his or her master."

Now, sir, if it was not the object and meaning of these laws to introduce, protect, and regulate slavery in the Territories of Indiana, Illinois, and Wisconsin, will you have the kindness to inform the public what object the legislature had in view in passing them? Although these enactments appear on the statute-book as having been passed and approved on the 17th of September, 1807, yet it may be proper to remark that most of the provisions had been in force for many years previous, and were collated, arranged, and re-enacted as of that date. Such was the condition of the laws in respect to slavery in all that district of country which embraces the present States of Indiana, Illinois, and Wisconsin. When the Indiana Territory was divided and the Territory of Illinois established in 1809, these laws were continued in force in the Illinois Territory, with perhaps some variations not important to the matters now in controversy, during the entire period of her Territorial condition, and until her admission into the Union as a State. The legislature, at its first session after the admission of Illinois into the Union, proceeded to revise all the laws then in force, and to make such changes as had been rendered necessary by the transition from a Territorial to a State government. Among these revised laws will be found, at page 354, "AN ACT RESPECTING FREE NEGROES, MULATTOES, SERVANTS, AND SLAVES," approved March 30, 1819. This act consists of twenty-five sections, no less than fifteen of which were copied almost word for word from those Territorial acts to which I have directed your attention. By comparing the provisions of this act with those of the Territorial laws, it will be observed that all the enactments in the Territorial statutes which were intended to protect and *maintain the rights of the master to his slaves are preserved and continued in force,* whether such slaves were held by the master under contracts and indentures, or otherwise. On the other hand, it will be remembered, by the same comparison, that those provisions in the Territorial statutes which *authorized* the INTRODUCTION OF SLAVES from the slaveholding States and Territories are *omitted.* This omission was not accidental, it was not the result of a mere oversight, but it was made advisedly, with the view of having the law conform to the first section of the sixth article of the constitution of the State, which is in the following words:

"Neither slavery nor involuntary servitude shall HEREAFTER be INTRODUCED into the State, otherwise than for the punishment of crimes whereof the party shall have been duly convicted; nor shall any male person, arrived at the age of twenty-one years, nor female person arrived at the age of eighteen, be held to serve any person as a servant, under any indenture HEREAFTER made, unless such person shall enter into such indenture while in a state of perfect freedom, and on condition of a bona fide consideration received or to be received for this service. Nor shall any indenture of any negro or mulatto HERE-AFTER made and executed out of this State, or, if made in this State where the term of service exceeds one year, be of the least validity, except those given in cases of apprenticeship."

The legislature having conformed to the letter and spirit of the constitution, by omitting all those provisions of the Territorial laws which authorized the introduction of slaves into the Territory, so that there should be no legal authority for the introduction of any more slaves into the State, proceeded to protect by legal enactment the rights of the owners to all the slaves in the State when the constitution was adopted, in obedience to what was conceived to be a clearly implied obligation in the section of the constitution which I have quoted.

In regard to the indentured slaves, however, there was an express stipulation in the constitution protecting the rights of the master or owner in the following words:

"Each and every person who has been bound to service by contract or indenture *in virtue of the laws of the Illinois territory heretofore existing,* and in conformity to the provisions of the same, without fraud or collusion, *shall be held to a specific performance of their contracts or indentures;* and such negroes and mulattoes as have been registered in conformity with the aforesaid laws *shall serve out the time appointed by such laws.*"

Thus it appears that these Territorial laws to which I have directed your attention, and under the authority of which slaves and slavery were introduced into the Territory and maintained and protected there, and even made hereditary, so far as to compel the children to serve the owners of their parents for twenty-eight or thirty years, according to their sex—these very laws, and the slavery introduced and established by them, to the extent necessary to protect the rights of the owners to all slaves in the Territory, were sanctioned and affirmed by the constitution, in defiance of the ordinance of 1787.

But I must return to the aforesaid act of 1819, and call your attention to some of its provisions, inasmuch as it was one of the laws which you deemed it so great an honor to carry into faithful execution, in obedience to the constitution and your oath when governor of Illinois.

Section 12th. "That any such servant being lazy, disorderly, guilty of misbehavior to his master or master's family, shall be corrected by STRIPES," &c.

Section 16th. "And if any master or *owner* shall put away any lame or sick servant, under pretence of freedom," &c., "such master or owner shall forfeit and pay thirty dollars," &c.

Section 17th. "That no *negro, mulatto, or Indian shall at any time purchase any servant* OTHER THAN OF *their own complexion;* and if any of the persons aforesaid shall nevertheless presume to purchase a *white servant*, such servant shall immediately become *free*, and shall be so held, deemed, and taken."

Section 18 provides that no person shall trade with "any servant or slave," &c., "and any person so offending shall forfeit and pay to the master or owner of such slave or servant four times the value," &c.

Section 19th. "That in all cases of penal laws where FREE persons are punishable by fine *servants shall be punished* BY WHIPPING, *after the rate of twenty lashes for every eight dollars*," &c.

Section 21st provides "that if any slave or servant shall be found at a distance of ten miles from the tenement of his or her master," &c., "without leave, to be punished with *stripes not exceeding thirty-five*," &c.

Section 22d. "That if any slaves shall presume," &c., without leave, to go upon the plantation of any person, the owner of the plantation may give "such slave or servant ten lashes on his or *her bare back*."

Section 23d provides that "unlawful assemblies, trespasses, seditious speeches," &c., "by any slave or slaves, servant, or servants, shall be punished with stripes," &c., "not exceeding thirty-nine."

Now, sir, I must be permitted to remind you again that these provisions recognising the existence of slavery stood upon the statute book in full force as a part of the laws of the State when you were governor of Illinois. You, if you performed your duties according to the constitution and your official oath, saw them faithfully executed. Yet you presume to arraign me for having alluded to a well-known historical fact in the course of a legitimate argument in the performance of my duties in the Senate. My statement was, that, although Congress had prohibited slavery by *the ordinance* in the Territories, it had not succeeded in excluding it *in fact;* that slavery existed there in defiance of the prohibition, and was recognised and protected by the Territorial legislation. I now affirm the remaining position which you have controverted, to wit: "It is a curious fact that, so long as Congress said the

Territory of Illinois should not have slavery, she actually had it; and on the very day when the Congressional prohibition was withdrawn the people of Illinois, of their own free will and accord, provided for a system of emancipation." The fact of the existence of slavery there, I trust, will no longer be denied. I have already shown that the constitution with which Illinois was admitted into the Union did not ABOLISH slavery, did not set at liberty the slaves then in the State, but provided that "HEREAFTER" no more should be introduced. It also provided that the "indentured servants," most of whom were also slaves, should be held to service for the entire period specified in their indentures.

It then provided for the emancipation of their children at an earlier period than that prescribed in the Territorial law under which they were born slaves. The law, as we have already seen, provided that the children of indentured slaves should remain slaves for thirty years if males, and twenty-eight years if females. The constitution shortened this period by the proviso "that the children *hereafter* born of such negroes or mulattoes shall become FREE, the males at the age of twenty-one years and the females at the age of eighteen years." Under this system of gradual emancipation the number of slaves in the State continued to diminish slowly but steadily until the adoption of the new constitution in 1847, when slavery may be supposed to have become extinct by virtue of the following proviso: "There shall be neither slavery nor involuntary servitude in this State, except as a punishment for crime," &c.

Now, sir, having vindicated every position in my speech which has been assailed by you, and established the correctness of every material fact and allegation by incontrovertible records, I trust I may be permitted to take leave of the subject, without being placed under the necessity, in self-defense, to recur to it again. Referring to these facts and allegations, you say "these assertions cast a mortifying reproach on our country;" "if faith is given to them the history of the country is made ludicrous:" "it shows that our greatest men and highest functionaries have been for seventy years under a most ridiculous and false delusion," &c. In all this you will permit me to suggest that you have fallen into a very natural error, in supposing that these well-authenticated facts were unknown to all intelligent men, merely because one of "our greatest men and highest functionaries" in Illinois' early history remains ignorant of them to this day. I have the honor to be, very respectfully, your obedient servant,

S. A. DOUGLAS

Reply of Senator Douglas to Ex-Governor Coles, of Illinois (n.p., n.d.). Edward Coles settled originally in Illinois in 1819, and was Governor of the state from 1822 to 1826. Six years later he moved to Philadelphia.

[1]See Edward Coles to Stephen A. Douglas, February 13, 1854, Washington *National Intelligencer*, February 18, 1854. In his letter, Coles disagreed with Douglas' assertion, made during the debates on the Kansas-Nebraska Act, that slavery had never been successfully excluded from Illinois by an act of Congress, and cited the Ordinance of 1787 as proof. Coles concluded that the fact that slavery did exist in some areas of Illinois during the territorial and early statehood periods was due to the laxity of the Federal and state governments rather than to the absence of laws against it.

To William L. Marcy

Dr Sir,   Senate March 16th '54

This note will be handed you by Senator Jones of Tenn.[1] We were in Paris together last Summer & became well acquainted with Mr Sanford (Secy of Legation).[2] I have no hesitation in saying that I think that it would be right that he should be allowed clerk hire. He could not have performed the duties without a clerk & I think the expense should be borne by the Government as the duties were entirely of a public character. Your obt servt

S. A. DOUGLAS

ALS, RG-59, National Archives.
[1]James C. Jones had been Governor of Tennessee from 1841 to 1845 and served in the United States Senate from 1851 to 1857.

[2]Henry S. Sanford, of Connecticut, was secretary of the legation in Paris from 1849 to 1854.

To George Nicholas Sanders

Washington

Dear Sir,   March 27th 1854

I have received your letter of the 3d inst. Your indignation at those whom you call conspirators against your character is natural. I am surprised only at the direction your wrath has taken. I am not in the habit of suspecting my friends—much less of condemning them on suspicion and without evidence. I cannot accept the forgiveness which you so graciously tender. I did not write you an account of the facts as they occured, for the reason that the rules of the Senate forbid it. Since you have chosen to disolve the kind relations which existed between us no explanation now or hereafter can be expected or desirable. But I have one thing to say to you which I wish you to remember. It is this; when, in the prossecution of your cherished purposes of revenge, you shall ascertain the true state of the facts and shall know who assailed you and who stood by you & defended you to the last, *you will feel more mortification and chagrine at having written your unkind letter to me than I did in reading it.* With this conviction I will venture to call myself your old friend

S. A. DOUGLAS

ALS, Illinois State Historical Library. Sanders was appointed United States Consul at London in November, 1853, but the Senate later refused to confirm the appointment. Sanders' discussion with European revolutionaries and his public "Address to the People of France," which appeared later in 1854, urging the French people to rise up against Napoleon III, aroused a great deal of adverse publicity.

To Howell Cobb

Washington

My Dear Sir,   April 2d 1854

I am greatly indebted to you for your kind letter[1] & regret that the pressure of business & multiplicity of engagements have rendered it impossible for me to answer letters, even from distinguished & esteemed friends among whom I am happy to rank you. I could not doubt that the Nebraska Bill & the principle asserted therin would meet your harty approval. It is the principle with which your public life is especially identified. It will triumph & impart peace to the country & stability to the Union. I am not detered or affected by the violence & insults of the Northern Whigs & abolitionists. The storm will soon spend its fury, and the people of the north will sustain the measure when they come to understand it. In the meantime our Southern friends have only to stand firm & leave us of the North to fight the great Battle. We will fight it boldly & will surely triumph in the end. The great principle of self government is at stake & surely the people of this country are never going to decide that the principle upon which our whole republican system rests is vicious & wrong.

I shall be glad to hear from you at all times & to receive suggestions from your pen as to the best mode of conducting the great movement in which we are all engaged. Very truly your friend

S. A. DOUGLAS

ALS, University of Georgia Library, Athens. Howell Cobb had represented Georgia in the lower house of Congress from 1843 to 1851, was Governor of Georgia from 1851 to 1853, and was elected to Congress again in 1854. He later served as Secretary of the Treasury in the cabinet of James Buchanan.
[1]Cobb wrote Douglas on February 5, 1854, endorsing the latter's course on the Kansas-Nebraska Act. "I hope to hear that the Administration & the entire democratic party are united in sustaining your position," he wrote; "I regard it as a crisis in the national democratic party and he who dallies is a dastard & he who doubts is damned" (Douglas Papers, University of Chicago Library).

To Twenty-five Chicago Clergymen

WASHINGTON, *April 6*, 1854.

REVEREND GENTLEMEN: I acknowledge your kind consideration, in sending me the proceedings of the public meeting composed of twenty-five clergymen of the city of Chicago opposed to the Nebraska bill.[1] These proceedings consist of a protest "in the name of Almighty God" against the passage of the Nebraska bill, and signed by yourselves "as citizens and as ministers of the Gospel of Jesus Christ;" and also of four resolutions, which are stated to have been adopted with but one dissenting voice. The last of these resolutions is as follows:

"4th. That in the debate recently held in the Senate of the United States upon the presentation of the memorial of the clergy of New England, we greatly deplore the apparent want of courtesy and reverence towards man and God manifest especially in the speeches of the senators from Illinois and Indiana;[2] and that we regard the whole tone and spirit of that debate, on the part of the opponents of said memorial, as an outrage upon the privileges of a large and respectable body of citizens, upon the dignity of the Senate, and upon the claims of the divine name, word, and institutions, to which we owe profoundest honor and reverence."

Here I am distinctly and "especially" charged with "the apparent want of courtesy and reverence towards man and God," in the performance of my public duties in the Senate. This is a grave charge, whether preferred against a private individual or a public man, and one which should not have been made recklessly and without sufficient authority. If unsupported by evidence and contradicted by the records, its enormity is greatly aggravated by the startling fact that it emanates from "ministers of the Gospel of Jesus Christ," professing to speak "in the name of Almighty God," and by his authority. When you shall read that debate carefully, you will be surprised at the injustice you have done me by attributing to me the language which I found it necessary to quote, for the purpose of comment, from the protest signed by the three thousand and fifty clergymen of New England. I agree that the language quoted was "wanting in courtesy and reverence to man and God," and it was for that reason that I called the attention of the Senate and the country to the astounding fact that any body of men, calling themselves clergymen, or by any other name, in this age and in this country, would presume to claim that they were authorized by the Almighty, and in his name, to pronounce an authoritative judgment upon a political question pending before the Congress of the United States. If you had attributed this language to its true authors and directed your censure against them, instead of me, who but quoted to expose it, I should have united with you in saying that it did manifest an "apparent want of courtesy" to the Senate and "reverence to God."

In the latter clause of the same resolution, you also say:

"That we regard the whole tone and spirit of that debate on the part of the opponents of said memorial, as an outrage upon the privileges of a large and respectable body of citizens," &c.

[301]

And in the third resolution, you say:

"That, in our office as ministers, we have lost none of our prerogatives, nor escaped our responsibilities as citizens," &c.

It is your obvious intention in these two resolutions to convey the impression to the world and induce the public to believe that I, and these senators who participated with me in the debate referred to, denied to the signers of that protest their right "as citizens," in consequence of their profession as "clergymen."

Unwilling as I am to believe that you, as the professed ministers of Jesus Christ, assembled in His holy name, could deliberately put forth a charge so unjust and unfounded, yet I am unable to put any other construction upon your language, or to conceive of any other object you could have had in passing these resolutions.

In vindication of my own character against the aspersions which you have so unjustly cast upon it, you must permit me to say to you, with the most profound respect for your "office as ministers," that, if you had read the debate yourselves before you pronounced judgment upon it, instead of following the lead of an unscrupulous partisan press, you would have known that the charge in any of its forms, and in all its length and breadth, was wickedly and wantonly untrue. So far from denying to the clergy of New England, or of any other portion of this country, any of their rights "as citizens," and so far from questioning their undoubted right to petition, protest, or remonstrate, in respect, to any measure coming or pending before Congress in the same manner, and by the same authority as other citizens under the Constitution, the debate shows that each and every senator against whom you have preferred this grave charge distinctly and expressly recognised and affirmed such right. In order to render my vindication complete, and to disabuse you of the error into which you have fallen—for, in your case, it must be error merely—I proceed to establish this position by extracts from the debate, as it appears in the *Congressional Globe*, and republished in pamphlet form at the abolition establishment in this city. At page 11 of that pamphlet, you will find that Mr. DOUGLAS said:

"The senator from Texas says the people have a right to petition. *I do not question it. I do not wish to deprive ministers of the Gospel of that right.* I do not acknowledge that there is any member of this body who has a higher respect and veneration either for a minister of the Gospel or for his holy calling than I have; but my respect is for him *in his calling.* I will not controvert what the senator from Massachusetts has said, as to there being, perhaps, no body of men in this country, three thousand in number, who combine more respectability than these clergymen."

Permit me to inquire of you, reverend gentlemen, whether you had read my speech, and particularly this portion of it, when you charged me with committing, in that debate, "an outrage upon the privileges of a large and respectable body of citizens," (referring to the clergymen who had signed that protest,) and when, in another resolution, you charged me and others, by implication, with the design of depriving you of your "prerogatives as citizens," on account of your "office as ministers!"

I now call on you, "as ministers of the Gospel of Jesus Christ," "as citizens," and as honest men, who are under a high moral and religious obligation to speak the truth and to do justice to all men, to withdraw this charge, and make an open and public confession of the injustice you have done me!

Again, in your resolutions, you do not confine your censure to myself, but you extend it to Senators Mason, Butler, Pettit, Adams, and Badger,[3] including all who participated in that debate in opposition to the propriety of the protest. Your language is, that you regard "the whole tone and spirit of that debate, on the part of the opponents of said memorial, as an outrage upon the privileges of a large and respectable body of citizens," &c.

Now, let us see whether your charge against Mr. MASON, that he committed an "outrage" on the rights of the memorialists "as citizens," be sustained by the record:

"Mr. MASON. That it is the right of the citizens of the United States to petition Congress, or either House of it, upon any subject that may be presented to them, is never denied, never should be denied; and such petition, upon any subject of public interest should be received and treated with the respect which is due to citizens. I trust I shall never see the day when the Senate of the United States will treat the authors of such petitions, upon any subject proper for legislation pending before the body, coming from the people of the United States, with aught but respect."

Thus it will be seen that Mr. Mason expressly affirmed the right of every citizen, whatever his profession or occupation in life, to petition Congress upon any subject pending before either house. In another portion of his speech in favor of the right of every class of our citizens to petition, he said:

"It is a respect due to them; but when they come here, not as citizens, but declaring that they come as ministers of the Gospel, and, as the honorable Senator from Texas declared them to be, vicegerents of the Almighty—so I understood him to declare, possibly he meant vice-regents, to supervise and control the legislation of the country— I say, when they come here as a class unknown to the government, a class that the government does not mean to know in any form or shape,

[303]

not to recommend or remonstrate, but to denounce our action as a great moral wrong, because they claim to be the "viceregents" of the Almighty, we are bound, not from disrespect to them as citizens, not from disrespect to the cloth which they do not grace, but from respect to the government, from respect to that sacred public trust which has been committed to us—to carry out the policy of the government and refuse to recognise them."

Mr. Mason expressly recognised and vindicated the full and equal rights of clergymen, in common with all other citizens, to petition government for the redress of grievances. His complaint was, that the protestants have not approached the Senate in their capacity as citizens; that they did not claim the right under the Constitution, or as being derived from any human authority or earthly tribunal; but, casting aside all human authority and constitutional right, they claim the divine prerogative as the "vice-regents" of the Almighty on earth to pronounce judgment in his name, and by his authority, upon a legislative question, which had been confided by the people, in obedience to the Constitution, to the decision of the Congress of the United States.

Senator Butler's speech comes next. Let us see if your charge be well founded against him:

"Mr. BUTLER. I have great respect, Mr. President, for the pulpit. I have such a respect for it that I would almost submit to a rebuke from a minister of the gospel, even in my official capacity; but they lose a portion of my respect when I see an organization, for, I believe, the first time in the history of this government, of clergymen within a local precinct, within the limits of New England, assuming to be, as the Senator from Texas said, the vicegerents of Heaven, coming to the Senate of the United States, not as citizens, as my friend from Virginia has said, but as the organs of God; for they do not come here petitioning or presenting their views under the sanction of the obligations and responsibilities of citizens under the Constitution of the United States, but they have dared to quit the pulpit, and step into the political arena, and speak as the organs of Almighty God. Sir, they assume to be the foremen of the jury which is to pronounce the verdict and judgment of God upon earth. They do not protest as ordinary citizens do; but they mingle in their protest what they would have us believe is the judgment of the Almighty. When the clergy quit the province which is assigned to them, in which they can dispense the gospel—that gospel which is represented as the lamb, not as the tiger or the lion—when they would convert the lamb into the lion, going about in the form of agitators, seeking whom they may devour, instead of meek and lowly representatives of Christ, they divest themselves of all respect which I can give them."

[304]

Here again you find that there was no disposition to deprive ministers of the gospel of any of their rights as citizens—no unwillingness to receive their petitions, memorials, or remonstrances, and to treat them with entire respect when presented in that capacity, and claiming no other or higher prerogatives than those secured to their fellow-citizens by the Constitution. But their divine right, emanating from a power higher than the Constitution, and above the sovereignty of the people and of the States of this Union, to decide a legislative measure, and issue command to the Senate in the name of the Deity, was seriously but respectfully called in question.

The speech of Senator Adams comes next in order. Let us see if your charge against him be sustained by the record. Did he commit "an outrage upon the privileges of a large and respectable body of citizens?" Did he propose to deprive you or any other body of clergymen of your "prerogatives as citizens?"

Mr. ADAMS said:

"I concur with my friend from South Carolina in regard to the petition which has been presented and ordered to lie on the table. It is addressed to the Senate and House of Representatives by a body of individuals as ministers of the Gospel. I trust I have as high a regard for their vocation as any other individual, and as much respect for the ministers of peace and good will on earth as any other individual; but when they depart from their high vocation, and come down to mingle in the turbid pools of politics, I would treat them just as I would all other citizens. I would treat their memorials and remonstrances precisely as I would those of other citizens. It is so unlike the apostles and the ministers of Christ at an early day, that it loses the potency which they suppose the styling themselves ministers of the Gospel would give to their memorials. The early ministers of Christ attended to their mission, one which was given to them by their Master; and under all circumstances, even when the Savior himself was upon earth, and attempts were made to induce him to give opinions with reference to the municipal affairs of the government, he refused. These men have descended from their high estate to assail the action of this body."

Where is the evidence of the truth of your charge against Senator ADAMS, that he meditated the design of depriving ministers of the Gospel of their rights of citizenship? Do you find it in the passage in which he declares that "*I would treat their memorials and remonstrances precisely as I would those of other citizens?*" Is it "an outrage upon their privileges" that they should be treated precisely like other citizens? If you think so, you will doubtless persevere in the course which you have commenced. If you think otherwise, you will hasten to withdraw the unjust imputations and repair the injury you have done.

[305]

Following the order of the debate, the next senator whom you have embraced in your charge of an outrage upon the privileges of the clergy, is Mr. PETTIT. The first paragraph of his speech on that occasion is in the following words:

"Mr. PETTIT. Mr. President, I am for the greatest liberty to the greatest number, and I will not deny to any class of my fellow citizens, under whatever name or denomination they may appear, the right to petition; and under the general term of 'petition,' provided for in the Constitution, I am willing to regard memorials and remonstrances, of whatever name, kind, or description, provided always they are respectful to the Senate."

In this speech you find no attempt to deprive the clergy of the rights of citizenship; no denial or limitation of their privileges as citizens. Their right to petition, memorialize, or remonstrate, "under whatever name or denomination," is conceded and affirmed in so many words. It is true, Mr. PETTIT spoke in very strong and decided terms upon the assumption of the reverend protesters to make known the mind and will of God concerning the Nebraska bill. He denied what they undertook to proclaim as a revelation by His authority, either prophetically of events to happen or judicially of judgments to be inflicted. But he spoke no word, he made no suggestion, against their full and uncontested rights, in their own names, as men and ministers, to remonstrate, to protest, and in the strongest terms, if respectful to the Senate, to declare their opinions of the nature and tendency of the legislation of which they disapproved. The only remaining speech, to which your censure can be supposed to apply, is that of Senator BADGER. He said:

"These gentlemen do not come here in the character of petitioners. These gentlemen do not come here in the character of remonstrants; they do not come here in the character of memorialists; but they come as protesters, not in their own name, not with the individual weight and authority which might be attributed to their protest on the ground of their own intelligence or worth, not merely with the weight and authority which might be superadded to this and other considerations from the fact of their being ministers of the Gospel. It is impossible to look at this paper without seeing that the honorable senator from New York has specially pleaded upon the subject, and that the reverend gentlemen who signed it will not thank him for assigning them in this paper the low position in which he wishes to place them. What is it?

" 'The undersigned clergymen of different religious denominations in New England, hereby, in the name of Almighty God, solemnly protest.'

" 'In their official characters as ministers of Almighty God, and in his name, they protest against the passage of the Nebraska bill.'

"Now, sir, these are educated gentlemen. They are men of experience in their vocation. They understand the true and solemn import of the words here used; and I have not the shadow of a doubt that they meant to enter a protest, as the language imports, as a protest, through them, of the Almighty God himself, speaking to this Senate."

In another portion of the same speech, he added:

"Well, then, sir, the whole paper proceeds in the same name and by the same authority; and, among other things, they protest against the measure as a great moral wrong, a breach of faith eminently injurious to the moral principles of the community, subversive of all confidence in national engagements, and as exposing us to the righteous judgment of the Almighty. All that is announced by these gentlemen, as ministers of God, affecting to speak in his name.

"The interpretation of the paper, sir, I think it is impossible to mistake; but I have said that I think too much importance has been attached to it. Whether this is to be understood as a denunciation of the judgments of God, or as a prediction of his judgments, I deny the authority to denounce, and I deny the gift of prophecy; and therefore I think we need not have troubled ourselves further on the subject."

I now pause for the purpose of inquiring of each of you, reverend gentlemen, in which one of these speeches was it proposed to deprive you, or any other clergymen, of your "prerogatives as citizens," in consequence of your "office as ministers?" In which one do you find "an outrage upon the privileges of a large and respectable body of citizens?"

I have proven affirmatively and conclusively that each and all of the senators against whom you made this serious charge did, in the debate to which you refer, distinctly recognise and concede to all clergymen, of whatever denomination, the undoubted right to "petition government for the redress of grievances," under the authority of the Constitution, in the same manner and with the same force as all other citizens. You will therefore permit me to suggest to you, with entire respect, that it is due to your own character, "as ministers of the gospel of Jesus Christ," as citizens, and as fair men who are bound by a high moral and religious obligation to do justice to all men, to withdraw the injurious imputations you have made upon the reputation of these distinguished senators, and to make an open and public confession of the injustice you have done them in connexion with myself. You must do this; you cannot fail to do it, unless you claim, by virtue of your "office as ministers," to be invested with civil and political rights and powers not possessed by citizens as such, not secured or conferred by the Constitution or any other human authority, but of divine origin, whereby you are empowered, "in the name of the Almighty God," to

[307]

command the Senate to decide a political and legislative question in the way you shall indicate!

After a careful and critical examination of your protest against the Nebraska bill, and of your resolutions in affirmance of your divine right to denounce that measure, in the name and by the authority of the Almighty, I fear that it is your purpose to claim and exercise this prerogative of the Deity upon legislative and political questions. Let me recall your attention to this remarkable protest:

"*To the honorable Senate and House of Representatives of the United States, in Congress assembled:*

"The undersigned, clergymen of different religious denominations in the northwestern States, as citizens, and as ministers of the Gospel of Jesus Christ, hereby, in the name of Almighty God, and in his presence, do solemnly protest against the passage of what is known as the 'Nebraska bill,' or any repeal or modification of existing legal prohibitions of slavery in that part of our national domain which it is proposed to organize into the territories of Nebraska and Kansas.

"We protest against it as a great moral wrong; as a breach of faith eminently injurious to the moral principles of the community, and subversive of all confidence in national engagements; as a matter full of danger to the peace, and even existence, of our beloved Union, and exposing us to righteous judgments of the Almighty.

"And your protestants, as in duty bound, will ever pray."

With the exception of the description of your locality "in the northwestern States" instead "of New England" and of the interpolation of the words "as citizens," this protest is an exact copy of the one presented to the Senate from the clergymen of New England upon which the debate occurred which you have condemned. After reading that debate and seeing the nature of the objections urged to the New England protest, it seems that you determined to present yourselves to the Senate in a two-fold capacity—the one "as citizens" and the other "as ministers of the Gospel of Jesus Christ." Nobody questions your right; no one denies the propriety of your exercising the constitutional right of petitioning government for redress of grievances in your capacity as citizens; nor can there be any well-founded objection to your adding these other words, "as ministers of the Gospel of Jesus Christ," if done only as illustrative of your relations to society and of your profession and occupation in life. This was not the obnoxious feature in the New England protest. The objection urged to that paper was, that the clergymen who had signed it, did not protest in their own names, as clergymen, or citizens, or human beings, or in the name of any human authority or civil right, but they assumed the divine prerogative and spoke to the Senate "in the name of Almighty God!"

With a full knowledge that senators in the debate to which you have alluded, understood the New England protest in this light—and as asserting a divine power in the clergy of this country higher than the obligations of the Constitution, and above the sovereignty of the people and of the States—to command the senators by the authority of Heaven and under the penalty of exposing them "to the righteous judgment of the Almighty," to vote in a particular way upon a given question, you now readopt the protest and repeat the command in the identical language in which it was originally issued. This looks as if it was your fixed and deliberate purpose, as clergymen, to force an issue upon this point with the civil and political authorities of the republic. If there were room for doubt or misapprehension, in this respect, on the face of the New England protest, you have removed all obscurity and avowed the purpose distinctly and boldly in the resolutions which you adopted at the time you signed your protest:

"*Resolved* 1st. That the ministry is the divinely appointed institution for the declaration and enforcement of God's will upon all points of moral and religious truth; and that as such, it is their duty to reprove, rebuke, and exhort, with all authority and doctrine."

This resolution appears to have been adopted by you at an Anti-Nebraska meeting, (composed exclusively of clergymen, twenty-five in number,) and called for the purpose of considering that question and none other. It was adopted in connexion with the protest, and forms a part of the same transaction. The protest denounces the Nebraska Bill "in the name of Almighty God" as "a great *moral wrong*" —"as a breach of faith eminently injurious to *moral principle* of the community," and, "as exposing us to the righteous judgments of the Almighty." The resolution declares "that the *ministry is the divinely-appointed institution for the declaration and enforcement of God's will upon all points of moral and religious truth!*" Do not the protest and resolution refer to the same question, to wit, the Nebraska bill now pending before Congress? Surely you will not deny that such was your understanding. You assembled to consider that question and none other. You acted upon that subject and that alone. Your resolutions were declaratory of the extent of your rights and powers as clergymen, and your protest was your action in conformity with those assumed rights and powers.

I understand, then, your position to be this: that you are "ministers of the Gospel;" that "the ministry is the divinely-appointed institution for the declaration and enforcement of God's will upon all points of moral and religious truth;" that this "divinely-appointed institution" is empowered "to declare" what questions of a civil, political, judicial, or legislative character, do involve "points of moral and religious

[309]

truth;" that the Nebraska bill does involve such "points," and is, there-fore, one of the questions upon which it is the duty of this "divinely-appointed institution" to "declare and enforce God's will;" and that, clothed with "all authority and doctrine," this "divinely-appointed in-stitution" proceeds to issue its mandates to the Congress of the United States "in the name of the Almighty God." This being your position, I must be permitted to say to you, in all Christian kindness, that I differ with you widely, radically, and fundamentally, in respect to the nature and extent of your rights, duties, and powers, as ministers of the Gos-pel. If the claims of this "divinely-appointed institution" shall be en-forced, and the various public functionaries shall yield their judgments to your supervision, and their consciences to your keeping, there will be no limit to your temporal power except your own wise discretion and virtuous forbearance. If your "divinely-appointed institution" has the power to prescribe the mode and terms for the organization of Nebraska, I see no reason why your authority may not be extended over the entire continent, not only to the country which we now pos-sess, but to all which may hereafter be acquired.

Nor do you propose to confine your operations to the supervision and direction of the action of Congress in the organization of territorial governments and the admission of new States into the Union. It is diffi-cult to conceive of any matter of private or public concern, pending before Congress, or in the legislatures of the different States, or in the judicial tribunals, which does not quite as much as the Nebraska bill "involve some point of moral and religious truth;" and we are in-formed, in your resolution, that "upon all points of moral and religious truth" the "ministry is the divinely-appointed institution for the dec-laration and enforcement of God's will." I do not wish to be under-stood as intimating that it is your present purpose, through the agency of this "divinely-appointed institution," to declare and enforce God's will" in all matters affecting our foreign policy and domestic concerns, nor that you intend to direct the movements of the political parties, and control the local and general elections throughout the country. It is enough to fill with alarm the mind of every patriot, and to bring sorrow and grief to the heart of every Christian, that you have asserted the right to do this in all cases, and have in one case attempted the exercise of this divine prerogative "in the name of Almighty God." It is true that, while you assert the right, in the broadest terms, and propose now to establish a precedent which will justify its exercise in all future time, in your second resolution you "disclaim all desire" to do certain things from which it might be inferred, on first view, that you do not intend to meddle with party politics, nor attempt to control the political movements of the day. This, however, turns out to be illusory, on a closer examination.

"*Resolved,* 2d, That while we disclaim all desire to interfere in questions of war and policy, or to mingle in the conflicts of political parties, it is our duty to recognise the moral bearing of such questions and conflicts, and to proclaim, in reference thereunto, no less than to other departments of human interest, the principle of inspired truth and obligation."

You do not "desire to interfere in questions of war and policy." Thus far I heartily approve. I rejoice to see that you are willing to leave the question of war where the Constitution has placed it—in the hands of Congress, as the representatives of the people and the States of the Union.

You "disclaim all desire," also, "to mingle in the conflicts of political parties." This sentiment is admirable. It will meet the cordial approbation of every patriot and Christian. But you immediately follow it with the declaration that "it is our duty to recognise the moral bearing of such questions and conflicts!" You do not desire to engage in war nor to fight the battles of your country, but you do claim that it is your right, and, if you please, your duty, by virtue of your office as ministers, through the agency of this divinely-appointed institution, to declare, in the name of Almighty God, a war, in which your country is engaged with a foreign power, to be immoral and unrighteous, although the representatives of the people and of the States, in pursuance of the Constitution, have declared it to be just and necessary. And this, not in the course of your ordinary pastorial duties to your several congregations, but as an organized body speaking to the constituted authorities of the nation. I cannot recognise the principle that, while you are protected in the enjoyment of all your rights as citizens, of all your just rights as ministers, you are yet released, by virtue of your office as ministers, from your allegience to the country during war, and from your obligation of obedience to the Constitution and laws and constituted authorities at all times.

You also say that you consider it your duty to take cognizance of "the moral bearing of the conflicts of the different political parties." The moral bearing of the democratic party, and of the whig party, and of the abolition party are each to be recognised by your divinely appointed institution; and you then add that it is your duty "to proclaim in reference thereunto the principle of inspired truth and obligation." You propose, through your divinely-appointed institution, to apply the test of "inspired truth" to each of the political organizations and to their respective conflicts, and "to reprove, rebuke, and exhort with all

[311]

authority and doctrine," in the name of the great Jehovah. With all due respect for you, as ministers of the Gospel, I cannot recognise in your divinely-appointed institution the power either of prophecy or of revelation. I have never recognised the existence of that power in any man on earth during my day. Only a few years since, and within the period of your own vivid recollection, the priesthood of a religious sect, calling themselves Latterday Saints, claimed for themselves the same right, by virtue of their divinely-appointed institution, to declare and enforce God's will on earth in respect to "all points of moral and religious truth." They also declared that it was their duty to recognise "the moral bearing of the conflicts of the political parties," and to "proclaim in reference thereunto the principle of inspired truth and obligation." When the Mormon prophet proclaimed the principle of inspired truth, "in the name of the Almighty God," and through the agency of his divinely-appointed institution, that it was the decree of heaven that STEPHEN A. DOUGLAS should be beaten, and his opponent elected to Congress in the Quincy district, the people of that portion of Illinois did not acknowledge the authority of the prophet, nor did the result of the election strengthen my opinion in the validity of his claims.

I have wandered over distant and extensive portions of the globe, during the past year, where the successor of Mahomet proclaimed and enforced God's will on earth, according to the principles of inspired truth and obligation, as recorded in the Koran; and, by the potency of his divinely-appointed institution, held, in the hollow of his hand, and suspended upon his breath, the lives, the liberties, and the property of millions of men, women, and children. When within his dominions and surrounded by his bayonets, I had neither the time nor the disposition to argue the question of his right to "reprove, rebuke, and exhort, with all authority and doctrine," in the name of the Almighty! But, when I set foot on the shores of my native land, under the broad folds of our national flag, and surrounded by the protecting genius of our American institutions, I did not feel like recognizing any such rightful authority of that divinely-appointed institution, in temporal affairs, here or elsewhere.

Your claims for the supremacy of this divinely-appointed institution are subversive of the fundamental principles upon which our whole republican system rests. What the necessity of a Congress, if you can supervise and direct its conduct? Why should the people subject themselves to the trouble and expense of electing legislatures for the purpose of enacting human laws, if their validity depends upon the sanction of your divine authority? Why sustain a vast and complex judicial system to expound the laws, administer justice, and determine all disputes in respect to human rights, if your divinely-appointed institution is invested with all authority to prescribe the rule of decision in the name of the Deity? If your pretensions be just and valid, why not dispense with all the machinery of human government and subject ourselves freely and unreservedly, together with all our temporal and spiritual interests and hopes, to the justice and mercy of this divinely appointed institution?

Our fathers held that the people were the only true source of all political power; but what avails this position, if the constituted authorities established by the people are to be controlled and directed—not by their own judgment, not by the will of their constituents, but by the divinely-constituted power of the clergy? Does it not follow that this great principle, recognised and affirmed in the constitution of the United States and of every State of this Union, is thus virtually annulled, and the representatives of the people converted into machines in the hands of an all-controlling priesthood?

The will of the people, expressed in obedience to the forms and provisions of the Constitution, is the supreme law of this land. But your "office as ministers" is not provided for in the Constitution. Your divinely-appointed institution is not recognised in that instrument. Nowhere in the Constitution or laws of any of the States, or of the United States, is there to be found a provision constituting or recognising you and your brethren "the divinely-appointed institution for the declaration and enforcement of God's will;" and therefore, in your character as a body of ministers, you cannot claim any political power under our system of government.

The persecutions of our ancestors were too fresh in the memories of our revolutionary fathers for them to create, recognise, or even tolerate, a church establishment in this country, clothed with temporal authority. So apprehensive were they of the usurpations of this, the most fearful and corrupting of all despotisms, whether viewed with reference to the purity of the church or the happiness of the people, that they provided in the Constitution that "no religious test shall ever be required as a qualification to any office or public trust under the United States." Still, fearful that, in the process of time, a spirit of religious fanaticism, or a spirit of ecclesiastical domination, (yet more to be dreaded, because cool and calculating,) might seize upon some exciting political topic, and in an evil hour surprise or entrap the people into a dangerous concession of political power to the clergy, the first Congress under the Constitution proposed, and the people adopted, an amendment to guard against such a calamity, in the following words:

"Congress shall make no law respecting an establishment of religion, or prohibiting the free exercise thereof."

[313]

The doctrine of our fathers was, and the principle of the Constitution is, that every human being has an inalienable, divinely-conferred right to worship God according to the dictates of his own conscience; and that no earthly institution, nor any "institution" on earth, can rightfully deprive him of that sacred and inestimable privilege.

However, it is no part of my purpose to inquire into the extent of your authority in spiritual affairs. That is a question between you and your respective congregations, with which I have neither right nor wish to interfere.

All that I have said, and all that I propose to say, has direct reference to the vindication of my character and position against the unjustifiable assaults which you have made in regard to my official action in the Senate. I repeat that your assumption of power from the Almighty, to direct and control the civil authorities of this country, is in derogation of the Constitution, subversive of the principles of free government, and destructive of all the guarantees of civil and religious liberty. The sovereign right of the people to manage their own affairs in conformity with the Constitution of their own making, recedes and disappears, when placed in subordination to the authority of a body of men, claiming, by virtue of their offices as ministers, to be a divinely-appointed institution for the declaration and enforcement of God's will on earth.

If your objection to the Nebraska bill consists in the fact that it asserts the great principle of self-government and declares the right of the people to regulate their domestic concerns in their own way, and thus, by implication, denies your right of supremacy, you are acting consistently with your own principles in opposing it.

Upon a careful examination of your protest, it is certain that you have acted under a total misapprehension of the principles and provisions of the bill, unless you object to it solely upon the ground that it recognises the propriety of leaving to the people of these Territories what is the undoubted right of the States to govern themselves in respect to their local and domestic concerns. On the supposition that you may have formed your opinions from unreliable sources of information, in the absence of the opportunity of reading the bill itself, I have copied, the only provision to which your protest can possibly be construed to refer:

"SEC. 14. That the Constitution, and all laws of the United States which are not locally inapplicable, shall have the same force and effect within the said Territory of Nebraska as elsewhere within the United States, except the eighth section of the act preparatory to the admission of Missouri into the Union, approved March 6, 1820, which, being inconsistent with the principle of non-intervention by Congress with slavery in the States and Territories, as recognised by the legislation of 1850, commonly called the compromise measures, is hereby declared inoperative and void; it being the true intent and meaning of this act not to legislate slavery into any Territory or State, nor to exclude it therefrom, but to leave the people thereof perfectly free to form and regulate their domestic institutions in their own way, subject only to the Constitution of the United States: *Provided,* That nothing herein contained shall be construed to revive or put in force any law or regulation which may have existed prior to the act of 6th March, 1820, either protecting, establishing, prohibiting, or abolishing slavery."

If the Nebraska bill shall become the law of the land, those of our fellow-citizens who may emigrate to that country, will find it, in respect to its jurisprudence, in precisely the same condition as our ancestors found Plymouth rock—with no code of laws, no system of political, civil, social, and domestic institutions, but with full power and authority to enact and establish for themselves such laws and institutions as they shall deem wise, just, and necessary; subject only to such limitation as is imposed by the Constitution. Do you wish to have the people of this country to understand that you claim the Divine authority for saying that it is "a great moral wrong," a violation "of God's will," and an infringement of His holy law, for Congress to allow the people of the Territories to enact and establish for themselves their own laws and institutions, in obedience to the Constitution their fathers have made, and to remove all legal obstructions in the way of the exercise of such rights? This is all that the Nebraska bill proposes to do. If, therefore, you continue to oppose it, you must confine your opposition directly and exclusively to this great principle of self-government, for you have neither pointed out nor intimated in your protest the existence of any other objections than those which stand as obstacles in the way of carrying this principle into complete effect.

Perhaps you will tell me that you are in favor of that principle which allows the people to enact such laws as they may choose, and that you oppose the bill only because it abrogates the eighth section of the act of 1820, sometimes called the Missouri compromise. Before you assume that position, I must be permitted to remind you that it is necessary, yea, absolutely indispensable, to render the eighth section of the Missouri act inoperative and void in order to enable the people to legislate for themselves freely upon all subjects touching their local interests and domestic concerns. You must therefore abandon your objections to the annulment of that section, or persevere in your opposition to the principle upon which the bill is founded.

In your protest, (alluding, I presume, to the annulment of the Missouri restriction,) you denounce the Nebraska bill "as a great moral wrong; as a breach of faith imminently injurious to the moral principles of the community, and subversive of all confidence in national engagements," and "exposing us to the righteous judgments of the Almighty!"

I am rejoiced to learn that the "clergymen of different denominations" in the city of Chicago have come to the firm conclusion that "a breach of faith," that the non-fulfillment of "national engagements" is "a great moral wrong," exposing the offenders "to the righteous judgments of the Almighty!"

I remember well my feelings upon this subject, in October, 1850. I should then have rejoiced with exceeding great joy to have heard from your lips, to have known that you were ready to proclaim in your pulpits and in public places, the sanctity of "national engagements," and the "great moral wrong" of their non-fulfillment; and especially when contained in the Constitution our fathers made for us, and upon which all patriots now look as the ark of our safety. I have no recollection that when the common council of the city of Chicago by resolutions, refused to carry into effect the "national engagements" contained in the Constitution of the United States, for the return of fugitives from service, when the council nullified an act of Congress passed for the purpose of carrying those national engagements into faithful execution; when the council called upon the police to refrain from rendering any assistance in executing the law; when public meetings were held, and speeches made proposing to defy death and the dungeon in resistance to the fulfillment of these "national engagements!" I say I have no recollection that, on the solemn and fearful occasion referred to, any one of your "divinely-appointed institution" appeared on the stand, or in the pulpit, or elsewhere to proclaim, "in the name of Almighty God," that the non-fulfillment of "national engagements was a great moral wrong, exposing us to the righteous judgments of the Almighty!" The particulars of that wild and terrific scene remain vividly impressed upon my memory; but I repeat, that I have not the slightest recollection that any one of you was ever suspected of a desire to see the law enforced, much less to contribute even moral aid to its execution.

There is, however, this difference in the two cases: the national engagement for the return of fugitives from service was incorporated into the Constitution of the United States, and therefore forms a part of the supreme law of the land; while the national engagements, to which you refer, as constituting what has been called an irrevocable compact, under the name of the Missouri compromise, have no existence in fact, are unsustained by the terms of the law and contradicted by the record of the transaction. You have, doubtless, been misled by the positive statements which have been solemnly put forth that the act of Congress of the 6th of March, 1820, constituted a sacred and irrevocable compact between the north and the south, whereby, in consideration of the admission of Missouri on an equal footing with the original States, it was stipulated that slavery should be forever excluded from all the residue of the country acquired from France north of latitude 36° 30′; and that the north has always been faithful in the performance of its part of the obligations, and that the south, having secured all its advantages, now seeks to be released from its incumbrances. I have the charity to believe that you have been misled by this erroneous and unfounded statement, which, in an imposing form, has been spread broadcast throughout the free States, and is now everywhere being circulated and repeated for partisan purposes; and, relying on the truth of the statement, and acting under that fatal delusion, you have had the misfortune to pronounce judgment "in the name of the Almighty God."

If you will condescend to listen to human authority, to legislative enactments, and congressional journals, in derogation of your divine testimony, you will find that Missouri was never admitted into the Union under the act of the 6th of March, 1820, called the Missouri compromise; that, if the said act was an irrevocable compact, it was disavowed and repudiated by the north within eleven months from its date; that Missouri, having formed a constitution conformable in all respects to said act, was denied admission into the Union in February, 1821, by northern votes; that the north, by a vote of 61 to 33, on motion of Mr. MALLORY, of Vermont,[4] refused to admit Missouri into the Union, with a constitution corresponding with the precise terms of the alleged compact, unless, "in addition" thereto, she would *"further provide, in and by said constitution, that neither slavery nor involuntary servitude shall ever be allowed in said State of Missouri;"* that, in consequence of the refusal of the representatives from the northern States to carry into effect what is known as the compromise of 1820, Missouri was compelled to submit to a new one, in the form of an irrevocable compact between that State and the United States, by the terms of which she was to be admitted into the Union on a new "condition," unlike anything contained in the act of 1820; that this compact was entered into and approved on the 2d of March, 1821; that Missouri complied with the condition in the month of June thereafter; and that, on the 10th of August, 1821, the President of the United States issued his proclamation declaring the fulfillment of the "condition" on the part of Missouri, and the admission of such State into the Union "in pursuance of the joint resolution" or "irrevocable compact" of March 2, 1821, and *not in conformity, with the act of* 1820. If there is any reliance upon human testimony, if there is any faith to be attached to historical and official records, these facts are true. Being true, there is no provision in the "national engagement," contained in the joint resolution of 1821, under which Missouri was admitted into the Union, whereby slavery was prohibited north of 36°30', or elsewhere in the Territories of the United States; nor does the Nebraska bill propose to repeal, impair, or in any manner affect that "irrevocable compact." Is it not manifest, therefore, according to all the evidences accessible to the human understanding, that you have labored under a lamentable delusion in supposing that the Nebraska bill involved "a breach of faith eminently injurious to the morals of the community and subversive of all confidence in na[tional en]gagements?"

When you shall have withdrawn the unfounded allegation that the bill involves "a breach of faith," and shall have made public confession of the injustice you have done the Senate in this particular, perhaps you will conceive it to be your duty to persevere in your opposition to its passage, upon the ground that it renders inoperative and void the eighth section of the act of 1820, in which Congress assumed the right to prohibit slavery in that country, not only while it should remain a territory, but in all time to come, after it shall have been sub-divided and admitted into the Union as sovereign and independent States. Reminding you again that it was necessary to render that section inoperative and void in order to recognise the great principle of self-government and State equality, and to leave the people free to regulate their local concerns and domestic institutions in their own way, you will discover that your opposition is confined exclusively to the principle of popular sovereignty. It does not vary the question in any degree, that human slavery is, in your opinion, a great moral wrong. If so, it is not the only wrong upon which the people of each of the States and Territories of this Union are called upon to act and decide for themselves. In the opinion of a large and respectable portion of our people, the manufacture and sale of ardent spirits and intoxicating drinks is a monstrous wrong, eminently injurious to the morals of the community. While these opinions are honestly entertained, and vigorous efforts are being made to induce the legislatures of the different States and Territories to pass laws for their enforcement, I have witnessed no attempt to induce Congress to declare the "Maine law" to be in force in all the Territories of the United States, and to remain in force forever in the States to be formed therefrom, regardless of the rights and wishes of the people to be affected thereby.

A very large and exemplary portion of our Christian community firmly believe that the practice of carrying the mails, of running stage-coaches for the conveyance of passengers, and of keeping open public houses and bar-rooms for gain on Sunday, is a great moral wrong; yet if Congress should propose to declare, by a fundamental and irrevocable act, that, in all time to come, such practices should never be tolerated in any of the territory which we now possess or may hereafter acquire, nor in any new State to be formed from such territory, it is possible that another portion of the Christian community, equally exemplary and sincere, might rise up and say that it is our firm conviction, after a thorough examination of the Holy Scriptures, that the seventh day, instead of the first day of the week, is the Sabbath which God has commanded us to keep holy; and that, if this law passes, you exclude us and our brethren and descendants forever from settling in those territories and States, or compel us to conform to an article of religious faith repugnant to our conscientious belief. Although you may be of the opinion, and doubtless are, that the practice of performing secular duties, and attending to worldly affairs on Sunday, is not in accordance with the divine law as recorded in the Holy Scriptures, it does not appear that you desire the interference of Congress in this particular to deprive the people of the Territories and new States of the privilege of regulating these matters in conformity with their sense of propriety and duty. I trust that the great body of the American people look upon the manufacture, sale, and use of instruments and implements of gaming as a wrong eminently injurious to the public morals; yet I have heard no objection to leaving the people of each State and Territory free to determine that question according to their sense of right and propriety.

I will not trouble you further with this class of cases, having cited enough to illustrate the principle. The entire criminal code of each State and Territory of the Union, and every section and provision thereof, is supposed to relate to some great moral wrong which the people in their sovereign capacity have deemed it their duty to prohibit, and, if possible, prevent by penalties and punishments. Inasmuch as you are willing to leave these questions, and all others which are supposed to be injurious to the morals of the community and prejudicial to the best interests of society, in the hands of the people of the respective States and Territories, would it not be better and wiser to entrust the slavery question to the arbitrament of the same authority, rather than to violate the great principle of self-government which lies at the foundation of all our free institutions? If I correctly understand your position, you do not object to permitting the people of the Territories, in the same manner as in the States, to exercise all rightful power and authority in all matters affecting the rights, interests, and happiness of white men. If the people are capable of self-government, I do not understand that it requires any higher degree of intelligence, virtue, or civilization, to legislate for the negro than for the white man. It will not be pretended

[319]

that the legislature of any Territory or State would or could, under the Constitution, deprive any freeman, black or white, of his liberty, except for crime; nor will it be insisted that Congress has the power to confer any such authority. Hence there is no possibility of a free man being reduced to slavery, or of the number of slaves in the United States being increased by the passage of the Nebraska bill. The only effect it could possibly have in respect to the slave is, that, in a certain contingency, he might be permitted to enter the country, and remain there as such, and in a certain other contingency he could not. If a slave should be removed from Kentucky to Nebraska, the effect would be to reduce the number on the east side of the Mississippi to the same extent that it was increased on the west, without enlarging the political power of the master or producing any injurious consequences to the slave; while, by the mere fact of his removal from an old country to a new one, from poor lands to rich ones, from a scarcity to an abundance of provisions, his temporal condition would be improved and his physical comforts increased. His presence in the new Territory could not in any mode or degree affect or injure any human being in any other Territory or State. If his presence should be offensive or injurious to any body it would be to the people of the Territory or State where he was located. Then, why not leave it to the people of such Territory or State to decide for themselves whether he shall be permitted to come or not? No body else has any interest in it; no other State or Territory would be affected by it. It is purely a question of domestic concern, which, for weal or for woe, affects the people of such Territory or State, and no body else. You think that you are abundantly competent to decide this question now and forever. If you should remove to Nebraska, with the view of making it your permanent home, would you be any less competent to decide it when you should have arrived in the country?

Thus, you see that the principle of the Nebraska bill is purely a question of self-government, involving the right and capacity of the people to make their own laws and manage their own local and domestic concerns. This is the only controverted principle involved in the bill. I am unwilling to believe that, upon mature reflection, and with all the advantages which your Christian character and experience may enable you to summon to your assistance, you will sanction the declaration that a proposition to carry this principle into effect is "a great moral wrong, exposing us to the righteous judgments of the Almighty."

It is the principle upon which the thirteen colonies separated from the imperial government. It is the principle in defence of which the battles of the Revolution were fought. It is the principle to which all our free institutions owe their existence, and upon which our entire republican system rests. This great principle is recognised and affirmed in the Constitution and bill of rights of every State in this Union as the corner-stone in the temple of our liberties. It was under the operation of this principle that slavery retired from the New England States. It was in obedience to its potential influence that slavery disappeared from New York, New Jersey, and Pennsylvania. It was by virtue of this principle that California came into the Union with her free constitution. It is in obedience to this principle that slavery is excluded from all the free States of this Union; and I trust that, whenever, in God's providence, it shall cease in the States where it now exists, it may cease under the operation of this principle, and **NONE OTHER!**

In conclusion, reverend gentlemen, permit me to say to you, in all kindness and sincerity, that it is with extreme reluctance that I submit this vindication of my character and position against the assaults which, I conceive, you have so unjustly made upon them. My respect for your holy calling would induce me to submit, in silence, even to an unmerited rebuke, in preference to engaging in a controversy with ministers of the Gospel in any case where duty did not compel me to speak. The acts for which you have arraigned me were a part of my official duty, in the performance of a high public trust, for which I am responsible to my State, to the Constitution, and to my God. The principle which it has been my aim to carry into effect, and for the support of which I have incurred your displeasure, is the one to which all the institutions of my State, and of each other State of this confederacy, owe their existence, and for the protection and preservation of which the Constitution of the United States was formed. With my conscientious convictions of the nature of the trust confided to my hands, I cannot doubt that fidelity to that principle and fidelity to that Constitution will carry with it the blessings of Heaven. I have the honor to be, very respectfully, your obedient servant,

S. A. DOUGLAS

To the Reverend Messrs. A. M. Stewart, Henry Klamer, A. Kengon, James E. Wilson, C. Wenz, Geo. L. Mulfinger, Timpson Guyer, R. H. Richardson, S. Bolles, T. V. Watson, W. A. Nichols, Joseph H. Leonard, J. McNamara, J. M. Weed, J. Sinclair, E. M. Gammon, John C. Holbrook, A. H. Eggleston, Paul Anderson, Harvey Curtiss, John Clark, R. F. Shinn, Luther Stone, A. W. Henderson, and ——— Fitch.

Letter of Senator Douglas, Vindicating His Character and His Position on the Nebraska Bill Against the Assaults Contained in the Proceedings of a Public Meeting Composed of Twenty-five Clergymen of Chicago (Washington, D.C., 1854).

[1]The meeting of the clergy of Chicago was held on March 27, 1854, "to take measures for a suitable expression of their sentiments upon the subject of the bill now pending in Congress, for the organization of the Nebraska and Kansas Territories." The proceedings

were reported in the Chicago *Tribune*, March 28, 1854.

²The memorial of the New England clergymen, signed by 3,500 ministers and dated March 1, 1854, was read before the Senate on March 13, by order of Douglas. In their memorial, the ministers protested against the repeal of the Missouri Compromise as "a great moral wrong, as a breach of faith eminently unjust to the moral principles of the community, and subversive of all

confidence in national engagements." Douglas and Senator John Pettit, of Indiana, spoke strongly against the memorial.

³James M. Mason of Virginia; Andrew P. Butler of South Carolina; John Pettit of Indiana; Stephen Adams of Mississippi; and George E. Badger of North Carolina.

⁴Rollin C. Mallary, a member of the House of Representatives at the time.

To Ninian W. Edwards

Washington
My Dear Sir,   April 13th 1854

I am greatly indebted to you for your kind letter. I was confined to my Room by sickness when it arrived; but the first time I went out I called at the War Departmt & found that the appointment was made of Veile[1] to West Point several days previous on the recommendation of Gen'l Shields & the members of the Ho of Reps. It would have afforded me great pleasure to have secured the appointmt for yourself, & I have no doubt it could have been done if your letter had been written two or three weeks sooner. I am very glad of your appointment by Gov Matteson.[2] Besides being in my opinion an admirable one for the state, it will enable you to exercise a good deal of influence in behalf of the great principle of the Nebraska Bill, which is the same asserted in your Resolution of 1851.[3]

I send you herewith my last Speech[4] & also my letter to the Clergy of Chicago. I see it stated that Col Bissel[5] is understood in Illinois to be opposed to the Nebraska Bill. I don't understand this, as he was very warmly in favor of the Bill before it passed the Senate & so declared himself to Shields, Richardson, Allen, & innumerable others (myself included).

Let what may happen I shall persevere & abide the consequences. I know the Bill is right & have full faith it will become a law this Session.

Let me hear from you often. Yours truly

S. A. DOUGLAS

ALS, Chicago Historical Society. Ninian W. Edwards had been Attorney General of Illinois from 1834 to 1835 and a Whig member of the state legislature for several terms. His father, Ninian Edwards, was Governor of the Territory of Illinois, Senator from Illinois after the state's admission to the Union,

and Governor of the state from 1826 to 1830.

¹"Veile" has not been positively identified. The only person of this name to graduate from West Point was Egbert Ludovicus Viele, of the class of 1847. For another Viele, see above, Douglas to French, June 29, 1851.

²In 1854, Edwards was appointed, as a Democrat, to the office of Superintendent of Public Instruction by Governor Joel A. Matteson.

³In January, 1851, Edwards, then a member of the Illinois House of Representatives, moved the adoption of a resolution rescinding the previous instructions of the legislature to the Congressional delegation to procure laws preventing the existence of slavery in the territories.

⁴*Speech of Hon. S. A. Douglas, of Illinois, in the United States Senate, March 3, 1854. On Nebraska and Kansas* (Washington, D.C., 1854).

⁵William H. Bissell, Representative from Illinois from 1849 to 1855, and later first Republican Governor of the state.

To Samuel Wolcott

Washington
April 26th 1854

Rev Sir,

Some kind but unknown friend has forwarded to me a copy of a Speech said to have been delivered by yourself at an anti Nebraska meeting at Providence R.I. on the 7th of last month, from which the following is an extract[1]

Rev. Mr. Wolcott's Speech.

At the Nebraska Meeting, Tuesday Evening.

I am compelled to rise, fellow-citizens, at a very unseasonable hour. If I can have your indulgence for a few moments, I shall regard it as a tribute not to the speaker, but to the cause of freedom.

It is now twenty years since I passed a day in the city of St. Louis, on my way to a home which had been transferred to the great West. While standing in a public room in one of the hotels in that city, a young man came up and introduced himself to me, remarking that he had observed on the books of the hotel my name and destination; that he also was from the East, had come to seek his fortunes in the West, and was wholly undecided where to locate himself. He added, that if agreeable to me, he would deem it a favor if he might accompany me to my friends in central Illinois, and he would seek a residence in that quarter. I assured him that I should be happy to have his company, and named the hour when I was to leave the city. He expressed a very lively satisfaction with the arrangement; and the first days and nights that he and I passed in the State of Illinois, we were fellow-travellers and fellow-lodgers.

I purposely omit those parts of the speech in which you indulge in coarse & insulting epithets towards myself for the reason that they involve matters of taste & properity which I chose to leave entirely between yourself & your audience. Nor are the facts stated of any material importance except as furnishing a graceful introduction to a clergyman's stump speech. I have the charity to believe that you are under the impression that the facts stated by you are true. I would not disturb your delusions upon this point but for the fact that I dwell with pleasure and perhaps with a pardonable pride upon the incidents connected with my early history in the West, and I am unwilling to have their truth destorted in such a manner as to efface the vivid impressions left on my mind. Permit me therefore to remind you that it is not true that you met me in St. Louis on your way to your home in the West twenty years ago—that it is not true that I came & introduced myself to you in a public room in one of the hotels in that city—that it is not true that I had observed or said that I had observed your name & destination on the books—that it is not true that I said to you that I would deem it a favor to accompany you to your friends in central Illinois—that it is not true that you assured me that you would be happy of my company and that you named the hour when you would leave the city—that it is not true that I expressed my lively satisfaction at the arraingement—that it is not true that we were fellow lodgers the first days & nights we spent in Illinois. I repeat that each one of these statements is a pure fiction—the result of a vivid imagination— but without a particle of foundation in truth. I happen to know how you got into the state of Illinois, but you have shown that you do not know how I got there. We did not enter the state together, nor at the same place, nor by the same means of conveyance, nor had we ever met or exchanged a word at St. Louis or elsewhere prior to our meeting in Illinois. Yet I have the charity to believe that under some strange hallucination you are under the impression that your statement is really true. It is a pitty to spoil so pretty a story, yet I will venture to do so by a statement of the facts of our first, and with one exception, I believe, our only interview. In the autumn of 1833 I landed at Alton in Illinois from a steam Boat. I was in extremely delicate health having been prostrate upon a sick bed for four or five months with the western fever, I had determined to proceed to Jacksonville & with that view requested the landlord to wake me in time for the stage which was expected from St. Louis. A little before daylight & on a very dark night I entered the stage which was very crowded & it was with some difficulty that I procured a seat. I was taken very sick, but soon fell to sleep, and awoke a little after sun rise on the prairie near where the Town of Jerseyville is now situated. It was the first time my eyes ever beheld a Prairie and I shall never forget the impressions & emotions produced by the scene. It was also the first time that I ever beheld the light of your countenance. When I awoke you were expounding fluently upon the glories & beauties of New England and her institutions & character in contrast with the wild and uncouth west. I did not introduce myself. I did not participate in your disquisitions, nor did you know who I was, or where I was from, or where I was going until

[324]

after dinner & when we were within a few miles of Jacksonville. In the meantime I had listened to the tale of your eventful history & that of your family in central Illinois and of your kindred in Connecticut. When I happened to ask some one what time we would probably

AL, owned by Martin F. Douglas. The letter is not complete. Reverend Samuel Wolcott was pastor of the High Street Congregational Church in Providence, Rhode Island. He had settled in Providence in 1853.

[1]The following extract from Wolcott's speech had been clipped from a newspaper and pasted on the sheet.

To Henry Augustus and Joseph C. Willard

Gentlemen   May 4th 1854

Doct Miller tells me that you have a fine article of Congress water & that he knows of no other place in the city where a good article can be had. The Doctor recommends the use of it in my family for sickness & suggested that probably you would furnish it for me. Can you spare me one Dozen Bottles at present.

Please send them by the bearer. Your friend

S. A. DOUGLAS

ALS, Library of Congress. In 1847, Henry Augustus Willard leased the City Hotel, in Washington, D.C., renaming it the Willard Hotel. Six years later he purchased the building and his brother, Joseph C. Willard, became a partner in the enterprise.

To James Buchanan

Washington

My Dr Sir,   July 21st 1854

Permit me to introduce to you the Rev Daniel Marvin, Jr a friend of an esteemed relative of mine, altho I have not the pleasure of his personal acquaintance. Any attentions and civilities shown him will be duly acknowledged by your friend

S. A. DOUGLAS

ALS, Historical Society of Pennsylvania. James Buchanan was United States Minister to Great Britain at this time.

To ———

[N.d., n.p.; AES, Kansas State Historical Society, Topeka. Endorsement by Douglas recommending the appointment of Robert L. Ream, a native of Pennsylvania, as chief clerk to the Surveyor General of Kansas and Nebraska territories. Ream received the appointment. The endorsement was written on a letter to Douglas by D. A. Starkweather, August 4, 1854, Canton, Ohio, and was probably forwarded to John Calhoun.]

To John Calhoun

Washington

My Dr Sir, Aug 10th 1854

I enclose to you a Letter from my friend the Hon C C Clay, Senator from Alabama,[1] recommending his friend Mr Elmore[2] for a Surveying contract or appointment in Kansas & Nebraska. Mr Elmore is the Brother-in-law of my friend Gov Fitzpatrick,[3] the other Senator from Alabama, and is a gentleman of high character & qualifications, with whose society you will be pleased. I shall be gratified to know that you have been able to comply with his wishes and grant the application he may make to you. Very truly your friend

S. A. DOUGLAS

ALS, Kansas State Historical Society. John Calhoun, of Springfield, Illinois, was a former member of the Illinois legislature and Mayor of Springfield. In 1854, he was appointed Surveyor General of Kansas and Nebraska territories.

[1]Clement C. Clay served in the United States Senate from 1853 to 1861.

[2]Rush Elmore, of Alabama, was later appointed an Associate Justice on the Kansas territorial Supreme Court.

[3]Benjamin Fitzpatrick was Senator from Alabama from 1853 to 1861. In 1860, he was nominated for the Vice-Presidency on the ticket headed by Douglas, but declined the nomination.

To John Calhoun

Washington

My Dr Sir, Aug 10th 1854

I herewith enclose a letter from the Hon Mr Henn of Iowa[1] recommending his friend for a clerkship.[2] Upon enquiry I learn that his friend possesses high qualifications for the office, and if consistent with your views & arraingements I should be glad to see Mr Henn gratified in this particular. I will here add that I should be glad if you would pay as much defference as possible to the wishes of Gen'l A. C. Dodge of Iowa[3] in awarding contracts to his friends where consistent with the public interests. Very truly your friend

S. A. DOUGLAS

ALS, Kansas State Historical Society.

[1]Bernhart Henn was Representative from Iowa from 1851 to 1855.

[2]Henn's friend, according to an endorsement on the letter, was E. F. Barnard.

[3]Augustus Caesar Dodge was Senator from Iowa from 1848 to 1855.

To John Calhoun

Washington

My Dr Sir, August 10th 1854

I herewith enclose to you a Letter of Judge Coskie of Virginia[1] recommending Major C. F. McDowell[2] of that state for assistant surveyor in Kansas or Nebraska. I take great pleasure in endorsing the Letter of my friend Judge Coskie and sincerely hope that his friend Major McDowell may be successful in his application to you. If you can give him the employment he seeks I shall not only be gratified, but shall esteem it a favor to myself. Very truly your friend

S. A. Douglas

ALS, Kansas State Historical Society.
[1]John Samuels Caskie was Judge of the Richmond and Henrico county circuit.
[2]McDowell has not been identified.

To J. A. Beckwith

My Dear Sir:—   Washington, Aug. 12, 1854.
I herewith send you a check on the Bank of Commerce, New York, for two hundred dollars, it being the balance of my subscription to Middlebury College, in my native State.[1] I leave for the West today, and will be obliged if you will acknowledge the receipt of the check by a letter addressed to me at Chicago, Illinois. I have the honor to be Very truly your obedient servant,

S. A. Douglas

Printed in "Illustrious Vermonters. Number One: Stephen Arnold Douglas," *The Vermonter*, II (January, 1897), 98. J. A. Beckwith was Treasurer of Middlebury College.

[1]In August, 1851, Douglas was awarded an honorary law degree by Middlebury College, at which time he pledged a donation of $500 to the college.

To Charles H. Lanphier

(Private)   Chicago
My Dr Sir,   Aug 25th '54
I speak to the people of Chicago on Friday next Sept 1st on Nebraska. They threaten a mob but I have no fears.[1] All will be right. Please give the notice in your paper as I have received many letters asking to be informed of the time of the meeting. Come up if you can & bring our friends with you. Your friend

S. A. Douglas

ALS, Illinois State Historical Library.
[1]The unpopularity of the Kansas-Nebraska Act in parts of the North resulted in a wave of anti-Douglas demonstrations. Douglas' speech in Chicago on September 1 became an additional opportunity for an expression of opposition against the "Little Giant." His speech was repeatedly interrupted by the hisses and cries of the audience, until he was forced to retire without completing it. It was at this time that Douglas was supposed to have observed, as he gave up the effort, "It is now Sunday morning—I'll go to church, and you may go to Hell!" Since the speech was delivered on a Friday evening, this remark could hardly have been uttered.

To ———

[September 4, 1854, Chicago; owned by Martin F. Douglas. Printed announcement to accompany the prospectus of the Chicago *Times*, "the only true and reliable Democratic Paper published in this City." By helping to give the paper a wide circulation, Douglas wrote, the recipient would be promoting "the cause of truth, justice, and sound Democratic principles." The establishment of the *Times* was the result of the defection of Chicago's Democratic papers from Douglas during the furor that followed the Kansas-Nebraska Act. Douglas made the arrangements for the establishment of the *Times* and persuaded James Washington Sheahan to be its first editor. The paper supported Douglas until its purchase by Cyrus Hall McCormick in 1860.]

To John C. Breckinridge

(*Confidential*)   Indianapolis
My Dr Sir,   Sept 7th '54

I deeply regretted not seeing you here as I expected. I had the pleasure of seeing Doct Rankin & Mr McGoffin,[1] & to receive your letter. I owe you an apology for not answering your letter sooner in regard to an interest on Lake Superior for Gov Powell.[2] I will part with one half of a share for ten thousand dollars cash, he paying his part of the expenses. I would not feel justified in selling for less. Indeed, I firmly believe that it is worth double that sum today as an investment. But I need that amount of money & must sell that amount of property somewhere. I have an offer of ten thousand for a lot in Chicago which cost me 1600 five years ago. I shall accept that offer unless our friend the Gov takes this. You will therefore notify me as soon as practicable whether he takes it or not that I may give an answer to the other party in Chicago in regard to the Lot. I learn from Mr Rice[3] that the "Squatter Claim" to three hundred acres has been awarded to us & that orders have [been] issued to that effect. Also that the certificates have been received at Washington for the other 21 tracts, & also to our additional tract since, making our lands amount to about 6,000 acres. I have heard nothing further from the military reservation.[4] Gov Bright[5] has sold one half of our share for ten thousand cash to Mr Riggs.[6] All the news is decidedly favorable from there—much more so than when I saw you.

I saw several gentlemen from the soo St Marie & they told me the canal is about done & will pass vessels through in a few weeks.[7] Rice writes me that there are five hundred inhabitants at our place. Robertson[8] writes Bright to the same effect.

[328]

Write me to Chicago immediately. We had a glorious meeting here yesterday. Indiana all right. In Illinois we will make all right. The row at Chicago is doing us immense good. We will carry the state. Yours truly

S. A. DOUGLAS

ALS, Library of Congress. John C. Breckinridge, of Kentucky, was a member of the House of Representatives from 1851 to 1855. In 1856, he was elected Vice-President of the United States.

¹Although the writing is not clear, McGoffin was possibly Beriah Magoffin, a member of the Kentucky Senate from 1850 to 1859. He was elected Governor of the state in 1859. Dr. Rankin has not been identified.

²Lazarus W. Powell was Governor of Kentucky from 1851 to 1855; he was later elected to the United States Senate. Douglas was a member of a syndicate organized for the purchase of land at the western tip of Lake Superior and for the development of the townsite of Superior, Wisconsin. Other members of the syndicate were Breckinridge, Jesse D. Bright, Henry M. Rice, and D. A. Robertson. The speculation was organized in anticipation of the construction of a railroad connecting Lake Superior with the Pacific coast and the completion of the Sault Ste. Marie Canal, connecting lakes Superior and Huron.

³Henry M. Rice was Delegate from Minnesota Territory from 1853 to 1857; when Minnesota was admitted to the Union in 1858, he was elected United States Senator.

⁴Probably Fort Snelling.

⁵Jesse D. Bright was Lieutenant Governor of Indiana from 1843 to 1845. He was elected to the United States Senate in 1845, where he remained until 1862.

⁶George W. Riggs, Washington banker and former banking partner of W. W. Corcoran.

⁷The Sault Ste. Marie Canal was not opened to traffic until April 19, 1855.

⁸D. A. Robertson, a member of the syndicate, was the agent for the purchase of the land at Superior, Wisconsin.

To John C. Breckinridge

Lasalle Ills

My Dr Sir,   Sept 14th 1854

I am now actively engaged in the canvass & shall remain on the stump until the November election. *We shall carry the State with a majority in the Legislature & of the Congressmen for Nebraska.* The Chicago mob has done us much good & we know what use to make of it. I left your friends McGoffin & Dr Rankin at Chicago.

I shall return to Chicago on Thursday night Sept 21st & remain until Monday morning the 25th. Can you not meet me there at that time as it will be the only opportunity I will have to see you. Will not our friend Gov Powell come with you so that we can arrainge that other matter at that time in case he accepts my offer.

My respects to Mrs B. Yours truly

S. A. DOUGLAS

ALS, Library of Congress.

To James Washington Sheahan

Lasalle

Sept. 14, 1854.

(Private)

We have had glorious meetings at Joliet, Morris, and Ottawa. I speak here today. The party are all right everywhere. We will gain more votes than we will lose on Nebraska and No Nothingism.[1] You ought to publish the exposition of No Nothingism from the Richmond Examiner and charge into them every day boldly and disputedly. That will bring the Germans and all other foreigners and Catholics to our side. Also make war on Wentworth[2] every good chance you get, for I shall attack him openly in my speech I make in his district. He must be beaten at all hazards.

Trust the Tribune, Dem. Press, & Chicago Democrats as allies & organ of the great abolition Party. Make no distinction between as respects their politics. This is the course I take in all my speeches. Mr. White[3] is getting more subscribers for you than any other Paper Bus. Your paper has not yet been read by the new subscribers, and they complain of this neglect. It will also be necessary to pay more attention to the market's Reports and the commercial articles. Let no expense be spared on this point. Tell Cook[4] that he must furnish all necessary funds for the paper and I will furnish money soon. I am making arrangements for that purpose. Excuse my direct mode of talking, but these things are necessary. We will carry our Legislative Tickets all along the Canal line and also this Congressional District if we make the right kind of a fight. Notice my meeting at Bloomington on the 26th of Sept. You will see it in the Joliet Signal. Yours truly,

S. A. DOUGLAS

P.S. Show this to Cook as I have not time to write to him.

Copy, University of Kansas Library, Lawrence. The original of this letter has not been located. A typewritten copy of the original was made by the late Professor Frank Heywood Hodder of the University of Kansas. The copy is obviously incomplete. George Fort Milton consulted the letters of Douglas to Sheahan while preparing his *Eve of Conflict: Stephen A. Douglas and the Needless War* (Boston, 1934), but the correspondence has since disappeared. James Washington Sheahan was a newspaper correspondent in Washington, D.C., until 1854, when he was induced by Douglas to undertake the editorship of the Chicago *Times*.

[1] The Illinois state election of 1854 was doubly significant to Douglas. He was concerned not only for the election of a Congressional delegation sympathetic to his position but also for a sympathetic state legislature. Since James Shields's Senate term had expired the new legislature would have the responsibility of electing a successor.

[2] John Wentworth, a member of Congress at this time, had broken with Douglas over the Kansas-Nebraska Act. He was not re-elected in 1854.

[3] Horace White, Chicago newspaperman, was associated with the Chicago *Evening Journal* at this time.

[4] Isaac Cook, former Sheriff of Cook County, was Postmaster of Chicago and a partner in the Chicago *Times*.

To Charles H. Lanphier

My Dr Sir,   Dec 18th 1854

I have just received your kind letter and will reply to it in the same
spirit of frankness & candor in which it is written. Upon mature reflection & after consultation with Richardson & other friends I am
confirmed in the opinion that our friends in the Legislature should
nominate Shields by acclamation, and nail his flag to the mast, and
never haul it down under any circumstances nor for any body. The
election of any other man would be deemed not only a defeat, but an
ungrateful dissertion of him, when all the others who voted with him
had been sustained. We are of the opinion also that the Whigs will
stick to Lincoln to the bitter end,[1] even if it resulted in no choice this
session & the consequent postponement of the election, under the
belief that they can carry the State next time for a Whig-Know-Noth-
ing candate for the Presidency and with him the Legislature. We also
think that Bessil[2] will be a candidate and will secretly urge his friends
to press his name. In that event, it is probable the free-soil or Anti
Nebraska Democrats will cling to him until the last with the hope of
bringing the Whigs over to Bissel. If this shall prove to be the position
of the Parties and the tactics of each, it would seem that, either there
would be no election, or that Bissel would be elected, which would
probably be equivalent to no election. Either of these events would
be better than the election of Lincoln or any other man spoken of. At
all events our friends should stand by Shields and throw the responsibility on the Whigs of beating him *because he was born in Ireland*.
The Nebraska fight is over, and Know Nothingism has taken its
place as the chief issue in the future. If therefore Shields shall be
beaten it will [be] apparent to the people & to the whole country that
a gallant Soldier & a faithful public servant has been stricken down
because of the place of his birth. Let this be made the issue in the
Newspapers & in the Legislature & everywhere; and with reference to
this issue let us rise or fall with Shields. This is the advice of our
friends here. We think that this line of policy will probably lead to a
postponement of the election, and in that event let evry paper in the
State put Shields name at the head of its columns for Senator & keep
it there until after the next legislative election. We are sure to triumph
in the end on this great issue. Our policy & duty require us to stand
firm by the issues in the late election, and to make no bargains, no
alliances, no concessions to any of the *allied isms*.[3]

Let this letter be strictly confidential & show it to Nobody except
our friend T L Harris.[4] I have no secrets from him. I have implicit
confidence in his discretion, firmness & fidelity. Tell him that he must

take personal charge of everything, and in no event leave Springfield even for a day during the Session. I will write to him in a day or two. Keep me fully advised of all matters. Yours truly

S. A. DOUGLAS

ALS, Illinois State Historical Library.

[1] Abraham Lincoln was one of the prominent contenders for the Senate seat held by Shields.

[2] Bissell was not a candidate for re-election in 1854 nor did he become a candidate for the Senate seat.

[3] The election for Senator took place on February 8, 1855. The Democratic members of the legislature voted for Shields until it was apparent that he could not be elected, whereupon they switched their support to Governor Matteson. In order to prevent Matteson's election, Lincoln was persuaded to instruct his following to vote for Lyman Trumbull. Trumbull, an anti-Nebraska Democrat, was elected.

[4] Thomas Langrell Harris had served one term in Congress from 1849 to 1851. He was elected again in 1854 and remained in Congress until his death in 1858.

To Franklin Pierce

[N.d., n.p.; LS, RG-59, National Archives. Recommending the appointment of Augustus Caesar Dodge to a "Foreign Legation of the first grade." The recommendation was signed by thirty-two members of the Senate, including Douglas. In February, 1855, Dodge resigned from the Senate to accept appointment as Minister to Spain, a post he held until 1859. The document is undated, although it is endorsed as having been received on December 29, 1854.]

To James Buchanan

Senate U.S.

My Dear Sir: Jany 1st 1855.

Permit me to present to you my friend Madame LaVert of Mobile, Alabama,[1] who makes the tour of Europe with her husband and charming Daughter on a trip of pleasure, and amusement. I need not inform you of a fact which will be so apparent when you form her acquaintance, that she is unrivaled even among the Ladies of our own country as an intelligent, fascinating, and charming woman.

I feel a patriotic pride in having her travel abroad as a specimen of what America can produce. I commend her to your kind attention, with the assurance that all civilties you may extend to her will be acknowledged as so many personal kindnesses to your friend

S. A. DOUGLAS

LS, Historical Society of Pennsylvania.

[1] Octavia Walton LaVert, of Mobile, was a novelist, and later author of *Souvenirs of Travel* (Mobile and New York, 1857), which resulted from the European trip referred to in the letter.

[332]

To James Washington Sheahan

January 18, 1855

I send you an extract from the New York Herald giving an outline of my Pacific Rail Road Bill. It has been agreed to by the Committees of both Houses & I hope it will pass.[1]

Copy, University of Kansas Library. This is probably but a fragment of the original letter.

[1]The New York *Herald*, January 15, 1855, described a bill introduced by Douglas on January 9 providing for the construction of northern, southern, and central Pacific railroads and a magnetic telegraph. The bill passed the Senate on February 19, but died in the House of Representatives.

To James Washington Sheahan

(Confidential)
My dear Sir:

Washington,
February 6, 1855.

Your letter written just after your return from Springfield was some ten days in reaching me so that it was too late to reply to it before the 31st, which been fine [?] for the Senatorial election. I had previously received and answered a letter from Maj. Harris on the same subject. My advice to him was that we should *stand by Shields to the last and make no compromises.* I am still of the same opinion. In the event the Legislature shall adjourn without electing a Senator, my opinion is that you and every Democratic editor in the State should at once hoist the name of James Shields for U.S. Senator in your paper and keep that flag at your mast head until after the election of '56. Good faith, honor and policy all dictate this course. I prefer no election under the circumstances to the election of any other man but Shields.

However, the question will have been decided and the Legislature adjourned by the time you receive this, so it is useless to say more upon the subject.[1]

I have seen the Committee upon your claim and they have authorized a favorable report which will be made and acted on in a few days. I trust I will be able to have the money subject to your draft soon. I shall not forget nor neglect what I promised you in regard to providing for your father if possible.

I send you an article from a Democratic Paper printed at Atlanta, Georgia, complimenting the present administration and nominating me for the succession. My determination not to be a candidate for President in '56 is well known to you and remains inflexable. But it might be well to copy the article with kind comments and at the same time say that my determination not to be a candidate has been known to all my intimate personal friends since the nomination of Gen'l Pierce in '52 and will be resolutely adhered to and refer to the article in the Sentinel[2] to that effect as having probably been published with my approbation etc., and avow the willingness of the Democracy of Illinois to unite cordially on Gen'l Pierce, or General Cass, or Mr. Buchanan or any other good man from the north, or on Mr. Hunter of Va. or Gen'l Houston of Texas or any other sound and reliable man from the South for the next Presidency; deprecating however the agitation of the question at this early day, and call on the Democratic Party to rally as a unit upon the Democratic platform in support of Democratic principles and the regular organization of the Party; and at the same time to cut loose now and forever from abolitionism— know nothingism—and all the other isms of the day as the allies of federalism and disunionism, etc., etc., I think a bold article of this kind would do good at this time. Say what you please about me, so that you say that I am not and will not be a candidate for the Presidency and that this fact has been well known to my friends for more than two years.

Copy, University of Kansas Library. This is not a complete copy of the original, since the closing and signature are missing.
[1]Lyman Trumbull was elected Senator by the Illinois legislature on February 8, two days after this letter was written.

[2]The article in the Washington *Sentinel*, edited by Beverley Tucker, stated that Douglas would not under any circumstances allow his name to be placed before the Democratic convention in 1856.

To Franklin Pierce

[N.d., n.p.; LS, RG-75, National Archives. Recommending the appointment of Thomas C. Shoemaker, formerly of Illinois but at this time a resident of Kansas Territory, to the office of Indian Agent for the Delaware Indian Agency in Kansas. The recommendation was signed by twelve individuals, including Douglas. The document was endorsed, "Recd. Febr. 9, '55." Shoemaker was appointed Receiver of Public Moneys for Kansas Territory on March 3, 1855, and served until 1857.]

To William Pitt Fessenden

Dr Sir,   March 2d 1855

As I have concluded with the assent of Mr Seward & Mr Brainard[1] as well as yourself to strike out of the report of my speech the other day so much as related to the interruptions which were interposed, I desire to say that the Telegraphic Reports in the New York papers do great injustice to you & to myself in attributing to me words disrespectful to yourself.[2] Nothing of the kind occured and no one in the Senate so understood it.

As the report is omitted solely for the reason that I have not time during these night sessions, I have no time to voice it, I deem this assurance due to yourself. Very truly yours

S. A. Douglas

ALS, Illinois State Historical Library. William Pitt Fessenden, of Maine, was elected as a Whig to the United States Senate in 1853 and served until 1864, when he was appointed Secretary of the Treasury by President Lincoln.

[1]William H. Seward, Senator from New York from 1849 to 1861, and Lawrence Brainerd, Free Soil Senator from Vermont from 1854 to 1855.

[2]On February 24, 1855, the New York *Herald* reported in detail a debate in the Senate on the previous day involving Douglas, Fessenden, Seward, and others, which was not included in the *Congressional Globe*. In the course of his remarks, according to the *Herald* report, Douglas stated, in reference to Fessenden, "A Know Nothing cannot be a Know Nothing without swearing to tell a lie."

To R. Hoe and Company

Washington
March 6th 1855

Sir,

This will be handed to you by Mr Cook who is Post Master at Chicago Ills and one of the owners of the Times Newspaper published in that city. He desires to purchase one of your Steam Presses & engines &c complete for his paper, and may find it convenient to get a reasonable time to make the payments. I desire to say to you that Mr Cook is abundantly responsible, being a man of large wealth and undoubted responsibility for his engagements. I will also add, if it will be of any service, that I will hold myself individually responsible that the notes for the Press shall be paid at maturity. Very respectfully

S. A. Douglas

ALS, Chicago Historical Society. R. Hoe and Company of New York city, headed by Richard and Robert Hoe, manufactured steam cylinder presses.

To James Washington Sheahan

March 10th, 1855

Cook left here for New York two days ago...

I will send you two short speeches made in the Senate in reply to Wade which I think it will be well to publish. You see that I put the matter right in regard to Negroes in Mississippi &c &c.[1] I like the tone of the Times. Keep up the fire....

Copy, University of Kansas Library. This is obviously a fragment of the original letter.

[1]Douglas' reply to Senator Benjamin F. Wade was made on February 23, 1855. Wade, Senator from Ohio

from 1851 to 1869, had earlier made certain charges against Douglas pertaining to the Mississippi plantation which Douglas' sons had inherited from their grandfather.

To John Wilson

My Dr Sir,   March 11th 1855

Illness has prevented me calling to see you for a few days in regard to certain appointment and removals from Ills. I would be glad if you would suspend all action in regard to them until I have an opportunity to be heard. Respectfully

S. A. Douglas

ALS, Chicago Historical Society. John Wilson was Commissioner of the General Land Office from 1852 to 1855.

To George C. Thomas

[March 13, 1855, Washington; ALS, Library of Congress. Notifying Thomas that he had not yet heard from the Governor of Illinois regarding Thomas' application for "Commissioner of Deeds &c." Thomas was a resident of Washington, D.C.]

To Jefferson Davis

Dr Sir,   March 30th 1855

Your letter of the 15th inst asking me to call & give you the requisite information in respect to the military services of the gentlemen recomme[nd]ed by me for appointment in the Army, was received night before last on my return from North Carolina. It would have afforded me pleasure to have furnished you satisfactory evidence of the gallant & honorable service of each of the gentlemen recommended by me, had I received your letter before the appointments were made. I perceive that you have honored Illinois with two appointments—both of the rank of Captain towit Captain Pickett of Richmond Va Virginia who never resided in Illinois,[1] and Mr Reynolds who I am informed, is a worthy non commissioned officer in the line of the Army & only asked for the Commission of a second Leutinant.[2]

I may be permitted to express my regret that those worthy & gallant officers who served with so much credit in the Mexican War and whom I recommended should have been overlooked. Very respectfully Your obet servt

S. A. Douglas

ALS, owned by J. M. Slechta, Jefferson, Wisconsin. Jefferson Davis, of Mississippi, had been a member of the House of Representatives from 1845 to 1846, had served in the Mexican War, and had been a member of the United

States Senate from 1847 to 1851, before being appointed Secretary of War in the cabinet of President Pierce.

¹George E. Pickett was promoted to captain on March 3, 1855. He later became a prominent officer in the Confederate Army.

²Possibly Charles Ambrose Reynolds, of Maryland, who was promoted to second lieutenant on March 3, 1855.

To Mason Brayman

Washington
Dr Sir,   April 3d 1855

I herewith enclose the Deed from me to the Ills Central Rail Road Com'y as per my promise to Mr Joy.¹ Please to deliver it to him on his arrival in Chicago. Very truly yours

S. A. DOUGLAS

ALS, Burton Historical Collection, Detroit Public Library. Mason Brayman was an attorney for the Illinois Central Railroad.

¹James F. Joy, Detroit lawyer and prominent railroad speculator, was general counsel for the Illinois Central in 1855.

To ———

[April 3, 1855, n.p.; ALS, Illinois State Historical Library. Douglas forwards a letter from A. J. Dickinson regarding the allegedly fraudulent entry of a quarter section of land. The bottom of the letter, bearing the name of the addressee, is missing. Three men by the name of A. J. Dickinson have been located: of Monroe County, who was a member of the state legislature in 1842; of Perry County, who was a justice of the peace in 1845; and of Randolph County, who held the position of County Clerk for several years in the early 1840's.]

To Charles H. Lanphier

Washington
My Dr Sir,   April 3d 1855

I received your letter in regard to the Clerkship of the U.S. District Court on my return from North Carolina, and would be glad to do anything in my power to carry out your wishes in this respect. But the appoint[ment] of the Clerk of the District Court lies exclusively with Judge Treat.¹ It is true that Judge McLean² can override him in regard to the Clerk of the *Circuit* Court if he chooses, but in that event there would be separate clerks for the two courts as is now the case in New York, Philadelphia, & several of the Northern cities. If Judge Treat makes an appoint[ment] promptly for the District Court & stands firm on the other, there is no danger of Judge McLean overuling him in the Circuit Court, but if he should, let him take the responsibility, & then each court will have a separate clerk.

[337]

I leave here for Chicago in a few days, and will recommend to Judge Treat for Clerk any man you, Harris, & McConnel[3] may agree upon. I have no personal choice except to gratify our friends who fight the battles. Your friend

S. A. DOUGLAS

ALS, Illinois State Historical Library.

[1]Samuel Hubbel Treat was an Associate Justice of the Illinois Supreme Court from 1841 to 1855, when he resigned to accept appointment as judge of the United States District Court for the Southern District of Illinois.

[2]John McLean, of Ohio, was Associate Justice of the United States Supreme Court.

[3]Thomas Langrell Harris and Murray McConnel.

To James Washington Sheahan

My dear Sir: Washington, April 6, '55.

I have just read your beautiful and touching notice in your paper of April 2 of my reply to Wade of Ohio in regard to my domestic affairs. It has occurred to me that Wentworth's unscroupulousness would prompt him to question the correctness of my statement and refer to the large amount of property I own in Chicago and inquire where the money came from to purchase it. The facts are as follows: The whole of my Chicago property cost me eleven thousand and three hundred dollars ($11,300) on a credit as is well known to many of my friends. I sold to the Illinois Central Rail Road the right of way to cross my land for twenty one thousand and three hundred dollars ($21,300) which enabled me to pay for the whole and have ten thousand left. I also sold to Col. Taylor,[1] or rather he sold for me and I ratified it, five thousand and four hundred dollars worth on the South branch of Chicago river. Thus I show fifteen thousand and four hundred dollars in addition to my pay and mileage as a Senator, which have gone into my personal and domestic expenses, after pay for the whole of my cheeings (sic)[2] for party. I have thought it prudent to furnish you with these facts to be used or not according to circumstances, but if used, to be done on your own authority and refer to the record and to rumor to sustain your statements. I have been unavoidably detained here much longer than I expected. I shall leave for Chicago in three or four days. It might be well to publish the whole of my speech in reply to Wade in broken doses as your space will permit.

Copy, University of Kansas Library. This is obviously an incomplete copy of the original.

[1]Probably Edmund Dick Taylor.

[2]The word "(sic)" appears on the typewritten copy.

To James C. Dobbin

[June 9, 1855, Chicago; ALS, RG-45, National Archives. Forwarding a letter from T. J. V. Owen, of Springfield, Illinois, asking that his brother, Elias Owen, then a student at the Naval Academy, not be sent to sea.]

To Charles H. Lanphier

Chicago

My Dear Sir, July 7th 1855

From some cause your letter dated the 3d and Post Marked at Springfield the 5th inst did not reach me until today. I have also received by todays mail a letter from Calhoun dated the 2d inst in which he stated that he should leave *that evening* for Fort Leavenworth. From these facts I infer that it is too late for my letter to be of any service to you even if I could furnish the information you desire. But I must plead ignorance on the subject of your enquiry. I would not know how to proceed to release myself from a Bond without first examining the act of Congress, nor am I certain that the statute says anything on the subject, as I have not the laws with me. If the law is silent on the subject my impression is that you would have to give notice to the Department in order that a new Bond might be required to be executed. I regret that I cannot be more specific on the subject.

I am glad to hear that everything looks well in Egypt[1] politically. The prospects were never brighter in this part of the state. It is evident that the reaction has extended over the whole Union. Under these circumstances I do not see how we can fail to elect the Dem nominee for President next year. Tell our friends in Egypt that I will visit them before the Summer is over. Your friend

S. A. DOUGLAS

ALS, Illinois State Historical Library.
[1] The name commonly applied to southern Illinois at this time.

To Franklin Pierce

Chicago

My Dear Sir, July 22d 1855

I have just been informed that there is a vacancy in the office of Consul at Tangiers by the death of the incumbent. You may possibly recollect that Gen'l Shields and myself as well as the representatives from this State united in recommending E B Ames Esq of this state for that office at the opening of your administration.[1] Mr Ames is now an applicant to fill the vacancy and I am anxious that he should succeed.

Unlike most of the disappointed applicants for office, he has remained faithful to his principles and Party not withstanding his disappointment. He is well qualified for the office and would attend to its duties punctually. I am not aware that Illinois has any one consular appointment abroad and the omission has caused some chagrin to our friends. I shall be extremely gratified at Mr Ames' success. You will find any quantity of recommendations for him on file in the State Department. I have the honor to remain Very truly your friend

S. A. DOUGLAS

ALS, RG-59, National Archives.
¹See above, March 5, 1853, and March 15, 1853.

To George P. Buell

Chicago
My Dear Sir, Aug 3d 1855

I have had an interview with Mr Sheahan in regard to your proposed connection with the Times. He has a high estimate of your talents as a writer and thinks you have few equals as an essayist. He does not feel authorized to invite you to Chicago for the reason that he has had correspondence with others & is under *conditional* obligations in certain contingencies which he did not explain. It is proper to say that I have no connection with nor, interest in, nor control over the paper. Yet I should be delighted to see you associated in the management of that paper. I believe that such an arraigment would be mutual[ly] benefifical to the paper, yourself & the Party, and I really hope that it may yet be brought about. I shall certainly be glad of an opportunity to aid in its accomplishment. I have the honor to be very truly your friend

S. A. DOUGLAS

ALS, owned by Martin F. Douglas. George P. Buell was a writer for the Cincinnati *Enquirer*.

To James W. Stone *et al.*

Chicago, Sept. 11, 1855.

Gentlemen: I have the honor to acknowledge the receipt of your polite invitation to deliver a lecture on the subject of slavery, at the Tremont Temple, in Boston, on the 7th of February next, or at such time during the next winter as my convenience will permit. Regarding slavery as a domestic regulation, which derives its existence and support from the local laws of the several States where it prevails, and with [which] neither the federal government nor the citizens or authorities of other States have any right to interfere, except to perform their constitutional obligations in reference to the rendition of fugitives, I have never deemed it my duty, as a citizen of a non-slaveholding State, to discuss the supposed advantages or evils, with the view of sustaining or destroying the domestic institutions of sister States, with which, under the Constitution and laws of the land, I have no right to interfere, and for the consequences of which I am in no wise responsible.

You will therefore permit [me] to say, with all due respect, that neither my tastes nor my public duties will permit me to accept your polite invitation. I have the honor to be, very respectfully, your obedient servant,

S. A. Douglas

Boston *Liberator*, October 5, 1855. James W. Stone was a Boston physician. Other members of the committee to which Douglas addressed his letter were Samuel Gridley Howe, Joseph Story, Nathaniel B. Shurtleff, Philo Sanford, Thomas Russell, John M. Clark, and Samuel May.

To Thomas A. Hendricks

Mt Vernon Ills

My Dr Sir, Sept 27th 1855

Permit me to introduce to you the Hon W B Scates, one of the Judges of the Supreme Court of this State.[1] The Judge visits Washington at the request of His Excellency Gov Matteson to consult with you in regard to the Swamp lands in this state.[2]

Our people think that great injustice is being done and inducements to innumerable & inormous frauds are being held out by the action of the Department in permitting evidence to be taken by individuals to disprove the legal evidence furnished to show what are swamp Lands. I have confered with Judge Scates fully upon the subject & fully concur with him in relation to it, & he will be able to put you in possession of all our views upon the subject. I invoke your prompt & favorable action in the premises. Very truly your friend

S. A. Douglas

ALS, RG-49, National Archives. Thomas A. Hendricks, of Indiana, was a member of Congress from 1851 to 1855. In 1854, he was defeated for reelection. President Pierce appointed Hendricks Commissioner of the General Land Office in 1855, a post he held until 1859.
[1] Walter Bennett Scates, a member of the Illinois Supreme Court from 1841 to 1847, and from 1853 to 1856, was Chief Justice in 1855 and 1856.
[2] In 1850, Congress passed an act granting to the states swampy and overflowed lands within their boundaries, provided these lands be reclaimed by the states.

To Howell Cobb

My Dear Sir,

With heartfelt joy I congratulate you on the glorious victory you
have achieved in the Empire State of the South.[1] True we have received but partial returns by Telegraph, but enouch to satisfy us that
your triumph is complete. I rejoice that the intrepid & gifted Stephens[2]
has been so nobly sustained and returned to the theatre of his usefulness in Congress. Victories are crowding upon us on all sides. The
tide is now completely turned. The torrent of fanaticism has been
rolled back almost everywhere. The allied army of *isms* is bound to be
routed & annihilated everywhere, north & South. Abolitionism, Know
Nothingism, and all the other isms are akin to each other and are in
alliance, some places secret and others open & avowed, but everywhere
in alliance against the national Democracy. We will be able to route
them in the north as completely as you have been in the South.

Your kind letter inviting me at Atlanta at the Great Mass Meeting
overtook me while making a tour through my state, but was not received until I had published my list of appointments, nor until after
the meeting had been held. I have not seen the proceedings of your
great meeting as I have been spending each day and traveling nights
to reach my next appointments. I have no doubt that you had a good
time, and I should have been delighted to have been with you. It
would have been exceedingly gratifying to have addressed the assembled Democracy of Georgia in order to demonstrate to the South
that Democratic principles were the same everywhere and could be
enforced by the same arguments in the Slave holding & non-slaveholding states. I regret however that I cannot claim the honor, as you
suggested I might of having contributed to the great victory you have
so gallantly won. In regard to the reward which you so generously
offered, I can only say that my position on that question is the same
as that of the slavery question—towit, non-intervention. I do not seek
the nomination—do not ask it at the hands of our friends. I have more
of pride, of feeling, of character, of patriotism in the success of the
course in which the best portion of our lives has been spent & to which
the residue is dedicated than I have in my own personal elevation.
Our first duty is to see that the organization of our Party is consolidated
and planted immoveably upon a sound, national, constitutional platform. Our Platform must be bold, unequivocal, & specific on all
controverted points. There must be no general highsounding phrases
meaning nothing—no equivocal terms—no doubtful meanings—no
double dealing for the benefit of timid & tricky politicians. We must
say precisely what we mean and say it in such language that it cannot

be construed one way south and another way north. We must make the next fight a fight for principles, and our triumph must decide the policy & the action of the government for at least four years. The new administration must not be a coalition of discordant materials nor a futile attempt to harmonize the chiefs of hostile factions; but it must be organized upon the principles avowed in the Platform and composed of men who are identified & bound by every tie to carry out those principles in their appointments as well as by their measures. Having these objects at heart to the end that the principles for which we are struggling may become the settled policy of the country in all future times & be engrafted upon our institutions as firmly as if they were incorporated into the constitution in terms instead of by inference, I desire our Party to assign me whatever position will make me most serviceable to the cause. The circumstances connected with the great Kansas & Nebraska struggle, and especially the course pursued by the allied factions & isms toward me individually will render the triumph of the cause my perfect & complete vindication. To this end all my energies will be directed. I ask no other reward—I seek no higher triumph.

From what I have said you will perceive that if my name shall be connected with the Presidential election it must be the voluntary act of our friends, prompted by an eye single to the success of the cause & the permanent triumph of our principles, without any reference to my personal wishes or aggrandizement, and especially without any agency on my part directly or indirectly, by word or deed.

I have felt this exposition due to the old friendship which has existed between us and which, I take pleasure in assuring you, has never been deminished in my breast—due to the identity of our political principles & patriotic objects, to the end that each may pursue his own line of policy with a distinct knowledge of the views of the other. I leave for Chicago on Monday morning where a letter will reach me at any time before the meeting of Congress. I am Dr Sir, very truly your friend

S. A. Douglas

ALS, University of Georgia Library.
[1]Among the successful Democratic candidates in Georgia's 1855 state elections were Herschel V. Johnson, who was elected to the governorship, and seven of the eight Congressmen, including Cobb himself.
[2]Alexander Hamilton Stephens served in the House of Representatives from 1843 to 1859.

To A. S. Williams

[October 14, 1855, Chicago; LS, Henry E. Huntington Library. Regrets that he cannot send Williams a copy of the *Congressional Globe*, as he had none on hand. Williams was a resident of Painesville, Ohio.]

[343]

To Charles H. Lanphier and George Walker

(*Private*)   Chicago
Dr Sirs   Oct 15th '55

I send you the Proceedings of our great meeting in this city. The Resolutions were adopted by acclamation.[1] They were prepared by several of us at Lexington & concurred in by men from Ohio, Ky, Indiana &c with the view of producing unity of action between the free & slave states at Cincinnati next Spring.

Can you not have them adopted in all of our County meetings & also by the State convention next Spring?

Illinois takes the lead & will have the honor of making the national Platform. The[y] should be treated as the "*Illinois Platform*" & get every county & Town to concur in them as such. We are all right now in Chicago. The Fusionists are *dead dead*. Let the fight go on. Trumbull can do no harm. He disgusted everybody here, & goes home mortified & chargrined. Your friend

S. A. Douglas

ALS, owned by William S. Walker, Chicago, Illinois.

[1] On October 12, 1855, Douglas addressed a large meeting in Chicago. The proceedings, copied from the Chicago *Times*, were published in the *State Register* on October 17. The resolutions referred to by Douglas, "The Platform of the Illinois Democracy," declared that Congress had no rightful authority to establish, abolish, or prohibit slavery in the states or territories and endorsed the principle of "non-intervention upon the subject of slavery" as embodied in the Kansas-Nebraska Act. Additional resolutions struck at the Know Nothing movement by declaring a natural right to freedom of religion, rejecting any distinction between naturalized and native-born citizens of the United States and warning that any secret association or brotherhood for political objects was dangerous to free institutions.

To George W. Jones

(*Private*)   Chicago
My Dr Gen'l   Oct 15th 55

I send you the Proceedings of a Great Mass Meeting in this city. The Resolutions were adopted by acclamation by about five thousand people. They will be adopted by every county in the State. They were prepared at Lexington by gentlemen from Ky, Tenn, Ohio, Indiana, Missouri and Illinois & we agreed to have them passed in all of those states as original, without stating where they come from, in order to show that Democracy was the same everywhere, in the free & slave states alike. Can you not have them adopted in Iowa, to show that she also belongs to the Democratic Line? I think they will suit your Democracy precisely. Let me hear from you. Your friend

S. A. Douglas

ALS, Iowa State Department of History and Archives.

To E. Randolph Smith

Chicago
Oct 17th 1855

My Dear Sir,

Will you have the Kindness to call at the Bank of H. A. Tucker & Co and deliver the enclosed acceptances and request him with the proceeds thereof to pay my note to the Bank of Peru for five thousand dollars and take up said note together with a certificate of stock for $5000 in the Bank of Peru[1] which is held as collateral for the payment of said note, and retain until my return the residue of the money for these acceptances.

I also owe Charles R. Starkweather[2] five thousand dollars for which he holds my note. I desire you to see him and if the money becomes due before my return I desire you to raise the money & take up the note. You can hypothecate the said certificate of Bank stock as collateral to raise the money, after applying the amount of Mr. Shelby's[3] draft (2625) herewith enclosed.

I also desire you to call on Mr R H Murray (Hardware Merchant on Lake Street a few doors east of Tremont on same side of same block)[4] and tender him fourteen hundred & eighty dollars & receive a Deed for the land described in the enclosed memorandum or bond. I herewith give you a check on H. A. Tucker & co for the money to make the payment. Receive the Deed & retain it until I return. Yours truly

S. A. DOUGLAS

ALS, owned by Martin F. Douglas. E. Randolph Smith, a partner in Smith, Bradley and Company, was a Chicago real estate broker and land agent.
[1] In Peru, Illinois. Attached to the letter is a certificate for fifty shares of stock in the Bank of Peru, valued at $5,000, and a promissory note for $5,000, dated October 26, 1855.

[2] Charles R. Starkweather was a Chicago real estate agent and a long-time resident of that city.
[3] Probably Isaac Shelby, Jr., a Chicago real estate dealer.
[4] Robert H. Murray was associated with the Chicago hardware firm of Hammill, Haight and Company.

To John Calhoun

Terre Haute Ind Nov 26th 1855

Dr. Sir: Permit us to urge on your attention, the claims of our sterling friend and colaborer in Democracy, W. D. Latshaw,[1] so well and familiarly known to you and other true men of Ills. After long years of labor in Support of National Democracy, Mr. L. is reduced to poverty, with a wife and several children dependent on him. He entertains the idea of emigrating and settling in Kansas, provided you will give him an opportunity to raise himself once more on the world, by giving him the appointment or contract for, running two or three

Corps of Surveyors, laying off townships into Section Lines. If you can do this, you will have conferred an obligation on us, and a favour on one, who is not onley worthy and deserving, but who will, in all probability make his professional mark in Kansas. We regret the necessity which compels Mr. L. to seek a new field, and causes us the loss of one of our ablest and most efficient Democratic Editors, whose faith and practice have ever been above suspicion.

We ask then that you will confer upon Mr. L. the appointment he desires, and notify him as early as possible, so that he may provide for the contingency. We are very respectfully Your most Obt Servents

S. A. DOUGLAS
THOS. L. HARRIS
ORLANDO B. FICKLIN
T. R. YOUNG[2]

LS, Kansas State Historical Society.
[1]William D. Latshaw had edited newspapers in Mt. Carmel and Charleston, Illinois. In January, 1855, he was defeated for secretary of the Illinois Senate. A year later, he was appointed agent for the Illinois Central Railroad.

The appointment referred to in this letter was never made.
[2]Timothy Roberts Young, of Marshall, Illinois, was a member of Congress from Illinois for one term from 1849 to 1851.

To James Washington Sheahan

[December 14, 1855, Terre Haute; ALS. This letter was sold at the galleries of W. D. Morley, Inc., Philadelphia, on May 29, 1942. It has not been located.]

To Henry M. Rice

[December 28, 1855, n.p.; ALS, owned by William H. Townsend, Lexington, Kentucky. This letter has not been located.]

To Howell Cobb

Cleaveland Ohio
My Dr Sir,   Jan'y 8th 1856

I have witnessed your course in the Democratic caucus with delight & admiration. It was just what I would have expected of you. Our success depends upon standing firmly by our organization and our Platform. Above all there must be no coalitions with any of the factions —no concessions to the enemy in any form. We can and will crush all our enemies by a bold avowal of & strict adherence to our principles.

Write me & give me an inside view of what is going on. I have been shut out from the political world for the last three months. My

[346]

general health is nearly restored, but my throat is still in a bad condition.[1] It is now very sore in consequence of the surgical operations recently performed, the last of which was a few days ago to cut off the *Uvula* or lower pallate. My Doctor (Dr Ackly) delights in running Probings down the windpipe, and cutting off pallates, & clipping Tonsils, and all such amusements. I confess that I do not enjoy the fun quite as well as he seems to do, but presume I will like it better when I get used to it. Write soon. Very truly your friend

S. A. DOUGLAS

ALS, University of Georgia Library.
[1]After campaigning strenuously for Democratic candidates in the 1855 Illinois state election, Douglas' voice failed and it became apparent that throat surgery would be necessary. He was taken to Terre Haute, Indiana (his last speaking engagement had been in Paris, Illinois), where he was placed under the care of a local doctor. In December, he traveled to Cleveland where he submitted to an operation on December 26 by Dr. Horace Ackley, Professor of Surgery at the Cleveland Medical College and one of Cleveland's leading surgeons. Douglas was unable to attend Congress until February.

To David S. Reid

Cleaveland Ohio
Jan'y 11th 1856

My Dr Sir,

I have intended writing you for sometime, but delayed as I hoped each week to get away. My health is improving, indeed I am well— all but my throat. My throat is still very sore, the result of Surgical operations. I am not permitted to leave the House during this cold weather, & it is with difficulty that I can swallow anything. My Doctor assures me that I will soon be able to resume my seat in the Senate. The disease has become Chronic and is very obstinate. I had the Uvula or lower Pallate cut off a few days ago & the present soreness is the result of that operation. I hope to be with you in a week or two. Present my kind regards to your good Lady & believe me truly your friend

S. A. DOUGLAS

P.S. Write me a good long letter & give me an inside view of politics. I have been shut out from the world & know not what has transpired.

ALS, North Carolina Department of Archives and History, Raleigh. Reid was elected to the United States Senate in 1854 and served until 1859.

To James Washington Sheahan

Cleveland, Ohio,
January 11, 1856.

I have as yet failed to receive the drafts I expected before this time. I have, however, attempted on assignments which I hope will succeed.

There is about ten thousand dollars in the hands of Smith Bradley & Co.[1] for Edmond Rice Esq. of Minnesota,[2] which is coming to Judge Granger[3] and myself from Mr. Rice. I have just received a letter from Mr. Smith[4] that they have received the money and are instructed by Mr. Rice to send him a certificate of Deposit for the same. I have just written to Smith that the money is coming to me from Rice—that I have three thousand dollars to pay in Chicago now due—that you are to attend it for me—that I have sent you a receipt for three thousand dollars signed by me for Mr. Price[5]—that you will present the receipt and receive the money—and that he can send the receipt to Mr. Price as money, etc.

I think he will pay you the money on this authority. Present the receipt and try it. Let me know the result at once. If this fails money shall come from some source. Let me know the precise amount you must have *now* and how much in 30 days and how much in 60 days and how much in 90 days. Let me know the worst and it shall be provided for.[6] I cannot fully understand the state of my own finances until I arrive at Washington. My papers have all been sent there under the impression that I would have arrived there long ago. It will probably be a week before I can leave here. My throat is still very sore. My Doctor does not allow me to leave the house at present, altho he says I am nearly well. The State Contests of this state passed off very well. Our friends have the entire and absolute control of the Delegation from this state. Ohio is as sure for us as Illinois. Our plan will be now to combine the whole North West as a unit if possible. The message will strengthen Pierce at the South.[7] That is all the better for us. The effect will be to hold the South uncommitted for the present. Push the Nebraska issue as prominently as possible as the main and only issue. Ohio has adopted it, and my state will do so. Buchanan will be compelled to define his position and take back his Harvest Home Letter.[8] No man can be nominated who is not identified with the Nebraska issue in the public mind and on the record.

Copy, University of Kansas Library. This is not a complete copy.

[1] Smith, Bradley and Company was a Chicago real estate firm.

[2] Edmund Rice was a St. Paul attorney, and, in 1856, a Ramsey County commissioner.

[3] Douglas' brother-in-law, Julius N. Granger.

[4] On January 8, 1856, E. Randolph Smith wrote to Douglas that he had carried out the latter's instructions (owned by Martin F. Douglas). See above, October 17, 1855.

[5] William Price was Postmaster of Chicago from 1857 to 1858, and later a partner with Sheahan in the publication of the Chicago *Times*.

[6] On March 8, 1856, Sheahan wrote to Douglas, "I wrote you at Cleveland a letter detailing our hardships, and your generous response enabled me to pay $1500 on the real estate,—the balance was consumed in paying a note of Cook's—his own which he had made no provision to meet. None of that sum which you loaned me—except a small amount went in to the *Times*"

(Douglas Papers, University of Chicago Library).

[7]President Pierce's third annual message to Congress, December 31, 1855.

[8]Buchanan wrote his "Harvest Home letter" on August 25, 1847, in response to an invitation to speak in Berks County, Pennsylvania. In the letter, which was Buchanan's opening bid for the 1848 Democratic Presidential nomi-

nation, he took a strong stand in favor of the extension of the Missouri Compromise line to the Pacific as the best means for settling the slavery agitation. Although Douglas had earlier stated that he would not seek the Democratic Presidential nomination in 1856, this letter to Sheahan indicates that he had changed his mind and was organizing his support for that office.

To Peter Harvey *et al.*

Washington City, Jan. 15, 1856.

Sir: Accept for yourself and the gentlemen of your committee the assurance of profound regret that it will not be in my power to avail myself of your kind invitation to the Webster Dinner to be given on the 18th instant.

The anniversary celebration of the birthday of Daniel Webster would be an occasion when with you I would respond, as would, I trust, all—North, South, East or West—to the noble sentiment of the illustrious Webster: *"One Country, one Constitution, and one Destiny."*

My duties here will, however, detain me. Meanwhile, with renewed assurances of regret at my enforced absence, accept for yourself and associates the respects of Yours,

S. A. DOUGLAS

Clipping-Photostat, Illinois State Historical Library. The newspaper in which this item was printed has not been identified. Peter Harvey was a Boston businessman, banker, and Treasurer of the Rutland Railroad. Earlier he had acted as Daniel Webster's financial adviser.

To James W. Singleton

My Dr Sir,   March 5th 1856

Accept my thanks for your kind letter of the 2d which for some cause did not reach me till this afternoon. Trumbull was admitted to his seat today I am told by a vote of 4 or 5 to one.[1] I was not there & have not been for some days. My throat is no better & I could not have said a word had I been there. No power on earth could have changed the result. *This I know.* Yet had I been in a condition to [influence?] the grounds of a vote I should have been present & took the lead in the fight on the side of our friends.

Make the acquaintance of my friend Disny of Ohio[2] at the Astor House. He may not talk freely to you at first, but when you tell him that I referred you to him he will do so. Altho not well, I am hard at work at my report & will have it out soon.[3] Don't fail to come back to Washington. Drop me a line & keep me posted. Your friend

S. A. DOUGLAS

ALS, owned by William H. Townsend. James W. Singleton, a Quincy, Illinois, lawyer, was a member of the Illinois state legislature from 1850 to 1854 and from 1861 to 1862.

[1] Lyman Trumbull, newly elected Senator from Illinois.

[2] David T. Disney, a Cincinnati, Ohio, lawyer, was a member of Congress from 1849 to 1855. With Singleton, Disney was working actively to promote Douglas' candidacy for the Democratic Presidential nomination later in the year.

[3] On March 12, 1856, Douglas presented the majority report on the Kansas troubles of the Senate Committee on Territories and announced his intention to introduce a bill enabling Kansas to become a state.

To James Guthrie

Sir   House of Reps. Mar. 13, 1856

We are strongly urged by Citizens of *Peoria* in the State of Illinois to have that City made a Port of delivery.

Allow us to State a few facts which in our judgment show the propriety of compliance with their wishes and wants.

Next to Chicago, Peoria is the largest City in Illinois. It is situated on one of the very best navigable Rivers of the Country, as is shown by the fact that the No. of Steam-Boat arrivals at its port in the last year was *1061*.

The Merchants of that City now import Hardware, Queensware &c from abroad, and are Rapidly Extending their trade. It may not be out of place to state that the Illinois River is connected with the Lakes by the Michigan & Illinois Canal, a work constructed in part by donations of land by the Genl. Govt. Through this Channel large quantities of Merchandize are shipt from Eastern Cities to St. Louis and other points of the Misspi River.

On the other hand goods are shipt from the lower Misspi *up the Illinois* & to LaSalle, and then sent by *R.Road* across the Country to Rock Island, thus proving the importance of the *Smaller* River.

As a Reason for the Speedy action of Congress it is said that there are now at New Orleans some Five thousand tons of R. Road Iron which is intended for the Peoria & Oquawka & Peoria & Logansport, R.Roads and which it is important to have landed at Peoria Early in the Spring (on account of Cheapness of freight at that time) although much of it will not be used until Summer. Other Iron, will also be needed for other Roads connecting with Peoria, and these Enterprises will be greatly promoted, if the duties on this Iron can be paid as it is needed to be laid down.

[350]

In view of these facts, it is hoped that you may Regard, as we do the propriety of making Peoria a port of delivery.

As your favorable opinion would essentially aid us in obtaining the necessary legislation, we hope you will not find it inconsistent with your views of propriety to Recommend the Measure desired.[1] Very Respectfully Your Obdt. Servts

S. A. Douglas
James Knox[2]
Thos. L. Harris
S. S. Marshall[3]
Wm. A. Richardson

LS, RG-56, National Archives. James Guthrie, of Kentucky, was Secretary of the Treasury in Franklin Pierce's cabinet.

[1]"An Act to constitute the cities of Hannibal, Missouri, and Peoria, Illinois, ports of delivery" was introduced in the House of Representatives by James Knox, of Illinois, and became law on April 5, 1856.

[2]James Knox, of Knoxville, Knox County, represented Illinois in the lower house of Congress from 1853 to 1857.

[3]Samuel Scott Marshall, of McLeansboro, was a member of Congress from Illinois from 1855 to 1859.

To James W. Singleton

(*Private*)

My Dr Sir,   March 16th 1856

I have just received your kind letter. I do not know of any Southern man of the kind you wish whom I could send on. You must leave that matter to our friend D[1] with whom you have been consulting. He is a discreet man, ful of talent & resources, and can judge on the ground better than I can advise at this distance. I will talk over Illinois affairs when you & Don come on here. All looks well & improving every day. Much depends on Virginia. Very truly your friend

S. A. Douglas

ALS, Illinois State Historical Library.

[1]David T. Disney. Singleton had written Douglas on March 5, urging him to send a Southern man to New York to help promote Douglas' support there.

To James Washington Sheahan

Washington, March 28th, 1856

I regret exceedingly the rupture between you and Cook.[1] He is wrong in trying to change the Paper and to turn you out and I have so written him. That must not be done.

On the other hand I regret to see you assailing him in the paper.[2] That looks like turning the party organ into a personal organ to fight a private feud. Such a use of the paper on either side will destroy its character. I beg of you to let Cook alone, and don't say a word about him in the paper. Of course because his friends will have a right to complain when they see a paper supported in part by his money assailing him.

I have spoken frankly. I approve heartily of your course in all other respects. I wish you success, and intend to stand by you. But the paper should be the organ of the party and not of a man. The feud must cease. You and Cook must close your quarrel. Let our friends take hold of it & settle it. I agree that you are entitled to control the paper & ought to control it. That is in your line of business which you understood perfectly, while Cook knows nothing about it and should not attempt it.[3]

Copy, University of Kansas Library. This is not a complete copy.

[1]The quarrel between Sheahan and Cook, both partners in the ownership of the Chicago *Times*, arose over the support of local candidates in Chicago and over the degree of ownership of the *Times* exercised by Sheahan. Sheahan wrote to Douglas on March 8, 1856, that Isaac Cook was trying to force him from the editorship. Since he had not heard from Douglas recently, Sheahan charged that Cook, as Postmaster of Chicago, may have intercepted Douglas' letters (Douglas Papers, University of Chicago Library). The next day, March 9, Cook wrote Douglas his side of the story (owned by Martin F. Douglas). Sheahan, he reported, had never given Douglas adequate credit for the support he had received from the Senator, and he accused Sheahan of using the cash sent by Douglas for his own private speculative purposes. "How can a man that you and I have treated so kindly act in this manner," Cook asked. He denied that he had tampered with Douglas' mail, and charged that Sheahan was trying to oust him from the partnership.

[2]On March 21, Sheahan wrote to Douglas again, accusing Cook of trying to dominate politics in Chicago and the county. "Unless you command him to be quiet, silent, & to follow & not lead," Sheahan wrote, "the party here will have to take action with him. . . . Unless you advise to the contrary the Times must take sides against him, & it will do so" (Douglas Papers, University of Chicago Library).

[3]Sheahan answered Douglas' letter bitterly on March 31: "You are altogether mistaken in supposing that *anybody* here regards the matter as a personal feud. . . . It is a struggle on his [Cook's] part to coerce the paper into a punishment of his personal opponents. . . . I was fighting your cause & not I. Cooks, I deny that they are identical . . . I do not intend to be forced out of this establishment by Cook, but I will quit it voluntarily if you say you insist upon it, or if you insist on his remaining in it. There can never again be any intercourse between us. He or I must leave, & your word is decisive as to my course. . . . Deserted by you, pursued by Cook, banished from my old home by the entire waste of all I have had, I see no recourse left me, but to start a new paper here" (Douglas Papers, University of Chicago Library). For Douglas' answer to this letter, see below, April 9, 1856.

To David Meriwether

[March 31, 1856, Senate Chamber; LS, Henry E. Huntington Library. Recommends the appointment of Julius R. Pomeroy, of Brooklyn,

New York, to the office of Commissioner of Deeds. David Meriwether, of Kentucky, was appointed to the United States Senate to fill the vacancy caused by the death of Henry Clay, and served for only a few months in 1852. In 1853, he was appointed Governor of New Mexico Territory by Pierce, and held that office until January, 1855. Although Douglas wrote to Meriwether as Governor of the territory, he no longer held that position.]

To James W. Grimes

[March 31, 1856, Senate Chamber; LS, Illinois State Historical Library. Recommends the appointment of Julius R. Pomeroy to the office of Commissioner of Deeds. James W. Grimes was Governor of Iowa from 1854 to 1858. In 1859, he was elected to the United States Senate.]

To James Washington Sheahan

Private   Washington, Wednesday, Apr. 9th, 1856

I have this moment received and answered your Telegraph. I have also sent the following telegraph dispatch to Cook:

"If you are my enemy you will continue your suit against the Times. If you are my friend you will dismiss it."[1]

I write him tonight to the same effect. I have also written him before in the strongest language of protest I could use. He thinks I run in concert with you and you seem to think that I have deserted you because I advised that you should not attack him in the columns of the paper.

You must retain the Times, and if you should be deprived of it by law, you must start another paper and I shall stand by you in so doing. Go ahead and have no fears. Your error is in supposing that I or anyone else can control Cook. He is the most obstinate man I ever saw. Notwithstanding his good feeling for me which I do not doubt, I have never been able to influence him against his will. Defend the suit to the last extremity and hold on to the paper if possible.

Copy, University of Kansas Library. This is not a complete copy.

[1]On April 5, 1856, Daniel Cameron, associated with Cook and Sheahan in the *Times,* wrote Douglas that Cook had tried to discharge Sheahan from the editorship (Douglas Papers, University of Chicago Library). Upon Sheahan's refusal to leave, Cook sought a court injunction to stop the publication of the newspaper. Crucial to

Cook's case was the question of whether Sheahan owned a half interest in the *Times,* as maintained by Sheahan and by Douglas (see below, April 11, 1856), or whether Sheahan's share was less than half, as argued by Cook. Cook's application for an injunction was dismissed by the court on April 16 (E. R. Hooper to Stephen A. Douglas, April 16, 1856, Douglas Papers, University of Chicago Library). Fear

[353]

was expressed by several of Douglas' associates that the Sheahan-Cook quarrel would have an adverse effect on Douglas and the party in Illinois, disastrous at a time when Douglas was a Presidential aspirant.

To James Washington Sheahan

Washington April 11th, 1856

Mr. Cameron has put your letter in my hands, and also related to me briefly the state of facts in regard to the Times. I can only repeat what I have written to you on more than one occasion, that you are by contract and by right owner of one half of the Times and sole editor of the paper, that in my opinion you ought to remain editor of the paper for the good of the party—that Mr. Cook's conduct in regard to the paper meets with my severest condemnation as I have repeatedly written him—that he must be acting under advice from the enemies of the party and of my enemies—that it is my wish that you should hold on to the paper and keep control of it if possible. I will now add that I cordially approve of your plan to start a new paper on the next day in the event that you loose possession of this one. I shall recognize your paper as the party organ and repudiate Cook's in the event that he gets possession and thus compels you to start a new one.

Mr. Cook understands these to be my opinions and has so understood them for many weeks. I have written my disapproval and condemnation of his conduct to him in plainer language and in stronger terms than I like to use to any one else. If things come to the worst he must be treated as an enemy, for his conduct can be regarded in no other light. Yet I would advise that no allusion be made to him in the columns of the paper if it can be avoided.[1]

Copy, University of Kansas Library. This is not a complete copy.

[1] The quarrel was finally settled through the intercession of Douglas' friend, Congressman Thomas Langrell Harris. Cook agreed to dispose of his interest in the *Times* to Sheahan and by the middle of May the deal had been concluded. Both Harris and Governor Matteson, who had assisted in the settlement, upheld Cook in the controversy. Harris wrote on May 18 that Cook had been "placed in a false position as to that controversy" (Douglas Papers, University of Chicago Library). Sheahan had the last word. Writing Douglas on May 19, he complained that Cook had destroyed the paper's credit and he found it impossible to raise the money necessary to buy Cook's share. He appealed to Douglas once again for funds (owned by Martin F. Douglas).

To Cooper Kinderdine Watson

Saturday, April 19, 1856.

Sir: I have examined the letter signed by your friend, James H. Lane, which you placed in my hands to-day, and will now give you my reasons for responding to you as its bearer, instead of him as its author.[1]

The letter is so equivocal in terms, and portions of it so irreconcilable with other portions, that it is impossible to determine, with any certainty, whether it is intended as a hostile message or a friendly note. It is true that the city is full of rumors that your friend, Col. Lane, intended to challenge me, and the letter-writers for those newspapers in the eastern cities most friendly to the revolutionary movements in Kansas; and most hostile to myself, not only announced the facts, some three or four days ago, but actually fixed the time when your friend intended to send the hostile message. The object of your friend in causing his intentions to be made known to the world and published in the newspapers is not for me to explain, when he and everyone must have known that the effect would inevitably be to have both parties arrested the moment he succeeded in making the public believe that he intended to invite a hostile meeting.

In the National Intelligencer of this morning I find a "card," published by your friend, in which he attempts to assail me personally, and to raise a question of veracity between us upon a point in reference to which he admits and affirmatively asserts the truth of my statement, but denies that he gave me or any other person a "shadow of authority for making any such statement." Having selected his tribunal, and removed his complaint from the jurisdiction to which public letter-writers in his confidence had declared he would bring it, and appealed to the public through the columns of the newspaper press, he is at liberty to prosecute it in that form as long as he pleases. Since the publication of this "card" in the newspapers, your friend, in a letter of which you are the bearer, and in which you are designated as his friend to receive my answer, referring to the debate on Monday last in the United States senate, on the fraudulent memorial of the spurious legislature of Kansas,[2] makes the following request of me: "I respectfully ask for such an explanation of your language upon that occasion as will remove all imputation upon the integrity of my action or motives in connection with that memorial."

The reason assigned for calling upon me to vindicate "the integrity of his actions and motives in connection with that memorial" are that "on Thursday of that week (the week previous to the debate of which he now complains) that memorial was the subject of severe criticism, and in connection with it charges of the most grave character were preferred against me," [your friend, Col. Lane.][3] It is not pretended that I made those charges against him in that debate. The published debate shows that "on Thursday of that week" no less than three or four senators did denounce that memorial as "an impudent forgery, attempted to be palmed off upon the senate of the United States through the hands of the venerable senator from Michigan;"[4] as "a paper which has reached the senate through fraud, which has stamped upon it every mark of forgery;" as "a forgery which has been palmed off on the senate;" and various other denunciations of a like character, all tending to stamp the memorial with fraud and forgery. I did not endorse these grave charges, on the one hand, nor repel them, on the other, for the reason that all the facts then known to the senate seemed to justify a strong suspicion, and, indeed, raise the presumption that they were true, yet the circumstances were not such as to render it my duty to do more than to reject the memorial upon the facts disclosed in the debate. In fact, I followed the lead of the illustrious senator from Michigan, who presented the memorial under the impression that it was a genuine paper by expressing a willingness to vote for his motion to print, as a matter of courtesy to him, so long as it involved no other consideration than the amount of money which the printing would cost. But when its reception and printing became the test of a principle which was to recognize and sanction the revolutionary proceedings in Kansas, I announced my purpose to vote against it for that reason. Subsequently such disclosures were made as to create doubts in the mind of Gen. Cass in respect to the authenticity of the paper, and he, after an interview with Col. Lane, from whom he had received it, made the following announcement to the senate, and voted for the resolution rescinding the action of the senate whereby the memorial was received and referred, and therefore withdrew it. Gen. Cass said:

"Within a few minutes I have had an interview with the gentleman who presented me with the petition, and I am bound to say to the senate that I am not satisfied that this paper is one which ought to be acted upon by the senate. This is all that it is necessary for me to say. I shall vote for the resolution of the senator from Virginia."

After the "memorial" had been denounced by several senators as a fraud and a forgery, and after Gen. Cass had thus announced his purpose to vote for its rejection for the reasons stated, Mr. Seward rose and stated that he had just conversed with Col. Lane on the subject, and he added:

"He tells me, and authorizes me to say, and requests me to say in the senate, as I do in his behalf, that before he left the state of Kansas he saw this paper, the same paper—he does not say that it is the identical paper in chirography—that he saw the memorial of which this is the substance and text, signed by all the members of the provisional legislature of Kansas, and that this is a true copy of that paper, as he had before stated to the honorable senator from Michigan, and I suppose the original is within his reach and available. This is in no substantial respect different."

Mr. Seward also further said that "this statement is due to him; and this statement is all I need say in justice to myself."

In reply to Mr. Seward a senator arose and said:

"I think, Mr. President, this debate will not be without its advantage to the country. We are beginning now to get the truth of this matter slowly, but it would seem securely."

"Where do we stand? A paper has been presented here, palmed upon the senator from Michigan, purporting to be a memorial from certain persons in Kansas who claim to be the senators and representatives of the state of Kansas. It is questioned; its authenticity is doubted; it is denounced as a forgery and a fraud. We learn now that it reached the honorable senator from Michigan at the hand of one who is sent here as a senator from Kansas. We learn from the senator from N.Y. that that paper, thus denounced on this floor as a forgery, and fraudulently done, came to the hands of the senator from Michigan by one of those men who is sent here as senator from the pseudo state of Kansas; and yet there is no man whom I have heard who undertakes to vindicate him. There is no gentleman who stands on this floor and says that the man who brought this paper here is what he claims to be—an honorable man—and that he brought a fair and honest paper. I do not understand the senator from New York to do that. Where are the gentlemen who claim to be here speaking for the oppressed people of Kansas? Sir, *noscitur sociis* is a safe maxim—the man is known by the company he keeps. If it be true that the man is known by the company he keeps, the company is known by the man who helps them."

After further discussion of a similar character, the resolution of Mr. Mason[5] was adopted by a vote of thirty-two in the affirmative to three in the negative, by which the order to refer the fraudulent paper to the committee on territories and printing were rescinded, and the paper was then withdrawn by Gen. Cass and returned to Col. Lane.

I have been thus minute in tracing the outlines of the debate which occurred on the first presentation of this fraudulent memorial, in order to show that I took no part in the discussion which questioned the authenticity of the paper or the conduct of Col. Lane in connection with it. Yet it will be observed that, in the letter which you bore from Col. Lane to me, it is stated, as the first cause of grievance, that "on Thursday of that week that memorial was the subject of severe criticism, and in connexion with it charges of a most grave character are preferred against me"—Col. Lane.

We have seen what these charges were:—They were no less than that of fraud and forgery. These charges were made and repeated by several senators in the course of that debate and received the sanction of the senate by a vote of 32 to [3] in the adoption of Mr. Mason's resolution. Your friend, Col. Lane rested under these charges until the next week, when he attempted to exculpate himself not by calling upon the senators who made the charges, for explanation, but by presenting a petition signed by himself, with the original memorial made a part of it, praying that the pretended copy, which had been rejected on the previous Thursday, might also be received, and inviting a comparison between the two, with a view of enabling the senate to determine whether the one which the senate had rejected was a copy or a forgery. As the chairman of the committee having charge of territorial affairs, it became my appropriate duty to institute the comparison which had been invited by Col. Lane in his petition, and to give the senate the result of my investigation. I found that while the rejected copy purported to be authenticated by the signatures (all in one handwriting) of the members of both houses of that spurious legislature, the original from which it was pretended to have been copied, had no signatures at all attached to it, and no authentication whatever, except an evasive affidavit taken that day before Judge McLean. I also found that the first three pages of the original were entirely suppressed in the pretended copy. I also found many other material omissions and suppressions, many interpolations and alterations, running all through the paper; and changing its whole character, not only in form, but in substance and principle. I exposed these things to the senate in plain and unmeasured terms, as it was my right and duty to do. I did not go out of my way to criminate or exculpate any one.—I dealt with the fraudulent paper as it came before me in the line of my duty, and left the authors of the iniquity free to pursue their own course. I showed that the original memorial, which it is alleged was adopted by the spurious legislature of Kansas, was based on the fundamental idea or principle that congress had no power to establish governments for the territories; that the Kansas-Nebraska act was unconstitutional and void for that reason; that the people of the territories owed no allegiance to the governments which had been or should be established by congress in the territories; and hence they had an inherent right to take the steps which they had taken to overthrow the territorial government without the consent and in defiance of the authority of congress. I also showed that in the pretended copy all this had been suppressed since the issue was made up between the two parties by the reports of the majority and minority of the committee on territories, and in lieu of it had been inserted an humble petition to congress recognizing its authority and praying for its interposition. In short, I showed and proved by a comparison of the two papers that the pretended copy was not a copy in any sense of the word, that it was a spurious fraudulent paper, in other words, that it was a base and impudent forgery. No senator did, no man, in or out of the senate, can vindicate the paper from this just condemnation. The severest judgment which I pronounced on this transaction is contained in the following extracts from my speech, which I now repeat as the only explanation I have to make of the matters to which they refer.

"I submit whether this does not make it a totally different document, affirming entirely different principles, in order to place their action in a totally different light. The Kansas legislature, in the original document, said they justified their acts because congress had no power over them. The memorial came in the other day recognising the power of congress. I ask, then, is it not a forgery thus to change the document in the most vitally important point upon which the whole proceeding rests? I do not say by whom the forgery was committed —I care not. The taint runs through this whole proceeding, and the affidavit does not cure or remedy it. Again:

"I can take up this memorial and show that, as I have exposed one heresy after another of their pretensions, they took the pen and ran through this memorial to get rid of the objection.

"It has been changed from time to time in material points, striking out and inserting until it has hardly a vestige of its original form. The very comparison which is here challenged between the pretended copy, presented the other day, and the original now, proved conclusively that such is the case. I then submit whether here was not evidence of the most glaring fraud ever attempted to be perpetrated upon a legislative body. After that fraud has been once detected and exposed, the question is, whether a second one is to be perpetrated upon us by taking the same spurious document and attaching it to a memorial, and thus dragging it into the senate?"

It should be borne in mind that the first time this fraudulent paper was presented to the senate, I pronounced no judgment upon the question of its authenticity, of the means by which it found its way to the secretary's table. Other senators did denounce it as "fraud and impudent forgery." I remained silent on these points, not from any sympathy with the fraud, but from my profound respect for the feelings of the illustrious senator from Michigan, whose confidence had been abased so far as to induce him to present it under the impression that it was an authentic memorial. When he discovered his mistake, I joined him in that vote of condemnation which the senate pronounced by 32 to 3 in the adoption of Mr. Mason's resolution.

The next week Col. Lane came to the senate, through Mr. Harlan, of Iowa,[6] and presented a memorial, in which he asks and challenges a comparison of the two papers, with the view of inducing the senate to reverse the judgment which had been so emphatically pronounced upon the authors of that fraud, at the same time avowing himself to be the person who perpetrated the act. I did make the comparison in pursuance of the request contained in his memorial, and stated the facts to the senate as I found them to exist, together with my opinions upon them. The senate ratified those opinions in the rejection of the memorial, by a vote of 30 to 11.

In the face of these facts, your friend, Col. Lane, calls upon me "for such an explanation of my language upon that occasion as will remove all imputation upon the integrity of his action or motives in connection with that memorial." My reply is, that there are no facts within my knowledge which can "remove all imputations upon the integrity of his action or motives in connexion with that memorial."

For the reasons which I have stated, I can have no correspondence with Col. Lane, and therefore address this note to you. Your obedient servant,

S. A. Douglas

Springfield *Illinois State Register*, May 5, 1856. Cooper Kinderdine Watson was a Free Soil member of Congress from Ohio from 1855 to 1857.

[1]Lane's letter to Douglas, written on April 18, 1856, had been delivered by Watson. Lane objected strongly to charges made against him by Douglas during a Senate debate and asked Douglas for an explanation. James H. Lane had been a Democratic member of Congress from Indiana from 1853 to 1855. In 1855, he moved to Kansas Territory where he assumed a significant and controversial role in the free-state movement. He was the presiding officer of the Topeka convention which drafted a free-state constitution for Kansas late in 1855. In 1856, he was elected to the United States Senate by the legislature that met according to the Topeka constitution but his election was not recognized.

[2]The "spurious legislature" was the body elected by the free-state element in Kansas under the Topeka constitution. On March 4, 1856, the legislature convened and prepared a memorial to Congress asking the admission of Kansas to the Union as a free state. Lane was commissioned to carry the memorial to the national capital. When it was presented to the Senate on April 7, it was discovered that all the signatures were written in the same handwriting and that the document had been revised following its passage by the legislature. Douglas charged that the memorial was fraudulent and held Lane responsible for the fraud.

[3]The brackets were supplied by Douglas.

[4]Lewis Cass had presented the Topeka memorial to the Senate.

[5]James M. Mason, Senator from Virginia from 1847 to 1861.

[6]James Harlan, Senator from Iowa from 1855 to 1865.

To William L. Marcy

[June 3, 1856, n.p.; ALS, RG-59, National Archives. Recommending that Louis Schade be appointed to a position in the State Department.

In 1855 and 1856, Schade was a Department of State translator. In 1856, he became editor of the Chicago *National Demokrat,* a German-language newspaper devoted to Douglas.]

To William A. Richardson

Washington
Hon W A Richardson June 3d 1856
I send by Telegraph a letter which you can read in the convention or not according to circumstances.

S. A. Douglas

ALS Copy, owned by Martin F. Douglas. In 1856, William A. Richardson repeated his role of four years before, that of leading the Illinois delegation in the Democratic national convention and managing the Douglas strategy. The convention opened at Cincinnati on June 2; the Douglas forces were headquartered at the Burnet House.

To William A. Richardson

Washington
Dear Sir, June 3d 1856
From the Telegraphic reports in the News papers I fear that an embittered state of feeling is being engendered in the convention which may endanger the harmony and success of our Party. I wish you and all my friends to bear in mind that I have a thousand fold more anxiety for the triumph of our principles than for my own personal elevation. If the withdrawal of my name will contribute to the harmony of our Party or the success of the cause I hope you will not hesitate to take the step. Especially it is my desire that the action of the convention will embody and express the wishes, feelings, and principles of the Democracy of the Republic, and hence if Mr Pierce or Mr Buchanan or any other eminent statesman who is faithful to the great issues involved in the contest, shall receive a majority of the convention, I earnestly hope that all of my friends will unite in ensuring him two thirds and then in making his nomination unanymous. Let no personal considerations disturb the harmony of the party or endanger the triumph of our principles.[1]

S. A. Douglas

ALS Copy, owned by Martin F. Douglas. This letter was printed, under date of June 4, 1856, in *Official Proceedings of the National Democratic Convention, Held in Cincinnati, June 2-6, 1856* (Cincinnati, Ohio, 1856), p. 46.
[1]Richardson nominated Douglas on the afternoon of June 5. Fourteen ballots were subsequently taken, the vote on the fourteenth being Buchanan, 152½; Pierce, 75; and Douglas, 63. The convention adjourned, to resume the balloting on June 6. Before the fifteenth ballot, Pierce's name was withdrawn and his support given to Doug-

las. On the sixteenth ballot, Buchanan received 168 votes to Douglas' 122. At this point, Richardson rose and read Douglas' letter. Buchanan was nominated on the next ballot.

To William A. Richardson

[June 5, 1856]

I send another Telegraphic Letter to be used in such manner as shall be deemed best. I leave evrything to the decision of our true friends. It may be well to read these two letters to the convention when the nomination is made, if not sooner.

June 5th 9 *a m*   S. A. DOUGLAS

ALS Copy, owned by Martin F. Douglas.

To William A. Richardson

Dr Sir,   June 5th, 9 *A. M.*

I have just read so much of the Platform as relates to the Nebraska Bill and slavery question. The adoption of that noble resolution by the unanymous vote of all the States accomplishes all the objects I had in view in permitting my name to be used before the convention.[1] If agreeable to my friends I would much prefer exerting all my energies to elect a tried Statesman on that platform to being the nominee myself. At all events do not let my name be used in such manner as to disturb the harmony of the party or endanger the success of the work so nobly begun.

S. A. DOUGLAS

ALS Copy, owned by Martin F. Douglas. Although Douglas suggested that this letter might be read to the convention, it was not done.
[1]The resolution referred to by Douglas declared, "The American Democracy recognize and adopt the principles contained in the organic laws establishing the Territories of Kansas and Nebraska as embodying the only sound and safe solution of the 'slavery question' upon which the great national idea of the people of this whole country can repose in its determined conservatism of the Union—NON-INTERFERENCE BY CONGRESS WITH SLAVERY IN STATE AND TERRITORY, OR IN THE DISTRICT OF COLUMBIA."

To William A. Richardson

June 5th 9½ *P M*

Mr Buchanan, having received a majority of the convention, is, in my opinion, entitled to the nomination.[1] I hope my friends will give effect to the voice of the majority of the Party

S. A. DOUGLAS

ALS Copy, owned by Martin F. Douglas.
[1]On the thirteenth and fourteenth ballots, the last two taken on June 5, Buchanan received a bare majority of the votes cast.

To John Pettit

My Dear Sir,   June 20th 1856

Accept my thanks for your kind letter.[1] I have no grievances growing out of the Cincinnati Convention and nothing to regret so far as
I am personal[ly] concerned. Our duty now demands our undivided
efforts to ensure the triumphant election of the Tickett chosen by the
convention. I take it for granted that Indiana is safe by an overwhelming majority, and will try to give a good account from Illinois.
Present my kind regards to Mrs Pettit. Very truly yours

S. A. DOUGLAS

ALS, Illinois State Historical Library.
John Pettit, of Lafayette, Indiana, had
been a member of Congress from 1843
to 1849 and of the Senate from 1853 to
1855. He was a delegate to the Cincinnati convention.

[1]On June 10, 1856, Pettit wrote to
Douglas, in an attempt to explain why
the Indiana delegation in the Cincinnati convention had voted consistently
for Buchanan. "To the Pennsylvania
Delegates & all others with whom I
conversed," he wrote, "I said my heart
was with Douglas but my head was

with Buchanan, or in other words I
preferred you for President but him
for a candidate, and I know that this
feeling was fully shared & entertained
by a large majority of our Delegates.
. . . The age and experience of Mr.
Buchanan tended not a little to produce
this result, and it was strengthened by
a large infusion of National Whigs
who agree with our platform & will
vote with us, but who begged that we
should give them a man of the olden
time" (Douglas Papers, University of
Chicago Library).

To ———

[June 25, 1856, Washington; AL Copy, owned by Martin F. Douglas.
The signature was omitted. Introducing Arthur G. Rose, of Charleston,
South Carolina, as "a gentleman of high standing and character and
in every respect worthy of your entire confidence."]

To Franklin Pierce

[July 1, 1856, Washington; ALS, RG-59, National Archives. Recommending Samuel P. Armstrong for appointment as United States Consul
at Matamoros, Mexico. Armstrong, a resident of Cincinnati although a
native of Kentucky, received the appointment at Matamoros on
July 21, 1856.]

To J. E. Roy

Washington
Sir,   July 4th 1856

I learn from the Newspapers that on Sunday the 1st day of June
in a Sermon preached by you in the Plymouth Congregational Church

of Chicago, you deemed it your duty to assail me personally and by name.[1] Referring to the affray between Mr. Sumner & Mr. Brooks[2] you say: *"Douglas, of giant Infamy* stood by with his hands in his pockett."

Altho I have no personal acquaintance with you or knowledge of your character as a citizen or minister of the Gospel, my respect for your profession and for those christian principles which it is your duty to proclaim and observe, induce me to take it for granted that you would not knowingly utter an unmitigated falsehood in the Pulpit on the Sabbath day with the intent to injure the character of a fellow citizen, and that, having committed such an act of injustice, you will feel it both a duty and a pleasure to repair the injury in the same place and before the same audience where the injury was done. With the view of enabling you to do me and yourself and the cause of truth the act of justice indicated, I now state to you that it is not true that I stood by with my hands in my pockett at the time—that I was not in the Senate chamber when the affray took place—that I did not witness any part of the transaction—that I was engaged in consultation on public affairs with several Senators and Representatives in another part of the Capital at the time, and had been so engaged for more than an hour previous—that I had no knowledge, intimation or belief that any such transaction was to take place at that or any other time—nor had I any knowledge or reason to believe that either Mr Sumner or Mr Brooks was in or near the capital at the time; and when I returned to the Senate chamber the affray had been over and quiet had been restored for some time. These facts are not only susceptible of proof by the Senators and representatives referred to, but are so well known to the Senate and to the whole community here, that no gentleman would hazard his character for truth and veracity by intimating his belief in the truth of the charge which you, under some strange misapprehension, have made against me in the Pulpit of a christian church on the Sabbath day.

You are also represented as having made another charge against me, equally unfounded and untrue, which I quote from the newspapers, not having seen a copy of the printed Sermon:[3]

"This and the Kansas crime reveal a new step in the policy of slavery; that *physical force* must and shall be used to carry out its measures.—The instigator of all this crime (Douglas) a short time since ventured to divulge the secret policy, when he declared to its first victim, 'We will subdue you sir,' and no one knows but this very thing was in his mind at the time."

In this passage you attribute to me language which I never uttered and a sentiment which I never conceived or harbored. It is true that

the New York Tribune and other unscrupulous partizan sheets attributed to me several months ago the same sentiment, but it is also true,
and the official debates of the Senate attest the fact, that I promptly
denied it in open Senate in the presence of Mr Sumner and all others
to whom it was alledged to have been directed, and not one of them
intimated or pretended, that the charge was true. Yet this same charge
which had been thus branded in open Senate as a base calumny, and
admitted to be such by the silence of all the Senators to whom it was
said to have been directed, is now repeated, after the laps of several
months, in the pulpit of the Plymouth Congregational Church of
Chicago; and made the foundation of a series of inferences equally
unfounded and unjust. I have never advised, or failed to rebuke, a
resort to physical force as a substitute for truth and reason in the
discussion and decision of public questions. Whether the Nebraska
Bill was a crime or a wise and just measure is a question which I have
always held myself ready to discuss calmly and dispassionately on all
proper occasions; and if physical force or mob violence, or any other
improper means have been used to destroy the freedom of speech,
either in Chicago[4] or elsewhere, it has not been approved by me or
my friends. I send this letter to you, instead of the news papers, for
the purpose of giving you an opportunity of doing justice to me and
to the cause of truth, which I trust you will regard a Christian duty,
in the same pulpit where the injury was committed. I have the honor
to be very respectfully your obedient servant

AL Copy, owned by Martin F. Douglas. Reverend J. E. Roy was pastor of
the Plymouth Congregational Church
in Chicago. This letter was published
in the Chicago *Times*, July 17, 1856.

[1]Roy's sermon was printed in pamphlet form and widely distributed
throughout Chicago.

[2]On May 22, 1856, Preston Brooks, a
member of Congress from South Carolina, attacked and caned Senator
Charles Sumner, while the latter sat
at his desk in the Senate chamber.
Brooks had been aroused by Sumner's
uncomplimentary remarks concerning

South Carolina and that state's Senator,
Andrew P. Butler, Brooks's kinsman,
and he determined to avenge the insults. Besides incapacitating Sumner,
the incident served to intensify sectional hostility to a fever pitch.

[3]The following extract from Roy's
sermon was not included in the original manuscript but was printed in the
newspaper version.

[4]Douglas here refers to the mob action which prevented him from defending the Kansas-Nebraska Act in
Chicago in 1854.

To James Washington Sheahan

Washington July 9, 1856

In reply to your enquiry I will state the memorandum or agree-
ment in regard to the German presses[1] was written in my room in the
Masonic Temple and locked up in my desk with other private papers.
No one was left in charge of the desk or papers for the reason that

when I left to canvass the Southern & eastern parts of the states, I expected to have returned to Chicago and to have there taken charge of all my papers. I have no knowledge or suspicion who has stolen the papers, if they have been stolen. The newspapers which published them should be held responsible for the robbery until they show where they got the papers.[2] Persons found in possession of stolen goods are justly held to be the perpetrators of the crime, until they show how they come into such possessions.

The opposition party shall be held accountable for using such means of warfare. It is a public, not a mere private affair, as the crime has been committed for the benefit of a political party and is being used for that purpose. Who is safe when his private desks may be robbed of his private papers, title deeds, letters &c &c. What honorable man can sustain a party which resorts to such means.

Do not allow your energies to be exhausted in a private quarrel, but make war upon the common enemy. I appreciate the difficulties and provocations which surround you, but still the wise course is to fight the common enemy for the triumph of our cause.

Copy, University of Kansas Library. This is not a complete copy.
[1]The agreement to which Douglas had reference was signed by five prominent Chicago Democrats, including Douglas, on September 12, 1855. The signers agreed to loan Michael Diversey $1,000 each, at 10 per cent interest, for the establishment of a Douglas Democratic German-language newspaper in Chicago. The paper was the *National Demokrat*, edited by Dr. Ignatius Koch. It was printed at the Chicago *Times* office.
[2]The newspapers in which the agreement was published were the Chicago *Democrat*, edited by John Wentworth, and the *Illinois Staats Zeitung*, a strong Republican German-language newspaper in Chicago. On July 10, 1856, Sheahan wrote in the Chicago *Times:* "We have heard...that the original agreement (which we have never seen) made by the several parties was left in the possession of Senator Douglas, and was by him locked up in a private drawer, in a desk used by him for keeping his business papers, in an office adjoining and communicating with office No. 6, Masonic Temple, Dearborn street."

To the Office of Indian Affairs

[August 4, 1856, Senate. Refers a letter from J. J. Smith regarding drafts drawn by Edward A. Bedell, former Indian Agent in Utah Territory. Douglas' referral was noted in Register #47 of Letters Received in the Office of Indian Affairs, RG-75, National Archives; the original has not been located.]

To George W. Riggs

[August 31, 1856]

I do hereby authorize George W Riggs to endorse my name on four notes signed by J Knox Walker[1] and one signed by Mr Magoffin now

disposited with Riggs & co for collection and to negociate and collect the same and do whatever is necessary for that purpose in my name.
Aug 31st 1856   S. A. DOUGLAS
Witness
J D Bright[2]

ANS, Library of Congress.
[1]J. Knox Walker was a prominent lobbyist and former private secretary of President James K. Polk.

[2]The word "Witness," as well as Bright's name, are in the hand of Jesse D. Bright, Senator from Indiana.

To Charles H. Lanphier and George Walker

Editors State Register: Joliet, Sep. 5, 1856.
Gen. Cass has authorized me to state that he will be present at the Democratic Mass Meeting to be held in your city on the 18th September.[1] You will please so state in the Register. Yours, &c.,

S. A. DOUGLAS

Springfield *Illinois State Register*, September 8, 1856.
[1]On September 16, 1856, the *State Register* announced that Cass would be unable to come to Springfield.

To Ephraim George Squier

Olney Illinois
My Dear Sir,   Sept 20th 1856
Permit me to introduce to you the bearer of the letter (Henry V. McCall Esq) of New Orleans,[1] who wishes to see you on business connected with Central American Officers. He comes to me highly recommended by several of my most intimate and valued friends as a Gentle man of integrity and honor, and I take great pleasure in introducing him to you as such, and commending him to your confidence and kind offices. I have the honor to remain very truly your obedient servant

S. A. DOUGLAS

ALS, Lincoln National Life Foundation. Ephraim George Squier was a noted archeologist and author of several books dealing with Central America. In 1849, he was Chargé d'Affaires to Central America, and in 1853 con-

ducted a survey for the Honduras Inter-Ocean Railroad.
[1]Henry V. McCall was a prominent New Orleans merchant and sugar planter.

To James Buchanan

Chicago Ills
My Dr Sir,   Sept 29th 1856
It was my intention to have visited you before I returned to the West, but the extra Session deprived me of that pleasure. We are in

the midst of the most exciting contest ever known in this State. The opposition are making desperate efforts, but I think you may rely upon this State with entire certainty. I have no doubt but that we shall give you a handsome and decided majority.[1] All the efforts of our Party should be concentrated on Penn at the State election. If you succeed on the 14th of Oct,[2] the battle is over—if we fail there, we will have a hard fight, but will give you Illinois at all events.

I start in a few moments for the Southern part of the State, and have only time to give assurances of the best wishes of your friend

S. A. Douglas

ALS, Historical Society of Pennsylvania.

[1]Buchanan carried the state of Illinois by more than 9,000 votes, over Fremont, although his vote was less than the Fremont and Fillmore vote combined.

[2]The date of the state election in Pennsylvania. Pennsylvania elected its Democratic state ticket by a small majority.

To James Washington Sheahan

Steam Boat
Nearing off St. Louis
Oct. 6th, 1856

My Dr. Sir:

I have just taken passage for Chester where I speak tomorrow. We had a good meeting at Belleville, and things look well in that county. Our friends feel certain of giving Richardson from 300 to 600 majority in St. Clair and about 3000 in that Congressional District. I have been reading Banks' speech at the Merchants Exchange in Wall Street N. York the 25th of Sept. & published in the N.Y. Times of the 26th.[1]

I send you an extract. You will see that he modifies the issues materially to get the votes of national men. He says the Fremonts do not raise the question whether slavery shall go into any Territories hereafter—That they do not propose to liquidate against the South on Slavery—That they do not propose *any legislation in regard to Kansas*—and hence they do not propose to restore the Missouri Compromise, nor pass the Wilmot Proviso, nor repeal the obnoxious laws, nor remedy any other alledged evils of which they complain.

All they propose to do is to elect Fremont *"so as to allow its people to settle the question for themselves"*. Read the whole speech. You will find it in the Tribune, Herald, & Times of Sept. 26th.

Would it not be well to prepare the minds of your readers for loosing the State election on the 14th of Oct? Benham's friends expect to loose it then, but carry the State by 20,000 in November.[2] We may have to fight against wind & tide after the 14th and hence our friends ought to be prepared for the worst. We must carry Illinois at all hazards and in any event. Your friend,

S. A. Douglas

Copy, University of Kansas Library.

[1] Nathaniel Prentice Banks, a member of Congress from Massachusetts from 1853 to 1857, was Speaker of the House of Representatives during the Thirty-fourth Congress, from 1856 to 1857.

[2] Spencer C. Benham was a Chicago land agent and a close confidant of Douglas. The Democratic state ticket in Illinois, led by William A. Richardson, candidate for governor, was defeated. William H. Bissell, the Republican candidate for governor, defeated Richardson by over 4,700 votes. The state was carried for Buchanan in the November election.

To the Office of Indian Affairs

[December 13, 1856, n.p. Submits letter of W. W. Davis, enclosing the petition of Allen Robinson and heirs, asking permission to sell the land granted to them as Indians. Noted in Register #47 of Letters Received in the Office of Indian Affairs, RG-75, National Archives; the original has not been located.]

To Samuel Treat

(*Confidential*)   Washington
My Dr Sir,   Dec 20th 1856

I have this moment received your letter of Dec 15th. Your previous letter reached here during my absence from the city and I received it a few days ago on my return. In the meantime I have been posting myself up in regard to the probable state of affairs. I do not think that things are in as bad a condition as you seem to consider, and as I confess the circumstances to which you refer would seem to indicate. I learn that the article in the Pennsylvanian was smuggled into that paper by Mr Fisk of Tyler notoriety and that he has been dismissed from [the paper] for that act.[1] I have no reason to believe that Benton is in favor or will be recognized by Mr Buchanan. On the contrary our friends here are in better spirits and look to the future with more hope then when I first arrived in the city. I have been quite active in preparing a movement in your favor and had already set down to write to you and report progress when the mail Boy brought me your letter forbidding the use of your name in any contingency. For, altho you judge rightly when you imagine that the Democracy of Ills sympathize keenly with Richardson in his defeat and are anxious to see him have a place in the Cabinet, and altho I heartilly sympathise with [th]em in that desire and will take great pleasure in doing all in my power to promote his wishes and interests in this respect, yet I do not think that this fact will militate against the propriety or feasibility

[369]

of putting you also into the Cabinet. In the first place I think the North West is entitled to two Cabinet appointments, and the North East to one. This will leave four to the South of whom Missouri may well claim one. By giving three to the North & three to the South, and one to Missouri as an extreme western as well as slave holding State, the geographical division would seem to be fair & just. Besides we may fail in getting a place for Richardson, and in that event we must have you. The indications are more favorable for him to go abroad than to receive a Cabinet appointment.[2] Under these circumstances I still insist that you must allow your name to be used as your friends here shall determine provided the policy of the administration is to be such as will make it proper and agreeable for you to be in the Cabinet. My present impression is that the Cabinet will be one with which and with whose policy you can harmonize with honor & pleasure. If so you must not restrain the action of your friends in your behalf. If on the Contrary our hopes in this respect shall prove adverse Col Richardson would be bound to decline on the same grounds that would control your action. I will not forget or neglect the Judiciary Bill to which you allude.[3] You may rely upon my best efforts in that respect.

But I repeat that you must leave me at Liberty to use your name in the other matter in the contingencies to which I have refered. It is not improbable that all may depend upon the right use of your name at the right time. Do not act rashly. Wait the developement of things, and let us survey the whole ground before we take a decisive step which may prove to be a false one. Had I written a few days ago I should have shared to some extent in your missgivings, but now the signs look brighter altho the mist still obscures the vision. I will write you again in a few days. I repeat, do not act hastily. Write me in full in entire confidence and give me your views of men and things. Truly your friend

S. A. DOUGLAS

ALS, Missouri Historical Society.

[1]Fisk was a member of the editorial staff of the Philadelphia *Pennsylvanian*. He was probably Theophilus Fisk, who two years later was assistant editor of the Philadelphia *Argus*. The article in question praised Thomas Hart Benton and endorsed his efforts to regain his Senate seat in Missouri. Treat, a member of the anti-Benton faction in Missouri, interpreted this endorsement as having been inspired by Buchanan. Treat wrote on December 30, 1856, in answer to Douglas' letter, that Fisk was not responsible for the article but that it had been inserted by William Rice, the editor of the *Pennsylvanian* (Treat Papers, Missouri Historical Society).

[2]Richardson was appointed Governor of Nebraska Territory, and served from January to December, 1858, when he resigned the office.

[3]A bill to divide Missouri into two judicial districts was discussed in Congress later in the session. This may be the bill referred to by Douglas. Treat was appointed a Federal district judge in 1857.

To John A. McClernand

Washington
Dec 23d 1856

My Dear Colonel,

I regret that I could not have met you at Chicago after the election as we had arranged when I last saw you. In regard to the land business to which we then directed our attention, I did nothing as there was not time to attend to it, and next Summer will do just as well. I would have been glad of the opportunity of advising with you in regard to political movements, both State and National. If there is anything in which I can gratify yourself or friends you must not hesitate to confer with me freely and in entire confidence. Will you not visit Washington at the Inauguration? Your position at the Seat of government[1] will enable you to cast your eye over the whole State and by your advice to give the right direction to the efforts of all our friends. What course will the national Whigs pursue now that the issue is distinctly made up between Fremont abolitionism on the one side and Constitutional–law-abiding-Union-loving men under the Democratic banner on the other side. So long as this issue is pending there can be no third party. Will not the Union men of the old Whig party go with us? Your position is favorable to aid in bringing about a cordial & honorable Union of all men who agree in principle to unite their efforts in the promotion of a common cause.

Let me hear from you on all points which concern the interest and welfare of the Democratic Party. Present my kind and respectful salutations to your good Lady and believe your friend truly

S. A. DOUGLAS

ALS, Illinois State Historical Library.
[1] In 1856, McClernand moved to Springfield, Illinois.

To ——

Washington
Jan'y 20th 1857

Gentlemen,

Accept my sincere thanks for your kind letter of invitation to be present at a Complimentary Dinner to be given to the Hon John B Weller[1] by citizens of California at the Kirkwood House on Thursday the 22d inst. I regret that a previous engagement, which I am not at liberty to disregard, will deprive me of the pleasure of assembling with you around the festive board on that occasion for the purpose of manifesting our regard and admiration for the character, talents and public services of a friend who has been my associate in both Houses of Congress and who has rendered the country such signal services in the field as well as the Council Chamber.

AL Copy, owned by Martin F. Douglas.

¹John B. Weller was a member of Congress from Ohio from 1839 to 1845, and United States Senator from California from 1852 to 1857. During the Mexican War, he served as a lieutenant colonel and colonel. From 1858 to 1860, he was Governor of California.

To James Buchanan

[January 28, 1857, n.p.; AES, RG-59, National Archives. Endorsement by Douglas on Sterling Price to James Buchanan, January 28, 1857, Brunswick, Missouri, concurring in Price's recommendation of Dr. Don C. Roberts, of Schuyler County, Missouri, for appointment as secretary to one of the territories. Roberts was a member of the Missouri state legislature. Sterling Price, a member of Congress from Missouri from 1845 to 1846, was at this time Governor of Missouri.]

To Samuel Treat

(*Private*)   Washington
My Dr Sir   Feby 5th 1857

Your kind letter is just received. Mr Buchanan has been here to consult & has returned to determine upon his Cabinet. I had a full & free conversation with him at his own request. He was diplomatic, and under all the circumstances the inference is irresistable that the patronage for the North West was disposed of before the nomination. Bright is the man who is to control it if they dare to carry out their designs. Slidel,¹ Bright & Corcoran (the Banker) assume the right to dispose of all the patronage. If this purpose is carried out & I am the object of attack I shall fight all my enemies and neither ask nor give quarter. I do not decline to urge friends, provided the opportunity is presented to do so under any prospect of success. At present, I am an out sider. My advice is not coveted nor will my wishes probably be regarded. I want nothing by [but] fair play. I ask nothing for myself. I want only a fair share for my friends. I desire the bold true men who fought the battle to be sustained. If this can be done I am content. If on the contrary the power of the administration is to be used either for plunder or ambition I shall return every blow they may give. Do not thing from the tone of this scrawl that I am discouraged. By no means. I am only in doubt, and prepared for any result. Very truly your friend

S. A. DOUGLAS

ALS, Missouri Historical Society.

¹John Slidell was United States Senator from Louisiana from 1853 to 1861. Both Bright and Slidell wielded strong influence in the Buchanan administration.

To James W. Singleton

(*Confidential*)   Washington
My Dear Sir,   Feby 14th 1857

Your kind letter of the 9th inst is duly received. In reply I can inform you that I have not declined being a candidate for the U.S. Senate in favor of the person named by you nor of any other person.[1] It is my purpose to submit my conduct to the approval or disapproval of the Democracy of the State for relection by the next Legislature. I am at a loss to know the meaning of your allusion and shall be glad to hear from you in full and in entire confidence. Very truly your friend

S. A. Douglas

ALS, Illinois State Historical Library.

[1]On February 9, 1857, Singleton wrote to Douglas, asking if Douglas had declined being a candidate for re-election to the United States Senate in favor of Governor Joel A. Matteson (owned by Martin F. Douglas).

To Thomas A. Hendricks

Senate U.S.

My Dr Sir,   Feby 17th 1857

Permit me to ask leave of absence for John Calhoun Esq. Surveyor General of Kansas & Nebraska, to visit his family at Springfield Ills. He has been constantly at his post in Kansas for nearly twelve months without visiting his family or attending to his private affairs, and a temporary absence is now indispensable for the reasons stated. I should [have] applied for this permission sooner as some weeks have now elapsed since he made the application through me. His present application seems to me so reasonable, in view of his strict attention to business, that I cannot doubt that you will take pleasure in granting it at once. Very truly your friend

S. A. Douglas

ALS, owned by Philip D. Sang, River Forest, Illinois.

To Thomas G. Young

Washington

My Dr Sir   Feby 22d 1857

I have just rec'd a letter from my friend T M Howell[1] enclosing a print and one from yourself respecting the P. O. in your place. It will afford me great pleasure to render you any service in my power, but I fear my right to interfere out side of my own state will not be recognized by the new administration. The Congressmen elect & leading men of the party in your own state will undoubtedly have control of the appointments and hence I would advise that you secure all the active cooperation you can in your own state. With this view I have advised our friend Howell to be here at the Inauguration or soon after to concentrate as much influence as he can in your behalf. Wishing you success I remain very truly your friend

S. A. DOUGLAS

ALS, William Henry Smith Memorial Library, Indiana Historical Society. Thomas G. Young has not been identified.
[1]Thomas M. Howell, one of Douglas' former classmates, was a lawyer in Canandaigua, New York.

To James Washington Sheahan

Washington Feby. 23rd, 1857

I have read your letter of the 26th inst. and fully appreciate the kind feelings which prompted it. The ridiculous story about Snowhook[1] and Cook is without a particle of foundation. I have no fear of any disclosure that anybody [may] have to make. If our friends would cease their personal quarrels and fight the common enemy of our principles with the same zeal & energy that they now fight one another, our party would be in the ascendant. If we fail to carry the State, we will owe our defeat to these miserable petty quarrels, strifes, and dissentions in our own ranks and not to the strength or skill of the abolitionists & Know Nothings. I shall not become a party to these feuds nor suffer myself to become the instrument of any faction to divide and destroy the party. I see no good cause for the present disorganized and demoralized condition of the party in Chicago. It is a melancholy spectacle to see the party which carried the Flag victorious in a fair fight with the combined enemies one year ago, so totally disorganized and demoralized that they are afraid to hold a convention or make a nomination at this time.

Never did a party throw away its favour & waste its strength so foolishly & uselessly by personal quarrels, resentments and desire for revenge. If this course is persisted in the consequences are obvious and inevitable. No party, no matter how patriotic its men, and how fine its principles can survive such a suicidal course.

In regard to the Post Office,[2] I have arrived at no conclusion. When the time comes for action I shall act promptly and for the best interest of the party and leave consequences to take care of themselves. Unless our friends will be more forbearing and conciliatory, and exert themselves to promote the unity & harmony of the party and the success of our principles, as predominant to all personal prejudices and jealous victory, and we will have nobody to blame but ourselves.[3]

[374]

Copy, University of Kansas Library. This is not a complete copy. [1]William B. Snowhook was Chicago Collector of Customs from 1853 to 1858. [2]Isaac Cook was removed as Postmaster of Chicago in March, 1857. [3]The wording of this last sentence indicates that several words may have been omitted in copying the letter.

To James Buchanan

[N.d., n.p.; LS, RG-59, National Archives. Recommending the appointment of John A. McClernand for appointment as Minister to Russia. The recommendation was also signed by Illinois Congressmen Thomas Langrell Harris, Isaac N. Morris, Robert Smith, Samuel Scott Marshall, and former Congressman James C. Allen. McClernand had served in the House of Representatives from 1843 to 1851, and had not been a candidate for renomination in 1850. His appointment to the office asked in this letter was not made. This and the following undated letters were probably written in March, 1857.]

To James Buchanan

[N.d., n.p.; LS, RG-59, National Archives. Recommending the appointment of Lafayette McCrillis, of Jerseyville, Illinois, to a first-class consulship. The recommendation was also signed by Harris, Smith, Marshall, and Allen. It was probably written in March, 1857. McCrillis was a member of the state legislature from 1854 to 1856, and early in 1858 was made a director of the Cairo and Fulton Railroad. The appointment was not made.]

To James Buchanan

[N.d., n.p.; LS, RG-59, National Archives. Recommending the appointment of William A. Richardson to a "first class mission." The recommendation was signed also by Harris, Smith, Allen, Morris, Marshall, and J. L. D. Morrison. Morrison had been elected to the House of Representatives to fill the vacancy in the Thirty-fourth Congress caused by the resignation of Lyman Trumbull, and served only from November, 1856, to March, 1857. Richardson had been the Democratic candidate for Governor of Illinois in 1856, but was defeated by William H. Bissell. He served as Governor of Nebraska Territory in 1858, although earlier, on September 7, 1857, President Buchanan wrote to Douglas, "I am truly sorry that Mr. Richardson did not accept the appointment of Governor of Nebraska; & after what passed between us, I was astonished to learn that he had been offended at the office" (owned by Martin F. Douglas).]

To James Buchanan

[N.d., n.p.; LS, RG-59, National Archives. Recommending the appointment of John P. Richmond, of Schuyler County, Illinois, for appointment to a first-class consulate. Richmond had been Speaker of the Illinois House of Representatives, a member of the state Senate, and a Presidential elector on the Buchanan ticket in 1856. The recommendation is also signed by Harris, Morris, Smith, Marshall, and Aaron Shaw. Shaw, of Crawford County, Illinois, had been a member of the state House of Representatives from 1850 to 1852. The appointment was not made.]

To Lewis Cass

[March 9, 1857, Washington; ALS. This letter has not been located. It is described in *A Catalogue of Lincolniana*, Thomas F. Madigan, New York, p. 43, #93. Recommending David T. Disney for a foreign diplomatic post, Douglas wrote in part: "Mr. Disney was for many years a distinguished member of Congress, and earned and maintained the reputation of one of the ablest men in the country. He is an accomplished scholar, a sound and reliable politician, a gentleman in all respects worthy of your confidence and esteem, and I should be particularly and especially gratified if you can grant the wishes of his friends." Disney was offered the appointment of Minister to Spain by President Buchanan but declined. He died soon after this letter was written, on March 14, 1857. Lewis Cass was Secretary of State in Buchanan's cabinet.]

To James Buchanan

[March 9, 1857, Washington; LS, RG-59, National Archives. Recommending the appointment of Henry A. Clark, a Chicago attorney and author, to a European consulate, preferably one on the Mediterranean. The recommendation was also signed by Harris, Morrison, Marshall, Allen, Morris, and Smith. The appointment was not made.]

To Howell Cobb

[March 9, 1857, Washington; LS, RG-56, National Archives. Asking that John S. Hacker, Collector at the port of Cairo, Illinois, be furnished with an office. Howell Cobb was Secretary of the Treasury in Buchanan's cabinet.]

To Lewis Cass

[March 12, 1857, Washington; ALS, RG-59, National Archives. Recommending the appointment of Patrick Golden, of Bangor, Maine, as United States Consul in Belfast, and asking Cass to "urge upon the President the propriety of his appointment." The appointment was not made.]

To James Buchanan

[N.d., n.p.; LS, Library of Congress. Recommending the appointment of Augustus M. Herrington, of Geneva, Kane County, Illinois, to the office of United States Attorney for the Northern District of Illinois. The recommendation was also signed by Marshall, Allen, Smith, Harris, and Morris. The recommendation was endorsed "Respectfully referred to the Atty General Dept of State 13th Mar. '57." Herrington, a Geneva attorney, had been a Democratic Presidential elector in 1856. He was appointed United States Attorney, but was later removed by Buchanan, reportedly because of his friendship for Douglas.]

To James Buchanan

[N.d., n.p.; AES, RG-59, National Archives. Endorsement on James Stephen Green et al. to James Buchanan, March 13, 1857, Washington City, concurring in the recommendation of Dr. Don C. Roberts for appointment as Secretary of Utah Territory. Green was United States Senator from Missouri. See also above, January 28, 1857.]

To Jeremiah Black

[March 19, 1857, Washington; LS, Illinois State Historical Library. Recommending the appointment of Augustus M. Herrington as United States Attorney for the Northern District of Illinois. Jeremiah Black, of Pennsylvania, was Attorney General in Buchanan's cabinet.]

To John B. Floyd

Saturday
My Dr Sir, March 21st 1857
This will be handed to you by my friend Elisha E Camp of Illinois who has been unanimously recommended by the Illinois delegation in Congress for a Leutenancy in the Army. He has seen a good deal of military service for a man of his age, having served in the Mexican War

as Leutenant in the 3d Dragoons (Temporary Army) and also having been since attached to the army as sutler. I understand that he has performed all his duties in the service with fidelity and honor, and would now like to enter the permanent army. His friends in Illinois take great interest in his success, and *I am particularly anxious to have him appointed.* Will you do me the favor to bear this matter in mind and give him the first vacancy if possible.[1] Very truly your friend

S. A. DOUGLAS

ALS, Illinois State Historical Library. John B. Floyd, of Virginia, was Secretary of War in Buchanan's cabinet.
[1] Elisha E. Camp was appointed Second Lieutenant of Infantry in May, 1857.

To [Horatio King?]

Tuesday night
My Dr Sir,   March 24th
Will you do me the favor to call & see me tonight. My Doctor will not allow me to go out at night, or I would come & see you. I desire to see you for a moment at any hour tonight. Your friend

S. A. DOUGLAS

ALS, Library of Congress. Since this letter is in the Horatio King Papers, it was probably written to King. Horatio King, of Maine, was First Assistant Postmaster General in Buchanan's cabinet.

To Lewis Cass

[March 27, 1857, n.p.; ALS, RG-59, National Archives. Supporting the recommendations for the appointment of Edward H. Wright, of New York, as Minister to Holland. Douglas wrote that "next to our Illinois recommendations to which I always give the preference, there is no one whose appointment would give me more pleasure." Wright had earlier been secretary of the legation in St. Petersburg, Russia. The appointment asked by Douglas was not made.]

To Lewis Cass

Washington
Dear Sir,   April 1st 1857
I herewith enclose a letter from John Ralli, U.S. Consul at Odessa in Russia.[1] He desires to retain the office and be permitted to continue his business as a merchant. I know him quite well, and take pleasure in assuring you that in my opinion the best interests of our country and especially of our countrymen abroad, require that he retain the office. It is a place of no profit and only valuable to him as a business man for

the protection it affords. Mr. Ralli is exceedingly polite, kind, and hospitable to all Americans visiting Odessa, and spends in that way and has done so for the last 25 years more than ten times the fees. I feel grateful to him for his attentions and services to me while in that Country, and feel a lively interest in his behalf.

Will you have the kindness to return me his letter and inform me what answer I may return to Mr. Ralli. Very respectfully your obt sevt.

S. A. DOUGLAS

ALS, RG-59, National Archives.
[1]John Ralli, a native of Odessa, was United States Consul at that place from 1831 to 1861.

To Lewis Cass

[April 7, 1857, n.p.; ALS, RG-59, National Archives. Recommending the appointment of General Ward B. Burnett as a commissioner "under the Reciprocity Treaty concerning the Brittish possessions." Burnett, a graduate of West Point, had been Dry Dock Superintendent at the Philadelphia and Brooklyn Navy Yards and Chief Engineer of the Brooklyn and Norfolk Water Works. The position asked for Burnett by Douglas was provided for in the "Treaty Regarding the North Atlantic Fisheries, Commercial Reciprocity with British North American Colonies, and Navigation of the St. Lawrence River, Lake Michigan, and Other Waters," signed in 1854 by Great Britain and the United States. Burnett was not appointed to this post, but in 1858 received appointment as Surveyor General of Kansas and Nebraska territories, succeeding John Calhoun.]

To Lewis Cass

[April 9, 1857, Washington; ALS, RG-59, National Archives. Recommending the appointment of Henry Owner, of California, as United States Consul at Tahiti. Owner was appointed Consul for Tahiti and the Society Islands in May, 1858, but held the post only until the following December, his appointment being rejected by the Senate.]

To Lewis Cass

[April 10, 1857, Washington; ALS, RG-59, National Archives. Recommending the appointment of Charles A. Leake as United States Consul in Cuba. Leake was at this time an officer in the United States Army in California. He was not appointed to the consulate.]

To James Buchanan

[April 14, 1857, n.p.; AES, RG-59, National Archives. Endorsement on Isaac Roland Diller to James Buchanan, n.d., n.p., in which Diller asked for appointment as United States Consul in Callao, Peru; Valparaiso, Chile; Lahaina, Sandwich Islands; or as Minister to Bolivia. Diller was Postmaster at Springfield from 1853 to 1857; as soon as his commission expired he was replaced. On March 24, 1857, he wrote to Douglas asking appointment to a foreign mission, preferably Naples, Portugal, or Switzerland (University of Chicago Library).]

To James Buchanan

[N.d., n.p.; AES, RG-59, National Archives. Endorsement on Isaac Roland Diller to James Buchanan, n.d., n.p., concurring in Diller's request for appointment as United States Consul at Bremen. Diller was appointed to the Bremen consulate in June, 1857, and held that post until 1861. His letter to Buchanan, on which Douglas' endorsement appeared, was probably written sometime after April 14 and before June, 1857.]

To James Buchanan

Washington
Sir,   April 25th 1857

Permit me to call your attention to the application of Elisha E Camp of Illinois for a 2d Liutenancy in the U.S. Army. While a mere Boy he enlisted as a private in the 2d Dragoons, that being the only mode by which he could participate in the Mexican War. After several months services in the ranks & as Sergent, he was promoted for gallant conduct to a 2d Liutenancy in the 3d Dragoons with whom he served to the close of the war, when the regiment was disbanded.

Since that time he has had three general warrants as sutler and under them served five years in Oregon and California. He now desires to return to the Army as 2d Liutenant, being the same rank he held during the Mexican War. Aside from his own services he might urge the military services of his father and grand father, but prefers to rely upon his own claims.

Permit me to express the great interest I feel in his appointment.
S. A. Douglas

ALS, Illinois State Historical Library. See above, Douglas to Floyd, March 21, 1857.

To John A. McClernand

Washington
My Dr Sir,   April 26th 1857

I received your letter two days ago in reference to the reappointment of our friend Capt Hunt.[1] I had supposed that the appointment had already been made, but went directly to the P.O. Dept and found that no action had taken place, but the Post Master General[2] assured me that Capt Hunt should be reappointed immediately. I presume he will receive his commission in a few days. Nothing is yet known about the foreign appointments. The President & Sec'y of State both tell me that they will not consider the subject for several weeks. Of course I can form no opinion what they intend to do. I shall leave for Chicago direct this week. Very truly your friend

S. A. DOUGLAS

ALS, Illinois State Historical Library.
[1]Samuel Hunt, former trustee of the Illinois Institution for Education of the Blind, was appointed Postmaster of Jacksonville, Illinois. Thomas Hunt, former captain in the Illinois militia and member of the state legislature, was appointed Postmaster of Ridott, Stephenson County, Illinois.
[2]Aaron V. Brown of Tennessee.

To Benjamin Franklin Angel

My Dr Sir,   Washington April 29, 1857.

As I am about to leave the city for my home in the West, I desire to say to you that I should be gratified at your appointment to some suitable mission abroad, and that last night in a frank and agreeable interview with the President I took occasion to say to him that I thought injustice had been done you by your rejection by the Senate, and that inasmuch as I had been in some degree instrumental in producing that result, I should be gratified at the opportunity of repairing the injury by moving your confirmation for a higher position. I also expressed to the President the deep interest our friend Judge Treat felt in your appointment. I am perfectly satisfied that the Explanations which have since been made if made to the Senate at the time, would have insured your unanimous confirmation instead of producing your rejection. I take pleasure in making this voluntary statement and shall be gratified if it shall in any degree aid in securing the appointment your friends are asking for you. Very truly your friend

S. A. DOUGLAS

Copy, RG-59, National Archives. Benjamin Franklin Angel, of Geneseo, New York, was United States Consul in Honolulu from 1853 to 1855, and Special United States Commissioner to China in 1855. In 1858, he was appointed Minister to Norway and Sweden, a post he held until 1862.

To James Buchanan

[May 10, 1857, Chicago; ALS, RG-59, National Archives. Recommending O. J. Rose, of Chicago, for appointment as United States Consul in Frankfort, Germany. Rose was a Chicago alderman from 1852 to 1853. He was not appointed to the consulate. See below, Douglas to Cass, January 2, 1858.]

To Lewis Cass

Chicago

My Dear General   May 11th 1857

Permit me to call your attention to the application of our friend Grund[1] for the Mission to Switzerland or the Consulate at Paris. I must confess that it seems almost senseless to remind you of a matter which I have become to know you have quite as much at heart as I have, yet the multiplicity of your public duties and engagements, render it impossible for you at all times to bear in mind all the obligations resting on you. You know the circumstances under which Mr Grund was induced to spend so much time in canvassing the frontier German settlements at the West, and you can bear testimony to the ability, fidelity, & efficiency with which he performed the duty. I think you will agree with me that it is a point of honor so far as Messrs Slidel & Bright, yourself & myself are concerned to see that a suitable place is tendered to him if it is in our form to command it. I must rely upon [you] however to represent me in this matter, having the fullest confidence in the kind feeling and good purposes of the President towards me. Mr. Grund is one of my constituents as well as my friend and I take pleasure in presenting him in both capacities. Public feeling towards the President & Cabinet in this part of the country is all that could be desired and much more flattering than we had a right to expect, judging from the vote at the Presidential Election. I shall be glad to hear from you. Your friend

S. A. Douglas

ALS, RG-59, National Archives.

[1]Francis J. Grund, born near Vienna, emigrated to the United States in 1827. Before his appointment in 1854 as United States Consul in Antwerp, Grund was a Philadelphia journalist and political correspondent of the Philadelphia *Public Ledger*. He held the Antwerp consulate from 1854 to 1860. Grund was the author of *The Americans in Their Moral, Social and Political Relations* (London, 1837).

To Lewis Cass

[May 16, 1857, Chicago; ALS, RG-59, National Archives. Recommending the appointment of Reverend Chauncey Eddy as United States

Consul in Beirut. Eddy was the brother of Dr. A. D. Eddy, a Chicago physician. The appointment was not made.]

To Lewis Cass

[May 16, 1857, Chicago; ALS, RG-59, National Archives. Recommending the appointment of Samuel Petersburger, a native-born German and a resident of Rockford, Illinois, to the post of United States Consul at Stuttgart. The appointment was not made.]

To Lewis Cass

[May 18, 1857, Chicago; ALS, RG-59, National Archives. Recommending Francis Frank, of Stephenson County, Illinois, for appointment "to some German Consulate." The appointment was not made.]

To Thomas A. Hendricks

[May 21, 1857, Chicago; ALS, RG-49, National Archives. Enclosing two duplicate receipts for land entered at the Chicago Land Office by Reverend Ichabod Clark of Rockford, Illinois, and asking that the patents for the land be sent to Mr. Clark immediately.]

To Lewis Cass

[May 22, 1857, Chicago; ALS, RG-59, National Archives. Recommending Augustus Weihe, a Chicago notary public, for appointment to a German consulate. The appointment was not made.]

To John Potts

Senate Chamber
Dr Sir,   Wednesday [May, 1857]
In reply to your note I have the honor to furnish the "Chicago Times" as the Newspaper in Chicago, which alone of all the papers printed in the English language, in that City is deserving of the patronage of the Federal Government. I recommend that paper for all advertisements in that part of the country. Very respectfully
S. A. DOUGLAS

ALS, RG-107, National Archives. The letter was undated but an endorsement indicates that it was received by the War Department in May, 1857. John Potts was chief clerk of the War Department.

To James Buchanan

[June 18, 1857, n.p.; AES, RG-59, National Archives. Endorsement on Nathaniel Paschall to James Buchanan, June 14, 1857, St. Louis, recommending the appointment of Henry A. Clark to a consulate. Paschall was editor of the St. Louis *Republican*. For Douglas' earlier recommendation of Clark's appointment, see above, March 9, 1857.]

To Lewis Cass

[June 23, 1857, Chicago; ALS, RG-59, National Archives. Recommending that Frederick W. Behn be retained as United States Consul at Messina, Kingdom of the Two Sicilies. Behn held the Messina consulate from 1848 to 1849 and from 1854 to 1859.]

Adele Cutts Douglas to her Mother

Chicago—

My dearest Mother   Wednesday June 24th

I have been thinking so much of home to-night and have just got a chance to write you after having talked myself to death over some very stupid women who honored me by calling socially—the object of most interest now in Chicago is a number of robberies which have set the world nearly crazy here and alarm me terribly of course all very needless they say—last night we had a serenade but a serenade looses its charm when you are obliged to ask the musicians in the house & give them a drink—which entirely destroys the sentiment. We dine here at 2 OC. and commence visiting at 11—the distances are so magnificent that I am kept busy from morning till night returning calls & somebody always to dinner so dear Mamma you see how little rest I have here to be very honest with you but you must never mention that I say so. I shall never breath freely in this atmosphere—you can never imagine until you come here how forlorn one feels after being accustomed to interesting & very refined people & how terribly ugly & dirty this City is. It has rained now for a fortnight & the roads are worse than any you can imagine—I am counting the days when I shall return—dear Mamma please write me what Mary the washerwoman has been doing to offend you—I got a note from her which I enclose to you together with $40 for Isaacs wages or Marys if it is convenient —I have not answered this note at all—but I wish you would speak to Father O'Toole about it—please write me about all you are doing and how every one is getting along in Washington. Does anyone remember me—I feel quite like an out cast & when you write about the friends and amusements at Washington I wish myself back in the old house on the hill. I enclose the money inside of the note from Mary—the children are well & happy they send a great deal of love to Grand Ma & Grand Pa and Mr. Douglas sends you his best love. I saw Corcoran at St Louis but he did not come to see me in Chicago. Gerrit Smith[1] dined with us yesterday & I went to hear him lecture though Douglas did not go of course. I was astonished at his Ultra views. Give my love to Mrs. Graham & ask if she got my letter & tell me if [Flan?] has returned. Ask Jeannie to write me. I am so anxious to hear some news of Washington. Good night dearest Mother best love to Papa & a thousand kisses to you. Your devoted daughter—

ADDIE DOUGLAS

Maddie[2] is well & seems content he is out tonight visiting some ladies please burn my letters. Don't let Papa keep them because I write many things I should not except in great confidence. I am trying to like this place but it is very difficult.

ALS, Chicago Historical Society. Adele Cutts Douglas was Douglas' second wife. Her father was James Madison Cutts, a nephew of Dolley Madison, and her mother was a member of the prominent Neale family of Maryland and a sister of the famous Mrs. Rose Neale Greenhow. Adele was raised in Washington, D.C., where her father held a government clerkship. A devout Roman Catholic, she married Stephen A. Douglas in a Catholic church on November 20, 1856, just prior to her twenty-first birthday.

[1]Gerrit Smith was a prominent New York abolitionist and member of Congress from 1853 to 1854, when he resigned his seat.

[2]James Madison Cutts, Jr., Adele's brother.

To Lewis Cass

[June 25, 1857, Chicago; ALS, RG-59, National Archives. Recommending Thomas Francis Meagher "for a suitable foreign appointment." Meagher, born in Ireland, had been an Irish revolutionary before his banishment to Tasmania in 1849. In 1852, he escaped to the United States, where he became a leader of the Irish element in New York and editor of the *Irish News*. In 1865, he was appointed Secretary and Acting Governor of Montana Territory.]

To Thomas B. Bryan

Washington
My Dr Sir,   July 11th 1857
I enclose to you a Deed for a Lot to Mr Healy[1] in accordance with an understanding with him. Not knowing where Mr H now is I send it to you with the request that you will deliver it to him. Tell Mr Healy that I will arrange all matters to his satisfaction when we meet. Very truly yours

S. A. DOUGLAS

ALS, Chicago Historical Society. Thomas B. Bryan was a Chicago attorney.

[1]George Peter Alexander Healy was an eminent portrait painter and resident of Chicago. He painted many leading figures of his day, including Cass, Audubon, Lincoln, Grant, Sherman, and, in 1857, Douglas.

To Lewis Cass

[July 16, 1857, n.p.; Copy, RG-59, National Archives. Letter attached to Joseph B. Austin to Lewis Cass, July 14, 1857, Chicago, in which Douglas attested to the reliability of Austin's character. Austin, a former United States Consul at Ciudad Bolivar, Venezuela, recommended the appointment of Juan Bautista Dalla-Costa, an American-educated merchant in Ciudad Bolivar, to that position. The appointment was not made.]

To Isaac Toucey

[July 16, 1857, Chicago; ALS, Chicago Historical Society. Recommending the appointment of Joseph B. Danforth, editor of the Rock Island (Illinois) *Argus*, for a pursership in the United States Navy. Isaac Toucey, of Connecticut, was Secretary of the Navy in Buchanan's cabinet. Danforth received his appointment and, after service off the African coast, resigned in October, 1858, to return to his newspaper. For a second letter recommending Danforth's appointment, see below, July 26, 1857.]

To Robert J. Walker

Chicago

My Dear Sir,   July 21st '57

I have just read your Proclamation to the people of Lawrence.[1] You have placed the Rebels[2] clearly in the wrong, and the whole country will sustain you in maintaining the supremacy of the laws. The justice of your course in insisting upon refering the constitution[3] to the people for ratification before it should be put in operation is so apparent that it has commanded the approbation of the whole country, with the exception of a small party at the South, and they are even now beginning to retrace their steps and join in their adhesion. The outbreak at the South was not produced so much by your course, as by the dissatisfaction felt by the formation of the Cabinet and the distribution of the patronage. They were in fact dissatisfied with the national administration, and seized upon the Kansas question as a pretext, and made you the scape goat. But the present state of the question will compel them to rally under your banner and vindicate your course from the beginning. I have never hesitated to express the opinion that the consti-

[386]

tution ought to be refered to the people for ratification. In fact you will recollect that we discussed that very point when you were here on your way to Kansas, and fully agreed on the course to be pursued. The only difficulty I have apprehended, was to define the qualifications of voters. But upon reflection I saw that it would be easy enough to determine that point, by first defining the qualifications of voters, in the constitution, for Governor, Legislature &c, and then provide that the same persons should be authorized to vote on the ratification of the constitution, who, by its terms, were qualified to vote for Governor, Legislature, & other officers to be elected under it. This rule would exclude all persons who have or shall rush into the Territory for the mere purpose of voting, but without intending to become permanent inhabitants of Kansas. The object should be to refer the constitution to the bona fide inhabitants of the Territory for their free acceptance or rejection, and to exclude all such as have gone there temporarily, for the mere purpose of participating in the contest, without becoming permanent citizens.

That the convention will adopt some just rule upon this subject and form such a constitution as a majority of the people will ratify I have never doubted. I take it for granted that the abolition or Republican party will vote against any constitution that may be made, even if it were a literal copy of their Topeka constitution;[4] but here they will find themselves in difficulty, for they cannot vote on the Constitution without recognizing the validity of the Territorial government under whose authority the convention is to assemble. If they do not vote, of course the new constitution will be adopted without serious oposition, but if they do vote, I still have faith that the law & order party[5] will be able to out vote them & adopt the constitution. It is all important that the convention shall make such a constitution as the people will ratify, and thus terminate the controversy. Write to me fully and in the fullest confidence. Very truly your friend

S. A. Douglas

ALS, New-York Historical Society, New York. Robert J. Walker, a native of Pennsylvania who had moved to Mississippi early in life, had been a member of the United States Senate from 1835 to 1845 and Secretary of the Treasury in President Polk's cabinet. In March, 1857, he was appointed Governor of the strife-torn Kansas Territory by President Buchanan. Persuaded that he could perform genuine national service by bringing order out of the chaos that characterized Kansas territorial affairs, Walker accepted the appointment partly at the urging of Douglas, one of his close friends. In his letter of acceptance, he expressed as one of the conditions of his appointment that Buchanan and his cabinet support him in his efforts to guarantee to Kansans the right to choose their own domestic institutions through free and fair elections. Because of these sentiments, Walker's appointment was greeted with widespread approval.
[1] The free-state citizens of Lawrence had adopted their own municipal charter, in defiance of the proslave territo-

rial legislature from which such charters emanated. On July 15, 1857, Governor Walker issued a proclamation to the people of Lawrence in which he argued the validity of the territorial laws, branded the action as rebellion, and urged them to abandon their course.

[2] Douglas was referring to the free-state element in Kansas Territory.

[3] In February, 1857, the Kansas territorial legislature provided for a convention to frame a state constitution, to meet in Lecompton, the territorial capital, the following September. The bill was vetoed by the territorial Governor, John W. Geary, but promptly passed over his veto. One of Geary's objections to the bill was the failure of the

legislature to insist on the submission of the constitution to a popular vote. The question of the submission of the constitution became the most controversial aspect of the statehood movement, even before the Lecompton convention met. Governor Walker was firm in his insistence that the proposed constitution be submitted in its entirety to the electorate for ratification or rejection.

[4] The free-state constitution, drafted in defiance of the territorial legislature in 1855.

[5] The "law & order" party was, in general, the Democratic party in Kansas Territory, including the proslave element.

To Ambrose Burnham

Chicago

Sir,   July 24th 1857.

I have received your notice on behalf of the Board of Health informing me that there is a nusance, produced by stagnant water on the North East fractional Quarter of Section 27 Town 39 N Range 14 West, belonging to me, and requiring said water to be removed. I have enclosed your notice to the President of the Illinois Central Rail Road, and called upon him to abate the nuisance, inasmuch as the stagnant water is mostly on the land belonging to said Road and used for their Track, and the water was made stagnant solely by the action of said company in making an embankment in the water of the Lake without any openings for fresh water to pass through. Before the Rail Road was made, the shore of the Lake was perfectly clean and free from all stagnant water or other nuisances, and such would be the case now, but for the action of said company in making a close embankment, without leaving passages for the water. I take the liberty, therefore, to suggest to the Board of Health, that the Illinois Central Rail Road Company should be called upon and required to remove the nuisance which they have created, instead of requiring the owners of the adjacent lands, whose property has been thus injured by the action of the Company, to abate the nuisance which that company has created to the injury and annoyance of private individuals. Very respectfully your obedient servt

S. A. DOUGLAS

ALS Copy, owned by Martin F. Douglas. Ambrose Burnham, a Chicago physician, was Chicago Health Officer.

To Isaac Toucey

Chicago

Sir,   July 26th 1857

You will pardon me for again calling your attention to the application of Col J. B. Danforth Jr of Ills for a Pursership in the Navy. I had reason to believe that he would fill the first vacancy after assigning one to Louisiana. The reason for giving Louisiana the preference over Illinois was that we had one Purser while Louisiana had none. Since that time no less than three vacancies have occured & been filled. And what makes the case more unpleasant, one of those vacancies was from Illinois and a man from another State was given the prefference, when it left our State without even one. It did occur to me that another state could not have much stronger claims than Illinois to fill a vacancy from this state when the effect was to leave us without any while other states had large numbers. However I will once more present the name of Col Danforth & hope for better luck. Very respectfully your friend

S. A. DOUGLAS

ALS, Chicago Historical Society. This letter was endorsed, apparently by Toucey, "Ans that there is no vacancy in the grade of Pursers but one is anticipated & when it occurs I will take pleasure in bringing the application to the consideration of the Presd." Danforth received this purser's appointment in August.

To John C. Burroughs

Chicago

My Dear Sir,   Aug 8th 1857

I have learned with surprise and regret that many persons and news papers, opposed to me in politics, have allowed their partizan feelings and prejudices to influence their action to the extent of endeavoring to injure and perhaps destroy the institution over which you have been chosen to preside, for no other reason than that the ground upon which it is to be established was owned and donated by me.[1]

So long as their efforts were interested in abusing me and maligning my motives by attributing to me the design of making a pecuniary speculation under the veil of benevolence I was content to remain silent, and trust to the people of Illinois with whom I have lived and whom I have endeavored to serve with fidelity and honor, for nearly a quarter of a century to do justice to my motives and vindicate my character. But when my enemies go so far as to assail the Institution itself and endeavor to marshall the forces and exert the influence of a powerful political party to destroy its usefulness merely because I donated the grounds and own the surrounding lands, I feel it my duty, so far as I have the power, to obviate the objections. With this view, I

[389]

propose to you as the President of the University of Chicago, and through you to the Board of Trustees, that in lieu of the lands which I have donated, I will refund all moneys which have been expended thereon, including the cost of laying the corner stone, and in addition I will subscribe and pay fifty thousand dollars toward establishing the University upon the plan which has been adopted on any other site which the Board of Trustees may select within the State of Illinois— the said sum of fifty thousand dollars to be expended in the endowment of a department or school of law in said University. In the event that the Board of Trustees, at their next meeting, shall accept this proposition as a measure more favorable to the success of the institution than the donation of the present site, I shall hold myself in readiness on one day's notice to give ample security for its faithful performance on my part.[2] I have the honor to be very respectfully your friend and obedient servant.

S. A. DOUGLAS

ALS Copy, owned by Martin F. Douglas. John C. Burroughs, a graduate of Yale and the Madison Theological Seminary, was pastor of the First Baptist Church in Chicago from 1852 to 1856, before becoming President of the new University of Chicago.

[1]In 1856, Douglas deeded ten acres of his Chicago lands to the Trustees of the University of Chicago, a newly organized Baptist institution, for use as a campus. Douglas' opposition accused him of making the donation solely in order to enhance the value of his adjoining property.

[2]Douglas' offer to withdraw the donation was not accepted. On August 11, 1857, Burroughs wrote Douglas that he saw no reason for changing the site of the university, and on September 2, the Board of Trustees formally declined Douglas' proposition. The following day, September 3, the Board wrote of its reasons for declining the offer: "No other site equally eligible for the purposes of a University can be found in Chicago or near enough to it to command the local patronage of the city, while a removal to any more remote point would involve a change of the corporate name of the University & invalidate a great proportion of all the subscriptions for the erection of its buildings & its endowment now amounting to more than $160,000." These documents (Burroughs to Douglas, August 11, 1857; the Resolution of the Board, September 2; and the letter from the Board to Douglas, September 3) are owned by Martin F. Douglas.

To Henry Hastings Sibley et al.

St Paul

Gentlemen   Aug 15th 1857

I have the honor to acknowledge your kind invitation, on behalf of my Democratic friends of this Territory, to partake of a Public Dinner, and also to address the citizens, on such day as may suit my convenience during my visit to this city. To say that I am grateful for this testimonial of your respect and confidence is but a feeble expression of my feelings. My object in visiting Minnesota at this time is to

[390]

witness the wonderful changes which have taken place in this beautiful country within the period of ten years, which has elapsed since I last saw it. My time is limited and will all be occupied in visiting a few of the many points of peculiar interest. Besides the people of Minnesota are now engaged in forming a constitution and organizing a state government preparatory to their admission into the Union on an equal footing with the original States. It is your right and duty, under the federal constitution, to determine for yourselves the fundamental principles upon which your local and domestic institutions shall rest. Having neither the right nor the disposition to influence the result, may I not hope that, upon reflection, you will approve of my resolution not to participate in any political discussions during my present visit, and that you will pardon me for declining your very kind invitation to a public Dinner.

Renewing my thanks for the flattering terms in which you have been pleased to speak of my action in the National Councils, I have the honor to be very truly your friend and obedient servant

S. A. DOUGLAS

Hon H H Sibley
  Ch of Dem Meeting
    &
Messrs
  M E Ames
  J B Brisbin
  Chas E Flandreau
  W W Kingsbury
Com of Arrangements

ALS, Minnesota Historical Society, St. Paul. This letter was published, under date of August 18, 1857, in the Chicago *Times*, August 26, 1857. Henry Hastings Sibley had been Delegate in Congress from Minnesota Territory from 1849 to 1853, and a member of the Minnesota territorial legislature. In 1857, he was president of the Minnesota constitutional convention. He later became Minnesota's first state Governor following the admission of that state into the Union in 1858.

To Henry Hastings Sibley

St. Paul, Aug. 18, 1857.

Dear Sir; I have the honor to acknowledge the receipt of your note of this date, enclosing a copy of preamble and resolutions of the Constitutional Convention, over which you have the honor to preside, inviting me to visit the Convention at any time during my stay in the city. It is with great pleasure that I accept the invitation, and will avail myself of the first convenient opportunity to visit the Convention informally and witness its proceedings. I trust you will do me the favor to express to the Convention my grateful acknowledgments for the very flattering terms in which they have been pleased to request my visit as a member of the Senate of the United States. I have the honor to be, very truly, your friend and obedient servant.

S. A. Douglas

Chicago *Times*, August 26, 1857.

To Amos Gaylord Throop

Chicago, Aug. 29, 1857.

Dear Sir: On my return home from Minnesota, last night, I received your letter of the 10th inst., which was left at my residence during my absence. I take great pleasure in responding to your inquiries, and furnishing all the information in my possession touching the subject to which you refer. The selection for the sight of the public buildings at the corner of Monroe and Dearborn streets, was made and confirmed by the department at Washington without my knowledge. I was not consulted, directly or indirectly, upon the subject, and when the fact became known that such a selection had been made, I did not hesitate to express my decided opinion that it was inconvenient, unwise, and unfortunate for this community. I did not attempt, however to have the site changed, for the reason that the proceedings of the meeting held in this city upon the subject were not sent to me, and my interposition was not requested.[1]

I had no interest in the matter, except a common interest with every citizen and property-holder in the city, and felt no other desire than to see the wishes of the people of the whole city consulted in the selection of a central, convenient, and proper site. Since the selection has been made, I am perfectly content to see it remain undisturbed so long as the people of Chicago are satisfied with it. If, on the contrary, a decided majority of our citizens are opposed to the present site, and will unite upon another more central and convenient, I will cheerfully do all in my power to carry out their wishes by having the site changed to such a point as they shall agree upon. It may be questionable whether the Department has the legal authority to change the site without the assent of Congress, since the present location has been sanctioned by two acts of Congress, making additional appropriations for enlarging and completing the building upon the site selected by the Department, and over which the jurisdiction had been ceded by the Legislature of Illinois; yet I have no doubt that Congress would give its assent to the change, provided that it shall be clearly shown that the public convenience requires it and the people of this city desire it.

[392]

In regard to your second inquiry, which involves the proposition to establish a branch post office, I take pleasure in saying that, in my opinion, the public convenience and interests would be promoted by establishing a branch post office in the West Division, and another in the North Division of the city, Chicago, being divided by the river and its branches into three distinct divisions, which are separated from each other by natural boundaries, would seem to require a post office in each. If the proper steps should be taken to demonstrate to the proper department the necessity of these branch offices, I cannot doubt the request of the citizens would be granted upon the same terms and conditions that branch offices are established in New York and the other principal cities of the Union. The necessity and propriety of these branch offices will not be materially affected by the location of the principal office, and hence can have but little influence in determining the question of the proposed change of site.

In conclusion, I take pleasure in assuring you, and those you represent, that I will cordially cooperate with you in effecting a change of the site whenever a clear majority of the people of the city shall select another and express their wish to have the change made, and also to secure the establishment of a branch office in either division, whenever a majority of the people of such division shall indicate their wish to have a branch office established.

Regretting the delay which has unavoidably occurred in answering your letter, I have the honor to be, very truly, Your fellow citizen,

S. A. Douglas

Chicago *Times*, September 3, 1857. This letter was reprinted by the *Times* from the Chicago *Daily Ledger*, a short-lived paper that ran only in 1857. Amos Gaylord Throop was a Chicago merchant and former alderman of the city.
[1]In 1854, the United States government purchased a lot at Dearborn and Monroe streets in Chicago for the construction of a post office. The selection of the site was vigorously opposed by Chicago citizens, who expressed their opposition in an indignation meeting shortly after the choice had become known. Notwithstanding this opposition, the post office was built at that location.

To the Editor of the Chicago *Times*

Chicago

Editor of Times   Aug 29th 1857

On my return from a short visit to Minnesota yesterday a friend called my attention to an extract from the New York Times in relation to the sale of the Fort Snelling Military Reservation, which is as follows:[1]

Other parties are in the back-ground, who participate in the whole-sale plunder; broken-down politicians who are to be provided for, and live politicians to be propitiated in the event of outcry and investigation. We do not know that Mr. Rice, or Mr. Douglas, or Mr. Orr,[2] had anything to do with the matter, though intimations to this effect have been thrown out, in the eastern newspapers. They have all been about St. Paul during the summer, and are known to be familiar with speculations in Government lands.—We are inclined to *believe this sale has been effected with their privity*, for they are well posted in these affairs, and they must have had their eyes opened by the passage of the law giving this important power to the Secretary. Whether or not they are among the participants in the fruits of the job, is a point on which we reserve our opinion till we are more fully enlightened as to the facts.

When the malicious insinuation contained in this paragraph first made its appearance in a Chicago Paper, whose daily avocation is to falsify my acts and traduce my character I treated it with indifference as I am in the habit of treating the calumnies which daily eminate from the same source. But when I find it repeated in so respectable a Paper as [the New York Times, written in an apparent spirit of fairness and connected with my recent visit to Minnesota in such a manner as to impart a show of plausibility to the story, I deem it proper at once to put an end to the slander. My recent visit to Minnesota had no reference to the Fort Snelling Reservation nor to any other land speculation.][3] I had no knowledge, information, or intimation that the Fort Snelling Military Reservation was to be sold until after the sale was made, and then only learned the fact by public rumor and news paper reports. I am not interested directly or indirectly in any land or property which the government of the United States has sold, either at private or public sale, out-side of the State of Illinois; and in this state I have no such interest except as to [the Tracts of land which I entered a few years ago and am now improving for a farm in this county.] When I became chairman of the Territorial Committee twelve years ago I determined that I would never purchase or own, or become interested in any land, town lots or other property in any of the Territories of the United States whilst I held that position, for the reason that I would not allow even an enemy the pretext for saying that my public action was influenced or stimulated by private interest. I have never departed from this rule in any one instance, and hence I am free to say that I do not now own and never have owned any lands, town lots, or other property in the Territory of Minnesota or any other Territory of the United States, nor have I any interest directly or indirectly in the sale, rents or proffits of any lands, lots, or property of any description in any of the Territories of the United States. [I trust that this unequivocal denial will put an end to the slanders which originated in the partisan press of this city and are now being circulated in other States. Very truly your fellow citizen

S. A. DOUGLAS

My opinions in regard to the expediency of selling Fort Snelling and the propriety of the mode of sale and the sufficiency of the compensation paid by the purchaser will be freely and fully expressed from my seat in the Senate should the question come before that body action.] Should any question connected with the sale of Fort Snelling come before the Senate for any legitimate action I shall then be ready to do full and ample justice to the distinguished gentleman who presides over the War Department and at the same time express my opinions freely in regard to the propriety of the sale and the sufficiency of the compensation paid by the purchaser.

S. A. DOUGLAS

ADfS, owned by Martin F. Douglas.
[1]The following extract was clipped from the newspaper and pasted to the letter sheet. In June, 1857, a contract was entered into by the United States government, represented by the Secretary of War, John B. Floyd, for the sale of the Fort Snelling military reservation. The proposed sale aroused considerable opposition and the entire matter became the subject of a Con-

gressional investigation during the next session of Congress.
[2]James L. Orr, of South Carolina, was a member of Congress from 1849 to 1859, and was Speaker of the House of Representatives during the Thirty-fifth Congress, from 1857 to 1859.
[3]This and the two following portions enclosed in brackets were lined out by Douglas in the original draft.

To the Editor of the Chicago *Times*

Chicago

Editor of Times   Aug 29th 1857

On my return from a short visit to Minnesota yesterday a friend called my attention to an article in the New York Times in relation to the sale of the Fort Snelling Military Reservation, in which my name among others is mentioned as one who is probably interested in the purchase

ADf, owned by Martin F. Douglas.

To the Editor of the Chicago *Times*

Chicago

Editor of Times   Aug 29th 1857

On my return Home yesterday from a short visit to the Upper Mississippi a friend called my attention to articles in various news papers associating my name with certain land speculations in our new Territories and plausibly connecting my recent visit to Minnesota with the sale of the Fort Snelling Military Reservation. While I am in the habit of treating the daily assaults of the partizan Press with indifference, relying upon the people who know me to do me justice, I deem it proper to say that my recent visit to Minnesota had no reference to the sale of the Fort Snelling Reservation nor to any other land speculation. When so many of our public men[1] visits our new territories and frontier settlements during the recess of Congress for the purpose of obtaining information which may be useful to them and to the country in the performance of their public duties, it is hardly just to assume that they are governed by no higher motive than [to] form combinations to defraud the government of its most valuable land

ADf, owned by Martin F. Douglas.

[1] The opening of this sentence originally read, "It is hardly just to assume that any public man who, during the recess of Congress" but was altered by Douglas to read as above.

To the Editor of the Chicago *Times*

Chicago, Aug. 29th, 1857.

Editor of Times:—Yesterday, on my return home from a short visit to the Upper Mississippi, a friend called my attention to articles in various newspapers, associating my name with certain land speculations in our new territories, and plausibly connecting my recent visit to Minnesota with the sale of the Fort Snelling Military Reservation. While I am in the habit of treating the daily assaults of the partizan press with indifference, relying upon the people, who know me, to do me justice, I deem it proper to say that my recent visit to Minnesota had no reference to the sale of the Fort Snelling Reservation nor to the sale or purchase of any land. When so many of our public men visit our new territories and frontier settlements during the recess of Congress, for the purpose of obtaining information which may be useful to them and to the country, in the performance of their public duties, it is hardly just to assume that they are governed by no higher motive than to form combinations to defraud the government of its most valuable lands.

I had no knowledge, information, or intimation that the Fort Snelling Reservation was to be sold until after the sale was made, and then only learned the fact by public rumor and newspaper reports. I am not interested directly or indirectly in any land or property which the Government of the United States has sold either at private or public sale, outside of the State of Illinois; and in this State I have no such interest except as to the tracts of land in this county which I entered a few years ago and am now improving for a farm. When I became chairman of the Territorial Committee of the Senate, twelve years ago, I determined never to purchase or own, or become interested in any land, town lots or other property in any of the territories of the United

States, whilst I held that position, for the reason that I would not allow an enemy even a pretext for saying that my public action was influenced or stimulated by my own private interest. I have never departed from this rule in any one instance, and hence I am free to say that I do not now own and never have owned any lands, town lots or other property in the territory of Minnesota or in any other territory of the United States, nor have I any interest directly or indirectly in the sale, rents or profits of any lands, lots, or property of any description in any of the territories of the United States.

Should any question connected with the sale of Fort Snelling come before the Senate for my legitimate action I shall then be ready to do full and ample justice to the distinguished gentleman who presides over the War Department, and at the same time express my opinions freely in regard to the propriety of the sale, and the sufficiency of the compensation paid by the purchasers.

S. A. Douglas

Chicago *Times*, August 30, 1857.

To James Buchanan

Chicago
Dear Sir,   Aug 31st 1857
I have just heard that you were in doubt in reference to the wishes of the delegation from State in our recommendations of persons for foreign appointments in consequence of our having recommended Col Richardson for a first Class Foreign appointment and also designated another person for Minister to Russia. I desire to state to you that while both recommendations were made in good faith under the belief that we were entitled to two, yet it was the distinct and express understanding with the entire delegation that Col Richardson should have the prefference over any Democrat in this State so far as we had a right to control the matter, and in the event you could give us but one mission, that he was to have that one. I desire to make this statement in order to put myself and my colleagues right with you. Very truly your friend

S. A. Douglas

ALS, RG-59, National Archives.

To James Buchanan

Chicago
My Dear Sir,   Sept 4th 1857
I enclose to you for your perusal a letter which I have just received from J N Granger Esq, who holds the position of recorder of the General Land Office. I will not conceal the deep mortification I feel in

[397]

having very respectable gentlemen believe that I would for a moment consent to the removal of Gen'l McConnel[1] or any other good Democrat in order to make room for any of my family relations. It is true that I should feel exceedingly gratified to see my father-in-law[2] promoted to the controllership, provided it was the voluntary act of the President, superinduced by the conviction that his high qualifications, his irriproachable character, and his long & faithful services in that Bureau indicate him out as the suitable and appropriate man for the place. But if his appointment is to be placed upon the ground of his relationship to me and is to be considered as cancelling any portion of the claim which Illinois may have to her just proportion of the federal patronage I do him no more than justice in assuming that he would be as prompt in declining as I would in withholding my assent to his appointment on those terms. I know my obligations to the people of Illinois and recognize the gratitude I owe her Democracy too well to allow any ties of blood or family or friendship outside of her limits to paralize or impair my efforts to secure a just & fair show of the federal appointments for the citizens of my own state. I rejoice to say that so far as I know I have but one relation from any state in the Union holding office under the federal government, and he was appointed through the influence of the late Wm L. Marcy from the state of New York where he was born and has always resided. I now desire to say that if Mr. Granger's appointment to office or his retention in office is dependent upon or affected by his relationship to me, or is taken into the account when the claims of Illinois are presented I feel bound to protest against the injustice done to me and to the people of the state I represent. Under past administrations I have felt keenly & deeply the neglect and injustice with which Illinois was treated in the distribution of the patronage. Other States could receive a Cabinet office, Foreign missions and several Bureau appointments all at the same time, while Illinois, a state which has never deserted the Democratic Banner, has been treated with a neglect which could not fail to wound the pride of all her working Democrats. Hence I feel bound to say to you in all frankness & kindness that any appointment you may make or person you may retain in office, other than the citizens of Illinois, no matter how near and dear they may be to me, must not be considered as any compensation for the omission to appoint such Democrats from this State as I in common with the rest of the Delegation have or may recommend. I have not yet felt dispose to complain of the apparent neglect of the just claims of this State in the distribution of the Patronage under your administration, having full faith that you would do us justice in the future appointments. I have the honor to be very truly your friend.[3]

S. A. Douglas

ALS Copy, owned by Martin F. Douglas.

[1]Murray McConnel, Douglas' early friend in Jacksonville, had been appointed Fifth Auditor of the Treasury by President Pierce in 1855.

[2]President Buchanan was contemplating the appointment of James Madison Cutts to the office of Second Comptroller of the Treasury Department.

[3]On September 7, 1857, President Buchanan replied to Douglas: "I have received your favor of the 4th Instant, by which you seem to apprehend that should I appoint Mr. Cutts 2d Comptroller, this appointment might be charged to Illinois. You need entertain no apprehensions on the subject. Should I make the appointment which is not improbable, it will be my own individual appointment proceeding entirely from my regard for Mr. Cutts & his family, & not because Senator Douglas has had the good fortune to become his son-in-law" (owned by Martin F. Douglas). Both Douglas' and Buchanan's letters were widely published in the press.

To Adele Cutts Douglas

Quincy
Sunday evening
My Dear Wife   Sept 6th 1857

I arrived here at half past ten last night in good health and without much fatigue. None of my friends expected me and hence my arrival took them all by surprise. A few however learned the fact in time to give me a charming serenade about twelve oclock, I had retired, but was still awake thinking of my dear wife, and wondering if you were as lonely and disconsolate, as sleepless and nervous without me as I was in consequence of your absence. The music was truly delightful and I should have enjoyed it exceedingly if I had only had my loved one to enjoy it with me. The boy awoke me this morning at seven in pursuance of my directions. I shaved, put on a clean shirt and dressed in time for Breakfast at eight. I have met with but few of my old friends— some being out of town and many not knowing of my arrival. However I have spent the day as pleasantly as could have been expected. I dined with a few friends at Gen'l Singleton's[1] and took tea with my old friend Doct S W Rogers[2] and family. They were all very anxious to see you and expressed the deepest regret that I did not bring you. I am resolved not to make another trip without you for everybody is more anxious to see you than me, and besides I am so lonely that I cannot enjoy my visit. I leave in the morning for Pittsfield, forty miles South of Quincy. My friend Judge Skinner[3] of the Supreme Court will take me down in his carriage so I anticipate quite a pleasant trip. I will write you again the first opportunity, altho you must not be surprised if I get home before my letters reaches you as the mails are very irregular the moment I leave the Rail Road lines. Give my love to Robert and Stephen and tell them that Papa never ceases to think of

[399]

them. Good night my Darling Wife, may God preserve and bless you is the constant prayer of your devoted and lonely husband.

S. A. DOUGLAS

ALS, owned by Martin F. Douglas.
[1] James W. Singleton.
[2] Samuel W. Rogers was a Quincy physician.

[3] Onias C. Skinner, of Quincy, was a Justice on the Illinois Supreme Court from 1855 to 1858.

To Lewis Cass

[September 23, 1857, Chicago; ALS, RG-59, National Archives. Recommending Dr. Albert H. Trapp, of Belleville, Illinois, for appointment as United State Consul in Hamburg. Trapp, a physician and surgeon, was a member of the Illinois state legislature from 1855 to 1857. He was not appointed.]

To Riggs and Company

Chicago

Dr Sir,   Sept 28th 1857

On return home Saturday night I received your letter of the 22d informing me of the nature of the remittances which you have received from Mr Rice.[1] I received also a letter from Mr Rice of similar purport as his letter to you, giving the assurance that the drafts would certainly be paid at maturity, and that he would pay the ballance at the earliest possible moment. I know Mr Stemson [?], the drawer of the draft, and have no doubt of the payment of them, judging from his character for punctuality and his large means. I regret exceedingly the disappointment as it has given me great uneasiness. I will see the money paid at the earliest possible moment, but must confess that my means of paying punctually depend upon my receiving sums due me and on which I have relied with entire confidence. The sudden change of monetary affairs has taken us all by surprise, and deprives us of the power of doing as we would like to do.[2] I can only say that I will see you paid at the earliest possible moment. Very truly your obedient servant

S. A. DOUGLAS

ALS, Library of Congress. George W. Riggs assumed full control of the Washington banking house, Corcoran and Riggs, in 1854. The firm was known from that time as Riggs and Company.
[1] Edmund Rice, former St. Paul, Minnesota, lawyer, was at this time Presi-

dent of the St. Paul and Pacific Railroad.
[2] The financial panic of 1857 reached its peak of severity in the early fall of that year. In late August and early September a large number of small Eastern banks and business houses were forced to close their doors, the stock market

dropped, and the loans of those banks which continued in operation were contracted. On September 25, banks in Philadelphia and Baltimore suspended specie payment.

To John B. Floyd

[October 5, 1857, Chicago; ALS, Illinois State Historical Library. Forwarding a petition for and recommending the appointment of Wimer Bedford, of Centralia, Illinois, to a lieutenancy in the United States Army. Bedford did not receive the appointment, but later served during the Civil War as a lieutenant in the Illinois Volunteers.]

To James Buchanan

Chicago
My Dear Sir,   Oct 8th 1857

It is due to you that I should explain the reasons which impelled me to furnish for publication a copy of my letter to you of the 4th and your reply of the 7th of Sept.[1] For several weeks the Washington correspondents of the New York Tribune and other papers kept "Senator Douglas' father-in-law" constantly before the public, and represented me as insisting upon his appointment to the office of 2d comptroller as a personal favor to myself, while the abolition news papers of this state repeated those statements and charged me with sacrificing the great claims of my democratic friends at home to a convenient family arraingement. So long as these statements had no higher authority then the anonymous correspondents of abolition newspapers I treated them with that silent contempt which they deserved. But I am now informed that on a recent occasion when a distinguished gentleman from this State called at the Treasury Department to see the Secretary on business and while waiting for that purpose the assistant Secretary inquired of him how many relatives Judge Douglas had, and on being asked what he meant by that inquiry, he stated that the administration expected to be called upon to provide offices for them all and hence would like to know how many he had. Rumors are ripe in this State that the case refered to is not the only instance in which similar remarks have been made, in the same department. Altho I had your authority for repelling the malignant calumnies implied in these inquiries and could not permit myself to believe that the Secretary of the Treasury had sanctioned them, yet there are those who were ungenerous enough to believe, or who at least profess to believe, that they reflect the feelings of the administration. Under these circumstances I have deemed it an act of justice to you as well as to myself to publish the correspondence in order to render harmless the intrigues of those

[401]

who hope to defeat the democratic party in this state by creating dessentions in our ranks. Trusting that you will approve the course I have pursued I have the honor to remain very truly and sincerely your friend.

S. A. DOUGLAS

ALS Copy, owned by Martin F. Douglas.
[1]See above, September 4, 1857.

To Horatio King

(*Confidential*) Chicago
My Dear Sir, Oct 9th 1857
I send today an official letter asking the removal of Mr Carpenter[1] and the appointment of the man whom I had promised the place. Mr Carpenter (Col R B) is disbursing agent for the new Post Office, Custom House &c in this city and boasts that he got it without the aid of the delegation in Congress in this state and that the administration will give him a place as my opponent when they would not as my friend. He has never mentioned to me the fact that his brother wanted the office & now claims the appointment as evidence that the administration is hostile to me. Hence I am compelled to make the distinct issue to ascertain whether the administration recognizes him or me as the organ of the Party. I am satisfied that the P M Genl did not intend to do an unkind act to me, but the result of it is looked upon as an act of hostility. There is no alternative, but his instantly removal. Ask Gov Brown to do it instantly & put the *sole responsibility on me*. To delay is to create mischief. Things cannot remain as they are. Very truly your friend

S. A. DOUGLAS

ALS, Library of Congress.
[1]R. B. Carpenter was appointed Disbursing Agent for the Chicago Custom House in February, 1857. He was removed from that office, as Douglas requested, but was immediately appointed Postmaster of Chicago in early 1858.

To Jonathan Baldwin Turner

Chicago
My Dear Sir, Oct 12th 1857
Accept my thanks for your kind note enclosing the pamphlett on Industrial Universities which I will take pleasure in examining with the view of forming a favorable judgment on the proposed movement.

I shall be happy to receive your work on the Races when completed.[1] Very respectfully your obedient servant

S. A. DOUGLAS

ALS, Illinois Historical Survey, University of Illinois. Jonathan Baldwin   Turner, a graduate of Yale and a professor at Illinois College, was a propagandist for the establishment of land-grant colleges.

¹Turner published, in 1851, *A Plan for an Industrial University for the State of Illinois, Submitted to the Farmer's Convention at Granville, Held, November 18, 1851, by Prof. J. B. Turner*, and, in 1861, *The Three Great Races of Men.*

To Lewis Cass

[October 26, 1857, Chicago; ALS, RG-59, National Archives. Recommending the reappointment of Max Stettheimer as United States Consul in Stuttgart, Germany. Stettheimer, of New York, held the consulate from 1854 to 1858.]

To William Weer

[November 22, 1857, n.p. This letter has been cited by Allan Nevins, *The Emergence of Lincoln* (2 vols., New York, 1950), I, 251, as having been printed in the Wyandotte (Kansas) *Western Argus*, October 22, 1860, but a search of the file of that paper has disclosed no such letter. According to Nevins, Douglas wrote Weer of his determination to oppose the Buchanan administration on the Lecompton Constitution issue, commenting, "I shall do this in a kind spirit towards the Administration and all my friends." Weer was United States Attorney in Kansas Territory.]

To John A. McClernand

(*Private*)   Chicago
My Dear Sir,   Nov 23d 1857

Your kind letter came to hand by due course of mail. I have not received a copy of the Kansas constitution, and hence cannot speak deffinitely upon the point of your enquiry, in regard to what is to be done. Of course we must stand firmly by the principle of the Kansas organic act, which guarantees the right of the people of each State & Territory to form and regulate their own institutions in their own way.¹

I repeat, we must stand on this principle and go wherever its logical consequences may carry us, and defend it against all assaults from any quarter. The only question is whether the constitution formed at Lecompton is the act & will of the people of Kansas, [or] whether it be the act and will of a small minority, who have attempted to cheat & defraud the majority by trickery & juggling. If it be the will of the people freely & fairly expressed it is all right, if not it must be rebuked. Of course I will not pronounce a final judgement on this point until I get the facts officially before me, altho the newspaper accounts look as if trickery & juggling have been substituted for fair dealing. If this shall turn out to be true we have but one course to pursue, and that is vindicate the principle of the organic act and the Cincinnati Platform by refering the whole matter back to the people. Let me hear from you soon. I leave for W the last of this week. Mrs D joins me in respects to Mrs Mc. Truly your friend

S. A. DOUGLAS

ALS, Illinois State Historical Library.
[1]The so-called Lecompton Constitution, providing for a slave state of Kansas, was drafted and signed by a convention meeting in the town of Lecompton, the capital of Kansas Territory. The most controversial aspect of the document was not its slavery provision, but rather its failure to provide for its submission to the voters of Kansas for ratification or rejection. This failure formed the basis for Douglas' opposition to the constitution.

To Edwin D. Morgan

Washington
My Dear Sir, Dec 4th 1857

Accept my thanks for your polite invitation on behalf of the New England Society of the City of New York to be present & participate in the festivities of the occasion on the 22d inst.

It affords me great pleasure to be able to accept the invitation. I have the honor to be very truly your obedient servant

S. A. DOUGLAS

ALS, New York State Library, Albany. Edwin D. Morgan was at this time New York State Commissioner of Immigration. He later served as Governor of New York from 1859 to 1862, and as a member of the United States Senate from 1863 to 1869. On December 2 Morgan invited Douglas to participate in the "Fore-fathers day" dinner at the Astor House on December 22 (Douglas Papers, University of Chicago Library).

To James Washington Sheahan

[December 6, 1857, n.p. This letter was cited by George Fort Milton, *Eve of Conflict: Stephen A. Douglas and the Needless War* (Boston, 1934), p. 275, n5. The original of this letter has not been located, nor has any copy been found in the notes taken from the Sheahan Papers by Professor Frank Heywood Hodder. This letter was probably an answer to two letters written to Douglas by Sheahan, November 30, 1857, and December 4, 1857, dealing with Kansas' Lecompton Constitution. In the latter letter, Sheahan urged Douglas to stand fast against the constitution. "To admit Kansas as a Slave State," he wrote, "would be destructive of everything in Illinois. We could never recover from it. ... Remember that the *only* fight of *1858* will be in Illinois" (Douglas Papers, University of Chicago Library).]

To Charles H. Lanphier and George Walker

(*Confidential*)   Washington
Dear Sirs   Dec 6th 1857.

The Battle will soon begin. We will nail our colors to the mast and defend the right of the people to govern themselves against all assaults from all quarters. We are sure to triumph. Keep the Ball rolling, & the Party united. It will be all right in the end. The Indiana Senators (Bright & Fitch[1]) are pledged to go for the Lecompton Fraud, but they will back down unless the South sustains them in their seats right or wrong. We can succeed without them, and, will have them when we do not need them.

Send me your paper. Your friend

S. A. Douglas

ALS, Illinois State Historical Library. [1]Graham N. Fitch, a medical doctor and former Professor of Anatomy at Rush Medical College, Chicago, served in the House of Representatives from Indiana from 1849 to 1853, and was elected to the United States Senate to fill a vacancy, serving from February, 1857, until 1861.

To James Madison Cutts

[December 10, 1857, n.p.; ALS, Chicago Historical Society. Introducing A. H. Coons, probably of St. Louis, Missouri, "who desires to see you on business."]

To Schuyler Colfax

(*Confidential*)   [December, 1857]
My Dr Sir,   Friday

I have just returned & received your note. Will be pleased to see you and Mr H. G.[1] any time this evening. Seven or eight oclock would suit me if agreeable to him & you & also Mr C.[2]

I will be at home all the evening and will see you privately at any time you may call. Yours truly

S. A. Douglas

ALS, Indiana State Library, Indianapolis. Schuyler Colfax, of Indiana, was a Republican member of Congress from 1855 to 1869. In December, 1857, Colfax made at least two visits to Douglas' home. The latter, on December 14, was in the company of Anson Burlingame, Massachusetts Congressman. The visit was described in detail by Colfax in a memorandum written after the meeting. According to Colfax, Douglas reiterated his determination to oppose the administration on the Lecompton issue and discussed the possibility of Republican support in this opposition (Indiana State Library). George Fort Milton, *Eve of Conflict: Stephen A. Douglas and the Needless War* (Boston, 1934),

p. 281, places the meeting between Colfax, Greeley, and Cochrane, referred to in this letter, before the visit of Colfax and Burlingame. Although undated, Douglas' letter to Colfax was thus written early in December, probably on December 4 or December 11, which fell on Friday. Congress convened on December 7.

[1]Horace Greeley, editor of the New York *Tribune*.

[2]Clark B. Cochrane, of New York, was a Republican member of Congress from 1857 to 1861.

To John B. Floyd

[N.d., n.p.; AES, Historical Society of Pennsylvania. Endorsement by Douglas on Jefferson Davis to John B. Floyd, December 16, 1857, asking the appointment of John Rogers Meigs to the United States Military Academy. Meigs, the son of Captain Montgomery C. Meigs, received the appointment in 1859 and graduated from West Point in 1863. He was killed in action in 1864.]

To Edwin D. Morgan

[December 21, 1857, Washington; Telegram, New York State Library. Informing Morgan of his inability to be in New York on December 22, because of his Senatorial duties.]

To Edwin D. Morgan

[December 21, 1857, Washington; Telegram, New York State Library. Expressing regret that it was impossible for him to be absent from the Senate on December 22.]

To Edwin D. Morgan

Washington
Dec 21st 1857

My Dear Sir,

I sincerely regret that my public duties will require my presence in the Senate tomorrow and thus deprives me of the pleasure of participating in the festivities of the New England Society, as I had intended and promised. I beg you to make my apology & express my regrets to your associates.[1] I am very truly your obedient servant

S. A. DOUGLAS

ALS, New York State Library.

[1]On December 22, 1857, Douglas moved that that portion of President Buchanan's message dealing with Kansas be referred to the Committee on Territories, thus touching off a long debate on the admission of Kansas to the Union under the Lecompton Constitution.

To Lewis Cass

Washington

My Dr General,   Jan'y 2d 1858

I feel it my duty to withdraw any letter of recommendation I may have signed in behalf of O J Rose of Chicago for any appointment at home or abroad under the federal Government. I make this withdrawal in consequence of disclosures which have been recently made of a character which would render his an unfit appointment.[1] Very truly your friend

S. A. DOUGLAS

ALS, RG-59, National Archives.
[1]Douglas had recommended Rose for the consulate in Frankfort, Germany (Douglas to Cass, May 10, 1857). Rose apparently defected from the Douglas ranks, for in June, 1858, he was a delegate to a Buchanan Democratic convention.

To Isaac V. Fowler *et al.*

Gentlemen,   Washington, Jan'y 7, 1858

Accept my thanks for your kind letter of invitation on behalf of the society of Tammany to attend and participate in the celebration of the 44th anniversary of the battle of New Orleans. I regret that my public duties will deprive me of the pleasure of being present on that occasion. No event in our history, since the days of the Revolution, has contributed so much to the honor and glory of this country as that which you propose to celebrate. While the memories of that day are the common inheritance of all patriotic citizens it is peculiarly proper that the Democracy, who achieved so many political victories under the lead of the immortal Jackson, should take especial pride in its commemoration. I have the honor to be, Very truly Your Obt Serv't

S. A. DOUGLAS

Messrs,
  I. V. Fowler
  D. E. Delevan
  W. D. Kennedy
  & others, Committee

LS, New York Public Library. Isaac V. Fowler was Postmaster of New York city.

To Lewis Cass

[January 18, 1858, Senate Chamber; ALS, RG-76, National Archives. Enclosing a letter "from one of my constituents, with the hope that you will furnish me with the information desired." Since this letter is among the Records of Boundary and Claims Commissions and

[407]

Arbitrations, the enclosure referred to by Douglas may have dealt with a private claim against a foreign government.]

To John W. Forney *et al.*

Washington City, *Feb.* 6, 1858.

Gentlemen: I regret that my public duties here will not permit me to be present and to participate with the Democracy of Philadelphia in their demonstration against the proposition to impose a constitution upon the people of Kansas against their will.

That the Lecompton constitution is not the act of the people of Kansas, and that it does not embody the popular will of that Territory, is now conclusively and undeniably established by a vote of the people, taken at a fair election, held on the 4th day of January, 1858, in pursuance of a law passed by the Territorial Legislature established by Congress.[1]

The idea that the Lecompton convention, clothed with no other authority than that which it derived from the Territorial Legislature, could ordain a constitution and put it in force without the consent of Congress, and in defiance and subversion of the authority of the Territorial Legislature established by Congress, is too preposterous to admit of argument.[2] Under our political system it requires sovereign power to ordain and establish constitutions and governments. While a Territory may and should enjoy all the rights of self-government, in obedience to its organic law, it is not a sovereign power. The sovereignty of a Territory remains in abeyance, suspended in the United States, in trust for the people when they become a State, and cannot be withdrawn from the hands of the trustee, and vested in the people of a Territory, without the consent of Congress. The last Congress having withheld this assent, by refusing to pass the bill recommended by President Pierce, to authorize the people of Kansas to form a constitution and State government when they should desire it and have the requisite population, the sovereignty of Kansas still remains in abeyance, without any authority of the Territorial Legislature to transfer it from the United States and vest it in the people of the Territory, without the consent of Congress.

Hence, I repeat, the Lecompton convention possessed just such authority as the Territorial Legislature was competent to confer, and, by the terms of the act, did confer upon it, and no more.

The Territorial Legislature did not endow the convention with sovereignty, for it had none to impart. It did not even bestow the power of legislation, for by the organic act it was vested with the legislative power of the Territory, without the right to delegate it to a convention of its own creation. Hence, the Lecompton Convention only possessed the authority, derived from the Legislature, to collect, ascertain, and embody the will of the people of the Territory upon the subject of admission into the Union, and to send the same as a memorial to Congress, under the clause of the Constitution of the United States, which secures the right peaceably to assemble and petition for a redress of grievances.

Such memorial, even if it embodied the form of a State constitution, Congress would be at liberty to accept or reject, according as it fairly represents, or misrepresents, the will of the people of the proposed State.

The Territorial Legislature, just elected by the voice and votes of the people of Kansas, believing this Lecompton memorial or constitution to be a fraud upon the wishes and rights of the people of Kansas, assembled and passed a law submitting the instrument to a fair vote of the people on the 4th of January last, at which election a majority of more than ten thousand votes was recorded against it.

With what show of justice or fairness can it be contended, in the face of this vote, that the people of Kansas do not, and have not, in the most solemn manner known to the laws, repudiated the Lecompton constitution as a wicked fraud upon their rights and wishes?

The enormity of this Lecompton scheme should not be concealed under the plea that the Convention declared the constitution to be in force, as the fundamental law of Kansas, without submission to the people, (except the slavery article,) and that, consequently, the authority of the Territorial Legislature was superseded on the 21st of December last. The Convention had no lawful authority to supersede the organic act of the Territory, by establishing a State constitution, without the consent of Congress. The attempt was not only unlawful, but if successful, would amount to rebellion against the lawful authority of the United States. The power of the Territorial Legislature was as complete on the 17th day of December last, when it passed the law submitting the Lecompton constitution to the vote of the people, as it was on the 19th of February, 1857, when it passed the act calling the Lecompton Convention.

As the Convention possessed no power, except what it received from the Legislature, it could do no act subverting or impairing the authority of the Legislature.

Hence, the act of the Legislature, submitting the whole constitution to the vote of the people, was just as valid and binding upon the subject-matter, as the act of the same Legislature calling the Convention into existence.

The conclusion is inevitable, that the Lecompton constitution does not, and never did, possess any vitality or authority, for two reasons: first, the Convention, not being vested with sovereign power, could not put it in operation; and, second, that the same legislative authority which called the Convention into existence, passed a law, before the constitution was to have taken effect by its own terms, for its submission to the people, and provided that if a majority of the votes should be cast against it at that election, it was to be null and void, not only as a constitution, but even as a memorial to Congress.

We are, therefore, forced irresistibly to the conclusion that the Lecompton constitution, whether viewed in a legal and technical sense or as a memorial professing to embody the popular will of Kansas, should be repudiated by every Democrat who cherishes the time-honored principle of his party, and is determined, in good faith, to carry out the doctrine of self-government and popular sovereignty, as guarantied in the Kansas-Nebraska act, and affirmed by the Cincinnati platform. I have the honor to be, your ob't serv't,

S. A. DOUGLAS

Messrs. John W. Forney, D. Webster, J. F. Johnston, E. G. Webb, John O'Brien, Dan'l Dougherty, B. D. Berry, Committee.

Letters to the Great Democratic Anti-Lecompton Meeting, Against the Lecompton Fraud, Held at Philadelphia, Pennsylvania, February 8, 1858 (Washington, D.C., 1858), pp. 9-10. The letter was published in the Springfield *Illinois State Register* on February 18, 1858. John W. Forney, a former clerk of the House of Representatives and editor of the Philadelphia *Press*, was chairman of invitation for the meeting. On February 5, he wrote Douglas, urging the Senator to attend the meeting "or send in a strong hearty letter" (Douglas Papers, University of Chicago Library). Letters from Henry A. Wise, Governor of Virginia; Charles E. Stuart, Senator from Michigan; and Representatives William Montgomery and John Hickman, of Pennsylvania, Thomas Langrell Harris, of Illinois, John G. Davis, of Indiana, and Samuel S. Cox, of Ohio, were also printed in the pamphlet.

[1]The Lecompton constitutional convention provided for two elections. The first was to be held on December 21, 1857, at which the electorate would vote, not on the entire constitution, but only on a separate schedule, "The constitution with slavery," or "The con-

stitution without slavery." It was this limited submission that created the storm of controversy over the Lecompton Constitution. The constitution itself guaranteed slave property; hence, no matter how the vote on the separate schedule resulted, Kansas would become a slave state. The second election was scheduled for January 4, 1858, at which time state officers under the new constitution would be elected. On December 1, Acting Governor Frederick P. Stanton called the newly elected free-state territorial legislature into special session. The legislature, convening on December 7, immediately provided for the submission of the entire constitution at the January 4 election. The first election, December 21, resulted in the acceptance of the "constitution with slavery," primarily because the vote was boycotted by the free-state element. The second election on the entire constitution resulted in its rejection by over 10,000 votes. It was this second referendum, representing the sentiment of all Kansans freely expressed, to which Douglas had reference.

[2]According to the Lecompton Constitution, a provisional government, with

John Calhoun, the president of the convention, as "regent," would supplant the territorial government on December 1, 1857. Calhoun was to supervise the elections for state officers and legislators, to appoint election judges, to count the returns, and to issue certificates of election to the successful candidates.

To George B. Butler

My Dr Sir, Feby 11th 1858

I have barely time to absent myself from the bed of my sick wife,[1] to write a hasty note in reply to the invitation to speak at your meeting. Please put it in form & give it the proper address.[2] Our friends here are in fine spirits, & are delighted to see the Democracy speak out against the monstrous fraud about to be attempted upon the people of Kansas. Please apologize to my friends for the meagre letter I send. Your friend

S. A. DOUGLAS

ALS, Massachusetts Historical Society, Boston. On February 9, 1858, Butler, a New York city lawyer and former editor of the New York *Journal of Commerce*, wrote to Douglas of a meeting to be held on Friday, February 12, in New York city, protesting against the Lecompton Constitution. He invited Douglas to speak at the meeting, or to send a letter expressing his views; George Bancroft was to preside (Douglas Papers, University of Chicago Library).

[1]Adele Cutts Douglas was recovering from a miscarriage.

[2]See below, Douglas to ——, February 11, 1858.

To ——

Washington

Gentlemen Feby 11th 1858

I have the honor to acknowledge the receipt of your kind invitation to address the Democracy of New York on Friday night in opposition to the effort being made to force Kansas into the Union with a constitution which the people of that Territory have repudiated and rejected at a fair and valid election by more than ten thousand majority. The time has now arrived when the Democracy of the whole country should hold meetings in the cities, towns, and counties, and proclaim in tones that will command respect their devotion to and determination to sustain and carry out in good faith the great principles of self government which lie at the foundation of all free institutions; and proclaim their determined and unyielding hostility to the consummation of a scheme so monstrous as to force a constitution at the point of the bayonet down the throats of an unwilling people.

I regret that my public duties as well as illness in my family demand my constant attention here, and thus deprive me of the pleasure which

I should otherwise enjoy in accepting your kind invitation. I have the honor to be very truly [your] obedient svt

S. A. Douglas

ALS, Massachusetts Historical Society.

To George Bancroft

Washington

My Dr Sir,
Feby 11th 1858

Accept my thanks for your kind note. I regret to inform you that Mrs Douglas is quite ill, and I am kept constantly at her bed side. I have written a hasty wrought outline of a letter to Geo B Butler Esq in reply to his invitation I wish you & he would look it over & put it in shape. I have but a minute to write as the mail is about to close.

Very kind regards to Mrs B & believe me truly yours

S. A. Douglas

ALS, Massachusetts Historical Society. On February 8, 1858, Bancroft wrote to Douglas, "We shall have a great meeting here on Friday next. You may be sure I shall do all in my power to give it a right direction, so that we may strengthen your hands & those of your friends in the house. You may judge that I am in earnest, when I tell you I have not attended a political meeting for many years" (Douglas Papers, University of Chicago Library).

Bancroft was the leading American historian of this day, as well as a devoted public servant and officeholder. During the administration of James K. Polk he held the post of Secretary of the Navy, and from 1846 to 1849 was United States Minister to Great Britain. In 1834, the first volume of his monumental *History of the United States* appeared, the publication of which extended over the next forty years.

To George Bancroft

Monday

My Dr Sir,
Feby 15th '58

Accept my thanks for your kind letter.[1] Mrs Douglas is doing as well as could be expected, & we hope she may be able to be out in a week or two. I regret that your meeting did not come.[2] Do not give it up, but call another. Keep the Ball rolling—arouse the country on the great issues of self government & all will end well. Very truly your friend

S. A. Douglas

ALS, Massachusetts Historical Society.

[1]Bancroft wrote Douglas on February 13 that support for Douglas' position on the Lecompton Constitution was increasing among New York Democrats, and he added, "Our watch word is Uncompromising hostility to the Lecompton Constitution because it is not the choice of the people" (owned by Martin F. Douglas).

[2]The meeting in New York city, scheduled for February 12, was to be

held at the New York Academy of Music, but the managers of the academy refused to turn on the lights since their charter forbade the use of the hall for political purposes.

To John W. Forney

Monday
My Dr Forney, Feby 15th

I have just rec'd your kind letter.[1] Mrs D is better & doing as well as could be expected. I am not dejected nor discouraged in the least. We will fight the battle out boldly & gallantly and triumph in the end. Let the enemy, threaten, proscribe & do their best or worst, it will not cause any honest man to falter or change his course. I am preparing a Report from the Territorial Committee on Lecompton.[2] It will be ready in two or three days. Let us stand by our colors, & make no compromise—no concession, and all will end well. My kind regards to Mrs F. Your friend

S. A. DOUGLAS

ALS, Historical Society of Pennsylvania.

[1] On February 14, 1858, Forney wrote to Douglas of his concern for Mrs. Douglas' health, and added, "You must not be cast down by these difficulties; upon you the whole heart of our nation reposes; a million of men look to you as their leader, and anything effecting you, affects them...we are ready to follow you wherever you may lead" (Douglas Papers, University of Chicago Library).

[2] Douglas' report from the Committee on Territories was one of three, Senator Green of Missouri reporting for the majority and Senators Collamer and Wade reporting for the Republican minority. On February 16, the day after Douglas wrote this letter, Green wrote Douglas that the majority of the committee had agreed to make the final report on Lecompton on February 18, two days hence (owned by Martin F. Douglas). Thus, it was thought, Douglas would be deprived of sufficient time to prepare his report, especially in view of his wife's illness. Douglas, however, worked steadily for two days and two nights and submitted his report on the appointed day.

To Charles J. Faulkner

Sir, [February 19, 1858]

In reply to your note propounding certain enquiries on behalf of the special committee appointed to investigate the recent sale of the Military Reservation of Fort Snilling I submit the following answers.[1]

In reply to Question first, I have no knowledge of the facts and circumstances connected with the recent sale of the military reservation at Fort Snelling; except from news papers and rumors subsequent to the sale. I did not know that the War Department had abandoned or intended to abandon the use of the Fort and reservation for Military purposes. Had never heard that the sale was to take place, and was surprised when I heard that it had been sold, and did not believe the report at first, for I was not aware that there was any law authorizing or permitting the sale.

In reply to the second Question I can state that I had never seen the Military Reservation but once, and that was in the summer of 1847, being ten years before the sale, and prior to the organization of the Territory of Minnesota, when I visited Fort Snelling and the surrounding country with a pleasure party, but paid no particular attention and formed no deffinite opinion about the value of the Reservation. Last summer, about a month after the sale of Fort Snilling I again visited that country for the first time in ten years. In making excursions into the country from St Paul, I crossed the Reservation twice from St. Antony & Meniopolis via Minnehaha (or little Falls) to Fort Snilling, and crossing the river at that point, returned to St Paul. In these trips, following each time on the same track and seeing but a small portion of the reservation, I could not form any deffinite opinion in regard to the value of the property or of its agricultural, manufacturing and commercial advantages. That portion of the tract over which I passed was beautifully situated, but I was not favorably impressed with the quality of the soil. Not know[ing] the selling price of the surrounding lands similar[ly] situated and having no reasons for making enquiries on the subject I am unable to fix a price per acre, and in regard to the gross amount for which the property ought to have sold, I can only say that the opinions which I heard expressed by others differed so widely that I placed very little reliance upon them. My impression then was and now is that public opinion attached a far greater value to the property than it was really worth.

In reply to the third Question, I must say that my opinion is of very little value in respect to what would be a fair price of the land for agricultural purposes, for the reason that I did not see but a small portion of the reservation and did not know the selling price of the surrounding agricultural lands; but if I were to hazard an opinion, I should say that I would not deem those lands worth more than ten dollars per acre for agricultural purposes, and doubt whether I would have deemed the [land] desirable for that purpose at that price.

In reply to the fourth Question. The site of the Fort and the land around it and running up the Mississippi towards Minnehaha was beautifully situated for a Town, and would have been of immense value for that purpose, had it been laid out and sold in Town lots some years ago, before the cities of St Paul, St Antony, and Minneopolis had become permanently established as manufacturing and commercial cities. But I think it is now too late to start a new town so near to those with the hope of fairly competing with them. The reservation is too near these other towns to become their rival, and too far off to be laid out as an addition to either of them. The Falls of Minnehaha are a charming resort as a watering place, and may become valuable on that account,—indeed I do not doubt that the lands immediately around those Falls would now command several hundred dollars per acre, but this consideration would extend to but a very small portion of the reservation.

In reply to the fifth Question, I must say that it is not my opinion that commissioners exercised a wise descretion in accepting $90,000 in gross for the whole reservation instead of subdividing it into small parcels and selling each seperately. It is possible and perhaps probable that if a uniform minimum of 7\frac{50}{100}$ had been fixed, and then the whole sold at public auction, combinations might have been formed so as to have prevented all competition; but I am equally well satisfied that if sealed proposals had been required on each forty acre tract seperately, or if the minimum price had been set on each forty acre tract according to its estimated value and then set up at public auction, the whole reservation would have brought a much higher sum than it sold for. I do not wish to be understood as expressing my opinion that the tract is worth[2] so much more than it sold for—I believe the value of it has been greatly over estimated. I would not deem it a very great speculation at $90,000 for the whole reservation, for I believe that a sagacious man could do quite as well with his money by making other purchases of private individuals. But while this was and is my opinion, it is certain that others persons attached a much higher value to it, and would probably have been glad of the opportunity of buying at a much higher price. But I do not deem it of so much importance whether the government should have received more or less for the land as it was that there should be no doubt of the entire disinterestedness and impartiality of the agents and the fairness of the sale; and for this reason particularly I regarded the sale as unfortunate, even if the purchaser paid all that it was worth, and as much as others would have given.

In reply to the sixth Question, I will state that I have no personal knowledge of the sale of any military or Indian Reservations, never having been present at any such sale or had any occasion to examine into the circumstances of such sale or the prices for which the lands were sold.

In reply to the seventh Question I will state that with great deferance for the opinion of the Secretary of War, I was surprised when I heard of the sale of Fort Snelling for the reason that I did not think it ought to have [been] abandoned and sold. My opinion was and now is that the government ought to have retained the Fort and fifty or an hundred acres of land at least around it, for a depot for arms, munitions, provisions & all kind of supplies to be forwarded up the Minnesota River to Fort Ridgely or up the Mississippi to for[t] Riply, or to the Red River of the North or wherever else the government might keep troops on the frontier beyond Fort Snilling. I thought Fort Snelling as important and even more important to be retained than Jefferson Barracks or Fort Leavenworth. I supposed that it was more convenient to receive & forward supplies to the Posts beyond than St Paul, being six miles further up and on the west side of the River, and having ample and convenient store houses and powder magazines and all the necessary conveniences for securing and forwarding supplies. But while this was and is my opinion on the subject, as it is a military question, I was not disposed to criticise the actions of those whose business it was to decide the question and who have decided it as they believe for the good of the service.

In reply to the Eighth question I will state that I do not know how the clause in the appropriation Bill authorizing the sale of Fort Snelling came to be incorporated in the act. I have no knowledge on the subject except what I have heard and seen in the newspapers since the sale. I presume I was not in the Senate when it was done as I have no recollection upon the subject, and did not know that any such law had passed until after the sale, and then expressed my belief that the report of the sale was unfounded for the reason that there was no law so far as I knew authorizing the sale. I presume that the clause must have been inserted in the appropriation Bill in my absence, as I was engaged on several committees of conference near the close of that Session which kept me away from the Hall when many of the appropriation [bills] were considered & most of the amendments adopted.

In reply to the ninth Question I can only say that[3] I have had no other opportunities of personal knowledge of the reservation & its use and value for any of the purposes named than those which I have stated—and those opportunities being so limited impart very little or no value to the opinions which I have expressed with so much diffidence, and which I would have withheld as being of no value in deciding the question of the propriety of the sale, if I could have done so without seeming to be disrespectful to a committee for whose members I have entire respect.[4]

Feby 19th 1858   S. A. DOUGLAS

ALS Copy, owned by Martin F. Douglas. Charles J. Faulkner was a member of Congress from Virginia from 1851 to 1859.

[1] On January 4, 1858, the House of Representatives resolved to investigate "the facts and circumstances connected with the sale of the military reservation at Fort Snelling." A committee of five was selected of which Faulkner was chairman. On June 6, 1857, a contract for the sale of the Fort Snelling

military reservation was made, under the authority of Secretary of War John B. Floyd, by which approximately 7,000 acres, comprising the entire reservation, were sold to a New York group for $90,000. Possession of the land was to be given as soon as the Secretary of War could dispense with it for military purposes. One-third of the purchase price was paid to the government, but the post was not abandoned by the time of the investigation. On February 17, 1858, Faulkner wrote Douglas a note, enclosing the inquiries and requesting answers as soon as possible. The note is in the Douglas Papers, University of Chicago Library, while a fragmentary manuscript of the inquiries, embodying the fifth, sixth, and seventh questions, is owned by Martin F. Douglas.

[2]The words "two or three times" were crossed out here.

[3]The words "it is fully answered by the answers which I have already made to the other questions" were crossed out here.

[4]The committee submitted two reports. The majority concluded that the sale of the reservation was without authority of law, and that Floyd's decision to sell the post "was a grave official fault." The minority, including Faulkner, failed to find any evidence that would "impeach the fairness of the sale or the integrity of any of the officers or agents of the government concerned in the same." The reports may be found in *House Reports*, 35 Congress, 1 Session, No. 351. Douglas' letter to Faulkner was printed in the report, pp. 392-395.

To John A. McClernand

Washington
My Dear Sir,   Feby 21st 1858

I have read your address to the people with pleasure and admiration.[1] It is a noble production, one that you may well be proud of, and of which your children will be proud. We are now engaged in a great struggle for principle which calls for all our energies and powers. The administration are determined to crush every public man who dissents from their policy of forcing a constitution on the people of Kansas against their will. I am glad to see with what gallanttry and boldness with which you put their threats at defiance. I am with you heart and soul in this great struggle, and you may rest assured that I will take no step backwards and abate not one iota of the position I have taken, let the consequences be what they may to me personally. I still have strong hopes that we will be able to lay the arm of power & save our cherished principles—the great fundamental right of every people to make their own constitution of government under our political system.

I have enclosed your letter[2] to the Hon R J Walker and presume you will hear from him on the subject.

Mrs Douglas is recovering from her illness and desires to be kindly remembered to Mrs McC. I am very truly you friend

S. A. DOUGLAS

ALS, Illinois State Historical Library.
[1]McClernand's "address," actually an undated public letter, reviewed the history of the Lecompton Constitution and was published in the *Illinois State Register* on February 12, 1858.
[2]McClernand wrote Douglas, on February 17, 1858, "Agitate! Rouse the

people! This must be our motto. If we can prevent a present defeat we will secure ultimately an overwhelming victory. Never before did any political struggle so thoroughly possess and sway the hearts of the masses" (Douglas Papers, University of Chicago Library).

To Samuel Treat

(*Private*)   Washington
My Dr Sir,   Feby 28th 1858

The great pressure of duties is the only apology I can offer for the delay in answering your kind & esteemed letters. I have conferred freely with our friend Green as you suggested,[1] but I fear there is no hope of an amicable adjustment of the Kansas Question. It has become apparent that the administration is more anxious for my distruction than they are for the harmony & unity of the Democratic Party. You have doubtless seen that they are removing all my friends from office & requiring pledges of hostility to me from all persons appointed to office. Of course my friends do not consider this course fair, honest, or Democratic, and will not be reconciled to the administration by this line of conduct. The administration is endeavering to form an alliance with the Republicans of Ills to beat me with a Republican.[2] While I can not say with certainty what the result will be, I am determined to stand firmly by my position and vindicate my principles and let the consequences take care of themselves. If the Party is divided by this course it will not be my fault. The Party in Ills is better united today than it ever was, and it remains to be seen how far they can succeed in dividing it for the benefit of the common enemy of our principles. The contest is a painful one to me, but I have no alternative, but to accept the issue and stand by what I deem to be my duty.[3]

I shall be glad to hear from you freely & fully and to avail myself of all suggestions you may do me the favor to make. I am very truly your friend

S. A. Douglas

ALS, Missouri Historical Society.

[1] On January 12, 1858, Treat wrote Douglas regarding the overwhelming vote of Kansans against the Lecompton Constitution on January 4: "Now, as there is, at length, a legal and authentic expression of the popular will against the Lecompton Constitution, a common ground is open for all Democrats. I trust that all further action will be matured *in* the Committee on Territories, and it will be such as all Democrats can readily adopt. If you and Green will set to work together, and get up a proper bill, harmony will be restored" (Douglas Papers, University of Chicago Library). Treat referred to James Stephen Green, Senator from Missouri from 1857 to 1861, and a member of the Senate Committee on Territories.

[2] Douglas was referring to the contest for his Senate seat which would take place in 1858.

[3] Douglas' position on the Lecompton Constitution ultimately triumphed. Al-

though the constitution was approved by the Senate, it failed in the House of Representatives. A committee of conference was appointed, and in the latter part of April reported the English Bill. By its terms, Kansas was to receive a land grant of nearly four million acres, plus 5 per cent of the proceeds from the sale of two million more, if its citizens approved immediate statehood under the Lecompton Constitution. If statehood should be rejected, Kansas would remain a territory at least two years longer, until its population should be larger. Actually, the voters of Kansas were to vote only on the acceptance or rejection of the land grant. The English Bill passed both houses of Congress by narrow margins, Douglas being among those who opposed it. On August 2, 1858, the land grant, and by implication the Lecompton Constitution, was rejected decisively by Kansas' electorate, by a margin of almost 10,000 votes.

To Riggs and Company

Messrs Riggs & co   Friday March 12th 58
    Mr Benham[1] will call on you for a statement of my acct with a view to ballancing it. I am sick or should call myself. Please send me a statement in detail showing the ballance, and the amount due on notes held for collection &c. Yours truly

S. A. Douglas

ALS, Library of Congress.
    [1]Spencer C. Benham acted as Douglas' financial agent.

To Lewis Cass

Senate Committee
on Territories.
Sir: April 22d /58
    I am directed by the Committee on Territories to enclose a copy of a Bill for running the boundary line between the United States and the State of Texas,[1] and to enquire whether any part of the line described in said Bill was ever run, either under the Treaty with Mexico or with Texas, and particularly whether so much of said line was run as lies on the 100th degree of longitude between Red River and 36°-30', of North latitude.
    I am also directed to enquire whether, in the opinion of the Department, an appropriation for this purpose is necessary and desirable, and, if so, what amount of money should be appropriated. Very respectfully

S. A. Douglas

LS, RG-59, National Archives.
    [1]A bill authorizing the President, in conjunction with the state of Texas, to run and mark the boundary between the United States territories and Texas passed the House of Representatives on February 9, 1858, and the Senate on May 18, 1858.

To Randal McLaughlin

[April 28, 1858, Washington City; Copy, University of Chicago Library. This letter, unsigned, is in the handwriting of James Madison Cutts, Douglas' father-in-law, who acted as Douglas' secretary at this time. In the letter, Douglas supported the application of Quincy McNeil, of Rock Island, Illinois, for commissioner to take the acknowledgment of deeds for the state of Pennsylvania. McLaughlin was a clerk in the state Treasury Department at Harrisburg, Pennsylvania.]

To ———

Washington City
Gentlemen   April 28, 1858.

I should gladly accept your invitation to attend the banquet to be given on 6th May next, by the Chicago Typographical Union to the Delegates to the National Convention of Printers, then to assemble, did my duties here admit of absence from my post.

At your hands, gentlemen, I am assured the members of a body representing so much of the worth, talent and patriotism of our country will meet with hospitable welcome in our youthful but already gigantic City of the West.

There too, I trust, as I believe, they will find abundant evidences of the vigorous growth of the arts and sciences as well as development of industry, enterprize and commerce, fully equal to the experiences they may bring from their homes in other parts of our inestimable Union.

With renewed regrets that I shall be unable to join you on the occasion I am &c.

Copy, University of Chicago Library. The copy is in the hand of James Madison Cutts.

To John B. Floyd

[May 1, 1858, Washington; RG-94, National Archives. This note, unsigned, is in the hand of James Madison Cutts. In it, Douglas tenders, through Floyd to the President, the services of the Fourth Brigade, Fifth Division of Illinois Militia. The troops might possibly have been offered for service in the campaign against the Mormons in Salt Lake City, the so-called "Mormon War."]

To C. J. Hedenberg

Washington, May 4, 1858
Judge Douglas finds himself precluded by pressing engagements, and has therefore requested me to reply to your letter of 29: ultimo.[1]

He desires me to say that you have chosen a striking and noble incident in the life of General Jackson—one full of dignity and honor to that illustrious patriot, as well as of moral to his fellow citizens—his appearance before, and submission to the fine imposed by Judge Hall at New Orleans in 1815; and that he cannot doubt but that if the artistical execution of the engraving equal the conception of the subjects as explained in your communication, the finished work will meet with just and general commendation.

Judge Douglas would have me add, that, for the purposes of the explanatory memoir, or key, you propose compiling, he accedes to your request, made at the suggestion, as you state, of his friends Gen'l Wm O Butler of Ky. and Col. Maunsell White of New Orleans,[2] so far as to enclose herewith a copy of his "Speech on refunding the fine assessed upon Gen: Jackson by Judge Hall in 1815"—and informing you that you will find—page 162 & 163—"Wheeler's Biographical and Political History of Congress, vol. 1—a fair detail of an occasion when he, Judge Douglas, felt himself highly honored by the thanks of General Jackson.

With best wishes for the speedy and successful completion of your undertaking—Respectfully Your Obedt Servt

J. MADISON CUTTS

University of Chicago Library. This letter was written and signed by James Madison Cutts.

[1]C. J. Hedenberg, a Philadelphia publisher, wrote Douglas on April 29 that he was going to execute an oil painting of Andrew Jackson submitting to the fine of Judge Hall in 1815. The painting would then be sent to London "to be engraved in the highest style of the art on steel." Hedenberg asked Douglas for a copy of the latter's speech on the remission of Jackson's fine, delivered in the House of Representatives on January 7, 1844 (Douglas Papers, University of Chicago Library).

[2]Maunsel White, a prominent New Orleans businessman, was a veteran of the Battle of New Orleans.

To Quincy McNeil

[May 10, 1858, Washington; Copy, University of Chicago Library. This letter, unsigned, is in the handwriting of James Madison Cutts. Douglas enclosed McNeil's commission, as commissioner to take the acknowledgment of deeds for Pennsylvania in Illinois. See above, Douglas to McLaughlin, April 28, 1858.]

To J. S. Ritterband *et al.*

Washington City
May 15, 1858

Gentlemen

I should be greatly pleased to be among my constituents in Illinois, and to avail myself of your polite invitation to be present at the Second

Anniversary Celebration of the Mendelssohn Literary Association of Chicago on Monday evening next, the 17th.

I trust you will kindly receive my regrets that this will be out of my power, & accept my best wishes for your enjoyment on the occasion.

Copy, University of Chicago Library. The copy is in the hand of James Madison Cutts; there is no signature. On May 11, 1858, J. S. Ritterband invited Douglas to the anniversary celebration on behalf of the Mendelssohn Literary Association of Chicago (Douglas Papers, University of Chicago Library).

To Strang, Chalfant and Company

[May 28, 1858, Washington City; Copy, University of Chicago Library. Testifying as to the respectability of the family of James Herrington, of Geneva, Illinois, but also stating his inability to judge, from insufficient knowledge, the pecuniary responsibility of Mr. Herrington. On May 26, Strang, Chalfant and Company, a Pittsburgh firm, wrote Douglas that Herrington had gone into the hardware business and wished to buy goods from them (Douglas Papers, University of Chicago Library). James Herrington had been County Clerk of Kane County for a number of years.]

To James Madison Cutts

Phil

My Dear Sir,   June 22d 1858

We arrived here safe last night and all well. I omitted several things before I left. 1st a blank Deed of Trust or mortgage which I may have use for or not in New York.[1] I left it in a cigar Box on the Table in the Library. Please send it by first mail to St. Nicholas N.Y. Also a letter from Mr. Vallandingham of Ohio.[2] Judge Mc Cook[3] spoke of it, but I did not see it. Please send it. Also such other Letters as come to me and you think I ought to see. I will send you a check from N Y for a $[. . .]oo[4] to pay clerks &c as promised. We leave at 2 oclock today for N.Y. Our love to Mother. Yours truly

S. A. DOUGLAS

ALS, owned by Martin F. Douglas.

[1]Correspondence to Douglas in the Douglas Papers, University of Chicago Library, in late June and July indicates that Douglas traveled to New York city in order to borrow money for his forthcoming Senatorial campaign in Illinois.

[2]On June 13, 1858, Clement L. Vallandigham wrote to Douglas urging him to stop in Columbus, Dayton, and Cincinnati on his way west to Illinois; "*Dont fail*—I have thrown out the hint, & you are expected" (Douglas Papers, University of Chicago Library). Vallandigham was a member of Congress

from Ohio from May 25, 1858, to 1863.

³Probably Daniel McCook, who remained in Washington during the summer of 1858, to assist in the handling of Douglas' correspondence, specifically to send out copies of Douglas' speeches and government publications in answer to requests. McCook had held a position in the Pension Office, but was dismissed, according to his statement, because of his criticism of Secretary of the Interior Jacob Thompson (McCook to Douglas, July 24, 1858, Douglas Papers, University of Chicago Library).

⁴The figure has been obscured by an ink blot and is illegible.

To Abraham Lincoln

Dear Sir: Chicago, July 24th, 1858

Your note of this date, in which you inquire if it would be agreeable to me to make an arrangement to divide the time and address the same audiences during the present canvass was handed me by Mr Judd.[1]

Recent events have interposed difficulties in the way of such an arrangment. I went to Springfield last week for the purpose of conferring with the Democratic State Central Committee upon the mode of conducting the canvass and with them and under their advice, made a list of appointments covering the entire period until late in October. The people of the several localities have been notified of the time and places of the meetings. These appointments have all been made for Democratic meetings and arrangements have been made by which the Democratic Candidates for Congress, for the Legislature and other offices will be present and address the people. It is evident, therefore, that these various candidates, in connection with myself, will occupy the whole time of the day and evening and leave no opportunity for other speeches.

Besides there is another consideration which should be kept in mind. It has been suggested recently that an arrangement had been made to bring out a third candidate for the U.S. Senate, who, with yourself, should canvass the state in opposition to me, and with no other purpose than to insure my defeat by dividing the Democratic party for your benefit.[2] If I should make this arrangement with you, it is more than probable that this other Candidate, who has a common object with you, would desire to become a party to it and claim the right to speak from the same stand; so that he and you in concert might be able to take the opening and closing speech in every case.

I cannot refrain from expressing my surprise, if it was your original intention to invite such an arrangement that you should have waited until after I had made my appointments, inasmuch as we were both here in Chicago together for several days after my arrival, and again at Bloomington, Atlanta, Lincoln and Springfield, where it was well known I went for the purpose of consulting with the State Central Committee and agreeing upon the plan of campaign.

[423]

While under these circumstances I do not feel at liberty to make any arrangement which would deprive the Democratic Candidates for Congress, state officers and the Legislature from participating in the discussion at the various meetings designated by the Democratic State Central Committee, I will, in order to accommodate you as far as it is in my power to do so, take the responsibility of making an arrangement with you for a discussion between us at one prominent point in each Congressional district in the state, excepting the second and sixth districts, where we have both spoken and in each of which cases you had the concluding speech. If agreeable to you I will indicate the following places as those most suitable in the several Congressional districts at which we should speak, to wit, Freeport, Ottawa, Galesburg, Quincy, Alton, Jonesboro' & Charleston.

I will confer with you at the earliest convenient opportunity in regard to the mode of conducting the debate and the times of meeting at the several places subject to the condition that where appointments have already been made by the Democratic State Central Committee at any of these places I must insist upon your meeting me at the time specified. Very Respectfully, Your Obedient servant

S. A. DOUGLAS

LS, Library of Congress. Lincoln had been nominated by the Republicans to oppose Douglas in the Senatorial election on June 16, 1858. Douglas returned to Chicago on July 9, and opened his campaign with a speech that day.

[1]Lincoln's note, dated July 24, Chicago, read: "Will it be agreeable to you to make an arrangement for you and myself to divide time, and address the same audiences during the present canvass? Mr. Judd, who will hand you this, is authorized to receive your an-swer; and, if agreeable to you, to enter into the terms of such arrangement" (Roy P. Basler, editor, *The Collected Works of Abraham Lincoln* [9 vols., New Brunswick, New Jersey, 1953], II, 522). Norman B. Judd was chairman of the Republican state central committee.

[2]Reports had circulated that Sidney Breese, then a Justice on the Illinois Supreme Court and a former United States Senator, would seek election to the Senate.

To Abraham Lincoln

Bement, Piatt Co. Ill.
July 30th, 1858

Dear Sir:

Your letter, dated yesterday, accepting my proposition for a joint discussion at one prominent point in each Congressional district as stated in my previous letter was received this morning.[1]

The times and places designated are as follows:

Ottawa,	Lasalle Co.	August 21st,	1858
Freeport,	Stevenson Co.	" 27th,	"
Jonesboro',	Union Co.	September 15 "	"
Charleston,	Coles Co.	" 18 "	"

Galesburg,	Knox Co.	October 7 " "
Quincy,	Adams Co.	" 13 " "
Alton,	Madison Co.	" 15 " "

I agree to your suggestion that we shall alternately open and close the discussion. I will speak at Ottawa one hour, you can reply occupying an hour and a half and I will then follow for half an hour. At Freeport you shall open the discussion and speak one hour, I will follow for an hour and a half and you can then reply for half an hour. We will alternate in like manner at each successive place.[2] Very resp'y Y'r ob't serv't,

S. A. DOUGLAS

LS, Library of Congress.

[1]Lincoln's letter to Douglas, July 29, 1858, is printed in Roy P. Basler, editor, *The Collected Works of Abraham Lincoln* (9 vols., New Brunswick, New Jersey, 1953) II, 528-530. The original, with signature and postscript only in Lincoln's hand, is owned by Martin F. Douglas. Lincoln concluded his letter with the statement: "I agree to an arrangement for us to speak at the seven places you have named, and at your own times, provided you name the times at once, so that I, as well as you, can have to myself the time not covered by the arrangement. As to other details, I wish perfect reciprocity, and no more. I wish as much time as you, and that conclusions shall alternate." In a postscript, he added: "As matters now stand I shall be at no more of your exclusive meetings, and for about a week from to-day, a letter from you will reach me at Springfield—."

[2]Lincoln replied to Douglas' letter on July 31: "Yours of yesterday, naming places, times, and terms, for joint discussions between us, was received this morning. Although, by the terms, as you propose, you take *four* openings and closes to my *three*, I accede, and thus close the arrangement. I direct this to you at Hillsboro; and shall try to have both your letter and this, appear in the Journal and Register of Monday morning" (Basler, II, 531).

To H. G. Crouch

My dear Sir:—   Winchester, Aug. 7, 1858.

Your letter of the 28th of July, communicating to me the fact that there is a rumor in circulation in Galena, supposed to have come from Gen. Jones, of Iowa, that pending the Illinois Central Railroad Grant in the Senate of the United States, an arrangement was made between him and me, by which the interests of Galena were sacrificed to those of Dubuque is received.[1] I have a distinct recollection of the facts of the case, and they are in substance as follows:—The bill, as drawn and introduced into Congress by myself, provided for a railroad from the southern terminus of the Illinois and Michigan Canal to the mouth of the Ohio River, with a branch to Chicago and another to Galena, the northwestern terminus of the road. General Jones, his colleague, and perhaps some others, objected to Galena as a terminus on the ground that the road would not connect with the Mississippi River, and thus a hiatus would be created between the east and the west side of the river. *I endeavored to dissuade them from their objections*, and to induce them to allow the bill to pass in the shape I had introduced it, *but they were immovable, and insisted on defeating the bill* unless we would extend the road to Dubuque. Upon full consultation with my colleagues in both houses of Congress, it was determined to permit the alteration to be made, under the belief that the whole bill would be defeated unless we consented to the change, and we thought it better to allow the change to be made than to lose the bill altogether, although we did not think that our Iowa friends were treating us kindly by attempting to defeat a great measure for our State on a point of the kind. Under these circumstances, I did cheerfully acquiesce and concur in the determination of the united delegation of the State, to agree to the change by which the road should be extended to Dubuque, but carefully omitting to provide at what point the crossing should be, whether at Dubuque, at Tete des Morts, or at any intermediate point. I will only add that any insinuation or intimation on the part of Gen. Jones, or any of his friends, that I had any collusion with him, and was willing to sacrifice the interests of Galena to those of Dubuque, or any other point, is basely and infamously false. Very respectfully, Your friend,

S. A. Douglas

John Carl Parish, *George Wallace Jones* (Iowa City, 1912), pp. 195-197. The letter was originally published in the Galena *Courier*, November 2, 1858. H. G. Crouch was editor of the *Courier*.

[1]George W. Jones, Democratic Senator from Iowa, took the side of the administration in the Douglas-Buchanan split and opposed Douglas' re-election to the Senate from Illinois in 1858. In his letter of July 28 to Douglas, Crouch reported that the Republicans were making use of Jones's statements (Douglas Papers, University of Chicago Library). For further developments in the controversy between Jones and Douglas, see below, Douglas to ———, [January, 1859].

To Charles H. Lanphier

My dear Sir— [August 15, 1858]

I find in the State Register of August 28th, 1856, a speech delivered by Major Harris in the House of Reps. on the 9th of August, 1856, in which is copied a resolution described as adopted at the first state convention of the Black Republican party as a part of their platform. I desire to know the time and place at which that convention was held, whether it was a mass meeting or a delegate Convention, whether Lincoln was present and made a speech and such other facts concerning the matter as you may be able to give. This information is very important and I want it immediately. Please consult Major Harris, hunt up the facts and write to me instantly directed to Ottawa. I must have it before next Saturday.[1]

Also telegraph me at Peoria the time & place of the convention which passed the resolution concerning no more slave states. Truly, Your friend,

S. A. DOUGLAS

P.S. The convention must have been held in Aug or Sept 1854— Lewistown

Aug. 15/58

LS, Illinois State Historical Library. Only the signature and the postscript are in Douglas' hand.

[1]The resolutions, alleged to have been adopted by a Republican meeting in Springfield in October, 1854, were read by Douglas in his first debate with Lincoln at Ottawa on August 21. In addition to calling for a reorganization of parties, they advocated the repeal of the fugitive slave law, the restriction of slavery to the states in which it existed, the abolition of slavery in the District of Columbia, and a prohibition on the admission of any more slave states. Lincoln denied any part in the drafting of the resolutions and later declared them to be fraudulent. The question of the validity of these resolutions and Lincoln's relationship to them provided one of the more important controversies between the two men during the debates. On August 26, 1858, Charles H. Lanphier wrote Douglas, "I see that your quotation from our old file has made an uproar. *I yet believe the resolutions there given* to be the genuine ones. Whether so or not, the point you made is not affected by their denial of the 'spot.' The resolution in dispute if I am not mistaken stood at the head of the Chicago Tribune, *as its platform*" (Douglas Papers, University of Chicago Library).

To Usher F. Linder

[August, 1858]

The hell-hounds are on my track. For God's sake, Linder, come and help me fight them.

Telegram, quoted in Albert J. Beveridge, *Abraham Lincoln, 1809-1858* (2 vols., Boston, 1928), II, 654-655. According to Beveridge, the telegraph operator sold a copy of this telegram to the Republicans. As a result, Linder became popularly known as "For-God's-sake-Linder." Linder, a former member of the Illinois state legislature, was a Charleston, Illinois, attorney.

To Usher F. Linder

[August 22, 1858, Chicago; ALS. This letter has not been located. It is described in *The Lincoln Collection Formed by Emanuel Hertz, New York City, Sold by His Order* (New York, 1927), p. 13. According to the description, the letter read in part: "Lincoln and myself hold a joint discussion at Freeport on Friday the 27th of this month. Our friends there tell me that the Republicans have made arrangements to have other speakers and among them Lovejoy to reply to me at night to help Lincoln." Owen Lovejoy, pastor of the Congregational Church in Princeton, Illinois, was a Republican member of Congress from 1857 until his death in 1864. On September 7, 1858, the Chicago *Daily*

[427]

Press and Tribune quoted an "extract from a recent letter" from Douglas to Linder: "For God's sake, Linder, come up into the Northern part of the State and help me. Every *dog* in the State is let loose after me—from the bull-dog Trumbull to the smallest canine quadruped that has a kennel in Illinois." This extract, if authentic, may have been part of Douglas' August 22 letter to Linder; it seems unlikely that he would have written an additional letter on this subject at this time.]

To Jacob I. Brown

My dear Sir: Chicago, August 29th, 1858

Your favor of the 26th inst. is received.[1] It is important that Gen. Linder should take the stump immediately, and the "genteel thing" will be done with him. Tell him to [meet?] me at my first appointment, wherever it may be, after his return from Indiana, prepared to take the stump from that time until the election. I have no such fears as you seem to entertain that it will not be possible for me to sustain my position against Trumbull, Lincoln, Carpenter, Breeze, Reynolds, Dougherty and the infamous sheet to which you allude.[2] The Democracy are thoroughly aroused, and well united, and a glorious triumph awaits us as certain as the day of election comes. Yet our friends should not be idle but should put forth efforts that will overcome those that are made against us. It is *all important* that we should carry the representative from your county and the senator from your district. I trust that our friends will spare no effort to secure a triumph. Very truly, Your friend,

S. A. DOUGLAS

LS, Illinois State Historical Library. Jacob I. Brown was Postmaster of Charleston, Coles County.

[1]Brown, a friend of both Douglas and Linder, had written to suggest that Linder's aid be enlisted in the Douglas campaign (Douglas Papers, University of Chicago Library).

[2]Sidney Breese, R. B. Carpenter, John Reynolds, and John Dougherty campaigned against Douglas on behalf of the administration Democrats. Reynolds, former Governor of Illinois, was nominated for superintendent of public instruction, and Dougherty, editor of the Jonesboro *Gazette* and a former member of the state legislature, was nominated for state treasurer. Both opposed Douglas candidates for these positions.

To Sydney Myers

[November 7, 1858, Chicago; LS. This letter has not been located. It is described in *A Catalogue of Lincolniana*, Thomas F. Madigan, New York, p. 43, #94. According to the description, Douglas wrote in part: "Accept my thanks for your kind congratulatory letter upon the result in this state. I remember with pleasure your zeal and active exertions in the good cause and feel grateful for the efforts and sacrifices which you made." Sydney Myers, a Galesburg, Illinois, attorney, wrote Douglas on November 5 (Douglas Papers, University of Chicago Library).]

To Henry A. Wise

My dear Sir: Chicago, Nov. 7th, 1858

Permit me to return to you my sincere thanks for the deep interest which you have felt and the encouragement you have afforded in the great contest which has just terminated in this state; and more especially for your eloquent and admirable address to the Illinois Democratic state Central Committee.[1] That letter touched the heart of every patriot and aroused every Democrat and every friend of the Constitution and the Union to renewed exertions. Pardon me for saying that it was a noble, patriotic letter and has done its work. You have doubtless learned the result of the fight by telegraph. We have carried both branches of the Legislature, securing a majority of ten on joint ballot over the combined forces of the Abolitionists and the federal office holders. Whatever may be the result in the other Northern states you may always rely upon Illinois as being faithful to the Democracy against the assaults and treasonable purposes of the Abolitionists and their allies. Very truly, your friend,

S. A. DOUGLAS

LS, Library of Congress. Henry A. Wise was at this time Governor of Virginia. He had been a member of the House of Representatives from 1833 to 1844.

[1]On October 13, 1858, Wise wrote John Moore, Douglas' campaign chairman, "I see you standing alone, isolated by a tyrannical proscription which would alike foolishly and wickedly lop off one of the most vigorous limbs of the National Democracy ... I see you, in spite of this imputation, firmly fronting the foe and battling to maintain conservative nationality against embittered and implacable sectionalism. ... Fight on, fight on, never yield but in death or victory" (Lanphier Papers, Illinois State Historical Library).

To the Committee of Invitation to the Pittsburgh Centennial Anniversary of the Capture of Fort Duquesne

Chicago

Gentlemen: Nov 17, 1858.

Accept my thanks for your polite invitation to be present at the centennial anniversary of the capture of Fort Duquesne, on the 20th inst. I regret exceedingly that my engagements are such as to deprive me of the pleasure which I should feel on being present on that interesting occasion. It is proper that so important an event in the history of this continent should be celebrated in a manner commensurate with the consequences which have resulted from it. Each succeeding century will add, as the past has added, grandeur to the scheme of the French Cabinet which contemplated a great North American empire, occupying the valley of the Mississippi, the Ohio, and the St. Lawrence, and confining the British Colonies to the Atlantic coast. That scheme was destroyed, and the hopes of its projectors dissipated by the campaign which resulted in the capture of Fort Duquesne. The great importance of this event will not be fully realized until the Mississippi valley shall have doubled and trebled its population, and become the heart of the Republic, more extensive, powerful and glorious than any empire that the world ever beheld. For these reasons the anniversary which you propose to celebrate is of peculiar interest to those of us whose fortune it is to have their homes in the valley of the Mississippi and the great lakes.

Renewing my regrets that I am not able to accept your polite invitation, and the assurance that I appreciate the honor which you have conferred upon me, I remain, very truly, Your friend and servant,

S. A. DOUGLAS

Chicago *Times*, December 3, 1858.

To Pierre Soulé *et al.*

[December, 1858]
St Charles
New Orleans

Gentlemen

Accept my sincere thanks for your kind favor testifying your approbation of my position in the late contest in Illinois and tendering your congratulations upon the glorious triumph acchieved by the Democracy of that State over the Enemies of the Constitution and the Union.

It will afford me great pleasure to comply with your request to address the people of New Orleans on Monday evening next at such place as you may designate.[1] Renewing my thanks to you and those you represent for the approval which you have been pleased to express of my political course I remain very truly your friend & obedient servant

S. A. DOUGLAS

Messrs Pierre Soulé
 J. R. Ward
 E H Dix
 B. S. Tappan
 & others
Committee

ALS Copy, owned by Martin F. Douglas. Pierre Soulé, former Senator from Louisiana and Minister to Spain, was practicing law in New Orleans at this time. On December 2, 1858, Soulé and several other citizens of New Orleans congratulated Douglas on his "able defence" of states' rights principles in the Illinois Senatorial contest, and invited him to speak in New Orleans "at such time and place as may suit your convenience" (Douglas Papers, University of Chicago Library).

[1]Douglas spoke at the Odd-Fellows Hall in New Orleans on December 6, 1858. He was en route from Illinois to Washington, D.C., by way of New Orleans, Cuba, and New York.

To ⸺

[On December 16, 1858, the Washington *States* reported the following: "Senator Douglas has recently written a private letter, in which he declares he is not a candidate for the Presidency. He states that the fight just ended had been one for principle, and of conscience and conviction, that the result has triumphantly vindicated his position in the eyes of his own people, than to represent whom in the confederated councils of sovereignties he has at present no higher ambition. He reiterates his adherence to the Democratic faith and organization, and vows his purpose to support the Charleston nominee. He will take an early occasion in the Senate to define his views, which he says have been the subject of much unjust misconstruction." This letter has not been located.]

To ⸺

[January, 1859]

Since my arrival in this city I have received a letter addressed by Geo. W. Jones to myself and purporting to have been written on the 9th of November, but post marked at the city of Washington on the ⸺ day of December 1858.[1] I say that the letter purports to have been written on the 9th of Nov. for the reason that it bears date on that day, and also has a certificate appended to it in the form of a postscript, certifying that it was actually written on the day of its date, notwithstanding that it contains an extract from a speech made by me in Chicago on the 17th of Nov. eight days after it was certified to have been written.

But it is a matter of entire indifference to me whether the letter was written by Mr Jones in Dubuque, Iowa, on the 9th of Nov. or whether it was concocted in the city of Washington by my confederated enemies after their arrival in that city as a part of their political campaign. My only object in noticing it is to explain to the public the reasons why I ever happened to refer to Mr Jones by letter or otherwise. Sometime in the month of July last, after the fierce struggle between the abolitionists and their allies on the one hand and the

[431]

regular organization of the Democratic party on the other had fairly commenced in Illinois I received a letter from Mr. Crouch, editor of the Galena Courier, informing me that Geo. W. Jones had been in Galena, electioneering for the abolition ticket and assisting the abolitionists to defeat the regular Democratic nominees by circulating the report that in the passage of the Illinois Central railroad bill in 1850 I had been unfaithful to the interests of Illinois by combining with him to promote the prosperity of Dubuque at the expense of the city of Galena. Whilst I did not attach the slightest importance to what Mr Jones might say or do I felt it to be my duty, as an act of Courtesy to Mr. Crouch, to reply to his letter and consequently did so in a letter of the 29th of July in which I stated that these insinuations, whether circulated by Mr Jones and his friends or by anybody else, were infamously false.[2] From that time the subject passed from my mind and I never had any knowledge that this harmless and inoffensive letter had been published until I received it in connection with Mr Jones epistle directed to myself. It now seems that the naughty words "infamously false" have been appropriated by Mr. Jones as personally offensive to himself and that he has sought a remedy for his wounded honor by publishing a letter addressed to me, dated on the 9th of November and mailed more than one month afterwards, his impatience not permitting him to wait twelve hours until I could receive it by the regular mail. In this letter he hurls back at me with unfeigned indignation the naughty words referred to, and deals in harsh terms and ugly denunciations in the hope of covering up the offensive words of my letter. I have no taste for this childish amusement and hence have nothing to say of Mr Jones, nor have I any vindication to make of the story which he now repeats, and attempts to prove by his own evidence, of my want of fidelity to the interests of my own state and his extraordinary services to the state of Iowa. I am willing to leave that question to the two states which are alone interested and authorized to decide. I am entirely content with the verdict which the people of Illinois have recently rendered upon my conduct and have no disposition to question the propriety and justness of the judgment which the people of Iowa have pronounced upon the services and conduct of Mr Jones.

Asking your pardon for occupying so much space in your valuable paper upon so small a matter I remain, Very truly, Y'r Ob't Serv't.

Copy, owned by Martin F. Douglas. This letter, obviously written to the press, was never published. It was probably composed sometime between December 28, 1858, when Douglas arrived in New York city from Havana, and January 10, when he took his seat in the Senate.

[1]The date is blank in the copy. Jones's letter has been published in John Carl

Parish, *George Wallace Jones* (Iowa City, 1912), pp. 197-202. In it Senator Jones objected bitterly to the tone and content of Douglas' letter to H. G. Crouch, editor of the Galena *Courier*, August 7, 1858 (see above), concerning the extension of the Illinois Central Railroad to Dubuque, Iowa.

²Douglas is in error on the date of his letter to Crouch. It was written from Winchester, Illinois, on August 7, 1858.

To Charles H. Lanphier

Jany 6 1858 [1859]

C. H. Lanphier
    Let the voice of the people rule.

Baltimore 5 1858 [1859]

S. A. DOUGLAS

Telegram, Illinois State Historical Library. This telegram was sent by Douglas upon receiving the news of his victory in the Illinois legislative election for United States Senator. The legislature balloted on January 6, 1859, Douglas receiving 54 votes to Lincoln's 46. Douglas had purposely delayed his trip to Washington, D.C., not wishing to take his seat in the Senate until the election had been decided. He first appeared in the Senate on January 10 and was formally sworn in on March 4, the first day of the third session of the Thirty-fifth Congress.

To the Editor of the Washington *States*

To the Editors of the States: [January 7, 1859]

Since my recent arrival in New York, I have seen, for the first time, a publication made by the Hon. John Slidell, denying positively that he authorized, or in any manner countenanced, the statement published in the Press and Tribune, of Chicago, just before the late Illinois election, to the effect that the slaves belonging to my children, in Mississippi, were cruelly and inhumanly treated.[1] In this denial, Mr. Slidell does justice to himself. He goes further, and says: "that the alleged statement, let it come from whatever source it may, is a base fabrication, in whole and in part, without a shadow of foundation in truth." In this he does justice to me; for, as the guardian of my children, I hold myself responsible for the manner in which these slaves are treated. I should not consider myself called upon to notice Mr. Slidell's publication had he paused here, and not have added the following paragraph:

"Mr. Douglas has, by authorizing and countenancing anonymous attacks on me, through a person officiating as his private secretary, lost all claim to the explanation that I would otherwise have promptly volunteered to give him."[2]

It is due to myself to publish an emphatic denial of the truth of the implication in the above paragraph. It is not true that I have authorized or countenanced anonymous attacks upon Mr. Slidell. It is true, however, that when the fact was first brought to my notice, that Dr.

[433]

Brainard,[3] a federal officer-holder and my enemy, had caused to be published, during my absence, in the Abolition organ of Chicago, this "base fabrication," with the name of the Hon. John Slidell as authority for its truth, I denounced it as such a calumny deserved, and expressed the opinion to my friends that it should be copied and circulated for the purpose of showing the base means employed to defeat my election, and also with the view of drawing forth such disclosures as would expose to public contempt the real author of the calumny, which object has been fully accomplished by the letter of Mr. Slidell. Jan. 7, 1850 [1859].   S. A. DOUGLAS

Washington *States*, January 11, 1859.

[1] The story that the slaves belonging to Douglas' children were mistreated appeared in the Chicago *Daily Press and Tribune*, November 1, 1858. Slidell's denial, written December 18 to the Washington *Union*, appeared in the *Press and Tribune* on December 24, 1858.

[2] In a letter to the Washington *Union*, written January 12 and published on January 13, Slidell explained the grounds of his charge that Douglas had authorized anonymous attacks on him: "During my visit to New Orleans in November last, an editor of a paper published there, who is a friend and partisan of Mr. Douglas, (but who at the same time is not unfriendly to me,) informed me that he had received an anonymous letter from Chicago for publication in his paper, commenting very severely upon me, and that he did not intend to publish it, but desired me to see it. He accordingly produced the paper, and read to me certain portions of it extremely vituperative. I told him that I had heard enough of it, and insisted on knowing the name of the author, and how the paper had been forwarded to him. To this he at first demurred, but on my urgent insistance that I had the right to know the name of the author, he said that it had been sent to him in the ordinary form of newspaper correspondence, either without signature or with an assumed one, and had been accompanied by a letter from Mr. James B. Sheridan. I requested him to give me the name in writing, which he did. I have it now in my possession. I had heard that this Mr. Sheridan acted as amanuensis for Mr. Douglas, had accompanied him through his late canvass, reported his speeches, &c., and I also asked the editor whether Mr. Sheridan did not stand in this relation to Mr. Douglas. His reply was that he so understood, having had other letters from him. I then declared to the editor in the presence of another person, and subsequently repeated the declaration to other friends, that on my arrival in Washington, where I expected, of course, to meet Mr. Douglas, I should call him for a categorical reply whether or not he had authorized this letter of his secretary, and should be governed in my course towards him by his manner."

[3] Dr. Daniel Brainard, of Chicago, was President and Professor of Surgery at Rush Medical College and Surgeon to the United States Marine Hospital in Chicago. The story of the mistreatment of the Douglas slaves had reportedly been told by Slidell to Brainard.

To David Gage

[January 13, 1859, Senate U.S.; ALS, Lincoln National Life Foundation. Introducing Colonel J. C. Walker, a friend of John Letcher of Virginia, who was visiting Chicago on business. Gage was part owner of the Tremont House in Chicago. John Letcher was at this time a member of Congress, but would soon be elected to the governorship of Virginia.]

To Graham N. Fitch

Washington, Jan. 21, 1859.

Sir: To-day, in secret session of the Senate, you offered me an affront so wanton, unprovoked, and unjustifiable that I am obliged to infer it must have been the impulse of momentary passion, and not of deliberate premeditation. This note is written for the purpose of affording you an opportunity of saying whether or not my conclusion is correct; and, further, of affording you an opportunity of retracting the offensive language which you thus gratuitously and unwarrantably applied to me.[1] Respectfully, &c.,

S. A. DOUGLAS

Washington *Union*, January 25, 1859.

[1]In reply, Fitch wrote Douglas on January 22: "Your note of yesterday was handed me this morning. In reply, I have to say that you yesterday made a charge that the lately-appointed federal officers in Illinois were corrupt, dishonest men or words to that effect. You knew my son to be one of those officers, and you could not expect me to hear such a charge without prompt denial of its truth. I pronounced it to be, to your knowledge, *untrue*. You subsequently so modified it as to satisfy me that you excepted my son from the general charge, although you did not name him, and I made no further issue with you on that subject. When, at a subsequent period of your remarks, you attributed to me statements which I had not made, I requested that in quoting me you would do so truthfully. These remarks were certainly not 'deliberately premeditated,' but they cannot be qualified correctly as the 'impulse of momentary passion.' The first was prompted by a determination to defend the honor and character of my son, as dear to me as my own, against an attack so general in its terms as necessarily to include him; and the second was the exercise of my right to rectify a misrepresentation of my own remarks" (Washington *Union*, January 25, 1859). Fitch's son, Henry S. Fitch, was appointed United States Attorney for the Northern District of Illinois in April, 1858.

To Graham N. Fitch

Washington, Jan. 22—9½, p.m.

Sir: Your note of this date has just been placed in my hands.[1] I admit, without hesitation, your right and duty to do justice to the reputation of your son. At the same time I maintain my right, in the discharge of my duty as senator, to comment freely and fully on the character of executive appointments, especially in my own State. I deny, however, that my general remarks in relation to the list of Illinois appointees, confirmed by the Senate during my absence, could be fairly interpreted to embrace your son. When you seemed so to construe them, I promptly replied that what I had said of the Illinois appointments was true as a *general rule*, but that there were exceptions,

among whom I recognised some of my own friends. Alluding particularly to your son, I added that I had nothing to say in regard to the
merits of his appointment, choosing to leave that question where I
placed it by my remarks to the Senate during the last session, in your
presence, at the time of his confirmation. You now admit that you
understood this explanation to exempt your son from the application
of my general remarks; and yet, you have failed to withdraw the
offensive language, but, on the contrary, at a subsequent stage of the
debate, when apologizing for a breach of senatorial decorum, you
expressly declared that you had nothing to retract—thus appearing, in
my apprehension, to reaffirm the objectionable words.

As to the other ground of offence admitted in your reply to my
note, I have to say that I did not understand you to assume to correct
me in a quotation of your language, as I was unconscious of making
any such citation, but to repeat the original offence in another form;
otherwise, I would have made a proper response on the instant.

This explanation, which is due alike to us both, on the points presented in your reply, affords you another opportunity of withdrawing
the offensive words which you admit you applied to me in yesterday's
debate.[2] Respectfully, &c.,

S. A. DOUGLAS

Washington *Union*, January 25, 1859.
[1]See above, January 21, 1859, n1.
[2]Fitch replied to this letter, January
23, 1859: "Your note of last evening
was handed me at 12, m., to-day. Your
explanation in regard to my son being
now explicit, I have no hesitation in
saying that if you had excepted him
from your charge, or not made it general, I would not have deemed myself
warranted in repelling it *in the words*
of which you complain as offensive,
and which, in *consequence of your
explanation*, I now withdraw.
"I am also informed by your note
that, if you had not been mistaken in
relation to my remarks on the subject
of your misrepresentation of my sentiments, you would at the instant have
made a proper response. This likewise
enables me to say that, in my closing
remarks explanatory to the Senate of
my share in an exciting debate upon a
subject not relevant to anything before
that body, and the responsibility for
the introduction of which rested solely
with you, I should have withdrawn, as
I now do, the second offensive remarks,
if you had made the same satisfactory
explanation *then* you have *now* made"
(Washington *Union*, January 25, 1859).

To Graham N. Fitch

Washington
Jan'y 24th 1859

Sir

Your note of yesterday has been received;[1] and while I accept your
withdrawal of the words to which I have taken exception, I owe it to
myself to protest against the idea you seem to entertain, that my note
of Saturday was intended as a precedent and enducing condition of
the redress, which I solicited, instead of being as I certainly designed

it, mere[ly] responsive to specifications in your reply to my first communication.

In regard to the introduction and relavancy of the matter in the debate out of which this difficulty arose, I cannot think that a proper subject of discussion in the present correspondence.[2] Respectfully &c

S. A. DOUGLAS

ALS Copy, owned by Martin F. Douglas. The letter was published as part of the Fitch-Douglas correspondence in the Washington *Union*, January 25, 1859.

[1]See above, January 22, 1859, n2.

[2]Fitch replied on the same day, January 24: "Your note of to-day was received at 11½, a. m. It is not for me to judge the motives which dictated yours of the 22d. I can only say that my answer was predicated upon the explanations it contained. If your explanations are disavowed, my withdrawal must likewise be disavowed" (Washington *Union*, January 25, 1859).

To Graham N. Fitch

Washington, Jan. 24, 1859.

Sir: I am averse to prolonging this controversy after gaining the substance of my demand; but I cannot close without responding to your last note[1] by saying that it is immaterial to me upon what you predicate your withdrawal, since I have guarded against a misapprehension of my position. Respectfully, &c.,

S. A. DOUGLAS

Washington *Union*, January 25, 1859.

[1]See above, January 24, 1859, n2.

To George H. Hull

Washington,
February 10 '59

My dear Sir—

I take pleasure in complying with your request to furnish you my autograph, with the sentiment that this Union can exist forever divided into free and slave states, as our fathers made it, if the Constitution be preserved inviolate. Very Resp'y Your Ob't Serv't,

S. A. DOUGLAS

LS, Illinois State Historical Library. George H. Hull was a Cincinnati grocery clerk and bookkeeper.

To Thomas A. Hendricks

My dear Sir—   Washington, February 10th '59

I have received a letter from E. M. Tucker, of Sugar Mound, Lynn county, Kansas Territory, informing me that his father, Christopher Tucker, is entitled to a quarter section of land, in the Military bounty land district in Illinois by virtue of having served in the Virginia militia in 1814, but they have lost their patent and have no means of ascertaining the numbers of the land which were assigned to them. Will you have the kindness to have the records searched and furnish me with the description of the land awarded to Christopher Tucker. Very truly, Your Ob't Serv't,

S. A. Douglas

LS, RG-49, National Archives.

To Charles H. Lanphier

Washington,
My dear Sir— Feb. 11, 1859.
I have not yet received my commission or certificate of election to the Senate of the United States. It so happens that at my reelection six years ago no certificate was sent to me. I desire to present it to the Senate this session, and I would be obliged to you if you would procure the certificate to be made out and send it to me immediately in order that it may be laid before the Senate before the adjournment. Very truly, Your friend,

S. A. Douglas

LS, Illinois State Historical Library.

To Thomas A. Hendricks

[March 8, 1859, Washington; LS, RG-49, National Archives. Enclosing a duplicate certificate for land filed on at the Danville, Illinois, Land Office and asking that the patent for the land be sent him in return.]

To ———

Washington, March 17, 1859.
Sir—Please make an exertion to obtain subscribers to this paper. Respectfully,

S. A. Douglas

Chicago *Daily Press and Tribune*, April 23, 1859. This apparently was a circular letter sent out to increase the circulation of the Washington *States and Union*, a Douglas organ.

To Charles Lanman

Washington,
My dear Sir— March 28, 1859
I have received a letter from my esteemed friend, Hon. N. W. Edwards, of Springfield, Ill. in which he states that he forwarded to you a biographical sketch of his late distinguished father, Ninnian

Edwards, for your Congressional Dictionary, and that he failed to retain a copy of that biography. He desires me to procure from you the original which he sent to you, in order that he may be able to retain a copy of it in his possession. You will therefore do me the favor to send me Mr Edward's manuscript at your earliest convenience. Very truly, Your Ob't Serv't,

S. A. Douglas

LS, New York State Library. Charles Lanman, of Georgetown, D.C., former newspaper editor, government librarian, and author, was private secretary to Daniel Webster in 1851.

To [James W. Singleton]

My dear Sir,   Washington, March 31, 1859.

Your kind letter of the 20th ult. arrived during the last days of the session when the pressure of business was so great that I was unable promptly to attend to my correspondence.[1] I have already sent you a copy of my speech, made after your letter was written, but before it was received, from which you will perceive a striking coincidence of the identity of our views.[2] We must meet the issue boldly which has been presented to us by the Interventionists from the North and from the South, and maintain with firmness a strict adherence to the doctrine of popular sovereignty and non intervention by Congress with slavery in the Territories as well as in the states. There is no other salvation for the Democratic party. I do not intend to make peace with my enemies, nor to make a concession of one iota of principle, believing that I am right in the position I have taken, and that neither can the Union be preserved or the Democratic party maintained upon any other basis. I agree with you fully in regard to the necessity of thorough organization of our friends preparatory to the great battle at Charleston. With a bold, honest platform, avowing our principles in unequivocal language, and a candidate standing upon that platform who is thoroughly identified with it, and whose past gives assurance that he will honestly carry it out, our success is certain. The time has arrived when our friends should prepare for energetic, organized action. I am, very truly, Your friend,

S. A. Douglas

LS, Illinois State Historical Library.
[1]On February 20, Singleton wrote Douglas concerning the efforts of Southerners to secure protection to slavery in the territories. "We are not in a condition to carry another ounce of Southern weight and I say so with a painful reluctance. We have essayed to vindicate their rights under the Constitution, we grant to them all we claim for ourselves, and we must now take our chances alike for the protection which the local laws will extend to our property in the territories; to go further and Legislate for one or every species of property in the terri-

tories—would be *inexplicable incon-sistency*, invoking the fatal acknowledgement *as eror* all our preconceived notions of the right and capacity of the people to regulate their domestic affairs in their own way.... The idea of an act of Congress to protect slavery in the territories is I doubt not intended to create a *dilemma* for your special distraction; hoping as you may be forced to choose the northern or South-ern [view], you will alienate the southern or Northern people.... That if you escape Cylla they will force you into Charybdis" (Douglas Papers, University of Chicago Library).

²*Speech of Hon. S. A. Douglas, of Illinois, in the Senate of the United States, February 23, 1859, in Reply to Hon. A. G. Brown, of Mississippi* (Washington, D.C., 1859).

To [James M. Scofield]

[March, 1859]

I sincerely regret that circumstances, over which I have no control, have rendered it impossible for me to visit Connecticut during your present canvass.¹ Your election this spring excites unusual interest, and involves important consequences. Upon it may depend the organization of the next Congress, and the ascendancy of the Democratic party in the House, in the election of speaker and the appointment of committees. The Democratic party is the only political organization, which can preserve the peace and harmony of the Union; and the integrity and ascendancy of the Democratic party can only be maintained by *an explicit and unequivocal recognition of the fundamental principle of* POPULAR SOVEREIGNTY *and* NON-INTERVENTION BY CONGRESS, WITH SLAVERY IN THE TERRITORIES *as well as in the States, as it was explained and understood in the great contest of 1854 and 1856.* I understand that the Democracy of Connecticut are now fighting the battle on this distinct issue, so far as federal politics are involved in the contest, and most heartily shall I rejoice in your success.

I regret that I am unable to participate in the conflict, and to argue before your people the great principle involved—"a principle as ancient as free government itself"—in defence of which the declaration of independence was proclaimed, and the battles of the Revolution were fought, and which now forms the basis of all our institutions. I repeat, I wish you complete success in the great conflict.²

Hartford *Post*, March 31, 1859. James M. Scofield was editor and proprietor of the *Post*. Only a portion of the letter was printed in the *Post*. Scofield had invited Douglas to visit Connecticut "to explain the Democratic principles of Popular Sovereignty and Non-intervention."

¹The 1859 spring elections in Connecticut attracted wide attention among national political leaders. Both the Democratic and Republican parties imported speakers of note and the campaign revolved principally about the question of slavery in the territories.

²The Republicans swept both the General Assembly and the Congressional races.

To John Pope

Washington
April 3—1859

My dear Sir:—

Accept my thanks for your kind letter of congratulation upon the result of the political campaign in Illinois. You will also pardon the delay in answering your letter as I found such a host of letters and such a pressure of business on my arrival here that it was impossible to attend to them during the session of Congress.

I trust that you are enjoying good health and are succeeding in your professional pursuits to your entire satisfaction. I shall always be happy to hear from you and to serve you whenever it is in my power. Very truly, your friend

S. A. DOUGLAS

ALS, Knox College, Galesburg, Illinois. John Pope, a captain in the United States Army, had been chief topographical engineer for the Department of New Mexico and had been engaged in the Pacific Railroad surveys during most of the 1850's.

To James Washington Sheahan

Washington,
April 8, '59

My dear Sir:

Your letter enclosed to Mr. Cutts, has just been handed to me. I certainly owe you an apology for not returning the first chapter which you sent me.[1] I have been so overwhelmed with other matters that it has escaped my attention but I will immediately revise it and return it to you. The difficulty I have is to know how to transmit it. I am satisfied the mails cannot be relied upon and as Benham will go out this week I think I had better reserve it and send it out by him. I have received no letter from you this winter except the one asking for a copy of the Globe, containing the debate in the Senate, which was immediately sent you. Mr. Sheridan[2] also informs me that he sent you several copies of my speech in pamphlet form, with the appendix, as soon as it was issued and before it was generally circulated, and to insure the Times receiving it sent copies to Mr. Price and Mr. Eastman, besides.[3] He has franked to you Price, Eastman, Daniels, Merrick[4] and others, the message and documents and other books. Please inform me whether these have been received. If my mail matter cannot pass through the Chicago post office it is time that the reason should be known. You can go on with your book as rapidly as you please and I will endeavor to be punctual hereafter in returning the proofs immediately after I have read them. I have made no arrangements and do not anticipate making any in reference to the large work to which you refer. I merely suggested the subject to Mr. Cooke, as a publishing house in Philada. (Smith & Co.) had applied to me for permission to get up such a work and I had said to them that I did not feel at liberty to give it fearing that they might interfere with the work which you and Mr. Cooke have undertaken.[5] For the present I am satisfied that the work in progress is all that is advisable. In conclusion permit me to assure you that nothing has occurred calculated in the slightest degree to impair these kind and confidential relations which exist between us.

Copy, University of Kansas Library. This copy is incomplete.

[1]Sheahan had been selected by Douglas to write his campaign biography, to be published by the firm of Derby and Jackson, New York. As portions of the manuscript were completed, they were submitted to Douglas for revision and correction. Although D. B. Cooke, representing the publisher, admonished Douglas with the need for haste (March 14 and 29, 1859, Douglas Papers, University of Chicago Library; March 26, 1859, owned by Martin F. Douglas), the book was subject to long delays. In the meantime, Henry M. Flint, a young Chicago lawyer, rushed a sketch of Douglas' life, which, with several of Douglas' speeches, was published anonymously in 1860 by Derby and Jackson as the *Life of Stephen A. Douglas . . . by a Member of the Western Bar.* Sheahan's work was eventually published, on the eve of the Charleston convention, by Harper and Brothers.

[2]James B. Sheridan was a reporter on John W. Forney's Philadelphia *Press* and an early expert in the art of "phonography," or shorthand. In 1858, he was employed by the Chicago *Times* to take verbatim accounts of Douglas' speeches in the debates with Lincoln.

[3]Zebina Eastman was a Chicago journalist.

[4]Elias Daniels and Richard T. Merrick were Chicago attorneys.

[5]A Philadelphia publishing house, Smith and Company, had expressed the desire to publish a volume of Douglas' speeches. Cooke, however, felt the greater demand to be for Douglas' biography, although he suggested that a "standard library volume of speeches" could be issued later (March 29, 1859, Douglas Papers, University of Chicago Library).

To George Bancroft

My dear Sir—   Washington, April 11, 1859

I am preparing an address upon the right of the people of the Territories to govern themselves in all their domestic relations, without the interference of the federal government, and the line of my argument requires me to trace the principle involved in the controversy between the colonies and the parent country.[1] I find that principle to have been that while the Colonists ceded to the imperial government the right to pass all laws which were imperial and not colonial, they claimed for themselves the exclusive right of legislation in respect to their internal polity, slavery included. In the enforcement of this argument I desire certain authorities which it has occured to me you could furnish with very little trouble. I perceive by an examination of a memoir prepared by Mr Jefferson to be presented to the Continental Congress in 1774, that he stated that the Colonial Legislatures repeatedly passed acts prohibiting the introduction of any more African slaves and that the King witheld his consent. Can you furnish me with a list of the enactments by Virginia, South Carolina and each of the other colonies prohibiting or excluding slavery, together with the dates of their enactment and the circumstances attending each, so far as is compatible with a brief statement. I refer to the enactments prior to 1774, for those of that year were merely retaliatory, and therefore, not the operation of a principle. I desire to show that our colonies claimed the right as Colonies to prohibit slavery. Any other facts or references to books which can be consulted here which you may be pleased to furnish me, will place me under peculiar obligations.[2] Very truly, Your friend,

S. A. DOUGLAS

LS, John Carter Brown Library, Brown University.
[1] Douglas was working on his study of popular sovereignty in the territories, published in *Harper's Magazine*, September, 1859, under the title, "The Dividing Line Between Federal and Local Authority: Popular Sovereignty and the Territories."

[2] Bancroft replied to Douglas on April 19, 1859, with references to actions taken by the Virginia and South Carolina colonial legislatures regarding the question of slavery and the slave trade (owned by Martin F. Douglas).

To James Washington Sheahan

Confidential   Washington, April 18, 1859

Last Thursday, when I enclosed you your first chapter with my corrections I supposed Mr. Benham had gone as he had told me that he certainly should start that morning. Supposing he had forgotten his promise to call & get a package for you I concluded to run the risk of sending it by mail. I trust you have received it by this time, and that you will not be offended at the way in which I have meditated by my corrections. The fact is I did not like the minute details, dates, names &c. about families which seem indelicate if not trifling, and may in some cases give offense and perhaps in some cases create controversy. But it has since occured to me that by erasures I may have destroyed the theme of your story without supplying the broken links. Thinking the subject all over last night, and having nothing more important to do, I sketched off rapidly a connected Biography, supplying the omissions to which you called my attention in your letter and which I feared I had failed to make in your chapter, and now enclose it to you in the rough draft as an outline of all you will need.[1] The personal Biography coming down to the time I first entered public life is the most difficult part of your work & the only part that will give you much trouble.

Permit me to suggest that you rewrite the first chapter, taking my sketch as the outline of facts, and elaborating such portions as you may see proper, but omitting those *minutiae* that may seem trifling & not worthy of record in a permanent work. Your introduction struck me as very fully, and yet I think is too much about "marriage to a principle" &c. repeating it too often. You will see that I have made this criticism on the margin of your printed slip in pencil mark merely for the purpose of calling your attention to it, but not to condemn. Pardon the freedom of my criticism for you know that I always invite criticism in my own productions as freely as I make them in others.

If you do not put the first chapter to press before I can collect the material, it is probable that I may be able to procure from New England some work giving a connected account of the Douglas family in America, altho I doubt whether [it] is desirable to do so. I leave this to your judgement. Benham will leave here tomorrow & will deliver to you this package and also a photograph of Brady which was I think the best yet taken.[2]

P.S. Mrs. D. desires you to return to her this rough sketch as she has a fancy to keep it in my hand writing. I have promised her that you will copy it and return her the original. Please redeem this promise for me. . . .

S. A. D.

Copy, University of Kansas Library. This copy is probably incomplete.

[1]See below, Autobiographical Notes, [April 17, 1859].

[2]Mathew Brady, the famed Civil War photographer, opened his Washington gallery in 1858. In February, 1859, Brady wrote Douglas for his order for photographs, so that it could be filled before the end of the Congressional session; he also wrote that he was allowing a liberal discount to members of Congress in order that Douglas' likeness could be distributed over the country (Douglas Papers, University of Chicago Library). Brady undoubtedly referred to the same photograph mentioned by Douglas in his letter to Sheahan.

Autobiographical Notes

[April 17, 1859]

Left N.Y. in June 1833 & went to Cleaveland Ohio & entered the office of S. J. Andrews Esq as a Student at Law—Taken sick soon after with the billious fever & confined to my bed till 1st Oct—

Had about $300 when I left home and between $30 & 40 when I left Cleaveland in Oct.

About the 1st Oct. left Cleaveland on a Canal Boat for Portsmouth,

Thence Cincinatti, Louisville, & St Louis, remaining a few days in each place—

About the 1st Nov, finding myself nearly out of money, I left & went to Jacksonville Ill & remaining 2 or 3 weeks went to Winchester to obtain a School in order to pay my expenses. At this time I have about $1.50 in money was in feeble health, and according to the best of my knowledge was miles from any person I had ever seen before. About the 1st Dec I obtained a School and taught 3 months making merely sufficient to pay expenses.

About the 1st March 1834 I returned to Jacksonville, obtained a License to practice Law, and opened an office. During the summer of 1834 I obtained a liberal share of law business, and took quite an active part in the political contests then pending.

In March there was much excitement respecting the removal of the Deposits by Gen Jackson—Public meetings &c &c—In the winter of 1834-5—I was elected States Atty for the 1st Circuit by the Legislature for two years—Objective of youth.

Conducted many important criminal trials & devoted myself to criminal Law & Practice.

In August 1836 was elected a member of the Legislature from the County of Morgan. On all political questions I acted with the Democratic Party & sustained the Administration of Gen Jackson. Was one of the committee that made a report defending the administration from the charges &c. Supported the Ill & Mich Canal, and a reasonable system of Internal Improvements, but objected to the extent of it & only voted for it reluctantly under instructions.

In March 1837 was appointed Register of the U.S. Land Office at Springfield by the President & Senate.

In March 1840 was appointed Secretary of State by Governor Carlin & was rejected by the Senate upon the ground that the Governor had not right to remove Col Field[1] the existing incumbent. This was strictly a party question, and one which produced much excitement over the whole State. The question was carried to the people & at the election which took place in August 1840 the Democratic Party obtained a majority in both branches of the Legislature. At the opening of the Legislature in Nov I was again appointed Secretary of State by the Governor & *confirmed* by the Senate.

In Feb'y 1841 I was elected by the Legislature a Justice of the Supreme Court & presiding Judge of the 5th Judicial Circuit & took my seat on the Bench.

[*Written across and in margin of pages*]
Lyceum[2]
[...] Meeting & discussion

Law cases before Magistrates &c &c

Letter to Sec of the Treasury in relation to opposing May's Election to Congress—[3]

Banks

Charters

Trial of Webber, Truett, Moffett, &c &c[4]

Secretary of [State] Case ⎱
Alien Case ⎰ in Supreme Court[5]

ADf, owned by Martin F. Douglas. These autobiographical notes were written on April 17, 1859, but enclosed and explained in Douglas' letter to Sheahan, April 18, 1859 (see above).

[1]Alexander Pope Field had been appointed Secretary of State in 1828 by Governor Ninian Edwards. Originally a supporter of Andrew Jackson, Field by 1838 had cast his lot with the Whig party. When Governor Carlin attempted to remove him, he refused to leave his office on the ground that the state constitution did not specify a term of office for Secretary of State. Field was supported in this position by the Whig majority in the upper house of the state legislature, and by two members of the state Supreme Court. The Democrats made a political issue out of this "life office question" in the election of 1840, carried both houses of the legislature, and successfully ousted Field in favor of Douglas.

[2]The Young Men's Lyceum of Springfield was founded in 1833, and soon became an important cultural force in the capital city.

[3]See above, Douglas to Woodbury, October 6, 1837.

[4]These were court cases argued by Douglas.

[5]For the "Secretary of State Case," see above, n1; for the "Alien Case," see above, Douglas to McClernand, January 29, 1841.

To J. B. Dorr

Washington, June 22, 1859.

My Dear Sir: I have received your letter inquiring whether my friends are at liberty to present my name to the Charleston Convention for the Presidential nomination.[1]

Before this question can be finally determined, it will be necessary to understand distinctly upon what issues the canvass is to be conducted.

If, as I have full faith they will, the Democratic party shall determine in the Presidential election of 1860 to adhere to the principles embodied in the Compromise measures of 1850, and ratified by the people in the Presidential election of 1852, and re-affirmed in the Kansas-Nebraska act of 1854, and incorporated into the Cincinnati platform in 1856, as expounded by Mr. Buchanan in his letter accepting the nomination, and approved by the people in his election —in that event my friends will be at liberty to present my name to the convention, if they see proper to do so.

If, on the contrary, it shall become the policy of the Democratic party, which I cannot anticipate, to repudiate these their time-honored principles, on which we have achieved so many patriotic triumphs; and, in lieu of them, the Convention shall interpolate into the creed of the party such new issues as the revival of the African slave trade, or a Congressional slave code for the Territories, or the doctrine that the Constitution of the United States either establishes or prohibits slavery in the Territories beyond the power of the people legally to control it as other property—it is due to candor to say that, in such an event, I could not accept the nomination if tendered to me.

Trusting that this answer will be deemed sufficiently explicit, I am, very respectfully, your friend,

S. A. DOUGLAS

Washington *National Intelligencer,* June 24, 1859. J. B. Dorr was editor of the Dubuque *Daily Express and Herald.* This letter was widely reprinted in the nation's press and created a considerable sensation as the first explicit statement of Douglas' plans for the Presidential nomination in 1860.
[1]On June 13, 1859, Dorr wrote to Douglas: "Permit me to say that your friends in this state of whom there are large numbers feel somewhat embarrassed by the want of definite knowledge of your position in relation to the Charleston Convention of 1860. The same cause has injured and if permitted to continue will injure the cause of *pure democracy* among the masses of the people while it can but operate against your personal interests should you be a candidate before the next National convention. The writer is perhaps asking too much but if agreeable to you will be greatly obliged by an answer touching this subject; and as the Democratic State Convention will assemble next week, will be further obliged by a reply by the 17th inst." (Douglas Papers, University of Chicago Library). The letter was endorsed in Douglas' hand, "Answered / The 'Dorr Letter.'"

To William T. Davis

Washington, July 8, 1859.

My Dear Sir: I have received the invitation of the Committee of Arrangements of the Pilgrim Society of Plymouth (which your letter of the 4th inst. informs me was sent to Chicago) to attend the celebration on the occasion of laying the corner stone of the national monument to the Pilgrim Forefathers. Not knowing, therefore, to whom to communicate my reply, I avail myself of your name for the purpose.

I can assure you, and through you, the Pilgrim Society, that it would give me great pleasure to meet the good people of Plymouth on the interesting occasion they will celebrate on the first Tuesday in August. They have a right to be proud of their forefathers, and so has Massachusetts and all New England. The history of the men of iron will, to comm[em]orate whose virtues a national monument will be erected, is a prominent feature in the history of the American colonies and the revolution which gave them independence. The principles enunciated by the Pilgrim Fathers lie at the foundation of popular government everywhere, and yet live in the constitution of our common country. The "Mayflower" brought with her to Plymouth the great principle of popular sovereignty, and the right of the people to govern themselves in their own way, and the life and conduct of the Pilgrim Fathers was, in all that pertained to civil government, a happy illustration of the principle which they first claimed in the cabin of that little vessel.

I repeat, my dear sir, that I should be most happy to meet the people of Plymouth at the time suggested, but such are the demands on my time that I am reluctantly compelled to deny myself that pleasure. With high respect, yours,

S. A. DOUGLAS

Chicago *Times*, August 6, 1859. William T. Davis was a member of a committee of arrangements appointed by the Pilgrim Society to invite Douglas to attend the laying of the cornerstone of the Pilgrim Monument in Plymouth. The invitation was extended on June 28, 1859 (Douglas Papers, University of Chicago Library).

To Mrs. Lucy Stone

Washington, July 14, 1859.

Mrs. Lucy Stone—Dear Madam:—Your kind letter of the 8th inst., wishing me to be present at a convention of the ladies of the Northwest, to be convened at Chicago on the 12th of Sept., to devise measures for the promotion of the happiness and the protection of the interests and rights of the female sex, has just been laid before me. You are right, dear Madam, when you say that I take a deep interest in all that concerns the ladies of our great and glorious country. And I need not now, after so many years of faithful labor in the cause of popular sovereignty, assure you that you have, in your endeavors *to obtain the liberty of governing yourselves in your own way, subject only to the Constitution of the United States, the full confidence of my undivided sympathy.* I regret, dear Madam, that business of great importance will prevent me from being present at your convention. I have the honor to remain, &c.,

S. A. DOUGLAS

Clipping, Illinois State Historical Library. The newspaper in which this letter was originally published has not been identified. Lucy Stone (Mrs. Henry Browne Blackwell), a native of Massachusetts and a graduate of Oberlin College, was a prominent reformer in the women's rights and antislavery movements. Commenting on this letter, the Cincinnati *Enquirer*, September 14, 1859, declared that it "is a forgery. It was a *canard* gotten up by a Republican editor in Maine, and bears the evidence of it in every line."

To William A. Seaver

Washington
July 17th 1859

My Dr Sir,

Your kind note was received this morning. I was surprised at the notice in the Tribune. I have not mentioned to mortal man the fact that I expected to make a publication in any paper, much less in the magazine.[1] Some of my friends know that I have been preparing a memoir on the subject of the "Dividing line between federal & local authority," called Popular sovrignty, *with a view to the debate which will take place in the Senate next winter,* but not one of them has the slightest suspicion that it is to be published before that time. Col Forney stated to me that you had mentioned to him at your Dinner that I thought of preparing an article for the magazine.[2] No one else knows the fact, and nobody will know it from me. I am making good progress with the paper, and *am well pleased with it thus far.* I will make it *suitable for the magazine,* and I am sure that my friend Fletcher Harper will never regret the favor to me in publishing it, while I claim it will help the magazine.[3] I think I will bring on the manuscript & stay one day, & have yourself, Fletcher Harper & Guernsey[4] to meet me at Breakfast the morning I arrive, and then read & criticize the paper.

Mrs D sends her friend[ly] regards. Yours truly

S. A. DOUGLAS

ALS, Illinois State Historical Library. Seaver, former editor of the Buffalo *Courier* and a supporter of Douglas, was at this time editing the *Churchman* in New York. He was a good friend of Fletcher Harper, of the publishing house, and helped to make arrangements for the publication of Douglas' article on popular sovereignty in *Harper's Magazine.*

[1]Seaver wrote Douglas, July 15, 1859: "While dining with Fletcher Harper, to day, mention was made of the paragraph that appears in the telegraphic despatches, of a forthcoming publication by you. That is very well, and the more of it, judiciously done, the better; but do not intimate to any one the *medium* through which you intend to get to the people. They are rather particular about these things at Harpers; and as your 'document' will be a somewhat noticeable innovation upon the ordinary run of their magazine articles, I think it would be well, under the circumstances, to let them have the full benefit of it" (Douglas Papers, University of Chicago Library). The newspaper notice in question appeared in the New York *Tribune,* July 15, 1859.

[2]Seaver had given a dinner party in New York earlier in the summer, to which Douglas, Fletcher Harper, John W. Forney, and others had been invited.

[3]The publishing firm later declared, "When Mr Douglas proposed to furnish us with a paper on 'Popular Sovereignty' we took the whole matter into careful consideration, and decided that, without reference to party politics, the subject was of such paramount interest that our readers would be glad to have, in permanent and accessible form, the carefully elaborated views of a statesman whose public experience had necessarily familiarized him with territorial jurisprudence" (Harper and Brothers to O. Jennings Wise, Septem-

ber 21, 1859, copy owned by Martin F. Douglas).

[4]A. H. Guernsey was one of the editors of *Harper's Magazine*.

To Sylvanus R. Lyman

Washington, July 18, 1859.

My Dear Sir: I received to-day, the duplicate of your letter addressed to me at Chicago: under date of the 6th inst., with respect to the invitation which the Democratic State committee honored me with to visit Maine, and address the people during the approaching political canvass. Your letter informs me of the action of the members of the state Committee, appointed by the state convention which assembled at Bangor on the 30th ult, whereby the invitation of their predecessors to me, was ratified, and a "sub-committee of seven appointed to make the necessary arrangements" for my visit, if the invitation should be accepted.

The proceedings of the authorized agents of the Democracy of Maine fill me with profound gratitude, and nothing but an imperative sense of duty which I owe to others could prevent an acceptance of the invitation which they have so generously tendered me. My private letter to you, under date of the 12th inst, informed you of the delicate health of my family, and expressed the fear that it would be impossible, under such circumstances, for me to leave them during the next month,—August—when the State committee require my services. A formal reply to the invitation of the committee was purposely withheld in the hope that I might after all, be enabled to accept it, as was, and still is, my cordial wish. My family physician now advises me that it would be highly imprudent for me to make the contemplated visit, and requires me to remain with my family, whose health has been, and is, such as to render our usual residence at Chicago during the recess of Congress impracticable.

I have read the resolutions adopted by your recent State convention with the liveliest satisfaction. The Democracy of Maine have planted themselves firmly on the grand principle of popular sovereignty, and, if they fight the battle manfully, as I am confident they will; success will crown their efforts. The odds are against them, I admit; but they can be and will be overcome by vigorous, energetic political action. Let them go into the contest with stout hearts and strong arms, resolved to win, and if they do not rout their opponents they will so cripple them at least, that they will put a Democratic triumph in Maine, in 1860, beyond contingency or dispute. I am, with the highest respect, Very truly yours,

S. A. DOUGLAS

Chicago *Times*, August 14, 1859. Sylvanus R. Lyman was chairman of the Maine Democratic state committee. His letter of invitation to Douglas was written on July 6, 1859 (Douglas Papers, University of Chicago Library). Lyman became a member of the Democratic national committee in 1860.

To Corydon Beckwith and Richard T. Merrick

Washington

Sirs   July 20th 1859

Just as I was leaving Chicago I was notified of a suit brought against me by Mr Gage of Mobile (Brother of Gage of the Tremont) on a covenant in a Deed for the property I sold him because of the Rail Road running across the tract, and no reservation of the right of way in the Deed. He had previously brought a suit against the Rail Road Company, but failing in that in consequence of my Deposition which you will find on the files of the Court, he now sues me on the warrants. W. D. Barry Esq of St Charles was the Attorney for the Rail Road company in that case, and inasmuch as he was familiar with all the facts I thought it best to retain him to assist you in the case.[1] When he called to see me just as I was leaving Chicago & stated the facts I told him I wished him to assist in the defense.

I therefore commit the case to your management and ask that you consult with Mr Barry. It seems to me that the law is in my favor as I am sure the justice of the case is, but it is a matter of importance in these times, I therefore ask for your best services.[2] Please let me hear from you & your opinion of the case. Very truly your friend

S. A. Douglas

ALS, Historical Society of Pennsylvania. Corydon Beckwith and Richard T. Merrick were Chicago law partners.

[1]William D. Barry was a St. Charles, Illinois, attorney and at one time a judge of the Kane County court. On July 11, 1859, Barry wrote Douglas that he had tried to have the case continued until the next term of the court but had not been successful. The court had given him until July 20 to file his pleas (owned by Martin F. Douglas).

[2]On July 23, Barry informed Douglas that the counsel for the plaintiff had demurred to the pleas which averred that Gage had purchased the land with a full knowledge and understanding of all the rights and privileges which the railroad had to it (owned by Martin F. Douglas).

To John L. Peyton

My Dear Sir: Washington, Aug. 2, 1859.

You do me no more than justice in your kind letter, for which accept my thanks, in assuming that I do not concur with the Administration in their views respecting the rights of naturalized citizens, as

[451]

defined in the 'Le Clerc letter,' which it is proper to observe, have been since materially modified.[1]

Under our Constitution there can be no just distinction between the right of native born and naturalized citizens to claim the protection of our government at home and abroad. Unless naturalization releases the person naturalized from all obligations which he owed to his native country by virtue of his allegiance, it leaves him the sad predicament of owing allegiance to two countries, without receiving protection from either—a dilemma in which no American citizen should ever be placed.

Neither have you misapprehended my opinions in respect to the African slave trade. That question seriously disturbed the harmony of the convention which formed the federal constitution. Upon it the delegates divided into two parties, under circumstances which, for a time, rendered harmonious action hopeless. The one demanded the instant and unconditional prohibition of the African slave trade on moral and religious grounds, while the other insisted that it was a legitimate commerce, involving no other consideration than a sound public policy, which each state ought to be permitted to determine for itself, so long as it was sanctioned by its own laws. Each party stood firmly and resolutely by its own position until both became convinced that this vexed question would break up the convention, destroy the Federal Union, blot out the glories of the revolution, and throw away all its blessings, unless some fair and just compromise could be formed on the common ground of such mutual concessions as were indispensable to the preservation of their liberties, union and independence.

Such a compromise was effected and incorporated into the constitution, by which it was understood that the African slave trade might continue as a legitimate commerce in those States whose laws sanctioned it, until the year 1808, from and after which time Congress might and would prohibit it forever throughout the dominion and limits of the United States, and pass all laws which might become necessary to make such prohibition effectual. The harmony of the convention was restored, and the Union saved by this compromise without which the constitution could never have been made.

I stand firmly by this compromise, and by all other compromises of the constitution, and shall use my best efforts to carry each and all of them into faithful execution, in the sense and with the understanding in which they were originally adopted. In accordance with this compromise, I am irreconcilably opposed to the revival of the African slave trade, in every form, and under any circumstances. I am, with great respect, yours truly,

S. A. DOUGLAS

Chicago *Times*, August 16, 1859. John L. Peyton, a native of Staunton, Virginia, and a writer, lived in Chicago for a time in the 1840's before returning to Virginia.

[1]The "LeClerc letter" was written by Secretary of State Lewis Cass on May 17, 1859, to Felix LeClerc, of Memphis, Tennessee. In the letter Cass wrote, "Your letter of the 13th instant has been received. In reply, I have to state that it is understood that the French Government claims military service from all natives of France who may be found within its jurisdiction. Your naturalization in this country will not exempt you from that claim if you should voluntarily return thither" (Chicago *Tribune*, July 15, 1859).

To Ninian W. Edwards

My dear Sir;   Washington, Aug. 11, 1859.

My attention had been given to a critical examination of the Ordinance of 1787, prior to the receipt of your's of July 11, 1859;—which I am none the less thankful for, because the same provisions to which you refer, had struck me with the force with which you were impressed by them.[1]

My engagements have been so many and so pressing, that it has been impossible to make an earlier acknowledgment of your very interesting letter, for which I again thank you, most kindly. Very truly Yours,

S. A. DOUGLAS

LS, Chicago Historical Society.

[1]On July 11, 1859, Edwards wrote Douglas of his interpretation of several of the sections of the Ordinance of 1787, especially those dealing with the power of the territorial legislature, in the hope apparently that the information might prove helpful to Douglas in the preparation of his essay on popular sovereignty (Douglas Papers, University of Chicago Library).

To the Editors of the San Francisco *National*

[August 16, 1859]

To the Editors of the "National," San Francisco, California: I am indebted to the kindness of an unknown friend for a copy of the *National* of the 16th July, containing a speech of the Hon. William M. Gwin[1] at Grass Valley, with black lines drawn around certain passages, for the purpose, I presume, of directing my attention especially to them. Inasmuch as your paper is the medium through which the assault on the political position which I have maintained in the Senate, and before the people of Illinois, was conveyed to the public, justice requires that you should publish such reply as my friends in California have a right, under the circumstances, to expect. Hence I address this letter to you.

After the defeat of the Lecompton Constitution in Congress, and the rejection by Kansas of the propositions contained in the "English Bill," all who felt a deeper interest in the peace and repose of the country than in the advancement of particular individuals, entertained the hope that the strife had ended, and that instead of new and odious tests of political fidelity to distract and divide, we should witness mutual desires and mutual exertions to present a united Democracy. If this just expectation has been disappointed, and the Democratic party, burdened with new tests, and demoralized by selfish rivalries and dissensions, have been defeated in States where they should and otherwise might have been successful, the responsibility must rest upon those who produced the unfortunate results. I shall not follow the example of these disturbers of Democratic harmony by reviving past issues, and indulging in criminations and recriminations; nor shall I stop to defend my action on the Lecompton question from their assaults. I am entirely content to rest my vindication on the verdict which the people of Illinois have already recorded, and trust to that enlightened public opinion of the whole country, which will, sooner or later, declare with emphasis and power that no constitution or institution should ever be forced upon a reluctant people, whether State or Territory.

Passing from his review of the Lecompton issue, Mr. Gwin said in his speech at Grass Valley:

"Near the close of the last session of Congress a debate was sprung upon the Senate upon the question of Territorial sovereignty. We had long expected such a discussion, because it was the duty of Mr. Douglas to give his reasons to the Senate and to the country for the line of policy he had considered it his duty to adopt in the Senatorial canvass in Illinois. The doctrines he had avowed in his Freeport speech had been condemned in the Senate by his removal from the Chairmanship of the Territorial Committee of that body, and it was expected that he would defend the position he had taken, and give ample time to those who differed from him to give the reasons that had influenced them in removing him from that important position at the head of the Territorial Committee he had filled for so many years in the Senate. But for reasons satisfactory to himself, he did not address the Senate until near the close of the session, when there was no time to give the subject that full consideration it deserved. He had asserted in his Freeport speech that a Territorial Legislature could *lawfully* by non-action or hostile legislation exclude slavery from such Territory.[2] Having always opposed this doctrine, I briefly announced my previous opinions, and declared that if such construction had been given to the Kansas-Nebraska act when it was under consideration in Congress in 1854, I should have voted against it."

Why was it "the duty of Mr. Douglas to give his reasons to the Senate and to the country for the line of policy he had considered it his duty to adopt in the Senatorial canvass in Illinois?" I had already given my "reasons" at Freeport, and at more than a hundred places during the canvass, and had been triumphantly sustained by the voice of the people and the vote of the Legislature against the combined forces of the Black Republicans and Federal office-holders and their allies and supporters in and out of the Senate. Why, I repeat, was it my duty to give my reasons to the Senate? The Senate is not my constituency. I am not responsible to the Senate, nor did any Senator venture to demand reasons for the line of policy which I had felt it my duty to pursue at home in a State canvass.

But if it *were* my duty, as Mr. Gwin states, to give my "reasons to the Senate" for the course which I pursued in the canvass, it necessarily follows that it *was the duty of the Senate to hear them* before they proceeded, as he alleges, to condemn me by my removal, during my absence, from the Chairmanship of the Committee on Territories which I had held for eleven years, and to which I was re-elected after my speech against the Lecompton Constitution.

The country is now informed for the first time that I was removed from the post of Chairman of the Committee on Territories because of the sentiments contained in my "Freeport speech." To use the language of Mr. Gwin, THE DOCTRINES HE HAD AVOWED IN HIS FREEPORT SPEECH HAD BEEN CONDEMNED IN THE SENATE BY HIS REMOVAL FROM THE CHAIRMANSHIP OF THE TERRITORIAL COMMITTEE OF THAT BODY. The country will bear in mind this testimony, that I was not removed because of any personal unkindness or hostility; nor in consequence of my course on the Lecompton question, or in respect to the Administration; but that it was intended as a condemnation of the doctrines avowed in my "Freeport speech." The only position taken in my "Freeport speech," which I have ever seen criticised or controverted, may be stated in a single sentence, and was in reply to an interrogatory propounded by my competitor for the Senate: That "the Territorial Legislature could lawfully exclude slavery, either by non-action or unfriendly legislation." This opinion was not expressed by me at Freeport for the first time. I have expressed the same opinion often in the Senate, freely and frequently, in the presence of those Senators who, as Mr. Gwin testifies, removed me "from the Chairmanship of the Committee on Territories," ten years after they knew that I held the opinion, and would never surrender it.

I could fill many columns of the NATIONAL with extracts of speeches made by me during the discussion of the compromise measures in 1850, and in defence of the principles imbodied in those measures in 1851 and 1852, in the discussion of the Kansas-Nebraska Bill in 1854, and of the Kansas difficulties, and the Topeka revolutionary movements in 1856, in all of which I expressed the same opinion and defended the same position which was assumed in the "Freeport speech." I will not, however, burden your columns or weary your readers with extracts of all these speeches, but will refer you to each volume of the Congressional Globe for the last ten years, where you will find them fully reported. If you cannot conveniently procure the Congressional Globe, I refer you to an editorial article in the Washington Union of October 5, 1858, which, it was reported, received the sanction of the President of the United States previously to its publication, a few weeks after my "Freeport speech" had been delivered. The Union made copious extracts of my speeches in 1850 and 1854, to prove that at each of those periods I held the same opinions which I expressed at Freeport in 1858, and, consequently, declared that I never was a good Democrat, much less sound on the slavery question when I advocated the compromise measures of 1850, and the Kansas-Nebraska Bill in 1854.

In the article referred to, the Washington Union said:

"We propose to show that Judge Douglas' action in 1850 and 1854 was taken with especial reference to the announcement of doctrine and programme which was made at Freeport. The declaration at Freeport was, that 'in his opinion the people can, *by lawful means*, exclude slavery from a Territory *before* it comes in as a State;' and he declared that his competitor had '*heard him argue the Nebraska bill on that principle* all over Illinois in 1854, 1855, and 1856, and had *no excuse to pretend to have any doubt on that subject.*' "

The Union summed up the evidence furnished by my speeches in the Senate in 1850 and 1854, that the "Freeport speech" was consistent with my former course, with this emphatic declaration:

"THUS WE HAVE SHOWN THAT PRECISELY THE POSITION ASSUMED BY JUDGE DOUGLAS AT FREEPORT HAD BEEN MAINTAINED BY HIM IN 1850, IN THE DEBATES AND VOTES ON THE UTAH AND NEW MEXICAN BILLS, AND IN 1854 ON THE KANSAS-NEBRASKA BILL; AND HAVE SHOWN THAT IT WAS OWING TO HIS OPPOSITION THAT CLAUSES DEPRIVING TERRITORIAL LEGISLATURES OF THE POWER OF EXCLUDING SLAVERY FROM THEIR JURISDICTIONS WERE NOT EXPRESSLY INSERTED IN THOSE MEASURES."

The evidence thus presented by the Washington Union—the evidence of an open enemy—is so full and conclusive, that I have uniformly advocated for ten years past the same principles which I avowed at Freeport, that I cannot refrain from asking you to spread the entire article before your readers as an appendix, if you choose, to this letter.

[456]

The question whether the people of the Territories should be permitted to decide the slavery question for themselves, the same as all other rightful subjects of legislation, was thoroughly discussed and definitively settled in the adoption of the compromise measures of 1850. The Territorial bills, as originally reported by the Committee on Territories, extended the authority of the Territorial Legislature to all rightful subjects of legislation consistent with the Constitution, *without excepting African slavery*. Modified by the committee of thirteen, they conferred power on the Territorial Legislature over all rightful subjects of legislation, *except African slavery*. This distinct question, involving the power of the Territorial Legislature over the subject of African slavery, was debated in the Senate from the 8th of May until the 31st of July, 1850, when the limitation was stricken out by a vote of yeas, 33; nays, 19; and the Territorial Legislature authorized to legislate on all rightful subjects, *without excepting African slavery*. In this form and upon this principle the compromise measures of 1850 were enacted.

When I returned to my home in Chicago, at the end of the session of Congress, after the adoption of the measures of adjustment, the excitement was intense. The City Council had passed a resolution nullifying the Fugitive Slave Act, and releasing the police from all obligations to obey the law or assist in its execution. Amidst this furious excitement, and surrounded by revolutionary movements, I addressed the assembled populace. My speech, in which I defended each and all of the compromise measures of 1850, was published at the time, and spread broadcast throughout the country. I herewith send you a copy of that speech, in which you will find that I said:

"These measures are predicated on the great fundamental principle *that every people ought to possess the right of forming and regulating their own internal concerns and domestic institutions in their own way.* It was supposed that those of our fellow-citizens who emigrated to the shores of the Pacific and to our other territories were as capable of self-government as their neighbors and kindred whom they left behind them; and there was no reason for believing that they have lost any of their intelligence or patriotism by the wayside, while crossing the Isthmus or the Plains. It was also believed that after their arrival in the country, when they had become familiar with its topography, climate, productions, and resources, and had connected their destiny with it, they were fully as competent to judge for themselves what kind of laws and institutions were best adapted to their condition and interests, as we were who never saw the country, and knew very little about it. To question their competency to do this was to deny their capacity for self-government. If they have the requisite intelligence and honesty to be intrusted with the enactment of laws for the government of white men, I know of no reason why they should not be deemed competent to legislate for the negro. If they are sufficiently enlightened to make laws for the protection of life, liberty, and property —of morals and education—to determine the relation of husband and wife, of parent and child—*I am not aware that it requires any higher degree of civilization to regulate the affairs of master and servant. These things are all confided by the Constitution to each State to decide for itself, and I know of no reason why the same principle should not be extended to the Territories."*

This speech was laid on the desk of every member of the Senate, at the opening of the 2d session of the 31st Congress, in December, 1850, when, with a full knowledge of my opinions on the territorial question, I was unanimously nominated in the Democratic caucus and re-elected by the Senate Chairman of the Committee on Territories. From that time to this I have spoken the same sentiments and vindicated the same positions in debate in the Senate, and have been re-elected Chairman of the Committee on Territories *at each session of Congress,* until last December, by the unanimous voice of the Democratic party in caucus and in the Senate, with my opinions on this territorial question *well known to and well understood by every Senator.* Yet Mr. Gwin testifies that I was condemned and deposed by the Senate for the utterance of opinions in 1858, which were put on record year after year so plainly and so unequivocally as to leave neither the Senate nor the country in doubt. Thus does Mr. Gwin, in his eagerness to be my public accuser, speak his own condemnation, for he voted for me session after session, with my opinions, the same that I spoke at Freeport, staring him in the face.

On the 4th of January, 1854, I reported the Nebraska Bill, and, as Chairman of the Committee on Territories, accompanied it with a special report, in which I stated distinctly *"that all questions pertaining to slavery in the territories, and in the new States to be formed therefrom, are to be left to the decision of the people residing therein, by their appropriate representatives to be chosen by them for that purpose."* And that the bill proposed "to carry these propositions and principles into practical operation in the precise language of the Compromise Measures of 1850." The Kansas-Nebraska act, as it stands on the statute book, does define the power of the Territorial Legislature "in the precise language of the Compromise Measures of 1850." It gives the Legislature power over all rightful subjects of legislation not inconsistent with the Constitution, *without excepting African slavery.* During the discussion of the measure it was suggested that it was necessary to repeal the 8th section of the Act of the 6th of March, 1850

[1820], called the Missouri Compromise, in order to permit the people to control the slavery question *while they remained in the territorial condition, and before they became a State of the Union.* That was the object and only purpose for which the Missouri Compromise was repealed.

On the night of the 3d of March, 1854, in my closing speech on the Kansas-Nebraska Bill, a few hours before it passed the Senate, I said: "IT IS ONLY FOR THE PURPOSE OF CARRYING OUT THIS GREAT FUNDAMENTAL PRINCIPLE OF SELF-GOVERNMENT THAT THE BILL RENDERS THE 8TH SECTION OF THE MISSOURI ACT INOPERATIVE AND VOID." The article of the Washington Union of October 5, 1858, to which I have referred, quotes this and other passages of my speech on that occasion, to prove that the author of the Nebraska Bill framed it with express reference to conferring on the Territorial Legislature power to control the slavery question. And further, that I boldly avowed the purpose at the time in the presence of all the friends of the Bill, and urged its passage upon that ground. I have never understood that Mr. Gwin, or any other Senator who heard that speech and voted for the Bill the same night, expressed any dissent or disapprobation of the doctrines it announced. That was the time for dissent and disapprobation; that was the time to condemn, if there were cause to condemn, and not four or five years later. The record furnishes no such evidence of dissent or disapprobation; nor does the history of those times show that the Democratic Party, in the North or in the South, or in any portion of the country, repudiated the fundamental principle upon which the Kansas-Nebraska Act is founded, and proscribed its advocates and defenders.

If Mr. Gwin did not understand the Kansas-Nebraska Bill when it was under consideration, according to its plain meaning as explained and defended by its authors and supporters, it is not the fault of those who did understand it precisely as I interpreted it at Freeport, and as the country understood it in the Presidential canvass of 1856. Mr. Buchanan, and leading members of his Cabinet, at all events, understood the Kansas-Nebraska Act in the same sense in which it was understood and defended at the time of its passage. Mr. Buchanan, in his letter accepting the Cincinnati nomination, affirmed that "this legislation is founded upon principles as ancient as free government itself, and, in accordance with them, has simply declared that the *people of a Territory*, LIKE THOSE OF A STATE, *shall decide for themselves whether slavery shall or shall not exist* within their limits." General Cass, now Secretary of State, has always maintained, from the day he penned the "Nicholson Letter" to this, that the people of the Territories have a right to decide the slavery question for themselves when-ever they please. In 1856, on the 2d day of July, referring to the Kansas-Nebraska Act, he said: *"I believe the original act gave the Ter-ritorial Legislature of Kansas* FULL POWER *to exclude or allow slavery."* Mr. Toucey, the Secretary of the Navy, interpreted that act in the same way, and on the same occasion in the Senate, said:

"The original act recognizes in the Territorial Legislature all the power which they can have, subject to the Constitution, and subject to the organic law of the Territory."

Mr. Cobb, the Secretary of the Treasury, in a speech at West Chester, Pennsylvania, on the 19th of September, 1856, advocating Mr. Buchanan's election to the Presidency, said:

"The Government of the United States should *not* force the institu-tion of slavery upon the people either of the Territories or of the States, against the will of the people, though my voice could bring about that result. I stand upon the principle—the people of my State decide it for themselves, you for yourselves, the people of Kansas for themselves. That is the Constitution, and I stand by the Constitution." And again, in the same speech, he said: "Whether they" (the people of a Territory) *"decide it by prohibiting it, according to the one doc-trine,* OR BY REFUSING TO PASS LAWS TO PROTECT IT, as contended for by the other party, *is immaterial. The majority of the people,* BY THE ACTION OF THE TERRITORIAL LEGISLA-TURE, *will decide the question;* and all must abide the decision when made."

Here we find the doctrines of the Freeport speech, including "non-action" and "unfriendly legislation" as a lawful and proper mode for the exclusion of slavery from a Territory clearly defined by Mr. Cobb, and the election of Mr. Buchanan advocated on those identical doc-trines. Mr. Cobb made similar speeches during the Presidential canvass in other sections of Pennsylvania, in Maine, Indiana, and most of the Northern States, and was appointed Secretary of the Treasury by Mr. Buchanan as a mark of gratitude for the efficient services which had been thus rendered. Will any Senator who voted to remove me from the chairmanship of the Territorial Committee for expressing opinions for which Mr. Cobb, Mr. Toucey, and Gen. Cass were re-warded, pretend that he did not know that they or either of them had ever uttered such opinions when their nominations were before the Senate? I am sure that no Senator will make so humiliating a confes-sion. Why, then, were those distinguished gentlemen appointed by the President and confirmed by the Senate as Cabinet Ministers if they were not good Democrats—sound on the slavery question, and faithful exponents of the principles and creed of the party? Is it not a significant fact that the President and the most distinguished and honored of his Cabinet should have been solemnly and irrevocably pledged to this monstrous heresy of "popular sovereignty," for asserting which the Senate, by Mr. Gwin's frank avowal, condemned me to the extent of their power?

It must be borne in mind, however, that the President and members of the Cabinet are not the only persons high in authority who are committed to the principle of self-government in the Territories. The Hon. John C. Breckinridge, the Vice President of the United States, was a member of the House of Representatives when the Kansas-Nebraska bill passed, and in a speech delivered March 23, 1854, said:

"Among the many misrepresentations sent to the country by some of the enemies of this bill, perhaps none is more flagrant than the charge that it proposes to legislate slavery into Kansas and Nebraska. Sir, if the bill contained such a feature it would not receive my vote. The right to establish involves the correlative right to prohibit, and denying both I would vote for neither.". . .

"The effect of the repeal, (of the Missouri compromise.) therefore, is neither to establish nor to exclude, *but to leave the future condition of the Territories dependent wholly upon the action of the inhabitants,* subject only to such limitations as the Federal Constitution may impose. . . . It will be observed that *the right of the people to regulate in their own way* ALL THEIR DOMESTIC INSTITUTIONS *is left wholly untouched,* except that whatever is done must be done in accordance with the Constitution—the supreme law for us all."

Again, at Lexington, Kentucky, on the 9th of June, 1856, in response to the congratulations of his neighbors on his nomination for the Vice Presidency, Mr. Breckinridge said:

"The whole power of the Democratic organization is pledged to the following propositions: That Congress shall not interpose upon this subject (slavery) in the States, in the Territories, or in the District of Columbia; *that the people of each Territory shall determine the question for themselves,* and be admitted into the Union upon a footing of perfect equality with the original States, without discrimination on account of the allowance or prohibition of slavery."

Touching the power of the Territorial Legislature over the subject of slavery, the Hon. James L. Orr, late Speaker of the House of Representatives, on the 11th of December, 1856, said:

"*Now, the legislative authority of a Territory is invested with a discretion to vote for or against the laws. We think they ought to pass laws in every Territory, when the Territory is open to settlement and slaveholders go there, to protect slave property. But if they decline to pass such law, what is the remedy? None, sir, if the majority of the*

[461]

people are opposed to the institution; and if they do not desire it in-grafted upon their Territory, all they have to do is simply to decline to pass laws in the Territorial Legislature for its protection, and then it is as well excluded as if the power was invested in the Territorial Legislature to prohibit it."

Mr. Stephens, of Georgia, in a speech in the House of Representatives on the 17th of February, 1854, said:

"The whole question of slavery was to be left to the people of the Territories, whether north or south of 36° 30', or any other line....

"It was based upon the truly republican and national policy of taking this disturbing element out of Congress and leaving the whole question of slavery in the Territories to the people there to settle it for themselves. And it is in vindication of that new principle—then established for the first time in the history of our government—in the year 1850, the middle of the nineteenth century, that we, the friends of the Nebraska bill, whether from the North or South, now call upon this House and the country to carry out in good faith, and give effect to the spirit and intent of those important measures of territorial legislation."

Again, on the 17th of January, 1856, he said:

"I am willing that the Territorial Legislature may act upon the subject when and how they may think proper."

Mr. Benjamin, of Louisiana, in a speech in the Senate on the 25th of May, 1854, on the Nebraska bill, said:

"We find, then, that this principle of the independence and self-government of the people in the distant Territories of the confederacy harmonizes all these conflicting opinions, and enables us to banish from the halls of Congress another fertile source of discontent and excitement."

On February 15, 1854, Mr. Badger, of North Carolina, said of the Kansas-Nebraska bill:

"It submits the whole authority to the Territory to determine for itself. That, in my judgement, is the place where it ought to be put. If the people of the Territories choose to exclude slavery, so far from considering it as a wrong done to me or to my constituents, I shall not complain of it. It is their business."

Again, on March 2, 1854, one day before the passage of the bill through the Senate, Mr. Badger said:

"But with regard to that question we have agreed—some of us because we thought it the only right mode, and some because we think it a right mode, and under existing circumstances the preferable mode —to confer this power upon the people of the Territories."

On the same day Mr. Butler, of South Carolina, said:

"Now, I believe that under the provisions of this bill, and of the Utah and New Mexico bills, there will be a perfect carte blanche given to the Territorial Legislature to legislate as they may think proper.... I am willing to trust them. I have been willing to trust them in Utah and New Mexico, where the Mexican law prevailed, and I am willing to trust them in Nebraska and Kansas, where the French law, according to the idea of the gentleman, may possibly be revived."

In the House of Representatives, June 25, 1856, Mr. Samuel A. Smith, of Tennessee, said:

"For twenty years this question had agitated Congress and the country without a single beneficial result. *They resolved that it should be transferred from these halls, that all unconstitutional restrictions should be removed, and that the people should determine for themselves the character of their local and domestic institutions under which they were to live, with precisely the same rights, but no greater than those which were enjoyed by the old thirteen States.*" And further: "In 1854, the same question was presented, when the necessity arose for the organization of the Territories of Kansas and Nebraska, and *the identical* principle was applied for its solution."

In the Senate, on the 25th of February, 1854, Mr. Dodge, of Iowa, (now Democratic candidate for governor of that State,) said: "And, sir, honesty and consistency with our course in 1850 demand that those of us who supported the Compromise measures should zealously support this bill, *because it is a return to the sound principle of leaving to the people of the Territories the right of determining for themselves their domestic institutions.*"

And in the House of Representatives, December 28, 1855, Mr. George W. Jones, of Tennessee, said:

"*Then, sir, you may call it by what name you please—non-intervention, squatter sovereignty, or popular sovereignty. It is, sir, the power of the people to govern themselves, and they, and they alone, should exercise it, in my opinion, as well while in a territorial condition as in the position of a State.*"

And again, in the same speech, he said:

"*I believe that the great principle—the right of the people in the Territories, as well as in the States, to form and regulate their own domestic institutions in their own way—is clearly and unequivocally imbodied in the Kansas-Nebraska act, and if it is not, it should have been. Believing that it was the living, vital principal of the act, I voted for it. These are my views, honestly entertained, and will be defended.*"

I could fill your columns with extracts of speeches of Senators and Representatives from the North and the South who voted for the

Kansas-Nebraska bill and supported Mr. Buchanan for the Presidency on that distinct issue; thus showing conclusively that it was the general understanding at the time that the people of the Territories, while they remained in a territorial condition, were left perfectly free, under the Kansas-Nebraska act, to form and regulate all their domestic institutions, slavery not excepted, in their own way, subject only to the Constitution of the United States. This is the doctrine of which Mr. Gwin spoke when he said:

"To contend for the power—and a sovereign power it is—of a Territorial Legislature to exclude by non-action or hostile legislation is pregnant with the mischiefs of never-ending agitation, of civil discord, and bloody wars. . . .

"It is an absurd, monstrous, and dangerous theory, which demands denunciation from every patriot in the land; and a profound sense of my duty to you would not permit me to do less than to offer this brief statement of my views upon a question so vital to the welfare of our common country."

Why did not the same "profound sense of duty" to the people of California require Mr. Gwin to denounce this "absurd, monstrous, and dangerous theory" when pronounced and enforced by General Cass, in support of the Compromise Measures of 1850, and thence repeated by that eminent statesman at each session of Congress until 1857, when Mr. Gwin voted for his confirmation as Secretary of State? Why did not Mr. Gwin obey the same sense of duty by denouncing James Buchanan as the Democratic candidate for the Presidency, when he declared in 1856 that "the people of a Territory, like those of a State, shall decide for themselves whether slavery shall or shall not exist within their limits?" Why did he not perform this imperative duty by voting against Mr. Cobb, who made Northern votes for Mr. Buchanan by advocating this same "absurd, monstrous, and dangerous theory of 'non-action' and 'unfriendly legislation'" when he was appointed Secretary of the Treasury? And, in short, why did he not prove his fidelity to a high sense of duty by protesting against my selection as Chairman of the Senate's Committee on Territories in the Democratic caucus by a *unanimous vote*, at every session that he has been a Senator, from 1850 to 1858, *with a full knowledge of my opinions?* The inference is, that Mr. Gwin, from his remarks on the "Dred Scott Decision," is prepared to offer it as an excuse for the disregard for so many years of that profound sense of duty which he owed to the people of California. It may be that before the decision his mind was not clear as to the sense of duty which now moves him. Of that decision he said:

"In March, 1857, the Supreme Court decided this question, in all its various relations, in the case of Dred Scott. That decision declares that neither Congress nor a Territorial Legislature possess the power either to establish or exclude slavery from the Territory, and that it was a power which exclusively belonged to the States; that the people of a Territory can exercise this power for the first time when they form a Constitution; that the right of the people of any State to carry their slaves into a common Territory of the United States, and hold them there during its existence as such, was guaranteed by the Constitution of the United States; that it was a right which could neither be subverted nor evaded, either by non-action, by direct or indirect Congressional legislation, or by any law passed by a Territorial Legislature."

Surely Mr. Gwin had never read the opinion of the Court in the case of "Dred Scott," except as it has been perverted for partisan purposes by newspapers, when he undertook to expound it to the good people of California.

It so happens that the Court did not decide any one of the propositions so boldly and emphatically stated in the "Grass Valley" speech!

The Court did *not* declare that "neither Congress nor a Territorial Legislature possessed the power either to establish or exclude slavery from a Territory, and that it was a power which exclusively belonged to the States."

The Court did *not* declare "that the people of a Territory can exercise this power for the first time when they come to form a Constitution."

The Court did *not* declare "that the right of the people of any State to carry their slaves into a common Territory of the United States, and hold them there during its existence as such, was guaranteed by the Constitution of the United States."

The Court did NOT declare "that it was a right which could neither be subverted nor evaded, either by non-action, by direct or indirect Congressional legislation, or by any law passed by a Territorial Legislature."

Neither the decision nor the opinion of the Court affirms any one of these propositions, either in express terms or by fair legal intrenchment.

This *version* of the "Dred Scott Decision" had its origin in the unfortunate Lecompton controversy, and is one of the many political heresies to which it gave birth.

There are other portions of Mr. Gwin's speech which are equally open to just criticism, and unwarranted by the facts to which they relate; but I refrain from commenting upon them, as I prefer to confine myself to those points upon which my political action, in common

[465]

with that of a large majority of the Democratic party, has been unjustly assailed before the people of California.

In faithful compliance with the pledges, creed, and platform of the Democratic party, I stand now as I did in 1850, in 1854, and in 1856, by the great cardinal principle that, under our political system, every distinct political community loyal to the Constitution and the Union is entitled to all the rights, privileges, and immunities of self-government, in respect to their internal polity and domestic institutions, subject only to the Constitution of the United States. Respectfully, your obedient servant,

WASHINGTON, *August* 16, 1859.   S. A. DOUGLAS

This letter was published in the San Francisco *National,* September 16, 1859, and shortly afterward as a pamphlet, under the title *Removal of Judge Douglas by the Senate as Chairman of the Committee on Territories. Letter of Judge Douglas in Reply to the Speech of Dr. Gwin at Grass Valley, Cal.* (n.p., n.d.).

[1]William M. Gwin was United States Senator from California from 1850 to 1855 and from 1857 to 1861. A native of Tennessee and a medical graduate of Transylvania University, he had served in the House of Representatives from Mississippi from 1841 to 1843.

[2]Douglas' so-called "Freeport Doctrine" was delivered on August 27, 1858, at the Freeport debate with Lincoln. In answer to a question from Lincoln, Douglas declared: "It matters not what way the Supreme Court may hereafter decide as to the abstract question whether slavery may or may not go into a territory under the Constitution, the people have the lawful means to introduce it or exclude it as they please, for the reason that slavery cannot exist a day or an hour anywhere, unless it is supported by local police regulations. Those police regulations can only be established by the local legislature, and if the people are opposed to slavery they will elect representatives to that body who will by unfriendly legislation effectually prevent the introduction of it into their midst. If, on the contrary, they are for it, their legislation will favor its extension. Hence, no matter what the decision of the Supreme Court may be on that abstract question, still the right of the people to make a slave territory or a free territory is perfect and complete under the Nebraska Bill." When Congress met in December, 1858, a Democratic party caucus removed Douglas from his chairmanship of the Senate Committee on Territories. Gwin's speech at Grass Valley, California, in July, 1859, was the first public statement of the reasons for Douglas' removal.

To William Dunbar

Washington, Aug. 31, 1859.

My dear Sir:—I have carefully read your letter of the 18th inst., and can perceive nothing in the interrogatories which you propounded to me, which I have not already expressed my opinion upon, and put it before the public.[1]

My speech in the Senate of February 23, 1859, in reply to Senator Brown, of Mississippi, and the article written by me for "Harper's Magazine," which you will find in the September number, discuss in a much more satisfactory manner than a letter will permit, the several questions which you submit to me. I refer you, therefore, to those sources of information for my opinions, and hope that you will be satisfied with my position as therein announced.

I have not a copy of the speech to send you; but it has been published in the *Cincinnati Enquirer*, (the weekly edition), and *Harper* you can readily procure. The re-publication of the article from *Harper* in the *Enquirer* last week, I wish to say, omitted a material portion. Yours truly,

S. A. DOUGLAS

Columbus *Ohio Statesman*, September 7, 1859. Dunbar was a Mount Vernon, Ohio, newspaper editor.

[1]On August 18, 1859, Dunbar wrote Douglas a letter (published also in the Columbus *Ohio Statesman*, September 7) setting forth his own position on the political questions of the day and asking Douglas to state his views on such questions as the constitutional power of Congress to legislate for the territories, the power of Congress to pass a slave code for the territories, and the right of the people of the territories to establish or prohibit slavery.

To James Lander

Washington
Aug't 31, 1859.

Dear Sir;

Your note of the 22d Inst, inquiring whether the "Young Men's Christian Association" of Jersey City can obtain my services to lecture before them during the Fall or Winter, is before me.

My time is almost constantly occupied either by my public duties, or with my private affairs. Hence, I am not at liberty to form any engagements to lecture before any Society or Association such as your Association proposes.

With my thanks to the Association which you represent for their courtesy, I am, Very respectfully Yours,

S. A. DOUGLAS

LS, Pierpont Morgan Library, New York. Lander, chairman of the lecture committee of the Jersey City Young Men's Christian Association, invited Douglas on August 22, 1859, to participate in a course of lectures by eminent men (Douglas Papers, University of Chicago Library).

To George Nicholas Sanders

(*Private*)

My Dr Sir,

Washington
Sept 22d 1859

I enclose you a letter to our friend Banks[1] of the kind you suggested. If this is not satisfactory tell me what you want said and I will say it, for he deserves it all. I cannot leave my family at present to come to New York. You & B must come & see me when you get the other matter arranged satisfactorily. I wish you and him God speed in the accomplishment of it. I have many things to say to you when I see you. All right in the West, and no mistake. Yours truly

S. A. Douglas

ALS, Watertown Library Association.

[1]A. D. Banks, formerly of Petersburg, Virginia, became an editor of the Cincinnati *Enquirer* in the spring of 1859. He was a strong supporter of Douglas' candidacy for the Presidential nomination in 1860. In the late summer of 1859, he opened an unofficial Douglas headquarters in New York city and later toured sections of the country in order to determine the extent of Douglas' support.

To Harper and Brothers

Washington
Messers Harper & Bros   Sept 24th 1859

Be pleased to accept my thanks for the 2500 copies of the Popular Sovereignty Pamphlet which you were so kind as to present. It is the finest specimen of the Printing art that I have ever seen. Renewing my thanks for your kindness I am very truly your friend

S. A. Douglas

ALS, University of Chicago Library.

To Henry K. McCoy

(Pr[ivate)][1]   Washington
My [Dear Sir,]   Sept 27th 1859

[The] delay in answering your kind letter of the 22d ult was caused to my absence from the city. It will be impossible for me to argue the *legal* points referred to by you within the limits of a private letter, nor do I deem it of material importance, for under the constitution all legal and judicial questions in regard to the powers of a Territorial legislature must be determined by the Courts, whose decisions all must respect and obey. The only political questions involved are that the whole question of slavery must be banished from the Halls of Congress, and referred to the people of the States and Territories interested in and to be effected by them. In the event that any citizen should feel agrieved by any local legislation whether State or Territorial, he must appeal to the courts for re[dress] and we are all bound by the decision when made. If the court decides that the laws are unconstitutional, they are void, and there is an end of the controversy. If on the contrary the courts decide the local enactment constitutional it must stand until repealed by the same power that passed it. Hence it is a matter of little consequence what you or I may think about the legal question before the court shall have decided it, when we both are willing as law-abiding citizens to respect and obey the judicial decision. This exposition of the Nebraska Bill was satisfactory to all

Southern men when it was passed. Pending the *Bill* I repeatedly expressed the same opinions in respect to the powers of the Territorial Legislature which I have since expressed at Freeport and in the Senate and in my recent article in Harpers Magazine. Mr Buchanan in his letter accepting the Cincinnati nomination expressed the same opinion —as did also Mr Cobb in his Speech at West Chester Pa in 1856 and in many other speeches—Gen'l Cass in a series of speeches running through a period of more than ten years, and a majority of all the leading Democratic Statesmen—North and South expressed the same sentiments. It is rather late in the day to make this issue on me, while sustaining & approving the course of those who were solemnly pledged to the same doctrine, and who are upheld in their high places without a word of dessent or complaint. The North western Democracy do not understand why this test is now made only upon me, while ninety nine out of every hundred of the sound Democracy are known to hold the same opinions. We have never made any test on others upon this question, but, if we are not now deemed sound enough to be voted for, it is asking a good deal of us to expect our support of those who thus proscribe us.

We stand by the Cincinnati Platform according to its obvious meaning, and are ready to reaffirm it at Charleston without the change of a word, and will then give it the same construction we have always given it. If this is not satisfactory to some of our Southern friends we shall regret but cannot avoid it. I have repeated the same opinions on this subject at each Session of Congress for ten years in succession & been reelected chairman of the committee of Territories each year with a full knowledge of my opinions on the subject of every man who voted for me until last year, when I was removed for avowing the same opinions which I had freely & uniformly avowed for ten years. I firmly believe I am right, and cannot change my opinions at this late day even to be President, much less to be chairman of the Committee on Territories. I am very respectfully your obedent servant

S. A. Douglas

ALS Copy, owned by Martin F. Douglas. Henry K. McCoy, a resident of Americus, Georgia, wrote Douglas on August 22, 1859, of his disagreement with the latter's position on the question of territorial power over slavery (Douglas Papers, University of Chicago Library).

[1]The words enclosed in brackets have been obscured by a blot.

Autobiographical Notes

[September–October, 1859?]

As chairman of the Territorial committee, first in the House of Representatives, and afterwards in the Senate, he reported and successfully carried through the Bills to organize the Territories of Minnesota, Oregon, New Mexico, Utah, Washington, Kansas, and Nebraska, and also the Bills for the admission into the Union of the States of Texas, Iowa, Wisconsin, California, Minnesota, and Oregon. So far as the question of slavery was applicable to the organization of Territories and the admission of new States on his first entrance into public life, he took the position that Congress should not interfere on the one side or the other, but that the people of Each Territory and State should be allowed to form and regulate their domestic institutions to suit themselves. In accordance with this principle he opposed the "Wilmott Proviso" as it is usually called, when first proposed in the House of Representatives in 1846 as an amendment to the Bill appropriating three millions of dollars to enable President Polk to make a Treaty of Peace with Mexico and afterwards in the Senate, when offered as an amendment to the Bill for the Organization of the Territory of Oregon. When he found the Southern Senators and Representatives unanymously supporting the Missouri Compromise line as a fair and just division of the common territory [between the two Sections of the Union][1] and the [Northern Senators and Representatives] great majority of northern Senators and Representatives insisting upon the Wilmot Proviso as [a substitute] applicable to all the territory of the United States as well south as north of 36 degres & thirty minutes, and was compelled to choose between these alternatives, he offered an amendment to the Oregon Bill in August 1848 to extend the Missouri Compromise line indeffinitely westward to the Pacific Ocean in the same sense and with the same understanding with which it was originally adopted in 1820 and extended through Texas in 1845—prohibiting slavery in all the territory north of the parallel of 36-30 and by implication recognizing its existence South of that line. This amendment was adopted in the Senate by a decided majority, receiving the support of every Southern Senator together with severall Northern Senators, but was defeated in the House of Representatives by nearly a sectional vote. [The defeat of rejection of the proposition to extend the Missouri Compromise in the House of Representatives and the defeat of the Wilmot proviso in the Senate] The refusal of the Senate to adopt the policy of Congressional prohibition of slavery in all the territories and the rejection in the House of Representatives of the proposition to extend the Missouri Compromise to the Pacific Ocean, gave rise to that fearful sectional aggitation which convulsed the whole country in 1849-50 and which was quieted by the legislation, known as the Compromise measures of 1850. Mr Douglas supported those measures with zeal and vigor, and on his return to Chicago, finding them assailed with great violence, he [made a speech in the city Hall]

[470]

defended the whole series of measures in a speech which is regarded by his friends as one of the ablest he ever made. In this speech he defined the principles on which the compromise measures of 1850 were founded and upon which he subsequently justified [the Kansas-Nebraska] and defended the Kansas-Nebraska Bill in these words:

"These measures are predicated on the great
"fundamental principle that every people
"ought to possess the right of forming
"and regulating their own internal concerns
"and domestic institutions in their own way."
Again
"These things are all confided by the
"constitution to each state to decide for
"itself, and I know of no reason why the same
"principle should not be extended to the
"Territories."

At the Session of 1853-4, he reported from the Senate Committee on Territories the celebrated Bill to organize the Territories of Kansas & Nebraska, which effectually revolutionized political parties in this country and formed the issues upon which the Democratic and Republican parties are now arrayed against each other. The whole controversy turned on the provision repealing the Missouri Compromise as being inconsistent with the principle of non-intervention by Congress with slavery in States and Territories. After repealing the Missouri restriction the Bill declared it to be the

"true intent & meaning of the act not to legislate
"slavery into any state or Territory nor
"to exclude it therefrom, but to leave the people thereof
"perfectly free to form and regulate their domestic
"institutions in their own way subject only to the
"constitution of the United States"

Whatever diversity of opinion may exist in regard to the correctness of this principle & the propriety of its application to the Territories, it must be admitted that Mr Douglas has proved faithful to it under all circumstances and defended it whenever assailed or violated.

He denounced & opposed with all his energy and ability the Lecompton Constitution upon the distinct ground that it was not the act and deed of the people of Kansas and did not embody their will. The ability and gallantry with which he conducted that memmorable contest against the whole forces and patronage of an administration of his own party exited the admiration of the whole country. Upon the adjournment of that Session of Congress he returned home to vindicate his action before the people [of Illinois in a reelection to the Senate] of Illinois in one of the most exiting & remarkable political canvasses ever known in this country. He had to encounter the bitter and determined hostility of the Federal Administration and all its patronage besides the solid & compact force of the Republican Party. He succeeded however in electing a majority of three in the Senate and five in the House, making eight on joint ballot in favor of his reelection, and was consequently reelected to the Senate for six years from the 4th of March 1859 by fifty four votes for him & forty six votes for Mr Lincoln his opponent. During the whole of that contest he maintained and defended the doctrine of non-intervention & popular sovreignty in the same sense in which he had previously proclaimed it in Congress. In a recent debate in the Senate (Feby 23) he boldly avowed and defended the same doctrine when assailed by several of the ablest Southern Senators. Hence it may be safely assumed that he will resolutely carry out his favorite theory that the people of the States and Territories shall form & regulate their domestic institutions to suit themselves subject only to the Constitution and the final decisions of the judicial tribunals, and that Congress must not intervene either to establish, [prohibit,] abolish, protect or exclude slavery.

Mr Douglas has been remarkably successful in promoting the local interests of his own State during his congressional career. To him, more than to any one individual is Illinois indebted for the magnificent grant of lands which secured the construction of the Illinois Central Rail Road, and contributed so much to restore the credit and develope the resources of that great state. While he has always taken a deep interest in protecting and fostering the inland commerce & navigation by River & Harbor improvements, he has not hesitated to declare that his experience has led him to the conclusion that those objects could be more certainly and effectually secured by a system of tonage duties than by the old plan of appropriations from the Federal Treasury. He was mainly instrumental in securing the passage of the law extending maratime and admiralty jurisdiction of the Federal Courts over the Great chain of Northern Lakes, having reported the Bill as a member of the Judiciary Committee & putt it on its passage when a member of the Ho of Reps.

He has always been a warm supporter & advocate of a Rail Road from the Mississippi River to the Pacific Ocean, having been a member of the various select committees on that subject and being the author of several Bills reported by those committees.

Mr. Douglas' views in regard to our foreign relations have seldom been in accordance with the policy of the administration. He opposed the Treaty with England limiting the Oregon Territory to the 49 parallel, contending that England had no rights on that coast and that the United States should never recognize her claim. He opposed the treaty of peace with Mexico upon the ground that the boundaries were unnatural & inconvenient, and that the provisions in regard to the Indians could never be executed. We have since paid Mexico ten millions of dollars to change the boundaries and release us from the stipulations in regard to the Indians. He opposed the ratification of the Clayton & Bulwer Treaty and endeavored to procure its rejection upon the ground, (among other things) that it pledged the faith of the United States in all time to come never to annex, colonize, or exercise dominion over any portion of Central America. He declared that he did not desire to annex the country at that time, but that the Istmus routes must be left open as highways to our Pacific possessions and that the time would come when we would be compelled to occupy the country, and that he would never pledge the faith of the Republic not to do in the future in respect to this continent what our interests and safety might compel us to do.

He is understood to advocate the acquisition of Cuba whenever the Island can be fairly obtained consistent with the laws of nations and the honor of the country.

Mr Douglas was married to Miss Martha D Martin, daughter of Col Robert Martin of Rockingham County N C on the 7th of April 1847, by whom he had [two children] three children, two of whom survive, Robert M, aged ten years, and Stephen A, aged eight years. The mother of these children died on the 19th of Jan'y 1853, and Mr D was again married to Miss [Addie] Adele Cutts, only daughter of the Hon James Madison Cutts of Washington D C on the 20th of Nov 1856.

ADf, owned by Martin F. Douglas. The draft is not complete, the pages being numbered 6 through 21. The first five pages of the manuscript have not been located. The purpose for which Douglas wrote this draft is not explicit. However, on September 12, 1859, Reverend William D'Arcy Haley, of Washington, D.C., wrote Douglas that he was preparing a book containing biographical sketches of all the Senators, and asked Douglas to send him an outline of his life, not to exceed twelve printed pages in length (Douglas Papers, University of Chicago Library). Several of Haley's sermons have been published but no record of the book referred to in his letter to Douglas has been located.

[1]These and the following words enclosed in brackets were lined out by Douglas in the original draft.

To John A. McClernand

(*Private*)   Washington
My Dear Sir,   Oct 1st 1859
    The Telegraph announces your nomination for Congress. I have not seen the particulars, but presume this intelligence is reliable, and there-

fore congratulate you on the strength of it, altho I was not aware that you were a candidate for the nomination.[1]

I trust that there are no defections or dissentions growing out of the disappointments of unsuccessful rivals. If I can be of any service to you in the Canvass, you can command my services in any way you may indicate, the moment the health of my family will permit me to leave them. Mrs Douglas is sick, and has a Daughter only *one day* old.[2] She is quite sick—was in a very critical condition yesterday, but is much better today. If I can do any good by letters, let me know to whom I shall write and what the difficulties are, if any. I have no fears about your election, but it is desirable that your majority should be large, overwhelming, on account of its effects at this time on other States. The importance o[f] a large majority cannot be over estimated. You should take the stump at once and so should all our friends, and *particularly the disappointed candidates.* They owe it to themselves as well as to the Party. I see that the Danites[3] are organizing for Charleston. They can do no harm [for] the whole country understand their character & weakness. Their pretensions will be treated with contempt by the Southern as well as northern Delegates. Our friends in the South are in fine spirits and gaining every day and confident of success. There will be no difficulty in Charleston. The election in Illinois last year settled that question, and all that now is necessary [is] that the majority shall not be proportionately diminished in your election. I do not expect that there will be a full vote at a special election, and therefore your majority may not be so large as the majority last year, but the proportion must be maintained if possible. Write & tell me what I can & ought to do.

Present my respectful regards to Mrs Mc C & believe me very truly yours

S. A. Douglas

ALS, Illinois State Historical Library.
[1]Thomas Langrell Harris died on November 24, 1858, having just been reelected to Congress. McClernand was elected to fill the vacancy caused by Harris' death and took his seat in the Thirty-sixth Congress in December, 1859.

[2]Douglas' daughter, Ellen, died when only about ten weeks old.
[3]The term "Danites" was applied by Douglas to those Democrats in Illinois who supported the Buchanan administration against him.

To Charles H. Lanphier

(*Private*)   Washington
My Dear Sir,   Oct 1st 1859
I see by the Telegraphic dispatches that the Danites have called a convention for January to appoint Delegates to Charleston. Is it not time the State Central Committee should call the Democratic State

Convention to appoint Delegates? It has occured to me that the convention should assemble in the Winter to appoint Delegates and adjourn until June to nominate candidates for Governor & State officers and Presidential electors. I throw out the suggestion for the reflection of our friends, without having fully considered it. The ground of the suggestion is that the party may not be ready to act on the nominations so early as January or even before the Charleston convention. Again if there should be a violent contest for Governor & State officers, possibly disappointed candidates might desire to make mischief between that time & the Charleston Convention. Think of these things and then decide. I shall be content with what our friends may think is best for the Party. Of course, we cannot in any contingency, recognize the Danites, as Democrats so long as they keep up a bolting, disorganizing opposition to the Party. Col Richardson told me at Chicago that his idea was that we should appoint 22 delegates for the State, all at large, and select the most prominent men with the best *political record on the slavery question* that could be found in the State—men well known to the whole country, and especially favorably known at the South. He feels right and will act efficiently. The prospects in the South are improving every day. We will have a strong party in the South when the convention meets. Do you exchange with the Mobile Register (Ala), if not you ought to do so? It is making a glorious fight on the right line.[1]

How does the nomination for Congress take? Is there any defection? I hope not. All discontents should be smothered for the good of the cause. I hope the party will rally as a unit for the nominee. A defeat would be ruinous to us. Its effect would be disastrous in the extreme. I have not heard a word, having only seen the result of the nominations announced by Telegraph. Write me in full, *and send me the Register*. I do not get [it]. Be sure to send it regularly to Washington. I hope to be able to come & help in the Canvass. Mrs Douglas is sick—has Daughter one day old—I will come as soon as it is prudent to leave her.

Present my kind regards to Mrs L & believe me yours truly

S. A. DOUGLAS

ALS, Illinois State Historical Library.

[1]The Mobile *Register* was edited by John Forsyth, one of Douglas' strong supporters in the South. On December 12, 1859, Forsyth wrote to Douglas: "Never in the history of our country, & in the course of this Western experiment of man's capacity to take care of & promote his own political well-being, have public men like yourself been so much needed. I am doing my poor endeavor to breast the storm of sectionalism *here*, as you have done in both sections of an exasperated union. ...I take the ground of popular sovereignty as the bond to which we have placed our seals & plighted our faith" (Douglas Papers, University of Chicago Library).

To George W. Manypenny

(*Private*)

My Dr Sir

Washington
Oct 1st 1859

I sincerely regret that I will not be able to visit Ohio again before the election.[1] Mrs Douglas is sick—has a Daughter only *one day old*, and I cannot leave her.

I do trust that you will be able to defeat the abolitionists in Ohio this year. It is an object dear to my heart. The importance of it cannot be over estimated. Ohio should lead the North West and I doubt not she will next year, if not this. Yet it would be a shame to see such a man as Chase again in the Senate.[2] I trust the rumors are not true that the Administration have issued orders to defeat the Democracy in Ohio this year. Such is the impression here, and Medil's[3] trip is understood to have such an object. Badly as I think of them and as I had a right to think of their conduct in Illinois last year I was not prepared to see them do the same thing in Ohio, Iowa, Wisconsin & Minnesota this year. And yet such is the impression here, and my letters from Iowa within a day or two express the same opinion. I have also received a letter from a prominent & influential Democrat from the Northern Part of your State expressing the same opinion and the writer thinks he has evidence of the fact. But still I have hopes of your success. You have now but a few days to work, and these should [be] well employed. I wish you would send me your paper. You did so during the winter, but I suppose it now goes to Chicago. Please change the direction to this place. I wish you would explain to our friends the reason why I cannot come and also how deeply I feel for their success.

Present my kind regards to Mrs M & believe me very truly your friend

S. A. Douglas

ALS, Library of Congress. George W. Manypenny was chairman of the Ohio Democratic state central committee and editor of the Columbus *Ohio Statesman*. He had been United States Commissioner of Indian Affairs from 1853 to 1857.

[1]Douglas made three speeches in September, at Columbus, Cincinnati, and Wooster, on behalf of Democratic candidates in the Ohio campaign of 1859. To offset the impact Douglas might have on the campaign, the local Republican organization invited Lincoln to speak in support of the Republican candidates. The speeches of Lincoln and Douglas in Ohio constituted an extension of their debates in Illinois the previous year.

[2]The Republicans swept the state election in October, achieving a majority in the state legislature and electing their state ticket. Salmon P. Chase, Ohio's Governor, was elected to the United States Senate by the legislature early in 1860.

[3]William Medill, former Representative from Ohio, Superintendent of Indian Affairs and Governor of the state, held the office of First Comptroller of the United States Treasury during the Buchanan administration.

To Fernando Wood

Washington
My Dr Sir,   Oct 3d 1859
  Your enclosing mortgage is duly received. The illness of Mrs Douglas will prevent its execution for a few days. She has a Daughter only
three days old and is very ill. Consider the mortgage executed and rely
upon receiving it in due time.[1] Yours truly

                                                    S. A. DOUGLAS

ALS, Illinois State Historical Library.
Fernando Wood, a New York shipping
merchant and former member of Congress, was Mayor of New York city
from 1855 to 1858 and in 1861 and 1862.
  [1]Wood had earlier assisted Douglas
in raising money for the 1858 Senatorial
campaign in Illinois. In August, 1858,
he and another New York party had
taken two three-year mortgages on
pieces of Douglas' land. The negotiation mentioned in this letter represented
either an extension of the earlier arrangement or a new arrangement
whereby Wood assumed still another
mortgage from Douglas. Douglas was
probably trying to raise money to fi-
nance his campaign for the Presidency
in 1860.

To the Democratic State Central Committee of Wisconsin

[On October 15, 1859, the Cincinnati *Enquirer* noted, "Senator Douglas has written a letter to the Democratic State Central Committee of
Wisconsin, informing them that it will be impossible for him to visit
their State and address the people during the present year." This letter
has not been located.]

To Reverdy Johnson

Washington
My Dr Sir,   Oct 21st 1859
  The extreme illness of Mrs Douglas is my apology for the delay in
answering your kind letter. She is better today, and we are greatly
encouraged in our hopes of her speedy recovery. My Reply to Black
is read[y] for the Press, with some slight corrections to be made in the
Proof sheets when finished.[1] I hope to be able to send you Proof sheets
in advance of publication on Monday or Tuesday. I regret I could not
have submitted it to you for revision, especially on the law points,
before publication. However I rest upon the decisions of the Supreme
Court on all law points. I am extremely gratified that you are replying
to Black.[2] Your great reputation as a lawyer will give authority to
your opinions throughout the Union. I am glad you have concluded
to withhold it until you see my reply, as I could not modify mine by
yours as I would have liked the privilege of doing on the legal points.

Present my kind regards to Mrs Johnson & accept assurances of my gratitude for your kindness to me. Very truly your friend

S. A. DOUGLAS

ALS, Library of Congress. Reverdy Johnson, one of the foremost constitutional lawyers of his time, had been a member of the United States Senate from Maryland from 1845 to 1849, and Attorney General of the United States in the cabinet of Zachary Taylor from 1849 to 1850. He represented the defense in the Dred Scott case and was one of the major influences in bringing about a decision against Scott.

[1] The publication of Douglas' essay in *Harper's Magazine* in September, 1859, was followed by an exchange of pamphlets between Douglas and Attorney General Jeremiah Black. Judge Black's anonymous *Observations on Senator Douglas' Views of Popular Sovereignty* was first published in the Washington *Constitution*, September 10, 1859, and later published in pamphlet form. Doug-

las replied with *Popular Sovereignty in the Territories: Judge Douglas in Reply to Judge Black* (Washington, D.C., 1859), the statement referred to in this letter.

[2] Reverdy Johnson, *Remarks on Popular Sovereignty, as Maintained and Denied Respectively by Judge Douglas, and Attorney-General Black* (Baltimore, Maryland, 1859). Johnson was in continuous correspondence with Douglas during the controversy with Black. On October 16, 1859, he wrote Douglas that he was preparing an answer to Black's pamphlet, and on October 18, he wrote that he would like to see Douglas' reply to Black before he released his pamphlet to the printer (Douglas Papers, University of Chicago Library).

To Henry J. Raymond

(*Private*)   Washington
My Dear Sir,   Oct 24th 1859

I send you in advance of publication the Proof sheets of my reply to Judge Black. It is the only copy sent to the New York Press. I have felt this act of courtesy due to the Times in consequence of the courtesy and kindness which it alone of all the New York journals, has shown me.[1] I fear that I will not be able to visit New York soon as I had hoped in consequence of the serious illness of Mrs Douglas. Altho a little better today, we are not without uneasiness, as she is so extremely feeble. Probably I will not be able to leave my House for some weeks. Very truly your friend

S. A. DOUGLAS

ALS, New York Public Library. Henry J. Raymond was editor of the New York *Times*.
[1] The New York *Times*, while not supporting Douglas politically, had re-

ported his campaigns fully and fairly, and Raymond, through his editorial columns, had expressed admiration and respect for the Illinois Senator.

To Reverdy Johnson

                                                                                 Washington
My Dr Sir,   Nov 4th 1859

Accept my thanks for your kind note of yesterday just rec'd.[1] I am happy to be able to inform you that Mrs Douglas is now decidedly better and our hopes are all revived. Her disease took a turn for the better yesterday and she has steadily improved ever since. The Doctors now think that she will certainly recover if she has no new attack which they do not anticipate.

I saw our friend Badger of North Carolina the other day and he expressed a stronger desire to see your pamphlet and I promised to send him one at Raleigh. He bears testimony to his understanding of the Nebraska Bill in the same way we now construe it. I suggested to him to address you a letter for publication expressing his concurence with you on all the legal points in the controversy and am inclined to think he will do so. Having offered the Badger Amendment and voted for the Bill his opinion on that question would command attention.[2]

All who have read your pamphlet concur in pronouncing it unanswerable. Mine was considered by my friends a very good argument before yours appeared. But without being envious I am truly grateful to you and feel great pride in being sustained by one whose legal authority none feel disposed to question. Renewing my thanks for your kind note I am very truly your friend

S. A. DOUGLAS

ALS, Library of Congress.
[1] Johnson's letter of November 3, 1859, has not been located. He wrote to Douglas, however, on October 25, 28, and 31, expressing satisfaction that Douglas was pleased with his pamphlet on popular sovereignty (Douglas Papers, University of Chicago Library).

[2] George E. Badger was a Whig Senator from North Carolina from 1846 to 1855. His amendment to the Kansas-Nebraska Act, adopted on March 2, 1854, provided that the repeal of the Missouri Compromise would not revive any prior law protecting, establishing, prohibiting, or abolishing slavery.

To John A. McClernand

December 7, 1859.

My Dear Sir:—Your note is just received, informing me that Mr. Kellogg, of Illinois,[1] in the course of a discussion in the House of Representatives today, made the following charge against me:

"Mr. Kellogg, of Illinois. I charge that Mr. Greeley was again and again, with others, in consultation in the parlor of Judge Douglas, planning and scheming the election of Judge Douglas to the Senate of the United States from the State of Illinois."[2]

Now, while it is true that men of all shades of political opinion have been in the habit of visiting at my house for the ten years I have kept house in Washington, and while it may be true that Mr. Greeley, among others, may have visited at my house within that time, it is wholly untrue that I ever planned or schemed, or had any arrangement whatever with Mr. Greeley, at my house or elsewhere, for the purpose of securing my re-election to the Senate of the United States. On the contrary, the charge, in all its parts and import, is utterly false. Very truly, your friend,

S. A. DOUGLAS

Chicago *Times*, December 16, 1859.

[1]William Kellogg, of Canton, Illinois, was a Republican member of Congress from 1857 to 1863.

[2]On December 7, 1859, McClernand wrote Douglas: "Mr Kellogg, of Illinois, in the course of remarks made by him, to the House, this morning, charged that you and Horace Greely, some two years ago this winter, at your house, in this city plotted and schemed together for the purpose of securing your re-election to the Senate. I write this note to inform you of the fact; leaving it to you to take such course, in the matter as you may think proper" (Douglas Papers, University of Chicago Library).

To John A. McClernand

My D Sir,   Dec 8th 1859

I should have answered your kind note last night but was too ill. Kelloggs charge that I ever formed or planned or contemplated an arraingement with Mr Greely in regard to the Illinois election, at my House or at any other place is an unmittigated falsehood. I have no recollection of Mr Greely having visited my House but once in ten years, and on that occasion the Illinois election was never alluded to. He called to pay his respects the same as any other visitor & talked freely on the current topics of the day in the presence of my family & others.

But I scorn to make any explanation or formal denial. Any man who will found a political charge on a pretended private conversation is not to be believed on oath.

You treated the matter perfectly right.

You will see that Mr Greely puts an end to the matter in his paper of today.[1] Very truly your friend

S. A. DOUGLAS

ALS, Illinois State Historical Library.

[1]In an undated letter to William Kellogg, printed in the New York *Tribune*, Greeley wrote, "Senator Douglas and I have been acquaintances for ten years or more.... Once only in our lives did we agree on a political question—that of resisting the attempt to force an abhorred Constitution on the People of Kansas.... And never did any letter, message, or word, pass between us implying a desire on his part that I should, or a promise on mine that I would, support him, at any time, for any office whatever."

To George Nicholas Sanders

                                                        Washington,
My dear Sir—   Dec. 15, 1859.

My health is improving so rapidly that I have given up the idea of going South, as advised by my physicians.[1] I hope to resume my seat in the Senate in the course of two or three weeks. It is possible, that in the meantime, Mrs Douglas and myself may make a visit to New York for a few days. This however, is not certain. I saw B to-day, and told him that you complained that he did not write.[2]

Present my kind regards to your family and believe me, Very truly, Your friend,

S. A. Douglas

LS, Library of Congress.
[1]As his wife recovered from her illness, Douglas himself fell ill around the middle of November. His "pamphlet war" with Attorney General Black was terminated in part because of the state of his health.
[2]"B" was probably A. D. Banks.

To Charles H. Lanphier

(*Private*)   Washington

My Dr Sir,   Dec 31st 1859

In compliance with your request the Democratic delegation have had a consultation and agreed upon some Resolutions *unanymously*, which are forwarded today in Duplicate,—one set by mail & the other by express—directed to you.[1] We have left you to frame such Resolution in regard to myself as you may think best. We think it will be adviseable to appoint Presidential electors as well as Delegates at this time for the reason that if you omit to do it the Danites will form an Electorial Tickett & then demand that we take theirs to prevent a division in the Party.

Prospects look bright & improving every day. Your friend

S. A. Douglas

ALS, Illinois State Historical Library.
[1]The resolutions were to be adopted by the state Democratic convention. On December 11, 1859, Lanphier wrote to Douglas urging that the resolutions be prepared with great care since they would be regarded as Douglas' platform. "Why not have [them] written under your own eye," Lanphier continued, "just as you want them? They should be brief and explicit, and handsomely expressed, and, I think, should include something in regard to our state matters" (Douglas Papers, University of Chicago Library).

To James Walker

[Letter of introduction, purportedly written by Douglas, to Dr. James Walker, President of Harvard College, for Robert Todd Lincoln. The young Lincoln was presented as the son of Douglas' friend Abraham Lincoln, "with whom I have lately been canvassing the State of Illinois." The sole source for this letter seems to be Edward Everett Hale, *James Russell Lowell and His Friends* (Boston, 1899), pp. 200-201, who heard the story from a Harvard professor of the time. Hale gives the date as 1860, but 1859 seems more likely since Robert Todd Lincoln attempted to enter Harvard in the fall of that year. Walker was President of Harvard from 1853 to 1860.]

To Charles H. Lanphier

Washington
My Dr Sir,   Jan'y 1st 1859 [1860]

The Resolutions were sent to you two days ago. I am informed that everybody wants to be delegate to Charleston, and that there will be much feeling and competition upon the subject. While I take no part & shall express no prefferences between friends it may be proper to suggest that after appointing the 22 delegates the convention might appoint as many assistant or consulting delegates as it chooses, or authorize the Central Committee to do it. In this way all of our friends can go in a quasi official capacity, and the more the better. It may not be politic to announce to the world that a large number is expected to go, but it is important that all our leading men in the State should be at Charleston. Perhaps it would be best to authorizing the State Central Committee to appoint as many consulting Delegates as they may see proper, and not announce their names publicly until about the time they start. Many will go when [they] are requested by the Central Committee who would no[t] otherwise do it, and in this way you can get the best men in the State. Everything looks well here & prospect better everyday. Very truly your friend

S. A. DOUGLAS

ALS, Illinois State Historical Library.

To Charles E. Stuart

(*Confidential*)
My Dr. Sir,   Washington January 15, 1860

Your kind letter was recd. yesterday, enclosing one from Mr Sherwood. You will find my reply to him enclosed.[1]

I am surprised and mortified at the rumors he and you report; there is not a word of truth in them. I never saw the articles to which you allude, neither before nor after the publication. I do not know what they were, or their author, although I infer from your [letter] that they were abusive of you.

I was applied to by one man from your state to know my wishes in regard to who should be the delegates. My reply was that I made it an invariable rule not to interfere with the matter in any state, not even in Illinois, but to have my friends in each state free to do as they pleased; that I was a stranger to the people of Michigan, and knew of but few of their public men; that I should be satisfied with whoever my friends might send to Charleston.

[482]

Your name was alluded to, and I was asked if I regarded you as my friend, and I replied I did; we had been on good personal terms; that during the Lecompton fight a strengthened friendship had grown up between us which remained unimpaired on my part, and I believed it was unchanged on yours. When he attempted to convince me that you ought not to be a delegate I replied that I had nothing to say on that point; that my friends in Michigan must do as they thought best in the choice of delegates; that I had been applied to by friends from other states to know my wishes and had refused to take part, and must do the same in Michigan.

I took it for granted that you would be appointed from Michigan, with as much certainty as Gov. Richardson would be in Illinois, without any request from me, and so stated in the conversation alluded to. But I have said more than was necessary on this subject. We know each other too well to allow mischief to be made between us.

I have no doubt of your election as a delegate, and Gov. Richardson was expressing his desire to me today to meet you at Charleston and expressing strong reasons why you should be there.[2] Let me, hear from you soon and frequently.

You are authorized in my name, to denounce the rumor that I am opposed to you. I would say more, but from the fact that I am not at liberty to express preferences, nor is there any necessity in your case; our friend Thompson tells me you will have no trouble in the convention.

Give my kind regards to Mrs S. in which Mrs D. joins me. Her health is improving; She is still weak and will be all winter. My health about as good as ever. Write often. Yours Truly

S. A. Douglas

Copy, Library of Congress. Charles E. Stuart was a member of Congress from Michigan from 1847 to 1849 and from 1851 to 1853, and served as United States Senator for one term from 1853 to 1859. During his Senate term and afterward, Stuart remained one of Douglas' devoted supporters.
[1]Stuart's letter, dated January 8, 1860, reported the rumor that Douglas did not want him to be a delegate to the Charleston convention. Stuart asked Douglas to write to Thomas R. Sherwood, who had expressed some concern over this report (Douglas Papers, University of Chicago Library). Sherwood himself wrote Douglas on January 9, and D. B. Cook, editor of the Niles (Michigan) *Republican*, wrote on January 10, both inquiring as to the truth of the rumor (*ibid.*).
[2]Stuart was elected delegate to the Charleston convention.

To William H. English

My Dr Sir,   Jany 20th 1860

I cordially recipr[oc]ate the kind sentiments expressed in your private note just received.[1] I will take pleasure in reading the speech you

have sent me & will then confer with you freely upon the subject refered to. Very truly yours

S. A. DOUGLAS

ALS, William Henry Smith Memorial Library, Indiana Historical Society.
¹English's note has not been located.

To ———

[January 31, 1860; ANS. This note has not been located. It was listed
in Stan. V. Henkels, compiler, *The Valuable Collection of Autographs
and Historical Papers Collected by the Hon. Jas. T. Mitchell . . . also
the Entire Lincoln Memorial Collection of Chicago, Ill. . . . to Be Sold
. . . Dec. 5th and 6th, 1894* (n.p., n.d.), p. 83.]

To J. ———

Washington

Dr Sir,   Feby 14th 1860

I beg you to present my kindest regards to Mrs & Miss Levin and
assure them that I should take great pleasure in complying with their
wishes to recommend Mr Dougherty if I felt at liberty to recommend
any one to the Clerk of the Ho of Reps for appointment; but the
rule is so well established at Washington that the patronage of the
House belongs to its own members & their friends that I have been
constrained to deny the requests of all of my friends for recommendations. With great respect I am very truly your obedient servant

S. A. DOUGLAS

ALS, Illinois State Historical Library. The name of the addressee is illegible.

To Fernando Wood

Dear Sir,   [February 16, 1860]

In reply to your note just received I take pleasure in stating that
there is not a particle of truth in the state[men]t published in the Constitution newspaper of this morning, that you had pledged the support
of the Delegates to Charl[es]ton to which you belong to me.¹ That
subject was not alluded to by either of us when I met you recently in
New York, nor have you ever given me any reason to believe that
your Delegates would support me in the event they were admitted
into the convention. Very respectfully
Feby 16th 1860   S. A. DOUGLAS

ALS, Henry E. Huntington Library.
¹Fernando Wood headed a rival delegation to the Charleston convention to that
endorsed by the Democratic organization in New York and led by Dean Richmond. Wood's group was anti-Douglas in the convention and was not seated.

[484]

To Peter Cagger

My Dear Sir,   Feby 19th 1860

My letters have accumulated so much recently that I could not properly reply to yours of the 14th inst at an earlier day. I very much regret not having seen you and Mr Richmond[1] at New York as I had anticipated. Should I again visit New York soon I will certainly let you know in advance. I will assure you however that the rumors to which you refer have never been credited by me and have not given me the slightest uneasiness. I think I understand fully your policy and the necessities which prompt it. I have had a free and satisfactory conversation with our friend Ludlow.[2] His visit here has done good and I doubt not you will be gratified with his report when he returns. Our friends are in the best of spirits here and have implicit confidence in the entire good faith of our friends in New York. There will be no serious difficulty in the South. The last few weeks has worked a perfect revolution in that section. They all tell me and write me that all will be right if our Northern friends will fearlessly represent the wishes and feelings of the Democracy in their own States. That such will be the case I have no doubt. Present my kind regards to my friends and believe me very truly yours

S. A. DOUGLAS

ALS, Illinois State Historical Library. Peter Cagger was a wealthy and politically powerful Albany attorney. He was a member of the New York delegation to the Charleston convention. On February 14, 1860, Cagger wrote to Douglas, "... do not let any rumors in regard to our delegation to Charleston, give you the slightest uneasiness. New York has no candidate in her own State for the Presidency" (Douglas Papers, University of Chicago Library).

[1]Dean Richmond, a prominent New York merchant and Vice-President of the New York Central Railroad, was chairman of the New York state Democratic committee and would lead the state's delegation to the Charleston convention.

[2]William H. Ludlow, of Sayville, New York, was also a member of the New York delegation to the Charleston convention.

To ———

Washington
Gentlemen   Feby 20th 1860

Accept my grateful acknowledgements for the rec'd Invitation which you have placed in my hands, inviting me on behalf of my political friends from all parts of Virginia to visit the metropolis of the old Dominion during the Session of the Sovereign convention.

I can assure you that I fully appreciate the honor, and would gladly accept the Invitation at once if I could do so consistent with my paramount duties here. The noble and patriotic position which Virginia has assumed in view of the dangers which threaten the existence of the Union and the peace of the country cannot fail to command the admiration of all conservative and Union-loving men. The unity of the States, the peace of the country, the hopes of all the friends of Constitutional government now depend upon the firmness, wisdom, and freedom of Virginia. So long as the Old Dominion stands by the Constitution and the Union I shall never despair of the Republic. You will accept for yourselves assurances of my thanks for the very agreeable measure in which you have performed the duty assigned you by those you represent. I am very truly your friend

AL Copy, owned by Martin F. Douglas.

To ———

[February 22, 1860]

I thank you, my Dear Madam, for the privilege of recording my name in your Album. Your graces and virtues are engraven upon the hearts of all your friends in language more eloquent and fervent than my pen can impart to paper. I am very truly your friend

Washington S. A. DOUGLAS

Feby 22nd 1860.

ALS, Illinois State Historical Library. Douglas received many requests for his autograph; those replies which have been located have, as a general rule, not been included in this collection.

To Shelton Mackenzie

(*Private*) Washington

My Dear Sir, Feby 22d 1860

Accept my thanks for your kind letter enclosing one from your friend in New York. My opinions on the subject referred to have [been] before the country for years and I do not deem it wise or necessary at this time to proclaim them over again. Any exposition of my view at this time, except in reply to assaults in the Senate, would be misconstrued. With many thanks for your kindness, I am very truly your friend

S. A. DOUGLAS

ALS, Historical Society of Pennsylvania. Robert Shelton Mackenzie, a native of Ireland and a medical graduate of Cork University, was a resident of Philadelphia. He was the author of several books, including a *Life of Charles Dickens*.

To Charles J. Faulkner

[March 24, 1860, Washington; ALS, Henry E. Huntington Library. Introducing Hudson E. Bridge, a St. Louis industrialist, "who visits

Europe with his family on a trip of Pleasure." Faulkner, formerly a member of Congress from Virginia, was United States Minister to France from 1859 to 1861.]

To Henry Cleveland

(*Private*)   Washington City

Dear Sir   March 31, 1860

I regret that very pressing engagements have prevented more prompt reply to your enquiries of the 25th instant.

You will find from my "Reply" and "Rejoinder" to Judge Black, and in my "Letter" to Dr Gwin, printed copies of which I have caused to be mailed to you, that I maintain Slave property stands on an equal footing with all other property, and is subject to the local law to the same extent and no further; and that, instead of being opposed to, I endorse the decision of the Court in the Dred Scott case.

Trusting that these views as repeatedly promulgated will meet your acquiescence. I remain, Yours respectfully

S. A. DOUGLAS

LS, New-York Historical Society. Henry Cleveland was on the staff of the Augusta (Georgia) *Constitutionalist*. On March 25, 1860, he wrote Douglas, asking the Senator to "give me your ideas upon popular sovereignty briefly expressed" (Douglas Papers, University of Chicago Library).

To ———

                                        Washington City

Gentlemen   March 31, 1860

Your communication announcing that the Ladies of Virginia propose inaugurating the marble statue of Henry Clay, by Heart, on the 12th of April next, in the City of Richmond, and that you have been appointed by them a Committee to invite me to attend and witness the ceremony, has been received by me with very high appreciation of the honor conferred by the invitation, of which you press acceptance.[1]

Be assured that though I may not promise myself the pleasure of being present at the instalation of the Statue from pressing engagements here of legislative duty, my earnest sympathy will attend every movement that will be made to raise in safety to its solid foundation the marble personation though far less durable than the undying fame of Henry Clay.

To the ladies of Virginia, the land of his birth, permit me to tender my thanks for their noble and successful efforts thus to cherish the memory of one, whom now that the animosities of party have passed away, all must owe truly & greatly honor.

With renewed thanks for the invitation with which I have been favored. Yrs Most Respy.

Copy, University of Chicago Library. The copy is in the hand of James Madison Cutts.
[1]The invitation, dated March 12, 1860, was sent by a committee headed by R. Ridgway, of Richmond (Douglas Papers, University of Chicago Library).

To Hendrick B. Wright

(Confidential)   Washington
My Dear Sir,   April 1st 1860
    I beg your pardon for the delay in acknowledging the receipt of your kind letter. I have been so overwhelmed with calls and letters that I have had no time to answer. I shall be glad to hear from you often and hope that you will keep me fully posted as I must necessarily rely in a great measure upon you in relation to matters in your vicinity. I have but few personal acquaintances in your part of Pennsylvania, nor indeed am I in correspondence with any. I regret that I could not have seen Mrs W before she left. Tell her she will receive a small package from me in a few days.[1] With many thanks for your kindness and a due appreciation of your talents, character and services, I am very truly your friend

S. A. DOUGLAS

ALS, Wyoming Historical and Geological Society, Wilkes-Barre, Pennsylvania. Hendrick B. Wright, of Wilkes-Barre, was a Democratic member of Congress from 1853 to 1855. He had been a delegate to the Democratic national conventions in 1844, 1848, 1852, and 1856.
[1]The package for Mrs. Wright contained a plaster bust of Douglas.

To D. M. Marshall

[April 8, 1860, Washington City; LS, Indiana State Library. Referring to a pension case and returning the papers pertinent to it. Since the Third Auditor's office was already in correspondence with Marshall on the case, Douglas wrote that he could not interfere in it. Marshall was a resident of La Grange, Lewis County, Missouri.]

To John F. Farnsworth

My Dear Sir,   [June, 1860]
    I regret that I will not be able to be in the Senate for some days in consequence of the condition of my throat. I may be compelled to go to New York and have an operation performed. Under these circum-

stances, I wish Mr Trumbull would give notice that he will call up the motion to reconsider, & then have it determined. He may also ask any one opposed to the Bill to pair off with me & say that I will deem it a favor to me to do so.

I am very anxious to have the Bill passed. Very respectfully

S. A. DOUGLAS

ALS, Library of Congress. John F. Farnsworth was a Chicago lawyer. He was elected to Congress as a Republican in 1856 and served two terms in the House of Representatives. Although the letter is undated, it seems likely that it was written early in June, 1860. On June 4, 1860, Farnsworth wrote Douglas, "What can we do about that Resolution in the Senate? ... I dislike to have any one else call up the motion to reconsider in your absence. When will you be able to be in the Senate again?" (Douglas Papers, University of Chicago Library). Although Douglas writes of his concern for the passage of a "Bill," he probably had reference

to his resolution, introduced in January, 1860, in favor of a "bill for protecting each State and Territory of the Union against invasion by the authorities or inhabitants of any other State or Territory, and for the suppression and punishment of conspiracies or combinations in any State or Territory with intent to invade, assail, or molest the government, inhabitants, property, or institutions of any State or Territory of the Union." The resolution, inspired by John Brown's raid at Harper's Ferry, was tabled on January 31, with the provision that Douglas could reintroduce it at any time.

To Follett and Foster Company

Washington—
Gentlemen—   June 9th 1860

I have received by Express one dozen copies of your publication of the joint Debates between Mr Lincoln and myself in 1858,[1] sent by order of the Hon Mr Cox,[2] who will pay you the amount of your bill.

I feel it my duty to protest against the unfairness of this publication, and especially against the alterations and mutilations in the Reports of my speeches. The original reports as published in the Chicago Times, altho' intended to be fair and just, were necessarily imperfect, and in some respects erroneous. The speeches were all delivered in the open air to immense crowds of people, and in some instances in stormy and boisterous weather, when it was impossible for the Reporters to hear distinctly and report literally. The reports of my speeches were not submitted to me or to any friend of mine for inspection or correction before publication; nor did I have the opportunity of reading more than one or two of them afterwards, until the election was over, when all interest in the subject had passed away. About one year ago a gentleman in Illinois wrote to me in this city for permission to publish these Joint Debates in book-form stating that Mr Lincoln had given his consent to their publication.[3] I did not retain a copy of my reply,

[489]

but according to my present recollection I stated that there were many errors in the reports of the speeches as published, and expressed my unwillingness to the publication unless I should have the opportunity of revising and correcting errors. I am not aware, however, that your publication has any connection with that application. Upon the slight examination of your publication which I have been able to make, I find that Mr Lincoln's speeches have been revised, corrected and improved since their publication in the newspapers of Illinois, while mine have been mutilated, and in some instances, the meaning changed by the omission of interrogatories and expressions of approbation and disapprobation by persons in the crowd to which my remarks were made responsive, but by the omission of which my replies seemed ambiguous, incoherent or unintelligible. The unfairness of these omissions and alterations is rendered more apparent by reference to the fact that similar interrogatories and expressions of applause or disapprobation are retained in Mr Lincoln's speeches in all cases where they add to their force, and omitted where they impair the effect of his argument. In short, I regard your publication as partial and unfair and designed to do me injustice by placing me in a false position. I saw in the preface to the first edition of your publication, which is omitted in the copy sent to me, a correspondence between Mr Lincoln and the Republican Committee from which it appears that Mr Lincoln furnished his speeches and mine for publication—his in the revised and corrected form and mine as they came from the hands of the Reporter without revision.[4] Being thus notified that his speeches had been revised and corrected, this fact ought to have reminded you that common fairness & justice required that I should have an opportunity of revising and correcting mine. But to deny me that privelege, and then to change and mutilate the reports as they appeared in the newspapers from which they were taken, is an act of injustice against which I must be permitted to enter my protest. In order that the injustice which you have done me may be in some degree diminished, I respectfully request that this letter, together with the correspondence between Mr Lincoln and the Committee which led to the publication, may be inserted as a Preface to all future editions of these Debates.[5] I have the honor to be, very respectfully your obdt servt,

S. A. DOUGLAS

Copy, Library of Congress. Follett and Foster Company was a Columbus, Ohio, publishing firm. This copy was enclosed in a letter from Follett and Foster Company to John G. Nicolay, June 12, 1860.

[1]*Political Debates Between Hon.*

Abraham Lincoln and Hon. Stephen A. Douglas, in the Celebrated Campaign of 1858 in Illinois (Columbus, Ohio, 1860). In December, 1859, the chairman of the Ohio Republican committee, George M. Parsons, asked Lincoln to send him copies of the Illinois debates, as well as of Lincoln's Ohio speeches, in September of that year, with a view to publishing them as a campaign document for the Republicans in 1860. Lincoln sent the speeches to Parsons, who turned them over to Follett and Foster for publication.

²Samuel S. Cox, a former owner of the Columbus *Ohio Statesman* and a member of Congress from 1857 to 1865, was one of Douglas' strong supporters in Ohio.

³On April 6, 1859, A. A. Couch, editor of the Washington (Illinois) *Investigator*, wrote Douglas of his plans to publish the joint debates. The plans were formulated by Couch, a Douglas supporter, and William A. Ross, a Republican. "The arrangement now contemplated," Couch wrote, "is to have the work open with Mr. Lincolns speech at Springfield; followed by yours at Chicago and Bloomington; Mr. Lincolns and yours at Springfield; the correspondence that led to the debate; the joint debate; closing with four or five administration speeches—entitling the work *'Illinois Politics.'* Mr. Lincoln has been consulted, approves the publication, and the above arrangement" (Douglas Papers, University of Chicago Library).

⁴In his letter to Parsons, December 19, 1859, Lincoln wrote: "The copies I send you are as reported and printed, by the respective friends of Senator Douglas and myself, at the time—that is, his by his friends, and mine by mine. It would be an unwarrantable liberty for us to change a word or a letter in his, and the changes I have made in mine, you perceive, are verbal only, and very few in number" (Roy P. Basler, editor, *The Collected Works of Abraham Lincoln* [9 vols., New Brunswick, New Jersey, 1953], III, 510).

⁵This Douglas letter was published in one of the several printings of the first edition. In their letter to Nicolay, the publishers wrote, "Enclosed is copy of letter received from Mr Douglas—we shall pay our respects to him to-morrow. It is pretty evident that the Judge thinks he suffers in comparison" (Library of Congress). On June 16, 1860, the publishers sent their reply to Douglas: "The speeches of Mr. Lincoln were

never 'revised, corrected, or improved' in the sense you use those words. Remarks by the crowd which were not responded to, and the reporters' insertions of 'cheers,' 'great applause,' and so forth, which received no answer or comment from the speaker, were by your direction omitted, as well from Mr. Lincoln's speeches as yours, as we thought their perpetuation in book form would be in bad taste, and were in no manner pertinent to, or a part of, the speech" (Edwin Erle Sparks, editor, *The Lincoln-Douglas Debates of 1858* [Springfield, Illinois, 1908], p. 594). The publishing company had earlier written to Cox that the edition of the debates contained "more of Lincoln than Douglas simply because the Rep. Committee desired it," but added that if Douglas should win the Democratic Presidential nomination, two of the Senator's 1859 Ohio speeches, as well as his speech in reply to Jefferson Davis in the Senate, would be added "to keep this book from being partizan" (May 23, 1860, Douglas Papers, University of Chicago Library). Douglas received the nomination but the edition of the debates remained unchanged. On July 16, 1860, Cox wrote Douglas: "It is within my personal observation & knowledge that large no's of these Debates are being sold—notwithstanding your protesting letter. Now it is for you to decide whether it is of consequence enough to you, to have the corrections made in the edition which may make your part of the discussion suitable and correct. Mr Foster proposed to remunerate you sufficiently by the sales, to pay for any labor of any one whom you might employ to fix the debates right. His idea is not to use your brain without in some way remunerating you. But I shut that up, by saying that you did not wish any pecuniary return for any *imprimatur*, which you chose to impress on the volume" (Douglas Papers, University of Chicago Library). Sparks concluded, from a careful comparison of the debates with the original newspaper reports, that the chief variations in Douglas' speeches involved only unimportant verbal changes and the omission of the crowd's interruptions.

To William A. Richardson

(*Private*)

My dear Sir,   Washington 11 PM. June 20th 1860.

I learn there is eminent danger that the Democratic party will be demoralized if not destroyed by the breaking up of the Convention. Such a result would inevitably expose the country to the perils of sectional strife between the Northern and Southern partizans of Congressional intervention upon the subject of Slavery in the Territories. I firmly and conscientiously believe that there is no safety for the country—no hope for the preservation of the Union, except by a faithful and rigid adherence to the doctrine of *non Intervention by Congress* with Slavery in the Territories.

Intervention means dis-union. There is no difference in principle between Northern and Southern Interventionists. The one intervenes for Slavery and the other against Slavery; but each appeals to the passions and prejudices of his own section against the peace of the whole country and the right of self government by the people of the Territories. Hence the doctrine of Non-Intervention must be maintained at all hazards.

But while I can never sacrifice the principle, even to attain the Presidency, I will cheerfully and joyfully sacrifice *myself* to maintain the principle. If therefore you and any other friends who have stood by me with such heroic firmness at Charleston and Baltimore shall be of the opinion that the principle can be preserved and the unity and ascendancy of the Democratic Party maintained, and the country saved from the perils of Northern abolitionism and Southern dis-union, by withdrawing my name and uniting upon some other non-Intervention and Union loving Democrat I beseech you to pursue that course.

Do not understand me as wishing to dictate to my friends. I have implicit confidence in yours, and their patriotism judgment and discretion. Whatever you may do in the premises will meet my hearty approval. But I conjure you to act with an eye single to the safety and welfare of the country, and without the slightest regard to my individual interests or agrandizement. *My* interests will be but promoted, and ambition gratified, and motives vindicated by that course on the part of my friends which will be most effectual in saving the country from being ruled or ruined by a sectional party.

The action of the Charleston convention in sustaining me by so large a majority on the Platform and designating me as the first choice of the Party for the Presidency is all the personal triumph I desire.[1] This letter is prompted by the same motives which induced my dispatch four years ago withdrawing my name from the Cincinnati Convention.[2] With this knowledge of my opinions and wishes you and other friends must act upon your own convictions of duty. Very truly your friend

S. A. DOUGLAS

LS, Duke University Library, Durham, North Carolina. The Democratic national convention met in Charleston, South Carolina, on April 23, 1860, but was unable to make a nomination. On April 30, several Southern delegations withdrew from the convention, climaxing a bitter fight over the party platform between the Douglas "popular sovereignty" forces and the Southern advocates of a Federal slave code. After an unsuccessful attempt to make a nomination, the remaining delegates adjourned for six weeks, to reconvene at Baltimore on June 18. This Douglas letter was written during the sitting of the Baltimore convention, but was never used by Richardson. Richardson assumed the leadership of the Douglas forces in both conventions, repeating the roles he had played in the 1852 and 1856 Democratic conclaves.

¹Following the withdrawal of the Southern delegations at Charleston, fifty-seven ballots for the Presidential nomination were taken. Douglas, on the final ballot, received 151½ votes, a majority of the full convention, but short of the two-thirds required for nomination.

²See above, June 3, 1856.

To Dean Richmond

Washington
June 22'd 1860.

10.0'clock The steadiness with which New York has sustained me will justify a word of counsel. The safety of the cause is the paramount duty of every Democrat. The Unity of the Party and the maintenance of its principles inviolate are more important than the elevation or defeat of any individual. If my enemies are determined to divide and destroy the Democratic Party and perhaps the Country rather than see me elected, and if the Unity of the party can be preserved and its time-honored principles maintained and its ascendency perpetuated by dropping my name and uniting upon some other reliable, Non-Intervention, and Union loving Democrat, I beseech you in consultation with our friends to pursue that course which will save the Party and the Country, without regard to my individual interests. I mean all this letter implies. Consult freely and act boldly for the right.

S. A. DOUGLAS

LS, University of Chicago Library. This second letter in which Douglas cleared the way for the withdrawal of his name from before the Baltimore convention was prompted by the fact that Richardson refused to use or make public his first statement (see above, June 20, 1860). Richmond likewise pocketed his letter and no move was made in the convention to withdraw Douglas' name. Douglas' supporters were so committed to his candidacy, at Charleston as well as Baltimore, that Douglas' withdrawal would have seriously jeopardized their political positions.

To August Belmont

Washington
My Dear Sir,   June 23d 1860

This will be presented to you by my friend McLean[1] who will express to you the obligation which I feel and am happy to acknowledge to the New York Delegation for their heroic firmness & fidelity to principle. I am, Dr Sirs, very truly your friend

S. A. DOUGLAS

ALS, Illinois State Historical Library. August Belmont, prominent New York banker, was a member of the New York delegation to the Charleston and Baltimore conventions. On June 23, the day this letter was written, Douglas was declared the unanimous choice of the Baltimore convention for the Presidential nomination.

[1]Possibly Washington McLean, editor of the Cincinnati *Enquirer* and a staunch supporter of Douglas. McLean was a member of the Ohio delegation to the conventions.

To William H. Ludlow, R. P. Dick, R. C. Wickliffe, *et al.*

Washington
Gentlemen   June 27th 1860

In accordance with the verbal assurance which I gave you when you placed in my hands the authentic evidence of my nomination for the Presidency by the [Regular][1] National convention of the Democratic Party, I now [place in your possession my formal acceptance of the nomination] send you my formal acceptance.

[After] Upon a careful examination of the Platform of principles adopted at Charleston and reaffirmed at Baltimore, with an additional resolution which is in perfect harmony with the others, [at Baltimore] I find it to be a faithful embodiment of the time-honored principles of the Democratic Party as the same were proclaimed and understood by all parties in the Presidential contests of 1848-'52-and '56.

Upon looking into the proceedings of the Convention also I find that the nomination was made with great unanimity, in the presence and with the concurence of more than two thirds of the whole number of delegates, and in exact accordance with the long established usuages of the Party.

My inflexible purpose not to be a candidate nor to accept a nomination in any contingency except as the regular nominee of the National Democratic Party; and in that case only upon the condition that the usuages as well as the principles of the Party should be [rigidly] strictly adhered to, had been proclaimed for a long time and become well known to the country.

These conditions having all been complied with, by the free and

[494]

voluntary action of the Democratic masses and their faithful representatives, without any agency, interference, or procurement on my part, I feel bound in honor and duty to accept the nomination.

In taking this step I am not unmindful of the responsibilities [which] it imposes; but, with a firm reliance upon Divine Providence, I have [full] faith that the people will comprehend the true nature of the issues involved and eventually maintain the right. The peace of the country and the perpetuity of the Union have been put in jeopardy *by the efforts [on the part of the Federal Government] to interfere with and control the Domestic* [relations] *affairs of the people in the Territories through* the agency of *the Federal Government.* If the power and duty of Federal Interference conceded, two hostile sectional parties [necessarily result as an inevitable consequence;] must be the inevitable result; the one inflaiming the passions and ambition of the North and the other of the South;—and each struggling to use the Federal power and authority for the aggrandizement of its own section at the expense of the equal rights of the other, and in derogation of those fundamental principles of self-government, which were firmly established in this country by the American Revolution as the basis of our entire republican system. During a memmorable period of our political history, when the advocates of Federal intervention upon the subject of slavery in the Territories [well nigh came near] had well nigh "precipitated the country into Revolution" —(the Northern Interventionists demanding the Wilmot Proviso for the prohibition of slavery and the Southern Interventionists[2] insisting upon Congressional Intervention for the protection of slavery, in opposition to the wishes of the people in either case) it will be remembered that it required all the wisdom, power, and influence of a Clay, and a Webster, and a Cass, supported by the conservative and patriotic men of the Whig and Democratic Parties of that day, to divise and carry out a line of policy which would restore peace to the country and [ensure perpetuity of] stability to the Union. The essential, living principle of that policy, as applied in the legislation of 1850, was and now is *Non-Intervention by Congress with slavery in the Territories.* The fair application of this great and equitable principle restored harmony and fraternity to a distracted country. If we now depart from that wise and just policy which [restored peace to the co[3] and security to the Republic] produced these happy results and permit the country to be again distracted, if not precipitated into revolution, by a sectional contest between [Northern and Southern] Pro-Slavery and Anti Slavery interventionists, where shall we look for another Clay, another Webster, or another Cass to pilot the ship of State [safely] over the breakers into the haven of peace and safety!

The Federal Union must be preserved. The constitution must be maintained inviolate in all its parts. Every right guarranteed by the constitution must be protected by law in all cases where legislation is necessary to its enjoyment. The judicial authority, as provided in the constitution, must be sustained, and its decisions implicitly obeyed and faithfully executed. The laws must be administered, and the constituted authorities upheld, and all unlawful resistance suppressed. These things must all be done with firmness, [energy] impartiality, and fidelity, if we expect to enjoy, and transmit unimparied to our posterity, that blessed inheritance which we have received in trust from the patriots and sages of the Revolution.

With sincere thanks for the kind and agreeable manner in which you have [communicated] made known to me the action of the convention I have the honor to be very respectfully your friend and fellow citizen.

AL Copy, owned by Martin F. Douglas. William H. Ludlow, of New York, Robert P. Dick, of North Carolina, and Robert C. Wickliffe, of Louisiana, were members of a committee appointed by the Baltimore convention to inform Douglas of his nomination. Douglas' reply, accepting the nomination, was widely published in the press. The version in Horace Greeley and John F. Cleveland, compilers, *Political Text-Book for 1860* (New York, 1860), pp. 212-213, differs from Douglas' draft only in minor word changes, punctuation, paragraphing, and date (the published letter bore the date June 29, 1860).

[1]All the words lined out by Douglas have been enclosed in brackets.

[2]In the published letter (Greeley and Cleveland, comps., *Political Text-Book for 1860*, p. 212) the words "then few in number, and without a single Representative in either House of Congress" were added here.

[3]Douglas had obviously started to write the word "country."

To James Madison Cutts

Washington
June 30th 1860

My Dear Sir

You will receive from Mr Charles Dewey of Raleigh North Carolina[1] checks or drafts on New York for me, which I wish you would forward to me in New York immediately as I need them to pay interest now about due. Please acknowledge them to Mr Dewey at the same time you send them to me. I also leave check of Mr Dickens[2] for $1220 99/100 which please place to my credit at Bank of Metropolis enough to pay all the checks I left unpaid, and send the ballance to me.

I will let you know what House I stop at in New York or you will learn it from the News papers.[3]

Please open all of my letters and attend to such as do not demand my personal attention, and send to me from time to time such as demand my personal attention. Very truly yours

S. A. DOUGLAS

ALS, owned by Martin F. Douglas.
[1]Charles Dewey was an agent for the State Bank of North Carolina.
[2]Possibly Asbury Dickens, Secretary of the Senate.
[3]Douglas was soon to leave for New York city, where he remained during the first half of July.

To Nathaniel Paschall

Fifth Ave Hotel
New York
July 4th 1860

(*Private*)

My Dear Sir,

Everything looks well in this State. Our friends here are confident of success. Gov Richardson[1] has just returned from a tour through the New England States. He reports things much better than we had hoped for. He thinks we will certainly carry Maine, New Hampshire, Rhode Island & Conn. Our friends in Penn & New Jersey are embarrassed by the action of the Central Committees of those States, but will form the Ticketts on our own Platform & fight boldly for the victory.[2] The reaction in our favor is immense, and we are gaining every day. Any Compromise with the Secessionists would be ruinous. An amalgation tickett with the bolters would desgust the people & give every Northern State to Lincoln.

We must trust to you to keep all right in Missouri. Yours truly

S. A. DOUGLAS

ALS, Maine Historical Society.
[1]William A. Richardson.
[2]Efforts were made in Pennsylvania and New Jersey to avoid a Democratic party split on the state level by fusing the Douglas and Breckinridge electoral tickets. In Pennsylvania, the electors had been chosen before the Charleston convention, thus including both Douglas and Breckinridge men. The Pennsylvania state committee urged all Democrats to support this electoral ticket on the understanding that the electors would vote for either Douglas or Breckinridge, depending upon which had the better chance to defeat Lincoln. The Democratic state committee of New Jersey met on July 2. A convention was summoned to select an electoral ticket that would include three electors pledged to Breckinridge and four pledged to Douglas. In both states, the Douglasites opposed the fusion efforts, refusing to join with the Breckinridge forces and insisting on a straight electoral ticket of their own. After later conventions in each state, however, fusion arrangements were developed in spite of this opposition.

To Charles H. Lanphier

(*Private*)

New York
July 5th 1860

My Dear Sir,

It will be necessary for me to remain here sometime to perfect our organization throughout the Union. In the meantime it is indispensable that our friends shall organize *every County* in Illinois thoroughly and open the canvass with vigor and energy.

[497]

No time must be lost, and no effort spared. Our friends here are in good spirits. We must make the war boldly against the *Northern abolitionists* and the Southern *Disunionists*, and give no quarter to either. We should treat the Bell & Everett[1] men friendly and cultivate good relations with them, for they are Union men. According to present appearances Breckenridge cannot carry a single State, except South Carolina, and perhaps Miss. Bell will probably carry Kentucky, Tennessee, North Carolina, Virginia, Maryland & Delaware. We shall probably carry Missouri, Arkansas, Louisiana, Texas, Alabama & Georgia in the South, and hope to get enough more in the free States to be elected by the people. *We can have no partnership with the Bolters.* If the election goes to the Ho of Reps, Lincoln, Bell and myself will be the *three* highest. If it goes to the Senate Hamlin & Johnson[2] will be the *two* highest. So you see that Breckenridge & Lane[3] can have no show in any event.

Richardson has just returned from New England, and reports *very favorable*. He thinks we will carry *Maine*, New Hampshire, Rhode Island & Conn. In New York our friends are confident of carrying the State, and also in New Jersey. We hope for the best in Penn. Now organize and rally in Ills & the North West. The changes in our favor are immense in the East. Organize the State. Yours truly

S. A. DOUGLAS

ALS, Illinois State Historical Library.
[1]John Bell, of Tennessee, and Edward Everett, of Massachusetts, were nominated President and Vice-President respectively by the Constitutional Union party on May 9, 1860.
[2]Hannibal Hamlin, of Maine, and Herschel V. Johnson, of Georgia, were the Vice-Presidential candidates of Lincoln and Douglas respectively.
[3]Joseph Lane, of Oregon, was Vice-Presidential candidate on the Breckinridge ticket.

To Elijah Purdy

[July 11, 1860, Fifth Avenue Hotel, New York; ALS. "Will you do me the favor to call on me at Parlor no. 58 at your earliest convenience today or tonight. I desire to consult you on matters of importance." The original of this letter has not been located. It has been described in *A Catalogue of Lincolniana*, Thomas F. Madigan, New York, p. 44, #95. Purdy was a New York city broker.]

To the Corresponding Secretary,
Lexington Monument Association

Boston, Thursday, July 19, 1860.

MY DEAR SIR: I have the honor to inclose my check on the Artisans' Bank, of New-York, for one hundred dollars, which you will do me a favor to hand to the proper officer, to be applied to the erection of the Lexington Monument. With my thanks for the civilities extended to me in my visit to-day to the birth-place of the American Revolution,[1] I am, very truly, yours,

S. A. DOUGLAS

New York *Times*, August 1, 1860.
[1]In the course of his New England campaign, Douglas had been taken on a tour of the Lexington battlefield.

To James B. Sheridan

New York

My Dear Sir   22 August 1860
   I wish you would meet me at Norfolk on Friday and go with me through North Carolina & Virginia, Maryland and Pennsylvania for about two weeks.[1] I leave tomorrow on the Roanoke. Your best route will be from Baltimore down the bay by steamer tomorrow night, if you do not join me here in time to go with me. Very truly Your friend

S. A. DOUGLAS

LS, Library of Congress.
[1]Having completed his campaign tour of the New England states, Douglas was about to begin his campaign swing through the states of the upper South.

To Ninety-six New Orleans Citizens

[November 13, 1860]

   GENTLEMEN: Your request to address the citizens of New Orleans "on the present condition of the affairs of our country," has just been placed in my hands. An invitation so numerously signed by the most eminent business men of this great commercial city, implies a compliment which I duly appreciate, and am exceedingly reluctant to decline.

   These are not the times for patriotic men to affect indifference, or to degenerate into despondency, or to rush madly into violent and extreme measures. Just in proportion as our common country is environed with peril, it becomes the imperative duty of every patriot in the land to increase his efforts and exert his utmost powers and energies to rescue the republic from the disasters which threaten its integrity.

   No man in America regrets the election of Mr. Lincoln more than I do; none made more strenuous exertions to defeat him; none differ with him more radically and irreconcileably upon all the great issues involved in the contest. No man living is [more?] prepared to resist, by all the legitimate means, sanctioned by the Constitution and laws

[499]

of our country, the aggressive policy which he and his party are understood to represent. But, while I say this, I am bound, as a good citizen and law-abiding man, to declare my conscientious conviction that the mere election of any man to the Presidency by the American people, in accordance with the Constitution and laws, does not of itself furnish any just cause or reasonable ground for dissolving the Federal Union.

It is not pretended, as far as I am informed, that any provision of the Constitution has been violated in the recent election. No act has been done which impairs or destroys the constitutional rights of any State or citizen. Nothing has yet occurred to release any citizen from his oath of fidelity to the Constitution of the United States, which is the *supreme law* of every State and of every citizen. But while it is conceded that no act has yet been done which impairs the rights or endangers the peace and safety of any portion of our country, it is *apprehended* that the election of Mr. Lincoln carries with it the assurance that the policy and principles of the party by which he was elected will prevail, and be carried into practical effect in every department of the Federal Government, and thereby *will* endanger the peace and safety of the slaveholding States. Is this apprehension well founded? Do the results of the recent election justify this apprehension? The President can do nothing except what the law authorizes. His duty is to see the laws faithfully executed. If he fails to perform this duty he will soon find himself a prisoner before the High Court of Impeachment. Fortunately that tribunal is so constituted as to command the confidence of the people of the entire South as well as of the conservative men of the North. We have this security that the *existing* laws will be faithfully executed. I have yet to learn that the people of the South complain of the acts of Congress *now* on the statute book, upon the subject of slavery, as applicable to the States or the Territories, or to the District of Columbia. These laws were enacted, mainly, if not entirely, by the joint action of the conservative members of the North and South, in opposition to the Abolitionists and Freesoilers, and have been acquiesced in by the Southern people as well as by their Senators and Representatives, under the present and preceding administrations of the Federal Government. Consequently, it is fair to presume that the South, so far from demanding the repeal of the existing laws upon the subject of slavery as essential to her safety and equality in the Union, will insist on their being retained upon the statute book, and faithfully executed. Nor are we permitted to infer that the Southern people require any additional legislation by Congress on this subject, for the reason that the Southern Senators and Representatives have not introduced and advocated any changes in the existing legislation upon the slavery question under the present Administration, and that of Mr. Pierce, when the Abolitionists and Free-soilers were in the minority in both Houses of Congress.

Assuming, therefore, that the Southern people and their Senators and Representatives deem their rights and institutions entirely safe under the Constitution and laws as they now stand, and only desire to be let alone, without any interference by Congress with their domestic concerns, the question arises whether Mr. Lincoln and any of his party will have the power, even if they have the disposition, to disturb or impair the rights and institutions of the South, either in the States or Territories, or in the District of Columbia? They certainly cannot do it under the existing laws. Will they have the power to repeal or change these laws, or to enact others? It is well known that they will be in a minority in both houses of Congress, with the Supreme Court against them. In the Northern States there have been elected already a sufficient number of Democratic members of Congress, bold and true national men, pledged to the Cincinnati platform and the doctrines of non-intervention by Congress with the question of slavery in the States and Territories, and the District of Columbia, who, added to the Southern Representatives, will give at least twenty majority against Mr. Lincoln and his party on all these questions. In the Senate there is also a decided and reliable majority. Hence, no bill can pass either house of Congress impairing or disturbing the rights or institutions of the Southern people in any manner whatever, unless *a portion of the Southern Senators and Representatives absent themselves so as to give an Abolition majority in consequence of their absence.*

In a minority in both houses of Congress, with the Supreme Court to expound the laws and restrain all illegal and unconstitutional acts, the President will be utterly powerless for evil, if he should have the disposition to do wrong. Even in the distribution of his patronage, he would be dependent upon the Senate for the confirmation of his nominees to office, so that he cannot appoint a bad man to office without the consent of those in whom the South confides. A partisan President, thus tied hand and foot, powerless for good or evil, without the consent and support of his political opponents, should be the object of pity and commiseration, rather than of fear and apprehension, by a brave and chivalrous people. What good or harm can he do to anybody, except to humble the pride and wound the sensibilities of a large portion of the American people by occupying the chair once filled by Washington, Jefferson, Madison and Jackson? Does this fact furnish sufficient cause for destroying the best government of which the history of the world gives an example? Four years will soon pass away, when the ballot-box will furnish a peaceful, legal and constitutional remedy for all the evils and grievances with which the country may be afflicted.

If, in the meantime, any act shall pe perpetrated which shall violate or impair the rights of any citizen or State, or shall endanger the peace and safety of any portion of our people, for which the Constitution and laws shall fail to provide adequate and efficient remedies, the time will then have arrived for those who think the Constitution has been disregarded and the Federal power perverted to purposes inconsistent with their safety, honor and equality, to consult and deliberate upon the nature, extent and mode of redress.

I do not anticipate, nor do I deem it possible in the present condition of the country, that, under the administration of Mr. Lincoln, any act can be perpetrated that would destroy or impair the constitutional rights of the citizen, or invade the reserved rights of the States upon the subject of slavery; but, if I should find myself painfully mistaken on this point, I have no hesitation in expressing my deliberate conviction that such an outrage would not only make the Southern people a unit, but would arouse and consolidate all the conservative elements of the North in firm and determined resistance, by overwhelming majorities.

In such an event, the South would occupy an impregnable position. With her own people united and animated by one sentiment—the unfaltering resolve to maintain and defend their rights and liberties as won by the blood of their fathers and guaranteed by the Constitution of their country, they could safely rely upon the justice of their cause, and confidently expect the sympathy of the civilized world, and the choicest blessings of Divine Providence while struggling for the right. Under these circumstances I can perceive no just cause, no reasonable ground for such rash and precipitate action as would plunge into the horrors of revolution, anarchy and bankruptcy, the happiest people, the most prosperous country and the best government the sun of Heaven ever shed his genial rays upon.

To those, if any such there be, who look upon disunion and a Southern Confederacy as a thing desirable in itself, and are only waiting for an opportunity to accomplish that which had been previously resolved upon—the election of Lincoln may furnish a pretext for precipitating the Southern States into revolution. But to those who regard the Union under the Constitution as our fathers made it, the most precious legacy ever bequeathed to a free people by a patriotic ancestry, and are determined to maintain it as long as their rights and liberties, equality and honor are protected by it, the election of Mr. Lincoln, in my humble opinion, presents no just cause, no reasonable excuse for disunion.

Having discussed all the questions at issue freely and elaborately in my addresses to the people during the recent canvass, I do not perceive that any patriotic objects can be advanced by any further public discussions on my part prior to resuming my seat in the Senate. That the passions and animosities engendered by recent contests may soon give place to reason and patriotism; that calm and wise counsels may prevail, and fraternal feeling be restored; that the Constitution may be preserved inviolate, and the Union maintained forever, is the ardent hope and fervent prayer of Your friend and fellow-citizen,

New Orleans, Nov. 13, 1860.   S. A. DOUGLAS

St. Louis *Republican*, November 17, 1860. During the latter weeks of the Presidential campaign, Douglas made a wide swing through the slave states, arguing strongly on behalf of the Union. He was in Mobile, Alabama, on election day. After receiving the news of Lincoln's election, he returned to Illinois. While stopping in New Orleans, he received an invitation to express publicly his "views on the present condition of the affairs of our country," signed by ninety-six New Orleans citizens. The above letter was Douglas' reply.

To James H. Lucas

Memphis Tenn
My Dear Sir,   Nov 26th 1860

Permit me to introduce to you my friend and Brother-in-law J. Madison Cutts Esq who is about to take up his residence in your City. You will find him a young man of Education, talent and integrity. I commend him to you as worthy of your entire confidence, and shall feel grateful for any courtesies and services you may render him. Very truly your friend

S. A. DOUGLAS

ALS, owned by Philip D. Sang. James H. Lucas was a St. Louis, Missouri, banker.

To William S. Prentice

(*Private*)   Washington
My Dr Sir,   Dec 5th 1860

In pursuance with your request I have caused to be copied from the Congressional Globe an abstract of the Debate to which you refer. I enclose it to you to be used as you think proper. I am grateful for the interest you take in my welfare & reputation.

I regret to say that our country is now in iminent danger. I know not that the Union can be saved. I am prepared to make any sacrifice consistent with patriotism & duty to save the republic. We must put our trust in God as our only hope. Very truly your friend

S. A. DOUGLAS

ALS, Illinois State Historical Library. Prentice was a Methodist preacher in Springfield, Illinois, and an early supporter of Douglas.

[503]

To Charles H. Lanphier

(*Private*)   Washington
My Dear Sir,   Dec 25th 1860

The prospects are gloomy, but I do not yet despair of the Union.[1] *We can never acknowledge the right of a State to secede and cut us off from the Ocean and the world, without our consent.* But in view of impending civil war with our breathren in nearly one half of the States of the Union, I will not consider the question of force & war until all efforts at peaceful adjustment have been made & have failed. The fact can no longer be disguised that many of the Republican Leaders desire war & Disunion under pretext of saving the Union. The[y] wish to get rid of the Southern Senators in order to have a majority in the Senate to confirm Lincolns appointments; and many of them think they can hold a permanent Republican ascendency in the Northern States, but not in the whole Union.

For partizan reasons therefore they are anxious to dissolve the Union, if it can be done without making them responsible before the people.

I am for the Union, and hence am ready to make any reasonable sacrifice to save it. No adjustment will restore & preserve peace *which does not banish the slavery question from Congress power* and place it beyond the reach of Federal Legislation. Mr Crittenden's proposition to extend the Missouri line accomplishes this object, and hence I can accept it now for the same reasons that I proposed it in 1848.[2] I prefer our own plan of Non Intervention & popular soverignty, however, & have proposed amendments to the Constitution on that basis, making some concessions for peace, which I send you.[3] Its chief merit is, that, while it takes the slavery question out of Congress forever, and secures the rights of self government to the white male inhabitants, it also covers all the points in controversy, and gives assurance of permanent peace. By confirming the existing *Status* in the Territories it affirms Popular Soverignty by confirming what the people have already done. In reference to new territory it is necessary to require fifty thousand people, in consequence of the Mexican population now inhabiting the country, being nearly that number in most of the Provinces. Show my proposition to our friends & give them, *privately*, my reasons for it, and let me know what they think of it. I have some faint hope of a satisfactory adjustment, but only faint hopes. Very truly your friend

S. A. DOUGLAS

ALS, Illinois State Historical Library.
[1]South Carolina seceded from the Union on December 20, 1860.

[2]The famous Crittenden Compromise, proposed by Senator John J. Crittenden, of Kentucky, provided for six amend-

ments to the Constitution, the most important of which was the extension of the Missouri Compromise line to California, with slavery prohibited north and protected south of the line. Other amendments would forbid Congress to abolish slavery in any of the States where it existed and to abolish slavery in the District of Columbia without the consent of the people and without compensation to the slaveowners; would protect the domestic slave trade from Federal interference; would provide for compensation to slaveowners whose fugitive slaves could not be recovered because of Northern rescue attempts; and would prevent further amendment of the Constitution in such a way as to tamper with the institution of slavery.

³Douglas' proposal would maintain the status of each existing territory until a population of 50,000 should be reached, when the territory could be admitted as a state with or without slavery and would forbid any further expansion of the nation except by a two-thirds vote in each house of Congress. Other features of Douglas' plan were similar to those proposed by Crittenden.

To August Belmont

Washington
Dec 25th 1860

My Dear Sir,

The prospects of our country are gloomy, but I do not entirely dispair of the Union. It is evident that many of the Republican leaders are anxious for disunion while professing intense devotion to the Union. This portion of them prefer their party to their country. They are afraid that some of Mr Lincoln's appointments would be rejected if all the Southern States are represented in the Senate. Think too that they may not be able to perpetuate the power of their Party in the whole Union, while they hope to be able to do so in the Northern half of it.

I am ready to make any reasonable sacrifice of party tenets to save the country. I must say however that I can never recognize or acquiesce in the Doctrine that any State can secede & separate from us without our consent. The States in the north west cannot consent to be cut off from the Ocean & the world by such a doctrine.

I can vote to extend the Missouri line as I proposed to do in 1848, and did so vote on Saturday last on Mr Crittenden's proposition. But I prefer another plan which I introduced yesterday and a copy of which I send you. It does not q[uite] suit anybody, but may possibly be taken by both parties as a compromise.

Nothing will do any good which does not take the *slavery question* out of Congress forever.

Let me hear from you & your views on my proposition.

Present my kind regards to Mrs B and the Boys. Very truly your friend

S. A. DOUGLAS

ALS, Chicago Historical Society.

To Alexander Hamilton Stephens

(*Private*)   Washington
My Dear Sir,   Dec 25th 1860

I have watched your noble & patriotic course with much interest. The prospects for saving the Union are indeed gloomy. We are now making an effort at Constitutional Amendments in our Committee of thirteen.[1] I fear we cannot carry Mr Crittenden's proposition to run the Missouri line. I send you a Proposition of mine. I think it can be carried, if the South will take it. Study it well, keeping in view the provisions of the laws of *Peon* Slavery in Mexico, and see if it is not all the South can wish.[2] I have endeavored to cover all the points in controversy. If you approve please call attention in the Press. I am willing to any modification in reason, which will take the subject out of Congress. Let me hear from you and believe me truly your friend

S. A. DOUGLAS

ALS, Library of Congress. Alexander Hamilton Stephens, of Georgia, had been a member of Congress from 1843 to 1859. Formerly a Whig, he was a candidate for Presidential elector on the Douglas ticket in 1860. Stephens was one of the most influential conservative Southerners during the sectional conflict. In 1861 he followed his state of Georgia out of the Union and was later elected Vice-President of the Confederate States of America.
[1]The Committee of Thirteen was organized by the Senate on December 18, and its members were named two days later. The committee was to receive proposals for settling the sectional difficulties and to report a compromise plan to the Senate.
[2]Douglas was referring here to the provision in his compromise plan that the existing status with regard to slavery of each territory would remain until the population of the territory reached 50,000.

To [William Ezzard *et al.*]

Washington
Dec 29th 1860

In reply to your enquiry, we have hopes that the rights of the South and of every State and Section may be protected within the Union. Don't give up the Ship. Don't despair of the Republic.

J. J. CRITTENDEN[1]
S. A. DOUGLAS

ALS Copy, owned by Martin F. Douglas. On December 26, 1860, a group of Georgians, headed by William Ezzard, wrote to Crittenden and Douglas: "Is there any hope for Southern Rights in the Union. We are for the Union of our Fathers, if Southern rights can be preserved in it. If not we are for Secession. Can we yet hope the Union will be preserved on this principle? You are looked to in this emergency. Give us your views" (copy, in Douglas' hand, owned by Martin F. Douglas). William Ezzard was Mayor of Atlanta.
[1]Crittenden's name was signed by Douglas in this copy.

To John E. Develin

[N.d., n.p.; ALS, Illinois State Historical Society. Introducing, at the "suggestion of Senator Seward," four members of the Illinois state legislature, Chauncey L. Higbee, James W. Singleton, William H. Underwood, and Samuel A. Buckmaster. Develin was a New York city attorney. Although the letter was undated, the year "1861" was added in pencil at a later time.]

To Joseph Wilson

[January 16, 1860 [1861], U S Senate Chamber; LS, RG-49, National Archives. Requesting information regarding certain land patents, on behalf of James Barnard, Postmaster at Wilkesboro, Illinois. Wilson was Commissioner of the General Land Office. The letter was post-marked January 16, 1861, indicating that it was misdated.]

To John Tyler

Washington

My Dear Sir   Feby 11th 1861

I have invited a number of friends to meet the President, members, and officers of the convention over which you have been chosen to preside to meet us in a social gathering on Tuesday the 12th inst, and hope that you and Mrs Tyler will do us the favor to join us on the occasion. I have made several attempts, but found it impossible, owing to the difficulty in finding the temporary residence of all the officers and members of the convention. I fear that some of our Invitations may not have reached their destination. Pray be so kind as to mention to the members and officers of the convention, if the opportunity occurs, that they are each and all expected on the occasion. I have the honor to be very respectfully your friend and obedient servant

S. A. Douglas

ALS, Essex Institute, Salem, Massachu-setts. On January 7, 1861, Governor John Letcher, of Virginia, proposed a national peace conference to consider means for settling the secession crisis and for averting war between the North and South. Officially sponsored by the state of Virginia, the convention met in Washington on February 4. Delegates from only twenty-one states were in attendance. The compromise plan proposed by the convention, strik-ingly similar to that offered by Crit-tenden earlier, was defeated in Con-gress and this last effort to avert war resulted in failure. John Tyler, of Virginia, ex-President of the United States, was the presiding officer in the convention.

To Jeremiah Black

[February 13, 1861, Washington; ALS, RG-59, National Archives. Requesting information on the memorial of Charles J. Helm, U.S. Consul at Havana, asking compensation for extra services and expenses incurred in the performance of his duties. Douglas wrote on behalf of the Senate Committee on Foreign Affairs, of which he was a member. Jeremiah Black, former Attorney General in Buchanan's cabinet, had been appointed Secretary of State on December 17, 1860.]

To William H. Seward

My Dear Sir,   March 21st 1861

Permit me to introduce to you my friend the Hon Alfred M Barbour of Harper's Ferry Virginia.[1] He is a bold, firm, & reliable friend of the Union and a member of the convention now in Session at Richmond. You can talk with him freely on the State of the Union and rely implicitly upon his discretion and honor. Very respectfully

S. A. DOUGLAS

ALS, Chicago Historical Society. Seward had just been appointed Secretary of State in Lincoln's cabinet.

[1]Alfred M. Barbour was a member of the Virginia secession convention, elected in February, 1861. Membership of the convention was dominantly conservative and Unionist and no action toward secession was taken at this time. In January, 1859, Barbour had been appointed Superintendent of the Arsenal at Harper's Ferry.

To James A. McHatton

My Dear Sir,   Washington April 4th 1861

The great pressure of public duties has deprived me of the time to attend to private affairs or friends correspondence. I have not heard or received a return of the amount of the proceeds of our crops, nor am I informed whether to enquire of Messrs Ward Hunt & co[1] or the new merchants. I should like to know how our account now stands, and what the ballance due us is, after paying our indebtedness, and in whose hands it is. The low price at which some lots of our cotton was sold is inexplicable to me. I cannot understand those sales when I compare the prices at which it was sold with other sales reported in the news papers of about the same date. I am exceedingly oppressed for the want of money, and do not know where I can get enough to pay my little Bills and current expenses, unless it can be got from our sales of cotton. Can you not arrainge to send me two thousand dollars —or even one thousand, to relieve my immediate necessities? Let me hear from you soon and direct to me at this place where I will remain until about the first of May.

Mrs Douglas joins in kind regards to yourself and your good Lady. I am very truly your friend

S. A. Douglas

ALS, owned by Martin F. Douglas. James A. McHatton, of Baton Rouge, Louisiana, had entered into a partnership agreement with Douglas in 1857 for the establishment and operation of a cotton plantation in Washington County, Mississippi. The plantation was established on 2,000 acres of McHatton's land. Douglas furnished the Negro slaves, stock, and items of equipment necessary to the operation. The slaves belonged to the estate of Robert Martin, the father of Douglas' first wife, and were held by Douglas in his capacity as executor of the estate and guardian of his two sons, who had inherited them, according to the terms of their grandfather's will, on the death of their mother. McHatton had been a member of the Louisiana delegation to the Charleston convention.

[1]Ward, Hunt and Company was the New Orleans commission house which handled the cotton from the plantation. On May 11, 1861, McHatton wrote Douglas, "As soon as the rest of the cotton is ship'd & sold, I will go to the City & have a settlement with Ward Hunt & Co. & see what arrangement I can make about sending you the money you want. The times are very hard, & really I believe every house in N. O. will stop payment" (owned by Martin F. Douglas).

To Ward Hill Lamon

Washington
My Dear Sir,   April 8th 1861

I cannot deny the request of the Reverend Mr Wigot,[1] so far as to enclose the within letter. I do not know the person recommended personally; but the Reverend Gentleman who writes the letter is a most estimably and worthy man, whom I should be delighted to gratify, if I felt at liberty to recommend any one, which I do not, under existing circumstances. I am very respectfully your obedient servant

S. A. Douglas

ALS, Henry E. Huntington Library. Ward Hill Lamon, a Bloomington, Illinois, attorney, was appointed by President Lincoln to be United States Marshal for the District of Columbia early in April, 1861.
[1]Reverend Wigot has not been identified.

Statement

[April 14, 1861]
Mr Douglas called on the President this evening and had an interesting conversation on the present condition of the country. The substance of the conversation was that while Mr D was unalterably opposed to the administration on all its political issues, he was prepared to sustain the President in the exercise of all his constitutional functions to preserve the Union, and maintain the government, and defend the Federal Capital. A firm policy and prompt action was necessary. The

Capital of our Country was in danger, and must be defended at all hazards, and at any expense of men & money. He spoke of the present & future, without reference to the past.

AD-Photostat, Illinois State Historical Library. This statement was written by Douglas for the press on April 14, 1861, the day of the surrender of Fort Sumter, following an interview with President Lincoln.

To Thomas E. Courtney

To T. E. Courtenay: Washington, April 15 [1861]
Without having been consulted or indorsing any particular measure, I am for my country and against all assailants.

S. A. DOUGLAS

Springfield *Illinois State Register*, April 22, 1861. Thomas E. Courtney was a prominent Chicago Democrat.

To James L. Faucett

To James L. Faucett: Washington, April 17 [1861].
I deprecate war, but if it must come, I am with my country and for my country, under all circumstances, and in every contingency. Individual policy must be subordinate to the public safety.

S. A. DOUGLAS

Springfield *Illinois State Register*, April 22, 1861. James L. Faucett was proprietor and editor of the St. Louis *Herald*. On April 16, 1861, he wrote to Douglas, asking, "Do you indorse Lincoln's war policy? Missouri will not" (Springfield *Illinois State Register*, April 22, 1861).

To Andrew Johnson

[April 17, 1861, Washington; LS, Library of Congress. Introducing Charles Henry Foster, of Murfreesboro, North Carolina, "a good democrat and a true friend of the Union." Foster was twice elected to the United States Congress in 1861 by loyal elements in North Carolina but was never able to take his seat. Andrew Johnson was at this time serving as United States Senator from Tennessee.]

To Charles H. Lanphier

Bellair [Ohio] Apl 22 1861
Mrs Douglas & myself leave here for Springfield tonight.

S. A. DOUGLAS

Telegram, Illinois State Historical Library. Not long after his conference with President Lincoln, Douglas left Washington for Illinois, where he would attend the opening of a special session of the state legislature. Along the way he spoke vigorously in behalf of the Union, urging support of the Lincoln administration in the crisis. Crowds gathered to hear him speak in Bellaire, Ohio, where he changed trains, Columbus, and Indianapolis. On April 25, he arrived in Springfield, and that night addressed the state legislature in one of his most stirring and impressive efforts.

To Abraham Lincoln

Springfield
My Dear Sir,   April 29th 1861
This letter will be delivered by J M Cutts Esq, the only Brother of Mrs Douglas, whom you may remember to have met some years ago at Chicago. He is a lawyer by Profession, a man of talents & attainments, and in every respect worthy of your confidence. He goes to Washington to take a hand in the defense of the Capital and the Government. He will be able to give you any information you may desire in regard to the public sentiment and condition of things in this State, as well Saint Louis, where he resides.

I found the state of feeling here and in some parts of our State much less satisfactory than I could have desired or expected when I arrived.[1] There will be no outbrake however and in a few days I hope for entire unanimity in the support of the government and the Union. I am very respectfully your obedient servant

S. A. DOUGLAS

ALS, Library of Congress.
[1]There were serious fears among state leaders that southern Illinois would not support the cause of the Union during the crisis. Douglas was summoned to Illinois in part to promote unity and support to the Lincoln administration in that area.

To Virgil Hickox

Chicago May 10th
My dear Sir   1861.
Being deprived of the use of my arms for the present by a severe attack of rheumatism I am compelled to avail myself of the services of an amanuensis in reply to your two letters.[1] It seems that some of my friends are unable to comprehend the difference between arguments used in favor of an equitable compromise with the hope of averting the horrors of war and those urged in support of the Government and Flag of our Country when war is being waged against the United States with the avowed purpose of producing a permanent disruption of the Union and a total destruction of its government.

All hope of compromise with the Cotton States was abandoned when they assumed the position that the seperation of the Union was complete and final and that they would never consent to a reconstruction in any contingency—not even if we would furnish them with a blank sheet of paper and permit them to inscribe their own terms.

Still the hope was cherished that reasonable and satisfactory terms of adjustment could be agreed upon with Tennessee North Carolina and the border States and that whatever terms would prove satisfactory to these loyal States would create a Union Party in the Cotton States which would be powerful enough at the ballot box to destroy the revolutionary Government and bring those States back into the Union by the voice of their own people.

This hope was cherished by the Union men North and South and was never abandoned until actual war was levied at Charleston and the authoritative announcement made by the Revolutionary Government at Montgomery that the Secession Flag should be planted upon the walls of the Capitol at Washington and a proclamation issued inviting the pirates of the world to prey upon the commerce of the United States.

These startling facts taken in connection with the boastful announcement, that the ravages of war and carnage should be quickly transferred from the Cotton fields of the South to the wheat fields and Corn fields of the North furnish conclusive evidence that it was the fixed purpose of the Secessionists utterly to destroy the government of our Fathers and obliterate the United States from the Map of the world.

In view of this State of fact there was but one path of duty left to patriotic men[;] it was not a party question nor a question involving partizan policy it was a question of Government or no Government —Country or no country and hence it became the imperative duty of every Union man—Evry friend of Constitutional liberty to rally to the support of our common country, its government and Flag as the only means of checking the progress of revolution and of preserving the Union of the States. I am unable to answer your questions in respect to the policy of Mr. Lincoln and his Cabinet. I am not in their confidence as you and the whole country ought to be aware. I am neither the supporter of the partizan policy nor the apologist for the errors of the Administration. My previous relations to them remain unchanged. But I trust the time will never come when I shall not be willing to make any needful sacrifice of personal feeling and party policy for the honor and integrity of my country.

I know of no mode by which a loyal citizen may so well demonstrate his devotion to his country as by sustaining the Flag, The Constitution, and the Union, under all circumstances and under evry Administration regardless of party politics against all assailants at home and abroad. The course of Clay and Webster towards the Administration of

General Jackson in the days of Nullification presents a noble and worthy example for all true patriots. At the very moment when that fearful crisis was precipitated upon the country partizan strife between Whigs and Democrats was quite as bitter and relentless as now between Democrats and Republicans. The Gulf which seperated party leaders in those days was quite as broad and deep as that which now seperates the Democracy from the Republicans. But the moment an enemy rose in our midst plotting the dismemberment of the Union and the destruction of the Government the voice of partizan strife was hushed in patriotic silence.

One of the brightest chapters in the history of Our Country will record the fact that during this eventful period the great leaders of the Opposition sinking the partizan in the Patriot rushed to the support of the Government and became its ablest and bravest defenders against all assailants until the Conspiracy was crushed and abandoned when they resumed their former positions as party leaders upon political issues. These acts of patriotic devotion have never been deemed evidences of infidelity or political treachery on the part of Clay and Webster to the principles and organization of the old Whig party. Nor have I any apprehension that the firm and unanimous support which the Democratic leaders and masses are now giving to the Constitution and the Union will ever be deemed evidences of infidelity to Democratic principles or a want of loyalty to the organization and creed of the Democratic party. If we hope to regain and perpetuate the ascendancy of our party we should never forget that a man cannot be a true Democrat unless he is a loyal patriot.

With the sincere hope that these my conscientious convictions may coincide with those of my friends I am very truly yours

S. A. Douglas[2]

LS, owned by Philip D. Sang. Virgil Hickox, a Springfield merchant, had long been prominent in Illinois Democratic politics. At this time, he was chairman of the state Democratic central committee.

[1]On May 4, 1861, Hickox wrote to Douglas: "You are supposed to be in the confidence of Mr Lincoln. The public desire *to know* why Congress was not called in extra session at an earlier day than the 4th of July." Hickox further advised Douglas "to make a full explanation, either in a speech to be published or in a letter" of his position on the developing crisis, since some of his supporters recognized a discrepancy between his atti-

tude on compromise during the secession crisis and his current support of the Lincoln administration in its effort to preserve the Union. "To save yourself with our friends," he added, "something must be done *immediately* in my judgment" (Hickox to Douglas, May 4, 1861, owned by Martin F. Douglas).

[2]This letter was forwarded by Hickox to Douglas' father-in-law, James Madison Cutts, in Washington, for publication in the Washington newspapers. Shortly afterward, however, Douglas and Hickox changed their minds regarding the propriety of publication. On May 13, Hickox wired Cutts to withhold publication and in a

letter written later in the day explained that "after consultation with him [Douglas] we concluded that the objects professed to be accomplished by it would not be attained by it but that perhaps silence was now his best course until he takes his seat in the Senate." Hickox went on to write, "The truth is that 99/100 of his political friends in Illinois distrust him on account of the great love that the Republicans profess now to have for him. Moreover they think they see a vast discrepancy between his present course and the one occupied by him in his speech on the inaugural and his positions taken on the 15 & 25 of March in the Senate. It was in view of this that I had written to him to say something that would save him his former friends. What he has written is all right but is only in substance what he said in his speech here and does not accomplish what we desired. The democrats here have been educated by reading his speeches to believe that Mr Lincoln has no constitutional right to pursue his present course. Hence they think the Judge in sustaining what is really thus the cause of his country & the flag of the Union, has gone over to the republicans. Time alone will remove the impression on the true democrats minds, and we concluded that we had better let it take its course" (Hickox to Cutts, May 13, 1861, owned by Martin F. Douglas). Cutts ignored Hickox's instructions and Douglas' letter was published in the Washington *National Intelligencer* on May 17.

The writing and publication of this letter to Virgil Hickox was the last significant act of Douglas' life. Following the severe attack of rheumatism mentioned in the letter, he fell gravely ill, and on June 3, 1861, Stephen A. Douglas was dead.

APPENDIX I

Fragmentary and Undated Letters

To Adele Cutts Douglas

Senate

My Dearest   Thursday

I will call myself in the course of the day & then write to you. I think you are right in not going today in the rain. I cannot leave the Senate at this time & will go as soon as I can leave. Do not expose yourself. I will make it all right. God Bless you my Dearest

S. A. Douglas

ALS, owned by Martin F. Douglas.

To John W. Forney

me to understand that he would.

Prospects look bright. Let our friends stand, firm, speak out bold, & act with energy and all will be well. Your friend

S. A. Douglas

ALS (fragment), Historical Society of Pennsylvania.

To the Mayor of Chicago

To the Mayor & Common Council of the City of Chicago.

The undersigned citizens of the city of Chicago who are liable to be assessed for streets & roads in said city, respectfully request that the street known as Cottage Grove Avenue & laid out by the Trustees of the Canal on Section 27 to the corporation line, be extended and opened as a street in a direct line until it intersects State Street at or near the North West corner of the South West Quarter of Section 22. The said Avenue has become the principal thoroughfare between the city & the Lake coast even as far as the Calumet river, and it has become necessary for the public convenience that it should be opened as a street so that the road may be put in good condition for travelling.

ADf, owned by Martin F. Douglas.

Letters Written by Stephen A. Douglas
as Register of the Springfield Land Office,
April 26, 1837–March 2, 1839

1. To James Whitcomb, Commissioner of the General Land Office. April 26, 1837; Copy, Illinois State Archives. Returning certain corrected certificates of purchase.

2. To James Whitcomb. April 26, 1837; Copy, Illinois State Archives. Transmitting the receipt of William L. May for a Chicago land patent.

3. To James Whitcomb. May 3, 1837; Copy, Illinois State Archives. Transmitting certificates of purchase and Receiver's receipts for lands sold during April, 1837.

4. To James Whitcomb. May 11, 1837; Copy, Illinois State Archives. Requesting a new book, Register of Certificates, since the old one is nearly filled.

5. To James Whitcomb. May 15, 1837; Copy, Illinois State Archives. Acknowledging the receipt of land patents in favor of Stephen S. Phelps and James Adams.

6. To James Whitcomb. May 23, 1837; Copy, Illinois State Archives. Returning a corrected certificate of purchase.

7. To James Whitcomb. N.d.; Copy, Illinois State Archives. Transmitting certificates of purchase, Receiver's receipts, and abstracts of sales for lands sold during May, 1837.

8. To ———. July 4, 1837; Copy, Illinois State Archives. Transmitting certificates of purchase, Receiver's receipts, and abstracts of sales for lands sold during June, 1837.

9. To Daniel Dunklin, Surveyor General of Illinois and Missouri from 1836 to 1841. July 7, 1837; Copy, Illinois State Archives. Transmitting an account of lands sold during the first two quarters of 1837.

10. To James Whitcomb. July 24, 1837; Copy, Illinois State Archives. Returning a corrected certificate of purchase.

11. To James Whitcomb. July 25, 1837; Copy, Illinois State Archives. Transmitting testimony in relation to the pre-emption right proved by Russel Fanshaw, an Indian trader with the American Fur Company, at Fort Edwards in 1829. The letter was also signed by John Logan, a member of the legislature from Jackson County who worked with Douglas in the Land Office at this time.

12. To James Whitcomb. August 2, 1837; Copy, Illinois State Archives. Transmitting certificates of purchase, Receiver's receipts, and abstracts of sales for lands sold during July, 1837.

13. To James Whitcomb. September 1, 1837; Copy, Illinois State Archives. Transmitting certificates of purchase, Receiver's receipts, and abstracts of sales for lands sold during August, 1837.

14. To James Whitcomb. October 2, 1837; Copy, Illinois State Archives. Transmitting certificates of purchase, Receiver's receipts, and abstracts of sales for lands sold during September, 1837.

15. To James Whitcomb. November 7, 1837; Copy, Illinois State Archives. Transmitting certificates of purchase, Receiver's receipts, and abstracts of sales for lands sold during October, 1837.

16. To James Whitcomb. November 14, 1837; Copy, Illinois State Archives. Acknowledging receipt of a letter, enclosing a patent in favor of Bartell Eads.

17. To James Whitcomb. December 1, 1837; ALS, RG-56, National Archives. Reporting the amount of public money in the possession of the Receiver of the Springfield Land Office as of this date, in accordance with Whitcomb's circular of September 30, 1837, requesting this information.

18. To James Whitcomb. December 2, 1837; Copy, Illinois State Archives. Transmitting certificates of purchase, Receiver's receipts, and abstracts of sales for lands sold during November, 1837.

19. To James Whitcomb. January 6, 1838; Copy, Illinois State Archives. Transmitting certificates of purchase, Receiver's receipts, and abstracts of sales for lands sold during December, 1837.

20. To James Whitcomb. January 8, 1838; ALS, RG-56, National Archives. Report of the amount of public money in the hands of the Receiver of the Springfield Land Office on January 1, 1838.

21. To James Whitcomb. February 6, 1838; Copy, Illinois State Archives. Transmitting certificates of purchase, Receiver's receipts, and abstracts of sales for lands sold during January, 1838.

22. To James Whitcomb. February 6, 1838; ALS, RG-56, National Archives. Report of the amount of public money in the hands of the Receiver of the Springfield Land Office on January 31, 1838.

23. To James Whitcomb. March 1, 1838; Copy, Illinois State Archives. Transmitting certificates of purchase, Receiver's receipts, and abstracts of sales for lands sold during February, 1838.

24. To James Whitcomb. March 2, 1838; Copy, Illinois State Archives. Report of the amount of public money in the hands of the Receiver of the Springfield Land Office on March 1, 1838.

25. To James Whitcomb. March 19, 1838; Copy, Illinois State Archives. Returning a corrected certificate of purchase.

26. To James Whitcomb. March 19, 1838; Copy, Illinois State Archives. Returning a large number of corrected certificates of purchase.

27. To James Whitcomb. March 31, 1838; Copy, Illinois State Archives. Report of the amount of public money in the hands of the Receiver of the Springfield Land Office.

28. To James Whitcomb. April 3, 1838; Copy, Illinois State Archives. Returning several land patents.

29. To James Whitcomb. April 6, 1838; Copy, Illinois State Archives.

Transmitting certificates of purchase, Receiver's receipts, and abstracts of sales for lands sold during March, 1838.

30. To James Whitcomb. May, 1838; Copy, Illinois State Archives. Transmitting certificates of purchase, Receiver's receipts, and abstracts of sales for lands sold during April, 1838.

31. To James Whitcomb. May 1, 1838; Copy, RG-56, National Archives. Report of the amount of public money in the hands of the Receiver of the Springfield Land Office.

32. To James Whitcomb. May 1, 1838; Copy, Illinois State Archives. Transmitting the bond of the Receiver of the Springfield Land Office.

33. To James Whitcomb. May 5, 1838; Copy, Illinois State Archives. Returning three land patents.

34. To James Whitcomb. May 10, 1838; Copy, Illinois State Archives. Returning several land patents.

35. To James Whitcomb. May 14, 1838; Copy, Illinois State Archives. Reporting inability to locate proof of the pre-emption of N. Lambert.

36. To James Whitcomb. May 15, 1838; Copy, Illinois State Archives. Reporting information in regard to the pre-emption entries of Peter and James Stewart.

37. To James Whitcomb. May 21, 1838; Copy, Illinois State Archives. Calling attention to an error in the entry of Richard Ayres and asking that attention be given to the case.

38. To James Whitcomb. May 24, 1838; Copy, Illinois State Archives. Enclosing proof of the entry of Alexander White.

39. To James Whitcomb. June 1, 1838; ALS, RG-56, National Archives. Report of the amount of public money in the hands of the Receiver of the Springfield Land Office.

40. To James Whitcomb. June 1, 1838; Copy, Illinois State Archives. Transmitting certificates of purchase, Receiver's receipts, and abstracts of sales for lands sold during May, 1838.

41. To James Whitcomb. N.d.; Copy, Illinois State Archives. Regarding several land patents.

42. To James Whitcomb. June 13, 1838; Copy, Illinois State Archives. Returning several land patents.

43. To James Whitcomb. July 6, 1838; ALS, RG-56, National Archives. Report of the amount of public money in the hands of the Receiver of the Springfield Land Office.

44. To James Whitcomb. July 6, 1838; Copy, Illinois State Archives. Transmitting certificates of purchase, Receiver's receipts, and abstracts of sales for lands sold during June, 1838.

45. To James Whitcomb. July 7, 1838; Copy, Illinois State Archives. Returning several certificates of purchase.

46. To James Whitcomb. August 3, 1838; ALS, RG-56, National Archives. Report of the amount of public money in the hands of the Receiver of the Springfield Land Office.

47. To James Whitcomb. August 3, 1838; Copy, Illinois State Archives. Transmitting certificates of purchase, Receiver's receipts, and abstracts of sales for lands sold during July, 1838.

48. To Levi Woodbury, Secretary of the Treasury. August 7, 1838; Copy, Illinois State Archives. Report of the amount of public money in the hands of the Receiver of the Springfield Land Office on August 1, 1838.

49. To James Whitcomb. August 14, 1838; Copy, Illinois State Archives. Acknowledging receipt of twelve bundles of land patents.

50. To James Whitcomb. August 29, 1838; Copy, Illinois State Archives. Transmitting a large number of certificates of purchase.

51. To Levi Woodbury. September 7, 1838; ALS, RG-56, National Archives. Report of the amount of public money in the hands of the Receiver of the Springfield Land Office on September 1, 1838.

52. To James Whitcomb. August [September] 7, 1838; Copy, Illinois State Archives. Transmitting certificates of purchase, Receiver's receipts, and abstracts of sales for lands sold during August, 1838.

53. To ———. N.d.; Copy, Illinois State Archives. Requesting the plats for lands which will soon be offered for sale.

54. To ———. October 9, 1838; Copy, Illinois State Archives. Transmitting certificates of purchase, Receiver's receipts, and abstracts of sales for lands sold during September, 1838.

55. To Levi Woodbury. November 15, 1838; ALS, RG-56, National Archives. Report of the amount of public money in the hands of the Receiver of the Springfield Land Office on November 1, 1838.

56. To James Whitcomb. November 15, 1838; Copy, Illinois State Archives. Transmitting certificates of purchase, Receiver's receipts, and abstracts of sales for lands sold during October, 1838.

57. To ———. November 22, 1838; Copy, Illinois State Archives. "We have the pleasure of informing you that we know of no such attempts or practices which would interrupt a fair and honest competition in the sale and disposition of public land at this office." The letter was signed also by the Receiver of the Land Office.

58. To ———. November 22, 1838; Copy, Illinois State Archives. Returning several corrected certificates of purchase.

59. To James Whitcomb. December 2, 1838; Copy, Illinois State Archives. Transmitting certificates of purchase, Receiver's receipts, and abstracts of sales for lands sold during November, 1838.

60. To Levi Woodbury. December 3, 1838; ALS, RG-56, National

Archives. Report of the amount of public money in the hands of the Receiver of the Springfield Land Office.

61. To Levi Woodbury. January 2, 1839; Copy, Illinois State Archives. Report of the amount of public money in the hands of the Receiver of the Springfield Land Office.

62. To James Whitcomb. January 2, 1839; Copy, Illinois State Archives. Transmitting certificates of purchase, Receiver's receipts, and abstracts of sales for lands sold during December, 1838.

63. To Levi Woodbury. February 7, 1839; Copy, Illinois State Archives. Report of the amount of public money in the hands of the Receiver of the Springfield Land Office.

64. To James Whitcomb. February 7, 1839; ALS, RG-56, National Archives. Report of the amount of public money in the hands of the Receiver of the Springfield Land Office on January 31, 1839.

65. To James Whitcomb. February 7, 1839; Copy, Illinois State Archives. Transmitting certificates of purchase, Receiver's receipts, and abstracts of sales for lands sold during January, 1839.

66. To Levi Woodbury. March 2, 1839; Copy, Illinois State Archives. Report of the amount of public money in the hands of the Receiver of the Springfield Land Office on February 28, 1839.

67. To James Whitcomb. March 2, 1839; Copy, Illinois State Archives. Submitting erroneous certificates of purchase for correction.

68. To James Whitcomb. March 2, 1839; Copy, Illinois State Archives. Submitting an erroneous certificate of purchase for correction.

69. To James Whitcomb. March 2, 1839; Copy, Illinois State Archives. Transmitting certificates of purchase, Receiver's receipts, and abstracts of sales for lands sold during February and March, 1839, "as my incumbency of this office will cease with today."

Index

Backenstos, Jacob B., 124

Badger, George E.: on ineligibility of Senator Shields, 173; and Kansas-Nebraska Act, 289, 462, 479; and protest of New England clergymen against Kansas-Nebraska Act, 303, 306-307; and Black-Douglas dispute on popular sovereignty, 479

Baker, Edward Dickinson: makes recommendations, 20, 153; and charges against Douglas, 190; and Compromise of 1850, 192; and Illinois Central Railroad, 214

Baltimore conventions, 1848, 1852, 1860. *See* Democratic party

Bancroft, George: letters to, 138, 412, 442; letters to Douglas, 412n, 443n; and Lecompton Constitution, 411n

Bank, United States: Douglas on, 15, 29-30, 44, 47; "Reign of Terror," 9, 15; and elections of 1834, 9; Andrew Jackson's policies defended, 62; and election of 1838, 69; and election of 1840, 85; bill vetoed by John Tyler, 99

Bank of Commerce (New York), 327

Bank of Metropolis (New York), 496

Bank of Peru (Illinois), 345

Banks and banking: Douglas on, 13-14, 39; in Illinois, 235; bill "disaffirming" Iowa and Wisconsin laws on, 142

Banks, A. D., 467, 481

Banks, Nathaniel Prentice, 368

Barbour, Alfred M., 508

Barlow, Nathan: letter to, 6

Barnard, E. F.: recommended, 326n

Barnard, James, 507

Barnburners, 157, 158-159

Barringer, Daniel Moreau, 265n

Barry, William D.: represents Douglas in lawsuit, 451; letters to Douglas, 451n

Bates, Edward, 60

Beck, ———, 150

Beckwith, Corydon: letter to, 451

Beckwith, J. A.: letter to, 327

Bedell, Edward A., 366

Bedford, Wimer: recommended, 401

Behn, Frederick W.: recommended, 384

Beirut, 383

Belfast (Ireland), 377

Belgium, 261

Bell, John, 194n; and election of 1860, 498

Belleville (Illinois): Democratic meeting in (1856), 368

Belmont, August: letters to, 494, 505

Benham, Spencer C., 368, 419, 441, 443-444

Benjamin, Judah P.: and Kansas-Nebraska Act, 462

Bennett, ———, 33

Benton, Thomas Hart, 14n; resolutions of, approved by Illinois legislature, 32; Douglas seeks advice of, 70n; and chairmanship of Senate Foreign Relations Committee, 184-186; and Compromise of 1850, 192; relations with Douglas, 257-258; and mail steamship subsidies, 257-258; and James Buchanan, 257, 369, 370n

Bents Fort, 139

Berdan, James, 72

Berlin (Germany), 265

Berry, B. D., 410

Berry, Dr. Isaac S.: recommended, 109

Billings, George W., 178, 180

Bird, Dr. J. Herman, 170

Bissell, William H.: and Illinois Central Railroad, 245; and Kansas-Nebraska Act, 322; and Illinois Senatorial election (1855), 331; elected Governor of Illinois, 369n

Black, Jeremiah: letters to, 377, 508; dispute with Douglas on popular sovereignty, 477, 478-479, 487

Black Hawk Indian War, 65, 155n, 194, 239

Blair, Francis Preston, 259n; letters to, 69, 158

[528]

Blair, Captain James D.: recommended, 162
Bledsoe, Albert Taylor, 190
Bloodgood, S. Dewitt, 74, 76
Bloomington (Illinois): Douglas meeting in (1854), 330; Lincoln and Douglas in (1858), 423
Board of Health, Chicago, 388
Bolivia, 380
Bolles, S., 321
Bond, Benjamin: recommended, 167n
Boston (Massachusetts): Douglas declines invitation to speak in (1855), 340-341
Boston and Portland Railroad, 127
Boston *Times*, 230-231
Boyd, Linn, 194
Bradbury, James W., 194n
Brady, Mathew, 444
Brainard, Dr. Daniel, 434
Brainerd, Lawrence, 334
Brandon (Vermont): Douglas' birth and early years in, 57-58
Brandon Academy, 58
Brayman, Mason: letter to, 337
Breckinridge, John C., 240n; letters to, 328, 329; land investment at Superior, Wisconsin, 329n; and Kansas-Nebraska Act, 461; and election of 1860, 498
Breese, Sidney, 169; letters to, 144, 147, 156, 198, 208; letter to Douglas, 208, 215n; letter to Thomas Ford, 117n; letter to James K. Polk, 107; letter to editors of *Illinois State Register*, 206n; makes recommendations, 109, 151, 152; elected United States Senator, 101; and Oregon question, 144; and River and Harbor Bill, 144; and Illinois Central Railroad, 198-206, 208-214; and bills granting lands to aid in railroad construction in Illinois, 199-204, 211-213; and Illinois Senatorial election (1858), 424n, 428
Bremen (Germany), 380
Bridge, Hudson E., 486
Bright, Jesse D.: witness, 367; land investment at Superior, Wiscon-

sin, 328, 329n; and patronage, 372, 382; and Lecompton Constitution, 405
Brisbin, J. B., 391
Brooks, Preston: affray with Charles Sumner, 364-365
Brown, Aaron V., 381, 402
Brown, Albert Gallatin, 466
Brown, B. Gratz, 259n
Brown, Jacob I.: letter to, 428; letter to Douglas, 428n
Brown, John, 489n
Brown, William: recommended, 38
Brown, William J.: letter to, 226
Brown, William Scott: recommended, 113, 144
Brown County (Illinois): and Mormon troubles, 122n
Browne, Thomas C., 95
Browning, Orville H., 102
Bryan, John A.: recommended, 151
Bryan, Thomas B.: letter to, 385
Bryant, Henry L., 33
Bryant, William P.: recommended, 162-163
Buchanan, Edward B.: recommended, 266
Buchanan, James, 460, 464; letters to, 107, 110, 150, 325, 332, 367, 372, 375, 376, 377, 382, 384, 397, 401; letters to Douglas, 375, 399n; relations with Douglas, 372, 397-398, 399n, 401-402, 403, 418, 476; and patronage, 372, 397-398, 399n, 401-402; on popular sovereignty, 469; and Thomas Hart Benton, 257, 369, 370n; and election of 1848, 157, 158-159; "Harvest Home letter" (1848), 348, 349n; and Compromise of 1850, 192; and election of 1852, 227, 233; and Baltimore convention (1852), 250-251, 252n; on Kansas-Nebraska Act, 459; and election of 1856, 334, 348, 349n, 361, 362; and Lecompton Constitution, 403, 406n
Buckmaster, Samuel A., 507
Buel, Alexander W.: makes recommendation, 265; recommended, 265

cinnati convention (1856), 344, 361-363, 492; and Lecompton Constitution, 404, 410, 411; and Illinois Senatorial election (1858), 423-424, 428, 429, 431-432; and elections of 1859, 440, 450, 476; Springfield state convention (1860), 475, 481-482; and election of 1860, 431, 446, 469; Charleston convention (1860), 431, 439, 446-447, 469, 474-475, 481, 482-483, 484-485, 492, 493n, 494; Baltimore convention (1860), 492-496; urged by Douglas to support Lincoln administration, 512-513

Democratic Press (Chicago), 330

Democratic Review, 216n, 233-234; and election of 1852, 237, 238n, 239-240, 246-247

Denman, Charles L.: recommended, 260

Denmark, 264

Dennis, Elias S., 166

Derby and Jackson (publishers): and biography of Douglas, 442n

Deseret. *See* Utah Territory

Detroit *Free Press*, 261

Develin, John E.: letter to, 507

Dewey, Charles, 496

Dick, Robert P.: letter to, 494

Dickens, Asbury, 233n, 496; letters to, 181, 195

Dickinson, A. J., 337

Dickinson, Daniel S.: letter to Zadoc W. McKnew, 215; at Baltimore convention (1852), 251

Diller, Isaac Roland, 258; letter to Douglas, 380; letter to James Buchanan, 380; recommended, 380

Diller, Jonathan R., 74, 82

Dillingham, Paul, Jr.: makes recommendation, 108-109

Dimmick, M. M.: letter to Franklin Pierce, 265

Disney, David T., 349, 351; recommended, 376

Diversey, Michael, 366n

Dix, E. H., 430

Dobbin, James C.: letters to, 263, 339

Dodge, A. R., 96n

Dodge, Augustus Caesar, 326; makes recommendation, 241; recommended, 332; and bill "disaffirming" Iowa and Wisconsin banking laws, 142; on Kansas-Nebraska Act, 463

Dodge, C. C.: recommended, 153

Dodge, Henry: and election of 1848, 159

Dorr, J. B.: letter to, 446; letter to Douglas, 447n

Dougherty, Daniel, 410

Dougherty, John, 145, 484; and Illinois Senatorial election (1846), 150; and Illinois Senatorial election (1858), 428

Douglas, Adele Cutts (second wife of Douglas), 481; letters to, 399, 517; letter to her mother, 384; marriage, 473; impressions of Chicago, 384-385; health, 411, 412-413, 417, 474, 475, 476, 477, 478-479

Douglas, Martha Denny Martin (first wife of Douglas), 164n, 171, 207, 219, 240; marriage, 473; inherits plantations in Mississippi and North Carolina, 161n, 190; health, 229; death, 267n, 473

Douglas, Robert Martin (son of Douglas), 171, 207, 399, 473

Douglas, Stephen A.: autobiographical sketches, 56-68, 102-103, 444-446, 469; makes recommendations, 20, 38, 103, 106-113, 133, 136, 138-139, 140, 144, 150, 151-152, 152-154, 161-163, 165-167, 177, 228, 241, 254, 260-266, 283, 325-327, 332, 334, 336, 339-340, 345-346, 352-353, 360-361, 363, 372, 375-378, 378-384, 385, 386, 389, 397, 400, 401, 402, 403, 406, 420

———, speeches: in defense of General Jackson, Jacksonville (1834), 15, 63; on railroads, Chicago (October 4, 1849), 178, 181n; on Wilmot Proviso, Springfield (October 23, 1849), 178, 181n, 182, 183n; on "Measures of Adjustment," Chicago

marriage to Adele Cutts, 385n; candidate for Presidential nomination (1856), 267, 333-334, 339, 342-343, 348, 349, 350n, 351; and Cincinnati convention (1856), 361-362; and election of 1856, 368-369; on party alignments, 371; report on Kansas troubles, 350; and memorial of Topeka (Kansas) statehood movement, 355-360; dispute with James H. Lane, 354-360; supports Governor Walker in Kansas, 386-387; relations with James Buchanan, 372, 397-398, 399n, 401-402, 403, 418, 476; on Dred Scott decision, 465, 487; visits Minnesota Territory, 390-391; on proposed sale of Fort Snelling, 393-397, 413-416, 417n; and Lecompton Constitution, 386-387, 403-404, 405, 406n, 408-410, 411-412, 412-413, 417, 418, 454, 471; candidate for re-election to United States Senate (1858), 373, 404, 418, 423-430, 431-433; debates with Lincoln, 423-425, 426-428; "Freeport Doctrine," 454-456, 460, 466n, 469; re-elected United States Senator (1858), 433, 471-472; removal from chairmanship of Committee on Territories, 454-455, 458, 460, 466n; dispute with Graham N. Fitch, 435-437; invited to campaign in Connecticut (1859), 440-441; invited to campaign in Maine (1859), 450; campaigns in Ohio (1859), 476n; article on popular sovereignty in *Harper's Magazine*, 442-443, 449, 466-467, 468, 469; dispute with Jeremiah Black over popular sovereignty, 477, 478-479, 487; denies arrangement with Horace Greeley for re-election to United States Senate, 479-480; resolution "against the invasion of States," 489n; biography of, by James Washington Sheahan, 441-442, 443-444; on publication of Lincoln-Douglas debates, 489-490, 491n; candidate for

Presidential nomination (1860), 431, 439, 446-447, 467-468, 468-469, 474-475, 481, 482-483, 484-485, 486-487; and Charleston convention (1860), 493n; and Baltimore convention (1860), 492-496; nominated for Presidency, 494-496; on Democratic platform, 494-495; and election of 1860, 497-498, 498-499; on election of Lincoln, 499-502; urges compromise in secession crisis, 504-506; confers with President Lincoln, 509-510; declares support of Lincoln administration, 509-510, 511-513; on Union sentiment in Illinois, 511; addresses Illinois legislature, 511n; death, 514n

Douglas, Stephen A., Jr. (son of Douglas), 399, 473

Douglass, Benajah (grandfather of Douglas), 5

Douglass, Beriah (uncle of Douglas), 5, 7

Douglass, Stephen A. (father of Douglas), 57

Downing, Major Jack, 2

Doyle, ———, 98

Dramatic Line, 259n

Dred Scott decision, 487; Douglas on, 465, 487; William M. Gwin on, 464-465

Dunbar, William: letter to, 466; letter to Douglas, 467n

Dunbar, William G.: recommended, 263

Duncan, Alexander: recommended, 107, 140

Duncan, Joseph, 12, 13n, 16, 64; petitions to, 20, 38

Dungan, C. B.: letter to, 94

Dunklin, Daniel: letter to, 521

Dunlap, Major Alexander, 154

Dunlap, James: letter to, 105

Dutcher, Frederick R.: letter to, 73

Duval, John P., 164

Dyer, Thomas, 201

Eads, Bartell, 522

Eames, Charles: recommended, 283

Hall, James, 34
Hall, Judge, 421
Hamburg (Germany), 400
Hamlin, Hannibal, 186n; makes recommendation, 266; and election of 1860, 498
Hancock County (Illinois): and Mormon troubles, 121-125
Hannegan, Edward A.: makes recommendation, 163
Hardin, John J., 16, 64-65, 67; letters to, 126, 137, 138, 139, 140; letters to Douglas, 137n, 138n, 140n; makes recommendation, 38; defeated by Douglas for States' Attorney, 12; opposes Douglas for state legislature, 36; commands militia in Mormon troubles, 120, 122, 123, 124, 125, 126; and Mexican War, 138n, 139, 140-141; on military policy toward Mexico and Great Britain, 137n, 138n; and Illinois Central Railroad, 214; killed at Battle of Buena Vista, 13n
Harlan, James: and memorial of Topeka (Kansas) statehood movement, 360
Harper, Fletcher: and Douglas' article in *Harper's Magazine*, 449
Harper and Brothers (publishers): letter to, 468; letter to O. Jennings Wise, 449n
Harper's Magazine: Douglas' article on popular sovereignty, 449, 466-467, 469, 478n
Harris, Thomas Langrell, 338; letter to Douglas, 354n; makes recommendations, 153, 346, 375-377; signs letter, 351; and Illinois Senatorial election (1846), 145; in Mexican War, 145; and Illinois Senatorial election (1855), 331, 333; and Sheahan-Cook feud, 354n; and Lecompton Constitution, 410n; speech in House of Representatives, 426; death, 474n
Harrison, William Henry: in election of 1836, 27, 45-46; candidate for President (1840), 74-80, 83-85, 90; fails to carry Illinois, 93;

and slavery in Indiana Territory, 293
Hart, Emmanuel B., 217, 219
Harvey, Peter: letter to, 349
Hawkes, Wright: recommended, 266
Healy, George Peter Alexander, 385
Hedenberg, C. J.: letter to, 420; letter to Douglas, 421n
Helm, Charles J., 508
Hempstead, Charles S.: letter to, 154
Henderson, A. W., 321
Henderson County (Illinois): and Mormon troubles, 122n
Hendricks, Thomas A.: letters to, 341, 373, 383, 437, 438
Hendrickson, John: letter to Douglas, 104
Henn, Bernhart: makes recommendation, 326
Henry, Anson G., 39
Herndon, Archer G., 148; letter to, 136
Herndon, William H., 136n
Herrington, Augustus M.: recommended, 377
Herrington, James, 422
Heslep, Joseph, 61; letter to, 105
Hewett, Josephus: makes recommendation, 20
Hickman, John: and Lecompton Constitution, 410n
Hickox, Virgil, 74, 82, 259; letter to, 511; letter to Douglas, 513n; letter to James Madison Cutts, 514n; and "alien case," 96n
Higbee, Chauncey L., 507
History of Congress, Biographical and Political . . ., by Henry G. Wheeler, 156, 421
Hodges, Edward F.: recommended, 108-109
Hoe, R., and Company: letter to, 335
Hoge, Joseph Pendleton: makes recommendation, 107; and Illinois Central Railroad, 214
Holbrook, Darius B.: and railroad promotion in Illinois, 178, 181n, 196, 199-202, 206n, 210-214

passage of act providing for, 196, 197-198; Douglas' promotion of, 472; Douglas-Breese letters on legislative history of, 198-206, 208-214; and connection with Michigan Central Railroad, 221-226, 244-245; and Douglas' Chicago property, 259, 337, 338; and Illinois Senatorial election (1858), 425-426, 432; involved in lawsuit, 451

Illinois legislature: passes act concerning states' attorneys, 16-17; elects Douglas States' Attorney, 11-12, 16-17, 64-65; Douglas elected to, 36n, 67, 445; nominates Hugh Lawson White for Presidency (1835), 32; and Illinois and Michigan Canal, 32, 67, 94, 176, 445; approves Thomas Hart Benton's "expungeing" resolutions, 32; removes capital from Vandalia to Springfield, 37, 38n; and internal improvements, 67-68, 176, 206n, 282; rumored resolutions supporting James K. Polk's veto of River and Harbor Bill, 148; rumored instructions on tonnage duties, 283; communications from Douglas as Secretary of State, 93-94; act reorganizing state Supreme Court, 96n; and Senatorial election (1842), 101n; endorses Asa Whitney's Pacific railroad plan, 133n; and Senatorial election (1846), 144-150, 151n; and power to elect successor to Senator Shields, 167-169, 172-173; special session (1849), 176; instructions on Wilmot Proviso, 189n, 191, 242; and Illinois Central Railroad, 178-181, 196-197; instructions on land grants to aid in railroad construction, 206n; instructions on Wilmot Proviso rescinded, 323n; and banking system in Illinois, 235; and Senatorial election (1852), 259n; special session (1854), 284n; rumored instructions on Nebraska bill, 283; and Kansas-Ne-

braska Act, 284n; and Senatorial election (1855), 331-332, 333; and Senatorial election (1858), 433n; Douglas addresses, 511n

Illinois Patriot (Jacksonville), 15, 63; letter to, 36

Illinois Republican (Springfield), 55n

Illinois River: surveys of, 104; improvement of navigation, 176

Illinois Staats Zeitung (Chicago), 366n

Illinois State Bank, 14

Illinois State Gazette (Jacksonville), 23

Illinois State Journal (Springfield), 425n

Illinois State Register (Springfield), 155, 177, 258, 267, 367, 425n, 426, 475; letters to, 74, 113; charges against Illinois delegation, 113-115; reply to Douglas' defense of Illinois delegation, 117n; and Kansas-Nebraska Act, 283-284

Indian Affairs, Office of, 236; letters to, 366, 369

Indian policy: Douglas on, 29, 269-270

Indian tribes: mentioned, 164, 236

Indiana: laws relating to slavery, 293-294; and Springfield Whig convention (1840), 88; politics in, 99, 329; and election of 1834, 9; and election of 1842, 99; and election of 1852, 234, 250-251; and election of 1854, 329; and election of 1856, 344, 363; and Lecompton Constitution, 405

Internal improvements, 10; in Illinois legislature, 67-68, 176, 206n, 282; bills vetoed by John Tyler, 114; and Pacific railroad, 132-133; River and Harbor Bill vetoed by James K. Polk, 148; rivers and harbors, 114, 144, 228, 268, 272-282, 472

Iowa: admission of, 470; and election of 1852, 233, 235, 236; and election of 1856, 344; and election of 1859, 476

Middlebury College: Douglas granted honorary degree, 229n; Douglas pledges donation to, 327

Miller, Dr., 325

Mills, Benjamin, 64

Milton, George Fort: on Douglas, ix

Minnesota (state): and election of 1859, 476

Minnesota Territory, 151, 165-166; organization of, 470; memorial of legislature, 189; Douglas' visit to, 390-391; constitutional convention in, 391-392; admission as state, 470

Mississippi: and election of 1848, 161; plantation in, belonging to Douglas' wife and children, 161n, 190-191, 335, 336n, 433, 434n, 508, 509n; and election of 1852, 236; and election of 1860, 498

Mississippi and Ohio Railroad, 220n

Missouri: and election of 1834, 9; troops for Mexican War raised in, 139; politics in, 184-185; and election of 1852, 233, 235, 236; and slavery agitation, 256; and election of 1856, 344; and patronage under Buchanan administration, 370; and election of 1860, 498

Missouri Compromise, 242, 255; repudiated by "Alabama resolutions" (1848), 161n; extension of, favored by Douglas, 242, 470; repeal of, 255, 286-287, 315-318, 458-459, 471; and election of 1856, 368; extension of, and secession crisis, 504-506

Missouri Democrat (St. Louis), 258

Mobile Register, 475

Moffett, ———, 446

Molony, R. S.: makes recommendation, 263; signs request, 247

Montgomery, William: and Lecompton Constitution, 410n

Moore, John: letter of Henry A. Wise to, 429n

Morgan, Edwin D.: letters to, 404, 406; telegram to, 406; letter to Douglas, 404n

Mormons: troubles in Illinois (1845), 120-127; exodus from Illinois, 137; Douglas and, 312

Moroney, Patrick, 247

Morris (Illinois): Democratic meeting in (1854), 330

Morris, Isaac N.: makes recommendations, 375-377

Morrison, J. L. D.: makes recommendations, 375-376

Morrison, John, 145, 148

Morrison, Joseph, 145, 148

Morse, James: letter to, 163

Morse, L. L., 5

Mulfinger, George L., 321

Murphy, Richard, 145

Murray, Robert H., 345

Myers, Sydney: letter to, 428; letter to Douglas, 429

Napier, Joseph, 68

Nashville (Tennessee): Douglas campaigns in (1844), 105n

National Demokrat (Chicago), 366n

National Intelligencer (Washington, D.C.), 290, 355

Nauvoo (Illinois), 120n; and Mormon troubles, 122, 125, 127

Nebraska Territory, 325, 326, 327; organization of, and Pacific railroad, 131; organization of, 268-271, 470

Nester, Patrick, 253

New England Society of New York City: invitation to Douglas, 404; Douglas declines invitation, 406-407

New Hampshire: and election of 1852, 233; and election of 1860, 497-498

New Jersey: and election of 1860, 497-498

New Mexico Territory: and Mexican War, 118n, 119-120; organization of, 187, 191-192, 244n, 470

Pratt, Orville C.: recommended, 161; and land grant to aid in railroad construction in Illinois, 202-203

Prentice, William S.: letters to, 99, 183, 503; recommended, 165; candidate for state legislature, 100

Price, Dr. Edward B.: recommended, 152

Price, Sterling: letter to James Buchanan, 372

Price, William, 348, 441

Providence (Rhode Island): anti-Nebraska meeting in, 323

Public and General Statutes Passed by the Congress of the United States of America ... [1789-1827], edited by Joseph Story, 247

Purdy, Elijah: letter to, 498

Quincy (Illinois): Douglas' visit to, 399-400; and Lincoln-Douglas debates, 424, 425

Quincy *Whig*, 190

Quitman, John A., 182-183

Railroads: in Illinois, 51, 67, 176, 178-181, 196-206, 208-214, 220, 221-226, 244-245, 259, 337, 338, 388, 425-426, 432, 451, 472; Pacific railroad, 127-133, 268, 270-271, 333, 472. *See also* names of individual railroad lines

Ralli, John: recommended, 378-379

Ralston, J. H.: and "alien case," 96n

Rankin, Dr., 328, 329

Raymond, Henry J.: letter to, 478

Ream, Robert L.: recommended, 325

Reed, James F.: recommended, 113

Reed, Silas: letter to, 104

Reid, David S., 227; letters to, 267, 347

Reid, Miss, 219

Reilly, Thomas Devin: recommended, 260

Republican party: 1854 Illinois platform, 426, 427n; and election of 1856, 368; and Lecompton Constitution, 387, 405n; and Buchanan administration, 418; and Illinois Senatorial election (1858), 426-428; and publication of Lincoln-Douglas debates, 489-490, 491n; and secession crisis, 504-505

Reynolds, Charles Ambrose, 336

Reynolds, John, 10n, 13n, 64; and Illinois Senatorial election (1858), 428

Reynolds, Samuel D.: recommended, 153

Rhode Island: and election of 1860, 497-498

Rhodes, Daniel P., 2n

Rice, Edmund, 348, 400

Rice, Henry M., 394; letter to, 346; land investment at Superior, Wisconsin, 328, 329n

Richardson, R. H., 321

Richardson, William A., 322, 331; letters to, 252, 361, 362, 492; signs letter, 351; recommended, 375, 397; at Baltimore convention (1852), 249, 252; at Cincinnati convention (1856), 361-362; campaign for Governor of Illinois, 368; defeated, 369; effort to secure appointment for, 370; appointed Governor of Nebraska Territory, 375; and election of 1860, 475, 497; at Charleston convention (1860), 483, 493n; at Baltimore convention (1860), 492, 493n

Richmond, Dean, 484n, 485; letter to, 493

Richmond, John P.: recommended, 376

Richmond *Enquirer*, 232

Richmond *Examiner*, 261, 330

Ridgway, R., 488n

Riggs, George W., 328; letters to, 155, 366

Riggs and Company, 367; letters to, 400, 419

Rio de Janeiro (Brazil), 263

Ritchie, Thomas, 249

Seminole Indian War, 164
Semple, James, 30, 135n, 144n; letters to, 36, 101; makes recommendations, 107, 109; candidate for United States Senate, 36; appointed to United States Senate, 102; and Mexican War, 141; and Illinois Central Railroad, 214
Senate: Douglas candidate for, 101; Douglas elected to, 151n, 259n, 433, 471-472; James Shields's election declared void, 167-169, 172-173; Thomas Hart Benton excluded from chairmanship of Foreign Relations Committee, 184-186; and Compromise of 1850, 191-193; election of Secretary of the Senate, 232-233; and Kansas-Nebraska Act, 283-284; and protest of Chicago clergymen against Kansas-Nebraska Act, 300-322; and memorial of New England clergymen against Kansas-Nebraska Act, 301-309, 322n; and memorial of Topeka (Kansas) statehood movement, 355-360; Sumner-Brooks affray, 364-365; and Lecompton Constitution, 405, 406n, 413, 419n; Douglas' dispute with Graham N. Fitch, 435-437. See also Congress
Settle, Thomas, 228n; letter to, 206
Seward, William H., 283, 334, 507; letter to, 508; and memorial of Topeka (Kansas) statehood movement, 356-357
Shaw, Aaron: makes recommendation, 376
Sheahan, James Washington, 340; letters to, 330, 333, 335, 338, 346, 347, 351, 353, 354, 365, 368, 374, 404, 441, 443; letters to Douglas, 348n, 352n, 354n, 404; persuaded to edit Chicago Times, 328; dispute with Isaac Cook, 351-354; writes biography of Douglas, 441-442, 443-444
Shelby, Isaac, Jr., 345
Shepley, George Foster, 253
Sheridan, James B., 434n, 441, 442n; letter to, 499

Sherwood, Thomas R., 482; letter to Douglas, 483n
Shields, James, 322; letter to, 98; letter to James K. Polk, 113; makes recommendations, 153, 262, 263, 264, 339; signs request, 247; appointed Commissioner of General Land Office, 113; appointed brigadier general in Mexican War, 140-141; elected to United States Senate, 169n; election to Senate declared void, 167-169, 172-173; special session of legislature to elect successor, 176n; re-elected to United States Senate, 169n; on Wilmot Proviso, 182-183; and Compromise of 1850, 192; and Illinois Central Railroad, 198, 205, 209, 214; and Illinois banking law, 235; and Thomas Hart Benton, 258; expiration of Senate term, 284n, 330n; and Illinois Senatorial election (1855), 331, 333
Shinn, R. F., 321
Shoemaker, Thomas C.: recommended, 334
Shunk, Francis R.: and election of 1848, 159
Shurtleff, Nathaniel B., 341n
Sibley, Henry Hastings: letters to, 390, 391
Sibley, Mark H., 59
Simms, Hall: letter to, 147
Sinclair, J., 321
Singleton, James W., 399, 507; letters to, 349, 351, 373, 439; letters to Douglas, 351n, 373n, 439n-440n
Skinner, Onias C., 399; recommended, 165-166
Slave code, 439-440n; Douglas on, 447
Slave trade, African: Douglas on, 447, 452
Slavery: Douglas on, viii, 182, 185, 190-191, 194, 241-243, 255-256, 291-298, 340-341, 470, 487, 500-502; enactments on, by colonial legislatures, 442-443; in Illinois, 291-298; in election of 1848, 161; and admission of California, 182;

and Thomas Hart Benton's exclusion from chairmanship of Senate Foreign Relations Committee, 184-185; and Mexican cession, 187-188, 189n; and Compromise of 1850, 192; no attempt at agitation in Congress (1850-51), 207; and election of 1852, 218; and organization of Nebraska Territory, 271; and Kansas-Nebraska Act, 284-290; and election of 1856, 362, 368; and election of Lincoln, 500-502; and secession crisis, 504-505. *See also* Popular sovereignty

Slaves: on Mississippi plantation belonging to Douglas' wife and children, 190-191; treatment of, on Mississippi plantation, 433-434

Slidell, John: letter to Washington *Union*, 434n; and patronage under Buchanan administration, 372, 382; and charges against treatment of slaves on Mississippi plantation belonging to Douglas' wife and children, 433-434

Slocumb, Rigdon B., 145

Smith, Benjamin F.: recommended, 265

Smith, E. Randolph: letter to, 345; letter to Douglas, 348n

Smith, Edward, 30

Smith, Gerrit: dines with Douglas, 385

Smith, J. J., 366

Smith, Robert: letter to, 163; makes recommendations, 107, 113, 140, 152, 165, 375, 376, 377; and Illinois Central Railroad, 214

Smith, Samuel A.: on Kansas-Nebraska Act, 463

Smith, Seba, 3n

Smith, Theophilus Washington: and "alien case," 95-96

Smith, Truman: and Kansas-Nebraska Act, 289

Smith and Company (publishers): and biography of Douglas, 442

Smith, Bradley and Company, 345n, 348

Smyrna and Muscat (Turkey), 152

Snowhook, William B., 374

Snyder, Adam W., 41

Soulé, Pierre: letter to, 430; letter to Douglas, 431n; at Baltimore convention (1852), 249, 251

South Carolina: and election of 1848, 160; and Compromise of 1850, 207, 208n; and election of 1860, 498

Southern Cross Railroad, 208n

Spalding, Josiah, 61

Spencer, Ambrose, 33

Spencer, John C.: letter to, 104

Spottswood, George W., 103

Spottswood, James H.: recommended, 103

Springfield (Illinois): state capital removed to, 37, 38n; Whig convention at (1840), 86-91, 92n-93n; Douglas speaks in (October 23, 1849), 178, 181n, 182, 183n; Lincoln and Douglas in (1858), 423

Springfield Land Office, 37, 38, 52-53, 94-95; Douglas appointed Register of, 37, 38n, 445

Squier, Ephraim George: letter to, 367

Stanton, Frederick P.: recommended, 263

Starkweather, Charles R., 345

Starkweather, D. A.: letter to Douglas, 325

State Capitol Reporter (Concord, New Hampshire): letter to, 284

Stemson, ———, 400

Stephens, Alexander Hamilton: letter to, 506; re-elected to Congress, 342; on popular sovereignty, 462

Stephens, John L., 259n

Stettheimer, Max: recommended, 403

Stevens, Isaac I.: recommended, 262

Stewart, A. M., 321

Stewart, James, 523

Stewart, Peter, 523

Stockholm (Sweden), 108